International Forum Selection

William W. Park
Professor of Law
Boston University

To Christine and Oliver Park,
who gave me a multitude of reasons to be grateful.

"O give thanks to the Lord for He is good.
His steadfast love endures forever."

Psalm 107

William W. Park is Professor of Law at Boston University,
Counsel to the firm of Ropes & Gray, and Vice President
of the London Court of International Arbitration.

ACKNOWLEDGMENTS

Special thanks are due to Mike Harrington for encouraging my initial questions about the relative reliability of different choice-of-forum devices. Bernard Audit, Michael Kerr, Jan Paulsson, Adam Samuel and Det Vagts generously looked at early drafts of the manuscript. Friends and colleagues who have contributed to my thinking about forum selection include Markham Ball, Axel Baum, Albert Jan van den Berg, Hal Berman, George Bermann, Jack Beermann, Thomas Bischof, Bob Bone, Bernd Busch, Christian Bühring-Uhle, Clark Byse, Tom Carbonneau, Daniela Caruso, Ron Cass, Laurie Craig, Alan Feld, John McGinnis, Berthold Goldman, Neil Hecht, Jack Hutchings, Gabrielle Kaufmann, Laurent Lévy, Andy Lowenfeld, Frank Macchiarola, Dan MacLeod, F.A. Mann, Claire Mansur, Martin Newhouse, Philippe Neyroud, Phil O'Neill, Dan Partan, Bill Patton, Otto Sandrock, Tom Reed, Michael Reisman, Paul Saba, Larry Sager, David Seipp, John Spencer, Avi Soifer, Johnny Veeder, Olivier Wehrli and Larry Yackle, as well as participants in faculty workshops at Boston University and Yeshiva University. Helpful research assistance came from Gaia Bernstein, Jacqui Fahey, Derek Footer, Alison Fox, Karen Goepfert, Bill Kaleva, Karl Ruping, Bennett Savitz and Paul Tutun.

TABLE OF CONTENTS

INTRODUCTION

Luke's gospel tells of a man who sought to have Jesus decide an inheritance dispute. "Rabbi," he said, "bid my brother divide the inheritance with me." Jesus dismissed the request for adjudication with a question of his own: "Who made me a judge or an arbitrator over you?"[1]

The question asked by Jesus about the source of adjudicatory authority lies at the heart of international forum selection analysis. Few of the legal dilemmas that vex international trade and investment have been more persistent than the matter of how and why an arbitrator or a judge ought to be empowered to hear a case with cross-border implications.[2]

Increasingly interdependent global marketplaces have led business managers to enter into agreements that create, allocate or limit judicial and arbitral power in cross-border commercial controversies. To enhance both efficiency and fairness in international relationships, such agreements direct litigation to particular tribunals, thereby reducing the risk that one side or the other will take unfair advantage of the uncertainties inherent in transactions with a foreign dimension.

Forum selection clauses inevitably create conflicts between the benefits of greater neutrality in dispute resolution and the costs inherent in relinquishing the right to sue and to be sued in courts that may later appear more convenient than the contractually-designated forum. Choice-of-forum clauses also implicate differences between the functions of courts and of arbitrators, between the concerns of merchants and those of consumers, and between efficient adjudication and the protection of basic community legal norms.

In its widest sense, forum selection includes all contractual choices of a binding mechanism to adjudicate present or potential disputes, whether by granting jurisdiction to courts or by consent to arbitration. Party choice and binding result constitute the defining characteristics of forum selection clauses. In these two respects, forum selection differs from many Alternative Dispute Resolution régimes currently in vogue, such as court-annexed arbitration, which is not consensual, or mediation and conciliation, which do not produce a result that is legally binding. As a practical matter, the rights of contracting parties will vary significantly depending on whether the choice-of-forum clause designates a nation's judicial system or provides for a private ("alternative") dispute resolution process. Court-designating agreements are usually

---

1. Luke 12:13-14.
2. Analogous questions of adjudicatory authority arise in public international disputes. *See generally* W. Michael Reisman, NULLITY AND REVISION (1971); W. Michael Reisman, SYSTEMS OF CONTROL IN INTERNATIONAL ADJUDICATION AND ARBITRATION (1992), at 11-45.

referred to as "jurisdiction clauses," in contrast to arbitration agreements that refer the parties to private dispute resolution.

The relative reliability of arbitration agreements as contrasted with court-designating jurisdiction clauses does not yield to facile analysis. Surprisingly perhaps, in some cases a commitment to private dispute resolution does a better job in promoting adjudicatory certainty than an agreement to litigate in a contractually designated court. Statutes and treaties require recognition of cross-border arbitration agreements and awards in situations where court-selecting jurisdiction clauses and judicial judgments are subject to enforcement only as a matter of judicial discretion and comity. Moreover, these arbitration treaties and statutes generally provide explicit grounds for annulment or nonrecognition of awards when the fairness and procedural integrity of the arbitral process has been compromised. Arbitration of international commercial controversies commends itself in many instances not by virtue of its speed or cost, but by reason of its neutrality and dependability.

While forum selection enhances international economic cooperation by providing a mechanism to reduce mutual distrust among trading partners, it is questionable whether a meaningful case can be made for enforcement of pre-dispute jurisdiction and arbitration clauses in consumer transactions. Although American law has often ignored this distinction between consumers and professionals, European legal régimes have generally required courts to disregard abusive prorogation agreements in consumer contracts. The European approach to forum selection provides a paradigm for a United States statute that would increase confidence in international economic commitments, while at the same time reducing the risk that consumers will be maneuvered into inaccessible or biased fora.

This book begins with a tale of forum selection gone awry, illustrating why some prorogation agreements do not always deliver the desired adjudicatory predictability. Chapters II and III contrast the relative reliability of jurisdiction clauses and arbitration agreements in an international context. Chapter IV explores drafting options and Chapter V examines judicial controls designed to safeguard the integrity of consensual dispute resolution. Chapter VI looks at European rules as models to promote a balanced enhancement of adjudicatory certainty with consumer protection. In Chapter VII a slight jurisprudential excursion considers the implications of international forum selection for the academic debate on legal certainty and neutrality. The final chapter of the book suggests several changes in the American legal framework for forum selection: a federal forum selection statute; a treaty network for enforcement of foreign judgments; and limitations on arbitration and jurisdiction clauses in consumer contracts.

International Forum Selection deals principally with commercial and financial disputes involving at least one private party. While similar questions arise in public arbitration between governments, the nature of the interests implicated in such inter-country arbitration differs dramatically from those legal concerns raised by business dispute resolution. Moreover, forum selection in commercial transactions usually occurs in the shadow of mandatory national court proceedings, changing significantly the procedural context in which disputes are submitted to arbitration.

The methodology of this study has been largely inductive. Questions and conclusions derive from particular problems or cases. Appendices supply documentary building blocks for analysis by both scholars and practitioners.

Notwithstanding its comparative elements, this book's perspective remains primarily North American. Particularly with respect to court-designating jurisdiction clauses, forum selection principles in the United States are more problematic than those of other Western legal systems. Limitations on judicial subject matter jurisdiction, the lack of any general statutory protection for consumers, and the absence of any multilateral jurisdiction and judgments treaty, all remain peculiarly American maladies.

These diverse elements of forum selection analysis affect both sound public policy and practical business planning. To begin refracting the various themes of inquiry, we shall now turn to a narrative about the way one hypothetical American company attempted to craft an adjudicatory régime for a multinational transaction.

WWP, Boston.
May 1995.

Chapter I

WHEN AND WHY FORUM SELECTION MATTERS

A. CAUTIONARY TALES ABOUT HOMETOWN JUSTICE.

1. Getting Into the Right Court.

Not long ago, a multinational enterprise with headquarters in Boston needed two cargo vessels to transport ore from its South American mines to its North American production facilities. A shipyard in a developing country with good harbors and cheap labor seemed the right place to build the vessels. Extended negotiations led to a contract between the shipyard and the multinational's Liberian shipping subsidiary, which was established to purchase and operate the vessels in a tax efficient manner. The multinational itself guaranteed its subsidiary's obligations. Interim payments were to be made as the vessels were built, with the final installment of the purchase price due at completion of both vessels.

When the shipyard notified the multinational that the vessels were completed, a dispute arose over the engine rooms and communication systems. The multinational maintained that the ships were not in fact finished according to contract specifications. The shipyard rejected these claims and filed suit to compel the final payment in a local commercial court.

Back in Boston, the lawyer who had advised the multinational during the contract negotiations congratulated herself on the foresight displayed in dealing with the shipyard. She had heard that courts in the shipyard's country lacked a tradition of judicial independence. Less courteous tongues had even characterized court proceedings there as auctions, with the judgment going to the highest bidder. Contemplating this unpleasant prospect, counsel had insisted that the contract designate courts in Boston as exclusively competent to settle any dispute.

The shipyard, of course, had protested that fairness required a more neutral solution. Its attorneys suggested settlement of any dispute through arbitration in Paris under the rules of the International Chamber of Commerce. The Boston lawyer, however, stood her ground. She had once been involved in a case where the arbitrator split the difference between the parties even though her client's case was clearly a winner. Arbitration, she said, injected too much uncertainty into the dispute resolution process. She noted that judges in Boston were trained to respect precedent, and that their decisions were subject to full appellate review.[3]

Hungry for business, the shipyard ceded to the Americans' superior bargaining power. The contract was drafted to include a clause providing that "all disputes arising out of this agreement will be subject to the exclusive jurisdiction of courts located within the Commonwealth of Massachusetts."

When the dispute over the contract specifications crystallized, things did not go according to plan. An action for damages filed by the multinational in the U.S. District Court for the District of Massachusetts was dismissed for lack of subject matter jurisdiction; the foreign subsidiary's presence as an indispensable party to the dispute defeated the requirement of complete diversity of citizenship. Jurisdiction could not be thrust upon the court. A subsequent action brought in Massachusetts state court was also dismissed on the basis of precedent holding jurisdiction clauses presumptively invalid, never explicitly overruled, notwithstanding scholarly opinion and judicial dicta saying earlier cases were out of step with the modern trend favoring jurisdiction clauses.[4]

In the next act of this troubling tale, the scene shifted to a court in the sleepy port town where the ships were being built. The chief judge owned a paint company whose principal customer was the shipyard. Since the United States was not a party to any judicial jurisdiction treaty, the local court felt free to evaluate the shipyard's commitment to litigate in American courts in light of the convenience of the American forum in the circumstances. The Massachusetts case law that had already caused problems back in Boston assisted the shipyard's argument that the prorogation clause was not enforceable. Fairness therefore required that the court give the parties some realistic hope of a remedy. After a hearing, the judge approved the sale of the vessels at a bargain price to a local buyer, who incidentally had been a substantial contributor to the election campaign of the current prime minister.

Back in Boston, the state court decision dismissing the action was appealed to the Massachusetts Supreme Judicial Court, which overruled the earlier precedent that had held jurisdiction clauses presumptively invalid. On rehearing, the court devoted considerable attention to the shipyard's argument that the action should be dismissed on *forum non conveniens* grounds, since the vessels and most of the witnesses were located abroad, and both the buyer and the seller were foreign corporations.

When the multinational finally obtained a favorable Massachusetts judgment, it moved to attach the shipyard's bank accounts. The Bostonians were surprised to learn

---

3. For a not dissimilar comparison of judges and arbitrators, see Justice Stevens's dissent in Mitsubishi Motors v. Soler Chrysler-Plymouth, 473 U.S. 614 (1985). In a case involving the arbitrability of anti-trust issues, Stevens lamented that the enforcement of arbitration clauses in international business would "dispatch an American citizen to a foreign land in search of an uncertain remedy." He continues: "Consideration of a fully developed record by a jury, instructed in the law by a federal judge, and subject to appellate review, is a surer guide to the competitive character of a commercial practice than the practically unreviewable judgment of a private arbitrator." *Id.* at 666.

4. *See* discussion of Nute v. Hamilton and Nashua River Paper Co. v. Hammermills, *infra* at note 133. Compare dicta in Jacobson v. Mailboxes and W.R. Grace v. Hartford Accident & Indemnity, *infra* at note 132.

that the country in which the accounts were located recognized foreign judgments only on the basis of a treaty obligation. The United States, of course, had never concluded a single enforcement-of-judgment treaty.

Several members of the legal community were secretly delighted with the opportunities presented by this trans-border drama. Three tenure-hungry academics began writing critiques of the Massachusetts judgment. One had a law and economics slant, applying the Coase theorem to the efficient enforcement of international commercial agreements. Another approached the problem from a law and literature perspective, comparing the uncertainties of forum selection with the chaotic forces facing Captain Ahab in Melville's *Moby Dick*. A left-leaning professor attacked the contract as a factor contributing to the oppression of disempowered workers at the shipyard.

The multinational's disappointed chief executive, however, was not amused. Efforts to secure a fair forum had misfired. Outside counsel was dismissed, and a rival law firm began negotiating the multinational's next overseas contract.

2. Staying Out of the Wrong Court.

Imagine, if you will, a rewrite of the shipbuilding misadventure. In the new narrative our American multinational focused less on getting into the "right" court (i.e., the one in Massachusetts) and more on staying out of the "wrong" court (i.e., the foreign tribunal), giving priority to minimizing its risks rather than maximizing its advantages. In the revised script the multinational accepted the shipyard's suggestion that any future controversy would be settled by arbitration in Paris under the Rules of the International Chamber of Commerce.

When the dispute arose, an arbitral tribunal (composed of a Belgian engineer, a Swiss professor and a French lawyer) had no problem accepting jurisdiction. The fact that International Chamber of Commerce arbitrators' fees are based on a healthy percentage of the amount in dispute made their task easier to contemplate.[5] The arbitrators found the ships had not been completed according to specifications. The shipyard was held liable to the Americans for damages incurred by the wrongful sale of the vessels. As required under the 1958 New York Arbitration Convention, the resulting award's *res judicata* effect was recognized in all countries where attachment of the shipyard's bank accounts was sought.[6]

As most scholars know, legal storytelling is problematic, because competing narratives evoke radically different sympathies.[7] Some business managers tell tales of

---

5. *See* W. Laurence Craig, William W. Park & Jan A.S. Paulsson, INTERNATIONAL CHAMBER OF COMMERCE ARBITRATION, Appendix I, Table 9 (2d ed. 1990).

6. *Compare* the arbitration in Case 723, Setenave v. Settebello, Netherlands Arbitration Institute, (Mssrs. Brunner, McCrindle and Vischer, arbitrators) *reported in* Financial Times, 27 Feb. 1986. Arbitral tribunal refused to recognize a Portuguese government decree designed to procure contract benefits to a state-owned shipyard in detriment of rights of foreign purchaser of supertanker.

7. A story about unemployed shoemakers in Massachusetts might elicit sympathy for tariffs, while a narrative about the poor shoemakers in Asia might be told to support the opposite position. On storytelling and legal scholarship, see generally Kathryn Abrams, *Heeding the*

excessive judicial review of arbitral awards at the place of proceedings. Others tell of unfair (from an American perspective) limits to discovery in arbitration, or of an idiosyncratic award rendered by a "wild card" arbitrator. An anecdote occasionally surfaces about an unprincipled compromise reminiscent of Solomon's suggested division of the baby.[8]

The elements of these competing adjudicatory narratives must be weighed carefully. Some aspects of arbitration enhance certainty and neutrality while others do not. As the analysis of the following chapters will show, the certainty-enhancing elements of arbitration are to some extent quantifiable. In particular, the New York Arbitration Convention binds almost a hundred countries to recognize and enforce arbitration agreements and awards. No similar multilateral treaty concluded by the United States will benefit American enterprises that rely on court-designating jurisdiction clauses. The book's final chapter will suggest that the United States should contemplate a network of jurisdiction and judgment treaties, as well as a federal statute to promote the reliability of jurisdiction clauses.

B. JURISDICTION BY CONTRACT.

1. Who Decides?

The absence of any non-national court with mandatory jurisdiction marks most international litigation.[9] In our legally and culturally heterogeneous world, judges sharing one party's nationality risk appearing biased to the other side. And judges from a relatively neutral third country generally will have no power to hear the dispute except as a result of the disputing parties' agreement.

Note 7, continued

Call of Stories, 79 Cal. L. Rev. 971 (1991); Jane Baron, *Intention, Interpretation and Stories,* 42 Duke L.J. 631 (1992); John Batt, *Law Science and Narrative: Reflections on Brain Science, Electronic Media, Story and Law Learning,* 40 J. Legal Ed. 19 (1990); Beryl Blanstone, *Teaching Evidence: Storytelling in the Classroom,* 41 Am. U. L. Rev. 453 (1992); Robert Chang, *Toward An Asian-American Legal Scholarship: Critical Race Theory, Post-Structuralism and Narrative Space,* 81 Cal. L. Rev. 1243 (1993); Daniel Farber & Suzanna Sherry, *Telling Stories Out of School: An Essay on Legal Narratives,* 45 Stanford L. Rev. 807 (1993); Samuel Gross, *Clinical Realism: Simulated Hearings Based on Actual Events in Students' Lives,* 40 J. Legal Ed. 321 (1990); Philip Meyer, *Convicts, Criminals, Prisoners and Outlaws: A Course in Popular Storytelling,* 42 J. Legal Ed. 129 (1992); Jeremy Paul, *A Bedtime Story,* 74 Va. L. Rev. 914 (1988); Carol Weisbrod, *Divorce Stories: Readings, Comments and Questions on Law and Narrative,* 1991 Brigham Young L. Rev. 143 (1991). *See generally, Symposium on Lawyers as Storytellers and Storytellers as Lawyers,* 18 Vt. L. Rev. 567 *et seq.* (1994).

8. *See* I Kings 3:24-25.

9. Notable exceptions include the European Court of Human Rights in Strasbourg, as well as the hybrid dispute resolution mechanisms of the U.S.-Iran Claims Tribunal in the Hague and the U.N. Compensation Commission (Iraq Claims) in Geneva. *See generally,* David Stewart, *The Iran-United States Claim Tribunal: A Review of Developments 1983-84,* 16 Law & Policy in Int'l Business 677 (1984); *Symposium on the Settlement with Iran,* 13 Lawyer of the Americas (U. Miami), No. 1 (1981), at 1 *et seq.,* Stewart Baker and Mark Davis, THE UNCITRAL

The consequences of this cross-border jurisdictional vacuum can be dramatic. Litigation may take place before courts of questionable independence, with procedural traditions radically different from those to which the litigant is accustomed. Proceedings may unfold not in a variant of the language of Shakespeare, but in the tongues of Molière, Cervantes, Demosthenes or Mohammed.

Jurisdictional preoccupations in international business will often eclipse the functionally related questions of choice of law and the enforcement of judgments.[10] Who makes the decision may be more vital to the outcome of a dispute than what rules apply.[11] If a dispute between an American buyer and an Algerian seller were to come before an Algerian court, the buyer would probably be less apprehensive about the substantive rules of the Algerian commercial code (which might actually favor the buyer in some cases) than the court's procedural, political and linguistic neutrality.

The business community has sought to enhance neutrality and certainty in cross-border dispute resolution through mutual agreements to mandatory jurisdiction. As a practical matter, consent to neutral adjudication must be obtained at the outset of the commercial relationship. After the dispute has arisen, an action in a court perceived as more favorable to one party will often reduce the other side's leverage in negotiating for a neutral forum. Once a South American distributor has begun litigation before its own national court, the distributor will normally be less inclined to accept Paris arbitration than it would have been when hoping to conclude the agreement with the United States manufacturer.

Note 9 continued

Arbitration Rules in Practice: The Experience of the Iran-United States Claims Tribunal (1994), William Lake and Jane Dane, *Judicial Review of Awards of the Iran-United States Claims Tribunal: Are the Tribunal's Awards Dutch?*, 16 Law & Policy in Int'l Bus. 755 (1984); The UN Compensation Commission (R. Lillich, ed., 1995); and Markham Ball, *The Iraq Claims Process — A Progress Report*, 9 J. Int'l Arb. (No. 1) 37 (1992). Recourse to the International Court of Justice rests on consensual foundations, usually a bilateral investment or commercial convention. *See e.g.*, International Court of Justice decision in Elettronica Sicula S.p.A v. Italy (the "ELSI Case"), *reported in* 1989 I.C.J. 15 and 28 I.L.M. 1109 (1989). See paragraph 48 of the I.C.J. opinion which recites the terms of Article 36 of the 1948 FCN Treaty between Italy and the United States. On the ELSI case, see generally F.A. Mann, *Foreign Investment in the International Court of Justice*, 86 Am. J. Int'l L. 92 (1992).

10. *See, e.g.* Friedrich K. Juenger, Choice of Law and Multistate Justice (1993). Professor Juenger writes: "Analytically these three categories [jurisdiction, choice of law and recognition of judgments] are distinct.... Functionally, however, the three topics are intertwined. An attorney will be hesitant to litigate in a forum whose choice-of-law rule invokes a law that defeats his client's claim, and he ought to advise against suing in a court whose judgment cannot be enforced in the forum and will not be recognized elsewhere." *Id.* at 3. For a French perspective on Professor Juenger's work, see Bernard Audit, *Revues*, in 76 Rev. Crit. Dr. Internat. Privé 245 (1987).

11. *See* Hanina Ben-Menachem, Judicial Deviation in Talmudic Law: Governed By Men Not Laws (1991, Jewish Law in Context, Neil Hecht, ed.). Professor Ben-Menachem writes, "No law in itself can prevent an unscrupulous judge from thwarting justice." *Id.* at 180.

2. Taxonomy.

Consent and bindingness define international forum selection, and distinguish the process from many of the Alternative Dispute Resolution ("ADR") schemes currently in vogue. Some ADR régimes, such as court-annexed arbitration, are not consensual.[12] Other ADR tools, such as mediation and conciliation, are not binding.[13]

While mediation and conciliation have a long tradition,[14] they will often require litigation or arbitration to achieve a relatively final resolution of the controversy.[15] Dispute resolution that is binding principally from a moral perspective will be more effective in a closely knit, ethnically homogeneous community with repeat dealings among community members.[16] It is questionable, however, whether "reputation-

---

12. On court-annexed arbitration, see Lisa Bernstein, *Understanding the Limits of Court-Connected ADR: A Critique of Federal Court-Annexed Arbitration Programs*, 141 U. Penn. L. Rev. 2169 (1993). *See also* the House of Representatives version of the "Court Authorization Act," HR 1102, passed by the U.S. House of Representatives on 12 October 1993, which would require all federal district courts to implement arbitration programs for federal courts in civil cases under $ 150,000. Other forms of statutory arbitration include arbitration under the Railway Labor Act. *See also* reference to the hybrid arbitral schemes of the Iranian Claims Tribunal in the Hague and the Iraq Compensation Commission in Geneva, *supra* note 9.

13. *See* Thomas Carbonneau, ALTERNATIVE DISPUTE RESOLUTION: MELTING THE LANCES AND DISMOUNTING THE STEEDS (1989); Stephen Goldberg, Frank E.A. Sander & Nancy H. Rogers, DISPUTE RESOLUTION: NEGOTIATION, MEDIATION AND OTHER PROCESSES (2nd ed. 1992); John S. Murray, Alan Scott Rau & Edward F. Sherman, PROCESSES OF DISPUTE RESOLUTION (1989), Chapters II & III; Leonard Riskin & James Westbrook, DISPUTE RESOLUTION AND LAWYERS (1987), Chapters III, IV & VI; Edward Brunet, *Questioning the Quality of Alternative Dispute Resolution*, 62 Tulane L. Rev. 1 (1987); Richard Delgado et al., *Finality and Formality: Minimizing the Risks of Prejudice in Alternative Dispute Resolution*, 1985 Wis. L. Rev. 1359 (1985); Harry T. Edwards, *Alternative Dispute Resolution: Panacea or Anathema*, 99 Harv. L. Rev. 668 (1986); Owen Fiss, *Against Settlement*, 93 Yale L.J. 1073 (1984); Tina Grillo, *The Mediation Alternative: Process Dangers for Women*, 100 Yale L.J. 1545 (1991); Richard Posner, *The Summary Jury Trial and Other Methods of Alternative Dispute Resolution: Some Cautionary Observations*, 53 U. Chicago L. Rev. 366 (1986); Judith Resnick, *Failing Faith: Adjudicatory Procedure in Decline*, 53 U. Chicago L. Rev. 494 (1986); Edward F. Sherman, *Court-Mandated Alternative Dispute Resolution: What Form of Participation Should Be Required?*, 46 S.M.U. L. Rev. 2079 (1993). For a European perspective on ADR, see Jacques Werner, *ADR: Will European Brains Be Set On Fire?*, 10 J. Int. Arb. (No. 4) 45 (December 1993).

14. The Talmud suggests that litigants attempt to settle disputes by conciliation at the outset of a trial. *See Code of Maimonides*, Book 14, BOOK OF JUDGES, at 66-67 (Yale University Press, 1949). The statutes of Ur, a foundation of Hammurabi's famous code, reportedly required that all controversies be submitted to a pre-trial conciliator. See Will Durant, OUR ORIENTAL HERITAGE (1935), at 127.

15. One European commentator has noted, "To put non-binding and binding processes in the same bag when their dynamics, parties' expectations and rules are so different, is bound to create a lot of confusion in the users' minds." Jacques Werner, *ADR: Will European Brains Be Set On Fire?*, 10 J. Int. Arb. 45 (No. 4, Dec. 1993).

16. *See* Jerold Auerbach, JUSTICE WITHOUT LAW (1983). *Compare* Lisa Bernstein, *Opting Out of the Legal System: Extralegal Contractual Relations in the Diamond Industry*, 21 J. Legal Studies 115 (1992). Religiously-based dispute resolution systems, considered to be "judicial" from

based" dispute resolution can be transplanted to controversies among culturally diverse and mutually suspicious (or even hostile) commercial actors. Jewish immigrants on New York's Lower East Side are more likely to resolve controversies among themselves than will the parties to a sale of natural gas by an Algerian state agency to an American multinational, or a joint venture between an Italian designer and a Japanese distributor.

Likewise, recourse to experts is not forum selection. The existence of a dispute distinguishes the exercise of judicial and arbitral jurisdiction from expert appraisement or valuation.[17] Two contracting parties may agree, for example, that certain matters of fact will be referred to a panel of experts. This does not mean, however, that the experts' decision will be enforceable as a judgment or an arbitral award. The role of experts is to avoid disputes, while the function of arbitrators and judges is to decide them.

Forum selection clauses operate in at least five different contexts. (1) The dispute may be domestic or international. (2) The clause may be tailor-made or contained in a standard form. (3) The agreement may cover a present or a future dispute. (4) The designated forum may be a public court or a private arbitral tribunal. (5) Finally, the forum selection clause may confer exclusive competence on a single tribunal, or may acknowledge the judicial power of one place without limiting the authority of another.

The rights of contracting parties will vary significantly depending on whether the choice-of-forum clause refers to a nation's judicial system or to a private dispute resolution process. The term "jurisdiction clause" (or sometimes "prorogation agreement"[18]) is generally used to describe a forum selection device that designates courts to hear a controversy, while reference to private dispute resolution is denominated as arbitration.

Note 16, continued

> within the religious context, will often be binding arbitration from the perspective of the secular legal system in whose shadow they unfold. *See* Avitzur v. Avitzur, 58 N.Y.2d 108 (1983), *cert. denied* 104 S. Ct. 76 (1983), enforcing a husband's agreement (contained in a marriage contract) to appear before a rabbinical tribunal (Beth Din) in the context of a divorce proceeding. *See generally* George Friedman, *A Look At Rabbinical Arbitration*, 1983 Arbitration and the Law 28, *reprinted from* New York Law Journal, 14 April 1983. On the Talmudic prohibition against Jews suing one another before gentile courts, see G. Horowitz, THE SPIRIT OF JEWISH LAW 650 (1963). On dispute resolution through church-related processes, see Matthew 18:15-17 and I Corinthians 6:1-7.

17. *See, e.g.*, the award rendered in I.C.C. Case No. 6535, involving a construction contract, discussed in 1993 Journal du Droit International (Clunet) 1024, *Observations* by Dominique Hascher. The general conditions applicable to the contract provided that certain disputes be referred first to an engineer, which is considered the inception of the arbitral process. On the use of experts within an arbitration proceeding, see discussion of the International Chamber of Commerce Institute Colloquium of 24/25 November 1993, in Charles Jarrosson, *Arbitrage et Expertise*, 1993 Revue de L'Arbitrage 779.

18. The verb "prorogate" sometimes causes confusion because it covers not only submission to a judge's jurisdiction by consent of the parties, but also a legislature's decision to adjourn (or prorogue) its session until a later date. Common to both types of prorogation is the notion of extension. By contract the parties extend the judge's jurisdiction, and by adjournment the parliament extends its debates until a later time. The forum selection usage comes to us from Scots law, and derives from the French *proroger*, meaning to prolong or to protract.

3. Consumer Transactions.

From a policy perspective, the most significant distinction to be made among forum selection agreements is between consumer and non-consumer transactions. Boilerplate forum selection clauses are often inserted in standard form sales, loan and equipment lease documentation, as well as in some international transactions such as ship charters. Negotiated prorogation clauses, however, are more common in more complex international contracts, tailored to a single commercial transaction and intended to protect the parties from being hauled into potentially inaccessible courts.

In international commercial relationships, sophisticated business managers with access to competent counsel look to forum selection clauses to remedy the gaps and overlaps of national jurisdiction. In contrast, a choice of forum or cognovit clause in the standard form consumer contract makes life simpler for the party with the dominant bargaining power.[19] Customer litigation is centralized in one judicial system convenient to the seller or lender. Therefore the even-handedness that commends forum selection clauses to international business managers is often lacking from the consumer's viewpoint. Unlike Western Europe, where statute and treaty generally restrict pre-dispute court selection in consumer and non-international transactions,[20] the United States has no comprehensive legislative scheme to protect against abusive forum selection.

4. Forum Shopping

Court selection and arbitration agreements differ from other varieties of forum shopping,[21] principally because the forum is in theory selected mutually by both parties. In most cases, a freely accepted prorogation agreement may mean no more than an attempt to find relatively neutral procedures and fair judges.

---

19. In the United States, such agreements may be linked to a *cognovit* clause (from the Latin *cognovit actionem,* meaning "he has confessed the action") by which a debtor authorizes an attorney appointed by the creditor to confess judgment on nonpayment. *See generally,* Howard Classen, Jeanne de Cervens, Robert Rowell & James Wise, *Survey of the Legality of Confessed Judgment Clauses in Commercial Transactions,* 47 Bus. Law. 729 (1992). In the United States, state statute and case law generally circumscribe such clauses; in consumer transactions confession of judgment usually will not be valid. *See id.* at 731, n.6 & 758-772. In commercial transactions, clauses freely bargained for have been upheld on waivers of due process rights when a contracting party has designated an out-of-state agent to accept service of process. *See* Overmeyer v. Frick, 405 U.S. 174 (1972); National Equip. Rental v. Szukhent, 375 U.S. 311 (1964).
20. European countries generally allow forum selection clauses in consumer contracts only after a dispute has arisen, when the contours of the controversy are visible and the weaker contracting party is less likely to give up rights without a proper *quid pro quo. See* Chapter VI.
21. The somewhat disparaging and reproachful term "forum shopping" has been applied to the behavior of litigants who seek advantage through lawsuit venue. *See generally,* Friedrich K. Juenger, *Forum Shopping, Domestic and International,* 63 Tul. L. Rev. 553 (1989). *See also Note, Forum Shopping Reconsidered,* 103 Harv. L. Rev. 1677 (1990). Exactly why forum shop-

Sometimes forum shopping is really law shopping: a search to avoid mandatory policy norms of the place of contract performance. For example, courts of one country might refuse to enforce exculpatory clauses limiting one side's liability, or might apply their own antitrust law notwithstanding the contracting parties' agreement to the contrary.[22] In such cases, merchants usually will choose a particular court for the dependability of these judges in enforcing the contract as the parties wrote it.

C. ADJUDICATORY NEUTRALITY [23]

In cross-border contract negotiations, the genesis of forum selection clauses derives from each side's concern about the fairness of the dispute resolution process, rather than from sensitivity to speed, cost or the proper application of national legal precedents. Merchants, manufacturers and bankers haunted by the specter of non-neutral foreign courts agree to the jurisdiction of a third-country court or arbitral tribunal in order to reduce the prospect of adjudication in the adversary's home country.

Anxiety over adjudicatory neutrality has both a political and a procedural aspect. Political neutrality relates primarily to the potential bias of the adjudicator. Concerns about procedural neutrality, however, center on awkwardly unfamiliar maneuvers before a foreign tribunal, regardless of the judge's impartiality. A Boston merchant who did not doubt a French judge's relative objectivity might still feel at a procedural disadvantage before the French court. The same Boston merchant, however, might worry about both the political predisposition of a judge in Baghdad (following the 1990-91 Gulf War) as well as the unfamiliarity of Iraqi civil procedure.

In a domestic consumer transaction, however, the neutrality factor often has an entirely different cast. A jurisdiction or arbitration clause contained in a standard form contract sometimes imposes a forum that may not prove accessible to the consumer. Ironically, the very value of fair adjudication that justifies enforcement of forum selection clauses in international business will often condemn such clauses in a domestic context.

D. CONTEMPLATING OPTIONS: COURTS OR ARBITRATORS?

A typical court-selecting jurisdiction clause in an international contract normally provides for the exclusive jurisdiction of courts in a country other than the residence of

Note 21, continued
    ping should be considered harmful remains obscure. The United States Supreme Court's disapproval of forum shopping was part of the justification for its 1938 decision in Erie v. Tompkins, 304 U.S. 64 (1938). Sometimes criticized as inefficient or even unethical, forum shopping opens the door to more than one possible adjudicator to hear a controversy. On the "*ex post* uniqueness" goal of conflicts resolution, *see* Joseph H. Sommer, *The Subsidiary: Doctrine Without A Cause?*, 59 Fordham L. Rev. 227, 247, 254 (1990).
22. *See* discussion of Bremen v. Zapata, *supra* note 43 and Mitsubishi v. Soler-Chrysler Plymouth, *supra* note 510.
23. *See also* discussion on the academic debate on neutrality *infra* at notes 726-760.

either party. For example, a contract between a Russian seller and an American buyer might provide that "any dispute arising out of the present agreement shall be decided exclusively by courts in Stockholm." Such a clause constitutes both a consent to suit in the chosen Swedish forum and a waiver of the right to bring an action in an otherwise competent court. A truly neutral third-country court, of course, might have no nexus to the parties or the dispute, raising a risk that the contractually-designated judge will refuse to hear the case.

A variation of the court-designating option, open to an enterprise with substantial economic leverage, lies in a jurisdiction agreement designating the dominant party's home tribunals. Frequently such jurisdiction clauses operate in tandem with a choice-of-law clause, providing that the contract will be interpreted according to the substantive rules of the dominant party's legal system.

Arbitration provides a third alternative. Business managers concluding a cross-border contract often agree to enhance neutrality and certainty by providing that controverted questions of fact and law arising out of their transaction will be settled by an arbitral tribunal. Arbitrators will have nationalities different from the parties and apply non-national procedures in a common language, thereby permitting a less biased deliberation than proceedings before one side's national judges. The panel might be constituted on an *ad hoc* basis, or could be convened according to the rules of an international arbitral institution such as the International Chamber of Commerce or the London Court of International Arbitration.

Given a choice, most American lawyers tend to recommend a clause granting jurisdiction to their clients' home courts. American judges, subject to appellate review, seem more likely to be faithful to the parties' *ex ante* expectations than foreign judges or undisciplined and unsupervised arbitrators. Most practitioners will have a story about an arbitrator who made good (in a commercial sense) on Solomon's threat to divide the baby in two by compromising the litigants' interests instead of rendering a principled decision squarely for the "right" side, usually the lawyer's client. Many lawyers also express fear that arbitrators lack sufficient respect for precedent, procedural safeguards and rules of evidence.

Although hometown justice permits a legal battle to be fought on familiar turf (at least if the hometown is our own), insistence on adjudication in the United States can backfire, bringing about the very evils that intelligent forum selection seeks to avoid: an unenforceable judgment or a decision by a less-than-neutral foreign judge. As discussed later, American courts generally do not treat jurisdiction clauses as dispositive, but consider them only as one factor to be weighed among many in the balance of public and private convenience. Moreover, no treaty network enforces American judgments abroad.

Such lack of clarity invites litigation. The observation that "nothing is final until it's right"[24] has a perverse counterpart in many business philosophies: "Nothing is final if it's not what we want." When one party has a strong interest in resisting the selected jurisdiction, its attorneys can be expected to invoke arguments about

---

24. *See* W. Michael Reisman, *The Breakdown of the Control Mechanism in ICSID Arbitration*, 1989 Duke L. J. 739 (1989) at 744, attributing the observation to Abraham Lincoln.

applicable law or the reasonableness of the designated forum. Even if quality lawyering after extended litigation delivers an appellate victory for a jurisdiction agreement, the intervening delay often will often reduce efficiency, one object of the forum selection exercise.

By giving the alternative forum an excuse to find the parties' agreement inoperative, these legal uncertainties may even assist a judicial hijacking to a foreign court. At the breakdown of a commercial relationship, the litigation strategy of a party seeking to avoid crossing the ocean would normally exploit the ambiguity of American forum selection principles. Old cases limiting the validity of jurisdiction clauses could lead a foreign court to take jurisdiction notwithstanding the choice of an American court. A French company might argue, on the basis of long-standing state law precedent invalidating prorogation agreements, that a jurisdiction clause was void under its applicable law,[25] and therefore ineffective to waive French jurisdiction based on plaintiff's citizenship.[26]

Arbitration will escape many of the limitations that plague court-selecting jurisdiction clauses.[27] National statutes and multilateral treaties provide for the recognition and enforcement of arbitral awards, as well as for the stay of litigation inconsistent with arbitration clauses. Moreover, the losers in a procedurally unfair arbitration will find that these arbitral statutes and treaties generally contain explicit grounds for annulment and nonrecognition of awards obtained through defective arbitral proceedings. In addition, arbitrators will almost invariably be found to hear a case if their fees are covered, and normally need not defer to foreign governmental decrees.

Although private adjudication suggests itself as a path to greater adjudicatory certainty in some contexts, it suffers from its own infirmities. Some subject matters have traditionally been deemed "non-arbitrable." Consolidation of multiparty proceedings may prove difficult or impossible. Furthermore, arbitrators are not subject to the type of appellate review that tends to expose sloppy reasoning and limit unprincipled adjudication.

Comparisons of the relative uncertainties of litigation and arbitration will change dramatically from a domestic to an international context, for the simple reason that the price of ambiguity is so much higher once a merchant has to consider litigation overseas. In a domestic context, the failure to get into a court in Massachusetts usually implicates no more dramatic an alternative than a court in New York or Miami, rather than Boston. Variations in language, Constitutional safeguards and basic notions of civil procedure will be slight. On the other hand, a failed jurisdiction clause in an international contract may mean xenophobic judges, a foreign tongue and markedly unfamiliar court procedures.

As the price of a failed forum selection clause becomes more costly, the practical reliability of an adjudicatory mechanism becomes more critical. A risk-averse

---

25. *See* discussion *infra,* note 131.
26. *See* French Code Civil Articles 14 and 15, attributing jurisdiction to French courts on the basis of the citizenship of either party.
27. As discussed more fully *infra* at notes 227-229, in this article, the term arbitration designates non-judicial procedures that are both consensual and binding. Mediation and court annexed conciliation are excluded from the scope of discussion.

American multinational will not readily accept potential litigation before a judge in Tripoli even if the chance is slight that the contract will go awry. When ambiguity in forum selection invites such dramatically disagreeable consequences, a business manager will normally want to maximize the prospects of a relatively neutral (albeit not perfect) forum, regardless of academic opinions on the doctrinally proper way to look at jurisdiction.

Chapter II

COURT-SELECTING JURISDICTION AGREEMENTS

A. SOURCES OF UNCERTAINTY — AN OVERVIEW

"An abstract term," De Toqueville observed, "is like a box with a false bottom: you may put in it what ideas you please, and take them out again without being observed."[28] The American approach to jurisdiction clauses has been marked by a significant level of such chameleon-like abstraction. Generalizations about the enforceability of court-selecting clauses obscure the radically divergent results obtained in different procedural contexts. Courts have abandoned much of their earlier hostility to contractual provisions that oust one state's judicial jurisdiction in favor of a rival forum.[29] Judges and commentators today tend to characterize choice-of-forum claus-

---

28. A. De Toqueville, DEMOCRACY IN AMERICA, Volume II, 1st Part, ch. 16 at 74 (Phillips Bradley ed., Vintage ed. 1945) (Henry Reeve trans. 1835 & 1840 ed.) (Francis Bowen Rev. 1862). In the original De Toqueville wrote, "Un mot abstrait est comme une boîte à double fond: on y met les idées que l'on désire, et on les retire sans que personne le voie." DE LA DEMOCRATIE EN AMERIQUE, Vol. II, 1ère Partie, Ch. XVI (Gallimard 1961), page 102. *Compare* Sylvia Plath's observation that "the concrete can save when the abstract might kill." Sylvia Plath, THE JOURNALS OF SYLVIA PLATH 287 (1982).

29. *See generally* Anne E. Covey & Michael S. Morris, *The Enforceability of Agreements Providing for Forum and Choice of Law Selection*, 61 Denv. L.J. 837, 839 (1988); Francis M. Dougherty, *Validity of Contractual Provision Limiting Place or Court in Which Action May Be Brought*, 31 A.L.R. 4th 404 (1984); Julia L. Erickson, *Forum Selection Clauses in Light of the Erie Doctrine and Federal Common Law: Stewart Organization v. Ricoh Corp.*, 72 Minn. L. Rev. 1090 (1988); Michael Gruson, *Forum Selection Clauses in International and Interstate Commercial Agreements*, 1982 U. Ill. L. Rev. 133 (1982), at 153-57; Walter Heiser, *Forum Selection in State Courts: Limitations After Stewart and Carnival Cruise*, 45 Fla. L. Rev. 361 (1993); Friedrich K. Juenger, *Supreme Court Validation of Forum Selection Clauses*, 19 Wayne L. Rev. 49 (1972); Friedrich K. Juenger, *General Course on Private International Law*, 193 Recueil des Cours 119 (1983); John McKinley Kirby, *Consumer's Right to Sue at Home Jeopardized Through Forum Selection Clause in Carnival Cruise Lines v. Shute*, 70 N.C. L. Rev. 888, 902-905 (1992); Leandra Lederman, *Viva Zapata: Toward a Rational System of Forum-Selection Clause Enforcement in Diversity Cases*, 66 N.Y.U. L. Rev. 422 (1991); Linda S. Mullenix, *Another Choice of Forum, Another Choice of Law: Consensual Adjudicatory Procedure in Federal Court*, 57 Fordham L. Rev. 291 (1988); Linda S. Mullenix, *Another Easy Case, More Bad Law: Carnival Cruise Lines and Contractual Personal Jurisdiction*, 27 Tex. Int'l L.J. 323 (1992); *Note, Enforceability of Forum Selection Clauses After Stewart Org. v. Ricoh Corp.*, 6 Alaska L. Rev.

es by terms such as "presumptively valid,"[30] "given effect,"[31] "enforceable unless unfair or unreasonable,"[32] and "recognized if freely negotiated."[33]

Nevertheless, choice-of-court clauses may be rendered ineffective due to (i) the lack of any clear enforcement criteria, (ii) the chosen court's refusal to hear the case, and (iii) the absence of any treaty network to enforce the resulting judgment. Moreover, the Act of State doctrine may impede American courts from effectively exercising their judicial power pursuant to jurisdiction clauses when to do so would

---

Note 29 continued

175 (1989); Richard A. Gantner, *Note*, 22 Seton Hall L. Rev. 505, 506 (1992); Ramon E. Reyes, *Medoil Corp. v. Citicorp: Uncertainty Requires an Indepth Inquiry into Forum Selection Clause Enforceability Issues*, 17 Brooklyn J. Int'l L. 687, 697-98 (1991). *See generally* Ved Nanda and David Pansius, LITIGATION OF INTERNATIONAL DISPUTES IN U.S. COURTS § 7.02(1)(e) (rev. 1993); Gary Born and David Westin, INTERNATIONAL CIVIL LITIGATION IN UNITED STATES COURTS 247-50 (2d ed. 1992).

30. *See* Bonny v. Society of Lloyd's, 784 F.Supp. 1350, 1353 (N.D. Ill. 1992); Karlberg European Transpa, Inc. v. JK-Josef Kratz Vertriebsgesellschaft, MBH, 618 F. Supp. 344, 347 (N.D. Ill. 1985); Forsythe v. Saudi Arabian Airlines Corp., 885 F.2d 285, 287 n.2 (5th Cir. 1989).

31. The Second Restatement on Conflicts summarizes the law as follows: "Parties' agreement as to the place of the action will be given effect unless it is unfair or unreasonable." Restatement (Second) Conflict of Laws, § 80. *Compare* the formulation of the RESTATEMENT (THIRD) ON FOREIGN RELATIONS LAW, § 421(2)(g), that a state's exercise of jurisdiction is "reasonable if . . . the person . . . has consented to the exercise of jurisdiction." *See also* § 421 cmt. "h" (a forum selection clause "generally confers on the chosen forum jurisdiction") and Reporters' Note 6 ("Courts in recent years have rarely taken jurisdiction over cases in which a different forum was chosen by the parties."); *Restatement (Third) Foreign Relations Law*, § 482(2)(f): Courts need not recognize judgments if "the proceeding was contrary to an agreement between the parties. . . ;" comment "h" and Reporters Note 5: "[t]he modern trend [is] to give effect to forum selection clauses."

32. *See* Fireman's Fund American Ins. Co. v. Puerto Rican Forwarding Co., 492 F.2d 1294, 1296-97 (1st Cir. 1974); Cuevas v. Reading & Bates Corp., 577 F. Supp. 462, 476 (S.D.Tex. 1983); Hoes of America Inc. v. Hoes, 493 F. Supp. 1205, 1208 (1979); Continental Grain Export Corp. v. Ministry of War-Etka Co., 603 F. Supp 724, 728 (1984); Prudential Resources Corp. v. Plunkett, 583 S.W.2d 97, 99 (Ky. Ct. App. 1979); Air Economy Corp. v. Aero-Flow Dynamics Inc., 300 A.2d 856, 857 (N.J. 1973); Reeves v. Chem Industrial Co., 495 P.2d 729, 731 (Or. 1972); High Life Sales Co. v. Brown-Forman Corp., 823 S.W.2d 493, 495 (Mo.banc 1992).

33. *See* Hamakua Sugar Co. v. Fiji Sugar Corp., 778 F. Supp. 503, 504 (D. Hawaii 1991); Phoenix Canada Oil Co. v. Texaco, Inc., 560 F. Supp. 1372, 1377 (Del. 1983); Exum v. Vantage Press Inc., 563 P.2d 1314, 1315 (Wash. App. 1977); Smith, Valentino & Smith, Inc. v. Superior Ct. of L.A. Cty., 551 P.2d 1206, 1208 (Cal. 1976); *Note, The Enforceability of Forum-Selection Clauses after Stewart Organization, Inc. v. Ricoh Corporation*, 6 Alaska L. Rev. 175, 180-181 & 185 (1989). *Compare* Burger King v. Rudzewicz, 471 U.S. 462 (1985) (forcing Michigan franchisee to defend a rent action in Florida where Florida choice of law clause ensured Florida district court's personal jurisdiction pursuant to the state's long-arm statute did not offend due process). The *Burger King* Court noted that "minimum requirements inherent in the concept of 'fair play and substantial justice' . . . defeat the reasonableness of jurisdiction even [though] the defendant has purposefully engaged in forum activities." Burger King, 471 U.S. at 477-78. For just such a case, see Asahi Metal Industry Co. v. Super. Ct., 480 U.S. 102 (1987).

call into question foreign governmental acts such as exchange controls.

In some cases these potential defects may matter little. For example, if the judgment debtor has assets within the chosen forum, the absence of a foreign judgments treaty may be irrelevant. In other cases, a desire for the safeguards of appellate review and public scrutiny of the adjudicatory process may outweigh the limitations of choice-of-court clauses. In most international transactions, however, the contracting parties will benefit from comparing the reliability of jurisdiction clauses with that of arbitration agreements, as discussed in Chapter III.

At present there exists no multilateral treaty comparable in scope to the New York Arbitration Convention, providing for recognition and enforcement of civil and commercial jurisdiction clauses and/or judgments. In June 1994, however, a Special Commission of the Hague Conference on Private International Law met to consider an international convention regulating jurisdictional matters and the recognition of foreign judgments.[34] Ultimately, this Convention may provide rules that would uphold the parties choice of forum. Until this project bears fruit, however, jurisdiction clauses and court judgments will often lack the treaty enforcement mechanism available to arbitration agreements and awards.

1. Enforcement Criteria.

Outside the contexts of admiralty and federal venue transfer, American courts have taken no uniform approach to standards for enforcement of jurisdiction clauses.[35] Unlike arbitration agreements, which are enforceable under federal statute and international treaty,[36] a court-selecting clause will be only one of several factors relevant to a court's jurisdictional analysis.[37] The enforceability of a jurisdiction clause will be controlled by what one federal court called "the totality of the circumstances mea-

---

34. For a discussion of this project, see Arthur von Mehren, *Recognition and Enforcement of Foreign Judgments: A New Approach for the Hague Conference?*, 57 Law & Contemporary Problems 271 (1994); Andreas Lowenfeld, *Thoughts About a Multinational Judgments Convention: A Reaction to the von Mehren Report*, 57 Law & Contemporary Problems 289 (1994). *See also* Catherine Kessedjian, *Towards a Worldwide Convention on Jurisdiction and Enforcement*, International Litigation News (I.B.A.), August 1994, at 8. For an earlier, now defunct, attempt by the Hague Conference at a jurisdiction treaty, see Convention of 25 November 1965 on Choice of Court, *reprinted in* Hague Conference on Private International Law, Recueil des Conventions, Item XV, at 96.

35. In only one American jurisdiction will choice-of-court clauses today be dispositive on the question of which court will hear the dispute. *See* N.Y. Gen. Obl. Law § 5-1402.

36. Federal Arbitration Act, 9 U.S.C. § 1 *et seq.*; 1958 New York Arbitration Convention, discussed *infra* in text accompanying notes 231-43.

37. *See* discussion *infra* at notes 67-69 and 141-46. One federal district court summarized the situation as follows: "Unlike [arbitration] there is no federal statute which provides an explicit answer to the validity of forum clauses...." Hoffman v. Minuteman Press Intern, 747 F. Supp. 552 (W.D. Mo. 1990) (Franchisor sought unsuccessfully to enforce a clause providing for litigation in New York).

sured in the interests of justice."[38]

When commercial controversies come into federal courts on the basis of diversity of citizenship, federal courts may be required to apply state law to the enforcement of jurisdiction clauses, which in some cases remains hostile to forum selection agreements. In cases where federal courts do adopt their own standards, they tend to rely on malleable considerations linked to the relative convenience of rival fora. No single federal motion exists to enforce a jurisdiction clause, whether by staying inconsistent litigation or by compelling the chosen court to hear the case. Enforcement of a jurisdiction clause in federal court usually will entail a delicate balancing of factors relevant to litigation convenience and fairness; the jurisdiction clause will be just one element to consider along with many others. The resulting uncertainty will invite litigation over the very issue of judicial competence that the parties had expected to settle in advance.

2. Judicial Refusal to Hear the Case.

Courts in the United States are rarely required to hear disputes just because the parties ask them to do so.[39] A contractually-designated court may have no subject matter jurisdiction notwithstanding an otherwise valid jurisdiction clause, or may find that personal jurisdiction cannot be based on a forum selection agreement alone.[40] Courts may also exercise discretion to refuse to hear cases for reasons of convenience and fairness. While one overworked American judge may enforce a jurisdiction clause to clear a crowded docket, an equally overworked judge in the contractually-selected jurisdiction may decline to hear the dispute on the basis that a more "convenient"

---

38. D'Antuono v. CCH Computax Systems, 570 F. Supp. 708, 712 (D.Rhode Island 1983), discussed *infra* at note 68. Rhode Island accountant bought computer system from California seller. Contract contained a clause providing for litigation in San Diego.

39. *See* discussion *infra* at notes 77-111 and 148-164. In this respect, the problematic nature of jurisdiction clauses has been noted in the American Bar Association Third Party Legal Opinion Accord, *reprinted in* 47 Business Lawyer 1 (1991). The ABA Accord provides in § 14(b) that opinions governed by the Accord will be deemed qualified, in that "forum selection clauses are not necessarily binding on the court(s) in the forum selected." See Scott FitzGibbon and Donald Glazer, LEGAL OPINIONS (1992), § 9.10, at 225.

40. Federal courts will lack subject matter jurisdiction, regardless of what the litigants agreed to, unless a dispute raises a question of federal law or implicates the requisite diversity of citizenship among the parties. *See infra* at notes 149-53. With respect to personal jurisdiction, see discussion *infra* at note 154, concerning a Florida decision which held that a prorogation clause was insufficient to create Florida jurisdiction over an out-of-state defendant because Florida's long-arm statute does not provide for creation of jurisdiction by contractual submission. *See* McRae v. J.D./M.D. Inc, 511 So.2d 540 (Fla. 1987), involving a Mississippi lawyer who contracted for the services of a Delaware corporation whose business was providing expert witnesses in malpractice actions. Other states, however, have taken a different view. *Compare* Vanier v. Ponsoldt, Supreme Court of Kansas, No. 66276, May 22, 1992, holding that by incorporating a forum selection clause into their contract parties waive any challenge to personal jurisdiction in the chosen forum.

forum may be found elsewhere. In practice courts may be more likely enforce jurisdiction clauses in order to send the dispute somewhere else than to increase their own workload.

3. Judgments Treaties.

The United States is not party to a single enforcement of judgments treaty in commercial matters.[41] In some cases foreign courts may enforce American judicial decisions as a matter of discretionary courtesy, or "comity." However, the international currency of American judgments can hardly be taken for granted. When claims must be satisfied by looking to assets abroad, creditors frequently learn too late that an American judgment in their favor will not necessarily secure attachment of a foreign defendant's property.[42]

B. THE ADMIRALTY CASES.

The landmark Supreme Court decision in *M/S Bremen v. Zapata Off-Shore Company*[43] enforced an agreement between an American and a German company to tow a drilling rig from Louisiana to Italy. The contract at issue contained a classic prorogation agreement: "Any dispute arising must be treated before the London Court of Justice."

When a storm damaged the rig, however, the Americans brought suit in Florida,[44] where the District Court refused to respect the jurisdiction clause. Prior to this time, American courts were generally hostile to pre-dispute agreements that ousted the jurisdiction of the otherwise competent court.[45] The United States Supreme Court, however, found that the District Court erroneously placed the burden of proof

41. The Hague Convention on Child Abduction is the only treaty ratified by the United States that requires deference to foreign judgments.
42. When courts and assets are more compatibly married, risks can be considerably reduced. For example, a prudent banker would normally take the precaution of securing loans to foreign borrowers with a pledge of assets in the bank's own jurisdiction, thus minimizing situations in which a local judgment would be ineffective for want of security. The loan documentation might provide for disputes arising out of the credit arrangement to be settled by courts of New York, while simultaneously the borrower collateralizes the loan with deposits or securities left with the same New York bank. Even complete collateralization does not always provide security, however. For example, a foreign bankruptcy court might be of the view that one creditor's security interest constituted a fraud on other creditors. The extraterritorial effect of such a foreign bankruptcy finding would depend on the facts of the case.
43. 407 U.S. 1 (1972).
44. The rig had been towed to Florida.
45. *See, e.g.* Carbon Black Export v. S.S. Monrosa, 254 F.2d 297 (5th Cir. 1958), *cert. denied*, 359 U.S. 180 (1959), stating that forum selection clauses were "contrary to public policy and unenforceable." *See generally* Friedrich Juenger, *Supreme Court Validation of Forum-Selection Clauses*, 19 Wayne L. Rev. 49 (1972).

on the German defendants to show that the "balance of convenience" was in favor of the London court.[46] Focusing on the needs of international commerce, the Court noted the value of a neutral forum:

Manifestly much uncertainty and possibly great inconvenience to both parties could arise if a suit could be maintained in any jurisdiction in which an accident might occur or if jurisdiction were left to any place where [the vessel or its owner] might happen to be found. The elimination of all such uncertainties by agreeing in advance on a forum acceptable to both parties is an indispensable element in international trade, commerce and contracting.[47]

The Court of course overstated the case. It is hardly imaginable that a jurisdiction clause could eliminate "all uncertainties" about the place of future litigation. Nor could a jurisdiction clause be characterized as "an indispensable element in international trade," given that a healthy volume of cross-border commerce existed even before the Supreme Court strengthened party autonomy by its decision in *Zapata*.[48]

The Supreme Court did not say that a jurisdiction clause determined which court should hear a case. Rather, it found that the lower court, in granting a *forum non conveniens* motion to decline jurisdiction, had abused its discretion by giving too little weight to the jurisdiction clause at issue. Other factors related to convenience and fairness might still tip the scales against enforcement of the prorogation agreement.

The opinion by Chief Justice Berger left open which national law (English, German or American) governed the choice-of-forum clause, seeming to assume that it would be governed by some sort of international law merchant applied by American courts. The Court also failed to resolve whether its decision was limited to admiralty cases, or applied as a matter of federal common law. It is far from clear whether federal or state law applies in cases lacking a substantive federal question or implicating a rule of federal procedure, or cases in which the contract designates a non-American forum.[49]

Almost twenty years after *Zapata*, another case within federal admiralty jurisdiction led the Supreme Court to reconsider the frontiers of forum selection. While *Zapata* involved a freely negotiated commercial agreement between sophisticated business managers from different continents, *Carnival Cruise Lines v. Shute*[50] involved

46. The judgment of the Court of Appeals was vacated and remanded for proceedings consistent with the Supreme Court opinion.
47. *Id.* at 13-14.
48. Compare the more temperate reasoning in Scherk v. Alberto-Culver, 417 U.S. 506 (1974), in which Justice Stewart referred to forum selection clauses as "an *almost* indispensable precondition to achievement of the orderliness and predictability essential to any international business transaction" (*id.* at 516, emphasis added). Stewart continued to note that "the dicey atmosphere of . . . a legal no-man's-land would surely damage the fabric of international commerce and trade, and imperil the willingness and ability of businessmen to enter into international commercial agreements." *Id.* at 517.
49. *See generally*, Friedrich Juenger, CHOICE OF LAW AND MULTISTATE JUSTICE (1993), at 213-16. For one case that applied the *Zapata* approach to selection of foreign fora, see Royal Bed & Spring Co. v. Famossul Industria e Comercio de Moveis Ltda, 906 F.2d 45 (1st Cir. 1990).
50. 499 U.S. 585 (1991). *Compare* Lauro Lines v. Chasser, 490 U.S. 495 (1989), arising out of the hijack of the *Achille Lauro* by Arab terrorists in 1985. Suit in the S.D.N.Y. for wrongful death

a consumer contract incorporating twenty-five paragraphs of fine print attached to the back of a passenger ticket. Through their local travel agent, a couple from the State of Washington purchased a one week vacation cruise ticket between Los Angeles and Mexico.[51] After the unfortunate wife slipped during a guided tour of the ship's galley, the couple filed suit in the U.S. District Court for the Western District of Washington: she for injuries, and he for loss of consortium.[52]

A sentence in one of the boilerplate clauses attached to the ticket provided that "all disputes...shall be litigated before a Court located in the State of Florida, U.S.A., to the exclusion of the Courts of any other state or country." After several trips through the federal and state court systems,[53] the U.S. Supreme Court finally decided that it was error for the Court of Appeals to refuse enforcement to a non-negotiated jurisdiction clause solely on the ground that such a clause was not the subject of bargaining.

The Supreme Court did not say that jurisdiction clauses are enforceable, but only that "a reasonable forum clause in a form contract ... well may be permissible," subject to "judicial scrutiny for fundamental fairness."[54] Justice Blackmun's opinion noted that the Shutes had apparently conceded receipt of notice of the forum clause, thus leaving open the possibility for judges in the future to find similar clauses unenforceable as to plaintiffs who did *not* in fact receive sufficient notice of the forum clause.[55]

Carnival Cruise has been subject to a thorough-going critique. Commentators have observed that the Supreme Court validated a jurisdiction clause in the very situation which should have made it unenforceable as an unconscionable clause contained in an adhesive consumer contract.[56] *Carnival Cruise* seemed not to recognize those

---

Note 50, continued

of passenger Leon Klinghoffer was resisted by Lauro Lines on the basis of a forum selection clause printed on the passenger ticket requiring that suit be brought in Italy. The Supreme Court held that a motion to dismiss based on a forum selection clause was not unappealable under 28 U.S.C. § 1291. *See* discussion in Lee R. Hardee, *Comment, Enforcing Forum Selection Clauses*, 1990 J. Disp. Resol. 401, 408-09; Edward Purcell, *Geography as a Litigation Weapon: Consumers, Forum-Selection Clauses and the Rehnquist Court*, 40 U.C.L.A. Law Rev. 423 (1992).

51. Carnival Cruise Lines Inc. had its principal place of business in Miami, although it claimed to be incorporated in Panama.

52. Shute v. Carnival Cruise Lines Inc., 1988 Am. Mar. Cases 591 (W.D. Wash. 1987).

53. The Court of Appeals at one point certified to the Washington Supreme Court the question of whether its long-arm statute reached Carnival Cruise's activities in the state, Shute v. Carnival Cruise, 783 P.2d at 79.

54. Carnival Cruise Lines, 499 U.S. 585, at 593 and 595.

55. *Id.* at 595. *See* Carnival Cruise Lines v. Superior Court of California, County of Los Angeles, 234 Cal.App.3d 1019, 286 Cal.Reptr. 323 (1991), involving more than two hundred cruise passengers who sought damages for injuries during a storm. On remand by the U.S. Supreme Court in light of Carnival Cruise v. Shute (111 S.Ct. 1614), the California Court of Appeal held that the forum selection clause would be unenforceable as to any plaintiff with insufficient notice of the clause prior to entering into the contract.

56. *See, e.g.*, Mullenix, *Another Easy Case, supra* note 29, at 359. *Compare* comment by Judge Posner in Northwestern Nat'l Ins. v. Donovan, 916 F.2d 372 (7th Cir. 1990): "If there ever was a case for stretching the concept of fraud in the name of unconscionability it was [*Carnival Cruise*]; and perhaps no stretch was necessary." *Id.* at 376. *See also* Note, *Carnival's Got the Fun ... And The Forum*, 53 U. Pitt. L. Rev. 1025 (1992).

normal contract doctrines that permit courts to disregard terms that are uncon-scionable[57] or contained in standard-form contracts.[58]

Legislators as well as scholars have been skeptical of the wisdom of *Carnival Cruise*. The year after the Supreme Court's decision, Congress inserted the adjective "any" before the word "court" in the 1936 Limitation of Shipowner's Liability Act.[59] The prior version of the Act made it unlawful for shipowners to "lessen, weaken or avoid the right of any claimant to a trial by court of competent jurisdiction" with respect to liability for loss or injury.[60] In *Carnival Cruise* the Court had reasoned that since litigation could go forward in Florida, the forum-selection clause in question did not lessen a right to "trial by [a] court of competent jurisdiction,"[61] a conclusion made possible by reading the indefinite article "a" into the statute. According to the legislative history of the 1992 amendment, addition of the word "any" before the ref-erence to "court," was intended to "overturn the result in *Carnival Cruise* ... [in order to] further the plaintiff's due process rights."[62]

One need not disapprove of all jurisdiction clauses in order to question the result in *Carnival Cruise*.[63] The true justification for prorogation agreements lies not so much in a theoretical assumption about the economic efficiency resulting from free-dom of contract, but in the practical enhancement of adjudicatory neutrality among parties from different countries. The Court in *Zapata* confronted a conflict between legal systems markedly different in language and procedures: Americans did not wish to litigate in Germany, and Germans wanted to avoid American courts. In *Carnival Cruise*, however, the dispute was between parties with substantial connections to the same country.[64] In this context, pre-dispute changes to normal jurisdictional rules might operate most fairly if combined with consumer protection measures giving commercially unsophisticated parties a non-waivable right to pursue claims in the court system of their domicile.

C. THE REGRETTED CHOICE.

When business managers have second thoughts about the wisdom of a jurisdiction clause, American case law provides an ample number of hooks on which to hang a challenge to the regretted choice. In deciding whether to honor a jurisdiction clause,

---

57. *See* RESTATEMENT OF CONTRACTS § 208. *Compare* U.C.C. § 2-302.
58. RESTATEMENT OF CONTRACTS § 211(3), dealing with terms contained in "standardized" writ-ten agreements when one party has reason to believe that the other party would not have assented had it been aware of the term's existence.
59. Marine Mammal Health and Stranding Response Act. P.L. 102-587 (Ocean Act of 1992) Title III, § 3006, 106 Stat. 5068.
60. 46 U.S.C. § 183c.
61. 499 U.S. 596.
62. CONGRESSIONAL RECORD, HOUSE, Oct. 5, 1992, H 11785, col. 2. (remarks by Mr. Studds).
63. *See* Mullenix, *Another Easy Case, supra* note 29 at 359, calling forum selection clauses "a bad idea."
64. The Shute household and the cruise line headquarters were both within the United States.

courts may balance factors related to the convenience of alternative fora. No statute mandates enforcement of the parties' agreement. The parties' contractual choice can be defeated by a finding that the jurisdiction clause is unreasonable, that subject matter jurisdiction is lacking, or that the contractually-designated forum is inconvenient.

1. Unreasonable Agreements.

In *Zapata* the Court made suitable reservations relating to the reasonableness of forum selection arrangements, saying that American courts would not enforce agreements that were "unreasonable or unjust, or ... invalid for such reasons as fraud or overreaching."[65] Since then, however, the Court has given little in the way of consistent guidance about what sort of agreement is "reasonable."[66] Any attempt to sketch the contours of reasonableness in forum selection will be less a guide to how courts necessarily behave than a laundry list of grounds on which a jurisdiction clause can be ignored.

Some courts are more systematic than others in their approach to the methodology used to determine "reasonableness." A case decided in the Southern District of New York, for example, listed only two factors (albeit broad ones) relevant to enforcement of a forum selection clause: the interests of the litigants and the public interest.[67] In contrast, the Federal District Court in Rhode Island has set forth nine factors relevant to the reasonableness of a forum selection clause: (1) the contract's substantive governing law; (2) the place of execution of the contract; (3) the place of performance of the relevant transactions; (4) the type of remedies available in the designated forum; (5) the public policy of the alternate forum; (6) the location of the parties, witnesses and evidence; (7) the relative bargaining power of the parties; (8) fraud, undue influence or "other extenuating or exacerbating circumstances;" and (9) the "conduct of the parties."[68] The Rhode Island Court emphasized a flexible approach, stating that what would ultimately control would be "the totality of the circumstances measured

---

65. 407 U.S. at 12. The Court noted in *Zapata* that the choice of forum was made "in arms-length negotiation by experienced and sophisticated businessmen." The Court assumed that the selection of a London court was "a reasonable effort to bring vital certainty to this international transaction and to provide a neutral forum experienced and capable in the resolution of admiralty litigation." 407 U.S. at 17. The English Court in the companion case accepted jurisdiction despite the absence of any connection between the transaction and the parties. *See* Unterwesser Reederei GmbH v. Zapata Off-Shore Company, [1968] 2 Lloyd's L. Rep. 158 (Ct. App.), stating that judicial discretion "will be exercised in favor of holding parties to their bargain." *Id.* at 163.

66. Compare the caveat about "reasonableness" in Bremen v. Zapata with the decision in Carnival Cruise v. Shute, *supra* note 50, where the Supreme Court refused to invalidate a jurisdiction stipulation in fine print on the back of a cruise line ticket, even though the ticket had not been seen by the consumers until *after* purchase, and sent a Washington couple to courts at the other end of the country from where they lived and bought their ticket.

67. Weiss v. Columbia Pictures Television, 801 F. Supp. 1276 (S.D.N.Y. 1992).

68. D'Antuono v. CCH Computax Systems, *supra* note 38, at 708.

in the interests of justice."[69]

The more frequent and straightforward defects in court-selecting jurisdiction clauses can be separated into three groups: (i) a clause is invalid in itself because it runs afoul of common law contract defenses such as fraud, lack of notice, or unequal bargaining power, (ii) a forum by its very nature proves to be remote, inconvenient or unfair, and (iii) a statute limits the application of a forum selection clause on public policy grounds.

a. Infirmities in the Jurisdiction Clause.[70]

One predicate for enforcement of a jurisdiction clause, according to the United States Supreme Court, is that the agreement itself be "freely negotiated" and "unaffected by fraud, undue influence or overweening bargaining power."[71] Elaboration of criteria by which to determine when a jurisdiction clause will be tainted by such fraud or unconscionability[72] has been left to the courts,[73] as have defenses based on the use of standardized agreements and contracts of adhesion.[74] In contrast to the decision in *Carnival Cruise*, at least two federal circuits have taken a more paternalistic approach to free bargaining for a litigation situs. In one case, a Massachusetts corporation entered into an equipment finance lease with an auto repair business in Georgia, containing a submission to jurisdiction of courts within the state of Oregon.[75] The jurisdiction clause was denied enforcement on the basis of evidence showing that there was in fact no bargaining for the forum in question. Likewise, in litigation arising out

---

69. *Id.* at 712.
70. *See generally*, Michael Gruson, *Controlling Site of Litigation*, in SOVEREIGN LENDING: MANAGING LEGAL RISK 29 (M. Gruson & R. Reisner, eds. 1984), at 33-38; Michael Gruson, *Forum-Selection Clauses in International and Interstate Commercial Agreements*, 1982 U. Ill. L. Rev. 133 (1982); James H. Carter, *Dispute Resolution and International Agreements*, in INTERNATIONAL ALTERNATIVE DISPUTE RESOLUTION, Chapter 4 (Business Laws Inc., William A. Hancock Editor 1983); David Epstein & Jeffrey Snyder, INTERNATIONAL LITIGATION: GUIDE TO JURISDICTION PRACTICE & STRATEGY (1989).
71. Bremen v. Zapata Off-Shore, 407 U.S. 1, 12 (1972). Similar limits on arbitration clauses were set forth by the Supreme Court in another landmark forum selection decision, Scherk v. Alberto-Culver, in which the Court said that an arbitration clause is "not enforceable if the inclusion of that clause in the contract was the product of fraud or coercion." *See* Scherk v. Alberto-Culver, 417 U.S. 506 (1974), at 519, n. 14.
72. *See* RESTATEMENT OF CONTRACTS, § 208. Compare UNIFORM COMMERCIAL CODE, § 2-302.
73. *See, e.g.*, Interamerican Trade Corp. v. Companhia Fabricadora De Pecas, (6th Cir. 1992); Royal Bed & Spring Co. v. Famossol Industria, 906 F.2d 45, 53 (1st Cir. 1990); Manrique v. Fabbri, 493 So.2d 437, 439 (Fla. 1986); Hauenstein & Bermeister Inc. v. Met-Fab Industries, Inc., 320 N.W.2d 886, 891 (Minn. 1982); Societe Jean Nicholas et Fils v. Mousseaux, 597 P.2d 541, 542 (Ariz. 1979).
74. The RESTATEMENT OF CONTRACTS § 211(3) provides that terms of a "standardized" contract are not part of the agreement if one party has reason to believe that another would not have assented if he/she knew that the writing contained the offensive term.
75. Colonial Leasing Co. of New England v. Pugh Brother Garage, 735 F.2d 380 (9th Cir. 1984).

of the 1985 terrorist attack on the cruise ship Achille Lauro, trial courts found that the thirty-two articles of fine print on the back of the ticket gave insufficient notice of the clause conferring jurisdiction on Italian courts in Naples.[76]

b. Convenience of the Chosen Forum.[77]

One might think that a litigant who had agreed to submit to the jurisdiction of a contractually designated court would be precluded from later arguing that his chosen forum was inconvenient.[78] Surprisingly, however, courts have not always adopted this "a deal is a deal" approach. Enforcement of a jurisdiction clause can be conditioned on a finding that the chosen forum is not substantially inconvenient or unfair.

Concerns related to the convenience of the designated court may be more disruptive than the common law defenses of fraud and overweening bargaining power in negotiation of the choice-of-forum clause. At the time of contract formation the parties may have trouble predicting what elements in the configuration of the as yet nonexistent dispute will cause a particular forum to seem unfair. Whereas fraud and bargaining power ought to be readily apparent at the time of negotiations, the same cannot always be said for the constellation of factors that inhere in notions of convenience,[79] including the future location of witnesses or potentially relevant documents, translation difficulties, and public policy.[80] A business manager's crystal ball will

---

76. *See* Chasser v. Achille Lauro Lines, 844, F.2d 50 (2d Cir. 1988) and Klinghoffer v. Achille Lauro Lines, 85 Civ. 9303 (S.D.N.Y. 21 Oct. 1987), aff'd Lauro Lines v. Chasser, 109 S.Ct. 1976 (1989). The Supreme Court decided that denial of a motion to dismiss on the basis of a jurisdiction clause was not immediately appealable as a collateral final order.

77. *See also* discussion *infra* at notes 155-64. *See generally* Andreas Lowenfeld, INTERNATIONAL LITIGATION AND ARBITRATION 263-80 (1993); Ved Nanda and David Pansius, LITIGATION OF INTERNATIONAL DISPUTES IN U.S. COURTS § 7.02(1)(e) (1993 Edition); Gary Born and David Westin, INTERNATIONAL CIVIL LITIGATION IN UNITED STATES COURTS 247-50 (2d ed. 1992); Mark D. Greenberg, *The Appropriate Source of Law for Forum Non Conveniens Decisions in International Cases: A Proposal for the Development of Federal Common Law*, 4 Int'l Tax & Bus. Law. 155 (1986); Hilny Ismail, *Forum Non Conveniens, United States Multinational Corporations, and Personal Injuries in the Third World: Your Place or Mine?*, 11 B.C. Third World L.J. 249 (1991); Harry Litman, Considerations of Choice of Law in the Doctrine of Forum Non Conveniens," 74 Cal. L. Rev. 565 (1986); Margaret G. Stewart, *Forum Non Conveniens: A Doctrine in Search of a Role*, 74 Cal. L. Rev. (1986).

78. At least some judicial and scholarly comment has argued for "placing a substantial burden on the party attempting to renege on its earlier acquiescence to location for suit." Linda J. Silberman, *Developments in Jurisdiction and Forum Non Conveniens in International Litigation: Thoughts on Reform and a Proposal for a Uniform Standard*, 28 Texas Int'l L.J. 501 (1993). Most of the discussion in Professor Silberman's article covers non-commercial litigation scenarios, in which the litigants, in Professor Silberman's words, "do not negotiate or plan in advance about forum choice." *Id.* at 528.

79. *See* factors listed in Copperweld Steel v. Demag-Mannesmann-Boehler, 578 F.2d 953 (3d Cir. 1978) (sale of casting machine; refusal to enforce a clause designating German courts).

80. *See* Union Ins. of Canton v. S.S. Elikon, 642 F.2d 721 (4th Cir. 1981) (actions to be brought in Bremen Germany under contract for shipment of air conditioners from Kentucky to

not always permit predictions about convenience of forum in a yet-to-be-born controversy.

Federal and state courts will generally refrain from exercising jurisdiction if to do so would result in substantial injustice or inconvenience. The doctrine of *forum non conveniens* permits courts to refuse to hear an action on the ground that it may be tried more conveniently or efficiently in an available alternate forum[81] indicated by the ends of justice.[82] By this discretionary escape hatch, a judge can give any of several elements decisive weight in declining to exercise jurisdiction.[83] The Uniform Model Choice of Forum Act (UMCFA), for example, requires dismissal of a case in favor of a contractually-selected forum only if the chosen state is not a "substantially less convenient" place for the trial.[84]

Claims of inconvenience in the contractually-designated forum ought to weigh differently according to whether they are presented by the plaintiff or the defendant. When a plaintiff wishes to renege on a choice-of-court commitment by bringing an action in a court other than the one designated by the jurisdictional submission, a

---

Note 80, continued

Kuwait; forum selection held contrary to Carriage of Goods by Sea Act (COGSA), 46 USC § 1303(8), prohibiting contract terms that result in a "lessening of liability"). *See* discussion *infra* at notes 112-16 and notes 605-07.

81. See Piper Aircraft v. Reyno, 454 U.S. 235 (1981); Gulf Oil Corp v. Gilbert, 330 U.S. 501 (1947). Foreigner's attraction to American courts due to pro-plaintiff tort laws and contingency fees created much of the backdrop for understanding American judicial attitudes toward "convenience" in forum selection.

82. *Forum non conveniens* considerations also interact with concerns about due process and personal jurisdiction. Asahi Metal Indus. Co. v. Super. Ct., 107 S.Ct. 1026 (1987). The Court held unconstitutional a state court's exercise of personal jurisdiction "[c]onsidering the international context, the heavy burden on the alien defendant, and the slight interests of the plaintiff and the foreign state."

83. Federal courts dismissal for *forum non conveniens* relies on concepts derived from Piper Aircraft v. Reyno, 454 U.S. 235 (1981) and Gulf Oil v. Gilbert, 330 U.S. 501 (1947). *See, e.g.,* Howe v. Goldcop, 946 F.2d 944 (1st Cir. 1991), *cert. denied* 112 S. Ct. 1172 (1992), dismissing a securities law action against a Canadian corporation, its officers and advisers for failure to disclose information related to corporate takeover efforts.

84. *See* 1968 HANDBOOK OF NATIONAL CONFERENCE OF COMMISSIONERS ON UNIFORM STATE LAWS (77th Year), MODEL CHOICE OF FORUM ACT, at 219: "A court should not exercise jurisdiction which is based on consent if to do so would result in injustice or in substantial inconvenience." The Model Act also qualifies the duty to stay actions inconsistent with a forum selection clause on a finding that the chosen court not be "a substantially less convenient place for trial" than the alternative forum. See UMCFA §§ 2(a)(2), 3(3) and 4(3). The 1966 draft Act was approved in 1968 by the National Conference of Commissioners on Uniform State Laws. The Act was adopted in two states — New Hampshire (N.H. RSA § 508-A) and Nebraska (Neb. Rev. Stat. § 25-413) — before being withdrawn by the Conference in 1975. *See generally*, PROCEEDINGS OF COMMITTEE OF THE WHOLE, UNIFORM CHOICE OF FORUM ACT, 5 August 1966. 1968 HANDBOOK OF NATIONAL CONFERENCE OF COMMISSIONERS ON UNIFORM STATE LAWS (77th Year) 219; 1975 HANDBOOK OF NATIONAL CONFERENCE OF COMMISSIONERS ON UNIFORM LAWS (84th Year) 142. The Conference explained the withdrawal by citing the Act's limited adoption as well as a constitutional question under Overmeyer v. Frick, 405 U.S. 174 (1971).

forum non conveniens claim should normally require a strong showing that the litigation in the chosen forum would be "so gravely difficult and inconvenient that [the plaintiff] will for all practical purposes be deprived of his day in court,"[85] at least if contract bargaining positions were relatively equal.[86] Yet courts often view the jurisdiction clause to be only one among several factors bearing on whether the contractually designated forum is appropriate.[87]

The Supreme Court has indicated that a domestic plaintiff's choice of forum will be entitled to more deference than the choice of a foreign plaintiff.[88] When it is the defendant who resists the jurisdiction clause, the parties' contractual choice may be given "some weight," but will not be dispositive of the action.[89]

An elaborate enumeration of forum-related criteria was proposed in the Conflict of Jurisdiction Model Act. Proposed in 1989 by a subcommittee of the American Bar Association Section on International Law and Practice,[90] the Model Act calls for designation of an "adjudicating forum." The fourteen factors to be considered in determining that forum include location of witnesses and documents, "interests of justice," "public policies of the countries having jurisdiction," and the "impact of litigation on the judicial systems involved."[91] While admirable as a jurisprudential exercise, the contemplated balancing of these factors is not likely to inspire party confidence in their forum selection agreement, and will put recognition of jurisdiction clauses in the

---

85. Bremen V. Zapata Off-Shore, 407 U.S. 1 (1972), at 17-18. *See also* Full-Sight Contact Lens Corp. v. Soft Lenses Inc., 466 F. Supp. 71 (S.D.N.Y. 1978), refusing to hear a plaintiff complain about forum inconvenience on a motion to transfer an action to the contractually-stipulated court.

86. *See* Kline v. Kawai AmericaCorp, 498 F. Supp. 868 (D. Minn. 1980), at 872.

87. *See, e.g.,* the Supreme Court opinion and the District Court decision on remand in Stewart v. Ricoh, discussed *infra* at note 137, where an equipment dealer brought an action in Alabama in disregard of the contractual stipulation providing for dispute resolution in Manhattan.

88. "When the home court has been chosen, it is reasonable to assume that this choice is convenient." *See* Piper Aircraft v. Reyno, 454 U.S. 235 (1981).

89. *See* National Equipment Rental v. Sanders, 271 F. Supp. 756 (E.D.N.Y. 1967) at 761: "The Court must no doubt give some weight to the agreement on the place of trial ... but it may not treat the parties' agreement on venue as depriving it of the power to change venue if the interests of justice require a transfer." *See also* National Equipment Rental v. Centra Cast Co., 270 F. Supp. 999 (E.D.N.Y. 1966); First National City Bank v. Nanz, 437 F. Supp. 184 (S.D.N.Y. 1975); Leasing Ser. Corp. v. Rich Indus. Supply, 456 F. Supp. 782 (S.D.N.Y. 1978); Coface v. Optique Du Monde, 521 F. Supp. 500 (S.D.N.Y. 1980); Plum Tree v. Stockment, 488 F.2d 754 (3d Cir. 1973). For a case in which the parties' agreement overcame at least some of the chosen forum's inconvenience, see New Amsterdam Casualty v. Estes, 353 Mass. 90, 94-96 (1967).

90. *See generally* Louise Teitz, *Taking Multiple Bites at the Apple: A Proposal to Resolve Conflicts of Jurisdiction and Multiple Proceedings,* 26 Int'l Law. 21 (1992).

91. Judgments arising out of the same transaction are enforced as if a timely designation of an adjudicating forum had been made. Connecticut became the first state to adopt the Act in 1991. *See* Act Concerning International Obligations and Procedures, Public Act 91-324.

shadow of a judge's right to dismiss cases notwithstanding a basis for jurisdiction.[92]

Challenge to courts designated by prorogation agreements can also be clothed in the garb of "public interests."[93] The strain on the court's own administrative system enters into consideration in determining whether a controversy may be better tried elsewhere.[94] The location and/or language of witnesses and evidence[95] may make litigation less expensive in what the court sees as a more appropriate place.[96] Public interests can derive from congested dockets,[97] the burden of jury duty,[98] the complexity of the conflict of laws issues,[99] and the substantive law applied in the competing jurisdiction.[100]

The Supreme Court has avoided deciding whether state or federal law applies to *forum non conveniens* motions in a diversity action.[101] Choice-of-law ambiguity

92. The only model act that does make forum selection clauses dispositive is the now defunct Hague Choice of Court Convention. Convention of 25 November 1963 on the Choice of Court. *See* Hague Conference on Private International Law, RECUEIL DES CONVENTIONS: 1951-1988, at 96. The Hague Choice of Court Convention limits the chosen court's discretion to decline jurisdiction to cases in which the parties would have been unable to exclude the jurisdiction of a particular court due to the subject matter of a dispute; for example, real estate or child custody disputes might be subject to the mandatory jurisdiction of a particular court or courts. Article 5 (by reference to Article 6(2)) provides that the chosen court will be "free to decline jurisdiction" (permissive not mandatory language) upon proof that "under the internal law of the State of the excluded court, the parties were unable, because of the subject matter, to agree to exclude the jurisdiction of the courts of that State."

93. For example, if foreign realty is at issue, the rival forum might have an interest in having its community values bear on what it views as a predominantly local dispute.

94. *See* Koster v. American Lumberman's Mut. Casualty Co., 330 U.S. 518, 524 (1947).

95. In at least one case a forum selection clause was refused enforcement because of translation difficulties for witnesses. *See* Copperweld Steel Co. v. Demag-Mannesmann-Boehler, 347 F. Supp. 53 (W.D.Pa. 1972), *aff'd* 578 F.2d 953 (3d Cir. 1978). In a dispute about the performance of a casting plant built by a Pennsylvania company, the clause designating German courts was characterized as unreasonable because witnesses spoke English, and the litigation in Germany would require translation and its "inherent inaccuracy."

96. *See*, for example, New Amsterdam Casualty v. Estes, 353 Mass. 90, 94-96 (1967).

97. *See* Gilbert v. Gulf Oil, 330 U.S. 510 (1947).

98. *Id.* at 508-09.

99. *See* Piper Aircraft v. Reyno, 454 U.S. 235 (1981). An aircraft crash in Scotland resulted in a wrongful death action against the manufacturer of the airplane and the manufacturer of the propeller. The District Court found that Pennsylvania law would apply to the suit against the manufacturer of the airplane, and Scottish law to the manufacturer of the propeller.

100. For example, the public policy of one forum, but not the other, might accept clauses that limit the defendant's liability. Normally, the change in substantive law applied by the rival forum would be given substantial weight only if the remedy in the alternate forum were "clearly inadequate or unsatisfactory." *See* Piper Aircraft, *supra* note 99, at 254. *See also* Stangvik v. Shiley, 54 Cal.3d 744, 819 P.2d 14 (1991), staying California products liability litigation with respect to products designed and manufactured in California, in order to allow the suits to be tried in the plaintiffs' home countries, Sweden and Norway. *Compare* Holmes v. Syntex Laboratories, 156 Cal. App. 3d 372, (1984), involving a product liability suit by British citizens against a California corporation.

101. *See* Piper Aircraft v. Reyno, *supra* note 99, at 248 n.13. The court assumed that state law and federal law on *forum non conveniens* were essentially identical.

therefore further frustrates the search for assurance that the parties' contractually selected neutral court will hear their dispute.

Decision-making based on open-ended and ill-determined factors such as convenience and justice may be appropriate for disputes implicating politically sensitive community values. Adjudicators considering hate crimes or free exercise of religion should probably be as concerned about the right result in the case as about consistency. In the global commercial community, however, the relative malleability of convenience and fairness notions defeats the certainty sought by business managers. Merchants who designate a neutral national court to hear future disputes arising out of their relationship will rarely be able to foresee the outcome of considerations related to location of witnesses, applicable legal norms, conflict of laws question, "vexation to a defendant," and the court's own administrative burden.[102]

To take an example, in one recent case[103] an agreement to run a casino in a Turkish hotel[104] provided that it would be subject to the jurisdiction of Turkish courts.[105] After a charge of attempted murder caused the casino operator to flee Turkey, the owners made other arrangements and the ex-operator filed a breach of contract suit in Massachusetts. The district court dismissed the action because of "public interests" that included a crowded docket and the application of a law unfamiliar to the federal judge.[106] The Court of Appeals had different ideas, however, and vacated the district court decision, citing Turkish counsel's failure to address fully the adequacy of Turkish justice.[107]

In a future case involving a dispute analogous to that of the Turkish hotel scenario, unpredictable variations in the fact pattern could affect an analysis of the chosen court's convenience. The private and public interests being considered by the alternative (non-contractual) forum would be weighed differently if the plaintiff was not accused of attempted murder in the chosen forum. Or the affidavit of foreign counsel might (or might not) contain clearer statements on the adequacy of the alternative court. Both aspects of the case will add a legal uncertainty likely to defeat attempts at reasonable risk management.

Political and cultural overtones permeate many cases where the inconvenience or remoteness of a foreign forum trump a prorogation agreement. Not all fora will

---

102. *See* Piper Aircraft, *supra* note 99, at 241.
103. Mercier v. Sheraton International, 935 F.2d 419 (1st Cir. 1991), *vacating* 744 F. Supp 380 (D. Mass. 1990).
104. The hotel was owned by a Turkish investment company and leased to the "Merkezi Boston Turkiye Subesi Istanbul division" of Sheraton hotels, a Delaware corporation with headquarters in Boston.
105. The agreement provided for "jurisdiction will [sic] Istanbul, Turkey." *Id.*
106. *Id.* at 386.
107. Turkish counsel by affidavit had opined that plaintiffs could prosecute "such commercial claims" in Turkish courts, but left out the magic words "for breach of contract and tortious interference with contract." *Mercier*, 935 F.2d 419, 425. The Court was also unsure whether one operator's flight from Turkey because of the murder charge would prevent another operator from bringing an action in Istanbul. *Id.*

appear as fair and accessible as, for example, Switzerland.[108] Iranian courts designated in a contract signed before the 1979 revolution have been found to be "gravely difficult and inconvenient" to the American contractor suing the Khomeini government.[109] In contrast, an employment agreement between two Americans provided that any disputes would be resolved solely by courts of the Kingdom of Saudi Arabia.[110] The court refused to presume a sufficient degree of inconvenience to warrant disregard of the jurisdiction clause, noting that the plaintiff had produced no "specific allegations as to travel costs, availability of counsel in Saudi Arabia, location of witnesses or his financial ability to bear such costs...."[111]

c. Statutory Limits.

A jurisdiction clause might be invalid by virtue of a statute that limits the application of forum selection on public policy grounds. For example, the Federal Employer's Liability Act[112] permits an action in courts at the defendant's residence or place of business, or at the place where the cause of action arose. Therefore courts will refuse to enforce agreements that by their terms exclude these statutorily designated fora.[113] Likewise, a jurisdiction clause may be invalid if the chosen court would result in a conflict with provisions of the Miller Act, which permits subcontractors on public works projects for the United States government to sue a general contractor on a surety bond in the federal court district "in which the contract was to be performed."[114]

Even a statute lacking any explicit jurisdictional provisions may operate to limit court selection clauses. The Carriage of Goods by Sea Act (COGSA) provides that

---

108. *See, e.g.,* Medoil Corp. v. Citicorp, 729 F. Supp. 1456 (S.D.N.Y. 1990) (dismissing the action in favor of the selected forum in Switzerland in a dispute arising out of a bank account agreement raising questions under the Securities Exchange Act of 1934 (15 U.S.C. §§ 78a-78o) and the Racketeer Influenced and Corrupt Organizations Act, 18 U.S.C. §§ 1861-68); Taag Linhas Aereas de Angola v. Transamerica, 915 F.2d 1351 (9th Cir. 1991), recognizing another Swiss forum in a controversy over air transport commissions.

109. *See* McDonnell Douglas v. Islamic Rep. of Iran, 758 F.2d 341 (1985) (The court found that "even if we assume for purposes of argument that the ... forum selection clause is mandatory, there is a 'compelling and countervailing reason' why the forum clause should not be enforced." This reason was found in affidavits concerning the lack of neutrality in Iranian courts at that time).

110. Spradlin v. Lear Siegler Management Services, 926 F.2d 865 (9th Cir. 1991).

111. *Id.* at 869.

112. 45 U.S.C. § 51-60.

113. *See* Boyd v. Grand Trunk Western Railroad, 338 U.S. 263 (1949). *See also* Aaacon Auto Transport, Inc. v. State Farm Mutual Auto Insurance Co., 537 F.2d 648 (2d Cir. 1976), *cert. denied* 429 U.S. 1042 (1977), applying the same principle to an arbitration clause that ran afoul of the Interstate Commerce Act, 49 U.S.C. § 20(11).

114. 40 U.S.C. § 270a-270d. *See* United States ex. rel. Gigliello v. Sovereign Constr. Co., 311 F. Supp. 371 (D.Mass 1970). *See also* United States ex. rel. Portland Construction Co. v. Weiss Pollution Control Corp, 532 F.2d 1009 (5th Cir. 1976), concerning an arbitration clause that was found not to prevent suit in federal court.

"any clause ... in a contract of carriage relieving the carrier or the ship from liability ... arising from negligence ... or lessening such liability otherwise than as provided in this chapter shall be null and void and of no effect."[115] Courts have sometimes interpreted this restriction to invalidate jurisdiction clauses in bills of lading that designate foreign courts.[116] In contrast, arbitration clauses in bills of lading have been able to withstand challenges before courts taking the view that the Federal Arbitration Act overrides application of COGSA.[117]

2. Applicable Procedural Law.

Since *Zapata* and *Carnival Cruise* were admiralty cases, they do not bind state courts. Moreover, in cases where federal jurisdiction in a cross-border commercial controversy rests on diversity of citizenship, it is not always obvious whether federal or state principles will govern the parties' prorogation agreement. Although federal law will control a motion to transfer venue from one federal court to another,[118] many international cases will not involve an American transferee court. A foreign court may be more appropriate either because of the configuration of the case (witnesses, applicable law, and related actions) or because the forum selection clause itself designates a foreign court.

Nothing in the Federal Rules of Civil Procedure requires a court to honor a court-selection agreement as such. There is as yet no "*Zapata* motion" to compel respect for a jurisdiction clause. When federal law governs forum selection, the standard for recognizing the parties' choice of court involves balancing several criteria that include location of witnesses, fairness to the parties and the burden on public resources. The court-selection clause may be characterized as the parties' invitation "asking the court to give effect to their agreement," but leaving open to either party "the opportunity to present whatever evidence will move a court in the particular circumstances not to decline to exercise its undoubted jurisdiction."[119]

115. COGSA § 3(8). 46 U.S.C. § 1300, at 1303(8). *See* discussion *infra* at notes 605-07.
116. *See* Indussa Corp. v. SS Ranborg, 377 F.2d 200 (2d Cir. 1967) (Norwegian carrier's bill of lading required suit in Norway for damages to cargo shipped from Antwerp to San Francisco); Union Ins. of Canton v. S.S. Elikon, 642 F.2d 721 (4th Cir. 1981) (actions to be brought in Bremen Germany under contract for shipment of air conditioners from Kentucky to Kuwait.) This interaction of choice-of-law and choice-of-forum clauses will be examined more fully in the discussion of mandatory national norms in Chapter V.
117. *See* Vimar Seguros y Reaseguros v. M/V Sky Reefer, 29 F.3d 727 (1st Cir. 1994), affirming stay of litigation pending arbitration of claims by owner of oranges against vessel and vessel owner for damage during voyage from Morocco to New Bedford.
118. 28 U.S.C. § 1404(a).
119. LFC Lessors v. Pacific Sewer Maintenance, 739 F.2d 4 (1st Cir. 1984) at 6, *quoting* Central Contracting Co. v. Maryland Casualty Co., 367 F.2d 341 (3d. Cir. 1966) at 345. *See generally* discussion of Stewart v. Ricoh, *infra* at note 137, and D'Antuono v. CCH Computax Systems, *supra* at note 68.

Federalism questions will generally serve to delight the party resisting the jurisdiction clause. The transferee forum might still be bound to apply the law that would have been applied by the transferor forum.[120] Moreover, state law governs recognition of foreign judgments,[121] and will often control amenability to suit in federal court.[122]

Absent preemption by Congress,[123] federal courts deciding contract disputes in diversity cases generally will follow the conflict of laws rules of the state in which the district court is sitting.[124] A jurisdiction agreement, of course, is a contract, albeit a contract whose enforcement could be characterized as a matter of either substantive law (creating rights and obligations among private parties) or procedure (determining where an action will be heard). When characterized as a substantive contract question, enforcement of a jurisdiction agreement in a diversity case might be subject to the state law governing the basic commercial document encapsulating the jurisdiction clause, as determined by relevant state conflict of laws principles.[125] The Third,[126] Fourth,[127] Eighth[128] and Eleventh[129] Circuits have followed this approach in diversity cases and applied state law to jurisdiction clauses. Other Circuits have assumed that federal law applies, often with little discussion, and sometimes on the assumption that federal and state law were similar.[130]

---

120. *See* van Dusen v. Barrack, 376 U.S. 612 (1961) and Ferens v. John Deere, 110 S. Ct. 1274 (1990), discussed *infra* at note 147.

121. Svenska Handelsbanken v. Carlsson, 258 F. Supp. 448 (D. Mass. 1966).

122. *See* Omni Capital Int'l v. Rudolf Wolff, 484 U.S. 97 (1987) (case arising under a statute that does not provide for service of process); *see also* United Rope Distributors, Inc. v. Kimberly Line, 770 F. Supp. 128 (S.D.N.Y. 1991), *decision adhered to on reconsideration*, 1992 WL 37644 (S.D.N.Y. Feb. 28, 1992).

123. No federal choice-of-forum statute or treaty analogous to the Federal Arbitration Act or the New York Arbitration Convention preempts state law for court selection clauses.

124. Klaxon v. Stentor, 313 U.S. 487 (1941). In Erie Railroad v. Tomkins, 304 U.S. 64 (1938), the Supreme Court stated, "Except in matters governed by the Federal Constitution or by acts of Congress, the law to be applied in any case is the law of the state." *Id.* at 78. On the *Erie* doctrine, see generally John B. Corr, *Thoughts On the Vitality of Erie*, 41 Am. U. L. Rev. 1087 (1992); Ralph Whitten, *Developments in the Erie Doctrine*, 40 Am. J. Comp. L. 967 (1992).

125. *See* John L. Erickson, *Forum Selection Clauses in Light of the Erie Doctrine and Federal Common Law: Stewart Organization v. Ricoh Corporation*, 72 Minn. L. Rev. 1090 (1988); Leandra Lederman, *Viva Zapata: Toward a Rational System of Forum-Selection Clause Enforcement in Diversity Cases*," 66 N.Y.U. L. Rev. 422 (1991). *See generally*, Linda S. Mullenix, *Another Choice of Forum, Another Choice of Law: Consensual Adjudicatory Procedure in Federal Court*, 57 Fordham L. Rev. 291 (1988); *See also Note, Forum Selection Clauses: Substantive or Procedural for Erie Purposes*, 89 Colum. L. Rev. 1068 (1989) (arguing that Stewart v. Ricoh itself was wrongly decided).

126. Diaz v. Nanco, 817 F.2d 1047 (3d Cir. 1987); Gen'l Engineering v. Martin Marrietta, 783 F.2d 352 (3d Cir. 1986) (state law governs unless significant federal interest implicated); Crescent Int'l v. Avatar Communities, 857 F.2d 943 (3d Cir. 1988).

127. Bryant Electric v. Fredericksburg, 762 F.2d 1192 (4th Cir. 1985).

128. Farmland Indus. v. Frazier-Parrott Commodities, 806 F.2d 848 (8th Cir. 1986).

129. Alexander Proudfoot Co. v. Tayer, 877 F.2d 912 (11th Cir. 1989).

130. In the First Circuit, *see* Rhodes v. Kalenuik, C.A. No. 92-10879-WF (D. Mass. May 24, 1994, available at 1994 U.S. Dist. LEXIS 8644), in which Judge Wolf applied the standards

Several states continue to consider jurisdiction clauses as presumptively invalid.[131] Other states suffer from a jurisdictional identity crisis on the issue. In Massachusetts, for example, dicta favorable to jurisdiction clauses[132] coexists with

Note 130, continued
established in Bremen v. Zapata and its progeny; LFC Lessors v. Pacific Sewer Maintenance, 739 F.2d 4 (1st Cir., 1984), discussed *infra* at note 119; D'Antuono v. CCH Computax Systems, 570 F.Supp. 708 (D.R.I. 1983); TUC v. Eagle Telephone, 698 F. Supp. 35 (D. Conn. 1988); Pappas v. E & J Gallo Winery, 565 F. Supp. 1015 (D. Mass. 1983). Cf. Lambert v. Kyser, infra note 136, where the Court of Appeals for the First Circuit avoided unfavorable Massachusetts precedent by finding the validity of the jurisdiction clause to be governed by Washington state law. In the Second Circuit, *see* Ritchie v. Carvel Corp., 714 F. Supp. 700 (S.D.N.Y. 1989). In the Seventh Circuit, *see* Northwestern Nat'l Ins. v. Donovan, 916 F.2d 372, 374 (7th Cir. 1990). In the Ninth Circuit, *see* Nanetti-Farrow v. Gucci Am. Inc., 858 F.2d 509, 512 (9th Cir. 1988).

131. At least eight jurisdictions restrict forum selection enforceability: Alabama, see Redwing Caniero v. Foste, 382 So. 2d 554 (Ala. 1980); Georgia, see Cartridge Rental Network v. Video Entertainment, 132 Ga. App. 748 (1974); Idaho, see McCerty v. Herrick, 451 Idaho 529 (1925); Iowa, see Davenport Mach. & Foundry v. Adolph Coors Co., 314 N.W.2d 432 (Iowa 1982); Maine, see Bartlett v. Union Mutual Fire Ins. Co., 46 Me. 500 (1859); Montana, see State *ex. rel.* Polaris v. Dist. Ct., 695 P.2d 471 (Mont. 1985); North Carolina, see Gaither v. Charlotte Motor Car Co., 182 N.C. 498 (1921); and Texas, see Fidelity Union Life Ins. Co. v. Evans, 468 S.W.2d 869 (Tex. Civ. App. 1971).

132. *See* Jacobson v. Mailboxes Etc., S.J.C. 2 March 1995, 1995 WL 86940 (Mass.), in which the court stated that it would "accept the modern view that forum selection clauses are to be enforced if it is fair and reasonable to do so." In Jacobson, however, the Court found (i) the contract was subject to California law (thus making the Massachusetts approach irrelevant), and (ii) the court selection clause was inapplicable to claims of fraud in the inducement of the contract. *See also* W.R. Grace v. Hartford Accident & Indemnity Co., 407 Mass. 572 (1990), 582 n. 13, in which the court emphasized that it faced a service of suit clause, *not* a court-selection clause, but added that it saw "nothing inherently inappropriate in a forum selection clause;" Graphics Leasing Corp. v. Y Weekly, 1991 Mass. App. Div. 110 (1991); Ernest and Norman Hart Brothers v. Town Contractors Inc., *infra* note 135; Cadillac Auto Co. v. Engeian, 339 Mass. 26 (1959). Connolly v. Rochester Shoe Tree Co. (Middlesex Superior Court, Civ. Action 93-5190-H, 1994) illustrates the confusion present in many court-selection cases. In enforcing an agreement designating courts in New Hampshire to hear a dispute about a bonus arising out of an employment contract, the Superior Court cited not a single Massachusetts precedent enforcing a jurisdiction clause governed by Massachusetts law; instead the Court looked to (i) a case governed by Washington law (Lambert v. Kysar, *infra* note 136), (ii) a case concerning the choice of applicable law, not the choice of a forum (Morris v. Watsco, 385 Mass. 672 (1982), finding Florida law to govern the rate of prejudgment interest), (iii) a case that in fact refused to enforce a court-selection clause (Ernest and Norman Hart Brothers v. Town Contractors, *infra* note 135) and (iv) the dicta in the footnote in W.R. Grace v. Hartford Accident and Indemnity, discussed earlier in this note.
Federal courts in the First Circuit have on occasion enforced jurisdiction clauses, either on the assumption (often with little discussion) that federal law applies (*see* cases cited *supra* at note 130), or alternatively by a choice-of-law analysis that applies the law of another state whose law looks more favorably on court-selection clauses (*see* discussion of Lambert v. Kysar, *infra* at note 136).

cases holding such clauses unenforceable,[133] subject to the law of another state,[134] or ineffective due to "equitable considerations."[135] In many cases the time and complexity of the court selection process defeats one object of the forum selection exercise: a reasonable measure of certainty that the chosen adjudicator will decide the case without undue delay.

A contract's choice-of-law clause will sometimes be subject to a legal system other than that of the forum. For example, maritime transactions often provide that the law of England will govern the parties' relationship. When an American court is called to enforce such a jurisdiction clause, it is not at all certain whether it should apply its own enforcement standards or those of the party-chosen law. Some courts apply a foreign (non-forum) law to determine the validity of a jurisdiction clause, an approach that may either validate or eviscerate the parties' choice of forum depending on the relevant legal regimes.[136]

133. Under Nashua River Paper Co. v. Hammermill Paper Co., 223 Mass. 8 (1916), confirming the rule in Nute v. Hamilton Mut. Ins. Co, 72 Mass. 174 (1856), Massachusetts courts long held court-selection clauses invalid. In New England Technical Sales Corp v. SEEQ Technology, Inc., 1992 Mass. App. Div. 248 (18 December 1992), the court refused to enforce a California jurisdiction clause in a contract between a New Hampshire plaintiff and a California defendant, noting that it was bound by prior case law unfavorable to forum selection "unless and until the issue of contractual forum selection clauses is reexamined by the Supreme Judicial Court of this Commonwealth." The court also noted that "even if the modern rule were adopted" the enforcement of the clause might have hinged on whether the choice of California courts frustrated a strong Massachusetts policy, such as the Commonwealth's statutory "regulation of fair trade and commerce." See also J.S.B. Industries v. Bakery Machinery Distributors, 1991 Mass. App. Div. 1 (2 January 1991), disregarding a New York choice-of-court clause.

134. *See* Jacobson v. Mailboxes Etc., *supra* note 132.

135. *See* Ernest and Norman Hart Brothers Inc. v. Town Contractors Inc., 18 Mass. App. Ct. 60 (1984). An electrical contractor brought suit in Massachusetts in disregard of a forum selection clause calling for disputes arising out of a works contract to be adjudicated in Connecticut. The Massachusetts court approved "the general attitude of courts toward contractual forum selection provisions [that] has changed in the direction of recognizing them." *Id.* at 65. Nevertheless, the court ignored the contract clause, citing "equitable considerations," which were nothing other than the fact that the lower court had already heard the case in disregard of the choice of forum clause. *Id.* at 67.

136. *See* Jacobson v. Mailboxes Etc., *supra* note 132. *See also* Lambert v. Kysar, 983 F.2d 1110 (1st Cir. 1993). Massachusetts buyer of Christmas trees brought action alleging breach by Washington sellers. The contract contained a jurisdiction clause designating Washington courts. Seller removed suit to federal court and there moved to dismiss for improper venue. The district court and the First Circuit upheld the forum selection clause, notwithstanding the cases cited, *supra* at note 133, on the grounds that the contract was governed by Washington law and therefore Washington law also governed the enforceability of the forum selection clause. *Cf.* Leasewell Ltd. v. Jake Shelton Ford, 423 F. Supp. 1011 (S.D.W.Va. 1976). *See also* Michael Gruson, *Forum Selection Clauses in International and Interstate Commercial Agreements*, 1982 U. Ill. L. Rev. 133, at 156 and n. 228.

3. Venue Transfer.

In *Stewart Organization Inc. v. Ricoh Corp.*[137] the Supreme Court decided that federal rather than state law would govern jurisdiction clauses involving transfer of venue from one federal court to another.[138] An Alabama corporation had entered into an agreement to market copier products for a manufacturer with its principal place of business in New Jersey. Controversies arising in connection with the dealership were to be adjudicated in Manhattan.

When the dealer disregarded the jurisdiction clause and filed its action for breach of the agreement in Alabama, the U.S. District Court for the Northern District of Alabama refused to transfer the case to New York. The Court reasoned that the question was controlled by Alabama law, which looked unfavorably on jurisdiction clauses. The Eleventh Circuit and the Supreme Court took a different view. Both held that transfer of venue from one federal court to another, pursuant to an explicit federal statute,[139] should be characterized as a procedural rather than substantive matter,[140] and therefore federal rather than state law controlled.

Application of federal law does not necessarily mean reliable criteria for enforcing the jurisdiction clause. The Supreme Court in *Stewart* stated that a jurisdiction clause was only one factor to be considered when courts entertain a motion to transfer venue. *Stewart* set up a balancing test, similar in methodology to *forum non conveniens* analysis, in which the parties' preference must be weighed in a case-by-case consideration of the convenience and fairness of a venue transfer.[141] The prorogation agreement might be outweighed by other elements such as the location of witnesses and a "public interest factor of systemic integrity and fairness."[142]

On remand in *Stewart* the District Court in Alabama did exactly what it had done before: the Court refused to transfer the case to New York. Applying the Supreme Court's balancing test, the District Court found Alabama "an entirely appropriate forum" for the action.[143] With due consideration to the availability of witness and

---

137. 487 U.S. 22 (1988).
138. "For the convenience of the parties and witnesses, in the interest of justice, a district court may transfer any civil action to any other district or division where it might have been brought." 28 U.S.C. § 1404(a). In cases other than venue transfer, however, the Supreme Court's decision did little to resolve the basic ambiguity about whether enforcement of forum selection clauses should be governed by state or by federal law. While some federal courts take *Stewart* to stand for the proposition that federal law generally governs forum selection in federal courts (*see, e.g.,* Northwestern Nat'l Ins. Co. v. Donovan, 916 F.2d 372 (7th Cir. 1990); Venners v. Kimball Int'l, 749 F. Supp. 714 (E.D. Va. 1990); Seward v. Devine, 888 F.2d 957 (2d Cir. 1989)), others are less certain that federal law should apply in diversity cases outside a motion to transfer an action from one federal court to another. *See* discussion *supra* at notes 126-29.
139. 28 U.S.C. § 1404 (a).
140. *See* discussion of Erie v. Tomkins, *supra* at note 124.
141. 487 U.S. 22, at 29 (citing Van Dusen v. Barrach, 376 U.S. 612 (1961)).
142. *Id.* at 30.
143. Stewart Org. v. Ricoh, 696 F. Supp. 591 (N.D. Ala. 1988).

documents, the Court in Alabama concluded that "both private and public interests militate against a transfer to Manhattan."[144]

The later District Court decision in *Stewart* underscores the insecurity of jurisdiction clauses under federal standards. Forum selection depends not on the contract clause, but on multiple transfer-related factors, including convenience to witnesses and parties, relative bargaining power, governing law, relevant activities, and congestion in transferee and transferor courts.[145] Prorogation agreements may turn out to be an invitation to adjudicatory foreplay, rather than a mechanism to provide for binding dispute resolution. The malleability and multiplicity of the factors weighed in deciding whether or not to transfer venue will often defeat firm predictions about forum[146] or applicable law.[147]

---

144. *Id.* at 591. The Court of Appeals, however, balanced the relevant factors differently, and reversed the district court for abusing its discretion. *See In re* Ricoh Corp., 870 F.2d 570 (11th Cir. 1989).

145. *See* discussion in Advent Electronics v. Samsung Semiconductor, 709 F. Supp. 843 (N.D. Ill. 1989).

146. *See* Red Bull Associates v. Best Western, 862 F.2d 963, 967 (2d Cir. 1988) (refusal to honor forum selection clause that would have transferred case to Arizona, on assumption that "outside the admiralty realm transfer motions are *not* governed by the standards articulated in *Bremen.*"); Page Construction v. Perini Construction, 712 F. Supp. 9 (D.R.I. 1989) (enforcing a forum selection clause by transferring a case from Rhode Island to Massachusetts); Advent Electronics v. Samsung Semiconductors, 709 F. Supp. 843, 845 (N.D. Ill. 1989) (transfer case from Illinois to California under forum selection clause that "weighed heavily" in favor of venue transfer.); Van's Supply & Equipment v. Echo, 711 F. Supp. 497 (W.D. Wisc. 1989) (refusal to enforce a forum selection clause that would have transferred case from Wisconsin to Illinois; suit involved construction of Wisconsin Fair Dealership Act); First Interstate Leasing v. Sagge, 697 F. Supp. 744 (S.D.N.Y. 1988) (vending machine lessor resists transfer from New York to California residence of lessee; choice of forum clause enforced). *Compare* Lexington Investment v. Southwest Stainless Inc., 697 F. Supp. 139 (S.D.N.Y. 1988), dismissing a complaint for improper venue under F.R.C.P. 12(b)(3), based on forum selection clause designating Ford Bend County, Texas.

147. In some cases, the chosen transferee court might be required to apply the law of the transferor court, thus defeating the object of the exercise. The rule announced in Van Dusen v. Barrack provides that a transferee federal district court must apply the state conflict-of-law rules that would have applied if venue had not changed. Venue transfer does not modify the applicable law. *See* Van Dusen v. Barrack, 376 U.S. 612 (1961). Airplane crash en route from Boston to Philadelphia resulted in forty wrongful death actions brought in Pennsylvania. Defendants moved to transfer action to District of Massachusetts where more than one hundred other actions arising from the same accident were pending. The Supreme Court held that a § 1404(a) transfer from Pennsylvania to Massachusetts should not result in a change of law. *See also* Feren v. John Deer, 110 S. Ct. 1274 (1990). Pennsylvania resident whose hand was caught in harvester sued in Mississippi where defendant did business. Transferor forum (Mississippi) statute of limitations applied in transferee forum (Pennsylvania) in action based on diversity. *See generally* Tom Fini, *The Scope of the Van Dusen Rule in Federal-Question Transfers*, 1992/1993 ANNUAL SURVEY OF AMERICAN LAW 49 (1993), discussing whether the Van Dusen rule applies to transfer of federal law claims.

4. Default by the Chosen Judge.

a. Subject Matter Jurisdiction.

As most American law students are taught, federal courts[148] are tribunals of limited jurisdiction.[149] Their power generally is limited to cases "arising under ... the laws of the United States" (federal question jurisdiction) and cases between citizens of different states or between a citizen of a state and an alien (diversity jurisdiction). When neither basis for jurisdiction exists, federal courts may be unable to hear a case regardless of how eager the litigants are to create judicial power.

Federal court power does not normally extend to suits between aliens.[150] The requirement of complete diversity of citizenship,[151] extended to international as well as domestic cases, means that unless a case raises a question of federal law, one foreigner generally may not sue another in federal court.[152] When a foreign company is an indispensable party on the wrong side of the litigation, the court may be required

---

148. Some state courts are also restricted by subject matter jurisdictional limits. *See, e.g.,* discussion *infra* at notes 184-85.

149. *See* U.S. Const. Article III, §2.

150. By way of exception one alien *may* sue another when a dispute arises under the Foreign Sovereign Immunities Act, discussed *infra* at notes 273-89. In Verlinden B.V. v. Central Bank of Nigeria, 461 U.S. 480 (1983), the United States Supreme Court considered the case of a Dutch plaintiff that asserted state law claims against a Nigerian government entity. The Court held that federal subject matter jurisdiction by virtue of 28 U.S.C. § 1330 (giving federal district courts "original jurisdiction ... of any nonjury civil action against a foreign state") satisfied Article III Constitutional requirement of a case "arising under" federal law. See discussion *infra* at — .

151. 28 U.S.C. § 1332. *See generally*, Charles Alan Wright, THE LAW OF FEDERAL COURTS § 24.

152. *See* Montalet v. Murray, 8 U.S. (4 Cranch) 46, 2 L.Ed. 545 (1807); Strawbridge v. Curtiss, 7 U.S. (3 Cranch) 267 (1806). *See also* Faysound Ltd. v. United Coconut Chems., 878 F.2d 290 (9th Cir. 1989); De Wit v. KLM Royal Dutch Airlines, 570 F. Supp 613 (S.D.N.Y. 1983); Corporacion Venezolana de Fomento v. Vintero Sales Corp., 629 F.2d 786, 790 (2d Cir. 1980) ("the presence of aliens on two sides of a case destroys diversity jurisdiction," quoting IIT v. Vencap Ltd, 519 F.2d 1001, at 1015); Field v. Volkswagenwerk AG, 626 F.2d 293 (3d Cir. 1980); Ed and Fred Inc. v. Puritan Marine Ins., 506 F.2d 757 (5th Cir. 1975); L'Européenne de Banque v. Republica de Venezuela, 700 F. Supp. 114, 125-27 (S.D.N.Y. 1988); Edilio Flores, Saulio Flores and Auto Partes Dominicana S.A. v. Citizens International Bank, S.D.N.Y. Memorandum Opinion, 92 CV 1692 (KMW), 14 October 1992. Complete diversity does not rise to the level of a Constitutional requirement. See cases cited in Gary Born & David Westin, INTERNATIONAL CIVIL LITIGATION IN U.S. COURTS 550 (2d ed. 1992). *Compare* Allendale Mut. Ins. v. Ball Data Systems, 10 F.3d 425 (7th Cir. 1993), where Judge Posner distinguished suits between foreigners from suits between U.S. citizens in which foreigners were also incidentally on both sides of the litigation. In Allendale the Court upheld a preliminary injunction against litigation in a French court in a dispute between American and British companies, on one side, and a French company and its American affiliate, on the other side. Citizens of different states must be on opposing sides of the litigation in order to satisfy the diversity requirement.

to dismiss the case.[153] Complete diversity as a predicate for federal court jurisdiction therefore can cause unpleasant home court surprises for American multinationals.

b. Personal Jurisdiction.

Some courts have required a jurisdictional nexus for personal jurisdiction in addition to the parties' consent. In *McRae v. J.D./M.D.*,[154] for example, a Florida court held that a jurisdiction clause was not sufficient to create jurisdiction over an out-of-state defendant because that state's long-arm statute does not provide for creation of jurisdiction by contractual submission. While the wisdom of this decision is open to question, it illustrates the risk of choosing a truly neutral judicial system to hear a dispute. While in some cases it may be possible to create a nexus with the chosen court by planning for some contract performance in the contractually designated forum, the fabrication of jurisdictional connections is not always a simple matter.

c. Crowded Dockets.

There was a time when judges were compensated according to the number of cases decided, in the form of fees paid by the parties.[155] This practice led to a lively struggle for business among the various courts.[156]

If such case-based judicial compensation had continued, one might well see

153. 28 U.S.C. § 1447(c) provides "If at any time before final judgment it appears that the court lacks subject matter jurisdiction, the case *shall* be remanded." (Emphasis added). On indispensable parties, see F.R.C.P. 19. Imagine that an American manufacturer and its British subsidiary enter into an agreement with a French distributor to sell goods produced by the British subsidiary. Superior bargaining power permits the American company to insist that any dispute arising out of the contract be submitted to federal courts within the United States. When the distributor fails to remit all of the sales proceeds to the manufacturer, the American company files a claim in a U.S. District Court. The British subsidiary's presence as an indispensable party might destroy diversity jurisdiction.

154 511 So.2d 540 (Fla. 1987). A Mississippi lawyer contracted for the services of a Delaware corporation whose business was providing expert witnesses in malpractice action. Other states, however, have taken a different view. *Compare* Vanier v. Ponsoldt, Supreme Court of Kansas, No. 66276, May 22, 1992, holding that by incorporating a forum selection clause into their contract parties waive any challenge to personal jurisdiction in the chosen forum. For a critique of the McRae decision, see Friedrich K. Juenger, *An International Transaction in the American Conflict of Laws*, 7 Florida J. Int'l L. 383 (1992), at 385..

155. On a per case basis English judges sealed judicial writs. *See generally*, Marjorie Blatcher, THE COURT OF KING'S BENCH: 1450-1550 at 39 (1978); Daniel Duman, THE JUDICIAL BENCH IN ENGLAND 1727-1875 at 111-26 (1982). Fees were eliminated by parliamentary acts in 1825 (for the common law courts) and 1832 (for the Court of Chancery). *Id.* at 123-24; Margaret Hastings, THE COURT OF COMMON PLEAS 83 (1971); 1 WILLIAM SEARLE HOLDSWORTH, A HISTORY OF ENGLISH LAW 252-64 (A. Goodhart and H. Hanbury, eds. 1969).

156. *See* John Hamilton Baker, AN INTRODUCTION TO ENGLISH LEGAL HISTORY 48 (1990).

greater judicial readiness to hear cases under prorogation agreements. Today, however, courts designated by forum selection agreements may find little incentive to close the loop and decide a case as directed by a jurisdiction clause. State and federal law do not normally provide for a motion to compel adjudication of a dispute because the parties have asked the court to do so.[157] In an era of court congestion, sending a case away is often considerably more attractive than hearing the dispute.

Most Anglo-American jurisdictions give their judges an escape hatch that will permit the contractually designated court to refuse to honor the parties' attempt to thrust jurisdiction upon the court. As already noted earlier in this chapter, considerations of fairness and convenience can trump an otherwise valid jurisdiction clause.[158] The discretion accorded by the doctrine of *forum non conveniens* generally permits both state or federal courts to invoke matters of public and private convenience to refuse to hear a case.

When one looks at random surveys of what American courts are really doing when enforcing jurisdiction clauses, it becomes apparent that prorogation agreements often serve as a vehicle to clear dockets by sending cases elsewhere. State court cases that commend enforcement of jurisdiction clauses frequently do so either in dicta only, or when dispatching the parties to another forum.[159] Similar patterns appear in federal cases, where many decisions that commend enforcement of prorogation agreements do so in order to send litigation to another court rather than to hear a dispute.[160] Many cases with dicta favorable to court-selection agreements refuse enforcement of the agreement in question due to the forum's inconvenience or unreasonableness.[161] In some federal cases, courts avoid enforcing prorogation agreements by construing them to be permissive rather than mandatory,[162] designating only one

---

157. New York state alone requires that its courts honor prorogation clauses by hearing the case presented. *See* discussion *infra* at notes 184-93. However, even the New York statute is circumscribed by boundaries related to the dollar magnitude of the dispute and the applicable law.

158. *See* discussion *supra* at notes 77-111.

159. *See* cases cited in Appendix K.

160. *See* cases cited in Appendix K.

161. *See* Red Bull Assoc. v. Best Western, 862 F.2d 963 (2d Cir. 1988) (allegation of discrimination); Union Ins. Soc. of Canton, Ltd. v. S.S. Elikon, 642 F.2d 721 (4th Cir. 1981) (despite forum selection clause in Bill of Lading that required litigation in Germany, Carriage of Goods Act applied where terms of forum selection clause represented an adhesion contract); Van's Supply & Equipment v. Echo, 711 F. Supp. 497 (W.D.Wis. 1989) (interpretation of Wisconsin Fair Dealership Act); Continental Grain Export Corp. v. Ministry of War-Etka Co., 603 F. Supp. 724 (S.D.N.Y. 1984) (forum selection clause not enforced where unreasonable and unjust to do so).

162. Courts have discerned ambiguity by playing with the absence of mandatory terms such as "shall" or "exclusive" in the forum selection clause. *See, e.g.*, Citro Florida v. Citrovale, S.A., 706 F.2d 1231 (11th Cir. 1985) (refusal to enforce a clause stating "place of jurisdiction is San Paulo, Brazil"); Keaty v. Freeport Indonesia Inc., 503 F.2d 955 (5th Cir. 1974) (clause that "the parties submit to the jurisdiction of the courts of New York" held ambiguous as to exclusivity).

place among many where litigation might be conducted.[163] Occasionally a dispute will have enough jurisprudential sex appeal that a neutral court will want to decide a case bearing little connection with the forum.[164]

5. The Alternative Court's Jurisdiction.

A court's readiness to hear a case rather than send the dispute to the contractually-designated forum will depend on the answers to multiple questions that judges ask themselves when determining jurisdiction.[165] What are the links between the court and the dispute or the defendant? Is the other forum more appropriate? Did the American lawmakers intend that American courts would apply American norms to the dispute?

A court's power to decide a dispute, often referred to as judicial jurisdiction, inevitably implicates fundamental questions about the reasonableness of national power to prescribe law. Legislative jurisdiction in turn implicates questions about the presumed intent of Congress, the law of nations, Constitutional due process requirements, and the court's own power over a third party recordholder.[166] For example,

163. *See generally*, Gary Sesser, *Choice of Law, Forum Selection and Arbitration Clauses in International Contracts: The Promise and the Reality, A U.S. View,*" 1992 Int'l Bus. Law. 397, noting that such decisions sometimes run counter to common sense, particularly when English might not have been the mother tongue of the clause's drafters.

164. *See* Rep. of Lebanon v. Sotheby's, and Marquess of Northampton Settlement, and Socialist Fed. Rep. of Yugo., 561 N.Y. Supp. 2d 566 (1990). When ancient Roman coins held by a Swiss auction house recently gave rise to a New York state action, the court refused to dismiss on *forum non conveniens* grounds, finding the alternative Swiss forum less conducive to the ends of justice than New York, in part because of perceived translation difficulties and less liberal discovery rules. Zurich was proposed as the alternative forum, presumably because the treasure was to be sent back to Sotheby's A.G. for auction. One wonders, however, whether the court would have been as eager to hear a routine dispute about a distributorship agreement or computer contract specifications. The coins (called the "Sevso Treasure") were contested by Lebanon and Yugoslavia on the basis that the treasure had been unearthed and stolen from these nations in the early 1970's. The dispute among Lebanon, Yugoslavia and the trustees of a British Marquess implicated what the court called the "mystery" of a theft of antiquities from several of the twenty-nine nations within the borders of the Fourth Century Roman Empire. The coins had been sent to New York as part of a marketing campaign intended to culminate in their sale at auction.

165. *See generally*, David Epstein & Jeffrey Snyder, INTERNATIONAL LITIGATION: GUIDE TO JURISDICTION, PRACTICE AND STRATEGY (1993), Chapter 6 ("Selected Issues of Personal Jurisdiction or Jurisdiction to Adjudicate and Limitations").

166. *See, e.g.,* Lea Brilmayer and Charles Norchi, FEDERAL EXTRATERRITORIALITY AND FIFTH AMENDMENT DUE PROCESS, 105 Harv. L. Rev. 1217 (1992). The authors of that article note that defenses in actions based on application of a federal statute that purports to apply "anywhere in the world" would include the argument that Congress did not intend the statute to apply in the particular fact pattern, or that extraterritorial extension of the statute violates international law. With respect to the extraterritorial application of state rather than federal law, there might be additional arguments raised relating to the Due Process Clause of the Fourteenth Amendment.

the power of a court in New York to decide a dispute arising out of fraud in the sale of American securities to a Geneva financial institution will depend on how U.S. law interacts with Swiss bank secrecy.[167]

The United States generally limits its judicial and legislative jurisdiction by reference to a nexus with the regulated person or activity. Even a legitimate basis for jurisdiction may not be exercised in a way that is "unreasonable." Factors bearing on the reasonableness of an exercise of jurisdiction include links with the territory of the regulating country, connections of nationality and residence, and the likelihood that one nation's lawmaking will conflict with that of another.[168]

The application of American economic law to foreign conduct[169] has been most often debated in the context of orders compelling production of documents and antitrust proceedings.[170] Complaints about extraterritorial assertion of jurisdiction, often combined with statutory retaliation from even close allies and trading partners,[171] have occasioned hundreds of law review articles exploring the right test for jurisdiction over foreign persons and activities,[172] either as a matter of law or of comity.[173]

---

167. For a fact pattern involving Swiss buyers and Swiss intermediaries in insider trading, see S.E.C. v. Banca Della Svizzera Italiana, 92 F.R.D. 111 (S.D.N.Y. 1981). For similar cases involving alleged violations of American law through banks located in other jurisdictions, see the two "Scotiabank" cases, U.S. v. Bank of Nova Scotia, 722 F.2nd 657 (11th Cir. 1983) and U.S. v. Bank of Nova Scotia, 691 F.2nd 1384 (11th Cir. 1982).

168. RESTATEMENT (THIRD) FOREIGN RELATIONS LAW, §§ 402 and 403 (1987).

169. *See* RESTATEMENT (THIRD) FOREIGN RELATIONS LAW, § 403. *See also* Timberlane Lumber Co. v. Bank of America, 549 F.2d 597 (9th Cir. 1976), *on remand* 574 F. Supp. 1453 (N.D. Cal 1983), *aff'd*, 749 F.2d 1378 (9th Cir. 1984), *cert. denied*, 472 U.S. 1032 (1985). *See generally* Gary Born, *A Reappraisal of the Extraterritorial Reach of U.S. Law*, 24 Law & Pol. Int'l Bus. 1 (1992); Lea Brilmayer, *The Extraterritorial Application of American Law: A Methodological and Constitutional Appraisal*, 50 Law & Contemporary Problems 11 (1987); Jay Westbrook, *Extraterritoriality, Conflict of Laws, and the Regulation of Transnational Business*, 25 Texas Int'l L.J. 71 (1990).

170. *See* Hartford Fire Insurance Co. v. California, 113 S. Ct. 2891 (1993), involving antitrust claims brought by nineteen states and numerous private plaintiffs for conspiracy among several insurance groups, including English reinsurers and brokers on the Lloyd's market in London. The majority opinion by Justice Souter affirmed the "effects test" for assertion of jurisdiction. The dissent by Justice Scalia approached the question as one of determining whether the antitrust statute itself provided for its applicability to the case. *See also* Laker Airways v. Pan American, 559 F. Supp 1124 (D.D.C. 1983); British Airways v. Laker Airways, [1983] 3 W.L.R. 545, [1984] Q.B. 142. For a survey of cases, see P.M. Roth, *Reasonable Extraterritoriality: Correcting the Balance of Interests*, 41 Int'l & Comp. L.Q. 245 (1992); INTERNATIONAL LITIGATION AND ARBITRATION 47-146 (Andreas Lowenfeld, ed., 1993).

171. *See* U.K. Protection of Trading Interests Act 1980; French Decree of 16 July 1980 (Law No. 80-538).

172. One author has counted over five hundred writings on the subject of extraterritorial application of American law. *See* Spencer Weber Waller, *Bringing Meaning to Interest Balancing in Transnational Litigation*, 23 Vand. J. Transnat'l L. 925, n.1 (1991).

173. Comity is an international version of the golden rule, by which one nation extends to another the type of deference that it would wish to receive for its own normative prescriptions. *See generally*, Joel Paul, *Comity in International Law*, 32 Harv. Int'l L.J. 1 (1991).

Many of the factors relevant to jurisdiction to prescribe law overlap those related to jurisdiction to adjudicate. Judicial jurisdiction generally must be justified by a relationship to a person or thing "such as to make the exercise of jurisdiction reasonable,"[174] including consent,[175] physical presence, nationality, and activity or effect within the state exercising jurisdiction.[176] Reasonableness in the form of minimum contacts with the forum has also been a matter of due process in American Constitutional law.[177]

How a jurisdiction clause will fare against jurisdictional claims of an alternative forum will often depend on the reasonableness of each forum in the context in which the clause is invoked. Jurisdiction may implicate a long-arm statute[178] or property within the forum,[179] or may raise questions of venue,[180] subject matter jurisdiction,[181] service of process,[182] and the convenience of the parties.[183] Whether business

174. RESTATEMENT (THIRD) FOREIGN RELATIONS LAW, § 421.

175. *Id.* § 421(2)(g), including comment "h" and Reporters' note 6.

176. *Id.* § 421(2).

177. Nearly half a century of Supreme Court decisions have required that exercise of jurisdiction not offend "traditional notions of fair play and substantial justice." International Shoe Co. v. Washington, 326 U.S. 310 (1945). *See* Shaffer v. Heitner, 433 U.S. 186 (1977); World Wide Volkswagen v. Woodson, 444 U.S. 286 (1980); Asahi Metal Industry v. Superior Court, 480 U.S. 102 (1987). In this last case, the Supreme Court found that the burden of litigating in the United States could render an assertion of jurisdiction unreasonable, even if minimum contacts with the forum (California) were established. *See generally* Harold G. Maier and Thomas R. McCoy, *A Unifying Theory for Judicial Jurisdiction and Choice of Law*, 39 Am. J. Comp. L. 249 (1991).

178. Recent cases, for example, have held that a foreign corporation's use of a New York bank constitutes a course of business that makes it reasonable for a court to assert personal jurisdiction under New York's long-arm statute. *See* United Rope Distrib. v. Kimberly Line, 770 F. Supp. 128 (S.D.N.Y. 1991). A third-party defendant shipowner (a Liberian corporation with its principal place of business in Greece) was sued for loss of cargo by a Delaware Corporation. The offending account in which the foreign company received payments for hire of its vessel was not its own, but rather the account of another company at the New York branch of Continental Bank International.

179. *See* Banco Ambrosiano, S.p.a. v. Artoc Bank & Trust Ltd., 464 N.E.2d (N.Y. 1984). This episode of the saga of the now famous Banco Ambrosiano scandal involved an action by the Italian bank against the Bahamian banking corporation begun by attachment of $ 8 million representing the balance of the Bahamian defendant's account with its New York correspondent bank, Brown Brothers Harriman.

180. Venue relates to the judicial district most geographically convenient for a suit.

181. Subject matter jurisdiction usually refers to a court's statutory authority to deal with a particular topic. For example, whether a court may enforce an administrative summons for documents, issued by tax authorities, will depend on the grant of authority in the Internal Revenue Code and related statutes. *See* I.R.C § 7402 & 28 U.S.C. § 1345.

182. Service of process is a concept relevant to whether a defendant has received notice of the litigation "reasonably calculated" to afford an opportunity to be present and to be heard.

183. The doctrine of *forum non conveniens* permits a court to dismiss an action, even when the court clearly has jurisdictional power to hear the case, when the relationship between the forum and the dispute is insufficient when compared to another more convenient relationship. *See* discussion *supra* at notes 77-111.

managers do in fact get their bargained-for forum will depend largely on how courts treat these jurisdictional configurations and questions.

D. THE NEW YORK FORUM SELECTION STATUTE.

The more a state limits the jurisdiction of its courts, the less the local bar will be able to sell opinions touting the enforceability of forum selection clauses. Such was the case in New York, where both the Business Corporation Law[184] and the Banking Law[185] restrict state court subject matter jurisdiction in international actions.[186]

In response to these jurisdictional limits,[187] as well as anxiety at uncertainties in predicting applicable law,[188] the New York legislature in 1984 moved to preserve New York's status as a center for international commerce and finance.[189] State courts are now required to respect a choice of New York law[190] and to honor a forum selection clause in a transaction involving not less than $1 million and subject to New York

184. N.Y. Bus. Corp. Law § 1314 (b) (1)-(5)..

185. N.Y. Banking Law § 200-b.

186. Grounds for subject matter jurisdiction in actions involving foreign corporations include a cause of action within the state, the contracts made or to be performed within the state, action involving property within the state, and doing business within the state or subject to state court jurisdiction.

187. Title 14, N.Y. Gen. Oblig. Law, 1984 N.Y. Laws ch. 421. To my knowledge, California is the only state which has had a statute similar to New York's Title 14. *See* Cal. Civ. Proc. Code, § 410.40, repealed by its own terms effective 1 January 1992; Cal. Stats. 1986, c. 968, § 5. For the legislative history of Title 14, see generally, NEW YORK STATE LEGISLATIVE ANNUAL 156 (1984) (Memorandum of Assemblyman Mark Alan Siegel).

188. Choice of law principles gave little weight to the parties' intent in determining the law applicable to agreements with multijurisdictional elements. *See* Auten v. Auten, 308 N.Y. 155 (1954). Rather, choice of law clauses were honored if the chosen law bore a "reasonable relationship" to the contract, similar to the approach of the RESTATEMENT (SECOND) CONFLICT OF LAWS § 187-88. The possibility that a choice of law clause would be ignored raised concern that parties to international contracts would be deterred from choosing the law of New York to govern their relationships, to the detriment of the standing of New York as a major commercial and financial center.

189. One can assume that the standing of New York affected fees paid to local lawyers who might be asked to opine on the validity of the contracts in question.

190. N.Y. Gen. Oblig. Law § 5-1401. The transaction must involve at least $250,000. *See generally,* Edith Friedler, *Party Autonomy Revisited: A Statutory Solution to a Choice-of-Law Problem,* 37 Kansas L. Rev. 471 (1989); Barry W. Rashkover, *Title 14, New York Choice of Law Rule for Contractual Disputes: Avoiding the Unreasonable Results,* 71 Cornell L. Rev. 227 (1985). For two cases arising under the new statute, see Credit Francais Int. v. Sociedad Financiera Commercio, 490 N.Y.S.2d 670 (1985) (Payments due defendant held by New York subsidiary of Marine Midland); Peter Lisec Glastechnisch GmbH v. Lenhardt Maschinebau GmbH, 172 A.D.2d 70 (1991) (German and Austrian companies sue over breach of settlement agreement).

law.[191] Dismissal of such actions on *forum non conveniens* grounds is prohibited.[192] California enacted similar provisions in 1986 which were repealed by their own sunset provisions as of 1 January 1992.[193]

E. The International Currency of Judicial Decisions.[194]

1. American Judgments Abroad.[195]

International business managers contracting with a foreign party will often be haunted by the prospect of a judgment that must be satisfied from property outside the jurisdiction of the competent judge. The United States is not party to a single enforce-

---

191. N.Y. General Obligation Law § 5-1402 (1) provides:

> [A]ny person may maintain an action or proceeding against a foreign corporation, non-resident, or foreign state where the action or proceeding arises out of or relates to any contract, agreement or undertaking for which a choice of New York law has been made in whole or in part pursuant to section 5-1401 and which (a) is a contract, agreement or undertaking, contingent or otherwise, in consideration of, or relating to any obligation arising out of a transaction covering in the aggregate, not less than one million dollars, and (b) which contains a provision or provisions whereby such foreign corporation or non-resident agrees to submit to the jurisdiction of the courts of this state.

192. *See* N.Y.C.P.L.R. Rule 327 (b). It provides:

> Notwithstanding the provisions of subdivision (a) of this rule [providing for stay or dismissal of an action when required by "substantial justice"], the court shall not stay or dismiss any action on the ground of inconvenient forum, where the action arises out of or relates to a contract, agreement or undertaking to which Section 5-1402 of the general obligations law applies, and the parties to the contract have agreed that the law of this state shall govern their rights or duties in whole or in part.

193. *See* discussion of California Senate Bill No. 1804, as amended 25 March 1992, proposing re-enactment of § 410.40 Cal. Code Civil Procedure, but without a sunset provision. In hearings before the Senate Committee on the Judiciary, 5 May 1992, concern was expressed that such measures would invite additional litigation into already overcrowded courts.

194. *See generally* materials cited in Robert Lutz, *Enforcement of Foreign Judgments, Part I: A Selected Bibliography on United States Enforcement of Judgments Rendered Abroad and Enforcement of Foreign Judgments, Part II: A Selected Bibliography on Enforcement of U.S. Judgments in Foreign Countries*, 27 International Lawyer 471 and 1029 (1993); *see also* Enforcing Foreign Judgments in the United States and United States Judgments Abroad (Ronald Brand, ed. 1992) and Ronald A. Brand, *Enforcement of Foreign Money Judgments in the United States: In Search of Uniformity and International Acceptance*, 67 Notre Dame L. Rev. 353 (1991).

195. On non-American recognition procedures, see Scoles & Hay, Conflict of Laws 967-71 (1984); Enforcement of Foreign Judgments Worldwide (C. Platto ed. 1989); Friedrich Juenger, *Recognition of Money Judgments in Civil and Commercial Matters*, 36 Am. J. Comp. L. 1 (1988); Robert Casad, Civil Judgment Recognition (1981).

ment of judgments treaty.[196] Therefore the practical effectiveness of a jurisdiction clause designating an American court might depend entirely on the domestic law of the foreign country where the debtor has property.[197]

Stubborn resistance to a judgments treaty even by close allies and trading partners of the United States is based on concern over extra-territorial application of American economic regulation, civil jury verdicts, multiple damage awards and strict product liability law.[198] A judgment treaty with the United States, ironically perhaps, raises for many foreigners fears about respect for basic procedural and economic fairness.[199] A treaty with Great Britain proved impossible due in part to British manufacturers' fears of multiple damages, notwithstanding Anglo-American cultural, linguistic and juridical affinities.[200]

196. The Hague Conference on Private International Law currently is working on a draft treaty that may, or may not, bear fruit in several years. *See* articles by von Mehren, Lowenfeld and Kessedjian, *supra* note 34; *see also* Michael Cohen, *Hague Conference to Draft Convention on Enforcing Foreign Judgments*, A.B.A. Newsletter for Section on Int'l Bus. L. 4 (Winter, 92/93).

197. A judgment creditor might not care about the other country's attitudes if the other party is unquestionably subject to the jurisdiction of an American court, and had substantial attachable assets within the United States. Thus, banks traditionally favor clauses that designate local courts when the borrower pledges funds on deposit with the bank, obviating the need to worry too much about recognition of a judgment abroad.

198. *See* discussion of U.S. Protection of Trading Interests Act of 1980, and parliamentary debate particularly critical of multiple damages in antitrust judgments. American damage awards may be considered excessive or unjust. In most countries, civil juries are unknown, and thus verdicts tend to be much lower than in the United States. Even in England the civil jury exists only for cases such as defamation, which were once common law crimes.

199. A recent decision refusing enforcement to an English libel judgment provides a reverse twist on foreign concerns about American judicial decisions. A New York state court refused to enforce the judgment on public policy grounds, because English libel law did not provide the media with the same level of First Amendment protection afforded by the U.S. Constitution. The offending article said that Swiss authorities had blocked plaintiff's bank accounts into which a Swedish arms manufacturer (Bofors) had deposited kickbacks. The New York court stated that British libel law places the burden on the defendant to prove the truth of the published statement, whereas in New York the plaintiff bears the burden of showing falsity and fault. *See* Bachchan v. India Abroad Publications, 585 N.Y.S. 2nd 661 (Sup. Ct. 1992).

200. In 1976 the United States and the United Kingdom initialed a draft "Convention for the Reciprocal Recognition and Enforcement of Judgments in Civil Matters," *reprinted in* 16 I.L.M. 71 (1977) (initialed at London, 26 October 1975) [hereinafter Convention]. *See generally*, Peter Hay and Robert Walker, *The Proposed Recognition-of-Judgments Convention Between the United States and the United Kingdom*, 11 Tex. Int'l L.J. 421 (1976); P.M. North, *The Draft U.K./U.S. Judgments Convention: A British Viewpoint*, 1 N.W. J. Int'l. & Bus. 219 (1979); *Comment, The Effect of the Proposed U.S.-U.K. Reciprocal Recognition and Enforcement of Civil Judgments Treaty on Current Recognition Practice in the United States*, 18 Colum. J. Transnat'l L. 119 (1979). After publication of the draft, changes were made in order to render the text more acceptable to British interests. The revised text is published in the Appendix to David Woodward, *Reciprocal Recognition and Enforcement of Civil Judgments in the United States*, 8 North Carolina J. Int'l Law & Com. Reg. 298, 322 (1983).

Lack of a judgment treaty network means that American business managers considering jurisdiction clauses designating American courts must consult foreign counsel about enforcement of judgment rules for each counterparty's country. This expensive venture will reveal that certain countries enforce foreign judgments on a discretionary basis, while others do not.

Some countries recognize foreign judgments on the basis of comity,[201] a judicially created golden rule of discretion and courtesy by which one country's courts respect decisions of another country's tribunals even though under no legal obligation to do so. Such recognition on a non-treaty basis has been the rule in France,[202] England,[203] Germany,[204] and Switzerland,[205] either with or without a requirement of reciprocity.[206]

Other jurisdictions may not always recognize a foreign judgment outside the context of a bilateral or multilateral convention. The statutory law of the Netherlands,[207] Denmark[208] and Sweden,[209] for example, provides no recognition to a foreign judgment in the absence of a treaty obligation.[210] In some countries, the

---

201. On comity, see generally, Joel R. Paul, *Comity in International Law*, 32 Harv. Int. L.J. 1 (1991); *Note, Foreign Judgments*, 20 Tex. Int'l L.J. 217, 219-22 (1985). *See also* cases cited in RESTATEMENT (THIRD) FOREIGN RELATIONS LAW § 481 Note 6.

202. Munzer v. Munzer-Jacoby, Cass., 7 Jan. 1964, 1974 Semaine Juridique II, 13590. *See generally*, Bernard Audit, DROIT INTERNATIONAL PRIVÉ §§ 440-485 at 363-395 (1991); Yves Loussouarn & P. Bourel, DROIT INTERNATIONAL PRIVÉ, §§ 491-509 at 612-631 (1978).

203. A.V. Dicey & J.H.C. Morris, THE CONFLICT OF LAWS 418-508, Rule 35-53 (L. Collins, ed., 11th ed. 1987); J. Morris, THE CONFLICT OF LAWS (1971) at 416-428 (Foreign Judgments Act of 1933) and 518-20 (comity).

204. Zivilprozessordnung § 328(5), requiring reciprocity for recognition of foreign judgments. *See* Peter Hay, *The Recognition and Enforcement of American Money Judgments in Germany*, 40 Am. J. Comp. L. 729 (1992).

205. Loi sur le droit international privé (1989), Articles 25-32. *See generally*, Pierre Karrer & Karl Arnold, SWITZERLAND'S PRIVATE INTERNATIONAL STATUTE OF 1987 50-56 (1989); Olivier Wehrli, *Recognition in Switzerland of Foreign Bankruptcy Judgments*, 2/3 European Report 5 (1992).

206. France, England and Switzerland do not seem to require reciprocity, while Germany does.

207. *See* Dutch Code of Civil Procedure, Article 431(1): "Except for provisions of Articles 985-94 [*re* treaties] decisions rendered by foreign judges or public deeds executed outside the Netherlands cannot be enforced in the Netherlands." (A.J. van den Berg trans.). In practice, foreign judgments may be given persuasive evidence as to the merits of a case in the Netherlands, particularly if based on a forum selection agreement. *See* authorities cited in Rene van Rooij and Maurice Polak, PRIVATE INTERNATIONAL LAW IN THE NETHERLANDS, at 58-75; Joseph Lookofsky, TRANSNATIONAL LITIGATION AND COMMERCIAL ARBITRATION (1992) at 496, n. 28.

208. *See, e.g.*, Danish Code of Civil Procedure § 223-a, and materials cited in J. Lookofsky, TRANSNATIONAL LITIGATION AND COMMERCIAL ARBITRATION 495-96 (1992).

209. Although the Swedish will review foreign judgments, they seem to give them weight as persuasive evidence in the case if predicated on a valid and exclusive forum selection clause. *See* Bogdon, *Recognition in Sweden of Money Judgments in Civil and Commercial Matters*, Nordisk Tidsskrift for International Ret 85 (1985).

210. *See generally* ENFORCING JUDGMENTS IN THE UNITED STATES AND UNITED STATES JUDGMENTS ABROAD (Ronald Brand, ed. 1992); ENFORCING MONEY JUDGMENTS (P.R. Wiener, ed., 1991).

enforcement forum must be officially "entrusted" with a judgment by the foreign court that renders it.[211]

If an American company's counterparty is resident in a country following common law legal tradition, guidance about recognition of judgment principles can be found in the latest edition of the Dicey & Morris conflicts treatise,[212] available in most university libraries. However, other countries present a less comfortable research experience with respect to attitudes toward recognition of foreign judgments. American multinationals doing business in Greece, Venezuela, Zaire or China will often face a daunting task in coming to grips with the relevant enforcement-of-judgment principles and practice.

2. Judicial Hijacking.

When commercial controversies heat up, one common litigation strategy is to raise objections to the jurisdiction or convenience of the contractually designated court in an attempt to hijack the dispute to a rival forum. Such competing judicial proceedings may put assets at risk at home as well as abroad,[213] since foreign judgments will generally be recognized in American courts as a matter of comity.[214] The Restatement (Second) on Conflicts provides that "a valid judgment rendered in a foreign nation after a fair trial in a contested proceeding will be recognized in the United States so far as the immediate parties and the underlying cause of action are concerned."[215] Similarly, the Restatement (Third) Foreign Relations Law provides that "[A] final judgment of a court of a foreign state granting or denying recovery of a sum of money

---

211. For example, Chinese procedure apparently conditions judgment enforcement on an explicit "judicial entrustment" of the judgment by a foreign court to a People's Republic of China tribunal. *See* Article 204, Foreign Economic Contract Law (Zhongua Renmin Gongheguo Guowuyuan Gongbao) published in the Peoples Republic of State Council Gazette, no. 6 207 (1982) (discussed in Andrew Kui-Nung Cheung, *Enforcement of Foreign Arbitral Awards in the People's Republic of China*, 34 Am. J. Compl. L. 295, 317 (1986)). *Compare with* W.D.W. Dennis, *China*, in ENFORCEMENT OF FOREIGN JUDGEMENTS WORLDWIDE 36-38 (Charles Platto ed. 1989) (discussing Chinese "entrustment" requirements).

212. A.V. Dicey & J.H.C. Morris, THE CONFLICT OF LAWS (L. Collins, 11th ed., 1987), Rules 35-53; *see also* J. Morris, CONFLICT OF LAWS 416 (1971), discussing Foreign Judgment (Reciprocal Enforcement) Act of 1933.

213. On recognition of foreign judgments in the United States, *see generally* ENFORCING FOREIGN JUDGMENTS IN THE UNITED STATES AND UNITED STATES JUDGMENTS ABROAD (Ronald Brand, ed. 1992); Ronald A. Brand, *Enforcement of Foreign Money Judgments in the United States: In Search of Uniformity and International Acceptance*, 67 Notre Dame L. Rev. 353 (1991); Arthur Von Mehren & Patterson, *Recognition and Enforcement of Foreign Judgments*, 16 Int'l Law. 425 (1982); *Note, Bachchan v. India Abroad Publications: The Clash Between Protection of Free Speech in the U.S. and Great Britain*, 16 Fordham Int'l L.J. 895 (1992-93). For a European perspective, see C. Kessedjian, LA RECONNAISSANCE ET L'EXÉCUTION DES JUGEMENTS EN DROIT INTERNATIONAL PRIVÉ AUX ETATS-UNIS (1987).

214. *See generally* R. Leflar, AMERICAN CONFLICTS LAW, § 74 at 171-74.

215. RESTATEMENT (2D) CONFLICT OF LAWS § 98.

... is conclusive between the parties and is entitled to recognition in courts in the United States."[216] In the twenty-two states[217] that have adopted the Uniform Foreign Money Judgments Recognition Act,[218] foreign money judgments must be recognized if "final and conclusive and enforceable where rendered."[219] Judgments generally may not be called into question for error of fact or law,[220] although non-recognition is mandated when due process, personal jurisdiction, or subject matter jurisdiction is lacking.[221] Discretionary grounds for non-recognition include insufficient notice, fraud, violation of public policy, conflict with another final judgment, inconvenient forum, and conflict with an agreement of the parties.

Courts generally need not recognize a foreign judgment rendered in disregard of a valid agreement between the parties.[222] The situation is not at all clear, however, when the jurisdiction clause fails to operate as intended. As we have seen, a jurisdiction clause may prove ineffective because of unfavorable state court decisions, indeterminate enforcement criteria or the designated court's refusal to hear the case.[223] For example, a French judgment in disregard of a jurisdiction clause designating Alabama courts might be enforced if the jurisdiction clause was inoperative under Alabama law, or was ineffective because of an Alabama court's refusal to hear the case on *forum non conveniens* grounds.

The absence of any federal statute covering court judgments analogous to the Federal Arbitration Act also means that the dilemma of federal-state controversies will continue to plague the enforcement of foreign judgments in the United States. Federal courts whose jurisdiction is based on diversity of citizenship must apply the foreign judgment recognition rules of the state in which they sit, absent federal preemption

---

216. RESTATEMENT (THIRD) FOREIGN RELATIONS LAW § 481.
217. Alaska, California, Colorado, Connecticut, Georgia, Idaho, Illinois, Iowa, Maryland, Massachusetts, Michigan, Minnesota, Missouri, New Mexico, New York, Ohio, Oklahoma, Oregon, Pennsylvania, Texas, Virginia, Washington.
218. Hereinafter "Judgments Act." 13 U.L.A. 261 (1962). Five states (Idaho, Georgia, Massachusetts, Ohio and Texas) have included lack of reciprocity as a ground for non-recognition of foreign judgments, making enforcement of American judgments rendered in those jurisdictions problematic or impossible in foreign countries that require proof of reciprocity for enforcement. For a recent case implementing the Act, as adopted in Massachusetts § 23A of M.G.L. c. 235, see Desjardins Ducharme v. Hunnewell, 411 Mass. 711 (1992) (Quebec judgment awarding court costs to a Canadian law firm). *See generally,* Alan Sorkowitz, *Enforcing Judgments Under the Uniform Foreign Money-Judgments Recognition Act,* 37 Practical Lawyer, No. 5, at 57; Brand, ENFORCING FOREIGN JUDGMENTS IN THE UNITED STATES, *supra* note 213, at 286-88. *Compare* Uniform Enforcement of Foreign Judgments Act, 13 U.L.A. 149, which applies to judgments of American courts entitled to full faith and credit.
219. U.F.M.J.A. § 4.
220. In some states, application of the Act on the basis of reciprocity opens the way to merits review of a foreign judgment.
221. Grounds for refusal of recognition listed by RESTATEMENT (THIRD) FOREIGN RELATIONS LAW are generally the same. The Restatement treats lack of subject matter jurisdiction as a discretionary rather than mandatory ground for refusal, and does not include *forum non conveniens.*
222. RESTATEMENT (THIRD) FOREIGN RELATIONS LAW § 482(2)(f); U.F.M.J. Act, § 4.
223. *See* discussion *supra* at notes 65-164.

by either treaty or legislation.[224] It is an open question, however, what rules a federal court should apply if asked to recognize a foreign judgment when jurisdiction is based on a federal question rather than on diversity of citizenship. For example, if a federal court were to take jurisdiction over an action against a foreign government, its jurisdiction might be based on the Foreign Sovereign Immunities Act,[225] suggesting that federal rather than state law would apply to recognition of a foreign judgment in the context of such litigation.

224. *See* Erie R.R. v. Tompkins, 304 U.S. 64 (1938). *See also* discussion in Svenska Handelsbanken v. Carlson, 258 F. Supp. 448, 450-57 (D. Mass. 1966). Massachusetts law rather than federal law applied in diversity action between Swedish bank and Massachusetts residents.
225. *See* Verlinden B.V. v. Centr. Bank of Nig., 461 U.S. 480 (1983).

Chapter III

PRIVATIZED DISPUTE RESOLUTION

A. THE CONTOURS OF ARBITRATION.

Surprisingly perhaps, reliability in forum selection can sometimes be enhanced significantly through a contractual exclusion of the jurisdiction of all courts in favor of private dispute resolution. Arbitration will escape many of the limitations that plague court-designating jurisdiction clauses, discussed in Chapter II.[226] Arbitrators rarely decline to hear a case if the claimant can provide an adequate deposit to cover costs. A network of multilateral treaties, reinforced by pro-arbitration national statutes, binds more than one hundred countries to enforce both the arbitration clause and the resulting award in all but the most limited of contexts. And arbitrators generally need not show the same deference as do courts when confronted with foreign governmental decrees such as exchange controls and expropriation orders.

Not all cases will be best served by arbitration, however. Honest judges with jurisdiction over attachable assets can normally deal adequately with disputes even in a court at the foreign party's residence. Routine financial transactions will usually (but not always — see *infra*, Chapter III-A-4) be adjudicated best by courts. An American bank, for example, will generally prefer to bring an action against a defaulting English borrower in the High Court of London, rather than arbitrate the loan default in Geneva or Paris. Likewise a Swiss financial institution will find enforcement of a pledge or other security agreement a more comfortable prospect before Swiss judges, a known quantity (at least to Swiss banks), rather than yet-to-be-appointed arbitrators. Arbitration generally will commend itself as an alternative to courts principally when one party has doubts about the attachability of the other side's assets or the integrity of the judges that might otherwise hear the case. It is not so much that parties to inter-

---

226. These limitations include (1) unclear criteria for enforcing jurisdiction clauses, (2) restrictions on subject matter jurisdiction, (3) judicial discretion to refuse to hear a case and (4) the absence of any multilateral treaty network for the enforcement of judgments. *Compare* Martin Hunter, Jan Paulsson, Nigel Rawding, & Alan Redfern, FRESHFIELDS GUIDE TO ARBITRATION AND ADR 1-2 (1993), which suggests several additional drawbacks to court proceedings as compared to arbitration: national judges may be untrained to deal with the foreign law governing the contract; courts may have difficulty with foreign languages and translation; and judicial proceedings are subject to public scrutiny.

national contracts choose arbitration, as that arbitration imposes itself *faute de mieux* in the absence of neutral national courts of compulsory jurisdiction.

Party choice and binding result distinguish arbitration from other forms of non-judicial dispute resolution. As a private alternative to government courts, arbitration binds the parties on the merits of either an existing dispute or a possible future dispute arising out of their contractual relationship. Procedures that are not consensual (such as court-annexed arbitration[227]) or not binding (such as conciliation[228]) either remain beyond the control of disputing parties or leave the parties free to seek a final and authoritative resolution of the dispute elsewhere.[229]

Arbitration must also be distinguished from reference to an expert.[230] Arbitrators are appointed to resolve disputes, while experts are hired to prevent them. Two con-

227. On court-annexed arbitration, see Lisa Bernstein, *Understanding the Limits of Court-Connected ADR*, *supra* note 9. The Iranian Claims Tribunal in the Hague and the United Nations Claims Commission in Geneva (*supra* note 9) are hybrid forms of dispute resolution often dealt with by arbitration lawyers notwithstanding the non-voluntary nature of their jurisdiction. The Iranian Claims Tribunal was imposed even on reluctant American claimants (*see* Dames & Moore v. Regan, 453 U.S. 654 (1981)) and the United Nations Claims Commission was forced on an unwilling Iraq. *Compare* bi-national anti-dumping review panels under Chapter 19 of the North American Free Trade Agreement.

228. *See* Thomas Carbonneau, ALTERNATIVE DISPUTE RESOLUTION: MELTING THE LANCES AND DISMOUNTING THE STEEDS (1989); Stephen Goldberg, Frank E. A. Sander, & Nancy H. Rogers, DISPUTE RESOLUTION: NEGOTIATION, MEDIATION AND OTHER PROCESSES (2nd ed. 1992); John S. Murray, Alan Scott Rau & Edward F. Sherman, PROCESSES OF DISPUTE RESOLUTION (1989), Chapters II & III; Leonard Riskin & James Westbrook, DISPUTE RESOLUTION AND LAWYERS (1987), Chapters III, IV & VI; Edward Brunet, *Questioning the Quality of Alternative Dispute Resolution*, 62 Tulane L. Rev. 1 (1987); Richard Delgado et al., *Finality and Formality: Minimizing the Risks of Prejudice in Alternative Dispute Resolution*, 1985 Wis. L. Rev. 1359 (1985); Harry T. Edwards, *Alternative Dispute Resolution: Panacea or Anathema*, 99 Harv. L. Rev. 668 (1986); Owen Fiss, *Against Settlement*, 93 Yale L.J. 1073 (1984); Tina Grillo, *The Mediation Alternative: Process Dangers for Women*, 100 Yale L.J. 1545 (1991); Richard Posner, *The Summary Jury Trial and Other Methods of Alternative Dispute Resolution: Some Cautionary Observations*, 53 U. Chicago L. Rev. 336 (1986); Judith Resnick, *Failing Faith: Adjudicatory Procedure in Decline*, 53 U. Chicago L. Rev. 494 (1986); and Edward F. Sherman, *Court-Mandated Alternative Dispute Resolution: What Form of Participation Should Be Required?*, 46 SMU Law Rev. 2079 (1993). *Compare* religious dispute resolution, *supra* note 16. *See also* critique of mediation by Alex Beam entitled *McJustice on Trial*, Boston Globe, 30 November 1992.

229. *See generally*, Derek Roebuck, *A Short History of Arbitration*, in HONG KONG AND CHINA ARBITRATION (Kaplan, Spruce & Moser, eds. 1994). One European commentator has noted, "To put non-binding and binding processes in the same bag when their dynamics, parties' expectations and rules are so different, is bound to create a lot of confusion in the users' minds." Jacques Werner, *ADR: Will European Brains Be Set On Fire?*, 10 J. Int. Arb. 45 (No. 4, Dec. 1993).

230. *See, e.g.*, the award rendered in I.C.C. Case No. 6535, involving a construction contract, discussed in 1993 JOURNAL DU DROIT INTERNATIONAL (Clunet) 1024, with *Observations* by Dominique Hascher. The general conditions governing the contract provided that certain disputes be referred first to an engineer, which is considered the inception of the arbitral process. On the use of experts in arbitration, see Jarrosson, *supra* note 17.

tracting parties may agree, for example, that certain matters of fact will be referred to a panel of experts. Without the defining element of a dispute, however, these decisionmakers will not benefit from arbitral immunity, and their decision will not be enforceable under the New York Arbitration Convention. In practice, of course, the way a contract is drafted can sometimes transform an expert into an arbitrator and vice versa. For example, a family business dispute among squabbling brothers and sisters could be resolved either by arbitration or, in the alternative, by a sale of commonly-held business interests from one group of siblings to another, pursuant to an agreement that left the purchase price to be determined by an expert.

1. Treaties.

Most of the world's trading nations have adhered to multilateral conventions that secure enforcement of bargains to arbitrate. Three major treaty networks to which the United States is party — the New York, Washington and Panama Conventions — enforce arbitration agreements and awards even in countries that have resisted similar treaties with the United States to cover court judgments, largely from concerns about the expensive nature of American punitive damage awards.[231]

The most important of these treaties is the Convention on the Recognition and Enforcement of Foreign Arbitral Awards, referred to as the "New York Arbitration Convention." Adopted in 1958, the New York Arbitration Convention was designed as a mechanism to make arbitration awards more "transportable" from the country where rendered to the country where the loser has assets. The Convention had its genesis in the inadequacies of the Geneva Conventions of 1923 and 1927,[232] which led the International Chamber of Commerce (I.C.C.) to draft a new treaty that would liberate international arbitration from burdensome enforcement procedures[233] and provide a more streamlined way to enforce both awards and agreements.[234]

The New York Arbitration Convention requires courts of almost one hundred contracting states to refer the parties to arbitration when a dispute is subject to a written arbitration agreement[235] not "null and void, inoperative or incapable of being

---

231. *See* discussion in Chapters II-E and VIII-B.

232. The New York Convention replaces the 1927 Geneva Convention as to the states that are parties to both Conventions. The 1923 Convention provided only for stay of court proceedings in the state where made, operating like a uniform law. *See generally*, Alan Redfern and Martin Hunter, INTERNATIONAL COMMERCIAL ARBITRATION 454-57 (2d ed. 1992).

233. In particular the requirement of "double-exequatur" (leave for enforcement in the award's country of origin) was read into the Geneva Convention of 1927. *See* I.C.C., *Enforcement of International Arbitral Awards: Report and Preliminary Draft Convention*, I.C.C. Brochure No. 174 (1953), *reproduced in* U.N. DOC. E/C.2/373.

234. *See* U.N. DOC E/CONF. 26/SR. 1-25, *reproduced in* Giorgio Gaja, NEW YORK CONVENTION, Part III (1987-88). *See generally*, Albert Jan Van Den Berg, THE NEW YORK ARBITRATION CONVENTION OF 1958 (1981).

235. Convention on the Recognition and Enforcement of Foreign Arbitral Awards, 330 U.N.T.S. 38, 21 U.S.T. 2517, T.I.A.S. No. 6997 (1958) [hereinafter New York Arbitration Convention] Article II.

performed," and concerning a subject matter "capable of settlement by arbitration."[236] The Convention-imposed duty to dismiss litigation inconsistent with an arbitration clause will not necessarily, however, bar administrative proceedings, such as a complaint before the International Trade Commission.[237]

After an award has been rendered, the New York Arbitration Convention requires that the foreign award be recognized and enforced as would a domestic award.[238] This Convention-mandated enforcement covers foreign awards, which is to say awards rendered outside the enforcing forum.[239] A court of a Convention state may refuse recognition and enforcement to awards only on the basis of a limited litany of procedural defenses that includes invalidity of the arbitration agreement, denial of an opportunity to be heard, arbitrator excess of jurisdiction, arbitral procedure contrary to the parties' agreement, and annulment of the award in the country where rendered.[240] These procedural defects, which must be asserted and proven by the resisting party, permit the court to avoid lending its power to support a fraudulent or unfair arbitration, but are

---

236. New York Arbitration Convention, Article II.

237. *See* Farrel Corp. v. International Trade Commission, 949 F.2d 1147 (Fed. Cir. 1991), *cert. denied*, 112 S. Ct. 1947 (1992). An American rubber and plastics manufacturer licensed an Italian corporation to use rubber and plastic mixing technology. When a dispute arose, the American licensor began litigation in Italy and the United States, notwithstanding the contract's arbitration clause providing for I.C.C. arbitration in Geneva. While judicial proceedings were dismissed (Farrel Corp. v. Pomini, Inc., No. C 88-2161A (N.D. Ohio, 10 Sept. 1990), a different treatment was given to a complaint against the Italian licensee alleging *inter alia* trade secret misappropriation and patent infringement, filed with the International Trade Commission. The Court interpreted Section 337 of the Tariff Act of 1930 (19 U.S.C. § 1337) to permit an International Trade Commission proceeding notwithstanding the arbitration clause, reasoning that arbitration agreements operate as a waiver of access only to a judicial, rather than administrative, forum.

238. New York Arbitration Convention, Article III provides that Convention states shall recognize foreign awards as "binding and enforce them in accordance with the rules of procedure of the territory where the award is relied upon," subject to no conditions more onerous than those imposed on domestic awards. It is of course possible that a country might adhere to the New York Convention and yet have a restrictive domestic arbitration law that does not provide an effective enforcement procedure for awards. The Panama Convention is more ambiguous. Article IV provides that an arbitral award shall have the force of a final judgment, but goes on to say only that the award "*may*" be enforced. The Panama Convention requires that the award be "not appealable," a concept of uncertain content in arbitration. The New York Convention permits (but does not mandate) refusal of recognition to an award that is "not binding ... or has been set aside," which is much narrower than "not appealable." In some countries there is New York Convention case law saying that an award may be binding even though subject to appeal.

239. The United States and many other countries have reserved application of the treaty on the basis of reciprocity, to awards rendered in the territory of another Convention party. The Convention may also apply to "non-domestic" awards, an obscure term that has only been interpreted once to my knowledge. Bergesen v. Muller, 710 F.2d 928 (2d Cir. 1983). In that case a U.S. court characterized an award rendered in New York as "non-domestic." The dispute involved a ship charter between Norwegian and Swiss parties for transport of chemicals between Europe, the Caribbean and North America.

240. New York Arbitration Convention, Article V(1).

not intended to permit judicial review of the merits of the dispute. Two additional defenses are open to a court on its own motion, without any proof by the party resisting the award: that the subject matter is not arbitrable, and that enforcement would violate the forum's "public policy."[241] While the first five Convention defenses relate generally to safeguards against injustice, the two final defenses serve as an explicit catch-all for the forum's particular substantive public policy.

To promote the international currency of arbitration awards, New York Arbitration Convention defenses have traditionally been given a narrow scope.[242] In the United States, for example, the Convention's public policy defense has been interpreted restrictively to include only violations of "our most basic notions of morality and justice."[243] A broad interpretation would defeat the Convention's purpose of permitting parties to international transactions to assure themselves of some measure of neutral dispute resolution.

In Latin American and Caribbean countries, the 1975 Inter-American Arbitration Convention (often referred to as the Panama Convention) mirrors much of the New York Arbitration Convention.[244] The Panama Convention's enforcement scheme, however, is more limited than that of the New York Arbitration Convention.

---

241. New York Arbitration Convention, Article V(2).

242. *See* Alan Redfern & Martin Hunter, LAW AND PRACTICE OF INTERNATIONAL COMMERCIAL ARBITRATION (2d ed. 1991), at 461-65. *See also* Albert Jan Van Den Berg, THE NEW YORK ARBITRATION CONVENTION OF 1958 (1981).

243. *See* Parsons & Whittemore v. Société Générale de l'Industrie du Papier (RAKTA), 508 F.2d 969 (2d Cir. 1974). American and European law give public policy a narrower scope in relation to transactions of an international character. There is less justification for a refusal to recognize foreign decisions when they affect controverted events that occur principally outside a country's own borders. Judicial decisions have construed the public policy defense narrowly in order to avoid disrupting the international dispute resolution process. An arbitrator's lack of independence from one of the parties has been held not to constitute a violation of public policy. Fertilizer Corp. of India v. IDI Management, Inc., 530 F. Supp. 542 (S.D. Ohio 1982). Participation in the Arab boycott of Israel has been held not to give rise to a public policy defense. Antco Shipping Co. v. Sidermar, 417 F. Supp. 207 (S.D.N.Y. 1976). Misleading the arbitral tribunal has been found not to trigger the public policy defense, although dicta in the same case states that active fraud, such as perjury, might cause enforcement of the award to violate public policy. Biotronik Mess-und Therapiegeraere GmbH & Co. v. Medford Medical Instrument Co., 415 F. Supp. 133, 139 (D.N.J. 1976). One case in which an award was refused enforcement on public policy grounds involved what the court deemed a penal provision of French law calling for a particularly high interest rate on late payment for goods, and must be viewed as an aberration. Laminoirs - Trefileries - Cableries de Lens, S.A. v. Southwire Co., 484 F. Supp. 1063 (N.D. Ga. 1980). *See generally* Robert Coulson, *So Far, So Good: Enforcement of Foreign Commercial Arbitration Awards in United States Courts*, in CONTEMPORARY PROBLEMS IN INTERNATIONAL ARBITRATION 353 (1986). For a contrasting view about the wisdom of a narrow public policy exception, see discussion in Andrew Arnfelt, *Avoiding the Arbitration Trap*, Financial Times, 27 October 1992, at 17, cols. 1-4, discussed *infra* at note 608.

244. Parties to the Panama Convention include Chile, Colombia, Costa Rica, El Salvador, Guatemala, Honduras, Mexico, Panama, Paraguay, Uruguay, the United States and Venezuela.

The Panama Convention is silent on orders to compel arbitration, stating only that an agreement to arbitrate is "valid," thus raising questions about whether courts must compel a recalcitrant party to arbitrate. Moreover, the Panama Convention provides only that execution and recognition of an award "may" be ordered, as contrasted with the New York Arbitration Convention's mandatory language providing that a contracting state "shall" recognize and enforce awards.[245]

The third major multilateral arbitration treaty to which the United States is party is the Convention on the Settlement of Disputes Between States and Nationals of Other States of 1965, usually referred to as the Washington Convention, and now ratified by more than one hundred countries. The Convention established the International Centre for the Settlement of Investment Disputes ("ICSID") as an organ of the World Bank.[246] Jurisdiction of ICSID is limited both with respect to the parties and subject matter. The dispute must arise directly out of an investment contract between a Convention contracting state and a national of another Convention contracting state.[247] Consent to ICSID jurisdiction may be given in an individual investment agreement, host state legislation or treaty obligations, but may not be withdrawn unilaterally.

The European Convention on International Commercial Arbitration[248] complements the New York Arbitration Convention. The European Convention applies only to relationships between parties resident in contracting states, including European subsidiaries of American companies, rather than to foreign awards generally. The European Convention's rigorous enforcement scheme limits the grounds on which an award may be set aside. Whereas the New York Arbitration Convention considers *any* annulment of an award where rendered as a basis on which recognition of an award may be refused, the European Convention permits annulment of an award in another contracting state to be a ground for non-recognition only if the annulment was for a Convention-enumerated reason. These grounds for annulment resemble the proce-

---

245. Inter-American Arbitration Convention, Article 4. The enforcement obligation applies only to awards that are "not appealable." No similar limitation is found in the New York Convention.

246. 575 U.N.T.S. 159. On ICSID, *see generally* W. Michael Reisman, Systems of Control in International Arbitration (1992), chapter 3, at 46-106; Moshe Hirsch, The Arbitration Mechanisms of the International Settlement of Investment Disputes (1993); W. Michael Reisman, *The Breakdown of the Control Mechanism in ICSID Arbitration,* 1989 Duke L. J. 739; Georges Delaume, *ICSID and the Courts,* 77 Am. J. Int'l L. 784 (1983); Georges Delaume, *ICSID Arbitration,* in Contemporary Problems in International Arbitration 23 (J. Lew, ed. 1987). For a spirited exchange on the finality of ICSID awards, see W. Michael Reisman, *Repairing ICSID's Control System: Some Comments on Aaron Broches' `Observations on the Finality of ICSID Awards,'* 7 ICSID Review 196 (1992); Aaron Broches, *On the Finality of Awards: A Reply to Michael Reisman,* 8 ICSID Review 92 (1993).

247. Washington Convention, Article 25.

248. European Convention on International Commercial Arbitration, Geneva, 484 U.N.T.S. 349 (1961). The Convention applies to international trade disputes between "physical or legal persons having, when concluding the agreement, their habitual place of residence or their seat in different Contracting states." Convention Article 1(a). Thus the 1961 Convention would cover disputes involving European subsidiaries of an American multinational.

dural defects set forth in the first four defenses to enforcement of awards in Article V of the New York Arbitration Convention, including an invalid arbitration agreement, denial of an opportunity to be heard, procedure contrary to the parties' agreement and arbitral excess of authority. For example, under the European Convention an award set aside in England for error of law could not, on that ground alone, be refused recognition in France. Error of law does not fall within the Convention-approved grounds for annulment. Nor could an award set aside by a French court for violation of public policy (*ordre public*) be refused recognition in London.

In the United States, the New York Arbitration Convention generally preempts inconsistent state law, giving arbitration agreements dispositive effect.[249] Convention-implementing legislation sweeps away much of the jurisdictional uncertainty that might otherwise plague aliens attempting to vindicate arbitral rights in the United States. Federal district courts have original jurisdiction over any action falling under the Convention,[250] regardless of the amount in controversy or citizenship of the parties.[251] Convention-related actions may be removed from state to federal court.[252]

Uncertainties about the interaction of federal and state law do exist at the margins, however. Although state arbitration law generally applies to international arbitration only to the extent not more restrictive than federal law, it is less than self-evident what sort of rules are or are not more restrictive.[253] For example, provisional measures such as pre-award attachment interject national court proceedings that parties intended to avoid, while at the same time increasing the winner's chances of enforcing the award. Courts have been divided on whether such measures are compatible with the New York Arbitration Convention.[254]

In addition to the New York, Panama and Washington Conventions, many bilateral commercial and investment treaties contain arbitration provisions.[255] For exam-

---

249. *But see* discussion of Volt v. Stanford, *infra* note 312. Some scholars have suggested, however, that state law be given a greater role in international arbitration. *See* Ian Macneil, AMERICAN ARBITRATION LAW (1992), proposing what he terms the "heretical" view that "modern state arbitration laws would govern in both state and federal courts." *Id.* at 179.

250. 9 U.S.C. § 203 provides that Convention actions shall be "deemed to arise under the laws and treaties of the United States."

251. Federal courts may confirm Convention awards even between aliens. *See* Bergesen v. Muller, 710 F.2d 928 (2d Cir. 1983) (charter party between Norwegian shipowner and Swiss company). Confirmation of "non-domestic" award rendered in New York under 9 U.S.C. § 207 provided for three year period for confirmation rather than one year limit for domestic awards.

252. 9 U.S.C. § 205.

253. *See* William W. Park, *National Legal Systems and Private Dispute Resolution*, 82 Am. J. Int'l L. 616, 617-18 n.5 (1988). *See also* Volt v. Stanford, 489 U.S. 468 (1989), discussed *infra* at note 312. A construction contract was interpreted as being governed by the law of California. State law provisions staying arbitration pending resolution of related litigation were held not to be preempted by federal law.

254. *See* discussion *infra* at notes 445-48.

255. For bilateral investment and commercial treaties concluded by the United States and containing arbitration clauses, see Appendix F-5 and Appendix F-6.

ple, the investment treaty between the United States and the Russian Federation[256] contains a consent to the jurisdiction of both the World Bank's Centre for the Settlement of Investment Disputes and arbitral tribunals established under the rules of the United Nations Commission on International Trade Law (UNCITRAL), and requires the place of arbitration to be a country that is a party to the New York Arbitration Convention.[257]

Finally, arbitration treaties provide a partial response to the problem of international *litis pendens*, or "prior action pending," when an action is brought in one country while proceedings are pending in another.[258] New York Arbitration Convention Article II clearly provides that a court seized of an action as to which an arbitration agreement exists *shall* refer the parties to arbitration, thus reducing the cost and potential inconsistency of parallel litigation.

2. Monetary Incentives.

When the parties can pay an arbitrator's fee, there is relatively little risk of not being able to find someone to hear the case.[259] Substantial financial disincentives argue against arbitrators refusing to hear a case for reasons of *forum non conveniens* or lack of subject matter jurisdiction. Arbitrator compensation in international cases can be substantial. For example, under the rules of the International Chamber of Commerce[260] arbitrators hearing a $1 million controversy (modest in international transactions) could each receive up to $30,000 in fees.[261] Many law professors supplement their academic stipends with service as an arbitrator.

Calculation of arbitrators' fees has been approached in two different ways: (i) an hourly rate or (ii) a percentage of the amount in dispute. The first approach is favored by the London Court of International Arbitration, which generally gives arbitrators between £ 600-£ 2000 for each day of meetings, and between £ 150- £ 375 per hour for other time spent.[262] The American Arbitration Association follows a similar approach to arbitrator remuneration. In contrast, the International Chamber of

---

256. Treaty Between the United States of America and the Russian Federation Concerning the Encouragement and Reciprocal Protection of Investment, Washington, 17 June 1992, *reprinted in* 31 I.L.M. 794 (1992) with introductory note by Herbert Golsong.
257. U.S.-Russian Investment Treaty, Article 3(b) and Article 3(d).
258. On *litis pendens*, see Bernard Audit, Droit International Privé (1991), Sections 558-59; George Delaume, Law and Practice of Transnational Contracts (1988), Section 5.20; Bruxelles and Lugano Conventions, *infra* notes 616-17, Articles 21-23.
259. There are, however, some limits. For example, the I.C.C. Rules restrict their scope to disputes that are "commercial" in nature.
260. The I.C.C. was recently described as "the most renowned of arbitral institutions." *See* Hall and Newton, "International Arbitration Bodies," N.Y. L.J., 16 June 1992, at 1, col.1.
261. *See* W. Laurence Craig, William W. Park and Jan A.S. Paulsson, International Chamber of Commerce Arbitration (2d ed. 1990) App. I, Tables 9A and 9B.
262. *See* Schedule of Costs in the London Court of International Arbitration Rules.

Commerce sets maximum and minimum fee limits based on the amount in dispute, calculated at varied rates applicable to each slice of the claim.[263]

Meaningful comparison of these two different approaches to arbitral fees will require assumptions as to both the amount in controversy and the time spent by the arbitrators. The most economical régime from the parties' perspective will depend on the complexity and the amount of damages claimed in each case. An I.C.C. arbitrator might be paid a relatively high fee in relation to time spent on the file if the parties settle the case early in the proceedings. On the other hand, the I.C.C. fee structure will turn out to be relatively inexpensive in cases whose factual and legal complexity require large amounts of time notwithstanding the modest damages claims.

3. State Contracts.[264]

Multinational enterprises sometimes enter into contracts with or within foreign states known for confiscatory policies. Chief among the multinational's concerns in such cases will be the Act of State doctrine, sovereign immunity and developing country attitudes toward compensation of foreign investors. In all three areas, arbitration agreements can enhance adjudicatory predictability substantially.

a. Acts of State.[265]

To avoid meeting obligations in hard currencies, foreign debtors will occasionally invoke exchange controls or payment moratoria imposed by their home countries. Under the Act of State doctrine, judges have sometimes felt prohibited from calling into question such foreign governmental acts even if contrary to the forum's public policy. The Restatement (Third) Foreign Relations Law sets forth the classic American formulation of the Act of State doctrine as follows:

> In the absence of a treaty or other unambiguous agreement regarding controlling legal principles, courts in the United States will generally

---

263. Under the fee schedule in effect as from 1 January 1993, fees run from $2000 minimum and a 15% maximum on amounts up to $50,000, but are calculated at between .01% to .05% on the amount of the dispute in excess of $100 million. For example, when the amount in controversy is $1 million, the fees of each arbitrator vary between $8,450 and $47,500. For a $100 million dispute the fees range spreads between $52,450 and $231,500. *See* I.C.C. Rules 20(2) and 20(3), and Internal Court Rule 18. The I.C.C. takes into account the complexity of the case in fixing the final fee amount. For example, in a consent award the fees might be quite small. *See generally,* W. Laurence Craig, William W. Park and Jan A.S. Paulsson, INTERNATIONAL CHAMBER OF COMMERCE ARBITRATION (2d ed. 1990), chapter 21.

264. *See generally,* Georges Delaume, *Enforcement of State Contract Awards: Jurisdictional Pitfalls and Remedies,* 8 ICSID Review (No.1) 29 (1993).

265. *See generally* Anne-Marie Burley, *Law Among Liberal States: Liberal Internationalism and the Act of State Doctrine,* 92 Columbia L. Rev. 1907 (1992); Daniel Chow, *Rethinking the Act of State Doctrine,* 62 Wash. L. Rev. 397, 444 (1987).

refrain from examining the validity of a taking by a foreign state of property within its own territory, or from sitting in judgment on other acts of a governmental character done by a foreign state within its own territory and applicable there.[266]

Exchange controls therefore may occasionally bar American courts from ordering payment of a foreign debt.

The early doctrinal underpinnings of the Act of State doctrine derive from a choice-of-law theory which holds that the law of the country where an act is performed determines its legitimacy. A more modern justification for the doctrine has been articulated in terms of the Constitutional separation of powers: courts should not risk hindering the executive's conduct of foreign affairs by passing judgment on foreign governmental acts affecting property within the foreign country's own territory.[267]

Courts sometimes avoid applying the Act of State doctrine by manipulating the situs of the property allegedly subject to the foreign government's power. For example, a debt may be deemed to be located outside the country of debtor's residence by a judicial finding that the debt was not governed by the law of the expropriating country.[268] However, such situs manipulation may come after several years of appellate litigation.[269]

American courts are not permitted to invoke the Act of State doctrine to refuse to enforce arbitral awards. After a judicial decision denying enforcement to a multi-million dollar arbitration award that arose out of nationalization of American-owned oil concessions,[270] the Federal Arbitration Act was amended to provide with elegant simplicity that "enforcement of ... arbitral awards and execution upon judgments based

---

266. RESTATEMENT (THIRD) FOREIGN RELATIONS LAW § 443.

267. *See* Banco Nacional v. Sabbatino, 376 U.S. 398 (1964).

268. *See* Allied Bank Int'l v. Banco Credito Agricola de Cartago, 757 F.2d 516 (2d Cir. 1985); Wells Fargo v. Citibank, *infra* note 269. *Compare* the seemingly irreconcilable results in Perez v. Chase Manhattan, 474 N.Y.S.2d 689 (1984) and Garcia v. Chase Manhattan, 735 F.2d 645 (2d Cir. 1984). Cf. Vischipco Line v. Chase Manhattan N.A., 660 F.2d 854 (2d Cir. 1980), *cert. denied* 459 U.S. 976 (1982) and Ngoc Quang Trinh v. Citibank N.A., 850 F.2d 1164 (6th Cir. 1988), *cert. denied* 496 U.S. 912 (1990). For some banks this matter has now been dealt with by the recently added § 25C of the Federal Reserve Act (12 U.S.C. 633), which provides that a bank may not be required to repay a deposit made at a foreign branch if repayment by the branch was prevented by an act of a government or instrumentality (de facto or de jure) in the country in which the branch is located unless the bank has expressly agreed in writing to repay the deposit under those circumstances. The Act applies only to deposits at Federal Reserve member banks, and does not address similar risks related to swaps or foreign exchange contracts.

269. *See* Wells Fargo v. Citibank, 852 F.2d 657 (2d Cir. 1988), *aff'd* 695 F. Supp. 1450, *rev'd* 110 S. Ct. 2034 (1990), *reconsidered* 936 F.2d 723 (2d Cir. 1991), *cert. denied* 22 June 1992. In the *Wells Fargo* saga there were no less than five different decisions spanning four years. Today *Wells Fargo* would be decided differently in light of the recently added Section 25C of the Federal Reserve Act, discussed *supra* note 268.

270. LIAMCO v. Libya, 482 F. Supp. 1175 (D.D.C. 1980), *vacated* as moot. The expropriation was considered an Act of State that would have been indirectly called into question by enforcement of the award.

on orders confirming such awards shall not be refused on the basis of the act of state doctrine."[271] Moreover, an arbitrator generally can be expected to feel less bound than a judge to defer to a government's conduct of foreign affairs.[272]

b. Sovereign Immunity.[273]

As with the Act of State doctrine, a plea of sovereign immunity is less likely to pose an obstacle to enforcement of an arbitral award than to enforcement of a judgment. Not only will courts generally recognize an arbitration clause as a waiver of immunity from jurisdiction, but execution of an arbitral award against government assets will in many cases be easier than execution of a court judgment.

Traditionally, one state will not haul into its courts a foreign government or governmental agency.[274] Such immunity from adjudicatory jurisdiction imposes limitations on the ability of an American court to vindicate contract rights against foreign state defendants in international transactions.

Most major legal systems follow a "restrictive" theory of sovereign immunity, which attempts to distinguish between commercial and public activities of a government or its agencies.[275] Immunity is said to attach only to activity of a public rather than commercial character.[276] The characterization of commercial activity, of course,

---

271. 9 U.S.C. § 15.

272. Even without a statute, arguments can be made that the LIAMCO case was wrongly decided. In enforcing foreign arbitral awards under the New York Convention a court does not run afoul of the Act of State doctrine for the simple reason that it does not call into question foreign governmental acts; the court merely enforces an award.

273. *See generally*, Mary Kay Kane, *Suing Foreign Sovereigns: A Procedural Compass*, 34 Stan. L. Rev. 385 (1982); Bruce Nichols, *Sovereign Debtors Under U.S. Immunity Law*, in Sovereign Lending: Managing Legal Risk 81 (M. Gruson & R. Reisner, eds. 1984); Ernest Patrikis, *Immunity of Central Bank Assets Under U.S. Law*, in Sovereign Lending: Managing Legal Risk 89 (M. Gruson & R. Reisner, eds. 1984). For a British perspective on sovereign immunity, see Francis A. Mann, *Sovereign Immunity Under English Law*, in Sovereign Lending: Managing Legal Risk 103 (M. Gruson & R. Reisner, eds. 1984). For an illustration of the practical difficulties created by sovereign immunity, see Michael Sher, *Can Lawyers Save the Rainforest: Enforcing the Second Generation of Debt for Nature Swaps*, 17 Harv. Envtl. L. Rev. 1 (1993).

274. The Supreme Court has interpreted the Foreign Sovereign Immunities Act as a grant of subject matter jurisdiction to federal courts; the enforcement action will constitute a federal question "arising under" the laws of the United States. *See* Verlinden B.V. v. Central Bank of Nigeria, 461 U.S. 480 (1983).

275. *See generally* authorities cited in William W. Park, *Legal Policy Conflicts in International Banking*, 50 Ohio St. L.J. 1067, 1079-81 (1989). For a recent case on the commercial certainty exception to immunity, see Argentina v. Weltover Inc., 112 S. Ct. 2160 (1992) (foreign state not immune from suit in U.S. courts for default on bonds).

276. *See* 28 U.S.C. § 1605 (a) (2). Compare other formulations of the doctrine. For Britain, see Charles J. Lewis, State and Diplomatic Immunity (3d ed. 1990); for France, see Bernard Audit, Droit International Privé §§ 402-06 (1991). *See generally*, Gamal Moursi Badr, State Immunity (1984); George R. Delaume, *Sovereign Immunity and Public Debt*, 23 Int'l Law. 811 (1989); Claude Reymond, *Souveraineté de l'Etat et Participation à l'Arbitrage*, 1985 Revue de L'Arbitrage 517 (1985).

is to a large extent culturally determined. Some commentators have recommended replacement of the public/commercial distinction with a "functional approach" that relies on a more explicit enumeration of immunity exceptions.[277]

A state's immunity from jurisdiction is distinct from its property's immunity from execution or attachment.[278] Therefore, effective vindication of contract rights against foreign sovereigns will often remain problematic even after a judgment on the merits, which may remain no more than a piece of paper.

United States courts generally permit execution against state property[279] only if there is a link between the property and the commercial activity on which the basic claim is based.[280] This nexus requirement may prove problematic when a foreign government default makes attachable assets scarce in the enforcement forum, frustrating vindication of contract rights notwithstanding a valid jurisdiction clause.[281]

Ironically however, in one particular fact pattern a defendant's sovereign status may actually create jurisdiction. Normally one alien may not sue another in federal court unless the litigation is based on a federal cause of action. The Supreme Court has held that the jurisdictional provisions of the Foreign Sovereign Immunities Act[282] operate to confer such federal question jurisdiction under Article III of the U.S. Constitution, regardless of the origin of the substantive legal claim.[283]

In 1988 the United States modified the requirement of a link between assets to be attached and the activity that gave rise to the underlying claim.[284] In the enforcement of arbitral awards, the only requirement for attachment is that the property serve in a

---

277. *See* Joan E. Donoghue, *Taking 'Sovereign' Out of the Foreign Sovereign Immunities Act: A Functional Approach to the Commercial Activity Exception,* 17 Yale J. Int'l L. 489 (1992).

278. Some countries also impose a general link between the forum and the subject matter or parties of the dispute. Switzerland, for example, requires a *Binnenbeziehung* ("internal connection") to justify attachment of a foreign government assets. *See* discussion *infra* at notes 703-07, and *Note, Social People's Libyan Arab Jamahiriya v. Libyan American Oil Company,* 75 Am. J. Int'l L. 153 (1981) (Geneva arbitral situs deemed insufficient connection).

279. With respect to property of autonomous state entities, agencies and instrumentalities, however, all property within the United States is subject to execution if the agency or entity is engaged in a commercial activity in the United States. 28 U.S.C. § 1610 (b). A waiver of immunity from attachment or from execution must be separate from the waiver of immunity from suit. *See* 28 U.S.C. § 1610. On the matter of piercing the corporate veil of a state-owned trading agency, see Hester Int. v. Fed. Rep. of Nig., 879 F.2d 170 (5th Cir. 1989).

280. 28 U.S.C. § 1610 (a)(2) provides that the property will not be immune if "the property is or was used for the commercial activity on which the claim is based." A similar nexus requirement is followed by other major jurisdictions. *See generally* George Delaume, LAW AND PRACTICE OF TRANSNATIONAL CONTRACTS §§ 8.09-8.12 (1988). In the United States, the provisions of the Hickenlooper amendment contained in § 1610(a)(3) remove immunity from attachment when what is at issue are rights in property which have been taken in violation of international law.

281. *See generally,* William W. Park, *L'arbitrage et le recouvrement des prêts consentis à des débiteurs étrangers,"* 37 McGill L.J. 375, 398-99 (1992).

282. 28 U.S.C. § 1330 (a) provides that district courts "shall have original jurisdiction ... of any nonjury civil action against a foreign state" as defined in 28 U.S.C. § 1603 (a).

283. *See* Verlinden B.V. v. Central Bank of Nigeria, 461 U.S. 480 (1983), in which a Dutch plaintiff asserted claims under state law against a Nigerian government agency.

284. *See* discussion of LIAMCO v. Libya, *supra* at note 270.

commercial activity in the United States which may be other than the activity giving rise to the claim. The Foreign Sovereign Immunities Act now provides that "property in the United States of a foreign state ... used for commercial activity in the United States, shall not be immune from attachment in aid of execution ... if [a United States] judgment is based on an order confirming an arbitral award rendered against the foreign State."[285]

Outside the United States arbitration clauses will also limit a sovereign's right to claim immunity from suit. Six months before a £ 182 million settlement between the International Tin Council (I.T.C.) and its creditors put an end to a dispute over the suspension of buffer stock operations,[286] the English House of Lords had interpreted the Council's Headquarters Agreement with the United Kingdom as granting immunity from suits arising out of the Council's creditors' claims.[287] The same Headquarters Agreement, however, had provided that the Council would not benefit from immunity in the enforcement of arbitration awards. Only those creditors who incorporated arbitration clauses in their agreements[288] had the benefit of waived immunity under the Headquarters Agreement and the British State Immunity Act.[289]

c. Expropriation.

Developing countries have sometimes taken the view that disputes over compensation for expropriated property must be decided by host state tribunals.[290] In some

---

285. 28 U.S.C. § 1610. In addition, the Foreign Sovereign Immunities Act generally denies a foreign state immunity in an attempt to avoid enforcement of either an arbitration agreement or confirmation of an arbitral award. *See* 28 U.S.C. § 1605 (a). An arbitration agreement will be enforceable notwithstanding a claim of sovereign immunity if (i) the arbitration takes place in the United States, (ii) the agreement or award is or may be governed by a treaty calling for the recognition and enforcement of arbitration awards, such as the New York or Panama Arbitration Conventions.

286. *See* International Tin Council Press Release of 30 March 1990.

287. J.H. Rayner Ltd. v. Dep't. of Trade, 3 W.L.R. 969, 3 All E.R. 523 (H.L. 1989).

288. For example, the London and Malayan Metal Exchanges had inserted arbitration clauses in their standard form metal trading contracts, as had one bank, according to the House of Lords. *See* J.H. Rayner, 3 W.L.R. at 999, 3 All E.R. at 542.

289. State Immunity Act, 1978, ch. 33, § 9. In an American compensation case, a New York State court enforced an agreement providing that controversies with the I.T.C. "shall be settled by arbitration in the City of New York." *See* Int'l Tin Council v. Amalgamate Inc., N.Y. L.J., 29 January 1988, at 14; *see also* A.H. Hermann, "U.S. Court Rejects ITC's Claim to Sovereign Immunity," Financial Times, 11 February 1988, at 9.

290. *See, e.g.,* 1974 Charter of Economic Rights and Duties of States, Article 2(2)(c): "In any case where the question of compensation [for expropriated property] gives rise to a controversy, it shall be settled under the domestic law of the nationalizing state and by its tribunals...." *See* William W. Park, *Legal Issues in the Third World's Economic Development*, 61 B.U. L. Rev. 1321 (1981); *see also* Robert F. Meagher, An International Redistribution of Wealth and Power (1979). On the Latin American attitude toward arbitration, see Horacio Grigera Naón, *Arbitration in Latin America: Overcoming Traditional Hostility*, 22 Inter-American Law Review 203 (1991).

countries this would have the practical consequence of permitting one party to a dispute to be the judge in its own case. The resulting bias would ultimately weaken the stability of private international investment and its attendant transfer of development technology. Arbitration reduces the prospect of such biased host-state determinations of compensation for expropriation. Arbitrators who have considered the Charter have rejected its effect with respect to arbitration agreements.[291] More significantly, ratification of the New York, Panama and Washington Conventions by many developing countries constitutes an explicit treaty obligation that on its face will trump the Charter's provisions.

4. Credit Arrangements.

The epidemic of lender liability litigation that began in the United States during the 1980's gives financial institutions an additional reason to look to arbitration clauses.[292] In lender liability claims, borrowers assert breach of banker-customer understandings in order to obtain damages for a banker's refusal to advance funds or extend repayment. An expression of catch-word quality, the term "lender liability" implicates a bank's implicit obligation of good faith in its dealings with customers. This populist concept in essence makes the financier a partner in the borrower's business venture.[293]

291. *See* Texaco Overseas Petroleum/California Asiatic Oil v. Libyan Arab Rep., 17 I.L.M 1 (1978). *See generally* discussion in W. Laurence Craig, William W. Park and Jan A.S. Paulsson, INTERNATIONAL CHAMBER OF COMMERCE ARBITRATION, Ch. 36, 643-57 (2d ed., 1990).

292. *See generally*, William W. Park, *L'Arbitrage et le recouvrement des prêts consentis à des débiteurs étrangères,"* 37 McGill L.J. 375 (1992); William W. Park, *Particularités de l'arbitrage en matière bancaire et financière,* 1994 Semaine Judiciaire 621; William W. Park, *When the Borrower and the Banker are at Odds,* 65 Tulane L. Rev. 1323 (1991); Otto Sandrock, *Internationale Kredite und die Internationale Schielsgerichtsbarkeit,* Zeitschrift für Wirtschafts- und Bankrecht (12 & 19 March 1994), pages 405 and 445. *See also* CITY DISPUTES PANEL HANDBOOK, London, 1994.

293. *See, e.g.,* Reid v. Key Bank, 821 F.2d 9 (1st Cir. 1987). The jury awarded $100,000 in compensatory damages and $500,000 in punitive damages (the punitive damages were struck down as impermissible under Maine law in contract actions), for the bank's breach of the implied obligation of good faith and fair dealing by terminating a line of credit to owners of a paint business, despite the right to do so under the loan agreement. *See also* KMC v. Irving Trust, 757 F.2d 752 (6th Cir. 1985). *See generally* Gerald L. Blanchard, LENDER LIABILITY LOAN PRACTICE & PREVENTION (1989); A. Barry Cappello & Frances Komoroske, LENDER LIABILITY (1987); Daniel R. Fischel, *The Economics of Lender Liability,* 99 Yale L.J. 131 (1989); Clayton P. Gillette, *Commercial Relationships and the Selection of Default Rules for Remote Risks,* 19 J. Legal Stud. 535, 565-74 (1990); Kenneth L. Goldberg, *Lender Liability and Good Faith,* 68 B.U. L. Rev. 653 (1988); Janine S. Hiller, *Good Faith Lending,* 26 Am. Bus. L.J. 783 (1988); David L. Johnson & Terrence J. Gaffney, *Lender Liability: Perspectives on Risk and Prevention,* 105 Banking L.J. 325 (1988); Dennis M. Patterson, *Good Faith, Lender Liability and Discretionary Acceleration,* 68 Tex. L. Rev. 169 (1989); Todd L. Pearson, *Limiting Lender Liability: The Trend Toward Written Credit Agreement Statutes,* 76 Minn. L. Rev. 295 (1991), noting that a majority of states have now added credit agreements to Statutes of Frauds in order to preclude lender liability claims based on oral contract claims.

To discourage what they consider to be excessive and unpredictable damage awards by juries in lender liability litigation, several American financial institutions now provide for arbitration in credit agreements.[294] From a lender's perspective, arbitration commends itself because an arbitral panel presumably will be less swayed by solicitude for the borrower than members of a civil jury whose own credit problems may make them empathize with the debtor.

The validity of arbitration clauses in consumer banking transactions has been subject to vigorous challenge. While some state court decisions have refused to enforce arbitration clauses invoked against borrowers under consumer loan contracts,[295] other decisions have upheld consumer finance arbitration.[296] Borrowers who resisted the arbitration agreement have argued that the arbitration agreements inserted into account statements were not genuinely consensual.[297] Such arguments about the voluntary nature of forum selection agreements may be highly fact-specific, depending on the mechanism by which the bank allegedly obtains a borrower's assent to an arbitration or jurisdiction clause.

294. *See, e.g.,* model clauses adopted by Bank of California and Bank of America, *reprinted in* James R. Butler, Arbitration in Banking (R.M.A. 1988). In its *Retail Investment Sales Guidelines for Banks,* The American Bankers Association has recommended arbitration under the rules of the American Arbitration Association for disputes arising from sales of mutual funds and other non-deposit investment products. *See* AAA, Dispute Resolution Times, Spring 1994, at 3. In June 1992, the Bank of America announced that it would require all deposit and bankcard agreements to be submitted to binding arbitration under the rules of the American Arbitration Association. *See* statement of Winslow Christien (Senior V.P. and Director of Litigation), *reported in* BNA World Arbitration & Mediation Report 135 (July 1992).

295. *See* Geneva Bell v. Congress Mortgage, Cal. App. 1st Dist., 17 May 1994, 24 Cal. App. 4th 1675 (1994), ordered depublished by Cal. Sup. Court on 18 July 1994, 30 Cal. Rep. 2d 205 (1994). The court in *Geneva Bell* refused to compel arbitration absent a "clear and informed" waiver of the right to a jury trial (homeowner claims against mortgage lenders for fraudulent business practices). *See also* ITT Consumer Financial Corp. v. Patterson, 14 Cal. App. 4th 1659, 18 Cal. Reptr. 2d 563 (1993), *petition for cert. denied,* U.S. Supreme Court No. 93-952, 7 March 1994, 114 S. Ct. 1217; California Court of Appeal held that the arbitration clause, used in documentation for relatively small loans, was an unconscionable limit on the borrower's opportunity to be heard. *Compare* Badie v. Bank of America, *infra* note 296.

296. Badie v. Bank of America, California Superior Court, San Francisco, No. 944916, decided 18 August 1994; bench opinion discussed in BNA Banking Report, Vol. 63, No. 8, at 293 (29 August 1994) and 5 World Arbitration and Mediation Report 231 (October 1994). Court upheld arbitration clause inserted into account statement where account agreement allowed bank to change terms of agreement at any time.

297. *See generally, Consumer Arbitration,* 4 World Arbitration and Mediation Report No. 7 (August 1993), at 192, *quoting* Patricia Sturdevant, chief attorney for the plaintiffs: "I like to say that ADR is like sex: it's great if both parties consent, but can't be allowed if one party is forced into taking part." *Id.* at 193. *See also Consumer Arbitration,* 5 World Arbitration and Mediation Rept. 231 (1994).

5. Interim Awards.

Arbitrators in international cases often sit in three-member tribunals with power to render interim awards that effectively divide a dispute into pieces to be decided one slice at a time. Depending on the particular arbitration rules applied, each interim award can become *res judicata* before the arbitration proceeds to its next stage.[298] In contrast, appellate court judges usually cast votes on the overall outcome of the case, regardless of decisions on particular issues.[299] Either an issue-by-issue or a case-by-case voting protocol may occasionally produce paradoxical results when compared with the other.

The effect of interim awards might be illustrated by the following configuration of case-by-case voting in a contract action to recover insurance proceeds on a building destroyed by fire.

Adjudicator (Judge or Arbitrator)	Issue I Was There a Contract?	Issue II Was There Loss?
1	Yes.	No.
2	No.	Yes.
3	Yes.	Yes.

In case-by-case voting, recovery would be denied, since only one adjudicator found both a contract and loss. Two out of three adjudicators would deny recovery, even though a majority had agreed that the contract had been concluded (adjudicators #1 and #3) and that the plaintiff had suffered loss (adjudicators #2 and #3).

In an arbitration involving an interim award, however, the decision about the existence of an insurance contract would become *res judicata* before the arbitrators

---

298. On interim awards, see W. Laurence Craig, William W. Park and Jan A.S. Paulsson, INTERNATIONAL CHAMBER OF COMMERCE ARBITRATION § 19.03 (2d ed. 1990). For a recent example of an arbitration involving an interim award, see Prudential-Bache v. Kyocera, award issued 25 August 1994, *reported in* 9 International Arbitration Report, No. 9 (Sept. 1994) at 3 and No. 10 (Oct. 1994) at 3, and 5 World Arbitration and Mediation Report No. 11 (November 1994) at 258. Normally, an interim award would become enforceable under Article III of the New York Convention. Interim awards should be distinguished from procedural orders that serve as efficiency devices to order debate.

299. *See generally*, Louis Kornhauser & Lawrence Sager, The *One and the Many: Adjudication in Collegial Courts*, 81 Cal. L. Rev. 1 (1993). With respect to U.S. Supreme Court practice, the authors note that "with few exceptions, each Justice on the Supreme Court has taken herself to be individually sovereign not only among the choice of rationales, but also over the choice among outcomes. [A]t the end of the day each Justice aligns herself with the outcome she would have chosen were she deciding the case alone." *Id.* at 13.

dealt with the question of loss. Arbitrators would vote first on whether a contract had been validly concluded and then would vote separately on the question of loss. Although arbitrator #2 might not believe a contract had ever been signed by the insurance company, he or she might nevertheless find that the house did in fact burn down. The interim award on the first matter (existence of a contract) would bind all arbitrators, resulting in recovery at a later stage of the proceedings.

The issue-by-issue adjudication to which international arbitration lends itself generally does a better job setting forth commercial norms to guide future business conduct. By helping commercial actors predict the outcomes of complicated business ventures, issue-by-issue adjudication enhances the business manager's ability to rely on the application of principled legal guidelines.

6. Rules and Reasons.

a. Institutional and Ad Hoc Rules.

The quality of an arbitration depends largely on the choice of the arbitrators who will find the facts of the case and weigh arguments of law. The procedural rules governing an arbitration will determine both how the arbitrators are selected and how they conduct the proceedings. In particular, these rules often set forth the process for selection of the chair of the arbitral tribunal when the parties or the party-nominated arbitrators are unable to agree on a mutually acceptable person.

Well-known arbitral institutions involved in international commercial disputes include the American Arbitration Association, the London Court of International Arbitration and the Paris-based International Chamber of Commerce. All three provide for careful constitution of the arbitral tribunal and even-handed supervision of an arbitration on basic procedural matters, including one party's delay in nominating an arbitrator or challenge to an arbitrator's independence. The International Chamber of Commerce Arbitration Rules are distinctive in two respects: (i) before the proceedings, arbitrators must establish "Terms of Reference" summarizing the parties' respective claims and defining the issues in the dispute, and (ii) awards are subject to the scrutiny of the I.C.C. Court for review of their form and for occasional comment on matters of substance.[300]

---

300. The ICC Court may modify matters of form, but only "draws [the arbitrator's] attention" to issues of substance. *See* International Chamber of Commerce Rules of Arbitration, Articles 13 and 21, and W. Laurence Craig, William W. Park and Jan Paulsson, INTERNATIONAL CHAMBER OF COMMERCE ARBITRATION (2nd ed. 1990), Chapters 15 and 20. The scope of the I.C.C. Court scrutiny is not always self-evident. For example, in Compagnie des Bauxites de Guinée v. Hammermills Inc., United States District Court for the District of Columbia, No. 90-0169, 29 May 1992, WL 122712 (D.D.C.), reported in 3 World Arbitration & Mediation Report (July 1992) at 167, an award was challenged because an arbitrator assessed $1 million in legal fees and costs after the award had been approved by the I.C.C. Court of Arbitration. The District Court confused the award after noting that the I.C.C. Rules "give rise to some ambiguity as to whether the assessment of legal costs must be included in the draft award submitted to the ICC Court."

Sometimes parties desire arbitration outside the framework of administrative supervision, due either to distrust or to ignorance of the available arbitral institutions. Such *ad hoc* proceedings can be conducted either pursuant to tailor-made contract stipulations, or by reference to standard arbitration rules such as those of the United Nations Commission on International Trade Law (UNCITRAL).[301] Under the UNCITRAL Arbitration Rules (not to be confused with the UNCITRAL Model Arbitration Law discussed *infra* at Section B-5 of this chapter), the parties name an "appointing authority" to select the sole arbitrator or tribunal chairman, as the case may be. When the parties fail to choose an appointing authority, the Secretary General of the Permanent Court of Arbitration at The Hague selects the appointing authority.

Ad hoc arbitration may be problematic due to the lack of institutional oversight. The supervisory vacuum will often serve to delight a defendant wishing to drag its feet. Moreover, courts asked to enforce awards obtained by default in an *ad hoc* arbitration may be more concerned that the defaulting party did in fact obtain proper notice of the proceedings than they would be if the award bears the imprimatur of an institution such as the International Chamber of Commerce, the London Court of International Arbitration or the American Arbitration Association. A procedural framework rooted in institutional rules does not preempt the mandatory arbitration law of the place of the proceedings or those of the forum called on to enforce the arbitration agreement or award. For example, some jurisdictions might hold a particular legal question (such as securities and antitrust law) non-arbitrable even though the subject matter posed no problems under the party-chosen (i.e., non-mandatory) arbitration rules.[302] Some issues, such as the independence of arbitrators, would normally be covered not only by institutional rules, but also by the laws of the arbitral situs and the enforcement forum.

Arbitration rules do not usually settle all internal procedural matters. Usually the arbitral tribunal will have discretion on questions related to standards of evidence and discovery, unless of course the parties have provided otherwise in their agreement. In commercial matters, European proceedings tend to rely more heavily on documents than Anglo-American legal actions, where live witnesses are heard and cross-examined. In some cases the parties themselves may stipulate that each side should have the

---

301. On the UNCITRAL Rules, see Isaak Dore, ARBITRATION AND CONCILIATION UNDER THE UNCITRAL RULES: A TEXTUAL ANALYSIS (1986); Isaak Dore, THE UNCITRAL FRAMEWORK FOR ARBITRATION IN CONTEMPORARY PERSPECTIVE (1993); Stewart Baker and Mark Davis, THE UNCITRAL ARBITRATION RULES IN PRACTICE (1994) and David Stewart, *The Iran-United States Claims Tribunal: A Review of Developments 1983-84,* 16 Law & Policy Int'l Bus. 677 (1984). For an example of the type of problems that can arise from *ad hoc* arbitration, see Intercarbon Bermuda v. Caltex Trading and Transport, 146 F.R.D. 64 (S.D.N.Y. 1993), where one party refused to proceed with an arbitration pursuant to an arbitration clause that provided for no institution to set the arbitration in motion. The claimant was required to spend seven years in litigation before obtaining a federal court order compelling arbitration. *See generally,* Robert Coulson, *The Practical Advantages of Administered Arbitration,* NIDR Forum 41 (Winter 1993).

302. *See* discussion *infra* at notes 345-417 and 531-579.

right to direct examination and cross-examination.[303] In most cases, however, arbitrators in cross-cultural disputes will have to decide on a compromise for evidentiary and discovery standards.

b. Reasoned Awards.

Reasoned awards are problematic. On the one hand, a written opinion adds rigor to the arbitral process. Sloppy arbitrating is generally more difficult when arbitrators must explain themselves. On the other hand, reasoned awards may detract from the finality of the arbitral process by giving the loser a hook on which to hang a court challenge to the award.

Reasoned awards are common in international arbitration. Opinions explaining the arbitrator's decision are the rule under procedures of both the International Chamber of Commerce and the London Court of International Arbitration, as well as the International Arbitration Rules of the American Arbitration Association.[304] In Continental Europe reasoned opinions are mandatory in many legal systems, at least in domestic arbitration.[305]

In the United States, however, the American Arbitration Association discourages reasoned awards in domestic cases.[306] Arbitrators who explain themselves will invariably expose the basis of their decision to greater scrutiny by judges looking to second guess the arbitral tribunal. Case law has held that arbitrators have no duty to explain their award.[307]

---

303. *See* Apple Stipulation, Clause VIII-D-3, discussed *infra* at notes 465-66.

304. L.C.I.A. Rule 16.1 provides that award must state "reasons upon which the award is based" unless all parties agree otherwise." I.C.C. Rule 20(1) requires the award to "deal with the merits of the case." Article 28(2) of the A.A.A. International Arbitration Rules provides that the tribunal shall state the reasons for its award "unless the parties have agreed that no reasons need be given."

305. French procedural law requires that arbitration awards contain reasons. N.C.PR.C. Article 1471 (Fr.). In an international arbitration, however, the parties may dispense with this requirement, which is not a matter of mandatory public policy (*ordre public international*). *See* cases discussed in Jean Robert & Thomas E. Carbonneau, THE FRENCH LAW OF ARBITRATION § 6.06, 610-13 (1983).

306. *See* Robert Coulson, BUSINESS ARBITRATION (4th ed., 1991), at 30: "Written opinions can be dangerous because they identify targets for the losing party to attack." *See also Q&A* in 48 Dispute Resolution J. (December 1993), at 63: "One reason for the lack of explanation in arbitration decisions is to avoid the opening of avenues for attacking the award."

307. *See* Sobel v. Herty Warner, 469 F.2d 1211 (2d Cir. 1972).

7. Governing Law.

a. Choice-of-Law Clauses.

The wide variety of choice-of-law clauses found in international contracts usually provide that the parties' rights and duties will be governed by a specific national legal system,[308] often supplemented by trade usage and/or mandatory norms of the place of performance.[309] Occasionally a contract will leave the arbitrators free to apply appropriate conflict-of-interest rules, or give arbitrators explicit power to decide without reference to any fixed national legal system.[310]

In federal systems such as the United States, the arbitration's procedural law must be distinguished from the legal régime governing the contract's interpretation and performance. If the contract does not make clear which law will apply to the arbitral proceedings, arbitration may be frustrated by a choice-of-law clause deemed to refer to provisions of state law. Although federal arbitration law generally preempts more restrictive state rules, it is not always self-evident which state rules are to be considered more restrictive than federal law.[311] In *Volt Information Sciences Inc. v. Board of Trustees of Leland Stanford Junior University*[312] a contract between Stanford University and an electrical contractor contained both an arbitration clause and a provision that the contract would be governed by the law of "the place where the project is located." After a dispute arose and the contractor filed a request for arbitration, Stanford sued two companies involved in the construction project that were not bound by arbitration clauses. The U.S. Supreme Court upheld a stay of arbitration under the California Arbitration Act, pending the outcome of related litigation, on the theory that the parties had submitted their arbitration to California law.

The wisdom and the limits of the *Volt* decision are open to question, in that the application of state law may become a backdoor method for obtaining waiver of rights otherwise guaranteed under the Federal Arbitration Act.[313] The practical lessons of the case are clear, however. Parties to international agreements who intend that their arbitration will be governed by federal arbitration law should say so explicitly.

---

308. *See generally* Friedrich Juenger, CHOICE OF LAW AND MULTISTATE JUSTICE (1993), at 54-57 and 216-18.

309. On choice of law in arbitration, *see* Yves Derains, *L'Application Cumulative par L'Arbitre des Systèmes de Conflit de Lois Intéressées au Litige,* 1972 Rev. Arb. 99.

310. *See* discussion of *lex mercatoria* and *amiable composition infra* at notes 314-30, and discussion of public policy implications for choice-of-law clauses, *infra* at notes 476-520.

311. State rules permitting pre-award attachment of assets have been a frequent source of controversy. *See generally* William W. Park, *National Legal Systems and Private Dispute Resolution,* 82 American J. Int'l Law 616 at 617-18 (1988).

312. 489 U.S. 468 (1989). Compare *Southland Corporation v. Keating,* 465 U.S. 1 (1984), holding that the Federal Arbitration Act applies in state courts, and *Prima Paint v. Flood & Conkling Mfg,* 388 U.S. 395 (1967) on the Act's applicablility in federal court diversity cases. *Compare* Securities Industry Ass'n v. Connolly, *infra* note 419.

313. *See Allied-Bruce Terminex v. Dobson,* 114 S.Ct. 834 (1995) and *Mastrobuono v. Shearson/ Lehman Hutton,* 11S S.Ct. 1212 (1995).

b. Lex Mercatoria and Amiable Composition.

Arbitrators occasionally purport to interpret a contract not according to a fixed national legal system, but according to principles of what has been called "the new law merchant," or *lex mercatoria*.[314] Some arbitrators will go even further, to render an award without regard to any legal system, national or international; this process is sometimes called *amiable composition*.[315] While there is nothing inherently wrong with *lex mercatoria* or *amiable composition*, both can be used to disguise an arbitrator's unauthorized imposition of personal preferences. Arbitrators may invoke either notion as a fig leaf to resolve a controversy according to idiosyncratic ideas of the right result, rather than the parties' shared *ex ante* contract expectations.

Amiable composition is a term of varied and not altogether precise meaning, used in Continental legal systems to refer to the power to decide a dispute without reference to any fixed system of law.[316] Normally an arbitrator will have power to decide as *amiable compositeur* only if explicitly so authorized by the parties. The French *Nouveau Code de procédure civile* describes *amiable composition* by contrasting it with rules of law: "The arbitrator decides according to the rules of law unless authorized by the arbitration clause to decide as *amiable compositeur*."[317] Some commentators have suggested that *amiable composition* gives the decisionmaker a "mandate to settle," while its Latin cousin *ex aequo et bono* involves only a discretional authority to mitigate "strict" law, whatever that might mean.[318]

The term *lex mercatoria* is also burdened with divergent content.[319] Some use the term to include trade usages helpful to fill the gaps in the party-selected law. Others

---

314. *See generally* references cited *infra* at note 319.

315. The term translates literally as "friendly compromise." The person who decides under such a régime of *amiable composition* is referred to as the *amiable compositeur*.

316. *See* Matthieu de Boisseson, Droit Français de l'Arbitrage §§ 354-377 (1983); Siguard Jarvin, *The Sources and Limits of an Arbitrator's Powers*, 2 Arb. Int'l 140 (1986). Article 13(4) of the Arbitration Rules of the International Chamber of Commerce (1986) [hereinafter I.C.C. Rules of Arbitration] provides for the arbitrator to assume the power of *amiable composition* only if the parties agree. On *amiable composition, see* Julian D. Lew, Applicable Law in International Commercial Arbitration 510-12 (1978); Jean Robert & Thomas E. Carbonneau, The French Law of Arbitration § 6.02 (1983). *See generally* Eric Loquin, L'Amiable Composition en Droit Comparé et International (1980).

317. "L'arbitre tranche le litige conformément aux règles de droit, à moins que, dans la convention d'arbitrage, les parties ne lui aient conféré mission de statuer comme amiable compositeur." N.C.P.C. Article 1474 (Fr.) (Translation by the author).

318. *See* Mauro Rubino-Sammartano, *Amiable Compositeur (Joint Mandate to Settle) and Ex Aequo et Bono (Discretional Authority to Mitigate Strict Law*, 9 J. Int'l Arb. 5 (No.1 1992). *See also* R.H. Christie, *Amiable Composition in French and English Law*, 58 Arb. 259 (1992).

319. *See generally* the essays contributed to Lex Mercatoria and Arbitration (Thomas E. Carbonneau, ed., 1990); Craig, Park and Paulsson, International Chamber of Commerce Arbitration, *supra* note 5, chapter 35; Georges Delaume, *The Proper Law of State Contracts and the Lex Mercatoria*, 3 For. Investment L.J. 79 (1988); Filip de Ly, International Business Law and Lex Mercatoria (1992); Feloc Dasser, *Internationale Schiedsgerichte und Lex Mercatoria*, Rechtsvergleichender Beitrag zür Diskussion über ein Nichtstaatliches Handelsrecht (Zurich, 1989), *reviewed by* Filip De Ly, 39 Am. J. Comp. L. 629 (1991);

use the term to indicate an autonomous legal order created through multiple, state-sanctioned, international economic relationships, or a multilateral treaty such as the United Nations (Vienna) Convention on the International Sale of Goods. *Lex merca-toria* may work its way into contract interpretation through the International Chamber of Commerce arbitration rules, which charge arbitrators in all cases to "take account of ... the relevant usages,"[320] or which (in cases where the parties have made no choice of law) call for application of "the law designated by those rules of conflict which [the arbitrator] deems appropriate."[321] Some arbitrators perceive their mission to include application of non-national customary international business law by dint of clauses expressly authorizing them to decide on the basis of "general principles of law" or "equitable considerations."

Little consensus exists about the substance of *lex mercatoria*. Among the principles said to constitute *lex mercatoria* are several time-honored generalities:[322] (i) *pacta sunt servanda* (contracts are to be enforced); (ii) *rebus sic stantibus* (a duty to adapt obligations to changed circumstances); (iii) *force majeure* ("impossibility" as a defense to contract performance); (iv) good faith; and (v) the presumption that a controlling interest of a group of companies contracted to arbitrate on behalf of all members of the group.

Although Continental courts have reacted favorably to *lex mercatoria*,[323] the English have been more dubious about an arbitrator's application of non-national

---

Note 319, *continued*
Bernardo Cremades & Steven Plehn, *The New Lex Mercatoria and the Harmonization of the Laws of International Commercial Transaction*, 2 B.U. Int'l L.J. 317 (1984); UNIDROIT PRINCIPLES OF INTERNATIONAL COMMERCIAL CONTRACTS (International Institute for the Unification of Private Law 1994).

320. I.C.C. Rules, Article 13(5).

321. I.C.C. Rules, Article 13(3).

322. *See* Rt. Hon. Lord Justice Mustill, *The New Lex Mercatoria: The First Twenty Five Years*, 4 Arb. Int'l 86, 110, *reprinted from* LIBER AMICORUM FOR LORD WILBERFORCE (Oxford Univ. Press 1987). Lord Mustill's now famous survey, included twenty notions that Lord Mustill had found characterized by various more or less convincing sources as "rules" of *lex mercatoria*. *See also* discussion in Craig, Park and Paulsson, *supra* note 5, at 621-30. The UNIDROIT PRINCIPLES OF INTERNATIONAL COMMERCIAL CONTRACTS, *supra* note 319, contain one hundred nineteen articles dealing with (1) General Provisions of Contract Law, (2) Contract Formation, (3) Contract Validity, (4) Contract Interpretation, (5) Contract Content, (6) Performance and (7) Non-Performance.

323. *See* French N.C.P.C. Article 1496 as amended, permitting application of *lex mercatoria* in the absence of choice of law by the parties. *See also* Norsolor v. Pabalk, Judgment of Oct. 9, 1984, Cass. civ. 1re, Fr., 10 D.S. Jur. 101, *reported in* 112 J. Dr. Dr. Int'l 679 (1985), 1985 Rev. Arb. 421, and XI Y.B.Int. Com. Arb. (Int'l Council Com. Arb.) 484 (1986). An arbitral tribunal decided a commercial agency termination dispute between a French and a Turkish company. The Turkish agent was awarded an indemnity of 800,000 French francs that was based on neither French nor Turkish law. The parties had provided for no national law to govern the merits of the dispute. The arbitrators selected *lex mercatoria* after applying "appropriate" conflict of law principles as allowed under article 13(3) of the Arbitration Rules of the International Chamber of Commerce. This award was ultimately upheld by the highest court in Austria (the seat of the arbitration).

principles to contract disputes.[324] In part this is because the content of *lex mercatoria* does not always permit much certainty about the outcome of an arbitration. For example, although *lex mercatoria* contains the principle of *rebus sic stantibus* (an implied condition that an agreement ceases to be binding if the facts upon which it was founded are radically changed), studies have concluded that arbitral awards are generally silent on the conditions for the principle's application.[325]

To be applied consistently, concepts such as good faith performance of contracts require the flesh of precedent on their doctrinal bones. While some institutions have published awards that might guide the application of *lex mercatoria*,[326] such publication is not always abundant.[327] This jurisprudential vacuum may lead some arbitrators to use transnational norms not to fill a gap in a contract according to a best guess about the parties' intent, but to justify application of private normative preferences.[328]

The goal of maximizing adjudicatory certainty will generally counsel against application of *lex mercatoria* or a grant of the power of *amiable composition*. In a cross-border business transaction among parties who lack the shared values of a relatively homogeneous community, fidelity to the parties' expectations is usually best secured by rights and duties delineated under a reasonably fixed legal system.[329] References to chameleon-like notions of *lex mercatoria* or *amiable composition* add a source of

---

324. *See* Mustill & Boyd, *infra* note 352, at 594-96. *See also* Eagle Star v. Yuval Ins. [1978] 1 Lloyd's Rep. 357, 362 and House of Lords decision in Amin Rasheed Shipping v. Kuwait Ins. Co., 1984 App. Cas. 50. An evolution in the English attitude, however, has been signaled by a Court of Appeal decision which recognized an award rendered in Switzerland in which the arbitrators applied no fixed national law. *See* Deutsche Schachtbau- und Tiefbohgesellschaft v. Ras Al Khaimah Nat'l Oil Co., [1987] 2 All E.R. 769, *reversed on other grounds* by House of Lords [1988] 2 All E.R. 833. Compare the French attitude in *Pabalk v. Norsolor*, *infra* note 566. *See generally* David Rivkin, *Enforceability of Arbitral Awards Based on Lex Mercatoria*, 9 Arb. Int'l 67 (1993).

325. *See* Denis Philippe, *'Pacta sunt servanda' et 'Rebus sic stantibus,'* in L'Apport de la Jurisprudence Arbitrale 181, 243 (1986): "La jurisprudence arbitrale est plutôt muette sur les conditions d'application de la clausula rebus sic stantibus." International Chamber of Commerce Pub. No. 440/1.

326. *See* Sigvard Jarvin, Yves Derains & Jean-Jacques Arnaldez (Eds.), Collection of ICC Arbitral Awards. Volume I — Awards 1974-85 (1990); and Volume II — Awards 1986-90 (1994).

327. *See* Gillis Wetter, *Review of W. Laurence Craig, William W. Park & Jan A.S. Paulsson, International Chamber of Commerce Arbitration* in Svensk Juristtidning 156, 161 (1984).

328. Arbitrators may be empowered to fill gaps either by the parties themselves, or by the properly applicable law. *See generally* Fritz Nicklisch, *Agreement to Arbitrate to Fill Contractual Gaps*, 5 J. Int'l Arb. 35 (1988); George Verveniotis, *Arbitration and Contractual Gaps*, 5 J. Int'l Arb.103 (1988). For an administrative law analogy, *see* Kenneth Culp Davis, *No Law to Apply*, 25 San Diego L. Rev. 1 (1988), arguing that the United States Supreme Court should not have denied review in Hecker v. Chaney, 470 U.S. 821 (1985), merely because there was "no law to apply." Davis argues for review to insure "justice, fairness and reasonableness." Davis, *supra*, at 11.

329. A different conclusion might obtain for arbitral régimes operating in relatively homogeneous communities. *See* Lisa Bernstein, *supra* at note 16.

uncertainty, and may lend themselves to abuse as a vehicle for the improper intrusion of an arbitrator's personal normative preferences into contract dispute resolution.[330]

B. THE ARBITRAL SITUS.[331]

The arbitral situs will influence the efficiency and fairness of an arbitration perhaps more than any other element within the parties' control at the time a pre-dispute arbitration clause is drafted.[332] The place of arbitration will affect three variables: the integrity of local judges who may be called to review an award; the availability of treaty enforcement mechanisms; and the finality of the arbitral award.

1. Judicial Integrity.

If the dissatisfied loser of an arbitration can have the award annulled by a corrupt judge, then as a practical matter the award will be very difficult to enforce. The New York and the Panama Conventions both provide for refusal to recognize an award that has been "set aside or suspended by a competent authority of the country in which...that award was made." The English version of the Convention uses the permissive "may," while the more forceful French text lends itself to a mandatory construction.[333] Since an enforcement forum rarely will second-guess courts at the place of arbitration by recognizing awards set aside where rendered,[334] maximizing certain-

---

330. *See* William W. Park, *Control Mechanisms in the Development of a Modern Lex Mercatoria,"* in LEX MERCATORIA AND ARBITRATION 109 (Thomas E. Carbonneau ed., 1990).
331. Chapter V explores in greater detail the public policy concerns that bear on judicial control over arbitration at the place of the proceedings. The balance between award finality and procedural integrity are there examined from the perspective of community interest rather than the goals of the business managers.
332. The selection of arbitrators, of course, is the single most important choice the parties make during an arbitration. However, the composition of the arbitral tribunal almost always takes place *after* the dispute arises, rather than when the arbitration clause is drafted.
333. Article V(1)(e). In French Article V reads, "La reconnaissance et l'exécution ne seront refusées que si...la sentence a été annulée par une autorité compétente du pays dans lequel la sentence a été rendue." ("Recognition and enforcement will not be refused unless ... the award has been set aside by a competent authority of the country in which that award was made.")
334. In theory, a court at another situs where the loser has assets could enforce an annulled award on a discretionary basis. Outside France (see discussion at notes 566-71) the author knows of only one case in which a court enforced an award annulled where rendered. Both presented peculiar circumstances. In Sonatrach v. Ford, Bacon & Davis (Tribunal de première instance de Bruxelles, 6 December 1988 and Cour d'appel de Bruxelles, 8ème chambre, 9 January 1990) a Bruxelles court ordered execution of an I.C.C. award that had been set aside after a merits review by an Algerian court at the seat of arbitration in Algiers. The Algerian defendant was the national gas agency, among the most powerful of state agencies in Algeria. The Belgian court likely suspected political interference at the arbitral situs. In the other decision, Pabalk v. Norsolor (Cour de Cassation, 9 October 1984, 1985 Revue de

ty involves choosing an arbitral situs where annulment of awards is not likely to be facilitated by a bribe to a local judge.

2. Treaty Coverage.

New York Arbitration Convention enforcement provisions generally apply to awards that are foreign from the perspective of the enforcement forum. Some countries, including the United States, grant treaty coverage on the basis of a reciprocity linked to the arbitral situs (party nationality being irrelevant), recognizing only awards rendered in another treaty country. The treaty's enforcement obligation normally does not apply as such at the arbitral seat.[335] While it might be possible for an award to come within the Convention's scope if characterized as "non-domestic," this concept is little-used and unfocused.[336]

Whether non-treaty enforcement mechanisms are available under national law will depend on the idiosyncracies of local statute. In some countries, it may matter very little whether the New York Arbitration Convention applies. For example, the Federal Arbitration Act provides for enforcement and confirmation of awards rendered in the United States regardless of Convention coverage. Not all countries, however, have legal systems that permit rapid and easy understanding of local (non-treaty) arbitral enforcement mechanisms.

3. Optimal Judicial Review.

a. Award Finality.

Finality in private dispute resolution requires that the parties assume some risk that the arbitrators will render a bad award. There is an assumption of risk that arbitrators will "get it wrong." Without finality on the merits of the dispute, arbitration becomes little more than polite foreplay to court litigation, or an interesting but unsuccessful attempt at settlement.

Arbitral finality should not mean, however, that the losing party must accept an arbitrator's refusal to respect the terms of the arbitral mission. Nor should finality be

Note 334, continued
l'Arbitrage 431) a French court recognized an Austrian award of an arbitral tribunal that had applied the "law merchant" (*lex mercatoria*), rather than any national legal principles. Ultimately, the Austrian lower court decision to annul the award was itself overturned.

335. The only significant differences in the United States between enforcing a New York Convention award and a domestic award are (i) a three year period (rather than one year period) for confirmation of the award, and (ii) additional grounds for refusal of confirmation drawn from Article V of the N.Y. Convention. The Convention Article V defenses are available in connection with a motion to confirm, but not to vacate. 9 U.S.C. § 207. In practice courts often confuse vacatur, refusal to confirm and refusal to recognize an award. *See, e.g.,* Northrop v. Triad, 811 F.2d 1265 (9th Cir.), *cert. denied,* 108 S.Ct. 261 (1987).

336. *See* Bergesen v. Muller, 710 F.2d 928 (2d Cir. 1983).

a license for a fundamental disaccord between how the arbitrators were authorized to decide and how they did in fact decide.[337]

From a legal perspective, the best place for international arbitration will be a country with a balanced approach to review of awards: where the judiciary promotes an arbitration's basic procedural integrity, but does not intervene to correct an arbitrator's honest mistake of law or fact. Judicial review on the merits of the dispute (as in England when the parties do not or cannot waive their right of appeal) will give clever counsel opportunities to disturb the award's *res judicata* effect. On the other hand, a total absence of any judicial review (as in Switzerland, when the right to challenge an award has been validly excluded by contract) will mean that the loser of a procedurally irregular arbitration must resist the defective award everywhere in the world that it had assets. A losing claimant in a defective arbitration may have no effective remedy at all (other than a new arbitration or litigation) since there will be no award to challenge.

b. Excess of Authority.[338]

Proper judicial supervision of arbitration requires a distinction between an arbitrator's clear excess of authority and an award that may be legally wrong but not *ultra vires*. The former should be reviewable; the latter not so. Yet the line between excess of authority and an error of law or fact is thin enough that any judge who ventures to correct excess of authority risks imposing his or her own judicial conclusions about the merits of the dispute. Even in a country whose arbitration statute limits judicial review to an examination of breaches of procedural integrity rather than error of law, room still exists for a judge to overreach in setting aside an award. Determining what constitutes an arbitrator's excess of authority often involves subtleties of characterization that in some cases may lead to vacatur of an award by a judge who disagrees with the arbitrator's conclusions, while in other cases may lead to recognition of an award arguably rendered in disregard of the contract terms.[339]

To illustrate the difficulties in limiting arbitral authority, imagine that two merchants agree that an arbitrator will settle disputes arising out of the sale of peaches. Another contract between the same merchants covers a sale of pecans but contains no arbitration clause. In such circumstances, an arbitral award purporting to cover the sale of pecans would normally be void. If the first arbitration agreement, however, referred to sales of "fruit," the scope of the arbitration agreement would be more problematic. A

---

337. *See generally* Adam Samuel, Jurisdictional Problems in Commercial International Arbitration (1989).

338. *See also* discussion *infra* at notes 358-61 and 393-96.

339. *See generally*, Mobil Oil v. Asamara Oil, 487 F.Supp. 63 (S.D.N.Y. 1980) and Inter-City Gas Corp. v. Boise Cascade Corp, 845 F.2d 184 (8th Cir. 1988). In the latter case the court said, "Although the arbitrator may interpret ambiguous language, the arbitrator may not disregard unambiguous contract provisions." *Id.* at 187. Yet the court wrote that it would "not set aside the arbitrator's award simply because . . . the arbitrator erred . . . in determining the facts." *Id.* at 189.

judge reviewing the award would be asked to consider whether "fruit" was used with its botanical meaning, comprising the contents of the developed ovary of any seed plant (including pecans) in which case the arbitrators would render an award about pecans within their authority. Similarly, arbitrators who apply provisions of United States antitrust law, notwithstanding the merchants' agreement that the contract shall be subject to the laws of Switzerland, might exceed their jurisdiction unless the mandatory norms of the place of performance preempt the contractually-designated law.[340]

The question of arbitrator authority may arise at the beginning as well as the end of an arbitration. The arbitrators' power to hear a dispute may be challenged, for example, on the basis that (i) the subject matter of the dispute is not capable of settlement by arbitration (*i.e.* not "arbitrable"), (ii) the arbitrators' contractually-defined mission does not permit adjudication of the dispute, or (iii) the arbitrators have no jurisdiction to determine the validity of the contract itself and/or the arbitration agreement.[341]

c. Public Policy and Due Process.

Judicial review on public policy grounds likewise can be problematic. Some countries, including France and Switzerland, have made public policy (*ordre public*) an explicit statutory ground for annulment of awards, although the constraints of this public policy may be different in international rather than domestic arbitration.[342] For example, usury limits and the requirement of reasoned arbitral awards have been included in domestic, but not international, public policy.[343] On the other hand, respect for the jurisdiction of bankruptcy courts has been held to constitute an element of international public policy.[344] Exchange controls, antitrust, customs and tax regulations probably implicate both domestic and international public policy, as do illegal arms deals and traffic in illicit drugs.

---

340. *See* the dicta in footnote 19 of Mitsubishi Motors v. Soler Chrysler Plymouth *infra* at note 510.

341. See discussion infra at notes 419-24 (arbitrability), notes 449-460 (contractually defined authority) and notes 359-61 and 396 (void and voidable contracts).

342. *See* discussion *infra* at notes 377-80 and 386-91.

343. *See* Judgment of June 9, 1983, Cour d'Appel, Paris, 1983 Rev. Arb. 497. An award was rendered in favor of a Liechtenstein company (Iso-Holding) that had assisted financing (through *portage d'action*) of Canadian operations of the loser. The transaction was attacked as a disguised loan at an interest rate (19.2%) in excess of the legal French maximum. Even if such a characterization were correct, the court held it would not violate *ordre public international*, and thus the award could not be annulled. *See id.* at 501 (commentary by Vasseur). On reasoned awards, see cases *cited in* Jean Robert & Thomas E. Carbonneau, THE FRENCH LAW OF ARBITRATION § 9.07(1) (1983). In addition, see the prohibition on arbitration by public entities, which does not apply to international arbitration. *See* Judgment of May 2, 1966, (Gelakis), Cass. civ. Ire, Fr., 1966 D.S. Jr. 575.

344. Judgment of March 8, 1988, (Thinet v. SRS), Cass. civ. Ire, Fr., 1988 D.S. Jur. (Information Rapides) 81. The court affirmed annulment of an arbitral award against a bankrupt company, granting damages in an amount different from the judgment of the bankruptcy court (*tribunal de commerce de Paris*). The award was found to violate *ordre public international* under

The contours of due process present special problems for international arbitration, principally because many legal concepts of fairness tend to be parochial notwithstanding claims to universality sometimes made by the legal profession. To the Continental business manager, for example, American-style discovery in civil cases will generally add unfamiliar complications rather than comfort.

4. National Models.

Although the New York Arbitration Convention permits refusal of recognition to an award set aside where rendered, the Convention establishes no criteria for proper or improper vacatur.[345] Thus judicial review of an award at the arbitral situs generally will be governed by the local arbitration law there in force.

Three statutory models have emerged for review of arbitral awards by courts at the seat of arbitration: (i) a right of appeal on the merits, (ii) a non-waivable right to challenge an award for defects of procedural integrity in the arbitration, and (iii) no judicial review at all.[346] From the perspectives of justice and the efficiency of international dispute resolution, the second alternative is preferable in that it permits challenge to awards for violations of fundamental fairness (such as bribery or excess of authority) but does not give the local judiciary the opportunity to interfere with the merits of the dispute.

A balance between award finality and procedural integrity will be found in arbitral régimes of most major arbitral centers, including England,[347] France,[348]

Note 344, continued

article 1502 of the French Nouveau code de procedure civile. The dispute, although between two French companies, was characterized as international because it arose from a contract for construction of buildings in Saudi Arabia. The case presents a different issue from whether bankruptcy courts themselves may as a matter of policy respect the bankrupt party's agreement to arbitrate. *See* SONATRACH v. Distrigas, 80 Bankruptcy Rep. 606 (D.Mass. 1987). However, even vital national and international public policies may sometimes be too ill-defined to be useful as a guide to arbitrators. *See* Northrop Corp. v. Triad Int'l Mktg., S.A., 811 F.2d 1265 (9th Cir.), *cert. denied,* 108 S. Ct. 261 (1987) (confirming an award of allegedly illegal commissions for arms).

345. *Compare* the approach of the European Arbitration Convention, discussed *supra* at note 248, which defines the "right" grounds for award annulment that will justify non-recognition.

346. This last model of "non-review" is discussed *infra* at notes 559-62. The first two approaches are dealt with *infra* at notes 347-417, in the discussion of arbitration law at major arbitral centers.

347. *See* discussion *infra* at notes 352-76. This assumes that the parties have excluded the normal right of appeal by contract. Section 23 of the 1950 Arbitration Act provides a non-waivable right to have an award set aside for arbitrator "misconduct." The right to opt out of appellate review by what the English call a pre-dispute "exclusion agreement" would be denied in cases dealing with commodities, insurance or admiralty matters governed by English law. The purpose of this carve-out is to keep English law in these areas fertilized by a stream of real live cases.

348. *See* discussion *infra* at notes 377-80.

Germany,[349] Switzerland[350] and the United States,[351] and as well as countries that have adopted the Model Arbitration Law of the United Nations Commission on International Trade Law. Each of these legal systems in its own way gives the loser of an arbitration a right to challenge an award obtained by a fundamentally unfair procedure. In addition to making sure that the arbitral tribunal was properly constituted pursuant to a valid arbitration agreement, courts will hear challenges to awards for (i) excess of authority by the arbitral tribunal, (ii) arbitrator bias, corruption or lack of independence or (iii) denial of one side's right to present its case.

The fashion in which these five national arbitral systems provide balanced judicial review at the place of arbitration will be sketched below. The goal of this section is not to provide an exhaustive or systematic analysis of the various national legal systems, but rather to highlight some of the more vital matters debated by scholars and practitioners.

a. England.[352]

Statutory Framework. Parties to international contracts[353] may conclude "exclusion agreements" that eliminate most judicial review of arbitration awards rendered in international disputes, as well as of interlocutory appeals on questions of law arising in the course of the arbitration. Absent an exclusion agreement, courts are empowered to hear appeals from an arbitrator's decision on matters of law.[354]

Even if an arbitration clause contains an exclusion agreement, English courts still have power to safeguard the basic procedural integrity of the arbitral process by set-

---

349. *See* discussion *infra* at notes 381-85.
350. *See* discussion *infra* at notes 386-91. However, the parties may choose cantonal rather than federal procedure, in which case Article 36(f) of the Inter-cantonal Concordat permits challenge to awards that are "arbitrary ... or constitute a clear violation of law or equity." Moreover, federal procedure (LDIP Article 192) permits the parties to exclude all review, thus putting themselves under the same regime of arbitral anarchy operating under the Belgian 1985 statute, discussed *infra* at notes 559-62.
351. *See* discussion *infra* at notes 392-416.
352. On English arbitration law, *see generally* Michael Mustill & Stewart Boyd, COMMERCIAL ARBITRATION (2d ed., 1989); Adam Samuel, *Developments in English Arbitration Law*, 5 J. Int'l Arb., Sept. 1988, at 9; Johan Steyn, *England's Response to the Model Law of Arbitration* (1993 Freshfields Arbitration Lecture) 10 Arb. Int'l 1 (1994). The provisions of the Arbitration Acts of 1950 and 1979 cover arbitral proceedings only in England and Wales. Scotland has its own arbitration regime, and has recently adopted the UNCITRAL Model Arbitration Law, discussed *infra* at note 417.
353. The 1979 Arbitration Act defines "domestic arbitration agreements," as to which exclusion agreements are not valid, as any agreement to arbitrate in the United Kingdom to which no foreign individual (non-citizen or non-resident) or corporation (determined with respect to either place of management or place of incorporation) is a party. In other words, an international agreement is defined as one including at least one foreign person. Compare definitions of international arbitration in the French and Swiss legislation, discussed *infra* at notes 377 and 386-91.
354. *See* Arbitration Act of 1979, Section 1.

ting aside an award for arbitrator "misconduct."[355] Recent court decisions have made clear that correcting arbitral misconduct will no longer serve as an excuse for back-door judicial tampering with the legal or factual merits of an arbitration.[356]

An exclusion agreement must be in writing. However, reference to appropriate institutional arbitration rules that stipulate waiver of the right to appeal will constitute the incorporation of a valid exclusion agreement into the basic contract.[357] Arbitration rules of the International Chamber of Commerce (Article 24) and the London Court of International Arbitration (Article 16.8) will operate to exclude appeal.

Exclusion agreements concluded before the beginning of an arbitration will not be valid when English law governs the contract and the controversy relates to the "special category disputes" of insurance, commodities, or admiralty matters. Parliament intended that commercial controversies should continue to fertilize the development of English law in areas in which it has long been preeminent.

Nor will pre-dispute exclusion agreements be valid if all parties are British residents or nationals. Non-international arbitration will normally be subject to the possibility of appellate review on the merits of the dispute, thereby protecting the perceived British interest in the proper application of the law in domestic cases.

Arbitral Jurisdiction. English courts have traditionally taken an activist approach to the question of how judges and arbitrators should interact concerning matters related to arbitral jurisdiction.[358] The last word on the subject will always be with the courts. However, the timing of recourse to courts on jurisdictional matters is open to debate. Continental legal systems often defer judicial review of arbitral jurisdiction until *after* an award has been rendered, whereas English judges allow a challenge to the arbitrator's competence to go straight to the courts at the initial stages of the proceedings.

The matter of the arbitrators' jurisdiction to determine the limits of their own authority is distinct from an arbitration clause's "separability" from the main contract in which it is contained. Separability reduces the potential for abuse by a party wishing to stop an arbitration before it has begun by asserting that the arbitration clause has been rendered invalid by some event discovered subsequent to signing the agreement. The arbitrator is thus able to rule on claims related to fraud in the inducement of the contract and other matters that might make the contract invalid.[359] The separa-

---

355. Arbitration Act of 1950, section 23.

356. *See* Bank Mellat v. GAA Development & Constr. Co., [1988] 2 Lloyd's Rep. 44, 45 (Q.B.) (majority arbitrators refuse to convene further meetings at request of dissenter).

357. Arab African Energy Corp. v. Olieprodukten Nederland B.V., [1983] Lloyd's Rep. 419 (Q.B.).

358. *See* discussion of arbitration of claims of fraud in the inducement, *infra* at note 460. *See also* discussion of the arbitrators' jurisdiction to determine their own jurisdiction, *infra* at note 360 and 396.

359. *See* cases in note 361. For American analogues, see Prima Paint Corp. v. Flood & Conklin Mfg. Co., 388 U.S. 395 (1967) and Nicaragua v. Standard Fruit Company, 937 F.2d 469 (9th Cir. 1991). In the latter case the Circuit Court reversed a lower court that improperly looked to a contract in its entirety in order to determine whether to enforce an arbitration clause.

bility doctrine serves some of the same purposes as the Continental doctrine known as *Kompetenz-Kompetenz*, or *compétence de la compétence*, which purports to give the arbitral tribunal initial power to determine its own jurisdiction, although courts may later review the award.[360]

The existence of a fully developed doctrine of separability has been elaborated in recent cases that have brought England closer in this respect to other major arbitral centers.[361] An arbitration clause can legally confer jurisdiction on an arbitrator to consider the legality of the main contract, even though the parties will have a right of recourse to courts on the question of arbitral jurisdiction.

The Courts' "Inherent Powers". Arbitration in England sometimes implicates the "inherent powers" of English courts to intervene in arbitral proceedings. A recent House of Lords decision examining the contours of such judicial powers arose from a dispute about the cost of alterations in construction of the Channel Tunnel between England and France. In *Channel Tunnel Group Ltd. ("Eurotunnel") v. Balfour Beatty Construction Ltd.*,[362] the disagreement over modifications led the general contractor to threaten to stop work. Eurotunnel's action against the builder for an injunction restraining suspension of work was met by the contractor's motion to stay court proceedings by virtue of a contract clause providing for arbitration in Bruxelles under the rules of the International Chamber of Commerce.

As a general matter, English courts must refer parties to arbitration when their dispute is covered by a valid international arbitration clause. However, the courts of England (like those of many other countries) may grant interim measures of protection in the event of emergencies. In an opinion by Lord Mustill, the House of Lords

---

360. *See, e.g.*, Article 1458 of the Nouveau code de procédure civile, providing that "When a dispute before an arbitral tribunal pursuant to an arbitration clause is brought before a court (*"juridiction de l'Etat"*), the latter must declare itself incompetent. If the dispute has not yet been put before the arbitral tribunal, the court must also declare itself to lack jurisdiction unless the arbitration clause is obviously invalid (*"manifestement nulle"*). In neither case can the court raise its lack of jurisdiction on its own motion. *See also* Article 16 of the UNCITRAL Model Law, providing that "a decision by the arbitral tribunal that the contract is null and void shall not entail *ipso jure* the invalidity of the arbitration clause." *See generally* C. Svernlov, *What Isn't, Ain't,* Volume 8, No. 4, J. Int'l Arb. 37 (1991); Andrew Rogers & Rachel Launders, *Separability — The Indestructible Arbitration Clause*, 10 Arb. Int'l (No. 1) 77 (1994). *See also* D. Rivkin and F. Kellner, *In Support of the FAA: An Argument Against U.S. Adoption of the UNCITRAL Model Law*, 1 Am. Rev. Int'l Arb. 535, at 547-48. *See also* discussion *infra* at notes 394-96.

361. *See* Ashville Investments Ltd. v. Elmer Contractors Ltd., [1988] 2 All England Reports 577 and Harbour Assurance Co. (U.K.) Ltd. v. Kansa General International Assurance Co. Ltd., [1993] Q.B. 70 and [1993] 3 All England Reports 897. *See generally* DTI Consultation Paper on 1994 Draft Arbitration Bill, *infra* note 370, at III, 3-7. *See also* D. Mark Cato, ARBITRATION PRACTICE & PROCEDURE (1992), Section 3.8, at 45-54.

362. [1993] 2 W.L.R. 270; [1993] A.C. 335. *See generally*, Claude Reymond, *The Channel Tunnel Case and the Law of Int'l Arb'n*, 109 L.Q.R. 337 (1993); V.V. Veeder, *Chronique de jurisprudence anglaise: L'Arret Channel Tunnel*, 1993 Revue de L'Arbitrage 705 (1993). It was announced on 5 April 1994 that the dispute was settled for an additional £ 70 to £ 85 million, for a total payment of £ 1.14 billion to the builders.

confirmed both a stay of the court action in light of the arbitration clause, and the principle that English courts possessed inherent power to grant an interim injunction against work stoppage notwithstanding the arbitration clause. Under the circumstances, the court refused to grant an injunction, but only as a matter of discretion, rather than from lack of authority.

The Arbitration's Curial Law.[363] In *Hiscox v. Outhwaite*,[364] a dispute concerning a reinsurance contract between two insurance syndicates was referred to arbitration pursuant to a clause stipulating London as the arbitral situs. The sole arbitrator, an English barrister practicing in France, conducted the arbitration in London but signed and dated the award when he returned home to Paris.[365] The loser applied to the High Court in London for leave to appeal a question of law.[366] Normally an English court can grant leave to appeal questions of law that arise in connection with arbitral awards made in England, assuming no written exclusion of the right of appeal. However, if the award was deemed to be rendered in Paris, then English courts arguably would have no jurisdiction to hear the appeal, and the award would be enforceable as foreign under the New York Arbitration Convention.[367] Therefore it became critical to determine whether the award was made in England or abroad.

The House of Lords held that for purposes of the New York Arbitration Convention the award was "made" in Paris, where it was perfected by the arbitrator's signature. Surprisingly however, the opinion by Lord Oliver of Aylmerton[368] went on to say that English courts could nevertheless exercise a curial jurisdiction to hear appeals, and could adjourn any decision on enforcement under the Convention until after the appeal had been heard. Because the arbitration had its seat in England, the applicable procedural law was English notwithstanding the place where the award was made.

The result in *Hiscox v. Outhwaite* may be satisfactory (in the sense that the English court's assertion of jurisdiction most likely fulfilled the parties' expectations), but the

---

363. *See also* the more general discussion of an arbitration's curial law *infra* at notes 541-79.

364. House of Lords Decision No. 1, 24 July 1991, [1991] All England Reports, 641. The case is reproduced in XVII ICC YEARBOOK OF COMMERCIAL ARBITRATION (1992) at 599. Commentaries on the case include Claude Reymond, *Where is an Arbitral Award Made?*, 108 Law Quarterly Review 1 (1992); John Timmons, *Where is an Arbitration Award Made and What Are the Consequences?*, Arbitration (May 1992), at 124; Fraser Davidson, *Where is an Arbitral Award Made?*, 41 International & Comparative Law Quarterly 637 (1992); Michael Schneider, *Le lieu où la jurisprudence est rendue*, 9 Bulletin de L'Association Suisse de L'Arbitrage 279 (1991).

365. The award in question, styled a "final interim award," rejected the contention that the contract had been effectively rescinded and determined preliminary issues related to the amount of damages.

366. Leave to appeal may be granted under § 1(3)(b) of the 1979 Arbitration Act. The loser also applied for an order directing the arbitrator to state reasons pursuant to 1979 Arbitration Act § 1(5) and for remission of the award pursuant to § 22 of the 1950 Arbitration Act.

367. *See* § 7(1) of the 1975 Arbitration Act, implementing the New York Convention in the United Kingdom.

368. The other Law Lords expressed agreement with the draft speech prepared by their "noble and learned friend Lord Oliver."

reasoning is open to question. Distinguished scholars have argued that an award should be considered made not by reference to a single geographical nexus such as the place of signature, but by its connection with the entire legal framework of the arbitration's procedural seat.[369] While this argument has some force, one must nevertheless question too great a gap between the contractually designated seat of arbitration and the place where the arbitral hearings actually take place. While the goals of the international arbitral system would hardly call for strict territorial formalism, it would defeat the parties' legitimate expectations if arbitrators went so far as to treat the seat of arbitration as only a legal fiction. If the parties provided for arbitration in London, presumably they do not want the arbitrators holding all the hearings and deliberations in Paris just because their palates prefer French cuisine. Indeed, too much deviation from the parties' expressed mandate could result in non-recognition of an award for excess of authority under New York Arbitration Convention Article V(1)(c).

Reform? Under the supervision of the Department of Trade and Industry, the British government published a draft arbitration bill that would consolidate into a single statute the arbitration provisions now contained in several different acts.[370] The bill proposes nothing radically different from current law with respect to judicial review of awards. Agreements excluding appeal on questions of law would continue to be permitted in international arbitration, except for pre-arbitration exclusion agreements covering the "special category disputes" related to maritime, insurance and commodities contracts governed by English law.[371] Notwithstanding an exclusion agreement, the High Court would still have power to set aside an award for arbitrator misconduct, which the bill now defines to include cases where "proceedings have been improperly conducted or a reference or award has been improperly procured."[372] The Court would not be authorized to set aside an award, however, if remission of the award to the arbitrators (a less drastic measure) would be appropriate.[373]

---

369. *See* Claude Reymond, *Where is an Arbitral Award Made?*, 108 Law Quarterly Review 1 (1992). Professor Reymond writes, "When one says that London, Paris or Geneva is the place of the arbitration ... one means that the arbitration is conducted within the framework of the law of arbitration of England, France or Switzerland, or to use an English expression, under the curial law of the relevant country." On the situs of awards, *see also* Francis Mann, 1 Arbitration International 107 (1985), and Johan Steyn and V.V. Veeder in INTERNATIONAL HANDBOOK ON COMMERCIAL ARBITRATION.

370. Hereinafter DTI 1994 DRAFT ARBITRATION BILL. The genesis of the Department of Trade and Industry bill can be traced to 1989, when the Departmental Advisory Committee on Arbitration Law (DAC), under the chairmanship of Lord Mustill, recommended that England not adopt the United Nations Committee on Trade Law (UNCITRAL) Model Arbitration Law, but instead adopt a new arbitration act of its own making. Subsequently a private working group (chaired by Mr. Arthur Marriott) and the Department of Trade and Industry, advised by the DAC (this time chaired by Lord Justice Steyn), produced a draft bill that was published in February of 1994. For a less than enthusiastic initial reaction to the bill, see A.H. Hermann, *Bill Pulls the Wrong Punches*, Financial Times, 15 February 1994, page 12.

371. DTI 1994 DRAFT ARBITRATION BILL, Section 33. In "special category disputes" exclusion agreements would be valid only if concluded after the beginning of the arbitration.

372. DTI 1994 DRAFT ARBITRATION BILL, Section 27(1)(b).

373. The High Court's power to remit an award to the arbitrators is not circumscribed by any requirement that the Court find proceedings improperly conducted or an award improperly

The much-debated matter of "security for costs" is one aspect of English arbitration law that may be ripe for reform. In *Coppée-Lavalin S.A./N.V. v. Ken-Ren Chemicals and Fertilizers Ltd.*,[374] the House of Lords in a three-two decision required the High Court to exercise its discretion to order security for costs in an I.C.C. arbitration.[375] The fact pattern of the case seems almost tailor-made to arouse sympathy for the fixing of costs: a bankrupt claimant (Ken-Ren) backed by the Kenyan government was willing to fund an arbitral proceeding but not necessarily to pay costs if it should lose the arbitration. Nevertheless, it is not clear that either the interests of international arbitration or the intention of the parties is furthered by such judicial intervention in a private procedure, even in the pursuit of making the parties play more fairly.[376]

b. France.

Statutory Framework. The French arbitration régime promotes the procedural integrity of arbitration without facilitating court second-guessing of arbitrators on matters of law or fact. Article 1502 to the *Nouveau Code de Procédure Civile*, applicable to arbitrations that "implicate international commerce,"[377] permits an international award rendered in France to be annulled when:

(1) the arbitrators decided in the absence of an arbitration agreement or on the basis of a void or expired agreement;

(2) the arbitral tribunal was improperly constituted or the sole arbitrator irregularly appointed;

(3) the arbitrators exceeded their mission;

(4) the adversarial principle [i.e., due process] was not complied with;

(5) the recognition or enforcement of the award would be contrary to international public policy (*ordre public international*).

Note 373, continued

procured. DTI 1984 Draft Arbitration Bill Section 27(1)(a). In its commentary on the draft bill the DTI mentions the four traditional grounds for remission of awards (arbitrator misconduct, an arbitrator's request to correct admitted mistake, "procedural mishaps," and material fresh evidence discovered after the award), as well as recent cases evidencing what it terms a "retrograde" trend toward expanding the grounds for remission and thereby reducing the finality of awards. *See* Department of Trade and Industry Consultation Paper, pages III: 14-15.

374. House of Lords, 5 May 1994, [1994] 2 W.L.R. 631. The case arose out of an arbitration pursuant to a contract for a chemical plant to be built in Kenya by a Belgian company. *See generally* Claude Reymond, *Security for Costs in International Arbitration*, 110 Law Quarterly Review 501 (1994).

375. The statutory basis for the High Court's power is found in Section 12(6) of the Arbitration Act 1950.

376. *See* dissenting opinion by Lord Justice Mustill.

377. Nouveau Code de Procédure Civile [hereinafter N.C.P.C.], Article 1492. *See also* discussion of French cases enforcing foreign awards, discussed *infra* at notes 566-71.

These five grounds for challenge come into play when an award rendered in France is attacked by means of a motion to set aside (*recours en annulation*) to the appropriate Cour d'Appel,[378] or when the prevailing party in the arbitration asks for judicial confirmation (*exequatur*) of the award in order to enhance its enforcement.

An award may be challenged for violation of international, rather than domestic, public policy (*ordre public*). While both international and domestic public policy are creatures of French jurisprudence, the former applies in international disputes while the latter is relevant only in domestic contexts. The requirements of domestic public policy are the more stringent, in order to permit French courts to protect French interests.[379]

Arbitral Jurisdiction. Shortly after its promulgation, the French decree was tested in a case in which a Hong Kong company had concluded a contract, signed by the Egyptian Minister of Tourism and the Egyptian General Organization for Tourism and Hotels (EGOTH), for a joint venture to develop a resort complex near the Pyramids.[380] It was uncertain whether signature of the Minister of Tourism had bound Egypt as a party to the arbitration clause, or whether the government had intervened only in a supervisory and regulatory capacity. Opting for the first interpretation, the arbitrators rendered a $12 million award against the Republic of Egypt. The Paris Cour d'Appel, affirmed by the Cour de Cassation, disagreed, and annulled the award against Egypt on the ground that the arbitrator decided in the absence of a valid arbitration agreement. The court thereby affirmed judicial power to scrutinize an award to determine whether the loser did in fact sign the arbitration agreement.

c. Germany.[381]

Statutory Framework. The German arbitration régime makes no distinction between domestic and international arbitration conducted under German procedural

---

378. N.C.P.C. Article 1504.

379. *See generally* H. Batiffol & P. Lagarde, Droit International Privé (5th ed. 1970), at § 366. *See also* cases discussed in W. Laurence Craig, William W. Park, Jan A.S. Paulsson & W. Michael Reisman, Cases and Materials on Commercial Arbitration, Chapter 9-E-5.

380. Egypt v. Southern Pacific Properties, Ltd., Judgment of July 12, 1984, Cour d'appel, Paris 1987 J.D.I. (Clunet) 129; 1986 Rev. Arb. 75. *See* 23 I.L.M. 1048 (E. Gaillard trans. 1984). Affirmed by Cour de Cassation Judgment of Jan. 6, 1987, Cass. civ. lre, 1987 J.D.I. (Clunet) 469 (with commentary by Ph. Leboulanger), *reprinted in* 26 I.L.M. 1004 (E. Gaillard trans. 1987). The I.C.C. award itself (Case No. 3493) is published in 22 I.L.M. 752 and 1986 Rev. d'Arbitrage 105. Following a subsequent ICSID award against Egypt (ICSID Case No. ARB/84/3, 20 May 1992), the parties reached a final settlement in December 1992. *See* 8 Int. Arb. Rep. 328 (Jan. 1993).

381. Special thanks are due to Christian Bühring-Uhle for help with these German materials. For an English language survey of German arbitration law, *see generally*, Otto Sandrock, *International Arbitration in the Federal Republic of Germany: A Hitherto Missed Opportunity*, 1 Am. Rev. Int'l Arb. 49 (1990).

law.[382] Enforcement of an award may be made if the award has been subject to judicial confirmation.[383] A court may vacate an award when confirmation is refused, or at the initiative of a losing party who has made a motion to set aside the award.

An award may be annulled or refused confirmation on the following grounds, set forth in the German Code of Civil Procedure (ZPO) Section 1041:

1. absence of a valid arbitration agreement, or violation of the applicable arbitral procedure;
2. violation of public policy;
3. improper representation of a party;
4. violation of the adversarial process (*Rechtliches Gehör*), implicating one party's right to be heard;
5. lack of a reasoned opinion, unless a statement of reasons has been waived;
6. any of the grounds that could lead to the setting aside of a final judgment, to the annulment of a judgment that has already become final.[384]

Reform? Germany has not yet developed its full potential as an arbitral situs, and has been described as "an elephant in international trade ... [but] a dwarf in international arbitration." Although Germans have been active as parties to arbitration under the Rules of the International Chamber of Commerce, arbitrating 60% as frequently as the French, Europe's regional leaders, Germany is chosen as an arbitral situs less than 10% as often as France.[385]

To remedy this situation, some scholars and practitioners have suggested adoption of the UNCITRAL Model Law. The issue has been subject to lively debate, but no concrete reform bills are now being debated in the German legislature.

382. *See* Sections 1025-1048 of the German Code of Civil Procedure (Zivilprozeßordnung-ZPO). The German Ministry of Justice is reportedly preparing draft legislation that would enact the UNCITRAL Model Law, discussed *infra* at note 417. See 9 International Arbitration Rept. (No. 12) 11 (1994). For an English translation, see CODE OF CIVIL PROCEDURE RULES OF THE FEDERAL REPUBLIC OF GERMANY OF JANUARY 30, 1877, translated by Simon L. Goren. For a commentary on the 1986 amendments, see Gerhard Wegen, *Introductory Note to German Action on the Revision of the Private International Law*, 27 I.L.M. 1 (1988). An arbitration is considered "foreign" if the procedure was governed by foreign law, regardless of the site. *See* German Supreme Court (Bundesgerichtshof) in BGHZ 21, 365. *See also* Geimer in Zöller (ed.), Zivilprozeßordnung (annotated code), Sec. 1044 n.4 (18th ed. 1993).
383. ZPO, Section 1042. The procedure for confirmation of domestic awards is set forth in ZPO Sections 1042a-1042d. The competent court is the regular court of first instance (Landgericht) which can decide in a simplified procedure without a hearing. However, there can be two levels of appeals.
384. *See* ZPO Sec. 580 no. 1-6, permitting vacatur of a judgment procured by criminal means (such as perjury, fraud, falsified documents) or based on a precedent that was subsequently annulled.
385. *See* Tables 6 and 7 of Appendix I, W. Laurence Craig, William W. Park & Jan A.S. Paulsson, INTERNATIONAL CHAMBER OF COMMERCE ARBITRATION (2d edition, 1990). From 1980 to 1988, Germans were involved in 522 I.C.C. arbitrations, compared the 892 arbitrations involving French parties. During the same period, Germany was chosen as an arbitral situs by the parties or the I.C.C. Court only 62 times, as compared to 646 for France. Compare similar statistics presented for the year 1988, suggested by Professor Sandrock, *id.*, at 49.

d. Switzerland.[386]

Statutory Framework. The Swiss federal conflict-of-laws code (generally referred to as the "*L.D.I.P.*") gives parties to international arbitration in Switzerland a choice between three régimes: (1) limited court review to ensure an arbitration's basic procedural fairness;[387] (2) complete autonomy, if the parties have concluded an explicit agreement to exclude court challenge;[388] or (3) broad judicial review for "violation of law or equity" under cantonal law.

If the parties neither elect cantonal procedure nor explicitly exclude judicial review, the *L.D.I.P.* provides five grounds for challenge of awards: (1) irregular composition of the arbitral tribunal; (2) erroneous decision by the arbitral tribunal with respect to its own jurisdiction; (3) award beyond the issues submitted to the arbitrators or failure to decide claims within the request for arbitration; (4) failure to respect the principle of equal treatment of the parties or the right to adversarial proceedings (*l'égalité des parties ou droit d'être entendu en procédure contradictoire*); (5) incompatibility of the award with public policy. Challenge to the award must be made before the Federal Supreme Court (*Tribunal fédéral*) in Lausanne unless the parties have expressly agreed to substitute review by the cantonal court of the arbitral seat.

Exclusion of Judicial Review. Review of awards may be excluded under Article 192 of the conflict-of-laws code by an explicit agreement (*déclaration expresse*). To be valid, waiver of the right to judicial review must be explicit, and no party may be a Swiss resident or have a Swiss permanent establishment. Reference to institutional arbitration rules containing renunciation of appeal (such as those of the International Chamber of Commerce or the London Court of International Arbitration) will not be sufficient to exclude review.

Normally, a party wrongfully joined to a Swiss arbitration under an arbitration clause it never signed (an affiliated corporation, for example) would still be able to challenge, in Switzerland, the arbitral tribunal's wrongful exercise of jurisdiction as to the non-signatory. In this respect the Swiss version of arbitral autonomy is superior to its analogue in Belgium.[389]

If the parties elect to apply cantonal rather than federal procedure,[390] the Intercantonal Concordat permits judicial review of awards on grounds that include "arbitrariness." Arbitrariness is defined to encompass an award "based on findings which were manifestly contrary to the facts appearing on the file, or one that constitutes a clear violation of law or equity."[391]

---

386. On the *Loi fédérale sur le droit international privé see generally* Marc Blessing, *The New International Arbitration Law in Switzerland*, 5 J. Int'l Arb. June 1988, at 9; Carlo Poncet & Emmanuel Gaillard, *Introductory Note and Translation to the Swiss LDIP*, 27 I.L.M. 37 (1988); LE DROIT DE L'ARBITRAGE (P. Lalive, J.-F. Poudret & C. Reymond, eds. 1989).
387. Swiss L.D.I.P. Article 190(2).
388. Swiss L.D.I.P. Article 192, permits exclusion of review only when both parties reside outside Switzerland.
389. *See* discussion of Article 1717, Belgian Code judiciaire, *infra* at note 559.
390. *See* L.D.I.P. Article 176(2).
391. Concordat Suisse sur l'Arbitrage, Article 36(f). *See* Philippe Neyroud & William W. Park,

e. The United States.

Legal Framework. A Federal District Court may vacate an award rendered in the United States in an international case only on the following enumerated grounds:
 (a) where the award was procured by corruption, fraud or undue means;
 (b) where there was evident partiality or corruption in the arbitrators;
 (c) where the arbitrators were guilty of misconduct by refusing to postpone the hearing or in refusing to hear evidence pertinent and material to the controversy, or of any other misbehavior by which the rights of any party have been prejudiced;
 (d) where the arbitrators exceeded their powers, or so imperfectly executed them that a mutual, final, and definite award upon the subject matter submitted was not made.[392]

The Federal Arbitration Act is drafted broadly enough to encompass arbitrator misconduct of the proceedings, for example by refusal to postpone hearings or to receive pertinent evidence, or when the bargained-for arbitral procedure was not followed by the arbitrators. The Uniform Arbitration Act generally parallels federal grounds for vacating an award, permitting vacatur only where an award was procured by fraud, or where arbitrators exceeded their authority, displayed partiality, or conducted the hearings so as to prejudice the parties' rights.

Excess of Authority. In the United States as elsewhere, the limits of an arbitrator's authority remain difficult to define. Courts asked to review awards have found no bright line to distinguish between an arbitrator's excess of authority, reviewable by courts, and a simple arbitrator error which neither the parties nor the legislators intended should lead to re-litigation on the merits. A Supreme Court opinion handed down over forty years ago contained dicta interpreting the Federal Arbitration Act to include the right to challenge an award for "manifest disregard of the law."[393] A concept fuzzy at best, "manifest disregard of the law" clearly presupposes something beyond an arbitrator's mistake or failure to understand and apply the law. It might include an arbitrator's intentional disregard of the correct governing law, but not an

---

Note 391, continued
   Predestination and Swiss Arbitration Law: Geneva's Application of the International Concordat, 2 B.U. Int'l L.J. 1 (1983-84). On the Concordat Suisse sur l'Arbitrage *see* P. Jolidon, Commentaire du Concordat Suisse sur L'Arbitrage (1984).
392. *See* 9 U.S.C. §10. Compare Uniform Arbitration Act §12 and N.Y. C.P.L.R. §7511. *See generally,* Ian MacNeil, Richard Speidel, & Thomas Stipanowich, Federal Arbitration Law (1994), Chapter 40.
393. Wilko v. Swan, 346 U.S. at 436 (1953). *See generally* Isabelle de la Houssaye, *Manifest Disregard of the Law in International Commercial Arbitration,* 28 Columbia J. Transnational L. 449 (1990). Illustrative cases in the area include Saxis S.S. Co. v. Multifacs Int'l Traders, Inc. 375 F.2d 577, 582 (2d Cir. 1967); San Martine Co. de Navigacion v. Saguenay Terminals, Ltd., 293 F.2d 796, 801 (9th Cir. 1961); Amicizia Societa Navegazione v. Chilean Nitrate & Iodine Sales Corp., 274 F.2d 805, 808 (2d Cir. 1960); Swift Indus. Inc. v. Botany Indus. Inc. 466 F.2d 1125 (3d Cir. 1972); Sea Dragon v. Gebr. Van Weelde Scheepvaartkantoor, 574 F. Supp. 367 (S.D.N.Y. 1983).

honest error in contract interpretation. Even a barely plausible explanation for an arbitrator's decision will often save a bad award from vacatur. One federal appellate judge has suggested that manifest disregard of the law may be found only "where the arbitrators understood and correctly stated the law but proceeded to ignore it."[394]

The limits of an arbitrator's authority can also be problematic at the beginning of an arbitration, for example when a court is asked to enjoin arbitration because of an alleged defect in the arbitrator's power to hear the case. Although an arbitration clause will be "separable" from the validity of the main contract in which it is contained,[395] troublesome distinctions arise when an arbitral tribunal is called to determine questions that might affect its own jurisdiction. The American approach to the timing of judicial intervention in this regard has generally been to allow an arbitration to go forward in the face of claims that the contract was induced by fraud (assuming a valid and sufficiently broad arbitration clause), or that contract rights and duties survive bankruptcy and assignment, but not when the contract and its arbitration clause were allegedly void *ab initio*, for example because of lack of authority to bind an alleged party to arbitration.[396] Thus in some situations the arbitrators may be permitted to deal with questions related to their own jurisdiction, even though courts will always have the last word on the matter when called to review an award.

Procedural Fairness. In an international dispute to be arbitrated in the United States, it is far from clear what aspects of procedural fairness ought to be considered essential. Some aspects of the Anglo-American adversarial process, such as the right to cross-examine witnesses, are usually seen by American lawyers and judges as basic to a fair arbitral hearing.[397] On other procedural matters, however, the right approach is less clear. For example, allowance ought to be made for the fact that to the European business manager American-style discovery may add unfamiliar complication rather than comfort.[398]

---

394. Merrill Lynch, Pierce, Fenner & Smith, Inc. v. Bobker, 808 F.2d 903 (2d Cir. 1986). *See* discussion of Mobile v. Asamera and Inter-City Gas v. Boise Cascade, *supra* note 339.

395. *See* discussion of separability *supra* at notes 358-61.

396. *Compare* Apollo Computer v. Berg, 886 F.2d 469 (1st Cir. 1989) and Hewlett-Packard v. Berg, 867 F.Supp. 1126 (D. Mass. 1994) (arbitrator entitled to consider post-bankruptcy assignment of rights to Swedish defendant) with Three Valleys Municipal Water District v. E.F. Hutton, 925 F.2d 1136 (1991) (courts must determine whether persons who signed contract containing agreement had authority to do so). *See also* note 460 *infra* concerning arbitrator's authority to deal with claims of fraud in the inducement. *Compare* discussion of *Kompetenz-Kompetenz* and separability, *supra* at notes 359-361.

397. Continental legal systems generally provide for more "inquisitorial" proceedings than Americans are comfortable with. On cross-examination in arbitration, see N.Y. Arbitration Law § 7506(c) (McKinney 1980); Nestel v. Nestel, 38 A.D.2d 942-43, 331 N.Y.S.2d 241, 243 (App. Div. 1972).

398. Foreign fears of extensive discovery may account for much reluctance to choose New York as an arbitral situs, even though courts in New York will ordinarily deny requests for discovery in arbitration. Steven J. Stein & Daniel R. Wotman, *The Arbitration Hearing, in* INTERNATIONAL COMMERCIAL ARBITRATION IN NEW YORK 87-98 (J. McClendon & R. Goodman eds., 1986).

Many questions of procedural fairness will become relevant in the arbitration endgame, when a court may be asked either to confirm or to vacate an award. Confirmation raises several of the same issues as vacatur, and then some. A United States court may vacate an award on the basis of the procedural defects set forth in Section 10 of the Federal Arbitration Act. Vacatur, however, is appropriate only when an award is rendered within the United States.[399] In the case of a foreign award covered by the New York Arbitration Convention, a court may refuse to confirm the foreign award[400] on any of the grounds for refusal of recognition set forth in Convention Article V.[401]

A question often arises as to whether the arbitration clause must contain a "consent to judgment" provision under Section 9 of the Federal Arbitration Act.[402] Many courts have skirted the issue by implying an entry of judgment stipulation on the basis of an arbitration clause providing for the finality of the award.[403]

Public Policy — Vacatur or Refusal to Enforce? Notwithstanding the broad invocation of public policy in labor arbitration, as well as in actions relating to the recognition and confirmation of foreign awards covered by the New York Arbitration Convention,[404] United States legislation says nothing about public policy as a ground

---

399. *See* International Standard Electric Corporation v. Bridas Sociedad Anonima Petrolera, Industrial Y Comercial, 745 F. Supp. 172 (S.D.N.Y. 1990), in which the court refused to vacate an award rendered in Mexico even though the contract was subject to New York law..

400. An award will be considered "made" at the time rendered by the arbitral tribunal, not when appeals have been exhausted under the applicable local law. *See* Seetransport Viking Trader v. Navimpex Centrala, 989 F.2d 572 (2d. Cir. 1993), in which a German vessel owner sought to enforce against a Roumanian shipbuilder a six million deutsche mark award rendered by an I.C.C. arbitral tribunal in Paris. The cause of action was time barred, the Court considering that the three year period began to run in 1987 when the final award was rendered, not in 1986 when the Roumanian challenge to the award was finally rejected by the Cour d'Appel de Paris.

401. 9 U.S.C. § 207. New York Convention Article V grounds for refusal of recognition include defects in procedural fairness (such as an invalid arbitration clause or an arbitrator excess of authority), non-arbitrability of subject matter and violation of public policy. *See* discussion *supra* notes 238-43.

402. 9 U.S.C. § 9 speaks of "parties in their agreement hav[ing] agreed that a judgment of the court shall be entered upon the award...."

403. *See* Daihatsu Motor Company v. Terrain Vehicles, 1993 U.S. App. Lexis 32987 (7th Cir. 1993). *Contra* Higgins v. U.S. Postal Service, 655 F. Supp 789 (D. Maine 1987). *Compare* Valley v. Tarrytown Associates, 477 F.2d 208 (2d Cir. 1973), deeming that reference to AAA arbitration rules was not in itself to imply entry of judgment. The AAA rules since that time have been amended to authorize award confirmation. *See generally* Gerald Palmer, *Enforcing Arbitral Decisions*, National Law Journal, 7 February 1994, at 25.

404. Under the New York Convention, foreign awards may be refused recognition, enforcement and confirmation on grounds which include violation of public policy. The New York Convention and its provisions with respect to recognition and enforcement of awards apply only to foreign awards and to a limited class of awards of uncertain scope referred to as "non-domestic." However, the United States implementing legislation for the New York Convention permits refusal to confirm a Convention award on Article V grounds. 9 U.S.C. § 207.

for annulment or vacatur of commercial awards rendered in the United States.[405] Therefore it is critical to distinguish between (i) vacatur of an award and (ii) judicial refusal to confirm or to recognize an award, even though not all courts have been clear on this.[406] Vacatur of an award at the place where rendered triggers the loss of its presumptive validity under the New York Arbitration Convention in actions to enforce the award abroad.

For example, imagine that an arbitrator in New York renders an award ordering an American multinational corporation to pay $5 million in damages to a French manufacturer. The multinational believes that the arbitrator intentionally disregarded applicable provisions of American antitrust law, and the award therefore violates a fundamental public policy of the United States. The American defendant is concerned that the French company will attempt to enforce the award outside the United States by attaching the multinational's assets held in countries that do not share the American vision of proper free competition policy. Therefore the American company wants to have the award set aside by courts in New York, in the hope of triggering application of Article V(1)(e) of the New York Arbitration Convention, which permits refusal of enforcement to awards set aside where rendered. This is not a case of asking the American court to refuse to recognize, enforce or confirm an award. Rather, the court is being asked to uproot the award by vacatur.

In this context, a quick examination of the Federal Arbitration Act reveals that a violation of public policy as such is not listed in Section 10 as a basis on which an award may be set aside. This lacuna contrasts with the arbitration statutes recently enacted in France, the Netherlands and Switzerland, as well as the UNCITRAL Model Law, which provide explicitly that commercial arbitration awards may be annulled for violation of public policy.

Public Policy — The Labor Analogy.[407] In American labor arbitration awards, the United States Supreme Court has long recognized a public policy ground for vacating arbitral awards. Congruence between standards for judicial review in labor and commercial arbitration cannot be assumed, however, and the implications for commercial arbitration of public policy vacatur in labor arbitration are unclear.[408] Judicial review of labor arbitration rests on a different statutory foundation than does commercial arbitration.[409] The Federal Arbitration Act specifically excludes from its coverage

---

405. Normally, vacatur under the Federal Arbitration Act is available only to awards rendered in the United States, notwithstanding that the contract dispute might be subject to a substantive American law. *See* International Standard Electric Corporation v. Bridas Sociedad Anonima Petrolera, Industrial Y Comercial, 745 F. Supp. 172 (1990), involving an award rendered in Mexico arising out of a contract dispute subject to New York law.

406. Northrop v. Triad, 811 F.2d 1265 (9th Cir. 1987).

407. Special thanks are due to Dan MacLeod for helpful conversations about the legal framework for labor arbitration in the United States.

408. *See* Revere Copper & Brass v. OPIC, 628 F.2d 81 (D.D.C. 1980); *See generally*, I. MacNeil, R. Speidel & T. Stipanowich, FEDERAL ARBITRATION LAW (1994), at chapter 11-6; DOMKE ON COMMERCIAL ARBITRATION, Ch. 33.03 (G. Wilner, ed., 1990).

409. As discussed below, the statutory foundation of labor arbitration lies in Section 301(a) of the 1947 Labor-Management Relations Act rather than the Federal Arbitration Act. 29 U.S.C.

"contracts of employment."[410] Moreover, labor arbitration has its roots in concerns quite apart from those that justify commercial arbitration.[411] While commercial arbitration is usually conceived of as a neutral method for vindicating particular private rights according to a defined legal standard, labor arbitration has been seen as a way to avoid class warfare through mediation.[412] The judicial hostility to commercial arbitration at the time the enforceability of labor arbitration was being tested in court led labor unions to rely on the Taft-Hartley Act,[413] arguing that labor arbitration was an

Note 409, continued

§185(a). *See* Textile Workers v. Lincoln Mills 353 U.S. 448 (1957). *See generally* Michael Harper, *Limiting 301 Preemption: Three Cheers for the Trilogy, Only One for Lingle and Lueck,* 66 Chi.-Kent L. Rev. 685 (1990); Kaden, *Judges and Arbitrators: Observations on the Scope of Judicial Review,* 80 Colum. L. Rev. 267 (1980); Kaster, *Note on the Consequences of a Broad Arbitration Clause Under the Federal Arbitration Act,* 52 B.U. L.Rev. 571 (1972); and the 1960 trilogy of *Steelworkers* cases, United Steelworkers v. Enterprise Wheel & Car, 363 U.S. 953 (1960), United Steelworkers v. Warrior & Gulf, 363 U.S. 574 (1960) and United Steelworkers v. American Mfg., 363 U.S. 564 (1960). *See also, Symposium on Labor Arbitration Thirty Years After the Steelworkers Trilogy,* 66 Chi.-Kent L. Rev. 531 (1990); Matthew Finkin, *Commentary on `Arbitration of Employment Disputes Without Unions'* 66 Chi. Kent L. Rev. 799 (1990); Samuel Estreicher, *Reply to Professor Finkin, Id.* at 817.

410. 9 U.S.C. § 1. The extent of this exemption is not entirely clear. *See* I. Macneil, R. Speidel & T. Stipanowich, *supra,* at Chapter 11 and Chapter 16. Professors Macneil, Speidel and Stipanowich note that the Federal Arbitration Act "does not govern [private sector collective bargaining] arbitration [although the Act] may be looked to for guidance by analogy in appropriate circumstances." *Id.* at § 11.3.1 They add that while it is not uncommon to find courts citing labor cases in connection with cases governed by the Federal Arbitration Act, with no overt recognition that they do not govern, "the practice is troublesome because it can easily lead to undesirable results where the two statutes differ." *Id.* at § 11.3.3. They also note that the Supreme Court has held that labor cases that deny preclusive effect to awards involving statutory rights do not control under the Federal Arbitration Act. *Id.* at § 16.5.1.2., citing Gilmer v. Interstate/Johnson Lane Corp., 111 S. Ct. 1647 (1991), a case involving an agreement to arbitrate an age discrimination dispute governed by the Federal Age Discrimination Employment Act.

411. The comparativist, of course, will contrast the American position with European labor law, where individual work-related disputes generally are considered non-arbitrable, and consigned to mandatory labor courts such as the *prud'hommes* tribunals of France. *See* Article 511, French Code du Travail, giving the *Conseils de Prud'hommes* exclusive jurisdiction to hear individual labor grievances. *See also* Wattelet c. Getaba & Lorquin, Cour d'appel de Paris (1re Ch. suppl.), 4 June 1992, 1993 *Rev. Arb.* 449. For an example of an Italian refusal to order arbitration of a labor dispute, see Pret. Genova, 30 April 1980, Quaglia v. Daros in Riv. Dir. Internaz. Priv. E. Proc. (1980) 458, *reprinted in* 7 YEARBOOK COMMERCIAL ARBITRATION 342 (1982).

412. *See* David Feller, *End of the Trilogy: The Declining State of Labor Arbitration,* 48 Arb. J. (No. 3) 18 (1993). *See also* American Arbitration Association, *Why Labor Management Use AAA Arbitration Services.*

413. § 301(a) of the Labor Management Relations Act of 1947 provides that "Suits for violation of contracts between an employer and a labor organization representing employees in an industry affecting commerce ... may be brought in any district court of the United States having jurisdiction over the parties, without respect to the amount in controversy or without regard to the citizenship of the parties." 29 U.S.C. § 185(a). *See* David Feller, *End of the Trilogy: The Declining State of Labor Arbitration,* 48 Arb. J. (No. 3) 18 (1993).

alternative to industrial strife and strikes rather than just a mechanism for adjudicatory contract disputes.[414]

Public Policy — Timing Court Inquiry in International Cases. In labor arbitration the Supreme Court has characterized vacatur for violation of public policy as "a specific application of the more general doctrine, rooted in the common law, that a court may refuse to enforce contracts that violate law or public policy."[415] One might argue that such an overarching public policy principle is not limited to labor matters, particularly at a time when labor and commercial arbitration have ceased to differ significantly.[416] Community force is rarely justified to sustain, directly or indirectly, private choices that violate public policy.

The precise configuration and timing of judicial invocation of public policy remains unclear, however, in international commercial arbitration. The question is not whether courts should intervene, but when. While courts must not *enforce* an award that violates a nation's law and fundamental notions of justice, it is open to question whether courts should *set aside* an award that violates public policy even before the award is presented for enforcement or recognition. In an international context vacatur of an award for violation of public policy injects into the arbitral process an unanticipated and possibly unnecessary degree of meddling by national

---

414. Messrs. Feller and Goldberg, counsel to the union, argued that only "as a back-up" that the exclusion of contracts of employment from the Federal Arbitration Act applied only to individual employment contracts, and not to collective bargaining agreements. *Id.* at 19. Presumably court litigation was not an alternative: partly due to time and cost constraints, partly because of perceived judicial hostility to employees, and partly because grievances subject to arbitration were often not major enough to merit court proceedings. The Supreme Court in *Lincoln Mills* interpreted Section 301(a) as more than a grant of jurisdiction, and said that Section 301 "authorizes federal courts to fashion a body of federal law for the enforcement of these collective bargaining agreements . . . ." 353 U.S. at 451.

415. United Paperworkers v. Misco, 484 U.S. 29 (1987) at 42.. *Misco* arose out of the vacatur of an arbitral award reinstating an employee dismissed for alleged possession of illegal drugs on plant premises, which arguably impaired the employee's ability to operate dangerous machinery used in cutting paper rolls. The Supreme Court admitted public policy grounds for setting aside labor awards, but reversed the lower court's vacatur of the award. In *Misco*, the Court found the award invulnerable to attack, both for the inadequacy of the asserted policy and the absence of conflict between the policy and the award. The Court stated that "the parties [to the arbitration agreement] did not bargain for the facts to be found by a court, but by an arbitrator chosen by them who had the opportunity to observe [the dismissed employee] and to be familiar with the plant and its problems." The doctrine derives, said the Court, "from the basic notion that no court will lend its aid to one who founds a cause of action upon an illegal or immoral act." Those who are troubled by the potential for broad court control of arbitration awards may be comforted by the Supreme Court's rejection of looseness in identifying public policy and in perceiving conflict between such policy and the award. The policy must be "well defined and dominant;" it is not to be drawn from "general considerations of supposed public interests," but from "laws and legal precedents," and "the violation of such a policy must be clearly shown if an award is not to be enforced. *Id.* at 43. *See generally* Bernard Meltzer, *After the Labor Arbitration Award: The Public Policy Defense*, 10 Indus. Rel. L.J. 241, 247-48 (1988).

416. On the rapprochement of labor and commercial arbitration, see David Feller, *End of the Trilogy: The Declining State of Labor Arbitration*, 48 Arb. J. (No. 3) 18 (1993).

courts at the arbitral situs. From the perspective of sound arbitration law, the better course will normally be to delay judicial inquiry into public policy until a court is asked to take positive action to enforce or recognize an award.

5. The UNCITRAL Model Law.

The United Nations Commission on International Trade Law (UNCITRAL) has drafted a model law that strikes a balance between arbitral autonomy on the merits of the dispute, and court control of the arbitration's procedural fairness.[417] Adopted in 1985 for consideration by national legislatures, the Model Law on International Commercial Arbitration gives parties freedom to choose their procedural arbitration rules within a framework of judicial review inspired by the New York Arbitration Convention. The Model Law has been adopted in a number of important jurisdictions, including Canada, Hong Kong and Scotland.

On the matter of award finality, Article 34 of the Model Law permits annulment of an award for essentially the same reasons that an award may be refused recognition under the New York Arbitration Convention. To secure annulment, the party making the application must furnish proof of one of the following defects:

(1) a party to the arbitration agreement was under some incapacity or the agreement is not valid under the law to which the parties have subjected it;

(2) one party was not given proper notice of the appointment of an arbitrator or of the arbitral proceedings, or was otherwise unable to present its case;

(3) the award deals with a dispute not falling within the terms of the submission to arbitration, or contains decisions on matters beyond the scope of the submission to arbitration;

(4) the composition of the arbitral tribunal or the arbitral procedure was not in accordance with the agreement of the parties.

An award may also be annulled at the place of arbitration if a court, even on its own motion, finds that the subject matter of the dispute is not capable of settlement by arbitration or that the award conflicts with the forum's public policy. However, Article 5 of the Model Law prohibits courts from exercising any powers not explicitly conferred by the law, such as those "inherent powers" exercised by English courts, as discussed above.

---

417. Adopted 21 June 1985 for consideration by national legislatures, *reprinted* 24 I.L.M. 1302 (1985). *See generally*, Howard Holtzmann & Joseph Newhouse, A GUIDE TO THE UNCITRAL MODEL LAW ON INTERNATIONAL COMMERCIAL ARBITRATION (1989); Gerold Herrmann, *UNCITRAL Adopts Model Law on International Commercial Arbitration*, 2 ARB. INT'L 2 (1986); Isaak Dore, ARBITRATION AND CONCILIATION UNDER THE UNCITRAL RULES: A TEXTUAL ANALYSIS (1986); Isaak Dore, THE UNCITRAL FRAMEWORK FOR ARBITRATION IN CONTEMPORARY PERSPECTIVE (1993). For contrasting views of the United Kingdom's response to the UNCITRAL Model Law, see articles by Lord Mustill and Lord Dervaerd at 10 Arb. Int. 3 and 63 (1990). *See also* Steyn, *England's Response to the Model Law on Arbitration, supra* note 352.

C. WILD CARDS.

Private adjudication falls prey to its own forms of unpredictability. An agreement to settle disputes through arbitration rather than in the courts may resolve some problems at the expense of creating others.

The catalogue of arbitration disadvantages might better be described as characteristics of arbitration which can work against some litigants in particular contexts. In addition to the perception that arbitrators tend to compromise on the merits of a dispute, problematic aspects of arbitration frequently cited by litigators include the undeniable facts that arbitrators are not bound by formal rules of evidence, that their awards are subject to only limited judicial review, and that there may be little pre-trial discovery. In the growing volume of arbitration literature, considerable ink has been spilled on several critical sources of uncertainty: (i) public policy limits on the enforceability of arbitration agreements and awards; (ii) arbitration involving more than two parties; and (iii) interim relief such as pre-award attachment of assets. As discussed below, in each of these areas judges, arbitrators and legislators are now struggling to invent what might be called the civil procedure of international arbitration.

1. Public Policy.[418]

a. Arbitrability.

At one time or another, courts in most jurisdictions have questioned the right of private litigants to oust judges of jurisdiction to hear disputes that raise sensitive public policy concerns, such as issues related to antitrust, securities regulation, patents, bankruptcy, the Commodities Exchange Act, civil rights, and state franchise statutes.[419] Courts reluctant to enforce an agreement to arbitrate such claims have limited the scope of the arbitration clause to basic contract matters.[420] The multilater-

---

418. *See also* discussion *supra* at notes 342-44, 404-16 and *infra* at notes 474-530, 587-612.
419. *See, e.g.,* Wilko v. Swan, 346 U.S. 427 (1953) (the 1933 Securities Act now overruled by Rodriguez de Quijas v. Shearson/American Express, *infra* note 424); Marchese v. Shearson Hayden Stone, Inc., 734 F.2d 414 (9th Cir. 1984) (the Commodities Exchange Act); Zimmerman v. Continental Airlines, 712 F.2d 55 (3d Cir. 1983), *cert. denied,* 464 U.S. 1038 (1984) (bankruptcy matters for which there is an automatic stay of all actions). *See generally* cases discussed in William W. Park, *Private Adjudicators and the Public Interest: The Expanding Scope of International Arbitration,* 12 Brook. J. Int'l L. 629 (1986); Andrew Rogers, Arbitrators, 10 Arb. Int'l 263 (1994). Richard E. Speidel, *Arbitration of Statutory Rights Under the Federal Arbitration Act,* 4 Ohio St. J. or Disp. Resol. 157 (1989). For an instance in which a state attempt to limit arbitrability failed, see Securities Industry Ass'n v. Connolly, 883 F.2d 1114 (1st Cir. 1989) (Massachusetts regulations requiring conspicuous disclosure of consequences of arbitration clause in securities brokerage agreements).
420. Surprisingly perhaps, sensitive claims of religious discrimination *are* arbitrable. *See, e.g.,* Felt v. Atchison, Topeka & Santa Fe Railway Co. (Civ. No. 92-4217, C.D. Cal., 18 August 1993), involving allegation by Seventh Day Adventist that his employer did not respect his

al treaty framework governing arbitration requires courts to enforce arbitration agreements and awards only if questions are "capable of settlement by arbitration."[421]

While most laws affect societal interests in one way or another, some statutes implicate public rights in a more vital way than others. For example, legislation that promotes a fair stock market or free competition creates direct benefits not only for the contracting parties, but also for the community at large.[422]

Suspicion of arbitrators has been at the heart of non-arbitrability cases. Like foxes guarding the chicken coop, arbitrators with a pro-business bias appear disposed to underenforcement of laws designed to protect the public. Lack of appeal on the merits of an award, as well as the absence of many Constitutional rights in arbitration,[423] has led some to compare arbitration to a black hole to which claims for vindication of fundamental rights are sent, never to be heard from again.

In the United States, judicial resistance to arbitration of public law claims has seen a steady erosion since the mid-1970's, particularly with respect to contracts containing an international element.[424] Although questionable in domestic transactions, where arbitration may lend itself to abuse in consumer contracts, this trend toward greater subject matter arbitrability justifies itself in an international context in which the divergence of the parties' nationalities can create a fear (sometimes legitimate) of biased foreign courts.

Arbitrability questions may create uncertainty not only when an arbitration agreement is presented for enforcement, but in the arbitration endgame, when the award is presented for enforcement. The New York Arbitration Convention permits refusal of recognition and enforcement to an arbitral award if a competent authority of the enforcement forum finds that the subject matter of the dispute is not capable of settlement by arbitration under the law of the place where enforcement or recognition is sought.

Note 420, continued

religious objection to working on Saturdays. On grievance arbitration involving allegations of religious discrimination, see Benjamin Wolkinson & Victor Nichol, *Religious Discrimination*, Dispute Resolution Journal, December 1993, at 54, discussing Section 701(j) of the 1972 Equal Employment Opportunity Enforcement Act, amending Title VII of the 1964 Civil Rights Act, 42 U.S.C. § 2000 e (J).

421. New York Convention Articles II(1) and V(2)(1).

422. Reference to "statutory claims" often serves as a functional equivalent of public law claims. Not all statutes, however, incorporate non-waivable rights of fundamental importance. In civil law systems, for example, basic contract law is statutory in much the same way the U.C.C. has codified the law of commercial transactions. Thus my preference for the term "public law right."

423. *See* Edward Brunet, *Arbitration and Constitutional Rights*, 71 North Carolina L. Rev. 81 (1992).

424. The line of Supreme Court cases in which arbitration clauses have been upheld in international contexts goes back to Scherk v. Alberto Culver Co., 417 U.S. 506 (1974), in which the Supreme Court explicitly extended its recognition to arbitration agreements that implicated securities regulation, even if the dispute could not have been arbitrated in a purely domestic transaction. *Id.* at 519-20. In 1985, the Supreme Court in the landmark case of Mitsubishi Motors v. Soler Chrysler-Plymouth, 473 U.S. 614 (1985), announced that arbitration agreements will be enforced in international contracts even if the claims relate to the fundamental,

b. Enforcing the Award.

The New York Arbitration Convention permits refusal of enforcement to an award whose enforcement would be contrary to the public policy of the country where recognition and enforcement is sought. In essence, courts may get a "second look" at the policies implicated by the arbitral process when an award is presented for enforcement.[425]

Most Western countries have tended to give the public policy defense of the New York Arbitration Convention a narrow scope. In *Parsons & Whittemore Overseas v. Societé Générale du Papier (RAKTA)*,[426] an American contractor sought to block the enforcement of an award in favor of an Egyptian corporation. The arbitration had resulted from abandonment, during and after the Arab-Israeli Six Day War in 1967, of the American company's obligation to build a paperboard mill in Alexandria, Egypt. The American company argued that the breach in diplomatic relations between the United States and Egypt at that time would make enforcement of the award contrary to United States public policy. The Second Circuit Court of Appeals rejected this argument, construing the public policy defense narrowly to incorporate only a violation of "the forum state's [i.e., the enforcement court's] most basic notions of morality and justice."[427] The Court reasoned that "to read the public policy defense as a parochial device protective of national political interests would seriously undermine the [New York Arbitration] Convention's utility."[428]

Not all agree with a narrow reading of the public policy defense, however. One commentator has suggested that a narrow notion of public policy "threatens the legitimate regulatory policies of both developed and developing countries," turning "a

---

Note 424, continued

or "core," public policy issues raised by antitrust laws that are not arbitrable in a domestic context. *See also* Gilmer v. Interstate/Johnson Lane Corp., 500 U.S. 20 (1991) (claims arising under the Age Discrimination Employment Act, 29 U.S.C. § 621); Rodriguez de Quijas v. Shearson/American Express, Inc., 490 U.S. 477 (1989) (Court overruled precedent, and held enforceable a pre-dispute agreement to arbitrate claims under the Securities Act of 1933); Southland Corp. v. Keating, 465 U.S. 1 (1984) (Federal Arbitration Act preempted state law and applied to state as well as federal claims; claims arising under the California franchise law were arbitrable); Société Nationale Algerienne (SONATRACH) v. Distrigas Corp., 80 Bankr. 606 (D. Mass. 1987) (contract for supply of liquified natural gas; arbitration ordered in Geneva between Algerian state agency and American company in chapter 11 reorganization). *See generally*, William W. Park, *Private Adjudicators and the Public Interest*, 12 Brooklyn J. Int'l Law 629 (1986); Jennifer Magyar, *Statutory Civil Rights Claims in Arbitration*, 72 B.U. L. Rev. 641 (1992). On French caselaw, see Jean Robert & Thomas Carbonneau, The French Law of Arbitration (1983), discussing the difference between domestic and international public policy constraints in French arbitration, at Part I, § 1.03, and Part II, §§ 2.03, 2.04, and § 9.03-9.08.

425. New York Arbitration Convention, Article V(2)(b). *See generally* discussion of Mitsubishi Motors, *infra* at note 510.

426. 508 F.2d 969 (2d Cir. 1974).

427. *Id.* at 974.

428. *Id.*

meaningful review of arbitral awards [into] a rubber stamp."[429] What this critique of the narrow view of public policy misses, however, is that a "meaningful review of arbitral awards" may eviscerate the independence of the entire process of cross-border arbitration. A broad view means more awards being set aside, and less of the reliability in international dispute resolution that promotes security in foreign investment.

2. Multiple Parties.

a. Parallel Adjudication.

In his "Macao Sardine Case," Sir Michael Kerr tells of a quarter million tins of sardines secretly filled with mud by a Macao canning company, sold and resold many times over throughout Asia.[430] Most of the claims gave rise to consistent judgments for damages, rendered in one consolidated action before the Hong Kong Commercial Court. However, the action against the Macao canning company itself ran into trouble. The contract for the initial sale was subject to an arbitration clause that precluded jurisdiction by the Hong Kong court. The duly constituted arbitral tribunal in the proceeding against the Macao company applied *lex mercatoria* to exonerate the supplier, leaving the original buyer with substantial damages to pay against the subsequent purchases but no hope of recovery against the real culprit.

Sir Michael's sardine narrative illustrates how parallel adjudication may yield inconsistent results on common issues of law and fact when two or more commercial agreements touch related parties or transactions. Judicial power to join claims can give litigation a considerable advantage over arbitration when multiple transactions raise the same issue, such as whether a particular event constitutes a *force majeure* defense to contract performance.

Although the rules of some arbitral institutions provide for joinder of parties even if resisted by one of the existing parties to the arbitration,[431] this does not deal with the need to obtain the consent of the party to be joined. In such a case, it may be necessary to have recourse to local courts to force consolidation.

The Federal Arbitration Act does not authorize forced consolidation of separate arbitration proceedings, even though the arbitrations present identical or similar questions of law and fact.[432] Some states do provide for statutory consolidation of

---

429. *See* Andrew Armfelt, *Avoiding the Arbitration Trap*, Financial Times, 27 October 1992, at 17, cols. 1-4. *Compare* Jan Paulsson's comment on two recent cases in which Indian courts annulled foreign arbitration awards, Jan A.S. Paulsson, *The New York Convention's Misadventures in India*, Int'l Arb. Rep. 3 (June 1992). For an Indian reaction, see Raghuraman, *International Jurist Flays India for Overstepping Bounds*, The Delhi Pioneer, 6 October 1992.

430. Michael Kerr, *Arbitration v. Litigation*, 3 Arb. Int'l 79 (1987).

431. *See* London Court of International Arbitration, 1985 RULES, Article 13.1.

432. *See* United Kingdom v. Boeing, 998 F.2d 68 (1993). The United Kingdom moved to consolidate arbitrations with Boeing and Textron, Inc., both of which had contracted with British Ministry of Defense to develop electronic fuel system called "fadec." The Court of Appeals

related arbitrations[433] under statutes that are not necessarily preempted by the Federal Arbitration Act.[434] The laws of several non-American jurisdictions, notably Hong Kong and the Netherlands, contain provisions authorizing court-ordered consolidation of different arbitrations.[435]

When arbitration does not take place in a jurisdiction that will force consolidation, careful drafting can promote effective joinder of related arbitrations.[436] The main objection to consolidation is that arbitrators who consolidate actions will thereby exceed their authority. However, if all relevant parties consent to the combination of two or more proceedings, it is difficult to see why one side should later be allowed to change its mind when the arbitral process runs counter to post-dispute preoccupations.[437]

When two parties are named as defendants, of course, they may face a dilemma in agreeing upon their party-nominated arbitrator. If the arbitration agreement provides for a three-member tribunal, the parties' options include compromise on a candidate or default in the nomination.[438]

b. Group Liability.

The theory of joint responsibility among related parties may permit consolidation through the back door. Principles said to constitute the "new international law

---

Note 432, continued

ruled that the district court cannot order consolidation of separate proceedings absent the parties' consent, distinguishing the Court's prior decision in Neurus Shipping, 527 F.2d 966 (2d Cir. 1975). *See generally* Comment, *Compulsory Consolidation of International Arbitral Proceedings*, 2 Tulane J. Int'l & Comp. L. 223 (1994). *See also* Paine Webber Inc. v. Fowler, 791 F. Supp. 821 (D. Kan. 1992) (denial of Paine Webber motion to consolidate arbitrations in which (i) employee alleges wrongful discharge related to sexual harassment and (ii) employer seeks to recover loans to employee which represented advances on salary); and Weyerhaeuser Co. v. Western Seas Shipping Co., 743 F.2d 635 (9th Cir. 1984) (court refuses motion of ship charterer to consolidate separate arbitrations between charter and shipowner and between charterer and subcharter.)

433. *See, e.g.*, Massachusetts Gen. Laws, c. 251, § 2A; California Code of Civil Procedure, § 1281.3.

434. New England Energy v. Keystone Shipping, 855 F.2d 1 (1st Cir. 1988).

435. *See* Section 6B of the Hong Kong Arbitration Ordinance, Ch. 351, applicable to domestic arbitration, but not contained in the UNCITRAL Model Law adopted for international arbitration. The Netherlands consolidation provisions are contained in Section 1046 of the Dutch Code of Civil Arbitration Law Procedure, discussed in Albert Jan van den Berg, R. van Delden and H.J. Snijders, ARBITRATION IN THE NETHERLANDS (1993).

436. All relevant arbitration clauses should provide for arbitration in the same country, according to the same substantive and procedural law, under the same institutional rules, and before a tribunal constituted of the same arbitrators.

437. *See generally* Sir Michael Mustill, *Multipartite Arbitration: An Agenda for Law-Makers*, 7 Arb. Int'l 393 (1991).

438. *See* Siemens and BKMI v. Dutco, Cour de Cassation (France), 7 January 1992, Chambre Civile No. 1, Cass., 1992 Rev. d'Arbitrage 470.

merchant," or *lex mercatoria*,[439] include group liability in arbitration implicating a corporate family. Factors relevant to a finding of group liability can include substitution of performance or other intervention in negotiations and contract communications; thin capitalization; intermixture of management; lack of separate administrative functions; pervasive control by shareholders; non-observance of corporate formalities; fraud; intermingling of assets and business activity; and use of the corporation for the purposes of the dominant shareholder.[440]

The place of incorporation provides a logical nexus by which to determine the law applicable to corporate personality.[441] Parent liability might also be based on an agency theory under the contract's governing law.[442] Arbitrators may find an affiliate to have represented a related company through a course of conduct during the contract negotiations or performance.[443] While arbitral joinder of companies within a

439. *See, e.g.*, Mustill, *supra* note 322, at 112 for item number 8 of Lord Mustill's list. This principle has been adopted in several arbitrations under the aegis of the International Chamber of Commerce Rules. *See e.g.* I.C.C. Awards 1434 and 2375, *reproduced in* 1976 J. Droit Int'l 978 (1976); I.C.C. Award No. 2291, 1975 J. Droit Int'l. 934; I.C.C. Award 4131, *discussed in* Craig, Park & Paulsson, I.C.C. ARBITRATION, *supra* note 5 at 95-102. Most of these awards could be decided on the basis of the parties' intent at the time of contracting as to which entities were to be bound. *See also* discussion of issue preclusion, *infra* at note 807.

440. For an excellent survey of elements courts consider when asked to disregard the separate identity of a subsidiary, *see* United Electrical, Radio and Machine Workers of America v. 163 Pleasant Street Corp and International Twist Drill (Holdings), 960 F.2d 1080 (1st Cir. 1992). The court was faced with the dilemma of whether to pierce the corporate veil between a Scottish parent corporation and its American subsidiary in order to permit satisfaction of workers' claims. While disregard of the corporate veil in this case would mean that a local subsidiary's debts could be paid, it could also send a signal to foreign investors about lack of respect for their legitimate corporate expectations, which in turn could chill job-creating investment. If potential investors cannot rely on the American corporate identity to limit their American exposure, investments may be fewer and the number of unemployed greater. If the veil is not pierced, a lack of investment may mean that some workers may lose jobs. If the veil is pierced, others will not have jobs to lose. *See generally*, Philip I. Blumberg, THE MULTINATIONAL CHALLENGE TO CORPORATION LAW: THE SEARCH FOR A NEW CORPORATE PERSONALITY (1993); Philip I. Blumberg, *The Corporate Entity in an Era of Multinational Corporations*, 15 Delaware J. Corp. Law 283 (1990); Philip I. Blumberg, THE LAW OF CORPORATE GROUPS (Vol. I, 1983; Vol. II, 1985). *See also* Catherine Mondange, LA TRANSPARENCE DE LA PERSONALITÉ MORALE DANS LE DROIT ANGLAIS DES SOCIÉTÉS ANONYMES (Paris 1979); REGULATING CORPORATE GROUPS IN EUROPE (D. Sugarman & G. Teubner, eds. 1990).

441. *See* RESTATEMENT (SECOND) OF CONFLICT OF LAWS, § 307. *See also* Pitts v. Ciba-Geigy, 616 F. Supp. 1495 (D. Mass. 1985).

442. The arbitrators might find that the course of conduct during the negotiations created an agency relationship between parent and subsidiary under the proper law of the contract (whether this be English, French, Swiss, or whatever), and that this is not an issue for the place of incorporation at all. For cases involving group liability, see Carte Blanche (Singapore) Ltd. v. Diners Club Int'l Inc., 2 F.3d 24 (2d Cir. 1993); Builders Federal Hong Kong Ltd. v. Turner Construction, 655 F.Supp. 1400 (S.D.N.Y. 1987); Société Nationale v. Shaheen Natural Resources, 585 F.Supp. 57 (S.D.N.Y. 1983).

443. For analogous issues involving state agencies and governments, *see* discussion of the SPP case in Albert Jan van den Berg, *The Efficiency of Awards in International Commercial Arbitration*, 58 Arb. 264 (1992).

corporate group will sometimes constitute a recognition of commercial reality, such non-consensual consolidation is not without its risks. The arbitrators' decision to make a parent answer for the debts of a subsidiary may constitute an excess of authority justifying vacatur of the award at the arbitral seat or refusal of its recognition by the enforcement forum.[444]

3. Interim Relief.[445]

No firm consensus exists yet on the availability of interim relief such as pre-award attachment. In the United States, pre-award attachment is permitted in maritime matters. However, with respect to non-maritime commercial arbitration, the circuits are divided.[446]

Some jurisdictions see interim relief in the form of pre-award attachment of assets as inconsistent with the goals of the New York Arbitration Convention. The argument runs that by bargaining for arbitration, parties to the contract have excluded intervention by national courts until an award is presented for enforcement. Other courts, however, accept pre-award attachment as a way to maximize enforceability of the arbitral process, entirely consistent with the objectives of the multilateral treaty network established by the New York Arbitration Convention.

The trend toward allowing interim measures of pre-award attachment has been promoted by state legislation.[447] However, state statutes may be of limited value when subject to challenge on grounds of federal preemption in cases falling under the New York Arbitration Convention.[448] To deal with this division of authorities, the arbitration agreement should explicitly provide for pre-award attachment, thereby rebutting any presumption that such interim measures are inconsistent with the parties' wishes.

---

444. *See, e.g.,* Vendome & Cartier v. Horowitz (Swiss Tribunal fédéral, J.T. 1981, at 61) (1979), *discussed in* Craig, Park, & Paulsson, I.C.C. ARBITRATION *supra* note 5, at 545.

445. *See generally* Alan Redfern, *Arbitration and the Courts: Interim Measures of Protection — Is the Tide About to Turn?, scheduled for publication in* Texas J. International Law (1994).

446. *Compare* McCreary Tire and Rubber v. CEAT, 501 F.2d 1032 (3rd Cir. 1974), which denied attachment, and Carolina Power & Light v. Uranex, 451 F. Supp 1044 (N.D.Cal 1977), where it was determined that nothing in the New York Convention precludes pre-award attachment. At least one First Circuit case is favorable to pre-award injunctions to preserve assets. Teradyne v. Mostek, 797 F.2d 43 (1st Cir. 1986), although it did not deal with a New York Convention context; *see also* Andros v. André & Cie., 430 F. Supp. 88 (S.D.N.Y. 1977). *See generally,* Joseph D. Becker, *Attachment in Aid of Arbitration: The American Position,* 1 Arb. Int'l 40 (1985).

447. *See, e.g.,* N.Y.C.P.L.R. §7502(c).

448. *See, e.g.,* Cooper v. Aleliers Motobecane, 57 N.Y.2d 408 (1982) (vacatur of attachment in support of I.C.C. arbitration in Zurich, on grounds that attachment was incompatible with New York Convention obligation of courts to refer the parties to arbitration); *see also* Drexel Burnham Lambert v. Ruebsamen, 3 N.Y. Law J. 17 (28 July 1988) (App. Div. 1st Dept. July 21, 1988).

Chapter IV

DRAFTING TO MITIGATE THE DOWNSIDE RISK

Many problematic aspects of both arbitration and litigation can be mitigated by intelligent crafting of the choice-of-forum agreement. Courts will inevitably look to the specific language of an arbitration or jurisdiction clause in determining the scope of an arbitrator's or a judge's authority.[449] A meaningful comparison of public and private dispute resolution therefore requires concrete drafting alternatives.

The cardinal rule of drafting an arbitration agreement or a jurisdiction clause is to avoid the type of ambiguity and equivocation that will later delight a party wishing to renege on its agreement. In some cases a defective choice-of-forum clause may be simply unenforceable.[450] Alternatively, courts occasionally will repair a defective clause by presuming an intent of the parties that is within the realm of reality.[451] Either way, the ambiguity adds an unnecessary layer of uncertainty and contention to business relationships.

A. COMBINING ARBITRATION AND LITIGATION.

In a multinational context, the intertwining of arbitration and choice-of-court agree-

---

449. *See, e.g.,* S.A. Minercao da Trinidad - Samitri v. Utah International, 745 F.2d 190 (2d Cir. 1984), discussed *infra* at note 460.
450. *See* National Iranian Oil Company v. Ashland Oil, 817 F.2d 326 (1987), in which the court deemed itself without power to "repair" an arbitration clause providing for arbitration in Iran. Iran was not a party to the New York Arbitration Convention, which the United States applies only on the basis of reciprocity to other Convention states.
451. *See* Rosgoscirc v. Circus Show Corp., 1993 WL 27733 (S.D.N.Y., 16 July 1993). A contract provision in an agreement intended to present the Moscow Circus in North America called for arbitration under the rules of a non-existent association, styled as "The International Arbitration in the Hague." After struggling with the parties' mutual mistake and the limits on the court's own power, the court ordered arbitration in New York under the rules of the American Arbitration Association. *Compare* Bauhinia Corporation v. China National Machinery & Equipment Import & Export, 819 F.2d 247 (9th Cir. 1987), in which the court ordered arbitration in California notwithstanding at least some indication in the contract that the parties intended arbitration in Peking.

ments can sometimes prove to be unworkable.[452] Or, an ill-drafted combination of court and arbitrator might deprive a party of the right to remove to federal court an action to enforce the arbitration commitment.[453]

Not all marriages of arbitration agreements and jurisdiction clauses, however, will prove pathological. Some practitioners counsel pre-dispute submission to the jurisdiction of a court for actions to compel arbitration.[454] Several recent cases arising out of insurance disputes have interpreted the choice-of-court portion of a joint litigation/arbitration clause as a limitation on the place where the parties may maintain an action to enforce the arbitration clause and to determine whether the dispute was subject to arbitration at all. In one case involving asbestos insurance claims, an Anglo-American reinsurance agreement contained a submission to "the jurisdiction of any court of competent jurisdiction within the United States of America," as well as provided that "any dispute [with respect to the interpretation of the policy] shall be referred to two arbitrators."[455] The court interpreted the submission to jurisdiction as a waiver of the foreign party's right to remove actions to federal court under the Federal Arbitration Act.[456]

In an analogous English case, the Commercial Court faced a dispute resolution clause that provided for adjudication under the arbitration rules of the International Chamber of Commerce as well as a submission to the "exclusive jurisdiction" of the Courts of England.[457] An opinion by Mr. Justice Steyn made sense of the two clauses by interpreting the jurisdiction of English courts as a specification of "the *lex arbitri*,

---

452. *See generally* W. Laurence Craig, William W. Park & Jan A.S. Paulsson, INTERNATIONAL CHAMBER OF COMMERCE ARBITRATION (2nd ed., 1990), § 9.02, at 158-160. One pathological clause provided that "in case of dispute the parties undertake to submit to arbitration but in case of litigation the *Tribunal de la Seine* shall have exclusive jurisdiction." *Id.* at 159, note 3. *See also* Frédéric Eiseman, *La clause d'arbitrage pathologique, in* ARBITRAGE COMMERCIAL: ESSAIS IN MEMORIAM EUGENIO MINOLI 129 (1974); H. Scalbert & L. Marville, *Les clauses compromissoires pathologiques,* 1988 Revue d'Arbitrage 117.

453. *See* Travelers Insurance Co. v. Keeling and Other Underwriters at Lloyd's of London, 199 WL 18909 and 1993 U.S. Dist. LEXIS 491 (S.D.N.Y, 19 January 1993), *aff'd* 996 F.2d 1485 (2d Cir. 1993). The right of removal for arbitration agreements and awards covered by the New York Arbitration Convention is provided by Section 205 of the Federal Arbitration Act.

454. *See e.g.* Jeffrey Barist, COMMERCIAL ARBITRATION LAW AND CLAUSES (1994), at § 15.01. Barist suggests a clause giving particular courts exclusive jurisdiction over an action to enforce rights and obligations arising from the arbitration agreement, subject to the right to apply to any court for enforcement of any related judgment.

455. Travelers Insurance Co. v. Keeling and Other Underwriters at Lloyd's of London, 199 WL 18909 and 1993 U.S. Dist. LEXIS 491 (S.D.N.Y., 19 January 1993), *aff'd* 996 F.2d 1485 (2d Cir. 1993).

456. The federal court remanded the case to New York State courts, where the American plaintiff began the action, reasoning that the Supreme Court of the State of New York is a "court of competent jurisdiction within the United States." *Compare* McDermott International v. Lloyd's Underwriters, 944 F.2d 1199 (5th Cir. 1991), in which a service of suit clause coupled with an arbitration agreement was held too ambiguous to constitute waiver of recourse to federal courts.

457. Paul Smith Ltd. v. H & S International Holding Inc., [1991] 2 Lloyd's Law Rep. 127 (1991), discussed *infra* at note 544.

the curial law or the law governing the arbitration."[458]

B. THE ARBITRATION CLAUSE.[459]

1. Essentials.

Arbitral tribunals are essentially creatures of the parties' mutual consent. Above all, therefore, business managers seeking a binding private dispute resolution mechanism should provide an unambiguous election to arbitrate all disputes arising from their particular contractual relationship. The language of standard arbitration agreements is not necessarily fungible; not all clauses, for example, will be broad enough to cover claims related to fraud in the inducement of the contract.[460] Five elements of an arbitration clause are vital: (i) applicable procedural rules with a workable mechanism for appointing the arbitrators; (ii) the mechanism for fixing the arbitrators' fees; (iii) the

458. *Id.* at 129-30. Mr. Justice Steyn noted that the law governing the arbitration itself concerns matters such as interim measures of protection, vacancies in the arbitral tribunal and the removal of arbitrators for misconduct.

459. *See* model clause in Appendix B. On drafting arbitration clauses, *see generally* W. Laurence Craig, William W. Park, Jan A.S. Paulsson, INTERNATIONAL CHAMBER OF COMMERCE ARBITRATION (2d ed. 1990) chapters 5-9; Jeffrey Barist, COMMERCIAL ARBITRATION LAW AND CLAUSES: A DRAFTER'S GUIDE (1994); J. Stewart McClendon, *Arbitration Clauses in International Contracts*, *in* SURVEY OF INTERNATIONAL ARBITRATION SITES (J.S. McClendon, ed., 3rd ed., 1993), p. 127; Robert Coulson, *The Practical Advantages of Administered Arbitration*, NIDR Forum 41 (Winter 1993); Markham Ball, *Just Do It — Drafting the Arbitration Clause in an International Agreement*, 10 J. Int'l Arb. 29 (No. 4, Dec. 1993); Piero Bernardini, *The Arbitration Clause of an International Contract*, 9 Journal of International Arbitration 45 (No, 2, 1992); Michael F. Hoellering, *How to Draft an AAA Arbitration Clause*, 1991-92 Arbitration and the Law 166 (1992); Stephen R. Bond, *How to Draft an ICC Arbitration Clause*, 7 ICSID Review — Foreign Investment Law Journal 153 (1992); International Chamber of Commerce, WORKING GROUP ON THE ICC STANDARD ARBITRATION CLAUSE, FINAL REPORT, COMMISSION ON INTERNATIONAL ARBITRATION, 1991 (Document No. 420/318 Rev.); David A. Hoffman, *Drafting ADR Contract Provisions: A Checklist and Sample Clauses*, 22 Mass. Lawyers Weekly 921 (1994); Marc Blessing, DRAFTING ARBITRATION CLAUSES, presented at Annual Meeting, Swiss Arbitration Association, Basel, 17 June 1994; Ewell Murphy, *How to Draft a Transnational Arbitration Clause: The Four Languages of Charles V*, *in* INTERNATIONAL ALTERNATIVE DISPUTE RESOLUTION, Chapter 3 (Business' Laws Inc. 1993); I.C.C. Commission on International Arbitration, FINAL REPORT, WORKING GROUP ON THE ICC STANDARD ARBITRATION CLAUSE, Doc. 420/318 Rev. (1991).

460. The question of whether the parties intended to arbitrate claims of fraudulent inducement may turn on eye-crossing subtleties in the way the arbitration agreement was drafted. *See* S.A. Mineracao da Trindade-Samitri v. Utah Int'l, Inc., 745 F.2d 190 (2d Cir. 1984). In holding the arbitration clause to cover claims of fraudulent inducement, the majority (opinion by Judge Swygert) felt that a clause referring to arbitration of "any question or dispute arising or occurring under the contract" was broader than one referring to "disputes or controversies under or arising out of the contract." The addition of "question ... occurring" did not move Judge Kearse, who saw no difference, and dissented, considering that in both cases fraud in the inducement fell outside of the scope of the clause. *Compare, e.g.*, Mediterranean Enterprises, Inc. v. Sangyong Corp., 708 F.2d 1985 (9th Cir.

place of arbitration; (iv) the language of the arbitration; and (v) the number of arbitrators. Additional elements that are often desirable include provisions concerning choice-of-law (both substantive and procedural), pre-award attachment and interim injunctive relief (by arbitrators and by courts), consolidation of parallel proceedings, punitive damages and a "last best offer" procedure.

Occasionally useful items include qualifications for arbitrators, time limits for constitution of the tribunal and rendering of the award, authority for the arbitrator to grant punitive damages, allocation of costs and attorneys' fees, and provision for reasoned awards. Most of these elements have already been discussed in Chapter III, and are included in the model clause contained in Appendix B. Many will represent a greater degree of detail than the corporate lawyer drafting the documents (or the client) will want to deal with at the end of the negotiating process. Three aspects of arbitration agreements not dealt with elsewhere deserve special attention at this point: (i) the number of arbitrators, (ii) baseball or "last best offer" arbitration and (iii) prophylactic measures against a "split the difference" award.

2. Number of Arbitrators.

International commercial arbitration rules usually provide for either a sole arbitrator or a three member tribunal. A single arbitrator will normally be cheaper. A three-member tribunal, however, makes for a more rigorous decision-making process. Most people behave differently in groups than they do alone. Arbitrators generally will be less prone to sloppy thinking if they must justify their conclusions in deliberations with others.

3. Baseball Arbitration.

In some arbitrations the parties may want to provide that each side will present a fixed monetary amount for consideration by the arbitrators, who will select either one or the other of the amounts presented. Sometimes called "baseball arbitration," because of its use to help set the compensation of major league baseball players in the United States,[461] the procedure restricts arbitrators to the parties' "last best" (*i.e.*, final) offers

---

Note 460, continued

1983) ("arising hereunder" seen as a narrow clause that was restricted to "disputes and controversies relating to interpretation of the contract and matters of performance." (*i.e.*, not to include fraud in the inducement); JJ Ryan & Sons, Inc. v. Rhone Poulenc Fibers S.A., 863 F.2d (4th Cir. 1988) ("in connection with this Agreement" construed to embrace "every dispute between the parties having a significant relationship to the contract regardless of the label attached to the dispute.").

461. The Basic Agreement between the Major League Baseball Players Association and the club owners provides for resolution of salary disputes under this "last best offer" arbitration. *See* American Arbitration Association, USING ALTERNATIVE DISPUTE RESOLUTION TO SETTLE SPORTS DISPUTES, at pages 8-11. *See generally* John Murray, Alan Rau & Edward Sherman, PROCESSES OF DISPUTE RESOLUTION: THE ROLE OF LAWYERS 591-94 (1989).

in settlement. Baseball arbitration encourages each side to move toward a middle ground.[462] A party that submits an unreasonably high or low figure risks rejection of its position, leaving the other side's submission as the only alternative.

Baseball arbitration may be particularly well-suited to disputes arising from commonly held business interests. For example, two siblings arguing over the price at which one should buy the other's interest in a family business might each submit to arbitrators an estimate of the fair market value of the commonly owned entity. Neither would want to propose too high or too low a figure, for fear that the arbitrators would take the other's estimate.

Baseball arbitration has also been used in tax disputes in which fiscal authorities and a taxpayer disagree on the correct "arm's length" price at which goods, services or intangibles should be transferred among related parties. One well-publicized intercompany transfer pricing dispute involved printed circuit boards manufactured by a Singapore affiliate of an American company.[463] The Internal Revenue Service sought to reallocate income to the American operations[464] from transactions that included sales, services and the use of intangibles.[465] The parties selected baseball arbitration under Tax Court Rule 124.[466]

4. Splitting the Difference.

Arbitrators will sometimes make a compromise award for a figure somewhere between the parties' competing positions, rather than rendering a principled decision

---

462. Each year in late February or early March in American newspapers one can find lists of those players (numbering about 150 per year now) who ask to have their salaries decided by arbitration, along with lists of those who settled before the arbitration (the vast majority of the cases) for something in between the two figures. For example in 1993, there were 118 players who went to arbitration. Six (6) won, (12) twelve lost and one hundred (100) settled by negotiations before the arbitration. This is an 85% settlement rate. *See Wrapping up Arbitration,* New York Times, 22 February 1993, page 2; *No Sacrifice for Players in Arbitration Hearings,* Chicago Tribune, 22 February 1993, page 9; M. Noble, *Players Cash In Big-Time,* Newsday, 21 February 1993, page 8.

463. The dispute covered the tax years 1984, 1985 and 1986. The case had been brought before Judge Julian Jacobs in the U.S. Tax Court. *See generally I.R.S. News Release IR 92-20,* 6 March 1992, *printed in* [1992] 13 CCH Standard Federal Tax Reporter, ¶ 46,217 at page 76,949. The parties stipulated that the three-member arbitral tribunal would consist of a retired judge, an economist and an industry expert.

464. In its deficiency notice the I.R.S. originally sought an allocation of $114 million. The stipulation stated that the range of possible income for Apple Singapore was between $16.3 million and $130.9 million.

465. Apple Computer Inc. and Consolidated Subsidiaries v. Commissioner of Internal Revenue, Docket No. 21781-90, Stipulation for Resolution of Issue Through Voluntary Binding Arbitration Under Tax Rule 124.

466. The arbitrators unanimously decided that the income of Apple Computer should be increased by $76 million, pursuant to the amounts submitted by the Internal Revenue Service. *See* award filed with Tax Court on 22 September 1993, BNA Daily Report for Executives, 27 September 1993, 1993 DER 185 d 59, Section on Taxation, Section G, 185.

based on the legal merits of the case. Whether in practice they do so more than judges is a matter of anecdotes rather than evidence.

To discourage an arbitral tribunal from such a Solomonic judgment, the parties normally should subject their contract to a fixed legal system rather than empowering the arbitrators to decide "in equity" or as *amiable compositeur*, or to apply *lex mercatoria*.[467] Such chameleon-like choice-of-law formulae may serve as a fig leaf to hide the substitution of an arbitrator's personal normative preferences for the parties' shared *ex ante* expectations. In addition, the contract should designate an arbitral situs where a losing party may challenge an award in court for an arbitrator's excess of authority.[468] Finally, the arbitrators should be required to render a reasoned award that will encourage them to articulate the legal and factual basis for their decision, thereby promoting principled awards.[469]

C. THE SUBMISSION TO JURISDICTION.[470]

Unlike arbitrators, judges usually receive their power from the state rather than the litigants. The parties' ability to circumscribe or enlarge this power by contract is therefore limited. Nevertheless, reliable forum selection can be enhanced through a jurisdiction clause such as the model in Appendix A, dealing with (i) limits on subject matter jurisdiction, (ii) *forum non conveniens* objections, (iii) notice and (iv) exclusivity of forum.

1. Subject Matter Jurisdiction.

If the parties select a forum in the United States, they may want the jurisdictional submission to refer to both state and federal courts in a particular locale. Although *personal* jurisdiction over the litigants generally will be conferred by the jurisdiction clause itself, no form of waiver or contractual submission can thrust *subject matter* competence on a federal court that would otherwise be unable to hear the case.[471] By providing for the jurisdiction of state as well as federal tribunals within a particular jurisdiction, contracting parties maximize chances that a jurisdiction clause will be workable notwithstanding limits on federal subject matter jurisdiction.

---

467. *See* discussion *supra* at notes 314-30. *See also* William W. Park, *Control Mechanisms in the Development of a Modern Lex Mercatoria*, in LEX MERCATORIA AND ARBITRATION 109 (T. Carbonneau ed., 1990).

468. *See* discussion *supra* at notes 347-417.

469. *See* discussion *supra* at notes 304-07.

470. *See generally* Lee Bucheit, *Negotiating the Submission to Jurisdiction Clause*, International Financial Law Review (November 1993) at 27.

471. In particular, federal courts generally will not be able to exercise jurisdiction over an action between two foreigners. As discussed supra at notes 149-52, exceptions to this limitation exist when the action raises a federal question, including an action covered by the Foreign Sovereign Immunities Act.

2. Forum Non Conveniens.

The best way to reduce the risk that a court action will be dismissed on grounds of *forum non conveniens* is to select a forum like New York State or Switzerland that treats jurisdiction clauses as dispositive and prohibits its courts from invoking considerations of inconvenient forum in cases covered by jurisdictional clauses.[472] Even if the parties cannot agree on such a jurisdiction, the submission clause should contain explicit waivers by the parties of any claim that the action be dismissed on grounds of inconvenient forum and/or improper venue.

3. Notice.

The jurisdictional clause should anticipate arguments about whether actual notice of the action was in fact received. Each party should appoint an agent for service of process within the chosen jurisdiction.

4. Exclusivity of Forum.

A non-exclusive jurisdictional clause will permit a claimant to bring an action in several of the locations where the defendant holds attachable assets. However, a jurisdiction clause is often needed to prevent an unwanted court from rendering a judgment, as much as to grant jurisdiction to desired tribunals. In one recent case brought in New York, the Second Circuit permitted dismissal on *forum non conveniens* grounds in favor of a Venezuela court, on the basis that the "permissive" (i.e., non-exclusive) forum selection clause operated only as a consent to jurisdiction and did not require the action to be brought in New York.[473] Whether the chosen forum should have exclusive or non-exclusive jurisdiction will depend on whether one expects to be a claimant or a defendant.

---

472. *See* discussion of N.Y. General Obligations Law § 5-1402 and N.Y.C.P.L.R. Rule 327, *supra* at notes 187-93, and Swiss L.D.I.P. Article 5, *infra*, notes 685-93.

473. Blanco v. Banco Industrial de Venezuela, 997 F.2d 974 (1993). Venezuelan bank guaranteed obligations of real estate developer under a loan agreement with a consortium of Middle Eastern banks. The forum selection provision stated that legal actions "may be brought in the High Court of Justice in England, the Courts of the State of New York, the Courts of the United States of America in New York or the Courts of the City of Caracas Venezuela...." *Id.* at 976.

Chapter V

PUBLIC CONTROL OF PRIVATE QUARRELS

Forum selection implicates public as well as private interests, particularly when jurisdiction or arbitration agreements are coupled with choice-of-law clauses in a way designed to defeat mandatory public policies or fundamental standards of procedural integrity. Legal systems that enforce commercial contracts therefore usually monitor the parties' choices with respect to forum and governing law, so as to safeguard substantive and procedural community norms.[474]

A. THE INTERACTION OF CHOICE OF LAW AND CHOICE OF FORUM.[475]

1. Party Autonomy and Its Limits.

Parties to international transactions generally have the right to choose the substantive law to govern their relationships.[476] Referred to as "party autonomy," this power to select the legal rules to be used to interpret commercial or financial arrangements has been recognized by national conflict-of-laws systems of most major international

---

474. The parties' choice of forum raises the centuries-old question of who is to guard the guards themselves: "Sed quis custodiet ipsos custodes?" Juvenal, SATIRES, II, 63.
475. *See generally*, Michael Gruson, *Controlling Choice of Law, in* SOVEREIGN LENDING: MANAGING LEGAL RISKS (M. Gruson & R. Reisner, eds. 1984); Michael Gruson, *Governing-Law Clauses in International and Interstate Loan Agreements: New York's Approach*, 1982 U. Ill. L. Rev. 207 (1982); Pierre Mayer, *Les Lois de Police Etrangères*," 1981 J. Dr. Int'l 277.
476. The parties might choose national law, the law of a country's political subdivision, or a set of principles referred to as *lex mercatoria*. The last of these is discussed *infra* at text accompanying notes 314-30.

trading nations, including the United States,[477] England,[478] France,[479] and Switzerland,[480] as well as in uniform statutes[481] and multilateral treaties.[482]

Predictability in multistate transactions has been invoked to justify party autonomy. By deferring to the parties' choice of the rules to govern their business relationship, courts augment the commercial players' ability to "foretell with accuracy their rights and liabilities under [their] contract."[483]

National legal systems limit this freedom of contract in order to protect a variety of vital community interests. For example, in the United States the Uniform Commercial Code requires a "reasonable relation" between a transaction and the state of the chosen law.[484] The Restatement on Conflict of Laws denies application of a law contrary to a fundamental policy of an otherwise applicable legal system with "a materially greater interest than the chosen state in the determination of the particular issue."[485] A directive of the European Union requires member states to insure that a choice-of-law clause does not deprive consumers of the protection of legislation restricting the effect of unfair contract terms.[486]

In general, the party-chosen law must not violate a public policy of the place of contract performance or of the forum asked to enforce the contract. Such policies

---

477. *See* RESTATEMENT (SECOND) CONFLICT OF LAWS § 187. The Supreme Court has emphasized the importance of contractual choice-of-law clauses in international cases in dicta contained in Scherk v. Alberto Culver, *supra* note 48, at 516, stating that "a contractual provision specifying in advance the forum in which disputes shall be litigated *and the law to be applied* is therefore an almost indispensable precondition to achievement of orderliness and predictability in any international business transaction." Emphasis added. For a brief survey of recent American cases on party autonomy, see Patrick Borchers, *Choice of Law in the American Courts in 1992: Observations and Reflections,* 42 Am. J. Comp. L. 125 (1994), at 135. For a cultural perspective on choice of law (juxtaposing "freedom of contract" and "justice in relationships"), *see* Joseph W. Singer, *Real Conflicts,* 69 B.U. L. Rev. 1, 110, 119-27 (1989).

478. *See* A.V. Dicey & J.H.C. Morris, CONFLICT OF LAWS Rule 180 (L. Collins ed., 11th ed. 1987).

479. *See* Bernard Audit, DROIT INTERNATIONAL PRIVÉ §§ 137-162 (1991); Pierre Mayer, DROIT INTERNATIONAL PRIVÉ § 575 at 419 (1987).

480. *See* Articles 116 and 187, Loi fédérale sur le droit international privé, discussed *supra* at note 386.

481. *See* UNCITRAL Model Law on International Commercial Arbitration, 21 June 1985, Article 34(2)(a).

482. *See* Article 3, European Convention on Law Applicable to Contractual Obligations, Rome, 19 June 1980, *reprinted in* 19 I.L.M. 1492 (1980). *See also* Article 6, Vienna Convention on Contracts for the International Sale of Goods, *reprinted in* 19 I.L.M. 672 (1980).

483. *See* RESTATEMENT (SECOND) CONFLICT OF LAWS § 187 Comment e.

484. *See* UNIFORM COMMERCIAL CODE § 1-105.

485. RESTATEMENT (SECOND) CONFLICT OF LAWS, § 187(2), set forth in Appendix I-2, provides that the party-chosen law will not apply if either (1) the chosen state has no substantial relationship to the parties and the transaction, and there is no other reasonable basis for the choice, or (2) the chosen law would violate the policy of a more vitally interested state..

486. Council of the European Communities, *Directive on Unfair Terms in Consumer Contracts,* No. 93/13/EEC, 5 April 1993, *published in* Official Journal of the European Communities, No. L 95/29, 21 April 1993.

may relate to fair securities markets,[487] free competition,[488] and exclusions of liability abusively imposed on weaker members of society.[489] The relationships of lender and borrower, franchisor and franchisee, landlord and tenant, all operate in a less than economically ideal world.[490] Thus some banks are prohibited from charging usurious rates of interest; franchisors must give adequate notice before terminating a franchise; and landlords have not always been allowed to charge residential tenants the market rate for an apartment.[491]

Choice-of-law clauses drafted to avoid such protective legislation are not difficult to imagine. A loan to a resident of New York, for example, might state that any dispute arising out of the credit facility will be subject to the law of a country notoriously lacking in any usury legislation. Or, a contract in restraint of trade might stipulate that it is to be governed by the law of a nation without rules promoting free competition.

In addition to public policy limits, conflict of laws sometimes deals with abuse of choice-of-law clauses by requiring a reasonable basis for the choice of law.[492] This reasonable basis for the choice of law will sometimes derive from the need for legal certainty and neutrality. When an African nation ships raw materials to an American buyer, the seller and the buyer may agree that "the laws of England" will govern their contract. In part this reflects a fear, rational or not, that the seller's law somehow will favor the seller, and vice versa. The party-chosen law may also justify its selection by its completeness. For example, English law would seem to provide more specific guidance for maritime transactions on the high seas than the law of a country like Switzerland, which has not possessed an ocean coastline since the Mesozoic age when the Alps rose from the Tethys Sea.

The following sections look deeper into the way that forum selection may interact with a fundamental policy of an otherwise applicable legal system. The vitality of such policies may be tested both before and after the arbitral process.

2. Prospective Waiver of Mandatory Norms.

Lawyers sometimes combine a contract's choice-of-law clause with a forum designation hospitable to the dominant side of the transaction. For example, lenders might

---

487. *E.g.*, S.E.C. Rule 10b-5.
488. *E.g.*, the United States' Sherman Act and Articles 85 and 86 of the European Union's Treaty of Rome.
489. The United Kingdom generally invalidates rules that would "unreasonably" exclude liability for negligence. Unfair Contract Terms Act of 1977, Section 2(2). This limit does not apply when the law of any part of the United Kingdom (i.e., England and Wales, Scotland or Northern Ireland) applies merely because of the parties' choice. Unfair Contract Terms Act of 1977, Section 27(1). *See also* discussion of European Communities Directive on Unfair Terms in Consumer Contracts, *supra* note 485.
490. For specific illustrations, see George P. Carpinello, *Testing the Limits of Choice of Law Clauses: Franchise Contracts As a Case Study*, 74 Marq. L. Rev. 57 (1990).
491. *See, e.g.*, Cal. Bus. & Prof. Code § 20020; Conn. Gen. Stat. § 424-133f, 1331; Ill. Stat. ch.1211, para. 1719; Ind. Code § 23-2-2.7-3; Minn. Stat. 80C.14; N.J. Stat. § 56:10-5.
492. *See* RESTATEMENT (SECOND) OF CONFLICT OF LAWS § 187(2), discussed *supra* at note 485..

subject a loan to the law of a country without a usury statute and also provide for arbitration of disputes with the borrower under the auspices of an institution known to appoint arbitrators untroubled by excessive interest charges.[493] Whether or not such choices will prevail depends in large measure on how arbitrators and judges balance party autonomy against the interest in application of what have been called "*lois de police*" or "mandatory public norms."

As mentioned in the preceding section, laws related to blockades, nationalization, currency controls, bankruptcies, competition law, securities regulation, environmental protection and boycotts usually will control particular aspects of a cross-border business relationship regardless of the legal régime chosen by the parties or by the forum's general conflicts rules. Such rules create direct benefits for members of society who never signed the forum selection agreement. Even if a freely accepted bargain will provide business partners with neutral dispute resolution, the chosen arbitrator or judge may not protect the public against under-enforcement of public norms.

First brought to scholarly attention by Continental jurists who described "police laws" (*lois de police*[494]), such mandatory norms supplant the otherwise applicable legal system in order to protect social and economic policies of a country with a vital interest in the questionable conduct.[495] *Lois de police* are spatially conditioned,[496] in

---

493. Differences in statutes of limitations or the validity of exculpatory clauses provide other illustrations. In *Bremen v. Zapata*, the American party's decision to ignore the contractually chosen forum in London commended itself because the contract included language purporting to exculpate the Germans from liability for damage to the rig. The Americans assumed that the exculpatory language had more chance of being upheld by an English court than an American one. In *Zapata*, the Supreme Court found the choice-of-law variation irrelevant to international towing contracts. Not all such public policy arguments, however, are so easily dismissed.

494. *See, e.g.,* Francescakis, *Quelques précisions sur les `lois d'application immédiate' et leurs rapports avec les règles de conflit de lois*, 1966 R.C.D.I.P. 1. Pierre Mayer, *Mandatory Rules of Law in International Arbitration*, 2 Arb. Int'l 274 (1986); *see also* Yves Derains, *Les Normes d'Application Immediate dans la Jurisprudence Arbitrale Internationale*," in DROIT DES RELATIONS ECONOMIQUES INTERNATIONALES: ETUDES OFFERTES À BERTHOLD GOLDMAN (P. Fouchard, P. Kahn & A. Lyon-Caen eds., 1982) at 29; Pierre Mayer, *Les Lois de Police Etrangères*, 1981 J. Dr. Int'l 277; *See generally,* Bernard Audit, DROIT INTERNATIONAL PRIVÉ §§ 92-113, 113, 92 (1991); Mohammad Reza Beniassadi, *Do Mandatory Rules of Public Law Limit Choice of Law in International Commercial Arbitration*, 10 Int'l Tax & Bus. L. 59 (1992); P.B. Carter, *Transnational Recognition and Enforcement of Foreign Public Law*, 1989 Cambridge L.J. 417 (1989); Thomas G. Guedj, *The Theory of the Lois de Police, A Functional Trend in Continental Private International Law—A Comparative Analysis With Modern American Theories*, 39 Am. J. Comp. L. 661 (1991).

495. *Compare* the related concept of "fraud on the applicable law." *See* Bernard Audit, FRAUDE À LA LOI §§ 485-502 (1974).

496. *See* Thomas G. Guedj, *The Theory of the Lois de Police, A Functional Trend In Continental Private International Law—A Comparative Analysis With Modern American Theories*, 39 Am. J. Comp. L. 661, 668 (1991). *Compare* Peter Hay's description of "self-limited rules of law" in Peter Hay, *Comments on `Self-Limited Rules of Law' in Conflicts Methodology*, 30 Am. J. Comp. L. 127, 129 (1982).

the sense that they apply to preempt the otherwise applicable law[497] only in the place of contract performance.[498]

Consumer protection statutes, for example, may override attempts to limit their provisions through choice of a foreign governing law. Protective legislation generally applies only in the territory of the consumer's residence, however. An English court hearing a dispute involving a French consumer might respect a clause designating French law even though it derogated from British consumer protection rules, whereas the derogation would be ignored as to a consumer resident in Britain.[499]

The conceptual ancestry of *lois de police* can be traced to a 1929 decision of the Permanent Court of International Justice in the Serbian Loan case.[500] French holders of bonds issued by the Kingdom of Serbia (as it then was) sought to enforce a "gold clause" prohibiting payment in paper currency. The court noted that the validity of the currency clause would be governed by French legislation (requiring creditors to accept payment in notes) even though the loan agreement was subject to Serbian law.[501] The Court went on, however, to hold that the invalidity of gold clauses under French currency laws was spatially conditioned to cover only domestic French transactions.[502]

At least one national statute[503] and four international treaties deal explicitly with *lois de police*.[504] The most important of these is the 1980 European Convention on the Law Applicable to Contractual Obligations,[505] which provides for recognition of the

---

497. See A.V. Dicey & J.H.C. Morris, 1 THE CONFLICT OF LAWS 21-25 (L. Collins ed., 11th ed. 1987).

498. For example, the Sherman Act is spatially conditioned in the sense that American antitrust law would normally be relevant only to American transactions. The law would normally apply "extraterritorially" only in the case of a foreign transaction that has a direct effect on the United States.

499. See, e.g., the United Kingdom Unfair Contract Terms Act 1977, which applies unless the contractual relationship is defined as an "international supply contract." *Id.* § 26. The Unfair Contract Terms Act states that it generally has effect notwithstanding any contract term purporting to apply the law of a country outside the United Kingdom (*i.e.*, other than English, Scots or Northern Irish law). See discussion in Dicey & Morris, *supra* note 497, at 23.

500. Payment of Various Serbian Loans Issued in France, 1929 P.C.I.J. No. 14, Series A No. 20/Series C No. 16-III. The case is reprinted in 1 Précis de la Jurisprudence de la Cour Internationale 452 (K. Marek, ed., 1974) (hereinafter "Marek"); *see also* Alexander Pandelli Fachiri, THE PERMANENT COURT OF INTERNATIONAL JUSTICE 289 (reprint 1980) (2d ed. 1932); 1 Edouard Hambro, CASE LAW OF THE INTERNATIONAL COURT 141 (1961).

501. "Every State is entitled to regulate its own currency," the court stated. Marek, *supra* note 500, at 294.

502. *Id.* at 295.

503. See Swiss *L.D.I.P.*, Article 19, discussed *supra* at note 386.

504. Rome Convention of 19 June 1980 on Law Applicable to Contractual Obligations; Hague Convention of 14 March 1978 on Law Applicable to Intermediary Agreements and Agency; Hague Convention of 20 October 1984 on Law Applicable to Trusts and their Recognition; Hague Convention of 30 October 1985 on the Law Applicable to International Agreements for the Sale of Goods.

505. 1980 O.J. (L 266) 1. Drafted under the aegis of the European Community, this treaty is sometimes referred to as the Rome Convention.

mandatory rules of a legal system having a "close connection" to the transaction.[506] The Convention will also permit courts to consider fundamental public policies of the place of performance if these do not conflict dramatically with those of the forum.[507] The Convention language is precatory rather than imperative, providing that "effect *may* be given to mandatory rules." The paradox of a mandatory norm whose application is permissive seems inevitable. Justice and comity often require public policies of one state to be balanced against competing norms of another jurisdiction.

While judges can hardly ignore the public norms of the communities that pay their salaries, the extent to which arbitrators may or must apply mandatory rules is open to question. From the parties' perspective, one might argue that an arbitrator's recognition of a *loi de police* constitutes an excess of authority contrary to the party-chosen substantive law. An arbitrator's power derives from the parties' contract, which rarely will allude to application of mandatory norms.[508] On the other hand, the arbitrator's own conscience or respect for international public order could impel departure from the parties' will. For example, an arbitrator might disregard a choice-of-law clause that led to enforcement of a contract for the sale of illegal drugs or payment of a bribe; or the arbitrator might decline jurisdiction to decide a dispute arising under such a contract.[509] Moreover, the international currency of arbitration awards requires that arbitrators be sensitive to the public policies of legal orders that support the arbitral process, at the risk of otherwise subjecting their awards to judicial annulment or non-recognition.

American law safeguards mandatory norms by asking whether a choice-of-forum clause is linked to a choice-of-law clause in such a way as to defeat fundamental policies of the place of contract performance. In the landmark United States Supreme

---

506. Article 7 provides: "When applying under this Convention the law of a country, effect may be given to mandatory rules of the law of another country with which the situation has a close connection, if and in so far as, under the law of the latter country, those rules must be applied whatever the law applicable to the contract. In considering whether to give effect to these mandatory rules, regard shall be had to their nature and purpose and to the consequences of their application or non-application."

507. The Hague Convention on Agency also provides that courts have discretion to take into account non-forum rules of a country with a close connection to the contract.

508. For an interpretation of a choice-of-law clause that permits an inference of the parties' acceptance of mandatory norms, see footnote 19 of *Mitsubishi Motors* discussed *infra* at note 510.

509. *See* Pierre Mayer, *Mandatory Rules of Law in International Arbitration*, 2 Arb. Int'l 274 (1986) (corruption as an excuse for ignoring the principle of *pacta sunt servanda*). *See also* I.C.C. Award No. 1110 (Argentina Bribery Case), 15 January 1963, discussed in Julian Lew, Applicable Law in International Commercial Arbitration (1978) at 553-55; *reprinted in* 10 ARBITRATION INTERNATIONAL 282 (1994), as an Annex to J. Gillis Wetter, *Issues of Corruption Before International Tribunals*, *id.* at 277. Judge Lagergren declined jurisdiction in an arbitral proceeding implicating illegal activity. *Compare* Westinghouse International Projects Co. v. National Power Corp., 7 Mealy's Int'l Arb. Report (No. 1), Section B-1 (1992), rejecting allegations of bribery.

Court decision in *Mitsubishi Motors Corp. v. Soler Chrysler-Plymouth*,[510] the parties had selected Swiss law to govern a dispute arising out of an automobile distribution agreement between a Japanese manufacturer and an American automobile dealer. The dispute also raised an American antitrust counterclaim under the Sherman Act. In ordering arbitration of the controversy, the United States Supreme Court assumed (perhaps naively) that the arbitrator would engage in choice-of-law *dépeçage* to apply the Sherman Act to the antitrust counterclaims notwithstanding the Swiss choice of law.[511] However, the Court went on to warn that it would not enforce an arbitration agreement that operated in tandem with a choice-of-law clause as a "prospective waiver" of the right to pursue Sherman Act claims. Writing for the majority, Justice Blackmun noted that "in the event the choice-of-forum and choice-of-law clauses operated in tandem as a prospective waiver of a party's right to pursue statutory remedies for antitrust violations, we would have little hesitation in condemning the agreement as against public policy."[512]

Blackmun's ideas were tested in a spate of litigation arising from financial losses incurred by the Lloyd's of London insurance exchange.[513] Investors in Lloyd's insurance syndicates (the investors being referred to as "Names" in Lloyd's parlance) brought actions in United States federal courts alleging violations of American securities laws.[514] The dispute resolution clauses in all relevant agreements contained choice-of-law clauses stipulating that the contracts would be construed in accordance

---

510. 473 U.S. 614 (1985). *See* William W. Park, *Private Adjudicators and the Public Interest*, 12 Brooklyn J. Int'l Law 629 (1986); *see also* Thomas E. Carbonneau, *Mitsubishi: The Folly of Quixotic Internationalism*, 2 Arb. Int'l 178 (1986); Andreas Lowenfeld, *The Mitsubishi Case: Another View*, 2 Arb. Int'l 116 (1986).

511. One scholar considers the heart of the Supreme Court ruling on arbitrability to be "mere *dictum*." He assumes that the arbitrators could have declined to adjudicate the antitrust claim. Hans Smit, *Mitsubishi: It Is Not What It Seems To Be*, 4 J. Int'l Arb. 7, 14-17 (Sept. 1987).

512. *Mitsubishi Motors*, *supra* note 510, 473 U.S. at 637 n.19. The scope of this "prospective waiver" dicta was tested in *In re* Hops, Antitrust Litigation, 655 F. Supp. 169, 172 (E.D. Mo. 1987), *appeal dismissed*, 832 F.2d 470 (8th Cir. 1987), involving a dispute between an American brewer and German hops merchants. The court found no reason to believe that application of German law in a Munich arbitration would deprive claimant of the opportunity to pursue antitrust claims.

513. *See When Names Are Mud*, The Economist, 27 July 1991, at 17, and *The Liquidity Gap at Lloyd's*, The Economist, 16 May 1992, at 101, discussing the losses for 1988 and 1989 announced in 1991 and 1992 respectively. Lloyd's profit and loss accounts are established three years in arrears.

514. *See, e.g.*, Roby v. Corporation of Lloyd's, 996 F.2d 1353 (2d Cir. 1993), aff'd 796 F. Supp. 103 and 824 F. Supp. (S.D.N.Y.); Riley v. Kingsley Underwriting Agencies, 969 F.2d 953 (10th Cir. 1992). *Compare* Bonny v. Society of Lloyd's, 1993 WL 292345 (7th Cir. 1993) in which the court affirmed the district court's dismissal of a motion for an injunction barring Lloyd's from drawing upon a letter of credit issued in connection with the plaintiffs' membership in Lloyd's.

with the laws of England,[515] and that disputes would be submitted to English courts[516] and to arbitration in London.[517] American courts upheld the jurisdiction and arbitration clauses, notwithstanding arguments that their enforcement would undermine the strong American public policy embodied in the securities laws. The American investors argued unsuccessfully that enforcement of the forum selection clauses would deprive them of remedies available under federal securities laws.[518]

In one decision[519] the court examined English common law and found that the plaintiffs had "adequate remedies in England to vindicate their substantive rights" and that American policies favoring "full and fair [securities] disclosure and deterring the exploitation of United States investors have not been subverted."[520] One wonders how feasible, in other cases, will be the judicial inquiry into whether the applicable foreign laws are compatible with American public policy. Sources on English law will likely be more accessible to an American judge than (for example) analogous legal provisions and practice in Iran, Libya, China or Zaire.

3. The Judge's Second Look at the Arbitration.[521]

In addition to considering the effect of mandatory public norms when called to enforce an agreement to arbitrate or litigate abroad, courts may decide to have a second look at public policy matters after the award or judgment has been rendered.[522]

---

515. The complex relationships implicated by membership in a Lloyd's syndicate usually involves a "General Undertaking" with Lloyd's itself and an agreement with the "Member's Agent" authorizing the conclusion of an agreement with the "Managing Agent" of a syndicate.
516. Under the relevant portions of the General Undertaking, "Each party hereto irrevocably agrees that the courts of England shall have exclusive jurisdiction to settle any dispute and/or controversy of whatsoever nature arising out of or relating to the Member's membership of Lloyd's."
517. The jurisdiction clause in the Managing Agency Agreement typically provides that each party "irrevocably submits for all purposes of and in connection with this agreement to the exclusive jurisdiction of the courts of England." *Id.*, at note 2. The arbitration clause in the Managing Agency Agreement generally provides that "any dispute, difference, question or claim relating to this agreement ... shall be referred at the request of either party to arbitration in London." In default of an agreement by the parties, the arbitrator is to be appointed by the Chairman or a Deputy Chairman of Lloyd's. *See* Riley. v. Kingsley Underwriting, *supra* note 514, at 995. n.3.
518. The U.S. Supreme Court had warned in its landmark 1985 *Mitsubishi* decision that American courts would condemn, as against public policy, a choice-of-forum clause that operated in tandem with a choice-of-law clause in such a way as to constitute a "prospective waiver" of American statutory rights. Mitsubishi Motors v. Soler Chrysler-Plymouth Inc., 473 U.S. 614 (1985), at 637, note 19, discussed *supra* at note 510. *See generally* William W. Park, *Private Adjudicators and the Public Interest*, 12 Brooklyn J. Int'l Law 629 (1986).
519. Roby v. Corporation of Lloyd's, *supra* note 514.
520. *Id.* at 1365.
521. *See generally* William W. Park, *Private Adjudicators and the Public Interest: The Expanding Scope of International Arbitration*, 12 Brooklyn J. Int'l L. 629 (1986).
522. Mitsubishi Motors Corp. v. Soler Chrysler-Plymouth, Inc., 473 U.S. 614, 637 (1985).

Relying on a problematic section of the New York Arbitration Convention,[523] the Supreme Court in *Mitsubishi* warned that American judges might be called to determine whether arbitrators in fact addressed American public law claims, which in that case related to antitrust law. The dicta reads in part as follows: "The national courts of the United States will have the opportunity at the award enforcement stage to ensure that the legitimate interest in the enforcement of antitrust laws has been addressed ... [and] to ascertain that the [arbitral] tribunal took cognizance of the antitrust claims and actually decided them."[524]

It is uncertain whether this "second look doctrine" calls for a broad examination of an arbitrator's decision, or only a mechanical examination of whether the arbitrator in fact did consider the statute. From a policy perspective, either option presents risks. A full judicial examination of an award could lead to review of the merits of the arbitration, impairing the arbitral autonomy sought by the parties initially. However, a look at an award to determine only whether the arbitrator in fact considered public law questions would be unlikely to prevent clever arbitrators from ignoring mandatory norms after having paid them enough passing lip service to satisfy a superficial judicial review.

In some cases the "second look doctrine" will put arbitrators in a double bind. An arbitrator who applies the parties' chosen legal system notwithstanding its conflict with a mandatory public norm may make the award unenforceable in the country of contract performance. However, an arbitrator who ignores the parties' choice of law in order to respect mandatory norms invites annulment of the award for excess of authority. For example, if a contract like the one litigated in *Mitsubishi* includes a choice-of-law clause explicitly selecting a legal system with no antitrust law, an arbitrator mindful of Justice Blackmun's caveat might decide an antitrust claim according to United States law. However, this departure from the parties' express choice of applicable law would increase the risk of challenge of the award outside the United States, where disregard of the Swiss choice-of-law clause would lend itself to a characterization as an excess of authority. The loser could challenge the award first at the place where rendered, on the theory that the arbitrator decided inconsistently with the arbitral agreement,[525] and then for arbitral excess of authority in the enforcement forum in which the loser's assets were located.[526]

---

523. New York Convention, Article V(2)(b) provides: "Recognition and enforcement of an arbitral award may also be refused if the competent authority in the country where recognition and enforcement are sought finds that: ... [t]he recognition or enforcement of the award would be contrary to the public policy of that country."

524. Mitsubishi Motors, *supra* note 510 at 638.

525. Analogous grounds for review exist in most major arbitral centers. *See* Wilko v. Swan, 346 U.S. 427, 436 (1953) ("manifest disregard of the law"); Federal Arbitration Act, 9 U.S.C. § 10(d) (1982) (arbitrators exceeded their power); French C. Pr. Civ. Article 1502 (decision in a manner inconsistent with the arbitrator's mission); Swiss L.D.I.P. Article 190(2)(c) (arbitral tribunal has gone beyond the claims submitted to it or failed to decide one of the claims); English Arbitration Act of 1950, § 23 (arbitrator "misconduct").

526. New York Arbitration Convention Article V(1)(c) permits refusal of enforcement to awards when arbitrators have decided matters not submitted to them.

The application of mandatory norms in international adjudication is not without its potential for abuse.[527] Imagine that an American construction company contracted with the Ruritanian Ministry of Education to build a university complex in Ruritania, and that the contract provided that it would be governed by English law. Subsequently the Ruler of Ruritania invoked a national economic emergency to invalidate contracts with foreign builders, thereby relieving the Ministry of Education of the obligation to pay the contractor. Normally, arbitrators would decide a dispute arising from that contract according to English law, as agreed by the parties. However, the imperative norms of the law most closely connected with the situation might include the Ruritanian emergency decree, thus opening the door to a decision frustrating the legitimate expectations that led the Americans to take the risk of building the university.

4. Timing of Judicial Intervention.[528]

Courts can safeguard the public interest by application of mandatory community norms in two ways: (1) by refusing to enforce the forum selection clause, thereby denying the contractually-selected court or arbitrator the right to hear the case, or (2) by reviewing the resulting judgment or award, either at the time when rendered (in an action for annulment) or when presented for enforcement or recognition. The former approach would prohibit forum selection in disputes that implicate sensitive public policies. The latter route would permit public claims to be decided in the chosen forum, but only on condition that judges later have the final word on enforcement of the decision.

There is a risk, of course, that judicial review of awards or judgments might come too late, and prove ineffective when the loser has assets in a third country willing to enforce the award or judgment without concern for the mandatory norms of the place of contract performance. In some cases, leaving review to the award stage will as a practical matter eliminate judicial review in the forum whose public policies are at issue. An American judge who compels arbitration in Geneva against a United States company may never have the chance to review the arbitral award, for the simple reason that the award might be enforced against assets of the loser located outside the United States.

In an international context, the importance of a relatively neutral forum argues for judicial intervention only after the award has been rendered, even at the risk that (for reasons mentioned above) some awards will escape serious judicial scrutiny. In a purely domestic context, an unenforceable arbitration or jurisdiction clause may result in a proceeding in Chicago rather than in Boston. In an international dispute, however, the alternative to the bargained-for adjudication may be a judicial proceed-

---

527. *See* F.A. Mann, *New Dangers of Arbitration in Switzerland*, Financial Times, 24 Nov. 1988, at 43.

528. *See also* discussion of the timing of judicial consideration of public policy challenges to awards in the United States, in text *supra* at notes 415-416.

ing in a foreign language before judges of a country in which graft or political influence makes basic procedural fairness problematic. To require parallel proceedings for public law issues frustrates the parties' fundamental expectations about the settlement of their differences. Having thought it agreed to arbitrate before a relatively neutral law professor in Paris or London, the claimant instead finds the dispute decided before a hostile judge in the defendant's country.

For these reasons, forum selection in cross-border disputes implicating mandatory national norms should be permitted, even if the recent trend toward allowing arbitration of public law claims[529] turns out to be a misguided experiment for domestic cases.[530] The factual and legal merits of the dispute will pass through the strainer of a neutral arbitrator or judge before judicial review of the award for conformity to public policy mandates. It is one thing to say that a judge can vacate an award or refuse to recognize a foreign judgment that violates the country's basic public order. It is quite another matter to say that a defendant should be able to move for a full trial on the merits in its home court by asserting a statutory counterclaim.

B. PROCEDURAL INTEGRITY.

1. Winners and Losers.

Recognizing that one person's delay is another's due process, most legal systems accommodate the low road of finality and the high road of fairness by giving the loser of an arbitration the right to challenge an award for violation of procedural regularities in the arbitral process. The desirable extent of such judicial control, however, has been the subject of lively exchanges. Protagonists of autonomous or "a-national arbitration"[531] have drawn a spirited reaction from those who argue that judicial review of awards is necessary to ensure the fair administration of justice.[532]

---

529. *See, e.g.,* Gilmer v. Interstate/Johnson, 500 U.S. 20 (1991) (age discrimination); Rodriguez de Cuellar v. Shearson, 490 U.S. 477 (1989) (securities); and Mitsubishi v. Soler Chrysler Plymouth, 473 U.S. 614 (1985) (antitrust).

530. *See generally* Edward J. Brunet, *Questioning the Quality of Alternate Dispute Resolution,* 62 Tul. L. Rev. 1 (1987).

531. The late Professor Berthold Goldman was among the first to urge that the nature of international arbitration leads to the necessity of a system that is "autonomous, not national." Berthold Goldman, *Les conflits de lois dans l'arbitrage international de droit privé,* II Recueil des Cours de L'Academie de Droit International de la Haye, 347, 379-80 (1963). *Compare* Jan Paulsson, *Arbitration Unbound,* 30 Int'l & Comp. L.Q. 358 (1981); Jan Paulsson, *Delocalization of International Commercial Arbitration: When and Why It Matters,* 32 Int'l & Comp. L. Q. 53 (1983). *Compare* Philippe Fouchard, L'ARBITRAGE COMMERCIAL INTERNATIONAL, (Dalloz, Paris 1964), at 22-23, emphasizing the search for "a really international framework [for commercial arbitration] where the particularities of the conflict of laws and substantive laws will no longer play any role."

532. The late Dr. Francis Mann's position was expressed most forcefully in F.A. Mann, *Private Arbitration and Public Policy,* 4 Civ. Just. Q. 257, 267 (1985); *see also* Francis A. Mann, *Lex Facit Arbitrum, in* INTERNATIONAL ARBITRATION: LIBER AMICORUM FOR MARTIN DOMKE 157, 159

Several arbitral centers have attempted to increase their shares of international arbitration by enacting reforms that free arbitrators from fear of judicial second-guessing. When in 1979 England moved to limit judicial review of arbitration awards rendered in London, Lord Cullen of Ashborne offered an estimate that this legislation would bring England £ 500 million of "invisible exports," a euphemism for arbitrators' and lawyers' fees.[533] Similar *laissez-faire* reforms followed in France in 1981, in Belgium in 1985 and in Switzerland in 1987.[534]

Delocalized arbitration sometimes promotes the parties' desire for privacy and finality in dispute resolution without necessarily violating the vital interests of the arbitral seat.[535] In a transnational dispute, the arbitration often will have its economic or social impact outside the borders of the place of the proceedings. Only if local substantive law applies to the merits of the dispute will detachment from the law of the place of the arbitration affect the country of the proceedings, and then only tangentially by removing from the courts some disputes that otherwise might have fertilized the local law's evolution.

The trend toward delocalization, however, has gone beyond merely taking from judges the power to hear appeals on substantive legal issues. Belgium has abolished all right to have an award set aside at the arbitral seat in some international

---

Note 532, *continued*
(1967) ("every arbitration is subject to a specific system of national law"). Dr. Mann's classic work was *reprinted in* 2 Arb. Int'l 241 (1986). *See also* Albert Jan Van den Berg, *The Efficiency of Awards in International Commercial Arbitration*, 58 Arb. 267 (1992); William W. Park, *National Law and Commercial Justice*, 63 Tulane L. Rev. 647 (1989); William W. Park, *The Lex Loci Arbitri and International Commercial Arbitration*, 32 Int'l & Comp. L.Q. 21 (1983).

533. 392 Parl. Deb., H.L. (5th ser.) 99 (1978); *see* William W. Park, *Judicial Supervision of Transnational Commercial Arbitration: The English Arbitration Act of 1979*, 21 Harv. Int'l L.J. 87, 96 & n.49 (1980).

534. *See* discussion *infra* at notes 377-80 (France), 559-61 (Belgium) and 386-91 (Switzerland).

535. On debate over delocalized arbitration and the *lex loci arbitri, see* Berthold Goldman, *Les conflits de lois dans l'arbitrage international de droit privé*, II Recueil des Cours de L'Academie de Droit International de la Haye 347 (1963); Alain Hirsch, *The Place of Arbitration and the Lex Arbitri*, 34 Arb. J. 43 (1979); Pierre Lalive, *Les Règles de Conflit de Lois Appliquées au Fond du Litige par L'Arbitre International Siégeant en Suisse*, 1976 Revue de L'Arbitrage 155; Francis Mann, *Lex Facit Arbitrum, in* INTERNATIONAL ARBITRATION: LIBER AMICORUM FOR MARTIN DOMKE 157 (1967); Francis Mann, *England Rejects `Delocalized' Contracts and Arbitration*, 33 Int'l & Comp. L.Q. 193 (1984); William W. Park, *The Lex Loci Arbitri and International Commercial Arbitration*, 32 Int'l & Comp. L.Q. 21 (1983); Jan Paulsson, *Arbitration Unbound: An Award Detached from the Law of its Country of Origin*, 30 Int'l & Comp. L.Q. 358 (1981); Jan Paulsson, *Arbitre et juge en Suède: Exposé générale et réflexions sur la delocalisation des sentences arbitrales*, 1980 Rev. Arb. 476; Jan Paulsson, *Delocalization of International Commercial Arbitration*, 32 Int'l & Comp. L.Q. 53 (1983); Arthur T. von Mehren, *To what Extent Is International Commercial Arbitration Autonomous? in* LE DROIT DES RELATIONS ECONOMIQUES INTERNATIONALES: ETUDES OFFERTES À BERTHOLD GOLDMAN (ed. P. Fouchard, P. Kahn & A. Lyon-Caen, Librairies techniques, Paris 1982) at 217.

arbitrations,[536] and Swiss legislation provides an option to waive any right of judicial challenge.[537]

Winners will approve of the speed and economy resulting from an adjudicatory system completely detached from national judicial control. Losers can be expected to show less enthusiasm. Total delocalization of arbitration would mean, for example, that the loser in a defective arbitration would be unable to litigate an arbitrator's excess of authority at the time the award is rendered. A corporation improperly joined to the arbitration (perhaps due to an overzealous arbitrator's decision to pierce the corporate veil of the defendant) may have to raise the matter in every country in which its assets are at risk in the execution of the award.[538]

When the victim of procedural irregularity is the claimant, the results of complete arbitral autonomy are even more dramatically unfair. If denied the opportunity to have the award set aside where rendered, the unsuccessful claimant will have no forum in which to contest the defective award, for the simple reason that there is nothing to enforce.

In private adjudication, there is an assumption of risk with respect to arbitrators who "get it wrong" as a matter of fact and law. This does not mean, however that a legal system should support arbitrators who render an award incompatible with the arbitrator's mission.[539] Judges must trace the thin line between what is simply an arbitrator error (a "bad award") and an arbitrator's excess of authority, even at the expense of inadvertently imposing their own conclusions about the merits of the dispute.[540]

536. On the Belgian statute, see *infra* notes 559-60.
537. On the Swiss federal statute, see *supra* notes 386-91.
538. In respect of piercing the corporate veil, the Swiss régime is marginally better than the Belgian, in that a parent corporation would not normally be bound by the waiver of recourse signed by a related company under L.D.I.P. Article 192, discussed *supra* at notes 386-91. On the other hand, if arbitrator fraud is alleged, it is difficult to see how the award could be challenged where rendered, unless the winner were to seek enforcement against assets within the jurisdiction, at which time the defenses of New York Convention Article V would come into play.
539. *See generally* Adam Samuel, JURISDICTIONAL PROBLEMS IN COMMERCIAL INTERNATIONAL ARBITRATION (1989).
540. *See generally* discussion *supra* at notes 338-40. *See* Mobil Oil v. Asamara Oil, 487 F. Supp. 63 (S.D.N.Y. 1980) and Inter-City Gas Corp. v. Boise Cascade Corp, 845 F.2d 184 (8th Cir. 1988). In Inter-City Gas Corp. v. Boise Cascade Corp., the Court noted: "Although the arbitrator may interpret ambiguous language, the arbitrator may not disregard unambiguous contract provisions." *Id.* at 187. Yet the court wrote that it would "not set aside the arbitrator's award simply because ... the arbitrator erred ... in determining the facts." *Id.* at 189.

2. Curial Law.

a. The Role of The Arbitral Seat.

The expression "curial law" is sometimes used to designate the legal régime governing the arbitration itself. Generally, the curial law will follow the place chosen for the proceedings (often referred to as the "arbitral seat" or "arbitral situs") and will usually (but not always) be the place where the award was rendered.[542] The arbitral seat may be selected by the parties themselves or designated by an arbitral institution. On occasion the arbitrators may for convenience hold hearings at places other than the arbitral seat.

The curial law is distinct from: (i) the law applicable to the substantive interpretation of the contract, (ii) the law that determines the validity of the arbitration agreement and (iii) the norms applied in enforcing the award. For example, a contract to be performed in part of the United States might provide that it will be interpreted under the laws of Switzerland, but that any disputes will be resolved by arbitration in London under the Rules of the International Chamber of Commerce. In this event, English arbitration law would be the curial law governing the arbitration itself on matters such as the setting aside of an award for misconduct, while Swiss law generally would govern the merits of the dispute. American law might be implicated if the defendant claimed that the arbitration agreement was invalid because it dealt with a "non-arbitrable" subject matter, as happened in the *Mitsubishi* case,[543] or that the award was unenforceable on public policy grounds.

English judges have examined in considerable depth the nature and implications of the curial law. In one case the Commercial Court has had to make sense out of a dispute resolution clause that provided for arbitration under the rules of the

---

541. *See generally* discussion *supra* at notes 337-46. *See also* W. Laurence Craig, William W. Park & Jan Paulsson, INTERNATIONAL CHAMBER OF COMMERCE ARBITRATION (2d ed. 1990), Chapter 28; Martin Hunter & Alan Redfern, INTERNATIONAL COMMERCIAL ARBITRATION (2d ed. 1991), at 297-302. Matters related more directly to the litigants' selection of a situs for the arbitration are discussed *supra* in Chapter III, which examines the place of the arbitral proceedings from the perspective of the business managers, as contrasted to the public policy focus of this section. On the influence of the arbitral situs on substantive legal choices generally, see Filip De Ly, *The Place of Arbitration in the Conflict of Laws of International Commercial Arbitration: An Exercise in Arbitration Planning*, 12 N.W. J. Int'l L. & Bus. 48 (1991).

542 Hiscox v. Outhwaite, 3 Weekly L. Rep. 297 (1991) (House of Lords), *reprinted at* XVII YEARBOOK OF INTERNATIONAL COMMERCIAL ARBITRATION 599 (1992) (award signed in Paris although arbitration deemed subject to English law), discussed *supra* at notes 364-69.. *See also* Naviera Amazonica Peruana S.A. v. Compania Internacional de Seguros del Peru, [1988] 1 pt. 2 Lloyd's Rep. 116 (C.A. 1987). The typed endorsement of an insurance policy between Peruvian shipowners and Peruvian insurers provided for "arbitration under the conditions and laws of London," but the printed conditions provided for "jurisdiction and competence of the city of Lima." On appeal it was held that the arbitration had its seat in London and thus English courts were competent to appoint an arbitrator, even though hearings might be held in Peru for convenience.

543. *See* discussion *supra* note 510.

International Chamber of Commerce *and* the "exclusive jurisdiction" of the Courts of England.[544] The plaintiff sought to enjoin the arbitration, arguing that arbitration was inconsistent with the reference to English courts. In an opinion by Justice Steyn (as he then was), the Court read the two clauses as compatible by interpreting the submission to jurisdiction of English courts as a reference to "the *lex arbitri*, the curial law or the law governing the arbitration."[545] The law governing the arbitration concerned matters such as interim measures of relief, vacancies in the arbitral tribunal and the removal of arbitrators for misconduct.

When the arbitration's curial law follows the arbitral situs, the curial law may remain undecided until the dispute is ripe for arbitration. For example, a charter party involving the Chinese National Foreign Trade Transportation Corporation contained a clause providing for disputes to be resolved by arbitration "in Beijing or London in defendant's option."[546] When the shipowner tried to bring litigation in England, the defendant moved to stay the action on the basis of the arbitration agreement. The Court of Appeal held the arbitration clause valid, notwithstanding what might seem to be the vagueness of the arbitral situs.

b. Award Annulment.

i. *The Perspective of the Arbitral Seat.*

Few disagree that some judicial review should be available in the jurisdiction in which the award is enforced.[547] Less consensus, however, exists on whether review should be available at the arbitral seat as well, in the form of judicial power to set aside awards.

The vital role of the arbitral seat in international arbitration derives in large measure from the enforcement scheme of the New York Arbitration Convention, which permits denial of recognition to an award set aside by a court of "the country in which [the] award was made."[548] The Convention therefore entrusts the place of arbitration with significant power to enhance, or to impair, the international effectiveness of an award rendered within its territory. The way courts at the arbitral seat exercise, or fail to exercise, their power to set an award aside generally will determine the award's international currency.

In the view of many scholars and practitioners, the power of the arbitral seat to affect the validity of an award carries with it an obligation to provide a judicial mechanism at the arbitral situs to control the arbitration's procedural fairness and integrity, but not to meddle with the arbitrator's decision on the substantive merits of the

---

544. Paul Smith Ltd. v. H & S International Holding Inc., [1991] 2 Lloyd's Law Rep. 127 (1991).

545. *Id.* at 129-30.

546. Star Shipping v. China National Foreign Trade Transportation Corporation (The "Star Texas"), [1993] 2 Lloyd's L. Rep. 445 (1993).

547. For a comprehensive analysis of the varieties of challenge to arbitral awards before national courts, see W. Laurence Craig, *The Uses and Abuses of Appeal from International Arbitration Awards, in* PRIVATE INVESTORS ABROAD ch. 14 (1987).

548. New York Convention, Article V(1)(e).

case.[549] Under the New York Arbitration Convention, however, the arbitral situs is free to set aside awards for any reason it sees fit, no matter how parochial.[550]

As mentioned earlier, judicial review of awards at the arbitral seat generally falls into three categories: full review of the legal merits; limited review related to matters of procedural fairness; and no review at all.[551] The first model seeks to maximize legal certainty at the expense of adjudicatory finality; the second looks to ensure an arbitration's integrity while minimizing judicial meddling with the arbitrator's substantive decision; the third model delivers finality without procedural safeguards.

As a matter of policy, the arbitral situs should provide grounds for review that are neither so excessive as to permit judicial intrusion into the merits of the dispute, nor so *laissez-faire* as to facilitate procedural unfairness. French,[552] German,[553] Dutch,[554] Swiss[555] and United States laws[556] follow such a balanced approach, by restricting review of awards to matters of basic procedural fairness. England provides for appeal on the legal merits of a dispute, but permits parties to exclude judicial review of international arbitration[557] except for matters of arbitrator "misconduct."[558] The UNCITRAL Model Law likewise strikes a balance between arbitral autonomy on the merits of the dispute and judicial control of the arbitration's procedural fairness.

In contrast, Belgium's *Code judiciaire* provides that awards rendered in Belgium in disputes between non-Belgians will be free from any action for annulment, regardless of whether the arbitrators took a bribe, exceeded their mission, or participated in

---

549. Alan Redfern & Martin Hunter, THE LAW AND PRACTICE OF INTERNATIONAL ARBITRATION 59-60 (2d ed. 1992).

550. In contrast, the European Convention limits the grounds on which an award's annulment will serve as a basis to refuse recognition. *See* discussion *supra* at note 248.

551. *See* discussion *supra* at notes 345-51.

552. On N.C.P.C. Article 1502, *see supra* at notes 377-80. Decree No. 81-500, May 12, 1981, applying specifically to arbitration that "implicates international commerce," adds articles 1442-1507 to Nouveau Code de Procédure Civile. *See generally* Bernard Audit, *A National Codification of International Commercial Arbitration: The French Decree of May 12, 1981*, *in* RESOLVING TRANSNATIONAL DISPUTES THROUGH ARBITRATION 117 (Thomas Carbonneau ed., 1984).

553. *See* discussion *supra* at notes 381-85.

554. The 1986 Dutch law, however, makes no distinction between review of domestic and international arbitration. *See* Pieter Sanders, *The New Dutch Arbitration Act*, 3 Arb. Int'l 194 (1987); Albert Jan van den Berg, R. van Delden and H.J. Saijders, NETHERLANDS ARBITRATION LAW (1994).

555. *See* discussion *infra* at notes 386-91.

556. United States Arbitration Act, 9 U.S.C. § 10 (1982).

557. 1979 Arbitration Act, § 3, applicable to awards rendered in England and Wales but not Scotland. Exclusion agreements entered into before the dispute arises will not be valid if all parties are British residents or nationals. Exclusion agreements will not be valid if English law applies to the substantive merits of the dispute *and* if the controversy relates to insurance, commodities, or shipping. Thus, current commercial controversies will continue to fertilize the development of English case law in areas in which it has long been preeminent.

558. 1950 Arbitration Act, § 23.

a fraud against one of the parties.[559] The Swiss federal conflict-of-laws code[560] in some cases accords parties an option to exclude court challenge entirely.[561] Swiss law is more sensitive than the Belgian statute, in that it permits — but does not impose — complete exclusion of review by consent of foreign parties.[562]

ii. The Perspective of the Enforcement Forum.

Questions asked at the arbitral seat intersect with those that will be asked later when the arbitrator's decision is presented for enforcement. For example, an arbitrator in London may render an award that as a practical matter must be enforced in New York, where the loser's bank accounts are located. While New York may impose its own standards with respect to claims such as excess of authority and arbitrator misconduct, both matters covered by the New York Arbitration Convention, it is less certain, however, whether New York courts should defer to an English decision setting aside the award.

Suppose, for example, that an arbitral award is set aside in London on the ground that the parties did not validly consent to arbitration. Should the award be enforced in the United States if the American court sees no reason to question the validity of the arbitration agreement? What should an American court do if an English judge set aside the award for reasons that are *not* grounds for annulment in the United States, such as error of law? Under the New York Arbitration Convention, deference to the

---

559. Article 1717 of the Belgian *Code judiciaire* provides:

> Courts of Belgium may hear a request for annulment only if at least one of the parties to the dispute decided by the award is either a physical person having Belgian nationality or residence, or a legal entity created in Belgium or having a Belgian branch or other seat of operation. *(Translation by the author)*

On Belgian arbitrator law, see generally Marcel Storme & Bernadette Demenlenaere, INTERNATIONAL ARBITRATION IN BELGIUM (1989); Guy Horsmans, *Actualité et évolution du droit Belge de l'arbitrage*, Revue de L'Arbitrage 417, 437-40 (1992).

560. Loi fédérale sur le droit international privé. *See generally* Marc Blessing, *The New International Arbitration Law in Switzerland*, 5 J. Int'l Arb. 9 (June 1988); Pierre Lalive, *The New Swiss Law on International Arbitration*, 4 Arb. Int'l 2 (1988); Charles Poncet & Emmanuel Gaillard, *Introductory Note and Translation*, 27 I.L.M. 37 (1988).

561. Loi fédérale sur le droit internationale privé (L.D.I.P.) Article 192, permitting exclusion of review by a "*déclaration expresse*" when parties reside outside Switzerland. Because waiver of the right to judicial review of the award must be explicit, reference to institutional arbitration rules containing renunciation of appeal provisions (such as article 24 of the International Chamber of Commerce Rules) will not be sufficient to exclude review. If the parties neither elect cantonal procedure nor explicitly exclude judicial review, the L.D.I.P. provides five bases for challenge of awards: (1) irregular composition of the arbitral tribunal or incorrect appointment of the sole arbitrator; (2) an erroneous decision by the arbitral tribunal with respect to its own jurisdiction; (3) a decision beyond the scope of issues submitted to the arbitrators, or failure to decide claims within the request for arbitration; (4) failure to respect the principle of equal treatment of the parties or the right to adversarial proceedings ("*droit d'être entendu en procédure contradictoire*"); (5) incompatibility of the award with public policy (*ordre public*). L.D.I.P. Article 190(2).

562. *See generally* discussion at notes 386 *et seq.*

London nullification would be permitted but not required. Convention Article V(1)(e) allows denial of recognition to an award set aside by a court of the arbitral seat. The English language version of article V(1)(e) is permissive, stating that an award "may" be refused recognition and enforcement if set aside "by a competent authority of the country in which, or under the law of which, that award was made." The equally authoritative French text, however, is more forceful, lending itself to an interpretation that mandates refusal of recognition.[563]

The 1961 European Convention on International Commercial Arbitration[564] provides that annulment of an award in its country of origin constitutes a ground for refusal of recognition only when the annulment was for a Convention-enumerated reason. These reasons generally follow the first four defenses to enforcement of awards in Article V of the New York Arbitration Convention, and include lack of proper notice, a void arbitration agreement, and arbitral excess of authority.[565]

An annulled award could also be recognized under the enforcement forum's domestic law, regardless of any Convention obligation. In *Pabalk v. Norsolor*,[566] a commercial agency agreement between a French company and a Turkish agent gave rise to an arbitration in Austria. Applying *lex mercatoria*, the arbitral tribunal rendered a "split the difference" award that was quashed by the Vienna Appeals Court.[567] This vacatur at the arbitral seat led the Paris *Cour d'appel* to refuse recognition (*exequatur*) to the award on the basis that annulment under the law of the arbitral situs rendered the award unenforceable in France. France's highest court, the *Cour de cassation*, reversed the *Cour d'appel*, directing it to determine whether the award would be enforceable under French *internal* law. The Court noted that New York Arbitration Convention Article VII explicitly provided that the Convention would not "deprive any interested party of any right he may have to avail himself of an arbitral award in

---

563. The French text of Article V(1)(e) states that recognition and enforcement will not be refused unless the award was annulled or suspended: "La reconnaissance et l'exécution de la sentence ne seront refusées que si ... la sentence ... a été annulée ou suspendue."

564. European Convention on International Commercial Arbitration, Geneva, 1961. The European Convention complements the New York Convention with respect to disputes among residents of European countries, and applies only to relationships between parties from contracting states, while the New York Convention applies to foreign awards generally.

565. For example, an award rendered in Paris in an arbitration between a French and an Italian company might be set aside by a French court for violation of French public policy (*ordre public*). Since violation of public policy is not listed in the recognized grounds for annulment in the Geneva Convention, the award would still be enforceable in Italy under the Convention. On the other hand, enforcement would not be assured to a similar award against the Italian company's American parent, since the United States is not a party to the Geneva Convention, and the New York Convention permits blanket refusal of recognition to awards set aside where rendered.

566. *See* Pabalk v. Norsolor, French Cour de Cassation, Judgment of Oct. 9, 1984, Cour de cassation, Cass. civ. 1re, Fr., 1985 Rev. Arb. 431, with commentary by Berthold Goldman, 112 J. Dr. Int'l (CLUNET) 679 (1985), with commentary by Philippe Kahn.

567. On *lex mercatoria*, see *supra* at notes 314-30. Later, the Vienna annulment was itself reversed by the Austrian Supreme Court.

the manner and to the extent allowed by the law ... of the country where such award is sought to be relied upon."[568]

In line with the position taken in *Norsolor*, the French *Cour de cassation* recently held in the *Hilmarton* case that an award set aside at the arbitral seat in Switzerland should nevertheless be recognized in France on the ground that the award was international in character and "not integrated into the [Swiss] juridical order."[569] A public works contract to be performed in Algeria led to an I.C.C. arbitration in Geneva in which the arbitrator refused a claim for payment of consulting services, having found the contract tainted by influence peddling, an activity contrary to public policy. This award was annulled by a Geneva cantonal court, whose decision was confirmed by Switzerland's highest court. The French *Cour de cassation* held that the Geneva award against the consultants was entitled to recognition (*exequatur*) notwithstanding its annulment in Switzerland.[570]

Parallel to these proceedings another French court recognized an award in favor of the consultants in the *Hilmarton* case, rendered by a second arbitral tribunal constituted in Switzerland after nullification of the first award.[571] The potential for com-

---

568. In light of Pabalk v. Norsolor and the subsequent enactment of Nouveau Code de procédure civile article 1502, the earlier French case of Berardi v. Clair must be considered effectively overruled. In Berardi v. Clair, Judgment of 20 June 1981, Cour d'appel de Paris, 1981 Rev. Arb. 424, a dispute between French and Canadian parties led to an award rendered in Switzerland that was recognized by the Paris Tribunal de grande instance. Three months later, the cantonal Cour de justice in Geneva annulled the award as "arbitrary" under Article 36 of the Intercantonal Concordat on Arbitration, then in force. The Geneva court action led the Paris Cour d'appel to quash the lower court decision, stating that "execution of an annulled award *must* be refused." ("L'exécution d'une sentence arbitrale *doit* être refusée.") *Id.* at 426. *See* discussion in William W. Park, *National Law and Commercial Justice: Safeguarding Procedural Integrity in International Arbitration*, 63 Tulane L. Rev. 647 (1989), at 682-83.

569. Société Hilmarton Ltd. v. Société Omnium de Traitement et de Valorisation (OTV), Cour de cassation, 23 March 1994, *reprinted in* 1994 Rev. de l'Arbitrage 327 (with commentary by Charles Jarrosson) and English translation in 9 International Arbitration Reports (Mealy Publications), No. 5, at E-3 (1994). Apparently, the contract to act as "intermediary" was illegal under Algerian law. However, the Geneva court found that illegality under Algerian law was not sufficient to constitute a violation of Swiss public policy, absent a showing of bribery, for which the arbitral tribunal found insufficient evidence. *See generally* Vincent Heuzé, *La Morale, L'Arbitre et Le Juge*, 1993 Revue de L'Arbitrage 179. The Swiss cases are reported in 1993 Revue de L'Arbitrage at 315 (Cour de Justice du Canton de Genève, 17 Nov. 1989) and at 322 (Tribunal fédéral, 17 April 1990).

570. The *Cour de cassation* used broad language, stating that "la sentence rendue en Suisse était une sentence international qui n'était pas intégrée dans l'ordre juridique de cet Etat, de sorte que son existence demeurait établie malgré son annulation et que sa reconnaissance en France n'était pas contraire à l'ordre public international." *Id.* at 484. For another case in which an award annulled where rendered was enforced in France, see Jolasry v. Polish Ocean Line, Cass. Civ. 1re, 10 March 1993, Bull. I, no. 99, page 66, with commentary by J. Paulsson & G. Coop in 1 Dispute Resolution Update (No. 2) 9 (I.B.A. Committee D, 1994). *Compare* Société Unichips Finanziaria v. Gesnouin, Cour d'appel de Paris, 12 February 1993, *in* 1993 Rev. de l'Arbitrage 255 at 259, with commentary by Dominique Hascher.

571. Tribunal de Grande Instance, Nanterre, 25 May 1993 discussed in Charles Jarosson, *supra* note 569 at 329. The Nanterre Tribunal de Grande Instance on 22 September 1993 (Jarosson, *id.* at 329; reprinted 9 INT. ARB. REP. B-1 (Jan. 1994)) also held that the judicial annulment in

plications arising from claims based on inconsistent awards argues for a general deference to award annulment at the arbitral situs, or at least clearer rules about when a court may enforce an award that is inconsistent with another award that has already received judicial recognition in the same country.

As a general rule, courts outside of France do not enforce awards annulled where rendered, at least not when pronounced by a judiciary with an established tradition of independence whose annulment criteria were consistent with the pro-arbitration goals and scheme of the New York Arbitration Convention.[572] However, enforcement of an award that had been annulled in its country of origin might be appropriate if there was reason to suspect that the annulment had been procured through corruption or undue political influence brought to bear on the local judiciary.

In addition to cases in which an enforcement forum is asked to recognize awards set aside where rendered, an enforcement forum might also have to grapple with the arbitral seat's explicit refusal to set an award aside. Imagine for example that an English judge rejected a losing defendant's allegation that an arbitrator in London took a bribe. Should this determination on the matter of bribery be *res judicata* in New York if the award is there presented for enforcement? Thus far there is little case law or doctrine on the effect of such a finding of "non-nullity" under the *lex loci arbitri*. The "right" answer, however, would seem to be that an enforcement forum should be free to exercise its own control over challenges to the integrity of the arbitral proceedings on grounds contained in New York Arbitration Convention Article V.

c. Multiple Curial Laws?

Conflict and accommodation between the curial law of different countries has arisen in several recent arbitrations conducted in London. In one case, an agreement calling for arbitration in London was combined with reference to the Indian Arbitra-

---

Note 571, continued

Switzerland would not be recognized under the Franco-Swiss Jurisdiction and Judgments Treaty (Convention Franco-Suisse sur la compétence judiciaire et l'exécution des décisions en matière civile et commerciale), abrogated effective 1 January 1992.

572. The author knows of only one non-French case in which an award annulled where rendered was enforced abroad. *See* Société Nationale Pour La Recherche, Le Transport et La Commercialisation des Hydrocarbures (SONATRACH) v. Ford, Bacon & Davis Inc., Tribunal de Première Instance de Bruxelles (12è Chambre), 6 December 1988, R.G. No. 45.818, affirmed by Cour d'Appel de Bruxelles (8è Chambre), R.G. No. 726/89, 9 January 1990. An I.C.C. award of $1.8 million was rendered in Algiers in favor of an American company against one of Algeria's most important state agencies. Subsequently, the award was vacated by an Algerian court. The Belgian courts permitted enforcement of the award notwithstanding the annulment, explicitly rejecting the argument that enforcement should be refused under the provisions of New York Convention Article V(1)(e). The Belgian court seemed to focus on the lack of any provision for retroactive effect of the New York Convention, noting *inter alia* that Algeria had not ratified the New York Convention until 12 July 1988, whereas the award in question was rendered on 29 December 1985.

tion Act of 1940.[573] The Commercial Court in London interpreted this designation of Indian law as indicating procedural rules "internal" to the arbitral tribunal, and not inconsistent with English arbitration law. The arbitration therefore continued to be subject to the supervisory jurisdiction of English courts. In another case, proceedings were commenced by the defendants in the High Court of Bombay to determine the scope of the arbitration.[574] The defendants argued that the parties' choice of Indian law to govern the substantive merits of the dispute deprived English courts of their jurisdiction. Here again, the Commercial Court affirmed its jurisdiction based on the London situs of the arbitration.

Decisions of courts in India have implicated jurisdictional questions similar to those raised before English courts. In *Oil & Natural Gas Commission v. Western Company of North America*,[575] Indian courts were held to have jurisdiction to hear an action brought by a losing Indian party to set aside an award on the basis that Indian law applied to the arbitration agreement notwithstanding the situs of the arbitration outside India. *National Thermal Power Corporation v. Singer Corporation*[576] similarly decided that Indian courts had jurisdiction to hear an action to set aside an interim award rendered in London, at least in a case where Indian law was the proper substantive law of the contract.

These Indian court decisions have been viewed with alarm by commentators[577] concerned about the proper treaty framework for international arbitration.[578] New York Arbitration Convention Article V(1)(e) allows non-recognition of awards set

---

573. Union of India v. McDonnell Douglas Corp., [1993] 2 Lloyd's L. Rep. 48 (Decided 22 December 1992).

574. Sumitomo Heavy Industries v. Oil and Natural Gas Commission, [1994] 1 Lloyd's Law Rep. 45 (Decided 23 July 1993).

575. 1987 All India Reports SC 674, *excerpted in* XIII Yearbook Commercial Arbitration 473 (1988).

576. *Reprinted in* 18 Yearbook of International Arbitration (I.C.C.A.) 403 (1993). *Compare* Renusager Power Co. Ltd. v. General Electric Co., 1993 (4) SCALE, *discussed in* Tony Khindria, *Enforcement of Arbitration Awards in India,* 23 Int. Bus. Lawyer 11 (January 1995).

577. *See* Jan Paulsson, *The New York Convention's Misadventures in India,* 7 International Arbitration Report, No. 6, at pp. 3-8 (June 1992). For the Indian reaction, see Raghuraman, *International Jurist Flays India for Overstepping Bounds,* The Delhi Pioneer, 6 October 1992. Ironically, several years earlier Paulsson suggested that developing nations could be made more acceptable as arbitration venues if the parties were to subject the arbitration to a procedural law other than that of the arbitral situs. *See* Jan Paulsson, *Extent of Independence of Arbitration from the Law of the Situs, in* Contemporary Problems in International Arbitration 141, at 148 (J. Lew ed. 1987). The problem of course, is that the application of an extra procedural law can backfire to subject an award to potential annulment actions at two places rather than one, which is exactly what happened in the Indian cases later criticized by Paulsson. *See* William W. Park, *National Law and Commercial Justice,* 63 Tulane Law Rev. 647 (1989), commenting on Paulsson's original procedural law thesis.

578. For a more optimistic view, see J. Gillis Wetter & Chad Priem, *The 1993 General Electric Case: The Supreme Court of India's Re-Affirm Pro-Enforcement Policy Under the 1958 New York Convention,* International Arbitration Reports (December 1993). *See generally,* F.S. Nariman, *Finality in India: The Impossible Dream,* 10 Arb. Int'l 373 (1994).

aside by "a competent authority of the country in which, or under the law of which, that award was made." Thus it is theoretically possible for an annulment by a court of a country other than the arbitral situs to produce effects under the Convention. This does not mean, however, that the exercise of jurisdiction by that country is sound policy.

American courts have refrained from exercising jurisdiction based solely on an applicable law clause. In *International Standard Electric Corporation (ISEC) v. Bridas Sociedad Anonima Petrolera, Industrial y Comercial.*,[579] an award was rendered in Mexico concerning a contract whose interpretation was subject to New York substantive law. The American party sought to have the award set aside in New York on the theory that courts of the country whose substantive law applied to the contract could vacate an arbitral award. The American party argued that authority for such vacatur could be found in the language contained in Article V(1)(e) of the New York Arbitration Convention, permitting refusal of recognition to an award set aside by courts of the country of "the law under which the award was made." The court found no justification for such a power to vacate the award. Distinguishing between the substantive and procedural law of an arbitration, the court concluded that "since the situs, or forum of the arbitration is Mexico, and the governing procedural law is that of Mexico, only the courts of Mexico have jurisdiction under the [New York Arbitration] Convention to vacate the award."

3. Geography and Judicial Integrity.

Determining how best to balance public and private interests in forum selection requires assumptions about the integrity of those national courts that may intervene in the arbitral process. In particular, a policy decision to allow a right to challenge awards at the arbitral situs assumes that courts there are basically honest. An arbitrator's knowledge that his or her decision may be subject to review by upright judges should promote the rigor and integrity of the arbitral process.

In some parts of the world, however, business managers will be more concerned about corruption of judges than of arbitrators. Not all places are blessed with relatively honest courts. In some countries a *laissez-faire* arbitration régime may well be the lesser of two evils. Bribery of state-selected judges, or their susceptibility to political influence, may be a more realistic fear than arbitral sloppiness.

C. A SPECIAL STATUS FOR INTERNATIONAL TRANSACTIONS.

In recent years, judicial controls over choice-of-forum clauses have tended to be less restrictive when applied to international rather than domestic transactions. Courts enforce international arbitration and jurisdiction clauses even with respect to "public law" claims that would normally be too sensitive for either arbitration or foreign courts.[580] Moreover, arbitral awards rendered in international disputes are often sub-

579. 745 F. Supp. 172 (S.D.N.Y. 1990).
580. *See* discussion *supra* at note 424.

ject to a more relaxed scope of judicial review than awards in domestic arbitration. English, French, and Swiss arbitration statutes all restrict (or permit waiver of) grounds for annulment of awards when the dispute is international.[581]

Some lawyers see no need for such separate treatment of international arbitration. No less a scholar than Lord Mustill has written that he has "never understood why international arbitration should be different in principle from any other kind of arbitration."[582] Yet the basis for the distinction should not be a mystery. Fairness and efficiency in international dispute resolution require sensitivity to adjudicatory neutrality to a far greater degree than in a domestic transaction.[583] This neutrality is compromised when courts too easily review awards or declare the subject matter of a particular counterclaim to be non-arbitrable. The consequences to a Boston company of ending up in litigation in Atlanta or Chicago are less fearsome than the prospect of court proceedings in Algiers or Chittagong. Judicial meddling with an arbitration award is more destructive to efficient dispute resolution when it occurs in a country with unfamiliar procedures and perhaps an unfamiliar language. While some wealth-creating international transactions will go forward even if the parties' aspirations to a neutral forum can be easily defeated, in many cases the risk will be unacceptable.

A special standard for enforcing and monitoring international arbitration requires definitional criteria to distinguish domestic and international transactions.[584] One approach lies in a party-oriented test that looks to the nationality and residence of the litigants. This method has been favored in different forms by Belgian, English, Swiss and American statutes.[585] A less mechanical test, which asks whether a transaction implicates international commerce, has been adopted by the French.[586]

---

581. *See* discussion *supra* at notes 352-76, 377-80 and 386-91.

582. Michael Mustill, *Cedric Barclay Memorial Lecture*, 58 Arbitration 159 (Aug. 1992) at 165.

583. Imagine a Libyan enterprise contracting with a Massachusetts corporation under an agreement that provided for arbitration of disputes in Paris under the International Chamber of Commerce Arbitration Rules. When the contract became onerous for the Libyan enterprise, a Libyan statutory claim was asserted before a Libyan court, which refused on public policy grounds to give effect to the agreement to arbitrate. The American company that had expected that the dispute would be arbitrated in Paris rather than litigated in Boston would be distressed to see their expectations defeated by assertions of Libyan public law. It would not be surprising if the Libyans reacted similarly when the shoe was on the other foot.

584. On characterization in conflict-of-laws, see Bernard Audit, *Qualification et Droit International Privé*, 18 Droits — Revue Française de Théorie Juridique 55 (1993).

585. On the Belgian, English and Swiss statutes, see discussion *supra* at notes 559, 352-76 and 386-91, respectively. The United States looks to the parties' nationalities in the sense that it excludes contracts between Americans from the scope of the New York Arbitration Convention unless there is a reasonable relationship with a foreign country (9 U.S.C. § 202) and applies the New York Arbitration Convention to non-domestic awards rendered in the United States if the award was with "made within the legal framework of another country (*e.g.*, pronounced in accordance with foreign law) or involving parties domiciled or having their principal place of business outside the performing jurisdiction (Bergesen v. Joseph Muller Corp., 710 F.2d 928 (1983) at 932).

586. *See* French Nouveau Code de Procédure Civile, Article 1492, discussed *supra* at note 377.

Focus on the parties' nationalities and residence would seem the optimal way to determine whether a dispute's international character should qualify the arbitration for special treatment. The consequences of a failed forum selection clause in contracts between residents of the same country usually are less dramatic, even if elements of the contract are performed abroad, than when one party is foreign. Neutrality is less of a concern, for example, when one American must sue another in the United States, than when an American must sue a Libyan in Tripoli.

D. Limits on the Right to Choose.

Like any freedom, the right to choose a forum justifies itself in part by the values and outcomes furthered by the exercise of the right.[587] Freedom to select a particular court or arbitration régime can promote fairer and more efficient dispute resolution, or it can degenerate into an instrument for depriving an unsophisticated party of basic procedural rights. Particularly when forum selection clauses operate in tandem with choice-of-law provisions, they can be tools used to defeat vital public policies of the country of contract performance.

As a general rule, commercial actors should have the right to contract for a predetermined court. Such private choices will increase public welfare by providing an efficient way of allocating judicial competence in advance of litigation. Bargains about forum selection maximize community well-being by reducing the costs of litigation uncertainty.

In a consumer context, however, theories about the economic utility of forum selection clauses run up against the reality that consumers usually do not read the secondary terms of standard form contracts before signing the agreement.[588] When a consumer buys a new car or washing machine, how realistic is it to say that he or she has knowingly waived her future right to a day in court by bargaining for the forum designated in a printed sales form? When consumers do study a printed form's conditions, they will rarely be in a position to evaluate the burdens imposed. A meaningful evaluation of a foreign forum requires an understanding of how *foreign* choice-of-law principles will operate to limit contract terms at variance with public norms, a task beyond the competence of many trained lawyers, not to mention the average consumer.

---

587. *See* Herbert Schönle, *Les Fondements Constitutionels de la Liberté Contractuelle, in* PRÉSENCE ET ACTUALITÉ DE LA CONSTITUTION DANS L'ORDRE JURIDIQUE 61 (Helbing & Lichtenhahn, Basel and Francfort-sur-Main 1991). Professor Schonle comments *inter alia* on Swiss draft legislation aimed at limiting freedom of contract in cases of abuse of bargaining power, quoting a parliamentary report: "Ce principe fondamental du droit contractuel ne peut prétendre à une pleine et légitime application que si les engagements dont on entend assurer le respect émanent d'une décision mûrement réfléchie et prise en toute liberté."

588. *See* Lee Goldman, *My Way and the Highway: The Law and Economics of Choice of Forum Clauses in Consumer Form Contracts*, 86 Northwestern Univ. L. Rev. 700 (1992); John Sampson, *Distant Forum Abuse in Consumer Transactions: A Proposed Solution*, 51 Tex. L. Rev. 269 (1973).

The absence of informed bargaining by the consumer is not necessarily fatal to an argument for enforcing forum selection clauses. One approach to forum selection clauses would be to focus on the willingness of the dominant party in a transaction to commit itself to the transaction without forum selection clauses. Imagine, for example, that Ruritanian courts were reputed for corruption of such magnitude that bankers refused to lend money to Ruritanian borrowers. A grant of jurisdiction to the courts of England or some other jurisdiction with relatively impartial judges, coupled with a pledge or mortgage of the debtor's attachable English assets, would contribute to the solution of this problem. An enforceable forum selection clause changes the litigation venue as a necessary precondition for the transaction itself.

The interests of fairness, however, may sometimes trump such efficiency considerations when forum selection impoverishes procedural integrity by imposing adjudication that as a practical matter will be unaccessible to the weaker party.[589] In contrast to transactions between sophisticated parties with access to competent counsel,[590] informed bargaining for remote locations is not common in consumer transactions.[591] A trial distant from the consumer's residence may involve extra costs for counsel at the litigation situs and witness travel expenses, as well as different choice-of-law principles and attitudes concerning contract terms such as exculpatory clauses and restraints of trade.

Typically, consumers waive jurisdictional rights before any dispute has arisen, at signature of the standard form sale, loan or lease containing the forum selection clause. The danger of abuse in forum selection is reduced significantly if the clause is signed *after* the dispute arises, when specific claims have been identified, and forum selection becomes a form of settlement.

589. *See, e.g.*, Geneva Bell v. Congress Mortgage, 24 Cal. App. 4th 1675 (1994), ordered depublished by Cal. Sup. Court, 30 Cal. Rep. 2d 205 (1994). Court refused to compel arbitration absent a "clear and informed" waiver of the right to a jury trial; homeowner claims against mortgage lenders for fraudulent business practices. *See also* Patterson et al. v. ITT Consumer Financial Corporation, 14 Cal. App. 4th 1659, 18 Cal. Reptr. 2d 563 (1993), *petition for cert. denied*, U.S. Supreme Court, No. 93-952, 7 March 1994, 114 S.Ct. 1217. Arbitration clause in loan agreement with California consumers provided for dispute resolution by arbitration firm in Minnesota; court refused to compel arbitration, finding clause "unconscionable" by virtue of its adhesive (take-it-or-leave-it) nature, as well as elements of "oppression," unequal bargaining power and surprise. *But see* Badie v. Bank of America, *supra* note 296, upholding arbitration clause inserted in monthly statement where account agreement allowed bank to change terms of agreement at any time. *Compare* Carnival Cruise Lines v. Shute, discussed *supra* at note 50.
590. Between sophisticated parties, the geographical remoteness of a potential litigation situs might be within the parties' mutual expectations. *See, e.g.* Tennessee Imports v. Filippi, 745 F. Supp. 1314 (M.D. Tenn. 1990) (enforcement of agreement between American distributor and Italian manufacturer providing for arbitration in Italy) and China Resource Products v. Fayda International, 747 F. Supp. 1101 (D.Del.1990) (enforcement of agreement between American company and agency of Chinese government providing for arbitration in China).
591. Even in international business forum selection clauses are not always freely negotiated. *See* Weidner Communications v. H.R.H. Prince Bandar Al Faisal, 859 F.2d 1302 (7th Cir. 1988) (forum selection clause giving exclusive competence to Saudi courts in agreement re-negotiated by threat and intimidation in palace of Saudi party).

Pre-dispute waiver of a fair trial is of a different order of magnitude from settlement or other economic compromises. Agreeing to accept an unfair trial long before any dispute arises is qualitatively more dangerous than a bargain about the price of an automobile or the interest rate on a mortgage. Society as a whole stands to suffer a loss of confidence in the adjudicatory process when take-it-or-leave-it contracts dispatch ordinary folks to distant lands. While the weaker party of a transaction must often accept contract terms not entirely to its liking, waiver of an accessible forum should not be among these.

On balance, sound forum selection policy requires that the presumptive validity of forum selection agreements in consumer transactions be limited to: (1) agreements concluded *after* the dispute arose (when knowing abandonment of rights is more plausible) and (2) agreements that grant consumers an option to sue and to be sued at their residence. While there may be nothing inherently improper about renouncing one adjudicatory system for another, pre-dispute waivers that implicate fundamental due process rights should be recognized only if they result from the type of mature reflection that is usually lacking in adherence to the boilerplate terms of standard form consumer leases and sales agreements.

A limit on pre-dispute forum selection clauses would seem appropriate to all consumer transactions, international as well as domestic, that have a significant relationship with the excluded forum. For example, a Greek shipping company actively soliciting American residents to take Aegean vacation cruises should not be able to require disputes to be settled in Athens. On the other hand, an American travelling in Greece who there buys a ticket for a similar cruise should normally not be able to claim a right of recourse to American courts.[592]

In Western Europe, several national statutes and two international treaties recognize the importance of an accessible forum by providing that pre-dispute forum selection clauses generally will be ineffective in consumer transactions.[593] Likewise, many American state arbitration statutes also reduce the impact of potentially unfair arbitration clauses through a wide range of consumer-protection provisions.[594] Some of these statutes invalidate agreements that call for arbitration outside the state of the consumer's residence[595] or are deemed unconscionable.[596] Other statutes specifically

---

592. Some countries, of course, do give their citizens a right of recourse to their courts on the basis of nationality. *See* French *Code civil* Article 14: "L'étranger, même non résident en France, pourra être cité devant les tribunaux français pour l'exécution des obligations par lui contractées [en France ou en pays étranger] avec un français." Even in France, however, a Frenchman can waive his right to French jurisdiction through a forum selection clause. *See* Civ. 1re, 25 novembre 1986, Rev. trim. dr. civ. 1987, 548, with commentary by Mestre.

593. *See* discussion *infra* in Chapter VI.

594. *See generally*, Jonathan Breckenridge, *Bargaining Unfairness and Agreements to Arbitrate: Judicial and Legislative Application of Contract Defenses to Arbitration Agreements*, 1991 ANNUAL SURVEY OF AMERICAN LAW 925 (1992). Such attempts at limiting arbitration are not always successful. *See* Rodriguez de Quijas v. Shearson/American Express, *supra* note 424.

595. Oregon Rev. Stat. § 36.305.

596. *See* Texas Rev. Civ. Stat. § 224.

prohibit adhesion agreements to arbitrate future disputes whose parameters are unknown at time of signature.[597] Several jurisdictions do not allow arbitration of specified subject matters such as insurance[598] and real estate[599] (except in contracts between professionals in the field), or require the arbitration agreement to be signed separately from the main contract.[600] In banking transactions, the validity of consumer arbitration clauses may be subject to judicial challenge when banks fail to obtain a borrower's informed assent to the chosen forum.[601]

No general federal consumer-protection statute governs arbitration or jurisdiction clauses in the United States. For better or for worse, the implementation of contract defenses to forum selection agreements covering matters such as duress, fraud and lack of consent is left to judicial elaboration, as are defenses based on unconscionability and the use of standardized contracts.[602]

As suggested earlier, this gap in American law might be remedied by a prophylactic measure that would prohibit pre-dispute forum selection clauses in consumer contracts unless the consumer has the right to sue and to be sued at the courts of his or her domicile.[603] In the alternative, a statute should limit forum selection clauses to contracts between merchants and professionals acting in the capacity of their trade or business.[604]

Communities jeopardized by the outcome of commercial litigation will sometimes want subject matter restrictions on the scope of forum selection clauses. Some questions by their very nature have been deemed too sensitive to be left to private

---

597. *See* Iowa Code Ann. § 679 A.1; Missouri Ann. Stat. § 435.350; Nebraska Rev. Stat. § 25-2602.

598. Arkansas, Kansas, Kentucky, Missouri, Montana, Oklahoma, South Carolina and South Dakota. Oklahoma and Montana, however, exclude from the prohibition contracts between insurance companies, which presumably are aware of the rules of the game.

599. Georgia Code § 9-9-2(c). This exclusion does not apply, however, as between real estate professionals.

600. Texas Rev. Civ. Stat. § 224(b).

601. *See* discussion *supra* at notes 295-97.

602. *See* discussion *supra* at 70-76. THE RESTATEMENT OF CONTRACTS § 211(3) provides that terms of a "standardized" contract are not part of the agreement if one party has reason to believe that another would not have assented if he/she knew that the writing contained the offensive term.

603. Such a legislative proposal, discussed in Chapter VIII and set forth in Appendix C, might also serve as the basis for amendment of the Federal Arbitration Act. Because the United States implementing legislation to the New York Convention restricts its application to international commercial contracts (likely to affect very few consumers), treaty amendments presumably are less critical than statutory reform.

604. Such a limitation would require the elaboration of a fairly wide concept of "merchant," similar to that prevailing in continental legal systems. *See* discussion, *infra* at notes 705-21.

adjudication. Although the scope of non-arbitrable subject matters is fast eroding,[605] courts still resist enforcing jurisdiction clauses likely to lessen liability under statutes such as the Carriage of Goods at Sea Act[606] or to interfere with state regulation of franchisor/franchisee relationships.[607]

The proper scope of public policy as a ground for non-recognition of arbitral awards remains problematic. Some have argued for a broad scope to the New York Arbitration Convention's public policy defense to enforcement of arbitral awards, as a way to permit host countries to further local regulatory policies.[608] On the other hand, public policy review of arbitral awards can be a back door to judicial meddling with the process of private dispute resolution on which the confidence of international investment depends, particularly when nations are tempted to expropriate property of a foreign investor in disregard of contractual commitments.[609] Whatever its short-term benefits, using public policy as an excuse to disregard freely-negotiated obligations will chill future infusions of wealth-creating capital and technology, and may backfire to inhibit international commercial and financial cooperation.

Enforcement of forum selection clauses should in all cases be conditioned on the independence of the chosen adjudicator. Economic cooperation through business relationships makes sense *ex ante* only if the person charged with interpreting the contract will be relatively impartial. Litigants will usually see bias in an adjudicator as a good thing only if it operates against the other side.[610] Therefore forum selection arrangements should be refused enforcement when they work to designate an adjudi-

---

605. For discussion of subject matter arbitrability, see discussion *supra* at notes 419-24 and notes 598-99.

606. *See* discussion *infra* at notes 112-16. *See generally* Alan Nakazawa and Alexander Moghaddam, *COGSA and Choice of Foreign Law Clauses in Bills of Lading*, Tul. Maritime L.J. 1 (1992); *see also* recent amendment to Limitation of Shipowner Liability Act, 46 U.S.C. 183c, discussed *supra* at notes 59-62, which overturns the result in *Carnival Cruise.*

607. *See* EEC Centers of Ill. v. Entre Computer Cent., 597 F. Supp. 1182 (N.D. Ill. 1984).

608. One commentator has suggested that a narrow view of public policy (which is to say, fewer annulments of awards) "threatens the legitimate regulatory policies of both developed and developing countries. What should be a meaningful review of arbitral awards has come to resemble a rubber stamp." *See* Andrew Armfelt, *Avoiding the Arbitration Trap*, Financial Times, 27 October 1992, at 17, cols. 1-4. *Compare* Jan Paulsson's comment on two recent cases in which Indian courts annulled foreign arbitration awards, J.A.S. Paulsson, *The New York Convention's Misadventures in India*, Int'l Arb. Rep. 3 (June 1992). For the Indian reaction, see Raghuraman, *International Jurist Flays India for Overstepping Bounds*, The Delhi Pioneer, 6 October 1992.

609. *See e.g.*, discussion of the *LIAMCO* cases *supra* at note 270 and *infra* at note 703.

610. Some scholarly attitudes toward bias in litigation seem to suggest not only that biased justice is what the law has produced, but also that biased justice is what we should have, albeit with the right types of bias. *See* discussion *infra* at notes 728-43.

cator lacking independence from one or the other of the parties, both in a domestic[611] and an international context.[612]

---

611. *See* Commonwealth Coatings Corp. v. Continental Casualty Co, 393 U.S. 145 (1968). A subcontractor sued the sureties on the prime contractor's bond to recover sums due for painting. The contractual arbitration clause provided for each party to appoint an arbitrator, who in turn would select the third member of the arbitral tribunal. This third arbitrator was an engineering consultant whose customers included the prime contractor. The Court reversed the lower court refusal to set the award aside. Section 10 of the Federal Arbitration Act provides for vacatur of an award "where there was evident partiality ... in the arbitrators" and the AAA rules require disclosure of circumstances likely to create a presumption of arbitrator bias. *Compare* Article 2(7) of the Arbitration Rules of the International Chamber of Commerce and Article 3.7 of the Arbitration Rules of the London Court of International Arbitration, both of which require that even party-nominated arbitrators should be independent and impartial. Domestic arbitration has often allowed party-nominated arbitrators to be *de facto* advocates for one side. *See, e.g.,* Astoria Medical Group v. Health Insurer Plan of N.Y., 11 N.Y.2d 128 (1962) allowing a member of one party's board of directors to serve as arbitrator. Attitudes are changing, however, to require independence of all arbitrators. *See* Canon VII of American Arbitration Association Code of Ethics for Arbitrators in Commercial Disputes. *See generally* A.A.A. REPORT, *Party Appointed Arbitrators,* 16 Lawyers' Arb. Letter No. 4, Winter 1992/93 at 1.

612. In international arbitration, most institutional rules require arbitrators to be independent of the parties, at least in the sense of having no financial interest in the dispute's outcome. *See, e.g.,* I.C.C. Rule 2(7), L.C.I.A. Article 3.

Chapter VI

EUROPEAN PARADIGMS

Like travelling, a comparative approach to law can enlighten as well as entertain. Some of the most critical insights into one's own law come only after a comparison with other legal systems reveals what one's own system is not.[613]

European legal traditions balance competing objectives in forum selection in a way that often differs markedly from the American approach. Treaties and statutes protect consumers from untoward waiver of jurisdictional rights while at the same time giving more sophisticated commercial players an assurance that they will get their bargained-for forum. In Europe the teachings of a case such as *Bremen v. Zapata*, drawn from an international maritime towing contract between German and American companies, would not likely have been invoked to justify enforcement of a boiler-plate prorogation clause in a standard form cruise ticket like the one at issue in *Carnival Cruise v. Schute.*[614]

A. THE CONVENTION FRAMEWORK.[615]

1. Jurisdiction.

The Treaty on Jurisdiction and Judgments in Civil and Commercial Matters, known generally as "the Bruxelles Convention,"[616] was adopted under the auspices of the

---

613. *See generally,* René David, INTRODUCTION TO INTERNATIONAL ENCYCLOPEDIA OF COMPARATIVE LAW; Mary Ann Glendon, Michael Wallace Gordon, & Chris Osakwe, COMPARATIVE LEGAL TRADITION (1982); Konrad Zweigert and Hein Kötz, INTRODUCTION TO COMPARATIVE LAW (Tony Weir, trans. 1987); Gunther Frankenberg, *Cultural Comparisons,* 26 Harv. Int'l L.J. 411 (1985). See also Michael Wells, *French and American Judicial Opinions,* 19 Yale J. Int'l L. 81 (1994), at 82.

614. *See* discussion of Bremen v. Zapata, *supra* at note 43 and Carnival Cruise v. Shute, *supra* at note 50.

615. For an American perspective on the approach of the Bruxelles and Lugano Conventions, see Arthur von Mehren, *Recognition and Enforcement of Foreign Judgments, supra* note 34, at 281-82. Professor von Mehren notes that the United States would find it offensive to standards of fair play to enforce judgments obtained on the basis of "exorbitant jurisdiction" against non-domiciliaries of Convention states.

616. Bruxelles Convention on Jurisdiction and Judgments in Civil and Commercial Matters, *signed* 27 September 1968, *entered into force* on 1 February 1973 among the six original mem-

European Community (as it then was) to provide a comprehensive framework for the enforcement of foreign judgments and the international allocation of judicial competence. A parallel treaty adopted twenty years later in Lugano[617] extends similar principles to nations outside the European Union that belong to the European Free Trade Association.[618]

The general rule of the Bruxelles and Lugano Conventions[619] is that residents of a contracting state may be sued only before the courts of their home state.[620] As to residents of contracting states, the Conventions prohibit assertions of "exorbitant" jurisdiction[621] based solely on the plaintiff's nationality,[622] temporary physical presence[623] and property.[624] Jurisdictional fine tuning under the Conventions provides additional options to claimants in special cases relating to contracts,[625] alimony,[626]

Note 616, continued

bers of the European Community: Belgium, France, Germany, Italy, Luxembourg and the Netherlands. By subsequent protocols, the treaty has been extended to newer members of the Community: Denmark, Ireland and the United Kingdom in 1978, Greece in 1982 and Portugal and Spain in 1989. *See generally,* Bernard Audit, LE DROIT INTERNATIONAL PRIVÉ (1991).

617. Lugano Convention of 16 September 1988. At present, the Convention has been signed by Belgium, Denmark, Finland, France, Germany, Greece, Ireland, Italy, Luxembourg, the Netherlands, Norway, Portugal, Sweden, Switzerland and the United Kingdom. The Bruxelles Convention builds to some extent on the work of the Hague Conference "Convention on the Choice of Court," concluded in 1965 but never ratified. *See Convention de La Haye sur les accords d'élection de for, 25 November 1965, in* RECUEIL DES CONVENTIONS DE LA HAYE, CONFÉRENCE DE LA HAYE DE DROIT INTERNATIONAL PRIVÉ, CONVENTION XV at 96 (Martinus Nijhoff, The Hague).

618. These countries now include Iceland, Liechtenstein, Norway and Switzerland.

619. To make description easier, citations in this section refer to the text of the more recent Lugano Convention [hereinafter Convention], which follows the Bruxelles text with minor exceptions.

620. Convention Article 2(1). Excluded from application of the Convention are matters relating to (i) arbitration, (ii) bankruptcy, (iii) social security and (iv) personal status (such as marriage and inheritance.). *See* Convention Article 1.

621. *Id.* at Article 3.

622. *See* French Code civil Article 14.

623. *See* Burnham v. Cal. Super. Ct., 495 U.S. 604 (1990).

624. German Zivilprozessordnung (ZPO), Article 23, provides for judicial jurisdiction over a non-resident defendant with assets in Germany, regardless of whether there is a connection between the claim and the assets, or between the claim and Germany. The practice of German courts has traditionally been to give a wide application to Article 23, justifying judicial competence on the basis of books or fruit baskets left behind by a foreign visitor. *See* Gerhard Dannemann, *Jurisdiction Based on the Presence of Assets in Germany: A Case Note,* 41 Int'l & Comp. L.Q. 632 (1992). The German Bundesgerichtshof recently narrowed the scope of Article 23, holding that a dispute must have some connection with Germany to justify jurisdiction. *See* Muduroglu Ltd. v. TC Ziraat Bankast, BGH 2.7.1991, Neue Juristische Wochenschrift (N.J.W.) 1991, 3092 (dispute between a Turkish bank and a Cypriot corporation arising out of a contract for construction of a harbor in Libya.)

625. Convention Article 5(1).

626. Convention Article 5(2).

tort,[627] insurance,[628] and consumer transactions.[629]

As long as one party is domiciled in a Convention state, contractually designated courts of a Convention state shall have exclusive jurisdiction.[630] Written agreements granting jurisdiction to courts of a contracting state generally must be honored both by the designated court and by the alternative forum. Oral agreements confirmed in writing benefit from the same dispositive effect. Where neither party is domiciled in a Convention state, other Convention state courts shall have no jurisdiction unless the chosen court declines to hear the case.[631]

The Conventions exclude arbitration from their scope,[632] in favor of other international treaties such as the New York Arbitration Convention that already mandate enforcement of arbitral proceedings.[633] The European Court of Justice has taken a broad view of this exclusion, interpreting it to carve out from Convention coverage all disputes related to an arbitration, including ancillary controversies concerning the validity of the agreement to arbitrate.[634] In *Marc Rich v. Societa Italiana Impianti*[635] a

627. Convention Article 5(3).

628. Convention Articles 7 - 12.

629. Convention Articles 13 - 15. With respect to corporate governance and realty, Article 16 of the Conventions provide exclusive and mandatory fora at the situs of the corporate seat or property. In addition, for labor matters some countries do not permit parties to contract out of the exclusive jurisdiction of labor courts (*Tribunal de Prud'hommes*) or exclusive venue at the place of the employment obligation. *See, e.g.,* the decision in Sanicentral v. Collin, [1980] 2 C.M.L.R. 164 (1979).

630. Convention Article 17. At least one case has held that a non-exclusive jurisdiction clause is also enforceable under Article 17. See Kurz v. Stella Musical Veranstaltungs GmbH [1991] 3 WLR 1046.

631. By contrast, the Hague Convention on Choice of Court, *supra* note 92, seems to impose no limit related to party residence or nationality. Rather, Article 5 by negative implication imposes an obligation on the chosen court to hear the case unless another court could claim exclusive jurisdiction based on the dispute's subject matter.

632 Article I (4) states that the "Convention shall not apply to ... arbitration."

633. The New York Convention of 1958, and the European (Geneva) Convention of 1961. The European Convention, intended to supplement rather than to compete with the New York Convention, covers arbitrations between residents of treaty countries. The New York Convention's broader scope looks to the place of arbitration rather than the residence of the parties, and includes all foreign awards, regardless of party residence; the New York Convention permits a reservation to limit coverage to awards rendered in other treaty countries.

634. A narrower view would make the Convention inapplicable only in litigation connected directly with an existing arbitration, such as judicial recognition of an award. For a discussion of the merits of these competing views, see His Hon. Judge Zuleeg, *Report for the Hearing,* 7 Arb. Int'l 187 (1991); Marco Darmon, Marc Rich Co., A.G. v. Societa Italiana Impianti P.A., Opinion of the Advocate General, *supra* at 197; Peter Schlosser, *1968 Brussels Convention and Arbitration, supra* at 227; Paul Jerard, *Opinion, supra* at 243.

635. Marc Rich & Co., A.G. v. Societa Italiana Impianti P.A., European Court of Justice, 25 July 1991, EC Case No. C-190/89, *reprinted in* 7 Arb. Int'l 251 (1991) and XVII YEARBOOK COMM. ARB. 2343 (A.J. van den Berg, ed. 1992). For an American report of the case, see Arb. Times, *Important Ruling for ADR in Europe,* Spring 1992, at 8. *See generally,* Bernard Audit, *Arbitration and the Brussels Convention,* 9 Arb. Int'l 1 (1993); Comment by Wolfran Krohn, 86 Am. J. Int'l L. 134 (1992).

Swiss buyer began arbitration against an Italian seller in London, as provided in the sale contract. The buyer claimed that oil transported on a vessel known as *The Atlantic Emperor*[636] was seriously contaminated. When an English court was asked to assist in the appointment of an arbitrator,[637] the sellers commenced a rival proceeding in Italy, claiming that under the Bruxelles Convention only courts at the Italian defendant's residence were competent to hear a dispute. The real dispute (said the Italian seller) was over the very validity of the arbitration clause. If this issue of the clause's validity would be decided in the negative by Italian courts, English courts arguably would have no jurisdiction to appoint an arbitrator, which of course is exactly what the Italian sellers wanted.

The European Court of Justice interpreted the Convention's scope solely by reference to subject matter (arbitration) rather than the procedural posture of the litigation. Consequently, preliminary issues related to whether an arbitration agreement exists at all were deemed to be excluded from the Convention's scope. The English proceeding for the appointment of arbitrators therefore could go forward, notwithstanding the Italian litigation. What the European Court called "the principle of legal certainty" served as the jurisprudential touchstone underpinning the decision. The Court reasoned that the reliability of arbitration would be reduced if the Convention scope could "vary according to the existence or otherwise of a preliminary issue that could be raised at any time by the parties."[638] More questions for lawyers to debate mean less certainty that the chosen arbitrators will hear the case. Moreover, to apply the Convention to arbitration-related court proceedings would deprive courts at the arbitral seat of their curial jurisdiction over local arbitral proceedings.

While supportive of arbitration, the *Marc Rich* decision does have its drawbacks. In particular, the ruling opens the door to possibly inconsistent findings on the validity of an arbitration agreement. For example, an Italian court competent to hear a dispute under normal Convention rules might find an arbitration clause void, while an English court at the arbitral situs might find the arbitration clause valid.[639]

The Conventions restrict recognition of forum selection clauses in consumer transactions. When concluded for a purpose outside the scope of the user's professional activity, contracts benefit from a special jurisdictional régime in three cases: (i) installment sales of goods, (ii) installment loans to finance the sale of goods, and (iii) contracts for the supply of goods or services resulting from a solicitation or publicity in the consumer's country of domicile.[640] In such cases consumers may be sued only in their home courts.[641] Plaintiff consumers, however, have the option to bring

---

636. For the English aspect of the case, see Marc Rich & Co. v. Societa Italian Impianti (The Atlantic Emperor) [1989] 1 Lloyd's Rep. 548. The Court of Appeal referred to question to the European Court of Justice under a Protocol to the 1957 Treaty of Rome establishing the Common Market.

637. *See* Arbitration Act of 1950 § 10(3).

638. ECJ Case C-190/89, *reprinted in* 7 Arb. Int'l 251, 256.

639. *See* Bernard Audit, *supra* note 635, at 8-9.

640. This third category includes only contracts as to which acts are taken to conclude the contract in the country of domicile. Convention Article 13.

641. *Id.* at Article 14.

actions in courts either at their own domicile or at the domicile of the other party. The Conventions permit waiver of the consumer's special jurisdictional protection only *after* the dispute has arisen or when jurisdiction is conferred on courts of a Convention state where both parties are domiciled.[642]

2. Judgments.

Effective forum selection implicates enforcement of foreign judgments as well as jurisdictional agreements.[643] The best rules allocating judicial competence are of limited value if decisions rendered by contractually-selected judges are ignored in jurisdictions where the parties have their assets.

The Bruxelles and the Lugano Conventions both require contracting states to recognize and execute each other's judgments[644] in a manner not unlike that of the United States' Constitution's full faith and credit clause.[645] Indeed, at its inception the Bruxelles Convention was conceived of principally as a judgments treaty.

The Conventions admit only limited exceptions to recognition, intended to insure procedural integrity.[646] Judgments rendered in other Convention states must be recognized even without any judicial confirmation.[647] Refusal of recognition is justifiable only for: (i) procedural irregularities (including lack of jurisdiction, lack of proper notice to defendant and the *res judicata* effect of another judgment),[648] (ii) violation of the public policy of the enforcement forum,[649] and (iii) disregard of subject matter jurisdictional limitations as to matters such as insurance, consumer contracts, *in rem* proceedings, patents and corporate dissolution.[650]

B. INCONVENIENT FORA.

European legal systems traditionally have resisted the doctrine of *forum non conveniens*. A contractually-designated judge in Europe normally will have little discretion to refuse to hear a case only because one party claims that the contractually chosen

---

642. *Id.* at Article 15.
643. *See generally*, Robert Reuland, *The Recognition of Judgments in the European Community: The Twenty-fifth Anniversary of the Brussels Convention*, 14 Michigan J. Int'l Law 599 (1993).
644. *Id.* at Article 26.
645. *See* U.S. Const. Article IV, § 1.
646. *Id.* at Articles 26 (*re* recognition) and 31 (*re* execution).
647. *Id.* at Article 26.
648. *See id.* at Article 27.
649. *See id.* Article 27 (1).
650. Convention Articles 27 and 28 use the mandatory "shall not" be recognized in referring to judgments rendered by a court other the exclusive forum. Article 28 provides that "a judgment shall not be recognized if it conflicts with the provisions of Sections 3, 4 or 5 of Title II" of the Convention, which deal with insurance, consumer contracts and "exclusive jurisdiction" for the special subjects mentioned in the text above.

forum is "inconvenient." French doctrine has been particularly firm in requiring courts to hear a case regardless of claims of inconvenience.[651] Referring to the possibility that concepts of *forum non conveniens* might be imported into Continental Europe, a French scholar has written: "We must kill this source of squabbling in its egg."[652] Another leading French scholar has written that the concept of *forum non conveniens* is "foreign to the French legal system" and "unknown in French law."[653] When a French judge declines to hear a case, the judge is not exercising any discretion, but rather stating that jurisdiction never existed.[654] French law contains only pale reflections of *forum non conveniens*, found in the rule of *lis alibi pendens*.[655]

The French attitude is illustrated by a case decided by the Paris *Cour d'Appel* involving in a contract between two non-French companies (one incorporated in Liechtenstein and the other in Mauritius) concerning a dispute unconnected with France. The agreement granted jurisdiction to the courts of either Paris or Vaduz. The *Cour d'Appel* held that the prorogation agreement operated notwithstanding the absence of any link between France and the parties or their dispute.[656] The court reasoned that in the absence of fraud and any statutory prohibition on competence, French courts would honor the court selection.

German law likewise lacks any general equivalent of the doctrine of *forum non conveniens*. A German court possessing jurisdiction will not normally refuse to hear a case covered by a jurisdiction clause on the ground that the dispute has little connection with Germany, nor fail to honor a designation of a foreign court on the ground that the case would best be litigated in Germany.[657]

---

651. *See generally* Hélène Gaudemet-Tallon, *Le forum non conveniens, une menace pour la convention de Bruxelles*, 80 Rev. Crit. Dr. Int. Privé 491 (1991), at 509-10. French courts hear a case if there exists a "ground of competence" (*chef de compétence*), which would include the parties' nationality, the place of contract execution or performance, or the situs of the wrongful act. *See generally* Bernard Audit, DROIT INTERNATIONAL PRIVÉ §§ 334-92 (1991).

652. "Il faut tuer dans l'oeuf cette source de chicane." Georges Droz, Compétence Judiciaire et Effets des Jugements dans le Marché Commun, § 206 (1972).

653. Hélène Gaudemet-Tallon, *Les régimes relatifs au refus d'exercer la compétence juridictionnelle en matière civile et commerciale*, 1994 REVUE INTERNATIONALE DE DROIT COMPARÉ (NO. 2) 423.

654. Nouveau Code de Procédure Civile, Article 92 provides, "L'incompétence peut être prononcée d'office en cas de violation d'une règle de compétence d'attribution lorsque cette règle est d'ordre public ou lorsque le défendeur ne comparaît pas."

655. When the same dispute has been brought before two courts of the same level, the second court to which the matter was referred must dismiss the action. *See* discussion *supra* at note 258. *See also* Nouveau Code de Procédure Civile Article 100. In French, the rule is usually referred to as "*litis pendens*" or "*litispendance*." Related to *lis alibi pendens* is the rule of "connexité" permitting one court to dismiss or transfer a matter to another court when a related action has been brought in the second jurisdiction.

656. Société Belle Vue Mauricia (Harel Frères) v. Société Canmaga Trade Corporation, Cour d'appel de Paris (1ère chambre), 10 October 1990, *reprinted in* 1991 Revue Critique de Droit Int'l Privé 605 (commentary by Hélène Gaudemet-Tallon).

657. *See* Reinhold Geimer, *Internationales Zivilprozessrecht*, Zivilprozessordnung §§ 62 & 78 (Richard Zoeller, ed., 17th ed. 1991). *But see* Gerhard Dannemann, *Jurisdiction Based on the Presence of Assets in Germany: A Case Note*, 41 Int'l & Comp. L.Q. 632 (1992). The German

Switzerland's conflict of laws statute, discussed more fully in the next section, requires Swiss judges to hear international cases pursuant to valid prorogation agreements as long as one party resides in Switzerland or Swiss law is applicable to the dispute.[658] When both parties are Swiss residents, the L.D.I.P. does not apply, and some courts seem to apply notions of *forum non conveniens* to decline to exercise jurisdiction purportedly conferred by a court-selection clause.[659]

Traditionally, English judges have been inclined to accept jurisdiction based on a contractual submission, regardless of the parties' or the dispute's link with England. Lord Denning once dismissed the policy concern over forum shopping with a boast. "You may call this 'forum shopping' if you please," wrote Denning, "but if the forum is England, it is a good place to shop in, both for the quality of the goods and the speed of the service."[660]

The recent appearance of *forum non conveniens* notions in English law has been noted in cases in which an "appropriate" alternate forum would argue against extraterritorial service of process as a basis for litigation in England. In a case usually referred to as *The Spiliada*, the House of Lords elaborated on notions of discretionary refusal to hear a case notwithstanding the presence of a clear basis for jurisdiction.[661] A Liberian shipowner sought leave to serve process on a Canadian in a case implicating bills of lading that were expressly made subject to English law. English law permits service of process on a defendant outside England in a contract action governed by English substantive law.[662]

The House of Lords affirmed the trial court's discretion to allow service of the writ, in large measure because the action would have been time-barred in Canada. However, several Lords noted the possibility to stay litigation when another available

---

Note 657, continued

Bundesgerichtshof recently narrowed the scope of ZPO Article 23, holding that a dispute must have some connection with Germany to justify jurisdiction based on the situs in Germany of assets owned by the defendant. *See* Muduroglu Ltd. v. TC Ziraat Bankast, BGH 2.7.1991, Neue Juristische Wochenschrift (N.J.W.) 1991, 3092. (Dispute between a Turkish bank and a Cypriot corporation arising out of a contract for construction of a harbor in Libya.)

658. *See* Article 5, Loi fédérale sur le droit international privé, discussed *infra* at notes 669-704. *See generally* François Knoepfler and Philippe Schweizer, Précis de Droit International Privé Suisse 198 (Bern 1990); Kaurt Siehr, *Rules for Declining to Exercise Jurisdiction in Civil and Commercial Matters: Forum Non Conveniens and Lis Pendens in Swiss Law, in* Rapports Suisses présentés au XIVeme Congres international du droit comparé 163, published by the Institut suisse de droit comparé (Schulthess, Zürich, 1994).

659. *See, e.g.*, Handelsgericht des Kantons Zürich, HG92127B/HG92, September 9, 1992 (Zurich commercial refusal to hear a dispute between two Swiss entities). *See generally* discussion in Siehr, *supra* note 658, at sections 23-25, pages 170-71. Siehr mentions particularly Zürich ZPO Section 11(2), permitting refusal to hear a case because of a court's work load.

660. *See* The Atlantic Star, 1973 Q.B. 364 (C.A. 1973). The case arose from a collision in Belgian waters between Dutch and Belgian vessels. *See* Dicey and Morris, Conflict of Laws 393-95 (11th ed. Supp. 1989).

661. Spiliada Maritime v. Cansulex, House of Lords, (1987) A.C. 460.

662. *See* Rules of the Supreme Court (RSC) Order 11.

forum exists where the case can be "tried more suitably for the interests of all the parties and the ends of justice."[663] This formulation of the *forum non conveniens* doctrine permits courts to shield defendants against proceedings in a remote forum, and also to protect plaintiffs from disadvantageous litigation, for example, in a forum where an action might be time-barred.[664] Because England has no system of federal courts similar to that of the United States, resort to *forum non conveniens* concepts sometimes also serves a function in connection with venue transfer among geographical districts.[665]

The Bruxelles and Lugano Convention generally leave British courts no discretion to decline to exercise their jurisdiction. The possibility that a court could refuse to hear a case notwithstanding the allocation of judicial competence under the Conventions has been excluded by both case law and commentary.[666]

When the alternate forum is outside a Convention state, however, the Convention rules do not necessarily apply. In *Matter of Harrods (Buenes Aires) Ltd.*,[667] a dispute arose concerning a company registered in England that was also named defendant. Normally the Bruxelles Convention would have designated British courts as competent to hear the dispute, based on the English defendant's domicile. Since 1979 the shares of the London department store had been divided between two Swiss entities, with control ultimately residing in Argentina. The Court of Appeal determined that it had discretionary power to refuse to hear the case if it would be more appropriately heard in Argentina. The Court of Appeal held that the Bruxelles Convention prevented the invocation of *forum non conveniens* only when the court wished to stay or dismiss proceedings in favor of an alternate forum inside the European Community.[668]

---

663. *See* speech of Lord Goff of Chieveley.

664. *See generally*, Richard Fentiman, *Jurisdiction, Discretion and the Brussels Convention*, 26 Cornell International Law Journal 59 (1993).

665. The Civil Jurisdiction and Judgments Act of 1982 applies the principles of the 1968 Bruxelles Convention to intra-United Kingdom jurisdictional allocation between the three legal systems of England/Wales, Northern Ireland and Scotland. In contrast, specific rules deal with the correct "divisions," such as probate or admiralty. Scottish law has more precise rules dealing with the proper "sheriffdom" for an action.

666. *See In re* Berisford, 2 All E.R. 321, at 332: "The [Bruxelles] Convention leaves no room for application of any discretionary jurisdiction by the courts of this country, the availability of such a discretion would destroy the framework of the Convention." *Compare In re* Arkwright, 2 All E.R. 335 (1990) and *In re* Berisford, 2 All E.R. 321 (1990). In both cases, the more appropriate forum was New York. *See also* DICEY & MORRIS, *supra* note 212, Rule 34, at 410: "Where Article 17 of the 1968 Convention applies the chosen court has no discretion to decline jurisdiction."

667. Matter of Harrods (Buenes Aires) Ltd., 19 Dec. 1990, [1991] 4 All E.R. 334, [1991] 3 WLR 397 (Harrods No. 1), and [1991] 4 All E.R. 348 (Harrods No. 2) *reported in* Financial Times 16 (26 March 1991). *See* discussion by Richard Fentiman, *Jurisdiction, Discretion and the Brussels Convention*, 26 Cornell International Law Journal 59 (1993); Collins 1990 Law Quart. Rev. 535; Hélène Gaudemet-Tallon, *Le Forum Non Conveniens: Une menace pour la Convention de Bruxelles?*, 80 Rev. Crit. Dr. Int. Privé 491 (1991).

668. The House of Lords has adjourned the English proceedings in order to refer the matter to the European Court of Justice.

C. THE HELVETIC MODEL.

1. Switzerland's Statutory Framework.

The Swiss federal conflict-of-laws code rationalizes the patchwork of procedural rules applicable in twenty-six cantons,[669] thereby enhancing the long-standing role of the Helvetic Confederation as a situs for resolution of international disputes.[670] Known as the *Loi fédérale sur le droit international privé* or "L.D.I.P.,"[671] the code sets forth relatively precise rules relating to jurisdiction, choice of law, judgments, and international arbitration.[672]

As discussed in the next section, the code provides conditions under which a Swiss court[673] must exercise jurisdiction conferred by contract.[674] The code also sup-

---

669. *See generally*, Alfred E. Von Overbeck, *Les élections de for selon la loi fédérale sur le droit international privé du 18 décembre 1987, in* FESTSCHRIFT FÜR MAX KELLER ZUM 65 GEBURTSTAG 609, 611-612 (1989). In twenty-six cantons, the three sets of "half-cantons" (Appenzell, Basel and Unterwald) are counted as six jurisdictionally distinct political subdivisions, notwithstanding their common ancestry.

670. One of the earliest major international arbitrations took place in Geneva to settle the so-called "Alabama Claims" arising out of the American Civil War depredations of the Confederate raider the C.S.S. Alabama. Built in Liverpool, the Alabama took more than sixty Union ships as prizes before being sunk off Cherbourg by the U.S.S. Kearsarge on 19 June 1864. After the war, the United States claimed compensation from Great Britain (supposedly a neutral in the Civil War) for having allowed one of the belligerents to use its ports as a naval base for operations against the other. By an accord signed in Washington in 1871, the United States and Britain agreed to have their controversy concerning the Alabama and other Confederate ships decided by arbitration in Geneva. A year later, a five member arbitral tribunal (composed of a Brazilian, an Italian and a Swiss, as well as appointments by Britain and the United States) rendered an award in favor of the United States that ultimately led to payment of $15.5 million in damages. *See* Reginald Wright, THE *ALABAMA* CASE (1927); ARBITRAGE DE L'ALABAMA (Edited by Chancellerie d'Etat, Geneva, 1991 edition).

671. Loi fédérale sur le droit international privé, 18 December 1987, *entered into force* 1 January 1989 [hereinafter "L.D.I.P."]. One hundred years prior to the L.D.I.P., Switzerland enacted a "Loi fédérale sur les Rapports de droit civil des citoyens établis ou en séjour" (L.R.D.C.), effective 25 June 1891, now abrogated; the law dealt with matters of family, personal status and inheritance. *See generally* discussion by Alfred E. von Overbeck, *in* LES LEGISLATIONS DE DROIT INTERNATIONAL PRIVÉ 167 (Asser Institute, ed. 1971).

672. L.D.I.P. Article 1 provides that the law applies "en matière internationale"/"im internationalen Verhältnis." *See* F. Knoepfler and Philippe Schweizer, PRÉCIS DE DROIT INTERNATIONAL PRIVÉ SUISSE 88-89 (1990).

673. In Switzerland, the federal judicial system is effectively limited to one court, the *Tribunal fédéral.*

674. L.D.I.P., Article 5 discussed *infra* at notes 685-97. Law prior to the entry into force of the federal statute was also welcoming to forum shoppers unless the forum selection clause served as a basis for provisional measures that could involve extraterritorial assertion of jurisdiction. In one case a Geneva cantonal court accepted to hear a dispute between a Bermuda company and a Liechtenstein entity (*Anstalt*) concerning a worthless chrome mine in Zimbabwe. *See* the Swiss Supreme Court's decision in Chalkwell Investment Co. v. Bolac Anstalt, Tribunal fédéral, 25 September 1987 (1ère Cour Civile), No. P 373/86.

plies a framework for international arbitration in Switzerland,[675] while leaving domestic arbitration to cantonal law.[676] Arbitral awards rendered abroad will continue to benefit from a presumptive validity, at least if not set aside where rendered or if not inconsistent with fundamental procedural fairness.[677]

While still leaving some questions open to debate,[678] the Swiss statute suggests a starting point for reducing adjudicatory ambiguities in forum selection.[679] The private interest in party autonomy has not obscured the public goal of protecting a community's weaker members from abusive clauses. Federal standards that preempt unsettling divergences among cantonal procedures[680] make the Swiss statute particularly attractive as a model to inspire an American statute rationalizing the treatment of jurisdiction clauses.

2. Honoring Agreements.

The Swiss conflict-of-laws code provides basic jurisdictional rules compatible with those of the Bruxelles and Lugano Conventions.[681] Courts at the defendant's domicile or habitual residence generally will have jurisdiction in contract matters.[682] When the defendant has no Swiss domicile or residence, the place of contract performance will normally determine the jurisdictional nexus.[683] The Swiss statute fixes not only the international allocation of competence between Switzerland and other countries, but

---

675. L.D.I.P., Articles 176-94. *See generally*, Pierre Lalive, Jean François Poudret and Claude Reymond, LE DROIT DE L'ARBITRAGE (1989); Adam Samuel, JURISDICTIONAL PROBLEMS IN INTERNATIONAL COMMERCIAL ARBITRATION (1989); Marc Blessing, *The New International Arbitration Law in Switzerland,* 5 J. Int'l Arb. 9 (June 1988); Emmanuel Gaillard, *A Foreign View of the New Swiss Law on International Arbitration,* 4 Arb. Int'l 25 (1988).

676. Intercantonal Arbitration Concordat, *Concordat sur l'arbitrage,* approved by the Conseil fédéral on 27 August 1969. *See generally*, Pierre Jolidon, COMMENTAIRE DU CONCORDAT SUISSE SUR L'ARBITRAGE (1984).

677. L.D.I.P., Article 194. On interpretation of the New York Convention by Swiss courts, see Pierre Lalive, Jean-François Poudret & Claude Reymond, LE DROIT DE L'ARBITRAGE 456-62 (1989).

678. For example, it is uncertain what the attitude of Swiss courts should be toward foreign judgments that have ignored a prorogation agreement valid under Swiss principles, when the defendant raised and lost the forum selection issue before the foreign court? *See* von Overbeck, *supra* note 669, at 624-26.

679. Von Overbeck, *supra* note 669, at 620.

680. Professor von Overbeck has referred to these as "the uncertainties of cantonal folklore" — *les incertitudes du folklore cantonal. See* von Overbeck, *supra* note 669, at 620.

681. *See generally*, François Knoepfler, *Le contrat dans le nouveau droit international privé suisse, in* LE NOUVEAU DROIT INTERNATIONAL PRIVÉ SUISSE 79, 83 (François Dessemontet, ed., 1989); *see also* François Knoepfler and Philippe Schweizer, PRÉCIS DE DROIT INTERNATIONAL PRIVÉ SUISSE 195-96 (1990).

682. L.D.I.P., Article 112.

683. *Id.* at Article 113 speaks of contract "execution," but in the sense of the place where performance is *executed* ("la prestation litigieuse doit être exécutée en Suisse").

also eliminates jurisdictional inconsistencies arising out of Switzerland's inter-cantonal federal system.[684]

Swiss courts must recognize jurisdiction clauses if the dispute involves a question related to property or pecuniary interests[685] and the agreement permits proof by a text, such as by fax or a telegram.[686] The choice of jurisdiction will be presumed exclusive unless the contract provides otherwise.[687]

The choice of forum must not "abusively" deprive a party of the protection of a forum provided by Swiss jurisdictional rules.[688] This general prohibition of abusive jurisdiction clauses was the subject of vigorous debate within the Swiss parliament. Certain legislators objected to the provision because of its tendency to reduce certainty, by giving lawyers an opportunity to put forum selection in doubt.[689] On the contrary, other legislators suggested an expansion of the scope of the provision to invalidate abusive waivers of foreign as well as Swiss jurisdiction.[690]

Consumers have a right to elect to sue either at their own or their supplier's residence,[691] and may not waive the jurisdiction of courts at their own residence except *after* a dispute has arisen.[692] Choice-of-law clauses in consumer contracts generally are invalid.[693]

The Swiss conflict-of-laws code circumscribes the contexts in which a Swiss court may refuse the jurisdiction thrust upon it by the parties. In an international case, a party-chosen judge may not decline to hear a dispute if (i) Swiss law governs the liti-

684. Before enactment of the L.D.I.P., cantonal law generally covered matters related to jurisdiction and judgments, and federal law governed matters related to choice of law. Cantonal law could be preempted by federal treaties and by the 1891 L.R.D.C. (discussed *supra* at note 671) on family, personal status and inheritance matters.

685. L.D.I.P. Article 5 speaks of "*matière patrimoniale*" in its French version and "*vermögensrechtliche Ansprüch*" in German. Similar limits are imposed on arbitrability in L.D.I.P. Article 177. Thus divorce disputes as such are excluded from the scope of the Article. Other portions of the L.D.I.P. carve out additional subject areas as to which the normally competent jurisdictional rules apply notwithstanding a choice of forum. These include determinations of title to Swiss realty (L.D.I.P., Article 97), actions concerning public securities issues (LDIP, Article 151(3)) and pre-dispute clauses in consumer transactions (L.D.I.P., Article 114).

686. L.D.I.P., Article 5(1).

687. L.D.I.P., Article 5. For Swiss case law considering the exclusivity of forum selection clauses, see cases discussed in Internationale Schiedsgerichtsbarkeit in der Schweiz (G. Walters, W. Bosch, & J. Brönnimann, eds., 1991), construing the term "to submit" (*unterwerfen*) as expressing exclusivity.

688. L.D.I.P., Article 5 (2) provides: "L'élection de for est sans effet si elle conduit à priver d'une manière abusive une partie de la protection que lui assure un for prévu par le droit suisse."

689. *See* von Overbeck, *supra* note 669, at 620-21.

690. The *Conseil des Etats* (analogous to the U.S. Senate) at first voted to eliminate the limitation, and reversed itself only after opposition from the more populist lower chamber, the *Conseil national. See* discussion *id.*, at 620, references to the Swiss Bulletin officiel *cited in* n. 29, 30 and 31.

691. L.D.I.P. Article 114(1). The concept of consumer is similar to that of the Lugano and Bruxelles Conventions: the supply of goods or services not linked to the user's trade or profession. L.D.I.P., Article 120(1).

692. *Id.* at Article 114(2).

693. *Id.* at Article 120(2).

gation or (ii) one of the parties is resident in Switzerland.[694] There would seem to be no reason why the first criterion (application of Swiss law) could not be satisfied by the parties' own choice, as allowed by LDIP Article 116.[695] Thus Swiss legislators have statutorily limited judicial abstinence under any analogue to *forum non conveniens*, except in cases where the controversy has no connection at all with Switzerland.[696] Contractually designated courts must hear the case when the dispute implicates Swiss law or a Swiss resident, regardless of how great the burden might be on public resources.[697]

3. Foreign Judgments.

The federal statute also provides a uniform scheme for recognition of foreign judgments.[698] Judicial decisions not subject to challenge where rendered[699] will benefit from recognition unless incompatible with Swiss public policy.[700] Violation of public policy may be raised by the Swiss court on its own motion. In addition, a judgment

---

694. *Id.* at Article 5, alinéa 3(b). A foreign entity with a Swiss branch (*établissement*) in the relevant canton would also give rise to mandatory jurisdiction.

695. *See* Kurt Siehr, *supra* note 658, Section 24, at 170-71.

696. A different standard would apply in a domestic (internal) case not covered by the L.D.I.P. *See, e.g.*, the Zurich commercial court to hear a dispute between two Swiss entities (from Altishofen and Vernier). Handelsgericht des Kantons Zürich, HG92127B/HG92, September 9, 1992. *See also* J & M Communications v. Seabay Corp., Geneva Cour de justice civile (1ère section), 8 February 1990, *reported in* Semaine Judiciaire, 196 Vol. 112, No. 13 (3 April 1990). A British Virgin Islands company had agreed to purchase, from a Cayman Islands company all of the share capital of a Dutch Antilles company. The relevant contract was governed by Swiss law, and provided for settlement of disputes by Geneva courts. Fearing that its counterparty was negotiating directly with a competing buyer, also outside Switzerland, the purchaser requested the Swiss court to block any negotiations between the seller and the rival purchaser. Both the lower court and the appellate courts refused to issue such orders, reasoning that the more appropriate forum for the matter was the court with powers to enforce its orders directly. *See generally*, Carlo Lombardini, *Jurisdictional Clause in Contract*, Financial L. Rev. 42 (Jan. 1991); Siehr, *supra* note 658, at 170-71.

697. The new statute follows the lead of some prior case law in which Swiss courts accepted jurisdiction when neither party was Swiss and the litigation had no connection with Switzerland. *See* Chalkwell Investment Co. v. Bolac Anstalt, Tribunal fédéral, 25 September 1986, confirming the decision of the Geneva Cour de justice, 11 April 1986, in litigation over a Zimbabwe chrome mine, opposing a Bermuda corporation with Kentucky shareholders (Ashland Oil) against a Liechtenstein *Anstalt*. The cantonal court accepted jurisdiction in a decision upheld by Switzerland's Federal Supreme Court (*Tribunal fédéral*).

698. *See* L.D.I.P. Articles 25-32; *see also*, Volken, *Conflits de juridictions, entraide judiciaire, reconnaissance et exécution des jugements étrangers*, in Le Nouveau Droit International Privé Suisse (Dessemontet, ed.), *supra* note 681, at 245-48; Knoepfler and Schweizer, *supra* note 681, at 222-28; Martin Bernet & Nicolas Ulmer, *Recognition and Enforcement of Foreign Civil Judgments in Switzerland*, 27 International Lawyer 317 (1993).

699. L.D.I.P., Article 25.

700. *Id.* at Article 27.

must be refused recognition if inconsistent with a valid prior judgment in Switzerland or abroad or if the foreign proceeding is tainted with lack of proper notice to the losing party or absence of due process.[701] Unlike some prior cantonal provisions, the federal statute does not require reciprocal treatment of Swiss judgments in the foreign country whose courts rendered the decision.[702]

4. Requiring a Nexus.

Swiss law will require a "sufficient connection" with Switzerland (usually referred to as *Binnenbeziehung*) before a judgment or award[703] will be enforceable against a foreign state or its assets.[704] This nexus requirement (which applies even when the foreign state is acting in a commercial rather than public capacity) might be satisfied if a party to the contract is resident in Switzerland or if Switzerland is the place of contract performance. From a diplomatic perspective this is entirely understandable. No country wants to anger foreign powers needlessly, especially a nation whose banking industry seeks to attract depositor states.

D. Merchants or Consumers?

Like Switzerland's code, the French[705] and German[706] court selection rules commend themselves for an equilibrium and precision far superior to the United States' approach. France and Germany both enforce court selection agreements against presumptively sophisticated business professionals, but not against consumers. Separate

701. "Violation de principes fondamentaux ressortissant à la conception suisse du droit de procédure, notamment que ladite partie n'a pas eu la possibilité de faire valoir ses moyens." *Id.* Article 27(2)(b).

702. *See* Volken, *supra* note 698, at 247.

703. The nexus requirement arises even when an arbitral award has been rendered in Switzerland. In the Swiss sequel to the *LIAMCO* proceedings (discussed *supra* at note 270), an arbitral seat in Geneva was insufficient by itself to provide a connection with the dispute that would justify enforcement of the award. Judgment of 19 June 1980, Swiss Tribunal fédéral, BGE 106-Ia at 142; 1982-II, Journal des Tribunaux at 66; English summary in VI Yearbook Commmercial Arbitration 15 (1981) and 79 Am. J. Int'l Law 153 (1981).

704. *See* Circulaire du Département fédéral de justice et police du 26 novembre 1979 aux Gouvernements cantonaux, 1980 Jurisprudence des Autorités Administratives de la Confédération (J.A.A.C.), no. 54, at page 224. The German version speaks of a "near connection" with Switzerland (*näheren Beziehung zum schweizerischen Hoheitsgebiet*), while the French version refers to "certain links" with Switzerland (*certains liens avec le territoire Suisse*). *See also* cases cited by Swiss Tribunal fédéral in its Judgment of 19 June 1980, *supra* note 703.

705. *See generally* Bernard Audit, *supra* note 651, at 323-24; Pierre Mayer, Droit International Privé (1987) 187-90; Yvon Loussouarn and Pierre Bourel, Droit International Privé §§ 454-55, 493-94 (1978).

706. For help with German materials discussed below, special thanks are due to Christian Bühring-Uhle.

procedures regulate transactions between "merchants," a term of art that includes both individuals and companies contracting in their commercial capacity.[707]

The French Civil Procedure Code provides as follows:

> Any clause which directly or indirectly derogates from territorial jurisdictional rules is to be considered void [non-written] unless it was concluded between persons who contracted in their capacity as merchant (*commerçant*) and was specified in an obvious way in the obligation of the party against whom it is invoked.[708]

When first enacted in 1972, the terse text of the provisions left some uncertainty about whether they covered international contracts, and caused commentators to speculate that they might allow forum selection clauses in international business only between persons possessing the status of *commerçant*.[709] Subsequent case law, however, has made clear that the statutory restrictions on forum selection clauses will not generally apply in international transactions.[710] International forum selection clauses will be honored even in contracts between persons who are not merchants,[711] as long

---

707. "*Commerçant*" in France; "*Kaufmann*" (*Kaufleute* plural) in Germany. Lawyers, however, are excluded from coverage of these commercial regimes. Many civil law jurisdictions make a dichotomy between "civil" and "commercial" acts, having a separate legal regime for contracts concluded between or among persons contracting as merchants or in the capacity of their trade or business. *See* Arthur Taylor Von Mehren and James Russell Gordley, The Civil Law System 100-02, 129-30 (1977); Mary Ann Glendon, Michael Wallace Gordon, & Chris Osakwe, Comparative Legal Traditions 112-14 (1982); Konrad Zweigert & Hein Kotz, Introduction to Comparative Law, Ch. 11-14 (Tony Weir, ed., 1987).

708. N.C.P.C. Article 48:

> Toute clause qui directement ou indirectement déroge aux règles de compétence territoriale est réputée non écrite à moins qu'elle n'ait été convenue entre des personnes ayant toutes contracté en qualité de commerçant et qu'elle n'ait été spécifiée de façon très apparente dans l'engagement de la partie à qui elle est opposée.

709. *See* Yvon Loussouarn and Pierre Bourel, Droit International Privé § 454 (1978): "Faut-il en déduire que les prorogations conventionnelles de compétence internationale sont désormais interdites, sauf entre commerçants? Une telle solution serait regrettable...." *Id.* at 573-74.

710. *See* C.S.E.E. v. SORELEC, Cour de cassation, 1re Ch. Civ., 17 Dec. 1985, *reprinted in* 1986 Revue Critique de Droit International Privé at 537, with commentary by Hélène Gaudemet-Tallon. Dispute between two French enterprises arising out of subcontract for construction project in Libya. Although the case itself involved merchants, the court announced its decision in broader language. "L'Article 48 du nouveau code de procédure civile doit s'interpréter en ce sens que doivent être exclues de la prohibition qu'il édicte les clauses qui ne modifient la compétence territoriale interne qu'en conséquence d'une modification de la compétence internationale." *See* discussion in Bernard Audit, Droit International Privé §§ 387-88 (1991); Bernard Audit, *Droit International Privé: Compétence Internationale, in* 1986 Recueil Dalloz Sirey, 26ème Cahier, Informations rapides, at 265; Bernard Audit, Observations Civ. 1re, 17 décembre 1985, C.S.E.E. v. SORELEC, D. 1986 I.R. 265, Grands Arrets de la Jurisprudence de Droit International Privé (22e Ed.) No. 68.

711. Farmers selling goods, for example, would be included in the category of non-merchant. However, consumer transactions presumably would *not* benefit from the liberal recognition of international forum selection clauses. *See* Bernard Audit. Droit International Privé (1991),

as they do not run afoul of a French court's mandatory "territorial" jurisdiction in matters such as bankruptcy and family law.[712] French judges will not normally have discretion to refuse jurisdiction under a prorogation agreement.[713]

German law also refuses to enforce a choice of forum clause (*Gerichtsstands-klausel*) except when concluded after a dispute has arisen, when the rights have been identified and the risk of abuse of bargaining power will be less.[714] Like the French, the Germans allow two important exceptions to the general invalidation of pre-dispute forum selection agreements. First, pre-dispute forum selection clauses are permitted in contracts among merchants,[715] a category that includes all corporations, partnerships and individuals carrying on business in one of the "basic trades."[716] Second, pre-dispute forum selection clauses may be contained in international contracts, defined to include agreements in which at least one party has no "jurisdictional residence"[717] in Germany.

The European Union added another layer of consumer protection with ramifications for forum selection clauses. A European Council Directive[718] requires Member States to establish national rules under which unfair contract terms will not be binding on consumers.[719] The Directive states that a term which has "not been individually negotiated shall be regarded as unfair if, contrary to the requirement of good faith, it causes a significant imbalance in the parties' rights and obligations arising out of the

---

Note 711, continued

at Section 388, suggesting that French law would prohibit jurisdiction clauses as needed to protect commercially weaker parties: "[D]es règles spécifiques font obstacle, en droit interne, à la prorogation de compétence en vue de protéger une partie réputée plus faible telle que l'assuré ou le salarié." *Id.* at page 327. It is highly unlikely that very many international consumer contracts involving French residents would not be covered by the Bruxelles or the Lugano Conventions (which *do* contain consumer protection provisions), since France is surrounded on all sides by countries that are party to either the Bruxelles or Lugano Conventions. *See also* Charoy v. Belmac Corp., Cour d'Appel de Versailles, 8 April 1993, *reported in* 5 Int'l Litigation Procedure 346 (1994), holding Article 48 inapplicable to an international employment agreement between a French sales manager and a Florida company; duties to be performed in Europe, the Middle East and Africa; designated forum before courts of Tampa, Florida.

712. "Compétence territoriale impérative." For example, public policy would seem to dictate that prorogation agreements be void or voidable if in conflict with a French court's exclusive jurisdiction (*e.g.*, a bankruptcy court's determination of priorities among creditors) or would interfere with the determination of personal status (*e.g.*, marriage, adoption or divorce).

713. *See* discussion of Belle Vue Mauricia Harel Frères v. Canmaga Trade Corporation, discussed *supra* at note 656. (Contract between Liechtenstein entity and Mauritius corporation.)

714. Zivilprozessordnung (ZPO), Article 38.

715. *Kaufmann*, or in the plural *Kaufleute.*

716. *Grundhandelsgeschaeft.*

717. *Allgemeiner Gerichtsstand.*

718. Directive 93/13/EEC, 5 April 1993, *Unfair Terms in Consumer Contracts,*" *published 21 April 1993 in* Official Journal of the European Communities, No. L 95/29.

719. *Id.* Article 6(1).

contract, to the detriment of the consumer."[720] A list of illustrative unfair terms annexed to the Directive includes conditions "which would have the object or effect of ... excluding or hindering the consumer's right to take legal action or exercise any other legal remedy, particularly by requiring the consumer to take disputes exclusively to arbitration not covered by legal provisions."[721] The Directive does not make clear exactly what is meant by arbitration provisions that are "exclusive" and "not covered by legal provisions." However, the import of the Directive would seem to impose substantial limitations on the use of arbitration clauses in consumer contracts unless the consumer has some right to challenge the award in court.

720. *Id.* Article 3.
721. Directive 93/13/EEC, *supra* note 718, Annex I, Section q.

Chapter VII

NEUTRALITY, PREDICTABILITY AND ECONOMIC COOPERATION

International business lawyers generally seek to minimize the uncertainty and impartiality inherent in the cross-border legal environment. These lawyers draft arbitration and jurisdiction clauses, sometimes linked to choice-of-law agreements and treaty enforcement mechanisms, in order to foster a more neutral and predictable mode of dispute resolution than otherwise available to their clients.

To some, the merit of these commitments to a relatively neutral forum and determinate substantive law would seem self-evident. No econometric model should be required for the proposition that merchants and investors will be less likely to enter into business transactions abroad if they fear that potential disputes will be settled by biased judges of the other side's home courts. While some deals may promise profits great enough to lure adventurous entrepreneurs to take wild litigation risks, other transactions will not. Less reliable forum selection mechanisms will mean either fewer cross-border ventures, greater costs or a temptation to sloppy contract performance for want of realistic enforcement sanctions.

In contrast to the predictability-maximizing approach of international business lawyers, many American legal scholars have been intrigued by methodologies that seem to reduce certainty and impartiality. Some conflict-of-laws scholars emphasize "choice-influencing considerations" and justice in the individual case,[722] or a search for a result that furthers the "inherent morality that should be part of the relationship between the parties."[723] Others favor a "government interest analysis" that requires courts to inquire into the reasonableness of applying policies behind foreign laws,[724] or a "teleological" approach that looks principally to the better law in the specific case.[725] Certain American jurisprudential thinkers have gone further and emphasized

---

722. *See e.g.* Leflar's "better rule of law," discussed *infra* at note 729.

723. *See* Joseph Singer, *Real Conflicts*, 69 B.U. L. Rev. 1, 37, discussed *infra* at note 729.

724. Brainard Currie, SELECTED ESSAYS ON THE CONFLICT OF LAWS (1963). *See generally*, David Cavers, THE CHOICE-OF-LAW PROCESS (1965); PERSPECTIVES ON CONFLICT OF LAWS (James Martin, ed. 1980), at 67-189; CONFLICT OF LAWS (W. Reese, M. Rosenberg, & P. Hay, eds., 9th ed. 1990), at 485-95; David Cavers, *A Critique of the Choice-of-Law Problem*, 47 Harv. L. Rev. 173 (1933). *See also* discussion *infra* at note 729.

725. *See* Friedrich K. Juenger, CHOICE OF LAW AND MULTISTATE JUSTICE (1993) at 104 (on Leflar's "better rule of law"), 156-57 ("the inevitability of hometown justice") and 169-190 ("teleology").

what they perceive to be the inevitability of law's uncertainty and bias.[726]

International forum selection provides a prism through which to refract many of these jurisprudential questions related to law's determinacy and neutrality. My purpose here is not to join the general debate about the nature of law,[727] but rather to suggest that insights from thinking about international forum selection can be brought home to inform our understanding of when and why legal certainty and neutrality matter. Cross-border transactions illustrate how relative measures of neutrality and determinacy can and do meaningfully exist, and why they ought to serve as aspirational models for authoritative adjudicatory systems.

---

726. *See, e.g.*, Joseph W. Singer, *The Player and the Cards: Nihilism and Legal Theory*, 94 Yale L.J. 1 (1984) ("Critical Legal Scholars ... have shown that legal reasoning is indeterminate and contradictory. By its own criteria, legal reasoning cannot resolve legal questions in an objective manner; nor can it explain how the legal system works or how judges decide cases. We have [also] argued that law is not neutral: It is a mechanism for creating and legitimating configurations of economic and political power." *Id.* at 5-6); Jack Beermann, Barbara Melamed and Hugh Hall, *The Supreme Court's Tilt to the Property Right*, 3 B.U. Public Interest L.J. 9 (1993) ("Once [legal doctrine] is exposed as indeterminate, the belief in its legitimacy evaporates. . . ; rather than feel anxious about [legal] contradiction we should glorify it. . . ." *Id.* at 33); David Kairys, *Law and Politics*, 52 Geo. Wash. L. Rev. 243 ("Legal reasoning does not provide concrete, real answers to particular legal or social problems. Legal reasoning is not a method or process that leads reasonable, competent and fair-minded people to particular results in particular cases." *Id.* at 244); Allan C. Hutchinson, INTRODUCTION TO CRITICAL LEGAL STUDIES (A. Hutchinson, ed., 1989) ("No objectively correct results exist, regardless of whether presented in terms of legal doctrine or policy analysis and no matter how skilled the judge or advocate." *Id.* at 7.). On the antecedents of the critical legal studies movement in the "legal realism" of the period between the two World Wars, see AMERICAN LEGAL REALISM (William W. Fisher, Morton J. Horowitz & Thomas A. Reed, eds. 1993). *See generally*, Christopher Lutz, *Just Disagreement: Indeterminacy and Rationality in the Rule of Law*, 102 Yale Law Journal 997 (1994). For a related perspective taken from religious law, see Hanina Ben-Menahem, JUDICIAL DEVIATION IN TALMUDIC LAW: GOVERNED BY MEN, NOT BY RULES (1991, Jewish Law in Context, Neil Hecht, ed.).

727. *See* works by Henderson, Hutchinson, Kairys, Minnow, Resnick, and Singer cited *supra* at note 726. *Compare* Kent Greenawalt, *How Law Can Be Determinate*, 38 UCLA L. Rev. 1 (1990), explaining how law is determinate in what he admits are the "easy" legal questions, by drawing on observations about shared understandings not only in contract (*e.g., id.* at 49), but also in analysis of literary and theological texts (*id.* at 65-73); Kent Greenawalt, *The Enduring Significance of Neutral Principles*, 78 Colum. L. Rev. 982 (1978); Fred Schauer, *Rules and the Rule of Law*, 14 Harv. J. L. & Pub. Pol'y 645 (1991), contrasting rule-based decision-making (derived from generalizations that may be under- or over-inclusive in particular cases) and "particularistic" judging that attempts to maximize the right result in each case.

A. Neutrality Revisited.[728]

1. Questioning Impartiality.

Anyone concerned about enhancing legal neutrality and predictability in dispute resolution must recognize that many scholars have launched a critique of determinacy and impartiality in the legal process. In the context of choice-of-law analysis, domestic conflicts scholarship has often emphasized methodologies that enhance social justice and the right result in an individual case at the expense of certainty-promoting rules.[729] More generally, critical legal studies,[730] feminist scholarship[731] and critical

---

728. For an earlier discussion of adjudicatory neutrality, see chapter I, *supra* at notes 3-11 and 23-27.

729. *See generally* survey of literature in Joseph W. Singer, *Real Conflicts*, 69 B.U. Law Rev. 1, 23-32, 110-27 (1989). Professor Singer focuses on choice-of-law rather than choice-of-forum. However, we have seen how law and forum are intertwined, particularly as forum selection can be a way to avoid application of mandatory norms of the place of contract performance. Other result-oriented choice-of-law methodologies include David Cavers' principle of preference (including "justice between the litigating individuals"), in David Cavers, THE CHOICE OF LAW PROCESS (1965), and David Cavers, *A Critique of Choice of Law Problems*, 47 Harv. L. Rev. 173 (1933) and Robert Leflar's choice-influencing considerations (including "the better rule of law"), Robert Leflar, *Choice Influencing Considerations in Conflicts Law*, 41 N.Y.U. L. Rev. 267 (1966) and Robert Leflar, *Conflicts Law: More Choice-Influencing Considerations*, 54 S. Cal. L. Rev. 1584 (1966). *Compare* Peter Hay, *Reflections on Conflict-of-Laws Methodology*, 32 Hastings L.J. 1644 (1981); Alfred Hill, *Judicial Function in Choice-of-Law*, 85 Colum. L. Rev. 1585 (1985); Maurice Rosenberg, *Comment on Reich v. Purcell*," 15 U.C.L.A. L. Rev. 641 (1968). To the extent that a judge's conclusions about the right law to apply will take into account "the inherent justice or morality that should be part of the relationship between parties" (Singer, *Real Conflicts, supra*, at 37), some fora can be expected to refuse to give effect to otherwise applicable rules of law that conflict with mandatory public norms. *See* discussion of *Mitsubishi* footnote 19 and "prospective waiver" *supra* at notes 510-12, and the "second look" doctrine, *supra* at notes 521-27.

730. *See* authors cited *supra* at notes 726-727. *See also* David Kairys, THE POLITICS OF LAW: A PROGRESSIVE CRITIQUE (David Kairys, ed., 1984); Mark Tushnet, "Critical Legal Studies: A Political History," 100 Yale L.J. 1515 (1991), describing critical legal studies as "less an intellectual movement in law . . . than a political location." *Id.* at 1515.

731. *See, e.g.*, Trina Grillo, *The Mediation Alternative: Process Dangers for Women*, 100 Yale L.J. 1545 (1991) ("The patriarchal paradigm [is] characterized by hierarchy, linear reasoning, the resolution of disputes through the application of abstract principles, and the ideal of the reasonable person."); Catherine MacKinnon, *Feminism, Marxism, Method and the State: Toward Feminist Jurisprudence*, 8 J. Women Culture and Society 635, 645 (1983) ("The whole structure of law...and its undeviating bias in favor of rationality over all other values...defines it as a fundamentally patriarchal institution."); Robin West, *Feminism, Critical Social Theory and Law*, 1989 U. Chi. Legal F. 59 (1989). *See generally*, Marion Crain, *Feminism, Labor and Power*, 65 S. Cal. L. Rev. 1819 (1992); Marion Crain, *Images of Power in Labor Law: A Feminist Deconstruction*, 33 B.C. L. Rev. 481 (1992); Susan G. Kupfer, *Anatomy and Community in Feminist Legal Thought*, 22 Golden Gate L. Rev. 583 (1992); Gillian Lester, *Toward the Feminization of Collective Bargaining Law*, 36 McGill L.J. 1181 (1991); SYMPOSIUM, *The Voices of Women*, 77 Iowa L. Rev. 1 (1991).

race theory[732] point out the effect of white, middle-class, and male perspectives in filling gaps in the law.[733] In the tradition of legal realism, Critical Theorists see something other than principle as driving judicial decisionmaking. Pretensions at objective application of the law, they say, reveal themselves as masks for preserving the status quo. Fear that rights-based discourse may lead to misleading categories[734] has led some scholars to favor communitarian justice,[735] or to take into account an "inherent justice and morality" that should be part of legal relationships.[736] Others reject objectivity[737] in order to deconstruct texts[738] or demythologize rights.[739]

Critical Theory has sensitized lawyers to the temptation to confuse preferences

---

732. *See* Derrick Bell, FACES AT THE BOTTOM OF THE WELL 144-46 (1992); *see also* John Calmore, *Critical Race Theory, Archie Shepp, and Fire Music: Securing an Authentic Intellectual Life in a Multicultural World*, 65 S. Cal. L. Rev. 2129 (1992). *See generally* works cited in Richard Delgado and Jean Stefancic, *Critical Race Theory: An Annotated Bibliography*, 79 Va. L. Rev. 461 (1993).

733. *See, e.g.,* Marlee Kline, *Race, Racism and Feminist Legal Theory*, 12 Harv. Women's L.J. 115 (1989) ("These [feminist] insights have been applied to reveal the incomplete and biased nature of masculinist theory and...the same insights apply equally to our own [white feminist] work—that it too is incomplete and biased." *Id.* at 149.).

734. *See, e.g.,* Martha Minow, MAKING ALL THE DIFFERENCE: INCLUSION, EXCLUSION AND AMERICAN LAW 164-72 (1990) ("Rights provide a way to pretend to resolve the problem, but the problem remains."); Peter Gabel, *The Phenomenology of Rights Consciousness and the Pact of the Withdrawn Selves*, 62 Tex. L. Rev. 1563 (1984); Mark V. Tushnet, *An Essay on Rights*, 62 Tex. L. Rev. 1363; *see also* Elizabeth M. Schneider, *The Dialectic of Rights and Politics: Perspectives From the Women's Movement*, 61 N.Y.U. L. Rev. 589 (1986). *Compare* the perspective of a scholar not associated with critical legal studies. *See* Mary Ann Glendon, RIGHTS TALK: THE IMPOVERISHMENT OF POLITICAL DISCOURSE (1991).

735. *See, e.g.,* Aviam Soifer, *Upsetting Rights: Woe to Them That Are At Ease,"* presented to PARADOXES OF RIGHTS CONFERENCE, Amherst, Massachusetts, November 1992.

736. *See* Joseph W. Singer, *Real Conflicts*, 69 B.U. L. Rev. 1, 37 (1989). Professor Singer applies his framework in a contract context at 110-19.

737. *See* Allan C. Hutchinson, *Identity Crisis: The Politics of Interpretation*, 26 New Eng. L. Rev. 1173, 1184-88 (1992); Judith Resnik, *On the Bias: Feminist Reconsideration of the Aspirations for Our Judges*, 61 S. Cal. L. Rev. 1877 (1988) ("Impartiality and disengagement can never be achieved, hence all judgment is (sub rosa) suspect, hence we are always living in a second best world in which we cover our tracks with doctrines of insulation. Judges are in a permanent state of apology, for judges can never completely fulfill the aspirations of otherness." *Id.* at 1943.).

738. *See, e.g.,* Jacques Derrida, DE LA GRAMMATOLOGIE (1967); Jacques Derrida, *Force de Loi: le Fondement Mystique de l'Autorité/ Force of Law: The Mystical Foundation of Authority*, 11 Cardozo L. Rev. 919 (1990) ("Deconstructive interrogation [of critical legal studies] starts ... by destabilizing, complicating or bringing out the paradoxes of values ... a through and through problematization of law and justice." *Id.* at 931.); *see also* Pierre Schlag, *Le Hors de Texte C'est Moi: the Politics of Form and the Domestication of Deconstruction*, 11 Cardozo L. Rev. 1631 (1990).

739. *See* Jane Rutherford, *The Myth of Due Process,"* 72 B.U. L. Rev. 1, 3 (1992), who writes: "If a text can be said to have any meaning at all, it is a multiple meaning which changes over time with the changing values readers bring to it." One might respond that to treat *all* texts in this fashion is a bit like reading a cookbook and a psalm in the same fashion.

with precedent, often providing a useful corrective to doctrinal smugness. On the other hand, some scholars have suggested that Critical Theory has overstated its case, leaping from realism about the difficulty of disinterested decisionmaking to a broad condemnation of the entire legal system.[740] Others have expressed concern that disparagement of principled decisionmaking could lead to oppression.[741]

What is interesting about Critical Theory in connection with international forum selection is how its reaction to bias differs from that of the international commercial community. While international lawyers elaborate specific mechanisms aimed at eliminating bias (choice-of-law clauses, forum selection agreements and arbitration treaties[742]), Critical Theorists suggest less rather than more neutrality, embracing empathy (the right kind of bias?) in its stead.[743] While many start with a concern about substantive rules rather than the adjudicatory forum, it is hard to imagine divorcing one from the other. If legal doctrine lacks determinacy, it is at least in part because adjudicators are not neutral.

---

740. Commenting on critical theorists one scholar has written:

> It is a big step, for example, from observing that there are certain leeways inherent in fact-finding and rule-application, to asserting that there is no such thing as a fact and that all rules are radically indeterminate and manipulable. It is another major leap from being realistic about the difficulties of disinterested decision-making to a condemnation of the entire legal system as fatally tainted with racism, sexism and other forms of hegemony. ... [B]y opting out of the ongoing argument embodied in living legal traditions, they are left to commune disjointedly with one another or with themselves.

Mary Ann Glendon, *Tradition and Creativity in Culture and Law*, 27 First Things 13, 18 (November 1992).

741. *See* Harold Berman, LAW AND REVOLUTION 40-41 (1983) ("What is to prevent discretionary justice from being an instrument of repression and even a pretext for barbarism as it became in Nazi Germany?"). Professor Berman's allusion is to German National Socialist legislation that punished violations of "sound popular instinct." The *Gesundes Volksempfinden* ("sound popular instinct") was said to reflect the Führer's will. *See* Law of 28 June 1935; Gesetz zur Änderung des Strafgesetzbuches, published 5 July 1935, Reichsgesetzblatt [RGB1] 1 No. 70, at 213 (Ger.). Article I, section 2, provides punishment for "anyone who commits an act . . . which deserves punishment under the basic philosophy of a criminal statute and sound popular instinct." *See* Hubert Schorn, DER RICHTER IM DRITTEN REICH 62-76 (1959); Hubert Schorn, DIE GESETZGEBUNG DES NATIONALSOZIALISMUS ALS MITTEL DER MACHTPOLITIK 9-84 (1963).

742. Lawyers from developing countries sometimes express the perception that the major international arbitral institutions are dominated by industrialized Western nations (the analogue to Critical Theory's concern over "white male bias") and tend to select arbitrators insensitive to the legitimate aspirations of Third World economies. One result has been the elaboration by the United Nations of *ad hoc* arbitration rules that arguably permit greater impartiality in arbitral procedures. No serious arbitration lawyer, however, has suggested that neutrality and independence be abandoned as aspirational models for arbitral tribunals.

743. *See* Lynne Henderson, *Legality and Empathy*, 85 Mich. L. Rev. 1574 (1987); Martha Minow, MAKING ALL THE DIFFERENCE 219-221 (1990).

2. The Internationalist Perspective.

The descriptive and normative perspectives of international lawyers are marked by more relativity of tone than the discourse of many Critical Theorists.[744] Assuming that some adjudicatory processes are more neutral and reliable than others, international business lawyers seek to emphasize the neutrality and predictability of one decision-making mechanism over another. Even if complete objectivity will be elusive, they see a measure of fairness through independent, relatively neutral tribunals as both possible and desirable.[745]

The type of neutrality sought by internationalists focuses on what might be described as "reversibility." An adjudication process is neutral if the parties' nationalities could be reversed (French plaintiff becomes American, and American defendant becomes French) without changing the result in the case.[746] In this respect, one judge or arbitrator will be neutral only in comparison with alternatives. In a dispute between an Israeli seller and an Egyptian buyer, a Swiss arbitrator can usually be characterized as more neutral than an Israeli or Egyptian. A Spanish buyer and a North African seller accept arbitration in Geneva as comparatively more neutral than litigation before national courts in Algiers or Madrid. In seeking compensation for a business nationalized by Iran, an American buyer will feel more comfortable before the Iran-U.S. Claims Tribunal in the Hague than before an Iranian judge in Teheran.

Critical Theory, on the other hand, has tended to characterize *all* decision-making as biased.[747] Some Critical Theorists assure us that when legal doctrine is "exposed" as indeterminate, its legitimacy will "evaporate."[748]

One explanation for the difference between the internationalist approach and Critical Theory might be that international business lawyers live in a world of greater adjudicatory poverty than domestic scholars. Language, procedural safeguards, and judicial independence are all up for grabs, and the costs of impartiality and uncertainty are therefore more dramatic. French commercial cases and Swiss procedural orders

---

744. In part this may be due to the absence of a comparative dimension to most American legal scholarship. And in part it may also be because practitioners play a much greater role than academics in writing about cross-border transactions.

745. One American historian has noted that "there is no such thing as objectivity, but there is fairness." *See* Martin Marty. *Quoted in* The World (Unitarian Universalist Association, Nov./Dec. 1992), at 26.

746. With respect to substantive norms, however, neutrality implicates absence of distortion with reference to some policy goal. For example, one may speak of taxes that are "export neutral" or "import neutral" depending on how they affect exports or imports, and whether they leave American manufacturers on an equal footing with foreign competition. *See* William W. Park, *Fiscal Jurisdiction and Accrual Basis Taxation: Lifting the Corporate Veil to Tax Foreign Company Profits*, 78 Columbia Law Rev. 1610 (1978), at 1627-29.

747. *See* Judith Resnik, *On the Bias: Feminist Reconsiderations of the Aspirations for Our Judges*, 61 S. Cal. L. Rev. 1877, 1943 (1988): "Impartiality and disengagement can *never* be achieved, hence *all* judgment is (sub rosa) suspect, hence we are always living in a second best world in which we cover our tracks with doctrines of insulation." (Emphasis added.)

748. *See* Beermann, Melamed and Hall, *supra* at note 726, at 33.

are not found in most firm or faculty libraries as easily as American court decisions. No supra-national marshals compel compliance with orders of supra-national commercial judges. Foreign courts will not deal with American judgments according to a federalism model, and American-style procedural safeguards can rarely be taken for granted in litigation abroad. The international business lawyer must call on the talents of an archaeologist to find legal sources, and on the skills of comparative anthropology to discern what judicial decisions will be enforced in a cross-border dispute.

In contrast, the more homogenous world of single-country legal scholarship in the United States contains relatively fewer linguistic, ethical and procedural variations. Libraries stock the latest Supreme Court advance sheets. Hundreds of years of case law and statutes delineate relatively precise rules for judicial jurisdiction and the recognition of sister state judgments.

In choice of law as well as forum selection, internationalists tend to think in relative terms. A rule is determinate in practice because it reduces the number and likelihood of alternate outcomes to a case,[749] not because it operates with perfect predictability.[750]

An agreement to apply a relatively developed legal system to a commercial agreement supplies a fairness otherwise absent in international adjudication.[751] Any legal system may on some issues work to one side's disadvantage in a particular case. However, an agreement to "play by the rules" of a more evolved or complete system of law will normally maximize both parties' *ex ante* expectation of fair treatment. For example, the laws of a land-locked country would rarely be chosen to govern an agreement implicating transport of goods on the high seas. Rather, charter parties and marine insurance contracts are subjected to the law of a maritime nation with enough sea traffic to generate predictability-enhancing precedents. Often this will be the law of England,[752] with its statutory framework[753] and centuries of precedent[754] on the duty of disclosure,[755] the definition of loss,[756] and the allocation of damage.[757]

---

749. Compare a rule that fixes a royalty at the contract rate of "3% of gross sales" with one calling for a fee that is "fair" and "in accord with Biblical principles of justice."

750. No rule could be absolutely determinate for the simple reason that some judges and arbitrators are open to bribery.

751. The late Dr. Francis Mann noted, "No merchant of any experience would ever be prepared to submit to the unforeseeable consequences which arise from application of undefined and undefinable standards described as rules of a lex of unknown origin." *Introduction* to Lex MERCATORIA AND ARBITRATION at xxi (Thomas Carbonneau, ed., 1990).

752. *See, e.g.,* 1 Dicey & Morris, ON THE CONFLICTS OF LAWS 549-51 (L. Collins 11th ed., 1987). *See also* SONATRACH v. Distrigas, 80 B.R. 606 (D. Mass. 1987), where a long-term supply contract for liquified natural gas sold by an Algerian state agency to a Boston buyer provided for its interpretation under "laws of the United Kingdom," intended to mean English law.

753. *See, e.g.,* Marine Insurance Act, 1906, Ch. 41 (6 Edw. 7).

754. The first Court of Admiralty cases were collected in The Black book of admiralty between 1332 and 1357. *See* 1 William Searle Holdsworth, A History of English Law 545 (7th ed.). For a recent survey of the history of admiralty law, see Chartwell Shipping Ltd. v. Q.N.S. Paper Co., 1989 Am. Maritime Cases 2798 (Sup. Ct. Canada, 1989).

National legal systems as well as private contracting parties look to the law of countries with developed precedents in a particular area. To continue with the maritime example, the navigational statute of landlocked Switzerland, covering river vessels, explicitly instructs Swiss judges to fill gaps in their own law by reference to "the custom, doctrine and case law of maritime states."[758]

In evaluating the fairness of international dispute resolution mechanisms, the concept of independence also may be useful. Whether an adjudicator is free from bias often matters less than whether the adjudicator is independent of the parties.[759] In an arbitration arising out of Libyan nationalization of American oil concessions, a French law professor chosen to calculate compensation for expropriated property might share biases common to European academics.[760] However, the professor will be more independent of the parties (and thus arguably fairer) than either a Libyan government official or an officer of the expropriated oil company.

755. Marine insurance contracts impose on the parties a duty of *uberma fides* that requires disclosure of any material information while negotiating coverage. Marine Insurance Act of 1906, *supra*, Section 18 ("assured must disclose to the insurer, before the contract is concluded, every material circumstance...."). See Putnam Resources v. Pateman and Pateman v. Frenkel & Co., No. 91-1307 and 91-1308, (1st Cir. 1992) at 45. (denial of claim for theft of gold arising out of Sammartino scam in Rhode Island).

756. For a case involving the definition of "total loss" to damaged vessels, see Edinburgh Assurance Co. v. Burns Corp, 1980 American Maritime Cases 1260 (Cent. Dist. Cal. 1979); off-shore drilling platform disabled off the coast of Madagascar, governed by Marine Insurance Act of 1906.

757. On the allocation of loss in the case of shared fault, see Perusahaan Umum Listrik Negara Pusat v. M/V Tel Aviv, 1985 American Maritime Cases 66 (5th Cir. 1983); collision on high seas near Gibraltar between Israeli and Indonesian ships; Fifth Circuit refused to retain U.S. jurisdiction in favor of alternative London court, even though English law, contrary to American law, would limit recovery because of fault shared by plaintiff's Indonesian carrying vessel.

758. See Swiss *Loi fédérale sur la navigation maritime sous pavillon suisse* (23 September 1953, R.O. 1956, 1395403), recognized under Article 107 of the Swiss L.D.I.P., discussed *supra* at note 386. Article 7 of the Navigation Statute provides: "Si la législation fédérale, notamment la présente loi, ainsi que les règles juridiques internationales auxquelles il est fait renvoi, ne contiennent pas de dispositions applicables, le juge prononce selon les principes généraux du droit maritime. Si ces principes font défaut, il prononce selon les règles qu'il établirait s'il avait à faire acte de législateur, *en tenant compte de la législation, de la coutume, de la doctrine et de la jurisprudence des Etats maritimes.*" (Emphasis added.)

759. On the requirement of arbitral independence, see I.C.C. Rule 2(4). *See generally* M. Scott Donahey, *The Independence and Neutrality of Arbitrators*, 9 J. Int'l Arb. 31 (1992). *See also supra* at note 611.

760. *See, e.g.*, Texas Overseas Petroleum Company/California Asiatic Oil Company v. Libyan Arab Republic, award *reprinted in* 17 I.L.M. 1 (1978). The arbitrator had to decide whether the 1974 U.N. Charter of Economic Rights and Duties of States Article 2(2)(c) represented international law, thus giving host state courts exclusive jurisdiction to decide controversies about compensation for expropriated assets.

B. Homogenous Communities and a Heterogeneous World.

1. The Counterpoise of Rules and Justice.

Tightly-knit homogeneous groups often find informal extralegal adjudication more appropriate than legally binding procedures.[761] In such dispute resolution, notions of fairness may be more important than strict application of rules. For example, the diamond industry is reported to rely on social and religious links, including a "Diamond Dealers Club" that functions like a Jewish mutual aid society, providing its members with kosher restaurants, a synagogue and neighborhood visits to sick members.[762] Even within such tightly-knit communities, however, there may be occasional calls for legally binding dispute resolution.[763]

When contracting partners are not repeat players from homogeneous groups, however, they can be expected to look for a more objective approach to dispute resolution. In a heterogeneous world, lack of reasonable certainty regarding the applicable norms will rarely enhance cross-border commerce, finance, or investment. While some deals may be consummated without regard to the competent forum and applicable law, others will not.[764] A banker and a borrower will both want to know how the loan agreement, pledge or third party guarantee will be enforced. Depositors will want to know when their monies will be repayable.[765] Neither the lender nor the borrower will want disputes resolved according to an adjudicator's intuitive sense of fairness. Rather, they desire reasonably precise rules to guide decisionmakers about applicable community norms and values.[766] The users of any dispute resolution system can generally be expected to seek balance in their adjudicatory frameworks,[767] resisting dra-

---

761. *See* Jerold Auerbach, JUSTICE WITHOUT LAW (1983), and discussion of religious dispute resolution *supra* note 16.

762. *See* Lisa Bernstein, *Opting Out of the Legal System: Extralegal Contractual Relations in the Diamond Industry*, 21 J. Legal Studies 115 (1992), at 138-43.

763. Professor Bernstein writes that Diamond Dealers Club arbitration "awards can only be vacated for procedural irregularities" (*Id.* at 125, and cases at n. 24), implying that courts may sometimes be called upon to recognize that DDC arbitration is legally binding on the merits of the case.

764. Of course, parties to international contracts sometimes do compromise on a forum or governing law without a great deal of research on how their choices will affect the outcomes in the spectrum of possible controversies. When getting ready to sign a contract after long discussions about price and delivery terms, haggling over a future disputes clause often seems a bit like planning for divorce at a wedding.

765. *See* Libyan Arab Foreign Bank v. Bankers Trust [1988] Lloyd's L. Rep. 259 (decided 1987).

766. *See generally* Detlev F. Vagts, *Dispute Resolution Mechanism in International Business*, 203 Recueil des Cours (Hague Academy) 19 (1987) (citing M. Weber, GENERAL ECONOMIC HISTORY 277 (F. Knight trans. 1966)).

767. *See generally* Eric Robine, *What Companies Expect of International Commercial Arbitration*, 9 J. Int'l Arb'n (No. 2) 31 (1992). For a more general discussion of the relationship of the legal process to the distribution of "the things people want," see Harold D. Lasswell & Myres S. McDougal, *Criteria for a Theory About Law*, 44 S. Cal. L. Rev. 362, 388-90 (1971). *See also* W. Michael Reisman & A. Schreiber, JURISPRUDENCE: UNDERSTANDING AND SHAPING LAW 1-20 (1987).

matic alteration in the risk calculus of commercial or financial transactions, while at the same time recognizing that concerns related to fairness and vital community interests may sometimes trump otherwise applicable rules.[768]

2. Good Faith and Fairness.

While no company opts for an unfair result applied to itself, it is rarely possible to predict in advance of the dispute who will get the rough side of the law. In the words put into the mouth of Adam Bede, "There's no rules so wise, but what it's a pity for somebody or other."[769] When legal rules lead to a result that an observer sees as inappropriate to a particular case, the rules are juxtaposed to concepts of good faith and fairness that reach toward general notions of what is right.[770]

Good faith and fairness are sometimes invoked to justify the disregard of the contractually designated forum or law.[771] Such notions have emotional and philosophic overtones that appeal to commands of morality or ethics beyond (or in conflict with) those expressed in court decisions and statutes. Courts often fill gaps in commercial agreements by implying a requirement that the parties execute their obligation in good faith,[772] or limit exercise of contract rights in bad faith. The concept of good faith is

768. Michael Reisman has reminded us that "[m]uch as lawyers cannot practice law without clients, so international tribunals cannot decide disputes without litigants. Litigants come on an entirely voluntary basis and have no reason to come to an uncontrolled process." W. Michael Reisman, SYSTEMS OF CONTROL, *supra* note 2, at 2-3.

769. George Eliot, ADAM BEDE (Signet Classics Edition, 1981), page 506. The background for Adam's jurisprudential foray was the decision of the Wesleyan (Methodist) Conference, during the first decade of the 19th century, to restrict preaching by women, who of course included his wife Dinah. Unlike her brother-in-law Seth, who wanted to leave the Wesleyans over the issue and join a body "that 'ud put no bonds on Christian liberty," Dinah submitted to denominational discipline and limited herself to "other sorts o' teaching."

770. Some religious thinkers have argued that even God's own laws are overbroad. *See* Richard Wurmbrand, SERMONS IN SOLITARY CONFINEMENT 16 (1969): "No law can be righteous, even if it is divine, because every law fixes equal standards for men of unequal abilities, who are put in unequal situations." Wurmbrand complains that the commandment "Honor your father and your mother" is given to those whose fathers are good men as well as to those whose fathers beat them unjustly. "Thou shalt not commit adultery" is said to a man who has a loving wife as well as to one whose spouse is unbearable.

771. *See generally*, E. Allen Farnsworth, CONTRACTS (2d ed. 1990), at 550-59; E. Allan Farnsworth, *Good Faith Performance and Commercial Reasonableness Under the Uniform Commercial Code*, 30 U. Chi. L. Rev. 666 (1963); Robert Summers, *Good Faith in General Contract Law and the Sales Provisions of the Uniform Commercial Code*, 54 Va. L. Rev. 195 (1968); *Symposium on Good Faith in the Law*, 16 William Mitchell L. Rev. 1105 (No. 5, 1990). *See also* Charles Fried, CONTRACT AS PROMISE: A THEORY OF CONTRACTUAL OBLIGATION (1981), at 74-91; discussion of *lex mercatoria*, *supra* at notes 314-30.

772. *See* RESTATEMENT (2D) CONTRACTS § 205: "Every contract imposes upon each party a duty of good faith and fair dealing in its performance and its enforcement." Cf. UCC § 2-103, imposing a duty of good faith that includes "observance of reasonable commercial standards of fair dealing in the trade."

perhaps most useful when a contract gives one party wide discretionary power.[773] On occasion the party-chosen law itself may incorporate imprecise terms such as good faith or fair play,[774] giving a judge or an arbitrator greater latitude to excuse performance or award damages notwithstanding the otherwise applicable rule.[775]

To the extent that commercial law lags behind standards shared by the business community, a requirement of good faith may occasionally promote the parties' expectations. However, to infuse contract enforcement with too much of a fairness requirement may chill rather than foster cooperative international wealth creation. In a contract between sophisticated merchants, a court's exercise of discretion[776] in order to refuse enforcement of a forum selection clause that the court considers unfair will usually run counter to both sides' *ex ante* expectations, no matter how distant the designated forum. To condition enforcement of forum selection agreements on the good faith of their execution may add fairness in some cases while reducing it in others.[777]

Some scholars have gone further than good faith, to suggest that law should

---

773. *See, e.g.,* Tymshare v. Covell, 727 F.2d 1145 (D.C. Cir. 1984). Although compensation agreement of computer timesharing service permitted discretionary retroactive changes in sales quotas, such discretion was not unlimited; company could not exercise discretion in such a way as to deprive representative of fair benefits for labor.

774. For example, in the emerging case law on lender liability, the banker may be held to an ill-defined standard of "fair play." *See* G.L. Blanchard, Lender Liability: Law, Practice & Prevention (1991); D.R. Fischel, *The Economics of Lender Liability,* 99 Yale L.J. 131 (1989); David L. Johnson & Terrence J. Gaffney, *Lender Liability: Perspectives on Risk and Prevention,* 105 Banking L.J. 325 (1988).

775. There may be a particular temptation to excuse nonperformance because of dramatic market fluctuations in long-term contracts for the supply of natural resources. *See generally* Wolfgang Peter, Arbitration and Renegotiations of International Investment Agreements (1986); Clayton P. Gillette, *Commercial Rationality and the Duty to Adjust Long-Term Contracts,* 69 Minn. L. Rev. 521 (1985); Robert E. Scott, *Conflict and Cooperation in Long-Term Contracts,* 75 Cal. L. Rev. 2005 (1987); Richard E. Speidel, *Court Imposed Price Adjustments Under Long-Term Supply Contracts,* 76 N.W. U. L. Rev. 369 (1981).

776. For a more general discussion of the role of discretion in the law, see Kenneth Davis, Discretionary Justice: A Preliminary Inquiry (1969).

777. *See* Clayton P. Gillette, *Limitations on the Obligation of Good Faith,* 1981 Duke L.J. 619, 649-64 (1981). "Superficially, it appears that good faith, however defined, is consistent with the objectives of a certain, predictable corpus of commercial law. To the extent that good faith fosters promise-keeping, commercial actors can rely more readily on each other's forthcoming performance....Existence of an enforceable good faith principle that discourages breach presumably reduces the uncertainty of performance and the costs of uncertainty." *Id.* at 651. Professor Gillette adds, however, that an "expansive definition of good faith [may] serve as a source of uncertainty if it permits judicial modification of legal rules relied on in the parties' contractual arrangements [which is] likely to increase risks and raise costs at the contract formation stage." *See also* Clayton P. Gillette, *Commercial Relationships and the Selection of Default Rules for Remote Risks,* 19 J. Legal Studies 535 (1990).

encourage "regard for a neighbor's interest."[778] Such an inherently chameleon-like concept is unlikely to prove useful in meeting the long-term needs of cross-border business, and will provide little predictability in evaluating risks relevant to commercial choices.[779] Those familiar with the original story of the Good Samaritan know how a lawyer's simple question ("Who is my neighbor"[780]) has vexed jurists,[781] psychiatrists[782] and theologians for almost two thousand years, principally because the interests of one neighbor often will run counter to the needs of another.[783]

In some cases, of course, the adjudicator may have no choice but to rebel against fidelity to the parties' expectations. Illicit arms-shipments, the sale of illegal drugs, or contracts procured by bribery, all invite conscience-based refusal to enforce bargains. Conscience challenges objectivity[784] most strikingly when the adjudicator's moral

778. *See* Duncan Kennedy, *Form and Substance in Private Law Adjudication,* 89 Harv. L. Rev. 1685 (1976) ("The law is certain when not the bad man but the *good* man is secure in the expectation that if he goes forward in good faith with due regard for his neighbor's interest as well as his own, and a suspicious eye to the temptations of greed, then the law will not turn up as a dagger in his back."). *Id.* at 1774.

779. Developing countries that seek "fairer" prices for their own exports rarely pay above-market prices for materials produced by poorer neighbors. *See* William W. Park, *Legal Issues in the Third World's Economic Development,* 61 B.U. L. Rev. 1321, 1330-32 (1981) (suggesting that "equity" may become an excuse for opportunistic programs of "he takes who can"). The author knows of a lawyer who was once consulted in an author/publisher dispute governed by an arbitration clause providing for application of "Biblical principles of the Old and New Testaments." Needless to say, the parties had little idea of their respective rights and duties.

780. *See* the account Luke 10: 25-37.

781. THE GOOD SAMARITAN AND THE LAW (J. Ratcliffe, ed., 1981). For an example of a criminal codification of the duty to rescue one's neighbor, see French Code pénal article 63: "Sera puni ... quiconque s'abstient volontairement de porter à une personne en péril l'assistance que, sans risque pour lui ni pour les tiers, il pouvait lui prêter, soit par son action personnelle, soit en provoquant un secours." For a classic tort law context in which courts had to determine which persons benefitted from a duty of care, see the House of Lords 3-2 split in Donoghue v. Stevenson, [1932] A.C. 562.

782. Françoise Dolto has reminded us of the perils of identifying with the helper rather than the needy. Françoise Dolto, L'EVANGILE AU RISQUE DE LA PSYCHANALYSE 143-74 (1977).

783. For example, tariffs that help the poor in Detroit may inflict great harm on those even poorer in Mexico.

784. *Compare* Aviam Soifer, *Is the Personal Partial?: Encumbered Judges and the Judicial Oath,* PAPER PRESENTED AT CONFERENCE ON JEWS AND THE LAW IN THE UNITED STATES, Madison Wisconsin, Nov. 1991 (1992 Draft). Soifer writes, "Judges fail when they are . . . so detached they begin to think they can fly above the communities that still encumber them as well as all the rest of us."

concerns have a religious aspect.[785] Loan recovery,[786] interest,[787] and fair prices[788] are the objects of specific Biblical economic injunctions.[789] While it may seem far-fetched that religious belief could enter an economic context, the worldwide rise of fundamentalism,[790] as well as an increased concern for economic justice among more mainline religious denominations,[791] should make scholars think hard about the problematic role of an adjudicator's private principles.[792]

C. Fidelity to Shared Expectations.[793]

As cooking usually comes before cookbooks, so practice ought to precede theory. In practice, economic cooperation rests upon a measure of confidence that an adjudicator will be relatively faithful to the parties' *ex ante* shared expectations. Business man-

785. *See* Stephen Carter on the problematic nature of resting judicial decisions on moral understandings. Stephen Carter, *The Religiously Devout Judge*, 64 Notre Dame L. Rev. 832 (1989): "The ideal of the objective judge was slain by the legal realists long before the critical legal studies movement resurrected it in order to kill it again. But the ghost of the objective judge refuses to go away.... [O]nce a judge's moral understanding is permitted to play a role, the liberal argument cannot distinguish religiously based knowledge from other moral knowledge, or at least, cannot do so without arguments that require a bit too much cognitive dissonance." *Id.* at 944. *See generally*, Stephen Carter, THE CULTURE OF DISBELIEF (1993).

786. *See* Luke 6:35 ("Lend expecting nothing.")

787. *See* Leviticus 25:36-37; Abraham Weingort, INTERET ET CRÉDIT DANS LE DROIT TALMUDIQUE (Paris 1979); Jacques Legoff, LA BOURSE ET LA VIE (Paris 1986).

788. *See* Leviticus 25:14. On the doctrine of unjust price in Jewish law, see Meir Tamari, WITH ALL YOUR POSSESSIONS: JEWISH ETHICS AND ECONOMIC LIFE 97 (1987). On the Medieval Christian analogue, see Harold Joseph Berman, LAW AND REVOLUTION 245 (1983); Harold Joseph Berman, *The Religious Sources of General contract Law: An Historical Perspective*, 4 J. Law & Rel. 103 (1986).

789. *See* William W. Park, *Spiritual Energy and Secular Power*, *in* THE INFLUENCE OF RELIGION ON THE DEVELOPMENT OF INTERNATIONAL LAW 171 (Mark Janis ed., 1990).

790. *See* Martin Martin and R. Scott Appleby, THE GLORY AND THE POWER (1992).

791. *See* UNITARIAN-UNIVERSALIST ASSOCIATION GENERAL ASSEMBLY 1993 RESOLUTION ON ECONOMIC RIGHTS AND RESPONSIBILITIES. *See also* CHRISTIAN FAITH AND ECONOMIC LIFE (A.C. Smock, ed.), prepared for the 17th Grand Synod, United Church of Christ (1987); THE DEBT CRISIS AND THE THIRD WORLD (World Council of Churches Commission on Churches' Participation in Development, 1986).

792. *See also* Suzanne Stone, *In Pursuit of the Counter-Text: The Turn to the Jewish Legal Model in Contemporary American Legal Theory*, 106 Harv. L. Rev. 813 (1993), arguing that no secular theory of justice can serve the function of the divine hierarchy in Jewish law.

793. On legal predictability and economic development, see Detlev Vagts, *Dispute Resolution Mechanisms in International Business*, 203 Recueil des Cours 18-21 (Hague Academy of International Law 1987) ("The writings of Max Weber are taken to show the linkage between capitalist rationality and a legal system that provides stability and predictability. Such a system is contrasted with a "kadi" system in which decisions are handed down under a shade tree according to the momentary impulses of the kadi." *Id.* at 19.); *see also* Sally Ewing, *Formal Justice and the Spirit of Capitalism: Max Weber's Sociology of Law*, 21 Law and Society Rev. 487 (1987).

agers usually enter into commercial agreements because they assume that performance according to contract terms will bring a profit. They agree to rules as an accepted calculus of justice, even though those rules may lead to disagreeable consequences when the rough contours of controversy reveal themselves.

Neutrality as an aspirational model in business adjudication enhances certainty in the application of substantive legal norms, which in turn promotes economic cooperation by increasing confidence that effort and risk will be rewarded. While business managers' *post*-dispute concern is to win the litigation, their *pre*-dispute planning calls for a reasonably unbiased dispute resolution mechanism.[794] An American buyer and an Algerian seller will both want to maximize litigation certainty with a contract provision for "I.C.C. arbitration in London" (or some other such forum selection clause), regardless of how much one side realizes *after* a dispute arises that London arbitration reduces room for maneuver.

While absolute legal predictability may be neither possible nor welcome, legal risks do affect the commercial desirability of business cooperation. The worse the legal system that will hear a potential dispute, the greater must be the payoff to justify the investment.[795] Agreements for economic cooperation are valued in part because their performance takes place in the shadow of potentially coercive measures pursuant to decisions of authoritative adjudicators.[796]

Imagine for a moment a world lacking any relatively predictable mechanism to enforce the basic elements of an international business relationship. While some transactions might be consummated even without reliable adjudicatory régimes, others would not. In those cases where business ventures are concluded notwithstanding the lack of an adjudicatory mechanism, the absence of effective sanctions for poor performance can be expected to lead to sloppier contract execution, or increased prices to include an "adjudicatory risk premium."

Productive commercial cooperation rests in part on reliable dispute resolution.[797] Although inter-personal trust certainly plays a substantial part in finance,

---

794. To take another example, when applied to a transaction on the high seas, the laws of a maritime nation such as England commend themselves as more certain than the understandably less developed maritime law of a land-locked country. *See* discussion *supra* at notes 752-57.

795. Professor Vagts suggests, for example, that "a country can enjoy a rather bad reputation among lawyers and still attract investors if it possesses a large and readily accessible deposit of a rare and useful mineral." *Id.* at 20.

796. The concept of "law" and its analogues in languages other than English ties together bundles of norms and moral claims whose common denominator could be capaciously defined as an authoritative process for resolving disagreements. *See* W. Michael Reisman, *Criteria for Use of Force in International Law*, 10 Yale J. Int'l L. 279 (1985). ("Law is made where . . . the more effective members of the group concerned impose [on a disagreement] their vision of common interest.") *Id.* at 279. *See generally*, W. Michael Reisman & Aaron Schreiber, JURISPRUDENCE 269-305 (1987); Frederick Schauer, PLAYING BY THE RULES (1991). *Compare* Alfred Rubin, *Enforcing the Rules of International Law*, 34 Harv. Int. L.J. 149 (1993).

797. *See* Richard Posner, LAW AND ECONOMICS (4th ed.), whose theory of contract enforcement derives from concepts of market wealth maximization and efficiency. Posner builds on

lenders usually extend credit[798] and depositors usually place savings with banks[799] on the assumption that they will have recourse to a non-biased adjudicator in the event of disagreement.[800]

The predicament of developing countries highlights the significance of dependable judicial systems to economic development.[801] Economic advancement generally proceeds best in a legal environment in which business disputes are decided with relative predictability, and where combatants in the commercial arena benefit from equal access to courts. Growth in many developing country capital markets has been inhibited by political instability and the resulting uncertainty about effective vindication of legal rights in these nations.[802] Capital tends to flee places where governments impose confiscatory exchange controls.[803] Debt moratoria and expropriation without effective compensation chill wealth-creating investment and technology transfer to the detriment of the host country as well as the investor.[804]

Note 797, continued

Ronald Coase's article *The Problem of Social Costs*, 3 J. Law & Econ. 1 (1960). In the well-known hypothetical about train sparks hurting farm crops, the Coase theorem says that initial allocation of legal entitlements will not matter if parties among themselves can bargain for a cost-effective way to prevent reduction in economic value: spark-catching equipment for the railroad, or the farmer's planting crops far enough from the tracks to avoid the sparks.

798. For a discussion of the risk-related variables in cross-border lending, see William W. Park, *L'arbitrage et le recouvrement des prêts consentis à des débiteurs étrangers*, 37 McGill L.J. 375 (1992).

799. For a recent analysis of international lending and Eurodollar deposits that incorporates such analysis, see Rachel Gerstenhaber, *Freezer Burn: United States Extraterritorial Freeze Orders and the Case for Efficient Risk Allocation*, 140 U. Penn. L. Rev. 2333 (1992). Gerstenhaber looks at risk-return tradeoffs in Eurodollar deposits, and notes that banks "bribe" depositors to assume greater political risks by paying higher interest rates. *Id.* at 2374-75.

800. Lawyers dealing with commercial loan documentation have noted the negative effects of denying dispositive effect to forum selection clauses. *See* discussion of *Stewart v. Ricoh,* in Perry B. Newman, *Forum Selection Clauses in Commercial Loan Documents: Unimpeachable or Unenforceable?* 107 Banking L.J. 547 (1990). The author counsels that lenders should ensure that their chosen forum satisfies a host of criteria related to convenience, relative congestion of the transferee and transferor court dockets, relative bargaining power, governing law, and situs of activities giving rise to the underlying claim. *Id.* at 557, referring to the standards for transfer enumerated in Advent Elecs. v. Samsung Semiconductor, 709 F. Supp. 843 (N.D. Ill. 1989).

801. *See generally,* William W. Park, *Legal Policy Conflicts in International Banking,* 50 Ohio State L.J. 1067 (1989).

802. For a study of one country's dilemma, see Ikomi Ngongi, PRIVATIZATION IN CAMEROON: LEGAL AND INSTITUTIONAL PREREQUISITES (1991).

803. *See generally* William W. Park, *Legal Policy Conflicts in International Banking,* 50 Ohio State L.J. 1067 (1989).

804. For another concrete example, Latin American mutual funds receive high yields because the risk is high. *See* Gould, *Not for the Faint at Heart: Latin Funds Yielding 11%,* International Herald Tribune, 14 Dec. 1992, at 15, col. 1 noting that risk factors for Latin American government securities included coup attempts, defaults and policy shifts on negotiation with the IMF.

Few commercial actors will be happy buying the proverbial pig in a poke. Adjudicatory neutrality promotes economic cooperation because a relatively neutral judge or arbitrator can be counted on to respect the expectations shared by the parties at the time their bargain was struck, rather than the *ex post facto* desires of one party when the deal has gone sour. In the world's culturally diverse transnational business community, a handshake assurance that "we'll treat each other fairly" will not long be adequate to encourage the type of commercial activity that increases global well-being. Credit will be extended at higher rates (or not at all) if lenders are unsure of a loan agreement's enforceability. Entrepreneurs will be less apt to commit time and resources to a project without some assurance that specifications will be met, supply contracts honored and construction projects performed.[805]

Greater risks must be justified by greater returns. Therefore litigation uncertainty will often determine a business manager's choice of one investment over another. Imagine that an American merchant has an opportunity for a profit of $100 in Ruritania, where the merchant sees a fifty percent chance of a fair hearing to enforce the contract in the event of a dispute, or a profit of $70 in London, where the American perceives there to be a near certainty of a fair hearing. The business manager will likely choose the less profitable but more secure English investment. Even if the expected return is only $50 in London, risk-averse business managers may chose the more predictable London venture because of the inherent value of lower aggregate disruption: a guarantee of $50 will be more attractive than a fifty percent chance of receiving $100.[806]

In an international context an academic celebration of indeterminacy will make little sense. The productive activity that increasingly involves cooperation between people from different parts of the globe requires confidence that cross-border business disputes will be settled by reference to the parties' shared *ex ante* expectations. Although these shared expectations will contain gaps no matter how well memorialized, the parties will usually hope (at least at the time of contract signature) that the gaps will be

---

805. Even academics who delight in ambiguity would be skeptical of a teaching post without the assurance of a fixed paycheck at the end of the month. On the other hand, financial predictability may be neither necessary nor sufficient to move a pastor to preach a sermon, a true scholar to write an article, or a patriot to fight for the homeland.

806. *See generally* discussion of risk in Richard A. Posner, Economic Analysis of Law 12-13 (4th ed. 1992); Charles Goetz, Cases and Materials on Law and Economics, 76-79 (1984); Note, *Settling for Less: Applying Law and Economics to Poor People,* 107 Harvard L. Rev. 442 (1993); A. Mitchell Polinsky, *Risk Sharing Through Breach of Contract Remedies,* 12 J. Leg. Stud. 427 (1983); Mark Machina and Michael Rothchild, *Risk, in* Utility and Probability — The New Palgrave Dictionary of Economics (J. Eatwell, M. Milgate, & P. Newman eds. 1990), at 277.

807. The value of fidelity to shared contract expectations also presents itself in basic concepts of res judicata and issue preclusion. To recognize an arbitrator's award against someone who was never a party to the arbitration would seem to deny one party's legitimate expectation that a court rather than an arbitrator interpret the sale contract. Nevertheless, courts have sometimes allowed issue preclusion effect to awards when the non-party's interests were "ade-

filled by relatively neutral adjudicators applying reasonably determinate rules.[807]

A vignette about a young lawyer faced with a career choice might illustrate the contrast between an aspiration to neutral adjudication based on relatively determinate rules, and a free-style model of decision-making based only on notions of fairness. One friend cautioned the lawyer against letting past experiences determine future choices: "We can never build tomorrow on the assumption of yesterday's permanence. Life's only true security lies in learning to celebrate uncertainty." Another equally close friend replied rhetorically, "If we cannot build the future on the past, then on what can we ever build it?"

Each friend was correct, although each insight pushed to excess would have become unworkable. In law and in life, a neutral application of past precedents will not always determine what we shall get, let alone what we shall or should want. However, an absence of certainty can be a cure worse than the malady. The ill effects of rule-based reliability must be weighed against the injury from an adjudicatory system that permits little ability to predict the future. The jurisprudential lesson of international forum selection is that when a reasonable measure of certainty and impartiality do not exist, they will need to be invented.

Note 807, continued

> quately represented" in the arbitration. *See e.g.*, Universal American Barge Corp. v. J. Chem Inc., 946 F.2d 1131 (5th Cir. 1991). On the effect of arbitration agreements on non-signatories, see discussion *supra* at notes 440-44. On issue preclusion generally, see Colin Buckley, *Issue Preclusion and Issues of Law: A Doctrinal Framework Based on Rules of Recognition, Jurisdiction and Legal History*, 24 Hous. L. Rev. 875 (1987); Gerard Sanders, *Rethinking Arbitral Preclusion*, 24 Law & Policy Int. Bus. 101 (1992). For a different perspective on non-party preclusion, see Robert G. Bone, *Rethinking the Day in Court Ideal and Nonparty Preclusion*, 67 N.Y.U. L. Rev. 193, 236-87 (1992).

Chapter VIII

WHENCE AND WHITHER?

The values that justify forum selection agreements in international business often call them into question in domestic transactions. In cross-border contracts, arbitration and jurisdiction clauses permit parties from different countries to reduce the prospect of biased adjudication. In a domestic context, however, forum selection agreements often appear in the fine print of a standard form contract that serves to maneuver an ill-informed consumer into a court which may be neither accessible to the consumer nor sensitive to mandatory community norms. Waiver of a consumer's right to litigate in an accessible forum will rarely be justified by reasons as compelling as the special need for neutrality in international litigation.

Western European legal systems generally have been more vigorous than the United States in reconciling the tension between the business community's desire for adjudicatory certainty and society's concern to protect its commercially weaker members from abusive forum selection. Treaties and statutes in Europe give jurisdiction clauses dispositive effect in international business contracts, while establishing a separate régime for domestic transactions in which consumers benefit from a non-waivable right to litigate in courts at their domicile.

The time has come to bring the European models of court selection law across the Atlantic in the form of a federal court selection act. The Act would give jurisdiction clauses much the same force as now accorded to arbitration agreements, but deny enforcement to pre-dispute jurisdiction clauses in consumer contracts unless they give the consumer a right to sue and to be sued in courts at the consumer's residence. The statute would exclude from its scope contracts entirely between American citizens and/or residents. In addition, the United States should attempt to negotiate a network of judgments treaties, limited in scope to the enforcement of court decisions based on valid jurisdiction clauses. These measures will both enhance predictability in international commercial dispute resolution and protect consumers against ill-informed waiver of their right to seek justice before accessible tribunals.

A. An International Court Selection Act.[808]

American courts should be required by federal statute to honor international jurisdiction clauses without regard to the convenience of the alternative fora. When at least one party to a court-selection agreement is a citizen of a country other than the United States,[809] the statute would mandate that courts in the United States stay actions inconsistent with the choice-of-court clause. A federal court selection statute along the lines set forth in Appendix C would preempt inconsistent state legislation in the same fashion as the Federal Arbitration Act now generally preempts more restrictive state arbitration law.

In addition, federal courts designated under an international jurisdiction clause should be prohibited from declining to hear cases on *forum non conveniens* grounds as long as one party to the controversy is a United States citizen or the dispute raises a federal question. Both of these criteria would supply a nexus consistent with Article III of the United States Constitution.[810] States would be left free to decide whether or not to follow the example of New York in likewise limiting judicial discretion to refuse to hear a case.[811]

It is tempting to go further and to suggest that federal courts should hear cases notwithstanding the absence of a federal question or an American party, at least if the law of a political subdivision of the United States applies to the controverted transaction. Judicial determination of state law cases would enrich not only legal development, but also members of the bar called to render opinions and argue cases. A statute of such broad scope, however, might raise constitutional difficulties related to subject matter jurisdiction in a suit between two aliens not based on a federal ques-

---

808. For a parallel initiative aimed at rationalizing domestic forum selection, see Patrick Borchers, *Forum Selection Agreements in the Federal Courts after Carnival Cruise,* 67 Wash. L. Rev. 55, 107 (1992).

809. There would seem to be no need for a more expansive coverage of contracts exclusively among American residents, even if the contracts implicate international commerce. The other side's courts should not be that frightening when the other party can be sued in the United States. *Compare* coverage of New York Arbitration Convention under 9 U.S.C. § 202.

810. These criteria would not impose on federal courts an obligation to hear cases exclusively between aliens in the absence of a federal question. While the requirement of "complete" diversity does not rise to Constitutional dimensions (*see* Ed and Fred v. Puritan Marine Ins., 506 F.2d 757, 758 (1st Cir. 1975)), the presence of an alien as an indispensable party on both sides of a dispute may at present defeat jurisdiction even as between citizens. *See* Faysoud v. United Coconut Chems., 878 F.2d 279 (9th Cir. 1989). *Compare* Allendale Mutual Ins. Co. v. Bull Data Systems, 10 F.3d 425 (7th Cir. 1993), discussed *supra* at note 154, permitting a suit between aliens as long as citizens of different states are on opposite sides of the litigation. Since the model statute would not apply to disputes *entirely* between or among American citizens, the existence of at least one American citizen as a party would meet the requirement of minimal diversity of citizenship.

811. An attempt by Congress to force state courts to decide cases might raise Constitutional quibbles. Cf. Testa v. Katt, 330 U.S. 586 (1947), holding that state courts may not decline enforcement of federal statutory rights on local policy grounds.

tion. While an argument could be made that the international court selection statute might in itself serve as a source of wider federal subject matter jurisdiction, in much the same manner as do the New York Arbitration Convention and the Foreign Sovereign Immunities Act,[812] there would seem to be no compelling reason for the United States to push its court selection mandates that far. The benefit derived from foreign fees for American lawyers would have to be weighed against the cost of greater strain on judicial resources.

The statute should exclude pre-dispute jurisdiction clauses in consumer transactions unless the clause gives consumers an option to sue and to be sued at their residence.[813] Only *after* the dispute arises, when specific claims have been identified, will consumers normally be able to evaluate realistically the costs and benefits of a proposed forum, much as they would consider a settlement offer.

The consumer protection provisions of the statute should probably be limited territorially (at least through judicial construction) to consumer transactions with a significant relationship with an American forum. A foreign company actively soliciting American residents to take Mediterranean vacation cruises should not be able to require disputes to be settled in Paris. On the other hand, New Englanders studying in Paris who go to a Champs-Elysées travel agent to buy train tickets to Vienna should normally not be able to claim a right of recourse to American courts merely by virtue of domicile or citizenship,[814] at least until the United States concludes a comprehensive jurisdiction and judgments treaty providing reciprocity for consumer protection measures.

As an alternative way to protect consumer interests, the statute's scope could be

---

812. *See* Bergesen v. Muller, 710 F.2d 928 (2d Cir. 1983) and Verlinden v. Cent. Bank of Nig., 461 U.S. 480 (1983). In *Verlinden* suit between Dutch and Nigerian parties was based on federal question jurisdiction under the 1976 Foreign Sovereign Immunities Act. In *Bergesen*, jurisdiction in a dispute between Norwegian and Swiss companies was founded on Chapter II of the Federal Arbitration Act (9 U.S.C. §§ 203 and 207), implementing the New York Arbitration Convention. In a domestic case, however, the Federal Arbitration Act does not confer jurisdiction on federal courts. *See* Garrett v. Merrill Lynch Pierce Fenner & Smith, 7 F.3d 882 (9th Cir. 1993) (motion to vacate arbitration award for arbitrator bias dismissed for lack of subject matter jurisdiction); Harry Hoffman Printing v. Graphic Communications International Union, 912 F.2d 608 (2d Cir. 1990) (dismissal of employers' petition to vacate award in collective bargaining dispute, pursuant to both § 301 of the Labor Management Relations Act and § 10 of the Federal Arbitration Act).

813. Such a clause would at least meet one objective of the dominant party, by limiting forum shopping options. Forum selection would be rationalized to some extent, even if not perfectly. *Compare* UNIFORM COMMERCIAL CODE Article 2A-106. If the forum chosen in a consumer lease "would not otherwise have jurisdiction over the lessee," the choice is not enforceable. *Id.* § 106(2).

814. Some countries, of course, do give their citizens a right of recourse to their courts on the basis of nationality. See French *Code civil* Article 14: "L'étranger, même non résident en France, pourra être cité devant les tribunaux français pour l'éxecution des obligations par lui contractées [en France ou en pays étranger] avec un français." Even in France, however, this right to French courts can be waived through a forum selection clause. *See* Civ. 1re, 25 novembre 1986, Rev. trim. dr. civ. 1987, 548, with commentary by Mestre.

limited to contracts between merchants and other professionals acting in the capacity of their trade or business.[815] Such measures would enhance the values of predictability, reliability and neutrality, while reducing the countervailing danger that abusively imposed prorogation agreements would impair fundamental rights of a party with little realistic bargaining power.[816]

B. Modest Treaties.

As discussed in Chapter II, the United States has been unsuccessful in concluding even a single judgments treaty. The explanation for this surprising situation lies principally in foreign fears of American tort judgments and the extraterritorial application of United States economic regulation.

To maximize the effectiveness of a federal court selection statute, the United States should seek to negotiate a treaty network that enforces foreign judgments to the same extent as arbitration awards. In the best of all worlds, one might hope for American accession to a comprehensive multilateral treaty on civil and commercial jurisdiction and judgments along the lines of some provisions of the Bruxelles and Lugano Conventions discussed earlier.[817] However, a more realistic approach would focus on a judgments treaty of modest scope, covering only court decisions based on the parties' consent in the form of a forum selection clause. Pre-dispute jurisdiction clauses in consumer transactions could presumably be excluded from the scope of such treaties, as suggested for the international court selection act discussed earlier. Such a treaty would enhance confidence that jurisdiction clauses would be effective, while raising fewer fears of "unreasonable" judgments against non-American corporations unwillingly hauled before a civil jury in contingency-fee driven tort litigation.

C. Costs and Benefits.

Although the Federal Arbitration Act and the New York Arbitration Convention already give contracting parties one way to select a neutral adjudicator, international commercial actors cannot always get what they want from arbitration. While some business managers may be willing to run the risk of having an arbitrator split the difference between the parties, others will want their cases heard by trained national

815. Such a limitation would require the elaboration of concepts of "merchant" and "professional," similar to those prevailing in Continental legal systems. *See* discussion *supra* at notes 705-17.

816. Consumer agreements with foreign suppliers will be relatively rare, and will usually be concluded with the supplier's domestic branch or subsidiary, thus permitting the transaction to be characterized as domestic. For example, a Massachusetts resident's deposit with the Boston branch of a British bank should not be treated differently than a deposit with a New England financial institution.

817. *See* Chapter VI, *supra*, as well as the critique of the Lugano Convention by Professor von Mehren at *supra* note 615.

judges in proceedings with constitutional safeguards and subject to appellate review.[818] Not all wealth-creating ventures that rely on cross-border cooperation will go forward if arbitration clauses remain the only dispositive dispute resolution mechanism.[819]

In domestic and consumer transactions a case can be made for allowing judges broad discretion in enforcement of jurisdiction clauses, looking to the convenience of the chosen forum in the particular case. Permitting courts to weigh multiple factors bearing on the fairness of a contractually stipulated court arguably fosters a fairer adjudicatory process than does a rigid deference to a contract's prorogation clause.[820] In consumer transactions, the danger that a jurisdiction clause could be imposed on a take-it-or-leave-it basis might even justify denying the enforceability of such clauses altogether on public policy grounds, since the right to present one's case in an accessible court arguably should be non-waivable unless justified by some reason as compelling as the need for neutrality in international dispute resolution.[821]

In international commercial transactions, however, the harm from potentially abusive prorogation agreements must be balanced against policy concerns not present in domestic litigation. If a Boston seller must sue its buyer in Atlanta (or vice versa) the dispute will take place within a relatively homogeneous linguistic and procedural context. The same cannot always be said of litigation against a seller in a part of the world that does not share the English language or the Federal Rules of Civil Procedure, or where court procedures raise questions of judicial independence to an extent far greater than in the United States. Without the relative jurisdictional certainty that enforceable jurisdiction clauses bring, many economic relationships either will not be consummated or will be concluded at a higher cost.[822] The prospect that economically desirable ventures will be discouraged for want of neutral adjudicatory mechanisms argues for a more hard-and-fast approach, mandating enforcement of otherwise valid jurisdiction clauses in international cases. Given the diverse topography of nearly two hundred national legal systems, the goal of reducing the uncertainty

---

818. *See* Edward Brunet, *Arbitration and Constitutional Rights*, 71 North Carolina L. Rev. 81 (1992).

819. A preference for courts rather than arbitration sometimes results from an information gap and learning costs linked to the legal profession's division of labor. The corporate lawyers who negotiate and draft acquisition contracts or distributorship agreements generally are unfamiliar with the New York Convention.

820. *See* discussion of *forum non conveniens*, *supra* at notes 77-111.

821. Some might even affirm that access to an otherwise competent court is an aspect of human dignity that ought never to be alienable. *See generally* Margaret Radin, *Market-Inalienability*, 100 Harv. L. Rev. 1849 (1987). A different policy should prevail, however, when a concrete dispute has arisen, and the "sale" of the right to trial involves settlement of a defined and proximate claim.

822. In some cases, of course, enforcing a forum selection clause may result in a less neutral forum. For example, Massachusetts courts may be imposed by an economically stronger Massachusetts party. However, allowing freedom to make "bad" contract bargains among sophisticated business managers is the price for the type of private choice that in the aggregate will maximize public welfare.

in cross-border business outweighs the policies behind more flexible domestically-nurtured forum selection rules.[823]

---

823. Countervailing concerns relevant to controverted events with a foreign dimension prevail in other litigation questions. For example, foreign arbitral awards receive judicial confirmation in circumstances even when confirmation of a domestic award would fail. *See* 9 U.S.C. § 207, granting a three year limitation for confirmation of awards under the New York Arbitration Convention. And international arbitrators may decide matters implicating sensitive public policies that would normally be characterized as non-arbitrable in domestic transactions. *See generally,* William W. Park, *National Law and Commercial Justice,* 63 Tulane L. Rev. 647, 699-705 (1989).

Conclusion

The text of a law is often less important than the context of its interpretation. Legal rules by themselves have no power to stop a biased or corrupt judge from rendering a wrong or unjust decision. Therefore choice of forum may determine the outcome of a dispute as much as the applicable substantive law. Particularly in disputes with foreign elements, *who* decides a controversy often matters more than *what* standards purport to be relevant. A cross-border business transaction gone sour will be especially alarming less because of possible quirks in the contract's governing law than because of unfamiliar language, inadequate procedural safeguards and a xenophobic judge.

In business relationships with an international dimension, choice-of-forum agreements can enhance significantly the prospect of fair and predictable dispute resolution. On the other hand, in domestic consumer transactions, boilerplate forum selection clauses frequently defeat the very goal of fair adjudication called to justify such clauses in an international setting. Jurisdiction and arbitration agreements may designate courts and arbitral tribunals which are inaccessible to the consumer, or which give little weight to fundamental public policies of the place of contract performance. The aggregate social and economic consequences of pre-dispute forum selection clauses therefore will depend largely on whether the controverted events arise in a domestic or an international setting.

In international business, a commitment to private arbitration will often outperform an insistence on court litigation, both in reducing the prospect of biased foreign litigation and in maximizing the international currency of honest adjudication. Jurisdiction agreements designating American courts benefit from not a single enforcement treaty, and may prove ineffective when judges are unable or unwilling to allow the parties to thrust jurisdiction upon the court. On the other hand, a multilateral treaty network and a statutory framework mandate enforcement of arbitration agreements and awards in both state and federal courts, while at the same time providing explicit grounds for nonrecognition or annulment of awards obtained in procedurally unfair arbitrations. In addition, arbitrators can usually be found to hear a case if the parties can cover the fees. In some situations, of course, the advantages of arbitration may be overshadowed by a concern for the perceived benefits of court proceedings, such as full appellate review and scrutiny of the decision-making process.

European approaches to forum selection generally do a better job than American law in promoting certainty in cross-border transactions, while at the same time protecting consumers against ill-informed waiver of basic jurisdictional rights. In Western Europe, national statutes and multilateral conventions vest jurisdiction clauses and court judgments with much of the same effect now attaching to arbitral agreements and awards. European law will also generally prohibit jurisdiction clauses that do not give consumers the option to sue and to be sued at their domiciles.

Switzerland's conflict-of-laws code presents a particularly appealing paradigm. Swiss courts must hear cases governed by jurisdiction clauses if one party is a Swiss resident or if the contract is governed by Swiss law. However, Swiss law prohibits what it calls "abusive" prorogation agreements, and invalidates pre-dispute consumer waiver of normal jurisdictional rules, thus reducing the prospect that the fine print of a standard form contract will impose an unfair forum on an unsophisticated commercial bit player.

The Swiss code commends itself as a model for a federal choice-of-court statute to replace the patchwork of American jurisdictional rules. Under the statute proposed in Chapter VIII, courts would stay litigation inconsistent with the parties' jurisdictional choice, and federal courts generally would hear international cases when designated by a valid jurisdiction clause. In consumer transactions, however, consumers would have recourse to courts at their domicile.

A statute mandating enforcement of jurisdiction clauses presumes that people are more likely to commit themselves to productive enterprises when they can predict with relative confidence how controversies will be resolved. Such codification of forum selection law will run counter to much of the progressive dialogue in American conflicts scholarship that has emphasized methodologies giving courts the discretion to seek the "right" result in individual cases.[824] Whatever the benefits of flexible principles within a federal system, a more rule-based approach in international adjudication justifies itself by the special need to reduce bias and enhance certainty of forum in cross-border business adjudication.

Thinking about forum selection in international transactions can also lead to broader insights about the nature of the legal process. The drawbacks of an attempt at neutral application of determinate rules must be weighed against the dramatically disagreeable consequences of infidelity to the contracting parties' shared expectations. Commercial dispute resolution that seeks principally an ideal justice for the particular case at hand may eventually increase legal risks and chill productive economic cooperation. While an absolutely determinate and neutral legal system is neither desirable nor possible, the intelligent balancing of costs and benefits should lead policy makers and attorneys to favor a dispute resolution framework in which adjudicators seek to maximize both predictability and neutrality. If international forum selection teaches legal scholars anything, it should be that certainty and neutrality remain vital aspirational models for authoritative dispute resolution.

---

824. One commentator suggested that a federal conflicts statute would be tantamount to scholasticide, the "truly unpardonable sin." *See* Michael H. Gottesman, *Draining the Dismal Swamp: The Case for Federal Choice of Law Statutes,* 80 Geo. L.J. 1, 51 (1991).

DOCUMENTARY APPENDICES

Appendix A

MODEL JURISDICTION CLAUSE

1. All disputes, differences, controversies or claims arising in connection with, or questions occurring under, this present Agreement, shall be subject to the exclusive jurisdiction of the courts in [_____].
2. With respect to any such action, each party hereby:
   (i) consents to the personal jurisdiction of the above-designated jurisdiction;
   (ii) agrees that venue properly lies in the above-designated jurisdiction;
   (iii) waives any claim that any such action should be dismissed on grounds of inconvenient forum or lack of jurisdiction, or that any such action should be transferred to any court or tribunal outside the above-designated jurisdiction.
3. The parties agree that a final judgment by any court in the above-designated jurisdiction covered by this Agreement shall be conclusive and may be enforced in other jurisdictions in any manner provided by law.
4. The parties hereby waive any claim that a judgment obtained in the above-designated jurisdiction is invalid or unenforceable.
5. This Agreement shall be governed and construed according to the laws of [_____], excluding its choice-of-law principles.

Appendix B

MODEL ARBITRATION CLAUSE

1. All disputes, differences, controversies or claims arising in connection with, or questions occurring under, the present Agreement shall be finally settled under the Rules of Arbitration of [_____] by an arbitral tribunal composed of three arbitrators appointed in accordance with said Rules.

2. Each party shall nominate one arbitrator. If a party fails to nominate an arbitrator within thirty (30) days from the date when the Claimant's Request for Arbitration has been communicated to the other party, such appointment shall be made by [_____].

3. The two arbitrators so appointed shall agree upon the third arbitrator who shall act as Chair of the arbitral tribunal. If said two arbitrators fail to nominate a Chair within forty-five (45) days from the second of the two appointments, the Chair shall be selected by the [_____].

4. In all cases the Chair of the arbitral tribunal shall be a lawyer fluent in English and not of the same nationality as either party.

5. The place of arbitration shall be [_____].

6. The language of the arbitration shall be English.

7. The parties hereby exclude any right of appeal to any court on the merits of the dispute.

8. Judgment on the award may be entered in any court having jurisdiction over the award or any of the parties or their assets.

9. This Agreement shall be governed and construed according to the laws of [_____], provided that any dispute relating to this arbitration agreement shall be governed by the [arbitration law of the arbitral seat]. The award may grant any relief appropriate under the applicable law, including without limitation declaratory relief and/or specific performance. The arbitral tribunal shall not decide in amiable composition.

10. Nothing contained in this arbitration clause shall prevent either party from seeking interim measures of protection in the form of pre-award attachment of assets, nor from seeking injunctive relief to enforce in courts of competent jurisdiction rights covered by Sections [_____] of this Agreement. [Insert appropriate reference to matters such as (i) non-competition obligations and (ii) pledges, mortgages and other security agreements.]

11. In the event that disputes arise under both this present Agreement and the [_____] Contract, such disputes shall be resolved in a consolidated arbitral proceeding by a single arbitrator appointed in accordance with the [___] Rules. The consolidation provisions of [relevant consolidation statute, if any] shall apply, notwithstanding reference to governing law provisions above.

MODEL INTERNATIONAL COURT SELECTION ACT

SECTION 1.

This Act shall apply to an agreement not otherwise null or void which provides that a dispute shall be subject to the jurisdiction of any court, domestic or foreign, except that it shall not apply to:

(a) an agreement in a consumer contract unless
  (i) concluded after the dispute has arisen, or
  (ii) at the consumer's option any action shall be brought in courts located at the consumer's residence;
(b) an agreement procured by fraud, coercion or duress;
(c) an agreement linked to a choice-of-law clause that operates to defeat mandatory policy norms of the place of contract performance; and
(d) an agreement entirely between or among residents and/or citizens of the United States.

SECTION 2.

In any action before a court within the United States, the court in which suit is pending shall stay proceedings upon an issue referable to another court under a jurisdiction agreement to which this Act applies.

SECTION 3.

In any action arising out of a jurisdiction agreement to which this Act applies, no United States district court shall stay or dismiss any action on the ground of inconvenient forum or lack of jurisdiction, nor transfer the venue of an action nor dismiss an action for improper venue, except in a manner consistent with a jurisdiction agreement covered by this Act, provided that:

(a) at least one party is a citizen of the United States; or
(b) the dispute raises a question arising under the laws or treaties of the United States.

SECTION 4.

As used in this Act:

(a) a corporation shall be considered a citizen of the United States if incorporated under the laws of the United States or of any State or if it has its principal place of business within the United States;

(b) an individual shall be considered a resident of the place in which the individual has a principal place of abode;

(c) an alien admitted to the United States for permanent residence shall be deemed a citizen of the United States;

(d) a consumer contract includes any agreement with an individual for the purchase or lease of property, the provision of services or the extension of credit, unless within the scope of that individual's trade, profession or business;

(e) courts at a consumer's residence shall include both state and federal courts of proper venue within the state.

Appendix D

INTERNATIONAL JURISDICTION TREATIES

1. BRUXELLES CONVENTION[1]

European Union:
Convention on Jurisdiction and the Enforcement
of Judgments in Civil and Commercial Matters.

TITLE I: SCOPE

Article 1

This Convention shall apply in civil and commercial matters whatever the nature of the court or tribunal. It shall not exceed, in particular, to revenue, customs or administrative matters.

The Convention shall not apply to:
1. the status or legal capacity of natural persons, rights in property arising out of a matrimonial relationship, wills and succession;
2. bankruptcy, proceedings relating to the winding-up of insolvent companies or other legal persons, judicial arrangements, compositions and analogous proceedings;
3. social security;
4. arbitration.

TITLE II: JURISDICTION

Section 1: General provisions

Article 2

Subject to the provisions of this Convention, persons domiciled in a Contracting State shall, whatever their nationality, be sued in the courts of that State.

---

1. Consolidated and updated version of the Brussels Convention of 1968 and the Protocol of 1971. Reprinted in 29 I.L.M. 1413 (1990).

Persons who are not nationals of the State in which they are domiciled shall be governed by the rulers of jurisdiction applicable to nationals of that State.

Article 3

Persons domiciled in a Contracting State may be sued in the courts of another Contracting State only by virtue of the rules set out in Sections 2 to 6 of this Title. In particular the following provisions shall not be applicable against them:
— in Belgium: Article 15 of the civil code (Code civil — Burgerlijk Wetboek) and Article 638 of the judicial code (Code judiciaire — Gerechtelijk Wetboek),
— in Denmark: Article 248 (2) of the law on civil procedure (Lov om rettens pleje) and Chapter 3, Article 3 of the Greenland law on civil procedure (Lov for Grønland om rettens pleje),
— in the Federal Republic of Germany: Article 23 of the code of civil procedure (Zivilprozeßordnung),
— in Greece, Article 40 of the code of civil procedure (Κωδικαζ πολιτικηζ δικουομιαζ),
— in France: Articles 14 and 15 of the civil code (Code civil),
— in Ireland: the rules which enable jurisdiction to be founded on the document instituting the proceedings having been served on the defendant during his temporary presence in Ireland,
— in Italy: Articles 2 and 4, Nos 1 and 2 of the code of civil procedure (Codice di procedura civile),
— in Luxembourg: Articles 14 and 15 of the civil code (Code civil),
— in the Netherlands: Articles 126 (3) and 127 of the code of civil procedure (Wetboek van Burgerlijke Rechtsvordering),
— in Portugal: Article 65 (1) (c), Article 65 (2) and Article 65A (c) of the code of civil procedure (Código de Processo de Trabalho),
— in the United Kingdom: the rules which enable jurisdiction to be founded on:
(a) the document instituting the proceedings having been served on the defendant during his temporary presence in the United Kingdom; or
(b) the presence within the United Kingdom of property belonging to the defendant; or
(c) the seizure by the plaintiff of property situated in the United Kingdom.

Article 4

If the defendant is not domiciled in a Contracting State, the jurisdiction of the courts of each Contracting State shall, subject to the provisions of Article 16, be determined by the law of that State.

As against such a defendant, any person domiciled in a Contracting State may, whatever his nationality, avail himself in that State of the rules of jurisdiction there in force, and in particular those specified in the second paragraph of Article 3, in the same way as the nationals of that State.

Section 2: Special Jurisdiction

Article 5

A person domiciled in a Contracting State may, in another Contracting State, be sued:
1. in matters relating to a contract, in the courts for the place of performance of the obligation in question; in matters relating to individual contracts of employment, this place is that where the employee habitually carries out his work, or if the employee does not habitually carry out his work in any one country, the employer may also be sued in the courts for the place where the business which engaged the employee was or is not situated;
2. in matters relating to maintenance, in the courts for the place where the maintenance creditor is domiciled or habitually resident or, if the matter is ancillary to proceedings concerning the status of a person, in the court which, according to its own law, has jurisdiction to entertain those proceedings, unless that jurisdiction is based solely on the nationality of one of the parties;
3. in matters relating to tort, delict or quasi-delict, in the courts for the place where the harmful event occurred;
4. as regards a civil claim for damages or restitution which is based on an act giving rise to criminal proceedings, in the court seised of those proceedings, to the extent that that court has jurisdiction under its own law to entertain civil proceedings;
5. as regards a dispute arising out of the operations of a branch, agency or other establishment, in the courts for the place in which the branch, agency or other establishment is situated;
6. in his capacity as settlor, trustee or beneficiary of a trust created by the operation of a statute, or by a written instrument, or created orally and evidenced in writing, in the courts of the Contracting State in which the trust is domiciled;
7. as regards a dispute concerning the payment of remuneration claimed in respect of the salvage of a cargo or freight, in the court under the authority of which the cargo or freight in question:
(a) has been arrested to secure such payment, or
(b) could have been so arrested, but bail or other security has been given; provided that this provision shall apply only if it is claimed that the defendant has an interest in the cargo or freight or had such an interest at the time of salvage;

Article 6

A person domiciled in a Contracting State may also be sued:
1. where he is one of a number of defendants, in the courts for the place where any one of them is domiciled;
2. as a third party in an action on a warranty or guarantee or in any other third party proceedings, in the court seised of the original proceedings, unless these

were instituted solely with the object of removing him from the jurisdiction of the court which would be competent in his case;
3. on a counter-claim arising from the same contract or facts on which the original claim was based, in the court in which the original claim is pending.

Article 6a

Where by virtue of this Convention a court of a Contracting State has jurisdiction in actions relating to liability arising from the use or operation of a ship, that court, or any other court substituted for this purpose by the internal law of that State, shall also have jurisdiction over claims for limitation of such liability.

Section 3: Jurisdiction in matters relating to insurance

Article 7

In matters relating to insurance, jurisdiction shall be determined by this Section, without prejudice to the provisions of Articles 4 and 5 (5).

Article 8

An insurer domiciled in a Contracting State may be used:
1. in the courts of the State where he is domiciled, or
2. in another Contracting State, in the courts for the place where the policy-holder is domiciled, or
3. if he is a co-insurer, in the courts of a Contracting State in which proceedings are brought against the leading insurer.

An insurer who is not domiciled in a Contracting State but has a branch, agency or other establishment in one of the Contracting States shall, in disputes arising out of the operations of the branch, agency or establishment, be deemed to be domiciled in that State.

Article 9

In respect of liability insurance or insurance of immovable property, the insurer may in addition be sued in the courts for the place where the harmful event occurred. The same applies if movable and immovable property are covered by the same insurance policy and both are adversely affected by the same contingency.

Article 10

In respect of liability insurance, the insurer may also, if the law of the court permits it, be joined in proceedings which the injured party has brought against the insured.

The provisions of Articles 7, 8 and 9 shall apply to actions brought by the injured party directly against the insurer, where such direct actions are permitted.

If the law governing such direct actions provides that the policy-holder or the insured may be joined as a party to the action, the same court shall have jurisdiction over them.

Article 11

Without prejudice to the provisions of the third paragraph of Article 10, an insurer may bring proceedings only in the courts of the Contracting State in which the defendant is domiciled, irrespective of whether he is the policy-holder, the insured or a beneficiary.

The provisions of this Section shall not affect the right to bring a counterclaim in the court in which, in accordance with this Section, the original claim is pending.

Article 12

The provisions of this Section may be departed from only by an agreement on jurisdiction:
1. which is entered into after the dispute has arisen, or
2. which allows the policy-holder, the insured or a beneficiary to bring proceedings in courts other than those indicated in this Section, or
3. which is concluded between a policy-holder and an insurer, both of whom are domiciled in the same Contracting State, and which has the effect of conferring jurisdiction on the courts of that State even if the harmful event were to occur abroad, provided that such an agreement is not contrary to the law of that State, or
4. which is concluded with a policy-holder who is not domiciled in a Contracting State, except in so far as the insurance is compulsory or relates to immovable property in a Contracting State, or
5. which relates to a contract of insurance in so far as it covers one or more of the risks set out in Article 12a.

Article 12a

The following are the risks referred to in Article 12 (5):

1. Any loss of or damage to
   (a) sea-going ships, installations situated off-shore or on the high seas, or aircraft, arising from perils which relate to their use for commercial purposes,
   (b) goods in transit other than passengers' baggage where the transit consists of or includes carriage by such ships or aircraft;
2. Any liability, other than for bodily injury to passengers or loss of or damage to their baggage,
   (a) arising out of the use or operation of ships, installations or aircraft as referred to in (1) (a) above in so far as the law of the Contracting State in which such aircraft are registered does not prohibit agreements on jurisdiction regarding insurance of such risks,
   (b) for loss or damage caused by goods in transit as described in (1) (b) above;
3. Any financial loss connected with the use or operation of ships, installations or aircraft as referred to in (1) (a) above, in particular loss of freight or charter-hire;
4. Any risk or interest connected with any of those referred to in (1) to (3) above.

Section 4: Jurisdiction over consumer contracts

Article 13

In proceedings concerning a contract concluded by a person for a purpose which can be regarded as being outside his trade or profession, hereinafter called 'the consumer', jurisdiction shall be determined by this Section, without prejudice to the provisions of Articles 4 and 5 (5), if it is:
1. a contract for the sale of goods on installment credit terms, or
2. a contract for a loan repayable by installments, or for any other form of credit, made to finance the sale of goods, or
3. any other contract for the supply of goods or a contract for the supply of services, and
   (a) in the State of the consumer's domicile the conclusion of the contract was preceded by a specific invitation addressed to him or by advertising, and
   (b) the consumer took in that State the steps necessary for the conclusion of the contract.

Where a consumer enters into a contract with a party who is not domiciled in a Contracting State but has a branch, agency or other establishment in one of the Contracting States, that party shall, in disputes arising out of the operations of the branch, agency or establishment, be deemed to be domiciled in that State.

This Section shall not apply to contracts of transport.

Article 14

A consumer may bring proceedings against the other party to a contract either in the courts of the Contracting State in which that party is domiciled or in the courts of the Contracting State in which he is himself domiciled.

Proceedings may be brought against a consumer by the other party to the contract only in the courts of the Contracting State in which the consumer is domiciled.

These provisions shall not affect the right to bring a counter-claim in the court in which, in accordance with this Section, the original claim is pending.

Article 15

The provisions of this Section may be departed form only by an agreement:
1. which is entered into after the dispute has arisen, or
2. which allows the consumer to bring proceedings in courts other than those indicated in this Section, or
3. which is entered into by the consumer and the other party to the contract, both of whom are at the time of conclusion of the contract domiciled or habitually resident in the same Contracting State, and which confers jurisdiction on the courts of that State, provided that such an agreement is not contrary to the law of that State.

Section 5: Exclusive jurisdiction

Article 16

The following courts shall have exclusive jurisdiction, regardless of domicile:
1. (a) in proceedings which have as their object rights *in rem* in, or tenancies of, immovable property, the courts of the Contracting State in which the property is situated;
   (b) however, in proceedings which have as their object tenancies of immovable property concluded for temporary private use for a maximum period of six consecutive months, the courts of the Contracting State in which the defendant is domiciled shall also have jurisdiction, provided that the landlord and the tenant are natural persons and are domiciled in the same Contracting State;
2. in proceedings which have as their object the validity of the constitution, the nullity or the dissolution of companies or other legal persons or association of natural or legal persons, or the decisions of their organs, the courts of the Contracting State in which the company, legal person or association has its seat;
3. in proceedings which have as their object the validity of entries in public registers, the courts of the Contracting State in which the register is kept;
4. in proceedings concerned with the registration or validity of patents, trade marks, designs, or other similar rights required to be deposited or registered, the courts of the Contracting State in which the deposit or registration has been

applied for, has taken place or is under the terms of an international convention deemed to have taken place;

5. in proceedings concerned with the enforcement of judgments, the courts of the Contracting State in which the judgment has been or is to be enforced.

Section 6: Prorogation of jurisdiction

Article 17

1. If the parties, one or more of whom is domiciled in a Contracting State, have agreed that a court or the courts of a Contracting State are to have jurisdiction to settle any disputes which have arisen or which may arise in connection with a particular legal relationship, that court or those courts shall have exclusive jurisdiction. Such an agreement conferring jurisdiction shall be either:
   (a) in writing or evidenced in writing; or
   (b) in a form which accords with practices which the parties have established between themselves; or
   (c) in international trade or commerce, in a form which accords with a usage of which the parties are or ought to have been aware and which in such trade or commerce is widely known to, and regularly observed by, parties to contracts of the type involved in the particular trade or commerce concerned.
   Where such an agreement is concluded by parties, none of whom is domiciled in a Contracting State, the courts of other Contracting States shall have no jurisdiction over their disputes unless the court or courts chosen have declined jurisdiction.

2. The court or courts of a Contracting State on which a trust instrument has conferred jurisdiction shall have exclusive jurisdiction in any proceedings brought against a settlor, trustee or beneficiary, if relations between these persons or their rights or obligations under the trust are involved.

3. Agreements or provisions of a trust instrument conferring jurisdiction shall have no legal force if they are contrary to the provisions of Article 12 or 15, or if the courts whose jurisdiction they purport to exclude have exclusive jurisdiction by virtue of Article 16.

4. If an agreement conferring jurisdiction was concluded for the benefit of only one of the parties, that party shall retain the right to bring proceedings in any other court which has jurisdiction by virtue of this Convention.

5. In matters relating to individual contracts of employment an agreement conferring jurisdiction shall have legal force only if entered into after the dispute has arisen or if the employee invokes it to seise courts other than those for the defendant's domicile or those specified in Article 5(1).

Article 18

Apart from jurisdiction derived from other provisions of this Convention, a court of a Contracting State before whom a defendant enters an appearance shall have jurisdiction. This rule shall not apply where appearance was entered solely to contest the jurisdiction, or where another court has exclusive jurisdiction by virtue of Article 16.

Section 7: Examination as to jurisdiction and admissibility

Article 19

Where a court of a Contracting State is seised of a claim which is principally concerned with a matter over which the courts of another Contracting State have exclusive jurisdiction by virtue of Article 16, it shall declare of its own motion that it has no jurisdiction.

Article 20

Where a defendant domiciled in one Contracting State is sued in a court of another Contracting State and does not enter an appearance, the court shall declare of its own motion that it has no jurisdiction unless its jurisdiction is derived from the provisions of this Convention.

The court shall stay the proceedings so long as it is not shown that the defendant has been able to receive the document instituting the proceedings or an equivalent document in sufficient time to enable him to arrange for his defense, or that all necessary steps have been taken to this end.

The provisions of the foregoing paragraph shall be replaced by those of Article 15 of the Hague Convention of 15 November 1965 on the service abroad of judicial and extrajudicial documents in civil or commercial matters, if the document instituting the proceedings or notice thereof had to be transmitted abroad in accordance with that Convention.

Section 8: Lis Pendens-related actions

Article 21

Where proceedings involving the same cause of action and between the same parties are brought in the courts of different Contracting States, any court other than the court first seised shall of its own motion stay its proceedings until such time as the jurisdiction of the court first seised is established.

Where the jurisdiction of the court first seised is established, any court other than the court first seised shall decline jurisdiction in favour of that court.

Article 22

Where related actions are brought in the courts of different Contracting States, any court other than the court first seised may, while the actions are pending at first instance, stay its proceedings.

A court other than the court first seised may also, on the application of one of the parties, decline jurisdiction if the law of that court permits the consolidation of related actions and the court first seised has jurisdiction over both actions.

For the purposes of this Article, actions are deemed to be related where they are so closely connected that it is expedient to hear and determine them together to avoid the risk of irreconcilable judgments resulting from separate proceedings.

Article 23

Where actions come within the exclusive jurisdiction of several courts, any court other than the court first seised shall decline jurisdiction in favour of that court.

Section 9: Provisional, including protective measures

Article 24

Application may be made to the courts of a Contracting State for such provisional, including protective, measures as may be available under the law of that State, even if, under this Convention, the courts of another Contracting State have jurisdiction as to the substance of the matter.

TITLE III: RECOGNITION AND ENFORCEMENT

Article 25

For the purposes of this Convention, `judgment' means any judgment given by a court or tribunal of a Contracting State, whatever the judgment may be called, including a decree, order, decision, or writ of execution, as well as the determination of costs or expenses by an officer of the court.

Section 1: Recognition

Article 26

A judgment given in a Contracting State shall be recognized in the other Contracting States without any special procedure being required.

Any interested party who raises the recognition of a judgment as the principal issue in a dispute may, in accordance with the procedures provided for in Sections 2 and 3 of this Title, apply for a decision that the judgment be recognized.

If the outcome of proceedings in a court of a Contracting State depends on the determination of an incidental question of recognition that court shall have jurisdiction over that question.

Article 27

A judgment shall not be recognized:
1. if such recognition is contrary to public policy in the State in which recognition is sought;
2. where it was given in default of appearance, if the defendant was not duly served with the document which instituted the proceedings or with an equivalent document in sufficient time to enable him to arrange for his defence;
3. if the judgment is irreconcilable with a judgment given in a dispute between the same parties in the State in which recognition is sought;
4. if the court of the State in which the judgment was given, in order to arrive at its judgment, has decided in a preliminary question concerning the status or legal capacity of natural persons, rights in property arising out of a matrimonial relationship, wills or succession in a way that conflicts with a rule of the private international law of the State in which the recognition is sought, unless the same result would have been reached by the application of the rules of private international law of that State;
5. if the judgment is irreconcilable with an earlier judgment given in a non-Contracting State involving the same cause of action and between the same parties, provided that this latter judgment fulfills the conditions necessary for its recognition in the State addressed.

Article 28

Moreover, a judgment shall not be recognized if it conflicts with the provisions of Section 3, 4 or 5 of Title II, or in a case provided for in Article 59.

In its examination of the grounds of jurisdiction referred to in the foregoing paragraph, the court or authority applied to shall be bound by the findings of fact on which the court of the State of origin based its jurisdiction.

Subject to the provisions of the first paragraph, the jurisdiction of the court of the State of origin may not be reviewed; the test of public policy referred to in point 1 of Article 27 may not be applied to the rules relating to jurisdiction.

Article 29

Under no circumstances may a foreign judgment be reviewed as to its substance.

Article 30

A court of a Contracting State in which recognition is sought of a judgment given in another Contracting State may stay the proceedings if an ordinary appeal against the judgment has been lodged.

A court of a Contracting State in which recognition is sought of a judgment given in Ireland or the United Kingdom may stay the proceedings if enforcement is suspended in the State of origin, by reason of an appeal.

Section 2: Enforcement

Article 31

A judgment given in a Contracting State and enforceable in that State shall be enforced in another Contracting State when, on the application of any interested party, it has been declared enforceable there.

However, in the United Kingdom, such a judgment shall be enforced in England and Wales, in Scotland, or in Northern Ireland when, on the application of any interested party, it has been registered for enforcement in that part of the United Kingdom.

Article 32

The application shall be submitted:
— in Belgium, to the Tribunal de première instance or Rechtbank van eerste aanleg,
— in Denmark, to the byret,
— in the Federal Republic of Germany, to the presiding judge of a chamber of the Landgericht,
— in Greece, to the Μονομελεζ Πρωτοδικειο,
— in Spain, to the Juzgado de Primera Instancia,
— in France, to the presiding judge of the Tribunal de grande instance,
— in Ireland, to the High Court,
— in Italy, to the Corte d'appello,
— in Luxembourg, to the presiding judge of the Tribunal d'arrondissement,
— in the Netherlands, to the presiding judge of the Arrondissementsrechtsbank,
— in Portugal, to the Tribunal Judicial de Circulo,

— in the United Kingdom:

1. in England and Wales, to the High Court of Justice, or in the case of a maintenance judgment to the Magistrates' Court on transmission by the Secretary of State;

2. in Scotland, to the Court of Session, or in the case of a maintenance judgment to the Sheriff Court on transmission by the Secretary of State;

3. in Northern Ireland, to the High Court of Justice, or in the case of a maintenance judgment of the Magistrates' Court on transmission by the Secretary of State.

The jurisdiction of local courts shall be determined by reference to the place of domicile of the party against whom enforcement is sought. If he is not domiciled in the State in which enforcement is sought, it shall be determined by reference to the place of enforcement.

Article 33

The procedure for making the application shall be governed by the law of the State in which enforcement is sought.

The applicant must give an address for service of process within the area of jurisdiction of the court applied to. However, if the law of the State in which enforcement is sought does not provide for the furnishing of such an address, the applicant shall appoint a representative *ad litem*.

The documents referred to in Articles 46 and 47 shall be attached to the application.

Article 34

The court applied to shall give its decision without delay; the party against whom enforcement is sought shall not at this stage of the proceedings be entitled to make any submissions on the application.

The application may be refused only for one of the reasons specified in Articles 27 and 28.

Under no circumstances may the foreign judgment be reviewed as to its substance.

Article 35

The appropriate officer of the court shall without delay bring the decision given on the application to the notice of the applicant in accordance with the procedure laid down by the law of the State in which enforcement is sought.

Article 36

If enforcement is authorized, the party against whom enforcement is sought may appeal against the decision within one month of service thereof.

If that party is domiciled in a Contracting State other than that in which the decision authorizing enforcement was given, the time for appealing shall be two months and shall run from the date of service, either on him in person or at his residence. No extension of time may be granted on account of distance.

Article 37

An appeal against the decision authorizing enforcement shall be lodged in accordance with the rules governing procedure in contentious matters:
— in Belgium, with the tribunal de première instance or rechtbank van eerste aanleg,
— in Denmark, with the landstret,
— in the Federal Republic of Germany, with the Oberlandesgericht,
— in Greece, with the Εφετειο,
— in Spain, with the Audiencia Provincial,
— in France, with the cour d'appel,
— in Ireland, with the High Court,
— in Italy, with the corte d'appello,
— in Luxembourg, with the Cour supérieure de justice sitting as a court of civil appeal,
— in the Netherlands, with the arrondissementsrechtsbank,
— in Portugal, with the Tribunal de Relaçao,
— in the United Kingdom:
   (a) in England and Wales, with the High Court of Justice, or in the case of a maintenance judgment with the Magistrates' Court;
   (b) in Scotland, with the Court of Session, or in the case of a maintenance judgment with the Sheriff Court;
   (c) in Northern Ireland, with the High Court of Justice, or in the case of a maintenance judgment with the Magistrates' Court.

The judgment given on the appeal may be contested only:
— in Belgium, Greece, Spain, France, Italy, Luxembourg and the Netherlands, by an appeal in cassation,
— in Denmark, by an appeal to the højesteret, with the leave of the Minister of Justice,
— in the Federal Republic of Germany, by a Rechtsbeschwerde,
— in Ireland, by an appeal on a point of law to the Supreme Court,
— in Portugal, by an appeal on a point of law,
— in the United Kingdom, by a single further appeal on a point of law.

Article 38

The court with which the appeal under Article 37 (1) is lodged may, on the application of the appellant, stay the proceedings if an ordinary appeal has been lodged against the judgment in the State of origin or if the time for such an appeal has not yet expired; in the latter case, the court may specify the time within which such an appeal is to be lodged.

Where the judgment was given in Ireland or the United Kingdom, any form of appeal available in the State in which it was given shall be treated as an ordinary appeal for the purposes of the first paragraph.

The court may also make enforcement conditional on the provision of such security as it shall determine.

Article 39

During the time specified for an appeal pursuant to Article 36 and until any such appeal has been determined, no measures of enforcement may be taken other than protective measures taken against the property of the party against whom enforcement is sought.

The decision authorizing enforcement shall carry with it the power to proceed to any such protective measures.

Article 40

If the application for enforcement is refused, the applicant may appeal:
— in Belgium, to the Cour d'appel or Hof van beroep,
— in Denmark, to the Landsret,
— in the Federal Republic of Germany, to the Oberlandesgericht,
— in Greece, to the Εφετειο,
— in Spain, to the Audiencia Provincial,
— in France, to the Cour d'appel,
— in Ireland, to the High Court,
— in Italy, to the Corte d'appello,
— in Luxembourg, to the Cour supérieure de justice sitting as a court of civil appeal,
— in the Netherlands, to the Gerechtshof,
— in Portugal, to the Tribunal de Relaçao,
— in the United Kingdom:
   1. in England and Wales, to the High Court of Justice, or in the case of a maintenance judgment to the Magistrates' Court;
   2. in Scotland, to the Court of Session, or in the case of a maintenance judgment to the Sheriff Court;

3. in Northern Ireland, to the High Court of Justice, or in the case of a maintenance judgment to the Magistrates' Court.

The party against whom enforcement is sought shall be summoned to appear before the appellate court. If he fails to appear, the provisions of the second and third paragraphs of Article 20 shall apply even where he is not domiciled in any of the Contracting States.

Article 41

A judgment given on an appeal provided for in Article 40 may be contested only:
— in Belgium, Greece, Spain, France, Italy, Luxembourg and the Netherlands, by an appeal in cassation,
— in Denmark, by an appeal to the højesteret, with the leave by the Minister of Justice,
— in the Federal Republic of Germany, by a Rechtsbeschwerde,
— in Ireland, by an appeal on a point of law to the Supreme Court,
— in Portugal, by an appeal on a point of law,
— in the United Kingdom, by a single further appeal on a point of law.

Article 42

Where a foreign judgment has been given in respect of several matters and enforcement cannot be authorized for all of them, the court shall authorize enforcement for one or more of them.

An applicant may request partial enforcement of a judgment.

Article 43

A foreign judgment which orders a periodic payment by way of a penalty shall be enforceable in the State in which enforcement is sought only if the amount of the payment has been finally determined by the courts of the State of origin.

Article 44

An applicant who, in the State of origin has benefitted from complete or partial legal aid or exemption from costs or expenses, shall be entitled, in the procedures provided for in Articles 32 to 35, to benefit from the most favourable legal aid or the most extensive exemption from costs or expenses provided for by the law of the State addressed.

However, an applicant who requests the enforcement of a decision given by an administrative authority in Denmark in respect of a maintenance order may, in the State addressed, claim the benefits referred to in the first paragraph if he presents a statement from the Danish Ministry of Justice to the effect that he fulfills the economic requirements to qualify for the grant of complete or partial legal aid or exemption from costs or expenses.

Article 45

No security, bond or deposit, however described, shall be required of a party who in one Contracting State applies for enforcement of a judgment given in another Contracting State on the ground that he is a foreign national or that he is not domiciled or resident in the State in which enforcement is sought.

Section 3: Common provisions

Article 46

A party seeking recognition or applying for enforcement of a judgment shall produce:
1. a copy of the judgment which satisfies the conditions necessary to establish its authenticity;
2. in the case of a judgment given in default, the original or a certified true copy of the document which establishes that the party in default was served with the document instituting the proceedings or with an equivalent document.

Article 47

A party applying for enforcement shall also produce:
1. documents which establish that, according to the law of the State of origin the judgment is enforceable and has been served;
2. where appropriate, a document showing that the applicant is in receipt of legal aid in the State in which the judgment was given.

Article 48

If the documents specified in Articles 46 (2) and 47 (2) are not produced, the court may specify a time for their production, accept equivalent documents or, if it considers that it has sufficient information before it, dispense with their production.

If the court so requires, a translation of the documents shall be produced; the translation shall be certified by a person qualified to do so in one of the Contracting States.

Article 49

No legalization or other similar formality shall be required in respect of the documents referred to in Article 46 or 47 or the second paragraph of Article 48, or in respect of a document appointing a representative *ad litem*.

TITLE IV: AUTHENTIC INSTRUMENTS AND COURT SETTLEMENTS

Article 50

A document which has been formally drawn up or registered as an authentic instrument and is enforceable in one Contracting State shall, in another Contracting State, be declared enforceable there, on application made in accordance with the procedures provided for in Article 31 *et seq*. The application may be refused only if enforcement of the instrument is contrary to public policy in the State addressed.

The instrument produced must satisfy the conditions necessary to establish its authenticity in the State of origin.

The provisions of Section 3 of Title III shall apply as appropriate.

Article 51

A settlement which has been approved by a court in the course of proceedings and is enforceable in the State in which it was concluded shall be enforceable in the State addressed under the same conditions as authentic instruments.

TITLE V: GENERAL PROVISIONS

Article 52

In order to determine whether a party is domiciled in the Contracting State whose courts are seised of a matter, the Court shall apply its internal law.

If a party is not domiciled in the State whose courts are seised of the matter, then, in order to determine whether the party is domiciled in another Contracting State, the court shall apply the law of that State.

Article 53

For the purposes of this Convention, the seat of a company or other legal person or association of natural or legal persons shall be treated as its domicile. However, in order to determine that seat, the court shall apply its rules of private international law.

In order to determine whether a trust is domiciled in the Contracting State whose courts are seised of the matter, the court shall apply its rules of private international law.

TITLE VI: TRANSITIONAL PROVISIONS

Article 54

The provisions of the Convention shall apply only to legal proceedings instituted and to documents formally drawn up or registered as authentic instruments after its entry into force in the State of origin and, where recognition or enforcement of a judgment or authentic instruments is sought, in the State addressed.

However, judgments given after the date of entry into force of this Convention between the State of origin and the State addressed in proceedings instituted before that date shall be recognized and enforced in accordance with the provisions of Title III if jurisdiction was founded upon rules which accorded with those provided for either in Title II of this Convention or in a convention concluded between the State of origin and the State addressed which was in force when the proceedings were instituted.

If the parties to a dispute concerning a contract had agreed in writing before 1 January 1987 for the United Kingdom that the contract was to be governed by the law of Ireland or of a part of the United Kingdom, the courts of Ireland or of that part of the United Kingdom shall retain the right to exercise jurisdiction in the dispute.

Article 54a

For a period of three years from 1 November 1986 for Denmark and from 1 June 1988 for Ireland, jurisdiction in maritime matters shall be determined in these States not only in accordance with the provisions of Title II, but also in accordance with the provisions of paragraphs 1 to 6 following. However, upon the entry into force of the International Convention relating to the arrest of sea-going ships, signed at Brussels on 10 May 1952, for one of these States, these provisions shall cease to have effect for that State.

1. A person who is domiciled in a Contracting State may be sued in the courts of one of the States mentioned above in respect of a maritime claim if the ship to which the claim relates or any other ship owned by him has been arrested by

judicial process within the territory of the latter State to secure the claim, or could have been so arrested there but bail or other security has been given, and either:

(a) the claimant is domiciled in the latter State; or

(b) the claim arose in the latter State; or

(c) the claim concerns the voyage during which the arrest was made or could have been made; or

(d) the claim arises out of a collision or out of damage caused by a ship to another ship or to goods or persons on board either ship, either by execution or non-execution of a manoeuvre or by the non-observance of regulations; or

(e) the claim is for salvage; or

(f) the claim is in respect of a mortgage or hypothecation of the ship arrested.

2. A claimant may arrest either the particular ship to which the maritime claim relates, or any other ship which is owned by the person who was, at the time when the maritime claim arose, the owner of the particular ship. However, only the particular ship to which the maritime claim relates may be arrested in respect of the maritime claims set out in (5) (o), (p) or (q) of this Article.

3. Ships shall be deemed to be in the same ownership when all the shares therein are owned by the same person or persons.

4. When in the case of a charter by demise of a ship the charterer alone is liable in respect of a maritime claim relating to that ship, the claimant may arrest that ship or any other ship owned by the charterer, but no other ship owned by the owner may be arrested in respect of such claim. The same shall apply to any case in which a person other than the owner of a ship is liable in respect of a maritime claim relating to that ship.

5. The expression 'maritime claim' means a claim arising out of one or more of the following:

(a) damage caused by any ship either in collision or otherwise;

(b) loss of life or personal injury caused by any ship or occurring in connection with the operation on any ship;

(c) salvage;

(d) agreement relating to the use or hire of any ship whether by charterparty or otherwise;

(e) agreement relating to the carriage of goods in any ship whether by charterparty or otherwise;

(f) loss of or damage to goods including baggage carried in any ship;

(g) general average;

(h) bottomry;

(i) towage;

(j) pilotage;

(k) goods or materials wherever supplied to a ship for her operation or maintenance;

(l) construction, repair or equipment of any ship or dock charges and dues;

(m) wages of masters, officers or crew;

(n) mater's disbursements, including disbursements made by shippers, charterers or agents on behalf of a ship or her owner;

(o) dispute as to the title to or ownership of any ship;

(p) disputes between co-owners of any ship as to the ownership, possession, employment or earnings of that ship;

(q) the mortgage or hypothecation of any ship.

6. In Denmark, the expression `arrest' shall be deemed as regards the maritime claims referred to in 5(o) and (p) of this Article, to include a `forbud', where that is the only procedure allowed in respect of such a claim under Articles 646 to 653 of the law on civil procedure (lov om rettens pleje).

TITLE VII: RELATIONSHIP TO OTHER CONVENTIONS

Article 55

Subject to the provisions of the second paragraph of Article 54, and of Article 56, this Convention shall, for the States which are parties to it, supersede the following conventions concluded between two or more of them:

— the Convention between Belgium and France on jurisdiction and the validity and enforcement of judgments, arbitration awards and authentic instruments, signed at Paris on 8 July 1899,

— the Convention between Belgium and the Netherlands on jurisdiction, bankruptcy, and the validity and enforcement of judgments, arbitration awards and authentic instruments, signed at Brussels on 28 March 1925,

— the Convention between France and Italy on the enforcement of judgments in civil and commercial matters, signed at Rome on 3 June 1930,

— the Convention between the United Kingdom and the French Republic providing for the reciprocal enforcement of judgments in civil and commercial matters, with Protocol, signed at Paris on 18 January 1934,

— the Convention between the United Kingdom and the Kingdom of Belgium providing for the reciprocal enforcement of judgments in civil and commercial matters, with Protocol, signed at Brussels on 2 May 1934,

— the Convention between Germany and Italy on the recognition and enforcement of judgments in civil and commercial matters, signed at Rome on 9 March 1936,

— the Convention between the Federal Republic of Germany and the Kingdom of Belgium on the mutual recognition and enforcement of judgments, arbitration awards and authentic instruments in civil and commercial mattes, signed at Bonn on 30 June 1958,

— the Convention between the Kingdom of the Netherlands and the Italian Republic on the recognition and enforcement of judgments in civil and commercial matters, signed at Rome on 17b April 1959,

— the Convention between the United Kingdom and the Federal Republic of Germany for the reciprocal recognition and enforcement of judgments in civil and commercial matters, signed at Bonn on 14 July 1960,

— the Convention between the Kingdom of Greece and the Federal Republic of Germany for the reciprocal recognition and enforcement of judgments, settlements and authentic instruments in civil and commercial matters, signed in Athens on 4 November 1961,

— the Convention between the Kingdom of Belgium and the Italian Republic on the recognition and enforcement of judgments and other enforceable instruments in civil and commercial matters, signed at Rome on 6 April 1962,

— the Convention between the Kingdom of the Netherlands and the Federal Republic of Germany on the mutual recognition and enforcement of judgments and other enforceable instruments in civil and commercial matters, signed at The Hague on 30 August 1962,

— the Convention between the United Kingdom and the Republic of Italy for the reciprocal recognition and enforcement of judgments in civil and commercial matters, signed at Rome on 7 February 1964, with amending Protocol signed at Rome on 14 July 1970,

— the Convention between the United Kingdom and the Kingdom of the Netherlands providing for the reciprocal recognition and enforcement of judgments in civil matters, signed at The Hague on 17 November 1967,

— the Convention between Spain and France on the recognition and enforcement of judgment arbitration awards in civil and commercial matters, signed at Paris on 28 May 1969,

— the Convention between Spain and Italy regarding legal aid and the recognition and enforcement of judgments in civil and commercial matters, signed at Madrid on 22 May 1973,

— the Convention between Spain and the Federal Republic of Germany on the recognition and enforcement of judgments, settlements and enforceable authentic instruments in civil and commercial matters, signed at Bonn on 14 November 1983,

and, in so far as it is in force:

— the Treaty between Belgium, the Netherlands and Luxembourg on jurisdiction, bankruptcy, and the validity and enforcement of judgments, arbitration awards and authentic instruments, signed at Brussels on 24 November 1961.

Article 56

The Treaty and the conventions referred to in Article 55 shall continue to have effect in relation to matters to which this Convention does not apply.

They shall continue to have effect in respect of judgments given and documents formally drawn up or registered as authentic instruments before the entry into force of this Convention.

Article 57

1. This Convention shall not affect any conventions to which the Contracting States are or will be parties and which, in relation to particular matters, govern jurisdiction or the recognition or enforcement of judgments.
2. With a view to its uniform interpretation, paragraph 1 shall be applied in the following manner:

   (a) this Convention shall not prevent a court of a Contracting State which is a party to a convention on a particular matter from assuming jurisdiction in accordance with that Convention, even where the defendant is domiciled in another Contracting State which is not a party to that Convention. The court hearing the action shall, in any event, apply Article 20 of this Convention;

   (b) judgments given in a Contracting State by a court in the exercise of jurisdiction provided for in a convention on a particular matter shall be recognized and enforced in the other Contracting State in accordance with this Convention.

   Where a convention on a particular matter to which both the State of origin and the State addressed are parties lays down conditions for the recognition or enforcement of judgments, those conditions shall apply. In any event, the provisions of this Convention which concern the procedure for recognition and enforcement of judgments may be applied.
3. This Convention shall not affect the application of provisions which, in relation to particular matters, govern jurisdiction or the recognition or enforcement of judgments and which are or will be contained in acts of the institutions of the European Communities or in national laws harmonized in implementation of such acts.

Article 58

Until such time as the Convention on jurisdiction and the enforcement of judgments in civil and commercial matters, signed at Lugano on 16 September 1988, takes effect with regard to France and the Swiss Confederation, this Convention shall not affect the rights granted to Swiss nationals by the Convention between France and the Swiss Confederation on jurisdiction and enforcement of judgments in civil matters, signed at Paris on 15 June 1869.

Article 59

This Convention shall not prevent a Contracting State from assuming, in a convention on the recognition and enforcement of judgments, an obligation towards a third State not to recognize judgments given in other Contracting States against defendants domiciled or habitually resident in the third State where, in cases provided for in Article 4, the judgment could only be founded on a ground of jurisdiction specified in the second paragraph of Article 3.

However, a Contracting State may not assume an obligation towards a third State not to recognize a judgments given in another Contracting State by a court basing its jurisdiction on the presence within that State of property belonging to the defendant, or the seizure by the plaintiff of property situated there:

1. if the action is brought to assert or declare proprietary or possessory rights in that property, seeks to obtain authority to dispose of it, or arises from another issue relating to such property, or,
2. if the property constitutes the security for a debt which is the subject-matter of the action.

TITLE VIII: FINAL PROVISIONS

Article 60

[Omitted in amended version]

Article 61

This Convention shall be ratified by the signatory States. The instruments of ratification shall be deposited with the Secretary-General of the Council of the European Communities.

Article 62

This Convention shall enter into force on the first day of the third month following the deposit of the instrument of ratification by the last signatory State to take this step.

Article 63

The Contracting States recognize that any State which becomes a member of the European Economic Community shall be required to accept this Convention as a basis for the negotiations between the Contracting States and that State necessary to ensure the implementation of the last paragraph of Article 220 of the Treaty establishing the European Economic Community.

The necessary adjustments may be the subject of a special convention between the Contracting States of the one part and the new Member States of the other part.

Article 64

The Secretary-General of the Council of the European Communities shall notify the signatory States of:
(a) the deposit of each instrument of ratification;
(b) the date of entry into force of this Convention;
(c) any declaration received pursuant to Article IV of the Protocol;
(d) any communication made pursuant to Article VI of the Protocol.

Article 65

The Protocol annexed to this Convention by common accord of the Contracting States shall form an integral part thereof.

Article 66

This Convention is concluded for an unlimited period.

Article 67

Any Contracting State may request the revision of this Convention. In this event, a revision conference shall be convened by the President of the Council of the European Communities.

Article 68

This Convention, drawn up in a single original in the Dutch, French, German and Italian language, all four texts being equally authentic, shall be deposited in the archives of the Secretariat of the Council of the European Communities. The Secretary-General shall transmit a certified copy to the Government of each signatory State.

In witness whereof, the undersigned Plenipotentiaries have signed this Convention.
Done at Brussels this twenty-seventh day of September in the year one thousand nine hundred and sixty-eight.

2. Lugano Convention[1]

Convention on Jurisdiction and the Enforcement of
Judgments in Civil and Commercial Matters, 16 September 1988

Title I: Scope

Article 1

 This Convention shall apply in civil and commercial matters whatever the nature of the court or tribunal. It shall not extend, in particular, to revenue, customs or administrative matters.
 The Convention shall not apply to:
1. the status or legal capacity of natural persons, rights in property arising out of a matrimonial relationship, wills and succession;
2. bankruptcy, proceedings relating to the winding-up of insolvent companies or other legal persons, judicial arrangements, compositions and analogous proceedings;
3. social security;
4. arbitration.

Title II: Jurisdiction

Section 1: General provisions

Article 2

 Subject to the provisions of this Convention, persons domiciled in a Contracting State shall, whatever their nationality, be sued in the courts of that State.
 Persons who are not nationals of the State in which they are domiciled shall be governed by the rules of jurisdiction applicable to nationals of that State.

Article 3

 Persons domiciled in a Contracting State may be sued in the courts of another Contracting State only by virtue of the rules set out in Sections 2 to 6 of this Title.

1. Reprinted in 28 I.L.M. 620 (1989).

In particular the following provisions shall not be applicable as against them:
— in Belgium: Article 15 of the civil code (Code civil — Burgerlijk Wetboek) and Article 638 of the judicial code (Code judiciaire — Gerechtelijk Wetboek),
— in Denmark: Article 246 (2) and (3) of the law on civil procedure (Lov om rettens pleje),
— in the Federal Republic of Germany: Article 23 of the code of civil procedure (Zivilprozeßordnung),
— in Greece: Article 40 of the code of civil procedure (Κωδικας πολιτικης δικουομιας),
— in France: Article 14 and 15 of the civil code (Code civil),
— in Ireland: the rules which enable jurisdiction to be founded on the document instituting the proceedings having been served on the defendant during his temporary presence in Ireland,
— in Iceland: Article 77 of the Civil Proceedings Act (lög um meðferð einkamala i heraði),
— in Italy: Articles 2 and 4, Nos 1 and 2 of the code of civil procedure (Codice de procedura civile),
— in Luxembourg: Articles 14 and 15 of the civil code (Code civil),
— in the Netherlands: Articles 126 (3) and 127 of the code of civil procedure (Wetboek van Burgerlijke Rechtsvordering),
— in Norway: Section 32 of the Civil Proceedings Act (tvistemålsloven),
— in Austria: Article 99 of the Law on Court Jurisdiction (Jurisdiktionsnorm),
— in Portugal: Articles 65 (1) (c), 65 (2) and 65A (c) of the code of civil procedure (Codigo de Processo Civil) and Article 11 of the code of labour procedure (Codigo de Processo de Trabalho),
— in Switzerland: le for du lieu du séquestre/Gerichsstand des Arrestortes/foro del luogo del sequestro within the meaning of Article 4 of the Loi fédérale sur le droit international privé/Bundesgesetz über das internationale Privatrecht/ legge federale su diritto internazionale privato,
— in Finland: the second, third and fourth sentences of Section 1 of Chapter 10 of the Code of Judicial Procedure (oikeudenkäymiskaari/rättegångsbalken),
— in Sweden: the first sentence of Section 3 of Chapter 10 of the Code of Judicial Procedure (Rättegångsbalken),
— in the United Kingdom: the rules which enable jurisdictions to be founded on:
(a) the document instituting the proceedings having been served on the defendant during his temporary presence in the United Kingdom; or
(b) the presence within the United Kingdom of property belonging to the defendant; or
(c) the seizure by the plaintiff of property situated in the United Kingdom.

Article 4

If the defendant is not domiciled in a Contracting State, the jurisdiction of the courts of each Contracting State shall, subject to the provisions of Article 16, be determined by the law of that State.

As against such a defendant, any person domiciled in a Contracting State may, whatever his nationality, avail himself in that State of the rules of jurisdiction there in force, and in particular those specified in the second paragraph of Article 3, in the same way as the nationals of that State.

Section 2: Special jurisdiction

Article 5

A person domiciled in a Contracting State may, in another Contracting State, be sued:

1. in matters relating to a contract, in the courts for the place of performance of the obligation in question; in matters relating to individual contracts of employment, this place is that where the employee habitually carries out his work, or if the employee does not habitually carry out his work in any one country, this place shall be the place of business through which he was engaged;
2. in matters relating to maintenance, in the courts for the place where the maintenance creditor is domiciled or habitually resident or, if the matter is ancillary to proceedings concerning the status of a person, in the court which, according to its own law, has jurisdiction to entertain those proceedings, unless that jurisdiction is based solely on the nationality of one of the parties;
3. in matters relating to tort, delict or quasi-delict, in the courts for the place where the harmful event occurred;
4. as regards a civil claim for damages or restitution which is based on an act giving rise to criminal proceedings, in the court seised of those proceedings, to the extent that that court has jurisdiction under its own law to entertain civil proceedings;
5. as regards a dispute arising out of the operations of a branch, agency or other establishment, in the courts for the place in which the branch, agency or other establishment is situated;
6. in his capacity as settlor, trustee or beneficiary of a trust created by the operation of a statute, or by a written instrument, or created orally and evidenced in writing, in the courts of the Contracting State in which the trust is domiciled;
7. as regards a dispute concerning the payment of remuneration claimed in respect of the salvage of a cargo or freight, in the court under the authority of which the cargo or freight in question:
   (a) has been arrested to secure such payment, or
   (b) could have been so arrested, but bail or other security has been given; provided that this provision shall apply only if it is claimed that the defendant has an interest in the cargo or freight or had such an interest at the time of salvage.

Article 6

A person domiciled in a Contracting State may also be sued:
1. where he is one of a number of defendants, in the courts for the place where any one of them is domiciled;
2. as a third party in an action on a warranty or guarantee or in any other third party proceedings, in the court seised of the original proceedings, unless these were instituted solely with the object of removing him from the jurisdiction of the court which would be competent in his case;]
3. on a counterclaim arising from the same contract or facts on which the original claim was based, in the court in which the original claim is pending;
4. in matters relating to a contract, if the action may be combined with an action against the same defendant in matters relating to rights *in rem* in immovable property, in the court of the Contracting State in which the property is situated.

Article 6A

Where by virtue of this Convention a court of a Contracting State has jurisdiction in actions relating to liability arising from the use or operation of a ship, that court, or any other court substituted for this purpose by the internal law of that State, shall also have jurisdiction over claims for limitation of such liability.

Section 3: Jurisdiction in matters relating to insurance

Article 7

In matters relating to insurance, jurisdiction shall be determined by this Section, without prejudice to the provisions of Articles 4 and 5 (5).

Article 8

An insurer domiciled in a Contracting State may be sued:
1. in the courts of the State where he is domiciled; or
2. in another Contracting State, in the courts for the place where the policy-holder is domiciled; or
3. if he is a co-insurer, in the courts of the Contracting State in which proceedings are brought against the leading insurer.

An insurer who is not domiciled in a Contracting State but has a branch, agency or other establishment in one of the Contracting States shall, in disputes arising out of the operations of the branch, agency or establishment, be deemed to be domiciled in that State.

Article 9

In respect of liability insurance or insurance of immovable property, the insurer may in addition be sued in the courts for the place where the harmful event occurred. The same applies if movable and immovable property are covered by the same insurance policy and both are adversely affected by the same contingency.

Article 10

In respect of liability insurance, the insurer may also, if the law of the court permits it, be joined in proceedings which the insured party has brought against the insured.

The provisions of Articles 7, 8 and 9 shall apply to actions brought by the insured party directly against the insurer, where such direct actions are permitted.

If the law governing such direct actions provides that the policy-holder or the insured may be joined as a party to the action, the same court shall have jurisdiction over them.

Article 11

Without prejudice to the provisions of the third paragraph of Article 10, an insurer may bring proceedings only in the courts of the Contracting State in which the defendant is domiciled, irrespective of whether he is the policy-holder, the insured or a beneficiary.

The provisions of this Section shall not affect the right to bring a counter-claim in the court in which, in accordance with this Section, the original claim is pending.

Article 12

The provisions of this Section may be departed from only by an agreement on jurisdiction:
1. which is entered into after the dispute has arisen; or
2. which allows the policy-holder, the insured or a beneficiary to bring proceedings in courts other than those indicated in this Section; or
3. which is concluded between a policy-holder and an insurer, both of whom are at the time of conclusion of the contract domiciled or habitually resident in the same Contracting State, and which has the effect of conferring jurisdiction to the courts of that State even if the harmful event were to occur abroad, provided that such an agreement is not contrary to the law of the State; or

4. which is concluded with a policy-holder who is not domiciled in a Contracting State, except in so far as the insurance is compulsory or relates to immovable property in a Contracting State; or
5. which relates to a contract of insurance in so far as it covers one or more of the risks set out in Article 12A.

Article 12A

The following are the risks referred to in Article 12 (5):
1. any loss of or damage to:
   (a) sea-going ships, installations situated off shore or on the high seas, or aircraft, arising from perils which relate to their use for commercial purposes;
   (b) goods in transit other than passengers' baggage where the transit consists of or includes carriage by such ships or aircraft;
2. any liability, other than for bodily injury to passengers or loss of or damage to their baggage;
   (a) arising out of the use or operation of ships, installations or aircraft as referred to in (1) (a) above in so far as the law of the Contracting State in which such aircraft are registered does not prohibit agreements on jurisdiction regarding insurance of such risks;
   (b) for loss or damage caused by goods in transit as described in (1) (b) above;
3. any financial loss connected with the use or operation of ships, installations or aircraft as referred to in (1) (a) above, in particular loss of freight or charter-hire;
4. any risk or interest connected with any of those referred to in (1) to (3) above.

Section 4: Jurisdiction over consumer contracts

Article 13

In proceedings concerning a contract concluded by a person for a purpose which can be regarded as being outside his trade or profession, hereinafter called 'the consumer', jurisdiction shall be determined by this Section, without prejudice to the provisions of Articles 4 and 5 (5), if it is:
1. a contract for the sale of goods on installment credit terms; or
2. a contract for a loan repayable by installments, or for any other form of credit, made to finance the sale of goods; or
3. any other contract for the supply of goods or a contract for the supply of services, and
   (a) in the State of the consumer's domicile the conclusion of the contract was preceded by a specific invitation addressed to him or by advertising, and
   (b) the consumer took in that State the steps necessary for the conclusion of the contract.

Where a consumer enters into a contract with a party who is not domiciled in a Contracting State but has a branch, agency or other establishment in one of the Contracting States, that party shall, in disputes arising out of the operations of the branch, agency or establishment, be deemed to be domiciled in that State.

This Section shall not apply to contracts of transport.

Article 14

A consumer may bring proceedings against the other party to a contract either in the courts of the Contracting State in which that party is domiciled or in the courts of the Contracting State in which he is himself domiciled.

Proceedings may be brought against a consumer by the other party to the contract only in the courts of the Contracting State in which the consumer is domiciled.

These provisions shall not affect the right to bring a counterclaim in the court in which, in accordance with this Section, the original claim is pending.

Article 15

The provisions of this Section may be departed from only by an agreement:
1. which is entered into after the dispute has arisen; or
2. which allows the consumer to bring proceedings in courts other than those indicated in this Section; or
3. which is entered into by the consumer and the other party to the contract, both of whom are at the time of conclusion of the contract domiciled or habitually resident in the same Contracting State, and which confers jurisdiction on the courts of that State, provided that such an agreement is not contrary to the law of that State.

Section 5: Exclusive jurisdiction

Article 16

The following courts shall have exclusive jurisdiction, regardless of domicile:
1. (a) in proceedings which have as their object rights *in rem* in immovable property or tenancies of immovable property, the courts of the Contracting State in which the property is situated;
(b) however, in proceedings which have as their object tenancies of immovable property concluded for temporary private use for a maximum period of six consecutive months, the courts of the Contracting State in which the defendant is domiciled shall also have jurisdiction, provided that the tenant is a natural

person and neither party is domiciled in the Contracting State in which the property is situated;

2. in proceedings which have as their object the validity of the constitution, the nullity or the dissolution of companies or other legal persons or associations of natural or legal persons, or the decisions of their organs, the courts of the Contracting State in which the company, legal person or association has its seat;

3. in proceedings which have as their object the validity of entries in public registers, the courts of the Contracting State in which the register is kept;

4. in proceedings concerned with the registration or validity of patents, trade marks, designs, or other similar rights required to be deposited or registered, the courts of the Contracting State in which the deposit or registration has been applied for, has taken place or is under the terms of an international convention deemed to have taken place;

5. in proceedings concerned with the enforcement of judgments, the courts of the Contracting State in which the judgment has been or is to be enforced.

Section 6: Prorogation of jurisdiction

Article 17

1. If the parties, one or more of whom is domiciled in a Contracting State, have agreed that a court or the courts of a Contracting State are to have jurisdiction to settle any disputes which have arisen or which may arise in connection with a particular legal relationship, that court or those courts shall have exclusive jurisdiction. Such an agreement conferring jurisdiction shall be either:
(a) in writing or evidenced in writing, or
(b) in a form which accords with practices which the parties have established between themselves, or
(c) in international trade or commerce, in a form which accords with a usage of which the parties are or ought to have been aware and which in such trade or commerce is widely known to, and regularly observed by, parties to contracts of the type involved in the particular trade or commerce concerned.

   Where such an agreement is concluded by parties, none of whom is domiciled in a Contracting State, the courts of other Contracting States shall have no jurisdiction over their disputes unless the court or courts chosen have declined jurisdiction.

2. The court or courts of a Contracting State on which a trust instrument has conferred jurisdiction shall have exclusive jurisdiction in any proceedings brought against a settlor, trustee or beneficiary, if relations between these persons or their rights or obligations under the trust are involved.

3. Agreements or provisions of a trust instrument conferring jurisdiction shall have no legal force if they are contrary to the provisions of Article 12 or 15, or if

the courts whose jurisdiction they purport to exclude have exclusive jurisdiction by virtue of Article 16.

4. If an agreement conferring jurisdiction was concluded for the benefit of only one of the parties, that party shall retain the right to bring proceedings in any other court which has jurisdiction by virtue of this Convention.

5. In matters relating to individual contracts of employment an agreement conferring jurisdiction shall have legal force only if it is entered into after the dispute has arisen.

Article 18

Apart from jurisdiction derived from other provisions of this Convention, a court of a Contracting State before whom a defendant enters an appearance shall have jurisdiction. This rule shall not apply where appearance was entered solely to contest the jurisdiction, or where another court has exclusive jurisdiction by virtue of Article 16.

Section 7: Examination as to jurisdiction and admissibility

Article 19

Where a court of a Contracting State is seised of a claim which is principally concerned with a matter over which the courts of another Contracting State have exclusive jurisdiction by virtue of Article 16, it shall declare of its own motion that it has no jurisdiction.

Article 20

Where a defendant domiciled in one Contracting State is sued in a court of another Contracting State and does not enter an appearance, the court shall declare of its own motion that it has no jurisdiction unless its jurisdiction is derived from the provisions of this Convention.

The court shall stay the proceedings so long as it is not shown that the defendant has been able to receive the document instituting the proceedings or an equivalent document in sufficient time to enable him to arrange for his defence, or that all necessary steps have been taken to this end.

The provisions of the foregoing paragraph shall be replaced by those of Article 15 of the Hague Convention of 15 November 1965 on the service abroad of judicial and extrajudicial documents in civil or commercial matters, if the document instituting the proceedings or notice thereof had to be transmitted abroad in accordance with that Convention.

Section 8: *Lis Pendens* — related actions

Article 21

Where proceedings involving the same cause of action and between the same parties are brought in the courts of different Contracting States, any court other than the court first seised shall of its own motion stay its proceedings until such time as the jurisdiction of the court first seised is established.

Where the jurisdiction of the court first seised is established, any court other than the court first seised shall decline jurisdiction in favour of that court.

Article 22

Where related actions are brought in the courts of different Contracting States, any court other than the court first seised may, while the actions are pending at first instance, stay its proceedings.

A court other than the court first seised may also, on the application of one of the parties, decline jurisdiction if the law of that court permits the consolidation of related actions and the court first seised has jurisdiction over both actions.

For the purposes of this Article, actions are deemed to be related where they are so closely connected that it is expedient to hear and determine them together to avoid the risk of irreconcilable judgments resulting from separate proceedings.

Article 23

Where actions come within the exclusive jurisdiction of several courts, any court other than the court first seised shall decline jurisdiction in favour of that court.

Section 9: Provisional, including protective, measures

Article 24

Application may be made to the courts of a Contracting State for such provisional, including protective, measures as may be available under the law of that State, even if, under this Convention, the courts of another Contracting State have jurisdiction as to the substance of the matter.

TITLE III: RECOGNITION AND ENFORCEMENT

Article 25

For the purposes of this Convention, 'judgment' means any judgment given by a court or tribunal of a Contracting State, whatever the judgment may be called, including a decree, order, decision or writ of execution, as well as the determination of costs or expenses by an officer of the court.

Section 1: Recognition

Article 26

A judgment given in a Contracting State shall be recognized in the other Contracting States without any special procedure being required.

Any interested party who raises the recognition of a judgment as the principal issue in a dispute may, in accordance with the procedures provided for in Section 2 and 3 of this Title, apply for a decision that the judgment be recognized.

If the outcome of proceedings in a court of a Contracting State depends on the determination of an incidental question of recognition that court shall have jurisdiction over that question.

Article 27

A judgment shall not be recognized:
1. if such recognition is contrary to public policy in the State in which recognition is sought;
2. where it was given in default of appearance, if the defendant was not duly served with the document which instituted the proceedings or with an equivalent document in sufficient time to enable him to arrange for his defence;
3. if the judgment is irreconcilable with a judgment given in a dispute between the same parties in the State in which recognition is sought;
4. if the court of the State of origin, in order to arrive at its judgment, has decided a preliminary question concerning the status or legal capacity of natural persons, rights in property arising out of a matrimonial relationship, wills or succession in a way that conflicts with a rule of the private international law of the State in which the recognition is sought, unless the same result would have been reached by the application of the rules of private international law of that State;
5. if the judgment is irreconcilable with an earlier judgment given in a non-contracting State involving the same cause of action and between the same parties, provided that this latter judgment fulfills the conditions necessary for its recognition in the State addressed.

Article 28

Moreover, a judgment shall not be recognized if it conflicts with the provisions of Sections 3, 4 or 5 of Title II or in a case provided for in Article 59.

A judgment may furthermore be refused recognition in any case provided for in Article 54B (3) or 57 (4).

In its examination of the grounds of jurisdiction referred to in the foregoing paragraphs, the court or authority applied to shall be bound by the findings of fact on which the court of the State of origin based its jurisdiction.

Subject to the provisions of the first and second paragraphs, the jurisdiction of the court of the State of origin may not be reviewed; the test of public policy referred to in Article 27 (1) may not be applied to the rules relating to jurisdiction.

Article 29

Under no circumstances may a foreign judgment be reviewed as to its substance.

Article 30

A court of a Contracting State in which recognition is sought of a judgment given in another Contracting State may stay the proceedings if an ordinary appeal against the judgment has been lodged.

A court of a Contracting State in which recognition is sought of a judgment given in Ireland or the United Kingdom may stay the proceedings if enforcement is suspended in the State of origin by reason of an appeal.

Section 2: Enforcement

Article 31

A judgment given in a Contracting State and enforceable in that State shall be enforced in another Contracting State when, on the application of any interested party, it has been declared enforceable there.

However, in the United Kingdom, such a judgment shall be enforced in England and Wales, in Scotland, or in Northern Ireland when, on the application of any interested party, it has been registered for enforcement in that part of the United Kingdom.

Article 32

1. The application shall be submitted:
— in Belgium, to the Tribunal de première instance or Rechtbank van eerste aanleg,
— in Denmark, to the Byret,
— in the Federal Republic of Germany, to the presiding judge of a chamber of the Landgericht,
— in Greece, to the Μονομελεζ Πρωτοδικειο,
— in Spain, to the Juzgado de Primera Instancia,
— in France, to the presiding judge of the Tribunal de grande instance,
— in Ireland, to the High Court,
— in Iceland, to the Héraðsdomari,
— in Italy, to the Corte d'appello,
— in Luxembourg, to the presiding judge of the Tribunal d'arrondissement,
— in the Netherlands, to the presiding judge of the Arrondissementsrechtsbank,
— in Norway, to the Herredsrett or Byrett as namstrett,
— in Austria, to the Landesgericht or the Kreisgericht,
— in Portugal, to the Tribunal Juricial de Circulo,
— in Switzerland:
   (a) in respect of judgments ordering the payment of a sum of money, to the juge de la mainlevée / Rechtsöffnungsrichter / giudice competente a pronunciare sul rigetto dell'opposizione, within the framework of the procedure governed by Articles 80 and 81 of the loi fédérale sur la poursuite pour dettes et la faillite / Bundesgesetz über Schuldbetreibung und Konkurs / legge federale sulla esecuzione e sul fallimento;
   (b) in respect of judgments ordering a performance other than the payment of a sum of money, to the juge cantonal d'exequatur compétent / zuständiger kantonaler Vollstreckungsrichter / guiudice cantonale competente a pronunciare l'exequatur,
— in Finland, to the Ulosotonhaltija /överexekutor,
— in Sweden, to the Svea hovrätt,
— in the United Kingdom:
   (a) in England and Wales, to the High Court of Justice, or in the case of a maintenance judgment to the Magistrates' Court on transmission by the Secretary of State;
   (b) in Scotland, to the Court of Session, or in the case of a maintenance judgment to the Sheriff Court on transmission by the Secretary of State;
   (c) in Northern Ireland, to the High Court of Justice, or in the case of a maintenance judgment to the Magistrates' Court on transmission by the Secretary of State.
2. The jurisdiction of local courts shall be determined by reference to the place of domicile of the party against whom enforcement is sought. If he is not domiciled in the State in which enforcement is sought, it shall be determined by reference to the place of enforcement.

Article 33

The procedure for making the application shall be governed by the law of the State in which enforcement is sought.

The applicant must give an address for service of process within the area of jurisdiction of the court applied to. However, if the law of the State in which enforcement is sought does not provide for the furnishing of such an address, the applicant shall appoint a representative *ad litem*.

The documents referred to in Articles 46 and 47 shall be attached to the application.

Article 34

The court applied to shall give its decision without delay; the party against whom enforcement is sought shall not at this stage of the proceedings be entitled to make any submissions on the application.

The application may be refused only for one of the reasons specified in Articles 27 and 28.

Under no circumstances may the foreign judgment be reviewed as to its substance.

Article 35

The appropriate officer of the court shall without delay bring the decision given on the application to the notice of the applicant in accordance with the procedure laid down by the law of the State in which enforcement is sought.

Article 36

If enforcement is authorized, the party against whom enforcement is sought may appeal against the decision within one month of service thereof.

If that party is domiciled in a Contracting State other than that in which the decision authorizing enforcement was given, the time for appealing shall be two months and shall run from the date of service, either on him in person or at his residence. No extension of time may be granted on account of distance.

Article 37

1. An appeal against the decision authorizing enforcement shall be lodged in accordance with the rules governing procedure in contentious matters:

— in Belgium, with the tribunal de première instance or rechtsbank van eerste aanleg,

— in Denmark, with the landsret,

— in the Federal Republic of Germany, with the Oberlandesgericht,

— in Greece, with the Εφετειο,

— in Spain, with the Audiencia Provincial,

— in France, with the cour d'appel,

— in Ireland, with the High Court,

— in Iceland, with the Héraðsdomari,

— in Italy, with the corte d'appello,

— in Luxembourg, with the Cour supérieure de justice sitting as a court of civil appeal,

— in the Netherlands, with the arrondissementsrechtsbank,

— in Norway, with the lagmannsrett,

— in Austria, with the Landesgericht or the Kreisgericht,

— in Portugal, with the Tribunal da Relaçao,

— in Switzerland, with the tribunal cantonal Kantonsgericht / tribunale cantonale,

— in Finland, with the hoviokeus / hovrätt,

— in the United Kingdom:

(a) in England and Wales, with the High Court of Justice, or in the case of a maintenance judgment with the Magistrates' Court;

(b) in Scotland, with the Court of Session, or in the case of a maintenance judgment with the Sheriff Court;

(c) in Northern Ireland, with the High Court of Justice, or in the case of a maintenance judgment with the Magisrates' Court.

2. The judgment given on the appeal may be contested only:

— in Belgium, Greece, Spain, France, Italy, Luxembourg and in the Netherlands, by an appeal in cassation,

— in Denmark, by an appeal to the højesteret, with the leave of the Minister of Justice,

— in the Federal Republic of Germany, by a Rechtsbeschwerde,

— in Ireland, by an appeal on a point of law to the Supreme Court,

— in Iceland, by an appeal to the Hæstiréttur,

— in Norway, by an appeal (kjæremål or anke) to the Hoyesteretts Kjæremålsutvalg or Hoyesterett,

— in Austria, in the case of an appeal, by a Revisionsrekurs and, in the case of opposition proceedings, by a Berufung with the possibility of a Revision,

— in Portugal, by an appeal on a point of law,

— in Switzerland, by a recours de droit public devant le tribunal fédéral / staatsrechtlich Beschwerde beim Bundesgericht / ricorso di diritto pubblico davanti al tribunale federale,

— in Finland, by an appeal to the korkein oikeus / högsta domstolen,

— in Sweden, by an appeal to the högsta domstolen,

— in the United Kingdom, by a single further appeal on a point of law.

Article 38

The court with which the appeal under Article 37 (1) is lodged may, on the application of the appellant, stay the proceedings if an ordinary appeal has been lodged against the judgment in the State of origin or if the time for such an appeal has not yet expired; in the latter case, the court may specify the time within which such an appeal is to be lodged.

Where the judgment was given in Ireland or the United Kingdom, any form of appeal available in the State of origin shall be treated as an ordinary appeal for the purposes of the first paragraph.

The court may also make enforcement conditional on the provision of such security as it shall determine.

Article 39

During the time specified for an appeal pursuant to Article 36 and until any such appeal has been determined, no measures of enforcement may be taken other than protective measures taken against the property of the party against whom enforcement is sought.

The decision authorizing enforcement shall carry with it the power to proceed to any such protective measures.

Article 40

1. If the application for enforcement is refused, the applicant may appeal:
— in Belgium to the cour d'appel or hof van beroep,
— in Denmark, to the landsret,
— in the Federal Republic of Germany, to the Oberlandesgericht,
— in Greece, to the Εφετειο,
— in Spain, to the Audiencia Provincial,
— in France, to the cour d'appel,
— in Ireland, to the High Court,
— in Iceland, to the Héraðsdomari,
— in Italy, to the corte d'appello,
— in Luxembourg, to the Cour supérieure de justice sitting as a court of civil appeal,
— in the Netherlands, to the gerechtshof,
— in Norway, to the lagmannsrett,
— in Austria, to the Landesgericht or the Kreisgericht,

— in Portugal, to the Tribunal da Relaçao,
— in Switzerland, to the tribunal cantonal / Kantonsgericht / tribunale cantonale,
— in Finland, to the hovioikeus / hovrätt,
— in Sweden, to the Svea hovrätt,
— in the United Kingdom:
    (a) in England and Wales, to the High Court of Justice, or in the case of a maintenance judgment to the Magistrates' Court;
    (b) in Scotland, to the Court of Session, or in the case of a maintenance judgment to the Sheriff Court;
    (c) in Northern Ireland, to the High Court of Justice, or in the case of a maintenance judgment to the Magistrates' Court.
2. The party against whom enforcement is sought shall be summoned to appear before the appellate court. If he fails to appear, the provisions of the second and third paragraphs of Article 20 shall apply even where he is not domiciled in any of the Contracting States.

Article 41

A judgment given on an appeal provided for in Article 40 may be contested only:
— in Belgium, Greece, Spain, France, Italy, Luxembourg and in the Netherlands, by an appeal in cassation,
— in Denmark, by an appeal to the højesteret, with the leave of the Minister of Justice,
— in the Federal Republic of Germany, by a Rechtsbeschwerde,
— in Ireland, by an appeal on a point of law to the Supreme Court,
— in Iceland, by an appeal to the Hæstiréttur,
— in Norway, by an appeal (Kjæremål or anke) to the Hoyesteretts kjæremålsutvalg or Hoyesterett,
— in Austria, by a Revisionsrekurs,
— in Portugal, by an appeal on a point of law,
— in Switzerland, by a recours de droit public devant le tribunal fédéral; staatsrechtliche Beschwerde beim Bundesgericht / ricorso di diritto pubblico davanti al tribunale federale,
— in Finland, by an appeal to the korkein oikeus / högsta domstolen,
— in Sweden, by an appeal to the högsta domstolen,
— in the United Kingdom, by a single further appeal on a point of law.

Article 42

Where a foreign judgment has been given in respect of several mattes and enforcement cannot be authorized for all of them, the court shall authorize enforcement for one or more of them.

An applicant may request partial enforcement of a judgment.

Article 43

A foreign judgment which orders a periodic payment by way of a penalty shall be enforceable in the State in which enforcement is sought only if the amount of the payment has been finally determined by the courts of the State of origin.

Article 44

An applicant who, in the State of origin, has benefitted from complete or partial legal aid or exemption from costs or expenses, shall be entitled, in the procedures provided for in Articles 32 to 35, to benefit from the most favourable legal aids or the most extensive exemption from costs or expenses provided for by the law of the State addressed.

However, an applicant who requests the enforcement of a decision given by an administrative authority in Denmark or in Iceland in respect of a maintenance order may, in the State addressed, claim the benefits referred to in the first paragraph if he presents a statement from, respectively, the Danish Ministry of Justice or the Icelandic Ministry of Justice to the effect that he fulfills the economic requirements to qualify for the grant of complete or partial legal aid or exemption from costs or expenses.

Article 45

No security, bond or deposit, however described, shall be required of a party who in one Contracting State applies for enforcement of a judgment given in another Contracting State on the ground that he is a foreign national or that he is not domiciled or resident in the State in which enforcement is sought.

Section 3: Common provisions

Article 46

A party seeking recognition or applying for enforcement of a judgment shall produce:
1. a copy of the judgment which satisfies the conditions necessary to establish its authenticity;
2. in the case of a judgment given in default, the original or a certified true copy of the document which establishes that the party in default was served with the document instituting the proceedings or with an equivalent document.

Article 47

A party applying for enforcement shall also produce:
1. documents which establish that, according to the law of the State of origin, the judgment is enforceable and has been served;
2. where appropriate, a document showing that the applicant is in receipt of legal aid in the State of origin.

Article 48

If the documents specified in Articles 46 (2) and 47 (2) are not produced, the court may specify a time for their production, accept equivalent documents or, if it considers that it has sufficient information before it, dispense with their production.

If the court so requires, a translation of the documents shall be produced; the translation shall be certified by a person qualified to do so in one of the Contracting States.

Article 49

No legalization or other similar formality shall be required in respect of the documents referred to in Articles 46 or 47 or the second paragraph of Article 48, or in respect of a document appointing a representative *ad litem*.

TITLE IV: AUTHENTIC INSTRUMENTS AND COURT SETTLEMENTS

Article 50

A document which has been formally drawn up or registered as an authentic instrument and is enforceable in one Contracting State shall, in another Contracting State, be declared enforceable there, on application made in accordance with the procedures provided for in Articles 31 *et seq.* The application may be refused only if enforcement of the instrument is contrary to public policy in the State addressed.

The instrument produced must satisfy the conditions necessary to establish its authenticity in the State of origin.

The provisions of Section 3 of Title III shall apply as appropriate.

Article 51

A settlement which has been approved by a court in the course of proceedings and is enforceable in the State in which it was concluded shall be enforceable in the State addressed under the same conditions as authentic instruments.

TITLE V: GENERAL PROVISIONS

Article 52

In order to determine whether a party is domiciled in the Contracting State whose courts are seised of a matter, the Court shall apply its internal law.

If a party is not domiciled in the State whose courts are seised of the matter, then, in order to determine whether the party is domiciled in another Contracting State, the court shall apply the law of that State.

Article 53

For the purposes of this Convention, the seat of a company or other legal person or association of natural or legal persons shall be treated as its domicile. However, in order to determine that seat, the court shall apply its rules of private international law.

In order to determine whether a trust is domiciled in the Contracting State whose courts are seised of the matter, the court shall apply its rules of private international law.

TITLE VI: TRANSITIONAL PROVISIONS

Article 54

The provisions of this Convention shall apply only to legal proceedings instituted and to documents formally drawn up or registered as authentic instruments after its entry into force in the State of origin and, where recognition or enforcement of a judgment or authentic instrument is sought, in the State addressed.

However, judgments given after the date of entry into force of this Convention between the State of origin and the State addressed in proceedings instituted before that date shall be recognized and enforced in accordance with the provisions of Title III if jurisdiction was founded upon rules which accorded with those provided for either in Title II of this Convention or in a convention concluded between the State of origin and the State addressed which was in force when the proceedings were instituted.

If the parties to a dispute concerning a contract had agreed in writing before the entry into force of this Convention that the contract was to be governed by the law of Ireland or of a part of the United Kingdom, the courts of Ireland or of that part of the United Kingdom shall retain the right to exercise jurisdiction in the dispute.

Article 54A

For a period of three years from the entry into force of this Convention for Denmark, Greece, Ireland, Iceland, Norway, Finland and Sweden, respectively, jurisdiction in maritime matters shall be determined in these States not only in accordance with the provisions of Title II, but also in accordance with the provisions of paragraphs 1 to 7 following. However, upon the entry into force of the International Convention relating to the arrest of sea-going ships, signed at Brussels on 10 May 1952, for one of these States, these provisions shall cease to have effect for that State.

1. A person who is domiciled in a Contracting State may be sued in the courts of one of the States mentioned above in respect of a maritime claim if the ship to which the claim relates or any other ship owned by him has been arrested by judicial process within the territory of the latter State to secure the claim, or could have been so arrested there but bail or other security has been given, and either;

   (a) the claimant is domiciled in the latter State; or

   (b) the claim arose in the latter State; or

   (c) the claim concerns the voyage during which the arrest was made or could have been made; or

   (d) the claim arises out of a collision or out of damage caused by a ship to another ship or to goods or persons on board either ship, either by the execution or non-execution of a manoeuvre or by the non-observance of regulations; or

   (e) the claim is for salvage; or

   (f) the claim is in respect of a mortgage or hypothecation of the ship arrested.

2. A claimant may arrest either the particular ship to which the maritime claim relates, or any other ship which is owned by the person who was, at the time when the maritime claim arose, the owner of the particular ship. However, only the particular ship to which the maritime claim relates may be arrested in respect of the maritime claims set out under 5. (0), (p) or (q) of the Article.

3. Ships shall be deemed to be in the same ownership when all the shares therein are owned by the same person or persons.

4. When in the case of a charter by demise of a ship the charterer alone is liable in respect of a maritime claim relating to that ship, the claimant may arrest that ship or any other ship owned by the charterer, but no other ship owned by the owner may be arrested in respect of such claim. The same shall apply to any case in which a person other than the owner of a ship is liable in respect of a maritime claim relating to that ship.

5. The expression 'maritime claim' means a claim arising out of one or more of the following:

   (a) damage caused by any ship either in collision or otherwise;

   (b) loss of life or personal injury caused by any ship or occurring in connection with the operation on any ship;

(c) salvage;

(d) agreement relating to the use or hire of any ship whether by charterparty or otherwise;

(e) agreement relating to the carriage of goods in any ship whether by charterparty or otherwise;

(f) loss of or damage to goods including baggage carried in any ship;

(g) general average;

(h) bottomry;

(i) towage;

(j) pilotage;

(k) goods or materials wherever supplied to a ship for her operation or maintenance;

(l) construction, repair or equipment of any ship or dock charges and dues;

(m) wages of masters, officers or crew;

(n) master's disbursements, including disbursements made by shippers, charterers or agents on behalf of a ship or her owner;

(o) dispute as to the title to or ownership of any ship;

(p) disputes between co-owners of any ship as to the ownership, possession, employment or earnings of that ship;

(q) the mortgage or hypothecation of any ship.

6. In Denmark, the expression 'arrest' shall be deemed as regards the maritime claims referred to under 5. (o) and (p) of this Article, to include a 'forbud', where that is the only procedure allowed in respect of such a claim under Articles 646 to 653 of the law on civil procedure (lov om rettens pleje).

7. In Iceland, the expression 'arrest' shall be deemed, as regards the maritime claims referred to under 5. (o) and (p) of this Article, to include a 'lögbann', where that is the only procedure allowed in respect of such a claim under Chapter III of the law on arrest and injunction (lög um kyrrsetningu og lögbann).

TITLE VII: RELATIONSHIP TO THE BRUSSELS CONVENTION AND TO OTHER CONVENTIONS

Article 54B

1. This Convention shall not prejudice the application by the Member States of the European Communities of the Convention on Jurisdiction and the Enforcement of Judgments in Civil and Commercial Matters, signed at Brussels on 27 September 1968 and of the Protocol on interpretation of that Convention by the Court of Justice, signed at Luxembourg on 3 June 1971, as amended by the Conventions of Accession to the said Convention and the said Protocol by the States acceding to the European Communities, all of these Conventions and the Protocol being hereinafter referred to as the 'Brussels Convention'.

2. However, this Convention shall in any event be applied:

(a) in matters of jurisdiction, where the defendant is domiciled in the territory of a Contracting State which is not a member of the European Communities, or where Article 16 or 17 of this Convention confer a jurisdiction on the courts of such a Contracting State;

(b) in relation to a *lis pendens* or to related actions as provided for in Articles 21 and 22, when proceedings are instituted in a Contracting State which is not a member of the European Communities and in a Contracting State which is a member of the European Communities;

(c) in matters of recognition and enforcement, where either the State of origin or the State addressed is not a member of the European Communities.

3. In addition to the grounds provided for in Title III recognition or enforcement may be refused if the ground of jurisdiction on which the judgment has been based differs from that resulting from this Convention and recognition or enforcement is sought against a party who is domiciled in a Contracting State which is not a member of the European Communities, unless the judgment may otherwise be recognized or enforced under any rule of law in the State addressed.

Article 55

Subject to the provisions of Articles 54 (2) and 56, this Convention shall, for the States which are parties to it, supersede the following conventions concluded between two or more of them:

— the Convention between the Swiss Confederation and France on jurisdiction and enforcement of judgments in civil matters, signed at Paris on 15 June 1869,

— the Treaty between the Swiss Confederation and Spain on the mutual enforcement of judgments in civil or commercial matters, signed at Madrid on 19 November 1896,

— the Convention between the Swiss Confederation and the German Reich on the recognition and enforcement of judgments and arbitration awards, signed at Berne on 2 November 1929,

— the Convention between Denmark, Finland, Iceland, Norway and Sweden on the recognition and enforcement of judgments, signed at Copenhagen on 16 March 1932,

— the Convention between the Swiss Confederation and Italy on the recognition and enforcement of judgments, signed at Rome on 3 January 1933,

— the Convention between Sweden and the Swiss Confederation on the recognition and enforcement of judgments and arbitral awards signed at Stockholm on 15 January 1936,

— the Convention between the Kingdom of Belgium and Austria on the reciprocal recognition and enforcement of judgments and authentic instruments relating to maintenance obligations, signed at Vienna on 25 October 1957,

— the Convention between the Swiss Confederation and Belgium on the recognition and enforcement of judgments and arbitration awards, signed at Berne on 29 April 1959,

— the Convention between the Federal Republic of Germany and Austria on the reciprocal recognition and enforcement of judgments, settlements and authentic instruments in civil and commercial matters, signed at Vienna on 6 June 1959,

— the Convention between the Kingdom of Belgium and Austria on the reciprocal recognition and enforcement of judgments, arbitral awards and authentic instruments in civil and commercial matters, signed at Vienna on 16 June 1959,

— the Convention between Austria and the Swiss Confederation on the recognition and enforcement of judgments, signed at Berne on 16 December 1960,

— the Convention between Norway and the United Kingdom providing for the reciprocal recognition and enforcement of judgments in civil matters, signed at London on 12 June 1961,

— the Convention between the United Kingdom and Austria providing for the reciprocal recognition and enforcement of judgments in civil and commercial matters, signed at Vienna on 14 July 1961, with amending Protocol signed at London on 6 March 1970,

— the Convention between the Kingdom of the Netherlands and Austria on the reciprocal recognition and enforcement of judgments and authentic instruments in civil and commercial matters, signed at The Hague on 6 February 1963,

— the Convention between France and Austria on the recognition and enforcement of judgments and authentic instruments in civil and commercial matters, signed at Vienna on 15 July 1966,

— the Convention between Luxembourg and Austria on the recognition and enforcement of judgments and authentic instruments in civil and commercial matters, signed at Luxembourg on 29 July 1971,

— the Convention between Italy and Austria on the recognition and enforcement of judgments in civil and commercial matters, of judicial settlements and of authentic instruments, signed at Rome on 16 November 1971,

— the Convention between Norway and the Federal Republic of Germany on the recognition and enforcement of judgments and enforceable documents, in civil and commercial matters, signed at Oslo on 17 June 1977,

— the Convention between Denmark, Finland, Iceland, Norway and Sweden on the recognition and enforcement of judgments in civil matters, signed at Copenhagen on 11 October 1977,

— the Convention between Austria and Sweden on the recognition and enforcement of judgments in civil matters, signed at Stockholm on 16 September 1982,

— the Convention between Austria and Spain on the recognition and enforcement of judgments, settlements and enforceable authentic instruments in civil and commercial matters, signed at Vienna on 17 February 1984,

— the Convention between Norway and Austria on the recognition and enforcement of judgments in civil matters, signed at Vienna on 21 May 1984, and
— the Convention between Finland and Austria on the recognition and enforcement of judgments in civil matters, signed at Vienna on 17 November 1986.

Article 56

The Treaty and the conventions referred to in Article 55 shall continue to have effect in relation to matters to which this Convention does not apply.

They shall continue to have effect in respect of judgments given and documents formally drawn up or registered as authentic instruments before the entry into force of this Convention.

Article 57

1. This Convention shall not affect any conventions to which the Contracting States are or will be parties and which in relation to particular matters, govern jurisdiction or the recognition or enforcement of judgments.
2. This Convention shall not prevent a court of a Contracting State which is party to a convention referred to in the first paragraph from assuming jurisdiction in accordance with that convention, even where the defendant is domiciled in a Contracting State which is not a party to that convention. The court hearing the action shall, in any event, apply Article 20 of this Convention.
3. Judgments given in a Contracting State by a court in the exercise of jurisdiction provided for in a convention referred to in the first paragraph shall be recognized and enforced in the other Contracting States in accordance with Title III of this Convention.
4. In addition to the grounds provided for in Title III, recognition or enforcement may be refused if the State addressed is not a contracting party to a convention referred to in the first paragraph and the person against whom recognition or enforcement is sought is domiciled in that State, unless the judgment may otherwise be recognized or enforced under any rule of law in the State addressed.
5. Where a convention referred to in the first paragraph to which both the State of origin and the State addressed are parties lays down conditions for the recognition or enforcement of judgments, those conditions shall apply. In any event, the provisions of this Convention which concern the procedures for recognition and enforcement of judgments may be applied.

Article 58

(None)

Article 59

This Convention shall not prevent a Contracting State from assuming, in a convention on the recognition and enforcement of judgments, an obligation towards a third State not to recognize judgments given in other Contracting States against defendants domiciled or habitually resident in the third State where, in cases provided for in Article 4, the judgment could only be founded on a ground of jurisdiction specified in the second paragraph of Article 3.

However, a Contracting State may not assume an obligation towards a third State not to recognize a judgment given in another Contracting State by a court basing its jurisdiction on the presence within that State of property belonging to the defendant, or the seizure by the plaintiff of property situated there:

1. if the action is brought to assert or declare proprietary or possessory rights in that property, seeks to obtain authority to dispose of it, or arises from another issue relating to such property, or
2. if the property constitutes the security for a debt which is the subject-matter of the action.

TITLE VIII: FINAL PROVISIONS

Article 60

The following may be parties to this Convention:

(a) States which, at the time of the opening of this Convention for signature, are members of the European Communities or of the European Free Trade Association;
(b) States which, after the opening of this Convention for signature, become members of the European Communities or of the European Free Trade Association;
(c) States invited to accede in accordance with Article 62 (1) (b).

Article 61

1. This Convention shall be opened for signature by the States members of the European Communities or of the European Free Trade Association.
2. The Convention shall be submitted for ratification by the signatory States. The instruments of ratification shall be deposited with the Swiss Federal Council.
3. The Convention shall enter into force on the first day of the third month following the date on which two States, of which one is a member of the European Communities and the other a member of the European Free Trade Association, deposit their instrument of ratification.
4. The Convention shall take effect in relation to any other signatory State on the first day of the third month following the deposit of its instrument of ratification.

Article 62

1. After entering into force this Convention shall be open to accession by:
   (a) the States referred to in Article 60 (b);
   (b) other States which have been invited to accede upon a request made by one of the Contracting States to the depository State. The depositary State shall invite the State concerned to accede only if, after having communicated the contents of the communications that this State intends to make in accordance with Article 63, it has obtained the unanimous agreement of the signatory States and the Contracting States referred to in Article 60 (a) and (b).
2. If an acceding State wishes to furnish details for the purposes of Protocol 1, negotiations shall be entered into to that end. A negotiating conference shall be convened by the Swiss Federal Council.
3. In respect of an acceding State, the Convention shall take effect on the first day of the third month following the deposit of its instrument of accession.
4. However, in respect of an acceding State referred to in paragraph 1 (a) or (b), the Convention shall take effect only in relations between the acceding State and the Contracting States which have not made any objections to the accession before the first day of the third month following the deposit of the instrument of accession.

Article 63

Each acceding State shall, when depositing its instrument of accession, communicate the information required for the application of Articles 3, 32, 37, 40, 41 and 55 of this Convention and furnish, if need be, the details prescribed during the negotiations for the purposes of Protocol 1.

Article 64

1. This Convention is concluded for an initial period of five years from the date of its entry into force in accordance with Article 61 (3), even in the case of States which ratify it or accede to it after that date.
2. At the end of the initial five-year period, the Convention shall be automatically renewed from year to year.
3. Upon the expiry of the initial five-year period, any contracting State may, at any time, denounce the Convention by sending a notification to the Swiss Federal Council.
4. The denunciation shall take effect at the end of the calendar year following the expiry of a period of six months from the date of receipt by the Swiss Federal Council of the notification of denunciation.

Article 65

The following are annexed to this Convention:
— a Protocol 1, on certain questions of jurisdiction, procedure and enforcement,
— a Protocol 2, on the uniform interpretation of the Convention,
— a Protocol 3, on the application of Article 57.

These Protocols shall form an integral part of the Convention.

Article 66

Any Contracting State may request the revision of this Convention. To that end, the Swiss Federal Council shall issue invitations to a revision conference within a period of six months from the date of the request for revision.

Article 67

The Swiss Federal Council shall notify the States represented at the Diplomatic Conference of Lugano and the States who have later acceded to the Convention of:
(a) the deposit of each instrument of ratification or accession;
(b) the dates of entry into force of this Convention in respect of the Contracting States;
(c) any denunciation received pursuant to Article 64;
(d) any declaration received pursuant to Article Ia of Protocol 1;
(e) any declaration received pursuant to Article Ib of Protocol 1;
(f) any declaration received pursuant to Article IV of Protocol 1;
(g) any communication made pursuant to Article VI of Protocol 1.

Article 68

This Convention, drawn up in a single original in the Danish, Dutch, English, Finnish, French, German, Greek, Icelandic, Irish, Italian, Norwegian, Portuguese, Spanish and Swedish languages, all fourteen texts being equally authentic, shall be deposited in the archives of the Swiss Federal Council. The Swiss Federal Council shall transmit a certified copy to the Government of each State represented at the Diplomatic Conference of Lugano and to the Government of each acceding State.

In witness whereof, the undersigned Plenipotentiaries have signed this Convention.

Done at Lugano on the sixteenth day of September in the year one thousand nine hundred and eighty-eight.

JURISDICTION STATUTES

1. FRANCE

Nouveau Code de Procédure Civile, Article 48

Any clause which, directly or indirectly, impairs or waives jurisdictional rules of a territorial nature will be deemed void [literally "non-written"] unless the clause was entered into between persons who have contracted in their capacity as merchants and the clause appears in a clearly noticeable fashion in the obligation of the party against whom the clause in invoked.

French original reads:
"Toute clause qui, directement ou indirectement, déroge aux règles de compétence territoriale est réputée non écrite à moins qu'elle n'ait été convenue entre des personnes ayant toutes contracté en qualité de commerçant et qu'elle n'ait été spécifiée de façon très apparente dans l'engagement de la partie à qui elle est opposée."

2. GERMANY

Code of Civil Procedure *(Zivilprozessordnung)*

§ 38. Agreement Concerning the Jurisdiction of the Courts

(1) A court of first instance, which in itself has no jurisdiction, becomes competent by express or implied agreement of the parties, if the parties to the agreement are merchants who do not belong to the traders designated in § 4 of the Commercial Code, juridical persons of public law or separate estates created under public law.

(2) An agreement conferring jurisdiction on a court of first instance may also be concluded if at least one of the parties has no general jurisdictional connection [allgemeinen Gerichtsstand] within the country. The agreement must be in writing or, if it was made orally, confirmed in writing. If one of the parties has a general jurisdictional connection within the country, the only court chosen within the country may be the one before which the such party has his venue or one which has special jurisdiction.

(3) Otherwise, an agreement on jurisdiction is only permitted if it is express and in writing:
1. made after the dispute arose, or
2. was concluded for the case in which the party sued transferred his residence or customary abode outside the territorial application of this law or his residence or customary abode is unknown when the claim is filed.

German original reads:
§ 38. Zugelassene Gerichtsstandsvereinbarung

(1) Ein an sich unzuständiges Gericht des ersten Rechtszuges wird durch ausdrückliche oder stillschweigende Vereinbarung der Parteien zuständig, wenn die Vertragsparteien Kaufleute, die nicht zu den in § 4 des Handelsgesetzbuchs bezeichneten Gewerbetreibenden gehören, juristische Personen des öffentlichen Rechts oder öffentlich-rechtliche Sondervermögen sind.

(2) Die Zuständigkeit eines Gerichts des ersten Rechtszuges kann ferner vereinbart werden, wenn mindestens eine der Vertragsparteien keinen allgemeinen Gerichtsstand im Inland hat. Die Vereinbarung muß schriftlich abgeschlossen oder, falls sie mündlich getroffen wird, schriftlich bestätigt werden. Hat eine der Parteien einen inländischen allgemeinen Gerichtsstand, so kann für das Inland nur ein Gericht gewählt werden, bei dem diese Partei ihren allgemeinen Gerichtsstand hat oder ein besonderer Gerichtsstand begründet ist.

(3) Im übrigen ist eine Gerichtsstandsvereinbarung nur zulässig, wenn sie ausdrücklich und schriftlich
a) nach dem Entstehen der Streitigkeit oder

---

1. Translated and annotated by Pierre A. Karrer, Karl W. Arnold and Paolo Michele Patocchi, SWITZERLAND'S PRIVATE INTERNATIONAL LAW (2nd ed., 1994). Footnotes have been omitted.

b) für den Fall geschlossen wird, daß die im Klageweg in Anspruch zu nehmende Partei nach Vertragsschluß ihren Wohnsitz oder gewöhnlichen Aufenthaltsort aus dem Geltungsbereich dieses Gesetzes verlegt oder ihr Wohnsitz oder gewöhnlicher Aufenthalt im Zeitpunkt der Klageerhebung nicht bekannt ist.

3. SWITZERLAND

Swiss Federal Conflict-of-Laws Act[1]

Article 5

1. For an existing or future dispute of financial interest arising from a specific legal relationship the parties may agree on a place of jurisdiction. The agreement may be made in writing, by telegram, by telex, telecopier or any other means of communication which permits it to be evidenced by a text. Unless otherwise provided by the agreement, the choice of jurisdiction is exclusive.
2. A choice of jurisdiction is ineffective if a party is abusively deprived of protection at a place of jurisdiction provided by Swiss law.
3. The court chosen may not decline jurisdiction:
   (a) if one of the parties has its domicile, habitual residence, or business establishment in the canton of the chosen court, or
   (b) if this Statute declares Swiss law applicable to the case.

Article 114 (Contracts with Consumers)

1. For a consumer's lawsuit based on contracts for which the prerequisites of Article 120 subsection 1 are fulfilled jurisdiction lies, at the option of the consumer, with the Swiss courts:
   (a) at the domicile of the consumer of his habitual residence, or
   (b) at the domicile or, if there is none, at the habitual residence, of the marketer.
2. A consumer may not waive in advance the jurisdiction of his domicile or habitual residence.

4. UNITED STATES

a. New York

(i) General Obligations Law

§ 5-1401. Choice of Law
1. The parties to any contract, agreement or undertaking, contingent or otherwise, in consideration of, or relating to any obligation arising out of a transaction covering in the aggregate not less than two hundred fifty thousand dollars, including a transaction otherwise covered by subsection one of section 1-105 of the uniform commercial code, may agree that the law of this state shall govern their rights and duties in whole or in part, whether or not such contract, agreement or undertaking bears a reasonable relation to this state. This section shall not apply to any contract, agreement or undertaking (a) for labor or personal services, (b) relating to any transaction for personal, family or household services, or (c) to the extent provided to the contrary in subsection two of section 1-105 of the uniform commercial code.
2. Nothing contained in this section shall be construed to limit or deny the enforcement of any provision respecting choice of law in any other contract, agreement or undertaking.

§ 5-1402. Choice of Forum
1. Notwithstanding any act which limits or affects the right of a person to maintain an action or proceeding, including, but not limited to, paragraph (b) of section thirteen hundred fourteen of the business corporation law and subdivision two of section two hundred-b of the banking law, any person may maintain an action or proceeding against a foreign corporation, non-resident, or foreign state where the action or proceeding arises out of or relates to any contract, agreement or undertaking for which a choice of New York law has been made in whole or in part pursuant to section 5-1401 and which (a) is a contract, agreement or undertaking, contingent or otherwise, in consideration of, or relating to any obligation arising out of a transaction covering in the aggregate, not less than one million dollars, and (b) which contains a provision or provisions whereby such foreign corporation or non-resident agrees to submit to the jurisdiction of the courts of this state.
2. Nothing contained in this section shall be construed to affect the enforcement of any provision respecting choice of forum in any other contract, agreement or undertaking.

(ii) Civil Practice Law and Rules

Rule 327. Inconvenient forum
   (a) When the court finds that in the interest of substantial justice the action should be heard in another forum, the court, on the motion of any party, may

stay or dismiss the action in whole or in part on any conditions that may be just. The domicile or residence in this state of any party to the action shall be preclude the court from staying or dismissing the action.

(b) Notwithstanding the provisions of subdivision (a) of this rule, the court shall not stay or dismiss any action on the ground of inconvenient forum, where the action arises out of or relates to a contract, agreement or undertaking to which section 5-1402 of the general obligations law applies, and the parties to the contract have agreed that the law of this state shall govern their rights or duties in whole or in part.

b. Foreign Sovereign Immunities Act

28 U.S.C. §§ 1330 and 1602-1611

§ 1330. Actions against foreign states

(a) The district courts shall have original jurisdiction without regard to amount in controversy of any nonjury civil action against a foreign state as defined in section 1603(a) of this title as to any claim for relief in personam with respect to which the foreign state is not entitled to immunity either under sections 1605-1607 of this title or under any applicable international agreement.

(b) Personal jurisdiction over a foreign state shall exist as to every claim for relief over which the district courts have jurisdiction under subsection (a) where service has been made under section 1608 of this title.

(c) For purposes of subsection (b), an appearance by a foreign state does not confer person jurisdiction with respect to any claim for relief not arising out of any transaction or occurrence enumerated in section 1605-1607 of this title.

§ 1602. Findings and declaration of purpose

The Congress finds that the determination by United States courts of the claims of foreign states to immunity from the jurisdiction of such courts would serve the interests of justice and would protect the right of both foreign states and litigants in United States courts. Under international law, states are not immune from the jurisdiction of foreign courts insofar as their commercial activities are concerned, and their commercial property may be levied upon for the satisfaction of judgments rendered against them in connection with their commercial activities. Claims of foreign states to immunity should henceforth be decided by courts of the United States and of the States in conformity with the principles set forth in this chapter.

§ 1603. Definitions

For purposes of this chapter —

(a) A "foreign state", except as used in section 1608 of this title, includes a political subdivision of a foreign state or an agency or instrumentality of a foreign state as defined in subsection (b).

(b) An "agency or instrumentality of a foreign state" means any entity —

(1) which is a separate legal person, corporate or otherwise, and

(2) which is an organ of a foreign state or political subdivision thereof, or a majority of whose shares or other ownership interest is owned by a foreign state or political subdivision thereof, and

(3) which is neither a citizen of a State of the United States as defined in section 1332 (c) and (d) of this title, nor created under the laws of any third country.

(c) The "United States" includes all territory and waters, continental or insular, subject to the jurisdiction of the United States.

(d) A "commercial activity" means either a regular course of commercial conduct or a particular commercial transaction or act. The commercial character of an activity shall be determined by reference to the nature of the course of conduct or particular transaction or act, rather than by reference to its purpose.

(e) A "commercial activity carried on in the United States by a foreign state" means commercial activity carried on by such state and having substantial contact with the United States.

§ 1604. *Immunity of a foreign state from jurisdiction*

Subject to existing international agreements to which the United States is a party at the time of enactment of this Act a foreign state shall be immune from the jurisdiction of the courts of the United States and of the States except as provided in sections 1605 to 1607 of this chapter.

§ 1605. *General exceptions to the jurisdictional immunity of a foreign state*

(a) A foreign state shall not be immune from the jurisdiction of courts of the United States or of the States in any case —

(1) in which the foreign state has waived its immunity either explicitly or by implication, notwithstanding any withdrawal of the waiver which the foreign state may purport to effect except in accordance with the terms of the waiver;

(2) in which the action is based upon a commercial activity carried on in the United States by the foreign state; or upon an act performed in the United States in connection with a commercial activity of the foreign state elsewhere; or upon an act outside the territory of the United States in connection with a commercial activity of the foreign state elsewhere and that act causes a direct effect in the United States;

(3) in which rights in property taken in violation of international law are in issue and that property or any property exchanged for such property is present in the United States in connection with a commercial activity carried on in the United States by the foreign state; or that property or any property exchanged for such property is owned or operated by an agency or instrumentality of the foreign state and that agency or instrumentality is engaged in a commercial activity in the United States;

(4) in which rights in property in the United States acquired by succession or gift or rights in immovable property situated in the United States are in issue;

(5) not otherwise encompassed in paragraph (2) above, in which money damages are sought against a foreign state for personal injury or death, or damage

to or loss of property, occurring in the United States and caused by the tortious act or omission of that foreign state or of any official or employee of that foreign state while acting within the scope of his office or employment; except this paragraph shall not apply to —

    (A) any claim based upon the exercise or performance or the failure to exercise or perform a discretionary function regardless of whether the discretion be abused, or

    (B) any claim arising out of malicious prosecution, abuse of process, libel, slander, misrepresentation, deceit, or interference with contract rights; or

(6) in which the action is brought, either to enforce an agreement made by the foreign State with or for the benefit of a private party to submit to arbitration all or any differences which have arisen or which may arise between the parties with respect to a defined legal relationship, whether contractual or not, concerning a subject matter capable of settlement by arbitration under the laws of the United States, or to confirm an award made pursuant to such an agreement to arbitrate, if (A) the arbitration takes place or is intended to take place in the United States, (B) the agreement or award is or may be governed by a treaty or other international agreement in force for the United States calling for the recognition and enforcement of arbitral awards, (C) the underlying claim, save for the agreement to arbitrate, could have been brought in a United States court under this section or section 1607, or (D) paragraph (1) of this subsection is otherwise applicable.

(b) A foreign state shall not be immune from the jurisdiction of the courts of the United States in any case in which a suit in admiralty is brought to enforce a maritime lien against a vessel or cargo of the foreign state, which maritime lien is based upon a commercial activity of the foreign state: *Provided*, That —

(1) notice of the suit is given by delivery of a copy of the summons and of the complaint to the person, or his agent, having possession of the vessel or cargo against which the maritime lien is asserted; and if the vessel or cargo is arrested pursuant to process obtained on behalf of the party bringing the suit, the service of process of arrest shall be deemed to constitute valid delivery of such notice, but the party bringing the suit shall be liable for any damages sustained by the foreign state as a result of the arrest if the party bringing the suit had actual or constructive knowledge that the vessel or cargo of a foreign state was involved; and

(2) notice to the foreign state of the commencement of suit as provided in section 1608 of this title is initiated within ten days either of the delivery of notice as provided in paragraph (1) of this subsection or, in the case of a party who was unaware that the vessel or cargo of a foreign state was involved, of the date such party determined the existence of the foreign state's interest.

(c) Whenever notice is delivered under subsection (b)(1), the suit to enforce a maritime lien shall thereafter proceed and shall be heard and determined according to the principles of law and rules of practice of suits in rem whenever it appears that, had the vessel been privately owned and possessed, a suit in rem might have been maintained. A decree against the foreign state may include costs of the suit and, if the decree is for a money judgment, interest as ordered by the court, except that the court may not award judgment against the foreign state in an amount greater than the value of the vessel or cargo upon which the maritime lien arose. Such value shall be determined as of the time notice is served under subsection (b)(1). Decrees shall be subject to appeal and revision as provided in other cases of admiralty and maritime jurisdiction. Nothing shall preclude the plaintiff in any proper case from seeking relief in personam in the same action brought to enforce a maritime lien as provided in this section.

(d) A foreign state shall not be immune from the jurisdiction of the courts of the United States in any action brought to foreclose a preferred mortgage, as defined in the Ship Mortgage Act, 1920 (46 U.S.C. 911 and following). Such action shall be brought, heard, and determined in accordance with the provisions of that Act and in accordance with the principles of law and rules of practice of suits in rem, whenever it appears that had the vessel been privately owned and possessed a suit in rem might have been maintained.

§ 1606. *Extent of liability*

As to any claim for relief with respect to which a foreign state is not entitled to immunity under section 1605 or 1607 of this chapter, the foreign state shall be liable in the same manner and to the same extent as a private individual under like circumstances; but a foreign state except for an agency or instrumentality thereof shall not be liable for punitive damages; if, however, in any case wherein death was caused, the law of the place where the action or omission occurred provides, or has been construed to provide, for damages only punitive in nature, the foreign state shall be liable for actual or compensatory damages measured by the pecuniary injuries resulting from such death which were incurred by the persons for whose benefit the action was brought.

§ 1607. *Counterclaims*

In any action brought by a foreign state, or in which a foreign state intervenes, in a court of the United States or of a State, the foreign state shall not be accorded immunity with respect to any counterclaim —

(a) for which a foreign state would not be entitled to immunity under section 1605 of this chapter had such claim been brought in a separate action against the foreign state; or

(b) arising out of the transaction or occurrence that is the subject matter of the claim of the foreign state; or

(c) to the extent that the counterclaim does not seek relief exceeding in amount or differing in kind from that sought by the foreign state.

§ 1608. *Service; time to answer; default*

(a) Service in the courts of the United States and of the States shall be made upon a foreign state or political subdivision of a foreign state:

(1) by delivery of a copy of the summons and complaint in accordance with any special arrangement for service between the plaintiff and the foreign state or political subdivision; or

(2) if no special arrangement exists, by delivery of a copy of the summons and complaint in accordance with an applicable international convention on service of judicial documents; or

(3) if service cannot be made under paragraphs (1) or (2), by sending a copy of the summons and complaint and a notice of suit, together with a translation of each into the official language of the foreign state, by any form of mail requiring a signed receipt, to be addressed and dispatched by the clerk of the court to the head of the ministry of foreign affairs of the foreign state concerned, or

(4) if service cannot be made within 30 days under paragraph (3), by sending two copies of the summons and complaint and a notice of suit, together with a translation of each into the official language of the foreign state, by any form of mail requiring a signed receipt, to be addressed and dispatched by the clerk of the court to the Secretary of State in Washington, District of Columbia, to the attention of the Director of Special Consular Services — and the Secretary shall transmit one copy of the papers through diplomatic channels to the foreign state and shall send to the clerk of the court a certified copy of the diplomatic note indicating when the papers were transmitted.

As used in this subsection, a "notice of suit" shall mean a notice addressed to a foreign state and in a form prescribed by the Secretary of State by regulation.

(b) Service in the courts of the United States and of the States shall be made upon an agency or instrumentality of a foreign state:

(1) by delivery of a copy of the summons and complaint in accordance with any special arrangement for service between the plaintiff and the agency or instrumentality; or

(2) if no special arrangement exists, by delivery of a copy of the summons and complaint either to an officer, a managing or general agent, or to any other agent authorized by appointment or by law to receive service of process in the United States; or in accordance with an applicable international convention on service of judicial documents; or

(3) if service cannot be made under paragraphs (1) or (2), and if reasonably calculated to give actual notice, by delivery of a copy of the summons and complaint, together with a translation of each into the official language of the foreign state —

(A) as directed by an authority of the foreign state or political subdivision in response to a letter rogatory or request or

(B) by any form of mail requiring a signed receipt, to be addressed and dispatched by the clerk of the court to the agency or instrumentality to be served, or

(C) as directed by order of the court consistent with the law of the place where service is to be made.

(c) Service shall be deemed to have been made —

(1) in the case of service under subsection (a)(4), as of the date of transmittal indicated in the certified copy of the diplomatic note; and

(2) in any other case under this section, as of the date of receipt indicated in the certification, signed and returned postal receipt, or other proof of service applicable to the method of service employed.

(d) In any action brought in a court of the United States or of a State, a foreign state, a political subdivision thereof, or an agency or instrumentality of a foreign state shall serve an answer or other responsive pleading to the complaint within sixty days after service has been made under this section.

(e) No judgment by default shall be entered by a court of the United States or of a State against a foreign state, a political subdivision thereof, or an agency or instrumentality of a foreign state, unless the claimant establishes his claim or right to relief by evidence satisfactory to the court. A copy of any such default judgment shall be sent to the foreign state or political subdivision in the manner prescribed for service in this section.

§ 1609. Immunity from attachment and execution of property of a foreign state

Subject to existing international agreements to which the United States is a party at the time of enactment of this Act the property in the United States of a foreign state shall be immune from attachment arrest and execution except as provided in sections 1610 and 1611 of this chapter.

§ 1610. Exceptions to the immunity from attachment or execution

(a) The property in the United States of a foreign state, as defined in section 1603(a) of this chapter, used for a commercial activity in the United States, shall not be immune from attachment in aid of execution, or from execution, upon a judgment entered by a court of the United States or of a State after the effective date of this Act, if —

(1) the foreign state has waived its immunity from attachment in aid of execution or from execution either explicitly or by implication, notwithstanding any withdrawal of the waiver the foreign state may purport to effect except in accordance with the terms of the waiver, or

(2) the property is or was used for the commercial activity upon which the claim is based, or

(3) the execution relates to a judgment establishing rights in property which has been taken in violation of international law or which has been exchanged for property taken in violation of international law, or

(4) the execution relates to a judgment establishing rights in property —

(A) which is acquired by succession or gift, or

(B) which is immovable and situated in the United States: *Provided*, That such property is not used for purposes of maintaining a diplomatic or consular mission or the residence of the Chief of such mission, or

(5) the property consists of any contractual obligation or any proceeds from such a contractual obligation to indemnify or hold harmless the foreign state or

its employees under a policy of automobile or other liability or casualty insurance covering the claim which merged into the judgment, or

(6) the judgment is based on an order confirming an arbitral award rendered against the foreign State, provided that attachment in aid of execution, or execution, would not be inconsistent with any provision in the arbitral agreement.

(b) In addition to subsection (a), any property in the United States of an agency or instrumentality of a foreign state engaged in commercial activity in the United States shall not be immune from attachment in aid of execution, or from execution, upon a judgment entered by a court of the United States or of a State after the effective date of this Act, if —

(1) the agency or instrumentality has waived its immunity from attachment in aid of execution or from execution either explicitly or implicitly, notwithstanding any withdrawal of the waiver the agency or instrumentality may purport to effect except in accordance with the terms of the waiver, or

(2) the judgment relates to a claim for which the agency or instrumentality is not immune by virtue of section 1605(a)(2), (3), or (5), or 1605(b) of this chapter, regardless of whether the property is or was used for the activity upon which the claim is based.

(c) No attachment or execution referred to in subsections (a) and (b) of this section shall be permitted until the court has ordered such attachment and execution after having determined that a reasonable period of time has elapsed following the entry of judgment and the giving of any notice required under section 1608(e) of this chapter.

(d) The property of a foreign state, as defined in section 1603(a) of this chapter, used for a commercial activity in the United States, shall not be immune from attachment prior to the entry of judgment in any action brought in a court of the United States or of a State, or prior to the elapse of the period of time provided in subsection (c) of this section, if —

(1) the foreign state has explicitly waived its immunity from attachment prior to judgment, notwithstanding any withdrawal of the waiver the foreign state may purport to effect except in accordance with the terms of the waiver, and

(2) the purpose of the attachment is to secure satisfaction of a judgment that has been or may ultimately be entered against the foreign state, and not to obtain jurisdiction.

(e) The vessels of a foreign State shall not be immune from arrest in rem, interlocutory sale, and execution in actions brought to foreclose a preferred mortgage as provided in section 1605(d).

§ 1611. Certain types of property immune from execution

(a) Notwithstanding the provisions of section 1610 of this chapter, the property of those organizations designated by the President as being entitled to enjoy the privileges, exemptions, and immunities provided by the International Organizations Immunities Act shall not be subject to attachment or any other judicial process impeding the disbursement of funds to, or on the order of, a foreign state as the result of an action brought in the courts of the United States or of the States.

(b) Notwithstanding the provisions of section 1610 of this chapter, the property of a foreign state shall be immune from attachment and from execution, if —

(1) the property is that of a foreign central bank or monetary authority held for its own account, unless such bank or authority, or its parent foreign government, has explicitly waived its immunity from attachment in aid of execution, or from execution, notwithstanding any withdrawal of the waiver which the bank, authority or government may purport to effect except in accordance with the terms of the waiver; or

(2) the property is, or is intended to be, used in connection with a military activity and

(A) is of a military character, or

(B) is under the control of a military authority or defense agency.

Appendix F

INTERNATIONAL ARBITRATION TREATIES

1. NEW YORK CONVENTION ON THE RECOGNITION AND ENFORCEMENT OF FOREIGN ARBITRAL AWARDS [1]

Article I

1. This Convention shall apply to the recognition and enforcement of arbitral awards made in the territory of a State other than the State where the recognition and enforcement of such awards are sought, and arising out of differences between persons, whether physical or legal. It shall also apply to arbitral awards not considered as domestic awards in the State where their recognition and enforcement are sought.
2. The term "arbitral awards" shall include not only awards made by arbitrators appointed for each case but also those made by permanent arbitral bodies to which the parties have been submitted.
3. When signing, ratifying or acceding to this Convention, or notifying extension under article X hereof, any State may on the basis of reciprocity declare that it will apply the Convention to the recognition and enforcement of awards made only in the territory of another Contracting State. It may also declare that it will apply the Convention only to differences arising out of legal relationships, whether contractual or not, which are considered as commercial under the national law of the State making such declaration.

Article II

1. Each Contracting State shall recognize an agreement in writing under which the parties undertake to submit to arbitration all or any differences which have arisen or which may arise between them in respect of a defined legal relationship, whether contractual or not, concerning a subject matter capable of settlement by arbitration.

---

1. New York, 10 June 1958, 21 U.S.T. 2518, T.I.A.S. No. 6997, 330 U.N.T.S. 38.

2. The term "agreement in writing" shall include an arbitral clause in a contract or an arbitration agreement, signed by the parties or contained in an exchange of letters or telegrams.

3. The court of a Contracting State, when seized of an action in a matter in respect of which the parties have made an agreement within the meaning of this article, shall, at the request of one of the parties, refer the parties to arbitration, unless it finds that the said agreement is null and void, inoperative or incapable of being performed.

Article III

Each Contracting State shall recognize arbitral awards as binding and enforce them in accordance with the rules of procedure of the territory where the award is relied upon, under the conditions laid down in the following articles. There shall not be imposed substantially more onerous conditions or higher fees or charges on the recognition or enforcement of arbitral awards to which this Convention applies than are imposed on the recognition or enforcement of domestic arbitral awards.

Article IV

1. To obtain the recognition and enforcement mentioned in the preceding article, the party applying for recognition and enforcement shall, at the time of the application, supply:
(*a*) The duly authenticated original award or a duly certified copy thereof;
(*b*) The original agreement referred to in article II or a duly certified copy thereof.

2. If the said award or agreement is not made in an official language of the country in which the award is relied upon, the party applying for recognition and enforcement of the award shall produce a translation of these documents into such language. The translation shall be certified by an official or sworn translator or by a diplomatic or consular agent.

Article V

1. Recognition and enforcement of the award may be refused, at the request of the party against whom it is invoked, only if that party furnishes to the competent authority where the recognition and enforcement is sought proof that:
(*a*) The parties to the agreement referred to in article II were, under the law applicable to them, under some incapacity, or the said agreement is not valid under the law to which the parties have subjected it or, failing any indication thereon, under the law of the country where the award was made; or

(*b*) The party against whom the award is invoked was not given proper notice of the appointment of the arbitrator or of the arbitration proceedings or was otherwise unable to present his case; or

(*c*) The award deals with a difference not contemplated by or not falling within the terms of the submission to arbitration, or it contains decisions on matters beyond the scope of the submission to arbitration, provided that, if the decisions on matters submitted to arbitration can be separated from those not so submitted, that part of the award which contains decisions on matters submitted to arbitration may be recognized and enforced; or

(*d*) The composition of the arbitral authority or the arbitral procedure was not in accordance with the agreement of the parties, or, failing such agreement, was not in accordance with the law of the country where the arbitration took place; or

(*e*) The award has not yet become binding on the parties, or has been set aside or suspended by a competent authority of the country in which, or under the law of which, that award was made.

2. Recognition and enforcement of an arbitral award may also be refused if the competent authority in the country where recognition and enforcement is sought finds that:

(*a*) The subject matter of the difference is not capable of settlement by arbitration under the law of that country; or

(*b*) The recognition or enforcement of the award would be contrary to the public policy of that country.

Article VI

If an application for the setting aside or suspension of the award has been made to a competent authority referred to in article V(1)(*e*), the authority before which the award is sought to be relied upon may, if it considers it proper, adjourn the decision on the enforcement of the award and may also, on the application of the party claiming enforcement of the award, order the other party to give suitable security.

Article VII

1. The provisions of the present Convention shall not affect the validity of multilateral or bilateral agreements concerning the recognition and enforcement of arbitral awards entered into by the Contracting States nor deprive any interested party of any right he may have to avail himself of an arbitral award in the manner and to the extent allowed by the law or the treaties of the country where such award is sought to be relied upon.

2. The Geneva Protocol on Arbitration Clauses of 1923 and the Geneva Convention on the Execution of Foreign Arbitral Awards of 1927 shall cease to have

effect between Contracting States on their becoming bound and to the extent that they become bound, by this Convention.

Article VIII

1. This Convention shall be open until 31 December 1958 for signature on behalf of any Member of the United Nations and also on behalf of any other State which is or hereafter becomes a member of any specialized agency of the United Nations, or which is or hereafter becomes a party to the Statute of the International Court of Justice, or any other State to which an invitation has been addressed by the General Assembly of the United Nations.
2. This Convention shall be ratified and the instrument of ratification shall be deposited with the Secretary-General of the United Nations.

Article IX

1. This Convention shall be open for accession to all States referred to in article VIII.
2. Accession shall be effected by the deposit of an instrument of accession with the Secretary-General of the United Nations.

Article X

1. Any State may, at the time of signature, ratification or accession, declare that this Convention shall extend to all or any of the territories for the international relations of which it is responsible. Such a declaration shall take effect when the Convention enters into force for the State concerned.
2. At any time thereafter any such extension shall be made by notification addressed to the Secretary-General of the United Nations and shall take effect as from the nineteenth day after the day of receipt by the Secretary-General of the United Nations of this notification, or as from the date of entry into force of the Convention for the State concerned, whichever is the later.
3. With respect to those territories to which this Convention is not extended at the time of signature, ratification or accession, each State concerned shall consider the possibility of taking the necessary steps in order to extend the application of this Convention to such territories, subject, where necessary for constitutional reasons, to the consent of the Governments of such territories.

Article XI

In the case of a federal or non-unitary State, the following provisions shall apply:

(*a*) With respect to those articles of this Convention that come within the legislative jurisdiction of the federal authority, the obligations of the federal Government shall to this extent be the same as those of Contracting States which are not federal States:

(*b*) With respect to those articles of this Convention that come within the legislative jurisdiction of constituent states or provinces which are not, under the constitutional system of the federation, bound to take legislative action, the federal Government shall bring such articles with a favourable recommendation to the notice of the appropriate authorities of constituent states or provinces at the earliest possible moment;

(*c*) A federal State Party to this Convention shall, at the request of any other Contracting State transmitted through the Secretary-General of the United Nations, supply a statement of the law and practice of the federation and its constituent units in regard to any particular provision of this Convention, showing the extent to which effect has been given to that provision by legislative or other action.

Article XII

1. This Convention shall come into force on the ninetieth day following the date of deposit of the third instrument of ratification or accession.

2. For each State ratifying or acceding to this Convention after the deposit of the third instrument of ratification or accession, this Convention shall enter into force on the ninetieth day after deposit of such State of its instrument of ratification or accession.

Article XIII

1. Any Contracting State may denounce this Convention by a written notification to the Secretary-General of the United Nations. Denunciation shall take effect one year after the date of receipt of the notification by the Secretary-General.

2. Any State which has made a declaration or notification under article X may, at any time thereafter, by notification to the Secretary-General of the United Nations, declare that this Convention shall cease to extend to the territory concerned one year after the date of the receipt of the notification by the Secretary-General.

3. This Convention shall continue to be applicable to arbitral awards in respect of which recognition or enforcement proceedings have been instituted before the denunciation takes effect.

Article XIV

A Contracting State shall not be entitled to avail itself of the present Convention against other Contracting States except to the extent that it is itself bound to apply the Convention.

Article XV

The Secretary-General of the United Nations shall notify the States contemplated in article VIII of the following:
(*a*) Signatures and ratifications in accordance with article VIII;
(*b*) Accessions in accordance with article IX;
(*c*) Declarations and notifications under articles I, X and XI;
(*d*) The date upon which this Convention enters into force in accordance with article XII;
(*e*) Denunciations and notifications in accordance with article XIII.

Article XVI

1. This Convention, of which the Chinese, English, French, Russian and Spanish texts shall be equally authentic, shall be deposited in the archives of the United Nations.
2. The Secretary-General of the United Nations shall transmit a certified copy of this Convention to the States contemplated in article VIII.

PARTIES TO THE 1958 NEW YORK ARBITRATION CONVENTION

Country	Signature	Ratification, accession or succession
Algeria		7 February 1989
Antigua and Barbuda		2 February 1989
Argentina	26 August 1958	14 March 1989
Australia		26 March 1975
Austria		2 May 1961
Bahrain		6 April 1988
Barbados		16 March 1993
Belgium	19 June 1958	18 August 1975
Benin		16 May 1974
Bolivia		28 April 1995

Country	Signature	Ratification, accession or succession
Bosnia Herzegovina		1 September 1993
Botswana		20 December 1971
Bulgaria	17 December 1958	10 October 1961
Burkina Faso		23 March 1987
Byelorus	29 December 1958	15 November 1960
Cambodia		5 January 1960
Cameroon		19 February 1988
Canada		12 May 1986
Central African Republic		15 October 1962
Chile		
China		22 January 1987
Columbia		25 September 1979
Costa Rica	10 June 1958	26 October 1987
Croatia		26 July 1993
Cuba		30 December 1974
Cyprus		29 December 1980
Czech Republic	3 October 1958	30 September 1993
Denmark		22 December 1972
Djibouti		14 June 1983
Dominica		28 October 1988
Ecuador	17 December 1958	3 January 1962
Egypt		9 March 1959
El Salvador		10 June 1958
Estonia		30 August 1993
Finland	29 December 1958	19 January 1962
France	25 November 1958	26 June 1959
Georgia		2 June 1994
Germany	10 June 1958	30 June 1961
Ghana		9 April 1968
Greece		16 July 1962
Guatemala		21 March 1984
Haiti		5 December 1983
Holy See		14 May 1975
Hungary		5 March 1962
India	10 June 1958	13 July 1960
Indonesia		7 October 1981
Ireland		12 May 1981
Israel	10 June 1958	5 January 1959
Italy		31 January 1969
Japan		20 June 1961
Jordan	10 June 1958	15 November 1979
Kenya		10 February 1989

Country	Signature	Ratification, accession or succession
Kuwait		28 April 1978
Lesotho		13 June 1989
Lithuania		14 March 1995
Luxembourg	11 November 1958	9 September 1983
Macedonia		10 March 1994
Madagascar		16 July 1962
Malaysia		5 November 1985
Mali		8 September 1994
Mexico		14 April 1971
Monaco	31 December 1958	2 June 1982
Mongolia		24 October 1994
Morocco		12 February 1959
Netherlands	10 June 1958	24 April 1964
New Zealand		6 January 1983
Niger		14 October 1964
Nigeria		17 March 1970
Norway		14 March 1961
Pakistan		30 December 1958
Panama		10 October 1984
Peru		7 July 1988
Philippines	10 June 1958	6 July 1967
Poland	10 June 1958	3 October 1961
Portugal		18 October 1994
Republic of Korea		8 February 1973
Romania		13 September 1961
Russia	29 December 1958	24 August 1960
Saudi Arabia		19 April 1994
San Marino		17 May 1979
Senegal		17 October 1994
Singapore		21 August 1986
Slovakia		28 May 1993
South Africa		3 May 1976
Spain		12 May 1977
Sri Lanka	30 December 1958	9 April 1962
Slovakia		28 May 1993
Sweden	23 December 1958	28 January 1972
Switzerland	29 December 1958	1 June 1965
Syrian Arab Republic		9 March 1959
Thailand		21 December 1959
Trinidad and Tobago		14 February 1966
Tunisia		17 July 1967
Ukraine	29 December 1958	10 October 1960

Country	Signature	Ratification, accession or succession
United Kingdom		24 September 1975
United Republic of Tanzania		13 October 1964
United States of America		30 September 1970
Uruguay		30 May 1983
Venezuela		8 February 1995
Yugoslavia (Serbia & Montenegro)		26 February 1982
Zimbabwe		29 September 1994

DECLARATIONS AND RESERVATIONS TO THE NEW YORK ARBITRATION CONVENTION

ALGERIA

Referring to the possibility offered by article I, paragraph 3, of the Convention, the People's Democratic Republic of Algeria declares that it will apply the Convention, on the basis of reciprocity, to the recognition and enforcement of arbitral awards made only in the territory of another Contracting State and only where such awards have been made with respect to differences arising out of legal relationships whether contractual or not, which are considered as commercial under algerian law.

ANTIGUA AND BARBUDA

"In accordance with article I, the Government of Antigua and Barbuda declares that it will apply the Convention on the basis of reciprocity only to the recognition and enforcement of awards made in the territory of another contracting state.

The Government of Antigua and Barbuda also declares that it will apply the Convention only to differences arising out of legal relationships, whether contractual or not, which are considered as commercial under the laws of Antigua and Barbuda."

ARGENTINA

On the basis of reciprocity, the Republic of Argentina will apply the Convention only to the recognition and enforcement of foreign arbitral awards made in the territory of the other Contracting State. It will also apply the Convention only to differences arising out of legal relationships, whether contractual or not, which are considered as commercial under its national law.

The Convention will be interpreted in accordance with the principles and clauses of the National Constitution in force or those resulting from modification made by virtue of the Constitution.

The declaration made upon signature and contained in the Final Act read as follows:

"If another Contracting Party extends the application of the Convention to territories which fall within the sovereignty of the Argentine Republic, the rights of the Argentine Republic shall in no way be affected by that extension."

AUSTRIA

In a communication received on 25 February 1988, the Government of Austria notified the Secretary-General of its decision to withdraw as from that date, the following reservation, made upon accession to Convention:

The Republic of Austria will apply the Convention, in accordance with the first sentence of article I(3) thereof, only to the recognition and enforcement of arbitral awards made in the territory of another Contracting State.

BAHRAIN

The accession by the State of Bahrain to the Convention on the Recognition and Enforcement of Foreign Arbitral Awards, 1958 shall in no way constitute recognition of Israel or be a cause for the establishment of any relations of any kind therewith.

In accordance with article 1(3) of the Convention, the State of Bahrain will apply the Convention, on the basis of reciprocity, to the recognition and enforcement of only those awards made in the territory of another Contracting State party to the Convention.

In accordance with article 1(3) of the Convention, the State of Bahrain will apply the Convention only to differences arising out of legal relationships, whether contractual or not, which are considered as commercial under the national law of the State of Bahrain.

BARBADOS

In accordance with article 1(3) of the Convention, the Government of Barbados declares that it will apply the Convention on the basis of reciprocity to the recognition and enforcement of awards made only in the territory of another Contracting State.

The Government of Barbados will also apply the Convention only to the differences arising out of legal relationships, whether contractual or not which are considered as commercial under the laws of Barbados.

BELGIUM

In accordance with article I, paragraph 3, the Government of the Kingdom of Belgium declares that it will apply the Convention to the recognition and enforcement of arbitral awards made only in the territory of a Contracting State.

BOTSWANA

The Republic of Botswana will apply the Convention only to differences arising out of legal relationship, whether contractual or not, which are considered commercial under Botswana law.

The Republic of Botswana will apply the Convention to the Recognition and Enforcement of Awards made in the territory of another Contracting State.

BULGARIA

Bulgaria will apply the Convention to recognition and enforcement of awards made in the territory of another contracting State. With regard to awards made in the territory of non-contracting States it will apply the Convention only to the extent to which these States grant reciprocal treatment.

BYELORUS

Byelorus will apply the provisions of this Convention in respect to arbitral awards made in the territories of non-contracting States only to the extent to which they grant reciprocal treatment.

CANADA

The Government of Canada declares that it will apply the Convention only to differences arising out of legal relationships, whether contractual or not, which are considered as commercial under the laws of Canada, except in the case of the Province of Quebec where the law does not provide for such limitation.

CENTRAL AFRICAN REPUBLIC

Referring to the possibility offered by paragraph 3 of article I of the Convention, the Central African Republic declares that it will apply the Convention on the basis of reciprocity, to the recognition and enforcement of awards made only in the territory of another contracting State; it further declares that it will apply the Convention only to differences arising out of legal relationships, whether contractual or not, which are considered as commercial under its national law.

CHINA

1. The People's Republic of China will apply the Convention, only on the basis of reciprocity, to the recognition and enforcement of arbitral awards made in the territory of another Contracting State;

2. The People's Republic of China will apply the Convention only to differences arising out of the legal relationships, whether contractual or not, which are considered as commercial under the national law of the People's Republic of China.

CUBA

Cuba will apply the Convention to the recognition and enforcement of arbitral awards made in the territory of another Contracting State. With respect to arbitral awards made by other non-contracting States it will apply the Convention only in so far as those States grant reciprocal treatment as established by mutual agreement between the parties. Moreover, it will apply the Convention only to differences arising out of legal relationships, whether contractual or not, which are considered as commercial under Cuban legislation.

CYPRUS

The Republic of Cyprus will apply the Convention, on the basis of reciprocity, to the recognition and enforcement of awards made only in the territory of another Contracting State; furthermore it will apply the Convention only to differences arising out of legal relationships, whether contractual or not, which are considered as commercial under its national law.

CZECH REPUBLIC

Czechoslovakia will apply the Convention to the recognition and enforcement of awards made in the territory of another Contracting State. With regard to awards made in the territory of non-contracting States it will apply the Convention only to the extent to which these States grant reciprocal treatment.

DENMARK

In accordance with the terms of article I, paragraph 3, [the Convention] shall have effect only as regards the recognition and enforcement of arbitral awards made by another Contracting State and [it] shall be valid only with respect to commercial relationships.

ECUADOR

Ecuador, on a basis of reciprocity, will apply the Convention to the recognition and enforcement of arbitral awards made in the territory of another contracting State only if such awards have been made with respect to differences arising out of legal relationships which are regarded as commercial under Ecuadorian law.

FRANCE

Referring to the possibility offered by paragraph 3 of article I of the Convention, France declares that it will apply the Convention on the basis of reciprocity, to the recognition and enforcement of awards made only in the territory of another contracting State.

In a communication received on 27 November 1989, the Government of France notified the Secretary-General of its decision to withdraw, with effect from that date, the second declaration made upon ratification. For the text of the declaration so withdrawn, see United Nations, *Treaty Series*, vol. 336, p. 426.

GERMANY

With respect to paragraph 1 of article I, and in accordance with paragraph 3 of article I of the Convention, the Federal Republic of Germany will apply the Convention only to the recognition and enforcement of awards made in the territory of another Contracting State.

GREECE

The present Convention is approved on condition of the two limitations set forth in article I(3) of the Convention.

GUATEMALA

On the basis of reciprocity, the Republic of Guatemala will apply the above Convention to the recognition and enforcement of arbitral awards made only in the territory of another contracting State; and will apply it only to differences arising out of legal relationships, whether contractual or not, which are considered as commercial under its national law.

HOLY SEE

The State of Vatican City will apply the said Convention on the basis of reciprocity, on the one hand, to the recognition and enforcement of awards made only in the territory of another Contracting State, and on the other hand, only to differences arising out of legal relationships, whether contractual or not, which are considered as commercial under Vatican law.

HUNGARY

The Hungarian People's Republic shall apply the Convention to the recognition and enforcement of such awards only as have been made in the territory of one of the other Contracting States and are dealing with differences arising in respect of a legal relationship considered by the Hungarian law as a commercial relationship.

INDIA

In accordance with Article I of the Convention, the Government of India declare that they will apply the Convention to the recognition and enforcement of awards made only in the territory of a State, party to this Convention. They further declare that they will apply the Convention only to differences arising out of legal relationships, whether contractual or not, which are considered as commercial under the law of India.

INDONESIA

Pursuant to the provision of article I(3) of the Convention, the Government of the Republic of Indonesia declares that it will apply the Convention on the basis of reciprocity, to the recognition and enforcement of awards made only in the territory of another Contracting State, and that it will apply the Convention only to differences arising out of legal relationships, whether contractual or not, which are considered as commercial under the Indonesian Law.

IRELAND

In accordance with article I(3) of the said Convention the Government of Ireland declares that it will apply the Convention to the recognition and enforcement of arbitral awards made only in the territory of another Contracting State.

JAPAN

Japan will apply the Convention to the recognition and enforcement of awards made only in the territory of another Contracting State.

JORDAN

The Government of Jordan shall not be bound by any awards which are made by Israel or to which an Israeli is a party.

In a communication received by the Secretary-General on 23 June 1980, the Government of Israel declared the following:

"The Government of Israel has noted the political character of the statement made by the Government of Jordan. In the view of the Government of Israel, this Convention is not the proper place for making such political pronouncements. Moreover, the said declaration cannot in any way affect whatever obligations are binding upon Jordan under general international law or under particular conventions.

"Insofar as concerns the substance of the matter, the Government of Israel will adopt towards the Government of Jordan an attitude of complete reciprocity."

KENYA

In accordance with article I(3) of the said Convention the Government of Kenya declares that it will apply the Convention to the recognition and enforcement of arbitral awards made only in the territory of another contracting state.

KUWAIT

The State of Kuwait will apply the Convention to the recognition and enforcement of awards made only in the territory of another Contracting State.

It is understood that the accession of the State of Kuwait to the Convention on the Recognition and Enforcement of Foreign Arbitral Awards, done at New York, on the 10th of June 1958, does not mean in any way recognition of Israel or entering with it into relations governed by the Convention thereto acceded by the State of Kuwait.

LUXEMBOURG

The Convention is applied on the basis of reciprocity to the recognition and enforcement of only those arbitral awards made in the territory of another Contracting State.

MADAGASCAR

The Malagasy Republic declares that it will apply the Convention on the basis of reciprocity, to the recognition and enforcement of awards made only in the territory of another contracting State; it further declares that it will apply the Convention only to differences arising out of legal relationships, whether contractual or not, which are considered as commercial under its national law.

MALAYSIA

The Government of Malaysia will apply the Convention on the basis of reciprocity, to the recognition and enforcement of awards made only in the territory of another Contracting State. Malaysia further declares that it will apply the Convention only to differences arising out of legal relationships, whether contractual or not, which are considered as commercial under Malaysian law.

MONACO

Referring to the possibility offered by article I(3) of the Convention, the Principality of Monaco will apply the Convention, on the basis of reciprocity, to the recognition and enforcement of awards made only in the territory of another contracting State; furthermore, it will apply the Convention only to differences arising out of legal relationship, whether contractual or not, which are considered as commercial under its national law.

MOROCCO

The Government of His Majesty the King of Morocco will apply the Convention to the recognition and enforcement of awards made only in the territory of another Contracting State.

NETHERLANDS

Referring to paragraph 3 of article I of the Convention on the Recognition and Enforcement of Foreign Arbitral Awards, the Government of the Kingdom of the Netherlands declares that it will apply the Convention to the recognition and enforcement of awards made only in the territory of another Contracting State.

NEW ZEALAND

In accordance with paragraph 3 of article 1 of the Convention, the Government of New Zealand declares that it will apply the Convention, on the basis of reciprocity, to the recognition and enforcement of awards made only in the territory of another Contracting State.

Accession to the Convention by the Government of New Zealand shall not extend for the time being, pursuant to article X of the Convention, to the Cook Islands and Niue.

NIGERIA

In accordance with paragraph 3 of article I of the Convention, the Federal Military Government of the Federal Republic of Nigeria declares that it will apply the Convention on the basis of reciprocity to the recognition and enforcement of awards made only in the territory of a State party to this Convention and to differences arising out of legal relationships, whether contractual or not, which are considered as commercial under the laws of the Federal Republic of Nigeria.

NORWAY

The Government of Norway will apply the Convention only to the recognition and enforcement of awards made in the territory of one of the Contracting States.

The Government of Norway will apply the Convention to differences where the subject matter of the proceedings is immovable property situated in Norway, or a right in or to such property.

PHILIPPINES

The Philippine delegation signs *ad referendum* this Convention with the reservation that it does so on the basis of reciprocity.

The Philippines will apply the Convention to the recognition and enforcement of awards made only in the territory of another contracting State pursuant to Article I, paragraph 3 of the Convention.

The Philippines, on the basis of reciprocity, will apply the Convention to the recognition and enforcement of awards made only in the territory of another Contracting State and only to differences arising out of legal relationships, whether contractual or not, which are considered as commercial under the national law of the State making such declaration.

POLAND

With reservations as mentioned in article I, para. 3.

REPUBLIC OF KOREA

By virtue of paragraph 3 of article I of the present Convention, the Government of the Republic of Korea declares that it will apply the Convention to the recognition and enforcement of arbitral awards made only in the territory of another Contracting State. It further declares that it will apply the Convention only to differences arising out of legal relationships, whether contractual or not, which are considered as commercial under its national law.

ROMANIA

Romania will apply the Convention only to differences arising out of legal relationships, whether contractual or not, which are considered as commercial under its legislation.

Romania will apply the Convention to the recognition and enforcement of awards made in the territory of another Contracting State. As regards awards made in the territory of certain non-contracting States, the Romanian People's Republic will apply the Convention only on the basis of reciprocity established by joint agreement between the parties.

SINGAPORE

The Republic of Singapore will on the basis of reciprocity apply the said Convention to the recognition and enforcement of only those awards which are made in the territory of another Contracting State.

SWITZERLAND

On 23 April 1993, Switzerland withdrew its reciprocity reservation by which it had applied the Convention to the recognition and enforcement of awards made only in the territory of another Contracting State.

TRINIDAD AND TOBAGO

In accordance with article I of the Convention, the Government of Trinidad and Tobago declares that it will apply the Convention to the recognition and enforcement of awards made only in the territory of another Contracting State. The Government of Trinidad and Tobago further declares that it will apply the Convention only to differences arising out of legal relationships, whether contractual or not, which are considered as commercial under the Law of Trinidad and Tobago.

TUNISIA

With the reservations provided for in article I, paragraph 3, of the Convention, that is to say, the Tunisian State will apply the Convention to the recognition and enforcement of awards made only in the territory of another Contracting State and only to differences arising out of legal relationships, whether contractual or not, which are considered as commercial under the Tunisian law.

UKRAINE

Ukraine will apply the provisions of this Convention in respect to arbitral awards made in the territories of non-contracting States only to the extent to which they grant reciprocal treatment.

UNITED KINGDOM

The United Kingdom will apply the Convention only to the recognition and enforcement of awards made in the territory of another Contracting State. This declaration is also made on behalf of Gibraltar, Hong Kong and the Isle of Man to which the Convention has been extended.

UNITED REPUBLIC OF TANZANIA

The Government of the United Republic of Tanganyika and Zanzibar will apply the Convention, in accordance with the first sentence of article I(3) thereof, only to the recognition and enforcement of awards made in the territory of another Contracting State.

UNITED STATES OF AMERICA

The United States of America will apply the Convention, on the basis of reciprocity, to the recognition and enforcement of only those awards made in the territory of another Contracting State.

The United States of America will apply the Convention only to differences arising out of legal relationships, whether contractual or not, which are considered as commercial under the national law of the United States.

YUGOSLAVIA

The Convention is applied in regard to the Socialist Federal Republic of Yugoslavia only to those arbitral awards which were adopted after the coming of the Convention into effect.

The Socialist Federal Republic of Yugoslavia will apply the Convention on a reciprocal basis only to those arbitral awards which were adopted on the territory of the other State Party to the Convention.

The Socialist Federal Republic of Yugoslavia will apply the Convention [only] with respect to the disputes arising from the legal relations, contractual and non-contractual, which, according to its national legislation are considered as economic.

Territorial Application of New York Arbitration Convention

Country	Date of Receipt of the Notification	Territories
Australia	26 March 1975	All the external territories for the international relations of which Australia is responsible other than Papua New Guinea
Denmark	10 February 1976	Faeroe Islands, Greenland
France	26 June 1959	All the territories of the French Republic
Netherlands	24 April 1964	Netherlands Antilles, Surinam
United Kingdom	24 September 1975 21 January 1977 22 February 1979 14 November 1979 26 November 1980 19 April 1985	Gibraltar Hong Kong Isle of Man Bermuda Belize, Cayman Islands Guernsey
United States of America	3 November 1970	All the territories for the international relations of which the United States of America is responsible

Declarations and Reservations Made on Notification of Territorial Applications

UNITED KINGDOM

Reservations Made On Behalf of Belize, Bermuda, Cayman Islands, Guernsey

The Convention will apply in accordance with article I, paragraph 3 thereof, only to the recognition and enforcement of awards made in the territory of another Contracting State.

2. European Convention on International Commercial Arbitration[1]

Article I. Scope of the Convention

1. This Convention shall apply:
    (*a*) to arbitration agreements concluded for the purpose of settling disputes arising from international trade between physical or legal persons having, when concluding the agreement, their habitual place of residence or their seat in different Contracting States;
    (*b*) to arbitral procedures and awards based on agreements referred to in paragraph 1 (*a*) above.
2. For the purpose of this Convention,
    (*a*) the term "arbitration agreement" shall mean either an arbitral clause in a contract or an arbitration agreement, the contract or arbitration agreement being signed by the parties, or contained in an exchange of letters, telegrams, or in a communication by teleprinter and, in relations between States whose laws do not require that an arbitration agreement be made in writing, any arbitration agreement concluded in the form authorized by these laws;
    (*b*) the term "arbitration" shall mean not only settlement by arbitrators appointed for each case (*ad hoc* arbitration) but also by permanent arbitral institutions;
    (*c*) the term "seat" shall mean the place of the situation of the establishment that has made the arbitration agreement.

Article II. Right of Legal Persons of Public Law to Resort to Arbitration

1. In the cases referred to in Article I, paragraph 1, of this Convention, legal persons considered by the law which is applicable to them as " legal persons of public law " have the right to conclude valid arbitration agreements.
2. On signing, ratifying or acceding to this Convention any State shall be entitled to declare that it limits the above faculty to such conditions as may be stated in its declaration.

Article III. Right of Foreign Nationals to be Designated as Arbitrators

In arbitration covered by this Convention, foreign nationals may be designated as arbitrators.

---

1. Geneva, 21 April 1961, 484 U.N.T.S. 349.

Article IV. Organization of the Arbitration

1. The parties to an arbitration agreement shall be free to submit their disputes:
    (*a*) to a permanent arbitral institution; in this case, the arbitration proceedings shall be held in conformity with the rules of the said institution;
    (*b*) to an *ad hoc* arbitral procedure; in this case, they shall be free *inter alia*
        (*i*) to appoint arbitrators or to establish means for their appointment in the event of an actual dispute;
        (*ii*) to determine the place of arbitration; and
        (*iii*) to lay down the procedure to be followed by the arbitrators.
2. Where the parties have agreed to submit any disputes to an *ad hoc* arbitration, and where within thirty days of the notification of the request for arbitration to the respondent one of the parties fails to appoint his arbitrator, the latter shall, unless otherwise provided, be appointed at the request of the other party by the President of the competent Chamber of Commerce of the country of the defaulting party's habitual place of residence or seat at the time of the introduction of the request for arbitration. This paragraph shall also apply to the replacement of the arbitrator(s) appointed by one of the parties or by the President of the Chamber of Commerce above referred to.
3. Where the parties have agreed to submit any disputes to an *ad hoc* arbitration by one or more arbitrators and the arbitration agreement contains no indication regarding the organization of the arbitration, as mentioned in paragraph I of this article, the necessary steps shall be taken by the arbitrator(s) already appointed, unless the parties are able to agree thereon and without prejudice to the case referred to in paragraph 2 above. Where the parties cannot agree on the appointment of the sole arbitrator or where the arbitrators appointed cannot agree on the measures to be taken, the claimant shall apply for the necessary action, where the place of arbitration has been agreed upon by the parties, at his option to the President of the Chamber of Commerce of the place of arbitration agreed upon or to the President of the competent Chamber of Commerce of the respondent's habitual place of residence or seat at the time of the introduction of the request for arbitration. Where such a place has not been agreed upon, the claimant shall be entitled at his option to apply for the necessary action either to the President of the competent Chamber of Commerce of the country of the respondent's habitual place of residence or seat at the time of the introduction of the request for arbitration, or to the Special Committee whose composition and procedure are specified in the Annex to this Convention. Where the claimant fails to exercise the rights given to him under this paragraph the respondent or the arbitrator(s) shall be entitled to do so.
4. When seized of a request the President or the Special Committee shall be entitled as need be:
    (*a*) to appoint the sole arbitrator, presiding arbitrator, umpire, or referee;
    (*b*) to replace the arbitrator(s) appointed under any procedure other than that referred to in paragraph 2 above;

(*c*) to determine the place of arbitration, provided that the arbitrator(s) may fix another place of arbitration;

(*d*) to establish directly or by reference to the rules and statutes of a permanent arbitral institution the rules of procedure to be followed by the arbitrator(s), provided that the arbitrators have not established these rules themselves in the absence of any agreement thereon between the parties.

5. Where the parties have agreed to submit their disputes to a permanent arbitral institution without determining the institution in question and cannot agree thereon, the claimant may request the determination of such institution in conformity with the procedure referred to in paragraph 3 above.

6. Where the arbitration agreement does not specify the mode of arbitration (arbitration by a permanent arbitral institution or an *ad hoc* arbitration) to which the parties have agreed to submit their dispute, and where the parties cannot agree thereon, the claimant shall be entitled to have recourse in this case to the procedure referred to in paragraph 3 above to determine the question. The President of the competent Chamber of Commerce or the Special Committee, shall be entitled either to refer the parties to a permanent arbitral institution or to request the parties to appoint their arbitrators within such time-limits as the President of the competent Chamber of Commerce or the Special Committee may have fixed and to agree within such time-limits on the necessary measures for the functioning of the arbitration. In the latter case, the provisions of paragraphs 2, 3 and 4 of this Article shall apply.

7. Where within a period of sixty days from the moment when he was requested to fulfil one of the functions set out in paragraphs 2, 3, 4, 5 and 6 of this Article, the President of the Chamber of Commerce designated by virtue of these paragraphs has not fulfilled one of these functions, the party requesting shall be entitled to ask the Special Committee to do so.

Article V. Plea as to Arbitral Jurisdiction

1. The party which intends to raise a plea as to the arbitrator's jurisdiction based on the fact that the arbitration agreement was either non-existent or null and void or had lapsed shall do so during the arbitration proceedings, not later than the delivery of its statement of claim or defence relating to the substance of the dispute; those based on the fact that an arbitrator has exceeded his terms of reference shall be raised during the arbitration proceedings as soon as the question on which the arbitrator is alleged to have no jurisdiction is raised during the arbitral procedure. Where the delay in raising the plea is due to a cause which the arbitrator deems justified, the arbitrator shall declare the plea admissible.

2. Pleas to the jurisdiction referred to in paragraph 1 above that have not been raised during the time-limits there referred to, may not be entered either during a subsequent stage of the arbitral proceedings where they are pleas left to the sole discretion of the parties under the law applicable by the arbitrator, or

during subsequent court proceedings concerning the substance or the enforcement of the award where such pleas are left to the discretion of the parties under the rule of conflict of the court seized of the substance of the dispute or the enforcement of the award. The arbitrator's decision on the delay in raising the plea, will, however, be subject to judicial control.

3. Subject to any subsequent judicial control provided for under the *lex fori*, the arbitrator whose jurisdiction is called in question shall be entitled to proceed with the arbitration, to rule on his own jurisdiction and to decide upon the existence or the validity of the arbitration agreement or of the contract of which the agreement forms part.

Article VI. Jurisdiction of Courts of Law

1. A plea as to the jurisdiction of the court made before the court seized by either party to the arbitration agreement, on the basis of the fact that an arbitration agreement exists shall, under penalty of estoppel, be presented by the respondent before or at the same time as the presentation of his substantial defence, depending upon whether the law of the court seized regards this plea as one of procedure or of substance.

2. In taking a decision concerning the existence or the validity of an arbitration agreement, courts of Contracting States shall examine the validity of such agreement with reference to the capacity of the parties, under the law applicable to them, and with reference to other questions

   (*a*) under the law to which the parties have subjected their arbitration agreement;

   (*b*) failing any indication thereon, under the law of the country in which the award is to be made;

   (*c*) failing any indication as to the law to which the parties have subjected the agreement, and where at the time when the question is raised in court the country in which the award is to be made cannot be determined, under the competent law by virtue of the rules of conflict of the court seized of the dispute.

   The courts may also refuse recognition of the arbitration agreement if under the law of their country the dispute is not capable of settlement by arbitration.

3. Where either party to an arbitration agreement has initiated arbitration proceedings before any resort is had to a court, courts of Contracting States subsequently asked to deal with the same subject-matter between the same parties or with the question whether the arbitration agreement was non-existent or null and void or had lapsed, shall stay their ruling on the arbitrator's jurisdiction until the arbitral award is made, unless they have good and substantial reasons to the contrary.

4. A request for interim measures or measures of conservation addressed to a judicial authority shall not be deemed incompatible with the arbitration agreement, or regarded as a submission of the substance of the case to the court.

Article VII. Applicable Law

1. The parties shall be free to determine, by agreement, the law to be applied by the arbitrators to the substance of the dispute. Failing any indication by the parties as to the applicable law, the arbitrators shall apply the proper law under the rule of conflict that the arbitrators deem applicable. In both cases the arbitrators shall take account of the terms of the contract and trade usages.
2. The arbitrators shall act as *amiables compositeurs* if the parties so decide and if they may do so under the law applicable to the arbitration.

Article VIII. Reasons for the Award

The parties shall be presumed to have agreed that reasons shall be given for the award unless they
(*a*) either expressly declare that reasons shall not be given; or
(*b*) have assented to an arbitral procedure under which it is not customary to give reasons for awards, provided that in this case neither party requests before the end of the hearing, or if there has not been a hearing then before the making of the award, that reasons be given.

Article IX. Setting Aside of the Arbitral Award

1. The setting aside in a Contracting State of an arbitral award covered by this Convention shall only constitute a ground for the refusal of recognition or enforcement in another Contracting State where such setting aside took place in a State in which, or under the law of which, the award has been made and for one of the following reasons:
(*a*) the parties to the arbitration agreement were under the law applicable to them, under some incapacity or the said agreement is not valid under the law to which the parties have subjected it or, failing any indication thereon, under the law of the country where the award was made, or
(*b*) the party requesting the setting aside of the award was not given proper notice of the appointment of the arbitrator or of the arbitration proceedings or was otherwise unable to present his case; or
(*c*) the award deals with a difference not contemplated by or not falling within the terms of the submission to arbitration, or it contains decisions on matters beyond the scope of the submission to arbitration, provided that, if the decisions on matters submitted to arbitration can be separated from those not so submitted, that part of the award which contains decisions on matters submitted to arbitration need not be set aside;
(*d*) the composition of the arbitral authority or the arbitral procedure was not in accordance with the agreement of the parties, or failing such agreement, with the provisions of Article IV of this Convention.

2. In relations between Contracting States that are also parties to the New York [Arbitration] Convention on the Recognition and Enforcement of Foreign Arbitral Awards of 10th June 1958, paragraph 1 of this Article limits the application of Article V (1) (*e*) of the New York [Arbitration] Convention solely to the cases of setting aside set out under paragraph I above.

Article X. Final Clauses

1. This Convention is open for signature or accession by countries members of the Economic Commission for Europe and countries admitted to the Commission in a consultative capacity under paragraph 8 of the Commission's terms of reference.
2. Such countries as may participate in certain activities of the Economic Commission for Europe in accordance with paragraph 11 of the Commission's terms of reference may become Contracting Parties to this Convention by acceding thereto after its entry into force.
3. The Convention shall be open for signature until 31 December 1961 inclusive. Thereafter, it shall be open for accession.
4. This Convention shall be ratified.
5. Ratification or accession shall be effected by the deposit of an instrument with the Secretary-General of the United Nations.
6. When signing, ratifying or acceding to this Convention, the Contracting Parties shall communicate to the Secretary-General of the United Nations a list of the Chambers of Commerce or other institutions in their country who will exercise the functions conferred by virtue of Article IV of this Convention on Presidents of the competent Chambers of Commerce.
7. The provisions of the present Convention shall not affect the validity of multilateral or bilateral agreements concerning arbitration entered into by Contracting States.
8. This Convention shall come into force on the ninetieth day after five of the countries referred to in paragraph 1 above have deposited their instruments of ratification or accession. For any country ratifying or acceding to it later this Convention shall enter into force on the ninetieth day after the said country has deposited its instrument of ratification or accession.
9. Any Contracting Party may denounce this Convention by so notifying the Secretary-General of the United Nations. Denunciation shall take effect twelve months after the date of receipt by the Secretary-General of the notification of denunciation.
10. If, after the entry into force of this Convention, the number of Contracting Parties is reduced, as a result of denunciations, to less than five, the Convention shall cease to be in force from the date on which the last of such denunciations takes effect.

11. The Secretary-General of the United Nations shall notify the countries referred to in paragraph 1, and the countries which have become Contracting Parties under paragraph 2 above, of

(*a*) declarations made under Article II, paragraph 2;

(*b*) ratifications and accessions under paragraphs 1 and 2 above;

(*c*) communications received in pursuance of paragraph 6 above;

(*d*) the dates of entry into force of this Convention in accordance with paragraph 8 above;

(*e*) denunciations under paragraph 9 above;

(*f*) the termination of this Convention in accordance with paragraph 10 above.

12. After 31 December 1961, the original of this Convention shall be deposited with the Secretary-General of the United Nations, who shall transmit certified true copies to each of the countries mentioned in paragraphs I and 2 above.

Composition and Procedure of the Special Committee Referred to in Article IV of the European Convention

1. The Special Committee referred to in Article IV of the Convention shall consist of two regular members and a Chairman. One of the regular members shall be elected by the Chambers of Commerce or other institutions designated, under Article X, paragraph 6, of the Convention, by States in which at the time when the Convention is open to signature National Committees of the International Chamber of Commerce exist, and which at the time of the election are parties to the Convention. The other member shall be elected by the Chambers of Commerce or other institutions designated, under Article X, paragraph 6, of the Convention, by States in which at the time when the Convention is open to signature no National Committees of the International Chamber of Commerce exist and which at the time of the election are parties to the Convention.

2. The persons who are to act as Chairman of the Special Committee pursuant to paragraph 7 of this Annex shall also be elected in like manner by the Chambers of Commerce or other institutions referred to in paragraph 1 of this Annex.

3. The Chambers of Commerce or other institutions referred to in paragraph 1 of this Annex shall elect alternates at the same time and in the same manner as they elect the Chairman and other regular members, in case of the temporary inability of the Chairman or regular members to act. In the event of the permanent inability to act or of the resignation of a Chairman or of a regular member, then the alternate elected to replace him shall become, as the case may be, the Chairman or regular member, and the group of Chambers of Commerce or other institutions which had elected the alternate who has become Chairman or regular member shall elect another alternate.

4. The first elections to the Committee shall be held within ninety days from the date of the deposit of the fifth instrument of ratification or accession. Chambers of Commerce and other institutions designated by Signatory States who are not yet parties to the Convention shall also be entitled to take part in

these elections. If however it should not be possible to hold elections within the prescribed period, the entry into force of paragraphs 3 to 7 of Article IV of the Convention shall be postponed until elections are held as provided for above.

5. Subject to the provisions of paragraph 7 below, the members of the Special Committee shall be elected for a term of four years. New elections shall be held within the first six months of the fourth year following the previous elections. Nevertheless, if a new procedure for the election of the members of the Special Committee has not produced results, the members previously elected shall continue to exercise their functions until the election of new members.

6. The results of the elections of the members of the Special Committee shall be communicated to the Secretary-General of the United Nations who shall notify the States referred to in Article X, paragraph 1, of this Convention and the States which have become Contracting Parties under Article X, paragraph 2. The Secretary-General shall likewise notify the said States of any postponement and of the entry into force of paragraphs 3 to 7 of Article IV of the Convention in pursuance of paragraph 4 of this Annex.

7. The persons elected to the office of Chairman shall exercise their functions in rotation, each during a period of two years. The question which of these two persons shall act as Chairman during the first two-year period after the entry into force of the Convention shall be decided by the drawing of lots. The office of Chairman shall thereafter be vested, for each successive two-year period, in the person elected Chairman by the group of countries other than that by which the Chairman exercising his functions during the immediately preceding two-year period was elected.

8. The reference to the Special Committee of one of the requests referred to in paragraphs 3 to 7 of the aforesaid Article IV shall be addressed to the Executive Secretary of the Economic Commission for Europe. The Executive Secretary shall in the first instance lay the request before the member of the Special Committee elected by the group of countries other than that by which the Chairman holding office at the time of the introduction of the request was elected. The proposal of the member applied to in the first instance shall be communicated by the Executive Secretary to the other member of the Committee and, if that other member agrees to this proposal, it shall be deemed to be the Committee's ruling and shall be communicated as such by the Executive Secretary to the person who made the request.

9. If the two members of the Special Committee applied to by the Executive Secretary are unable to agree on a ruling by correspondence, the Executive Secretary of the Economic Commission for Europe shall convene a meeting of the said Committee at Geneva in an attempt to secure a unanimous decision on the request. In the absence of unanimity, the Committee's decision shall be given by a majority vote and shall be communicated by the Executive Secretary to the person who made the request.

10. The expenses connected with the Special Committee's action shall be advanced by the person requesting such action but shall be considered as costs in the cause.

PARTIES TO THE EUROPEAN CONVENTION

Country	Signature	Ratification or accession
Austria	21 April 1961	6 March 1964
Belgium	21 April 1961	9 October 1975
Bulgaria	21 April 1961	13 May 1964
Byelorussian SSR	21 April 1961	14 October 1963
Czechoslovakia	21 April 1961	13 November 1963
Denmark	21 April 1961	13 November 1963
Finland		21 December 1961
France	21 April 1961	16 December 1966
Germany	21 April 1961	27 October 1964
Hungary	21 April 1961	9 October 1963
Italy	21 April 1961	3 August 1970
Luxembourg		26 March 1982
Poland	21 April 1961	15 September 1964
Romania	21 April 1961	16 August 1963
Russia (Successor to U.S.S.R.)	21 April 1961	27 June 1962
Spain	14 December 1961	12 May 1975
Turkey		21 April 1961
Ukraine (Successor to Ukrainian SSR)	21 April 1961	18 March 1963
Yugoslavia	21 April 1961	25 September 1963

DECLARATIONS AND RESERVATIONS TO EUROPEAN CONVENTION

BELGIUM

In accordance with Article II, paragraph 2, of the Convention, the Belgium Government declares that in Belgium only the State has, in the cases referred to in Article I, paragraph 1, the faculty to conclude arbitration agreements.

LUXEMBOURG

Except where otherwise expressly provided for in the arbitration agreement, the presiding judges of the local courts shall assume the functions entrusted to the presidents of the chambers of commerce under Article IV of the Convention. The presiding judges shall hear the disputes in chambers.

3. INTER-AMERICAN CONVENTION ON INTERNATIONAL COMMERCIAL ARBITRATION [1]

The Governments of the Member States of the Organization of American States, desirous of concluding a convention on international commercial arbitration, have agreed as follows:

Article 1

An agreement in which the parties undertake to submit to arbitral decision any differences that may arise or have arisen between them with respect to a commercial transaction is valid. The agreement shall be set forth in an instrument signed by the parties, or in the form of an exchange of letters, telegrams, or telex communications.

Article 2

Arbitrators shall be appointed in the manner agreed upon by the parties. Their appointment may be delegated to a third party, whether a natural or juridical person.

Article 3

In the absence of an express agreement between the parties, the arbitration shall be conducted in accordance with the rules of procedure of the Inter-American Commercial Arbitration Commission.

Article 4

An arbitral decision or award that is not appealable under the applicable law or procedural rules shall have the force of a final judicial judgment. Its execution or recognition may be ordered in the same manner as that of decisions handed down by national or foreign ordinary courts, in accordance with the procedural laws of the country where it is to be executed and the provisions of international treaties.

Article 5

1. The recognition and execution of the decision may be refused, at the request of the party against which it is made, only if such party is able to prove to the

1. Panama, 30 January 1975.

competent authority of the State in which recognition and execution are requested:

a. That the parties to the agreement were subject to some incapacity under the applicable law or that the agreement is not valid under the law to which the parties have submitted it, or, if such law is not specified, under the law of the State in which the decision was made; or

b. That the party against which the arbitral decision has been made was not duly notified of the appointment of the arbitrator or of the arbitration procedure to be followed, or was unable, for any other reason, to present his defense; or

c. That the decision concerns a dispute not envisaged in the agreement between the parties to submit to arbitration; nevertheless, if the provisions of the decision that refer to issues submitted to arbitration can be separated from those not submitted to arbitration, the former may be recognized and executed; or

d. That the constitution of the arbitral tribunal or the arbitration procedure has not been carried out in accordance with the terms of the agreement signed by the parties or, in the absence of such agreement, that the constitution of the arbitral tribunal or the arbitration procedure had not been carried out in accordance with the law of the State where the arbitration took place; or

e. That the decision is not yet binding on the parties or has been annulled or suspended by a competent authority of the State in which, or according to the law of which, the decision has been made.

2. The recognition and execution of an arbitral decision may also be refused if the competent authority of the State in which the recognition and execution is requested finds:

a. That the subject of the dispute cannot be settled by arbitration under the law of that State; or

b. That the recognition or execution of the decision would be contrary to the public policy ("ordre public") of that State.

Article 6

If the competent authority mentioned in Article 5.1,e has been requested to annul or suspend the arbitral decision, the authority before which such decision is invoked may, if it deems it appropriate, postpone a decision on the execution of the arbitral decision and, at the request of the party requesting execution, may also instruct the other party to provide appropriate guaranties.

Article 7

This Convention shall be open for signature by the Member States of the Organization of American States.

Article 8

This Convention is subject to ratification. The instruments of ratification shall be deposited with the General Secretariat of the Organization of American States.

Article 9

This Convention shall remain open for accession by any other State. The instruments of accession shall be deposited with the General Secretariat of the Organization of American States.

Article 10

This Convention shall enter into force on the thirtieth day following the date of deposit of the second instrument of ratification.

For each State ratifying or acceding to the Convention after the deposit of the second instrument of ratification, the Convention shall enter into force on the thirtieth day after deposit by such State of its instrument of ratification or accession.

Article 11

If a State Party has two or more territorial units in which different systems of law apply in relation to the matters dealt with in this Convention, it may, at the time of signature, ratification or accession, declare that this Convention shall extend to all its territorial units or only to one or more of them.

Such declaration may be modified by subsequent declarations, which shall expressly indicate the territorial unit or units to which the Convention applies. Such subsequent declarations shall be transmitted to the General Secretariat of the Organization of American States, and shall become effective thirty days after the date of their receipt.

Article 12

This Convention shall remain in force indefinitely, but any of the States Parties may denounce it. The instrument of denunciation shall be deposited with the General Secretariat of the Organization of American States. After one year from the date of deposit of the instrument of denunciation, the Convention shall no longer be in effect for the denouncing State, but shall remain in effect for the other States Parties.

Article 13

The original instrument of this Convention, the English, French, Portuguese and Spanish texts of which are equally authentic, shall be deposited with the General Secretariat of the Organization of American States. The Secretariat shall notify the Member States of the Organization of American States and the States that have acceded to the Convention of the signatures, deposits of instruments of ratification, accession, and denunciation as well as of reservations, if any. It shall also transmit the declarations referred to in Article 11 of this Convention.

PARTIES TO THE PANAMA CONVENTION

Signatories	Ratification
Argentina	
Bolivia	
Brazil	
Chile	17 May 1976
Columbia	29 December 1986
Costa Rica	20 January 1978
Dominican Republic	
Ecuador	23 October 1991
El Salvador	11 August 1980
Guatemala	20 August 1986
Honduras	22 March 1979
Mexico	27 March 1978
Nicaragua	
Panama	17 December 1975
Paraguay	15 December 1976
Peru	22 May 1989
United States	27 September 1990
Uruguay	25 April 1977
Venezuela	16 May 1985

United States Reservations to the Panama Convention

1. Unless there is an express agreement among the parties to an arbitration agreement to the contrary, where the requirements for application of both the Inter-American Convention on International Commercial Arbitration and the Convention on the Recognition and Enforcement of Foreign Arbitral Awards are met, if a majority of such parties are citizens of a state or states that have ratified or acceded to the Inter-American Convention and are member states of the Organization of American States, the Inter-American Convention shall apply. In all other cases, the Convention on the Recognition and Enforcement of Foreign Arbitral Awards shall apply.
2. The United States of America will apply the rules of procedure of the Inter-American Commercial Arbitration Commission which are in effect on the date that the United States of America deposits its instrument of ratification, unless the United States of America makes a later official determination to adopt and apply subsequent amendments to such rules.
3. The United States of America will apply the Convention, on the basis of reciprocity, to the recognition and enforcement of only those awards made in the territory of another Contracting State.

4. CONVENTION ON THE SETTLEMENT OF INVESTMENT DISPUTES BETWEEN STATES AND NATIONALS OF OTHER STATES [1]

CHAPTER I: International Centre for Settlement of Investment Disputes

SECTION 1: Establishment and Organization

Article 1
> (1) There is hereby established the International Centre for Settlement of Investment Disputes (hereinafter called the Centre).
> (2) The purpose of the Centre shall be to provide facilities for conciliation and arbitration of investment disputes between Contracting States and nationals of other Contracting States in accordance with the provisions of this Convention.

Article 2
> The seat of the Centre shall be at the principal office of the International Bank for Reconstruction and Development (hereinafter called the Bank). The seat may be moved to another place by decision of the Administrative Council adopted by a majority of two-thirds of its members.

Article 3
> The Centre shall have an Administrative Council and a Secretariat and shall maintain a Panel of Conciliators and a Panel of Arbitrators.

SECTION 2: The Administrative Council

Article 4
> (1) The Administrative Council shall be composed of one representative of each Contracting State. An alternate may act as representative in case of his principal's absence from a meeting or inability to act.
> (2) In the absence of a contrary designation, each governor and alternate governor of the Bank appointed by a Contracting State shall be *ex officio* its representative and its alternate respectively.

Article 5
> The President of the Bank shall be *ex officio* Chairman of the Administrative Council (hereinafter called the Chairman) but shall have no vote. During his absence or inability to act and during any vacancy in the office of President of the Bank, the person for the time being acting as President shall act as Chairman of the Administrative Council.

---

1. Washington, D.C., 1965.

Article 6
 (1) Without prejudice to the powers and functions vested in it by other provisions
 of this Convention, the Administrative Council shall
   (a) adopt the administrative and financial regulations of the Centre;
   (b) adopt the rules of procedure for the institution of conciliation and arbitration proceedings;
   (c) adopt the rules of procedure for conciliation and arbitration proceedings
   (hereinafter called the Conciliation Rules and the Arbitration Rules);
   (d) approve arrangements with the Bank for the use of the Bank's administrative facilities and services;
   (e) determine the conditions of service of the Secretary-General and of any
   Deputy Secretary-General;
   (f) adopt the annual budget of revenues and expenditures of the Centre;
   (g) approve the annual report on the operation of the Centre.
    The decisions referred to in sub-paragraphs (a), (b), (c) and (f) above shall be
 adopted by a majority of two-thirds of the members of the Administrative
 Council.
 (2) The Administrative Council may appoint such committees as it considers necessary.
 (3) The Administrative Council shall also exercise such other powers and perform
 such other functions as it shall determine to be necessary for the implementation of the provisions of this Convention.

Article 7
 (1) The Administrative Council shall hold an annual meeting and such other
 meeting as may be determined by the Council, or convened by the Chairman,
 or convened by the Secretary-General at the request of not less than five members of the Council.
 (2) Each member of the Administrative Council shall have one vote and, except as
 otherwise herein provided, all matters before the Council shall be decided by a
 majority of the votes cast.
 (3) A quorum for any meeting of the Administrative Council shall be a majority of
 its members.
 (4) The Administrative Council may establish, by a majority of two-thirds of its
 members, a procedure whereby the Chairman may seek a vote of the Council
 without convening a meeting of the Council. The vote shall be considered valid
 only if the majority of the members of the Council cast their votes within the
 time limit fixed by the said procedure.

Article 8
    Members of the Administrative Council and the Chairman shall serve with-
 out remuneration from the Centre.

SECTION 3: The Secretariat

Article 9
> The Secretariat shall consist of a Secretary-General, one or more Deputy Secretaries-General and staff.

Article 10
    (1) The Secretary-General and any Deputy Secretary-General shall be elected by the Administrative Council by a majority of two-thirds of its members upon the nomination of the Chairman for a term of service not exceeding six years and shall be eligible for re-election. After consulting the members of the Administrative Council, the Chairman shall propose one or more candidates for each such office.

    (2) The offices of Secretary-General and Deputy Secretary-General shall be incompatible with the exercise of any political function. Neither the Secretary-General nor any Deputy Secretary-General may hold any other employment or engage in any other occupation except with the approval of the Administrative Council.

    (3) During the Secretary-General's absence or inability to act, and during any vacancy of the office of Secretary-General, the Deputy Secretary-General shall act as Secretary-General. If there shall be more than one Deputy Secretary-General, the Administrative Council shall determine in advance the order in which they shall act as Secretary-General.

Article 11
> The Secretary-General shall be the legal representative and the principal officer of the Centre and shall be responsible for its administration, including the appointment of staff, in accordance with the provisions of this Convention and the rules adopted by the Administrative Council. He shall perform the function of registrar and shall have the power to authenticate arbitral awards rendered pursuant to this Convention, and to certify copies thereof.

SECTION 4: The Panels

Article 12
> The Panel of Conciliators and the Panel of Arbitrators shall each consist of qualified persons, designated as hereinafter provided, who are willing to serve thereon.

Article 13
    (1) Each Contracting State may designate to each Panel four persons who may but need not be its nationals.

    (2) The Chairman may designate ten persons to each Panel. The persons so designated to a Panel shall each have a different nationality.

Article 14

(1) Persons designated to serve on the Panels shall be persons of high moral character and recognized competence in the fields of law, commerce, industry or finance, who may be relied upon to exercise independent judgment. Competence in the field of law shall be of particular importance in the case of persons on the Panel of Arbitrators.

(2) The Chairman, in designating persons to serve on the Panels, shall in addition pay due regard to the importance of assuring representation on the Panels of the principal legal systems of the world and of the main forms of economic activity.

Article 15

(1) Panel members shall serve for renewable periods of six years.

(2) In case of death or resignation of a member of a Panel, the authority which designated the member shall have the right to designate another person to serve for the remainder of that member's term.

(3) Panel members shall continue in office until their successors have been designated.

Article 16

(1) A person may serve on both Panels.

(2) If a person shall have been designated to serve on the same Panel by more than one Contracting State, or by one or more Contracting States and the Chairman, he shall be deemed to have been designated by the authority which first designated him or, if one such authority is the State of which he is a national, by that State.

(3) All designations shall be notified to the Secretary-General and shall take effect from the date on which the notification is received.

SECTION 5: Financing the Centre

Article 17

If the expenditure of the Centre cannot be met out of charges for the use of its facilities, or out of other receipts, the excess shall be borne by Contracting States which are members of the Bank in proportion to their respective subscriptions to the capital stock of the Bank, and by Contracting States which are not members of the Bank in accordance with rules adopted by the Administrative Council.

SECTION 6: Status, Immunities and Privileges

Article 18

The Centre shall have full international legal personality. The legal capacity of the Centre shall include the capacity

(a) to contract;
(b) to acquire and dispose of movable and immovable property;
(c) to institute legal proceedings.

Article 19

To enable the Centre to fulfil its functions, it shall enjoy in the territories of each Contracting State the immunities and privileges set forth in this Section.

Article 20

The Centre, its property and assets shall enjoy immunity from all legal process, except when the Centre waives this immunity.

Article 21

The Chairman, the members of the Administrative Council, persons acting as conciliators or arbitrators or members of a Committee appointed pursuant to paragraph (3) of Article 52, and the officers and employees of the Secretariat
(a) shall enjoy immunity from legal process with respect to acts performed by them in the exercise of their functions, except when the Centre waives this immunity;
(b) not being local nationals, shall enjoy the same immunities from immigration restrictions, alien registration requirements and national service obligations, the same facilities as regards exchange restrictions and the same treatment in respect of travelling facilities as are accorded by Contracting States to the representatives, officials and employees of comparable rank of other Contracting States.

Article 22

The provisions of Article 21 shall apply to persons appearing in proceedings under this Convention as parties, agents, counsel, advocates, witnesses or experts; provided, however, that sub-paragraph (b) thereof shall apply only in connection with their travel to and from, and their stay at, the place where the proceedings are held.

Article 23

(1) The archives of the Centre shall be inviolable, wherever they may be.
(2) With regard to its official communications, the Centre shall be accorded by each Contracting State treatment not less favourable than that accorded to other international organizations.

Article 24

(1) The Centre, its assets, property and income, and its operations and transactions authorized by this Convention shall be exempt from all taxation and customs duties. The Centre shall also be exempt from liability for the collection or payment of any taxes or customs duties.

(2) Except in the case of local nationals, no tax shall be levied on or in respect of expense allowances paid by the Centre to the Chairman or members of the Administrative Council, or on or in respect of salaries, expense allowances or other emoluments paid by the Centre to officials or employees of the Secretariat.

(3) No tax shall be levied on or in respect of fees or expense allowances received by persons acting as conciliators, or arbitrators, or members of a Committee appointed pursuant to paragraph (3) of Article 52, in proceedings under this Convention, if the sole jurisdictional basis for such tax is the location of the Centre or the place where such proceedings are conducted or the place where such fees or allowances are paid.

CHAPTER II: Jurisdiction of the Centre

Article 25

(1) The jurisdiction of the Centre shall extend to any legal dispute arising directly out of an investment, between a Contracting State (or any constituent subdivision or agency of a Contracting State designated to the Centre by that State) and a national of another Contracting State, which the parties to the dispute consent in writing to submit to the Centre. When the parties have given their consent, no party may withdraw its consent unilaterally.

(2) "National of another Contracting State" means:

(a) any natural person who had the nationality of a Contracting State other than the State party to the dispute on the date on which the parties consented to submit such dispute to conciliation or arbitration as well as on the date on which the request was registered pursuant to paragraph (3) of Article 28 or paragraph (3) of Article 36, but does not include any person who on either date also had the nationality of the Contracting State party to the dispute; and

(b) any juridical person which had the nationality of a Contracting State other than the State party to the dispute on the date on which the parties consented to submit such dispute to conciliation or arbitration and any juridical person which had the nationality of the Contracting State party to the dispute on that date and which, because of foreign control, the parties have agreed should be treated as a national of another Contracting State for the purposes of this Convention.

(3) Consent by a constituent subdivision or agency of a Contracting State shall require the approval of that State unless that State notifies the Centre that no such approval is required.

(4) Any Contracting state may, at the time of ratification, acceptance or approval of this Convention or at any time thereafter, notify the Centre of the class or classes of disputes which it would or would not consider submitting to the jurisdiction of the Centre. The Secretary-General shall forthwith transmit such notification to all Contracting States. Such notification shall not constitute the consent required by paragraph (1).

Article 26

Consent of the parties to arbitration under this Convention shall, unless otherwise stated, be deemed consent to such arbitration to the exclusion of any other remedy. A Contracting State may require the exhaustion of local administrative or judicial remedies as a condition of its consent to arbitration under this Convention.

Article 27

(1) No Contracting State shall give diplomatic protection, or bring an international claim, in respect of a dispute which one of its nationals and another Contracting State shall have consented to submit or shall have submitted to arbitration under this Convention, unless such other Contracting State shall have failed to abide by and comply with the award rendered in such dispute.

(2) Diplomatic protection, for the purposes of paragraph (1), shall not include informal diplomatic exchanges for the sole purpose of facilitating a settlement of the dispute.

CHAPTER III: Conciliation

SECTION 1: Request for Conciliation

Article 28

(1) Any Contracting State or any national of a Contracting State wishing to institute conciliation proceedings shall address a request to that effect in writing to the Secretary-General who shall send a copy of the request to the other party.

(2) The request shall contain information concerning the issues in dispute, the identity of the parties and their consent to conciliation in accordance with the rules of procedure for the institution of conciliation and arbitration proceedings.

(3) The Secretary-General shall register the request unless he finds, on the basis of the information contained in the request, that the dispute is manifestly outside the jurisdiction of the Centre. He shall forthwith notify the parties of registration or refusal to register.

SECTION 2: Constitution of the Conciliation Commission

Article 29

(1) The Conciliation Commission (hereinafter called the Commission) shall be constituted as soon as possible after registration of a request pursuant to Article 28.

(2) (a) The Commission shall consist of a sole conciliator or any uneven number of conciliators appointed as the parties shall agree.

(b) Where the parties do not agree upon the number of conciliators and the method of their appointment, the Commission shall consist of three conciliators, one conciliator appointed by each party and the third, who shall be the president of the Commission, appointed by agreement of the parties.

Article 30

If the Commission shall not have been constituted within 90 days after notice of registration of the request has been dispatched by the Secretary-General in accordance with paragraph (3) of Article 28, or such other period as the parties may agree, the Chairman shall, at the request of either party and after consulting both parties as far as possible, appoint the conciliator or conciliators not yet appointed.

Article 31

(1) Conciliators may be appointed from outside the Panel of Conciliators, except in the case of appointments by the Chairman pursuant to Article 30.

(2) Conciliators appointed from outside the Panel of Conciliators shall possess the qualities stated in paragraph (1) of Article 14.

SECTION 3: Conciliation Proceedings

Article 32

(1) The Commission shall be the judge of its own competence.

(2) Any objection by a party to the dispute that that dispute is not within the jurisdiction of the Centre, or for other reasons is not within the competence of the Commission, shall be considered by the Commission which shall determine whether to deal with it as a preliminary question or to join it to the merits of the dispute.

Article 33

Any conciliation proceeding shall be conducted in accordance with the provisions of this Section and, except as the parties otherwise agree, in accordance with the Conciliation Rules in effect on the date on which the parties consented to conciliation. If any question of procedure arises which is not covered by this Section or the Conciliation Rules or any rules agreed by the parties, the Commission shall decide the question.

Article 34

(1) It shall be the duty of the Commission to clarify the issues in dispute between the parties and to endeavour to bring about agreement between them upon mutually acceptable terms. To that end, the Commission may at any stage of the proceedings and from time to time recommend terms of settlement to the parties. The parties shall cooperate in good faith with the Commission in order to enable the Commission to carry out its functions, and shall give their most serious consideration to its recommendations.

(2) If the parties reach agreement, the Commission shall draw up a report noting the issues in dispute and recording that the parties have reached agreement. If, at any stage of the proceedings, it appears to the Commission that there is no likelihood of agreement between the parties, it shall close the proceedings and shall draw up a report noting the submission of the dispute and recording the failure of the parties to reach agreement. If one party fails to appear or participate in the proceedings, the Commission shall close the proceedings and shall draw up a report noting that party's failure to appear or participate.

Article 35

Except as the parties to the dispute shall otherwise agree, neither party to a conciliation proceeding shall be entitled in any other proceeding, whether before arbitrators or in a court of law or otherwise, to invoke or rely on any views expressed or statements or admissions or offers of settlement made by the other party in the conciliation proceedings, or the report or any recommendations made by the Commission.

CHAPTER IV: Arbitration

SECTION 1: Request for Arbitration

Article 36
(1) Any Contracting State or any national of a Contracting State wishing to institute arbitration proceedings shall address a request to that effect in writing to the Secretary-General who shall send a copy of the request to the other party.
(2) The request shall contain information concerning the issues in dispute, the identity of the parties and their consent to arbitration in accordance with the rules of procedure for the institution of conciliation and arbitration proceedings.
(3) The Secretary-General shall register the request unless he finds, on the basis of the information contained in the request, that the dispute is manifestly outside the jurisdiction of the Centre. He shall forthwith notify the parties of registration or refusal to register.

SECTION 2 : Constitution of the Tribunal

Article 37
(1) The Arbitral Tribunal (hereinafter called the Tribunal) shall be constituted as soon as possible after registration of a request pursuant to Article 36.
(2) (a) The Tribunal shall consist of a sole arbitrator or any uneven number of arbitrators appointed as the parties shall agree.
(b) Where the parties do not agree upon the number of arbitrators and the method of their appointment, the Tribunal shall consist of three arbitrators,

one arbitrator appointed by each party and the third, who shall be the president of the Tribunal, appointed by agreement of the parties.

Article 38

If the Tribunal shall not have been constituted within 90 days after notice of registration of the request has been dispatched by the Secretary-General in accordance with paragraph (3) of Article 36, or such other period as the parties may agree, the Chairman shall, at the request of either party and after consulting both parties as far as possible, appoint the arbitrator or arbitrators not yet appointed. Arbitrators appointed by the Chairman pursuant to this Article shall not be nationals of the Contracting State party to the dispute or of the Contracting State whose national is a party to the dispute.

Article 39

The majority of the arbitrators shall be nationals of States other than the Contracting State party to the dispute and the Contracting State whose national is a party to the dispute; provided, however, that the foregoing provisions of this Article shall not apply if the sole arbitrator or each individual member of the Tribunal has been appointed by agreement of the parties.

Article 40

(1) Arbitrators may be appointed from outside the Panel of Arbitrators, except in the case of appointments by the Chairman pursuant to Article 38.

(2) Arbitrators appointed from outside the Panel of Arbitrators shall possess the qualities stated in paragraph (1) of Article 14.

SECTION 3: Powers and Functions of the Tribunal

Article 41

(1) The Tribunal shall be the judge of its own competence.

(2) Any objection by a party to the dispute that that dispute is not within the jurisdiction of the Centre, or for other reasons is not within the competence of the Tribunal, shall be considered by the Tribunal which shall determine whether to deal with it as a preliminary question or to join it to the merits of the dispute.

Article 42

(1) The Tribunal shall decide a dispute in accordance with such rules of law as may be agreed by the parties. In the absence of such agreement, the Tribunal shall apply the law of the Contracting State party to the dispute (including its rules on the conflict of laws) and such rules of international law as may be applicable.

(2) The Tribunal may not bring in a finding of *non liquet* on the ground of silence or obscurity of the law.

(3) The provisions of paragraphs (1) and (2) shall not prejudice the power of the Tribunal to decide a dispute *ex aequo et bono* if the parties so agree.

Article 43

Except as the parties otherwise agree, the Tribunal may, if it deems it necessary at any stage of the proceedings,

(a) call upon the parties to produce documents or other evidence, and

(b) visit the scene connected with the dispute, and conduct such inquiries there as it may deem appropriate.

Article 44

Any arbitration proceeding shall be conducted in accordance with the provisions of this Section and, except as the parties otherwise agree, in accordance with the Arbitration Rules in effect on the date on which the parties consented to arbitration. If any question of procedure arises which is not covered by this Section or the Arbitration Rules or any rules agreed by the parties, the Tribunal shall decide the question.

Article 45

(1) Failure of a party to appear or to present his case shall not be deemed an admission of the other party's assertions.

(2) If a party fails to appear or to present his case at any stage of the proceedings the other party may request the Tribunal to deal with the questions submitted to it and to render an award. Before rendering an award, the Tribunal shall notify, and grant a period of grace to, the party failing to appear or to present its case, unless it is satisfied that that party does not intend to do so.

Article 46

Except as the parties otherwise agree, the Tribunal shall, if requested by a party, determine any incidental or additional claims or counter-claims arising directly out of the subject-matter of the dispute provided that they are within the scope of the consent of the parties and are otherwise within the jurisdiction of the Centre.

Article 47

Except as the parties otherwise agree, the Tribunal may, if it considers that the circumstances so require, recommend any provisional measures which should be taken to preserve the respective rights of either party.

SECTION 4: The Award

Article 48

(1) The Tribunal shall decide questions by a majority of the votes of all its members.

(2) The award of the Tribunal shall be in writing and shall be signed by the members of the Tribunal who voted for it.

(3) The award shall deal with every question submitted to the Tribunal, and shall state the reasons upon which it is based.

(4) Any member of the Tribunal may attach his individual opinion to the award, whether he dissents from the majority or not, or a statement of his dissent.

(5) The Centre shall not publish the award without the consent of the parties.

Article 49

(1) The Secretary-General shall promptly dispatch certified copies of the award to the parties. The award shall be deemed to have been rendered on the date on which the certified copies were dispatched.

(2) The Tribunal upon the request of a party made within 45 days after the date on which the award was rendered may after notice to the other party decide any question which it had omitted to decide in the award, and shall rectify any clerical, arithmetical or similar error in the award. Its decision shall become part of the award and shall be notified to the parties in the same manner as the award. The periods of time provided for under paragraph (2) of Article 51 and paragraph (2) of Article 52 shall run from the date on which the decision was rendered.

SECTION 5: Interpretation, Revision and Annulment of the Award

Article 50

(1) If any dispute shall arise between the parties as to the meaning or scope of an award, either party may request interpretation of the award by an application in writing addressed to the Secretary-General.

(2) The request shall, if possible, be submitted to the Tribunal which rendered the award. If this shall not be possible, a new Tribunal shall be constituted in accordance with Section 2 of this Chapter. The Tribunal may, if it considers that the circumstances so require, stay enforcement of the award pending its decision.

Article 51

(1) Either party may request revision of the award by an application in writing addressed to the Secretary-General on the ground of discovery of some fact of such a nature as decisively to affect the award, provided that when the award was rendered that fact was unknown to the Tribunal and to the applicant and that the applicant's ignorance of that fact was not due to negligence.

(2) The application shall be made within 90 days after the discovery of such fact and in any event within three years after the date on which the award was rendered.

(3) The request shall, if possible, be submitted to the Tribunal which rendered the award. If this shall not be possible, a new Tribunal shall be constituted in accordance with Section 2 of this Chapter.

(4) The Tribunal may, if it considers that the circumstances so require, stay

enforcement of the award pending its decision. If the applicant requests a stay of enforcement of the award in his application, enforcement shall be stayed provisionally until the Tribunal rules on such request.

Article 52

(1) Either party may request annulment of the award by an application in writing addressed to the Secretary-General on one or more of the following grounds:
(a) that the Tribunal was not properly constituted;
(b) that the Tribunal has manifestly exceeded its powers;
(c) that there was corruption on the part of a member of the Tribunal;
(d) that there has been a serious departure from a fundamental rule of procedure; or
(e) that the award has failed to state the reasons on which it is based.

(2) The application shall be made within 120 days after the date on which the award was rendered except that when annulment is requested on the ground of corruption such application shall be made within 120 days after discovery of the corruption and in any event within three years after the date on which the award was rendered.

(3) On receipt of the request the Chairman shall forthwith appoint from the Panel of Arbitrators an *ad hoc* Committee of three persons. None of the members of the Committee shall have been a member of the Tribunal which rendered the award, shall be of the same nationality as any such member, shall be a national of the State party to the dispute or of the State whose national is a party to the dispute, shall have been designated to the Panel of Arbitrators by either of those States, or shall have acted as a conciliator in the same dispute. The Committee shall have the authority to annul the award or any part thereof on any of the grounds set forth in paragraph (1).

(4) The provisions of Articles 41-45, 48, 49, 53 and 54, and of Chapters VI and VII shall apply *mutatis mutandis* to proceedings before the Committee.

(5) The Committee may, if it considers that the circumstances so require, stay enforcement of the award pending its decision. If the applicant requests a stay of enforcement of the award in his application, enforcement shall be stayed provisionally until the Committee rules on such request.

(6) If the award is annulled the dispute shall, at the request of either party, be submitted to a new Tribunal constituted in accordance with Section 2 of this Chapter.

SECTION 6: Recognition and Enforcement of the Award

Article 53

(1) The award shall be binding on the parties and shall not be subject to any appeal or to any other remedy except those provided for in this Convention. Each party shall abide by and comply with the terms of the award except to the

extent that enforcement shall have been stayed pursuant to the relevant provisions of this Convention.

(2) For the purposes of this Section, "award" shall include any decision interpreting, revising or annulling such award pursuant to Articles 50, 51 or 52.

Article 54

(1) Each Contracting State shall recognize an award rendered pursuant to this Convention as binding and enforce the pecuniary obligations imposed by that award within its territories as if it were a final judgment of a court in that State. A Contracting State with a federal constitution may enforce such an award in or through its federal courts and may provide that such courts shall treat the award as if it were a final judgment of the courts of a constituent state.

(2) A party seeking recognition or enforcement in the territories of a Contracting State shall furnish to a competent court or other authority which such State shall have designated for this purpose a copy of the award certified by the Secretary-General. Each Contracting State shall notify the Secretary-General of the designation of the competent court or other authority for this purpose and of any subsequent change in such designation.

(3) Execution of the award shall be governed by the laws concerning the execution of judgments in force in the State in whose territories such execution is sought.

Article 55

Nothing in Article 54 shall be construed as derogating from the law in force in any Contracting State relating to immunity of that State or of any foreign State from execution.

CHAPTER V: Replacement and Disqualification of Conciliators and Arbitrators

Article 56

(1) After a Commission or a Tribunal has been constituted and proceedings have begun, its composition shall remain unchanged; provided, however, that if a conciliator or an arbitrator should die, become incapacitated, or resign, the resulting vacancy shall be filled in accordance with the provisions of Section 2 of Chapter III or Section 2 of Chapter IV.

(2) A member of a Commission or Tribunal shall continue to serve in that capacity notwithstanding that he shall have ceased to be a member of the Panel.

(3) If a conciliator or arbitrator appointed by a party shall have resigned without the consent of the Commission or Tribunal of which he was a member, the Chairman shall appoint a person from the appropriate Panel to fill the resulting vacancy.

Article 57

A party may propose to a Commission or Tribunal the disqualification of any of its members on account of any fact indicating a manifest lack of the qualities required by paragraph (1) of Article 14. A party to arbitration proceedings may, in addition, propose the disqualification of an arbitrator on the ground that he was ineligible for appointment to the Tribunal under Section 2 of Chapter IV.

Article 58

The decision on any proposal to disqualify a conciliator or arbitrator shall be taken by the other members of the Commission or Tribunal as the case may be, provided that where those members are equally divided, or in the case of a proposal to disqualify a sole conciliator or arbitrator, or a majority of the conciliators or arbitrators, the Chairman shall take that decision. If it is decided that the proposal is well-founded the conciliator or arbitrator to whom the decision relates shall be replaced in accordance with the provisions of Section 2 of Chapter III or Section 2 of Chapter IV.

CHAPTER VI: Cost of Proceedings

Article 59

The charges payable by the parties for the use of the facilities of the Centre shall be determined by the Secretary-General in accordance with the regulations adopted by the Administrative Council.

Article 60

(1) Each Commission and each Tribunal shall determine the fees and expenses of its members within limits established from time to time by the Administrative Council and after consultation with the Secretary-General.

(2) Nothing in paragraph (1) of this Article shall preclude the parties from agreeing in advance with the Commission or Tribunal concerned upon the fees and expenses of its members.

Article 61

(1) In the case of conciliation proceedings the fees and expenses of members of the Commission as well as the charges for the use of the facilities of the Centre, shall be borne equally by the parties. Each party shall bear any other expenses it incurs in connection with the proceedings.

(2) In the case of arbitration proceedings the Tribunal shall, except as the parties otherwise agree, assess the expenses incurred by the parties in connection with the proceedings, and shall decide how and by whom those expenses, the fees and expenses of the members of the Tribunal and the charges for the use of the facilities of the Centre shall be paid. Such decision shall form part of the award.

CHAPTER VII: Place of Proceedings

Article 62
>Conciliation and arbitration proceedings shall be held at the seat of the Centre except as hereinafter provided.

Article 63
Conciliation and arbitration proceedings may be held, if the parties so agree,
(a) at the seat of the Permanent Court of Arbitration or of any other appropriate institution, whether private or public, with which the Centre may make arrangements for that purpose; or
(b) at any other place approved by the Commission or Tribunal after consultation with the Secretary-General.

CHAPTER VIII: Disputes between Contracting States

Article 64
>Any dispute arising between Contracting States concerning the interpretation or application of this Convention which is not settled by negotiation shall be referred to the International Court of Justice by the application of any party to such dispute, unless the States concerned agree to another method of settlement.

CHAPTER IX: Amendment

Article 65
>Any Contracting State may propose amendment of this Convention. The text of a proposed amendment shall be communicated to the Secretary-General not less than 90 days prior to the meeting of the Administrative Council at which such amendment is to be considered and shall forthwith be transmitted by him to all the members of the Administrative Council.

Article 66
(1) If the Administrative Council shall so decide by a majority of two-thirds of its members, the proposed amendment shall be circulated to all Contracting States for ratification, acceptance or approval. Each amendment shall enter into force 30 days after dispatch by the depositary of this Convention of a notification to Contracting States that all Contracting States have ratified, accepted or approved the amendment.
(2) No amendment shall affect the rights and obligations under this Convention of any Contracting State or of any of its constituent subdivisions or agencies, or of any national of such State arising out of consent to the jurisdiction of the Centre given before the date of entry into force of the amendment.

CHAPTER X: Final Provisions

Article 67

This Convention shall be open for signature on behalf of States members of the Bank. It shall also be open for signature on behalf of any other State which is a party to the Statute of the International Court of Justice and which the Administrative Council, by a vote of two-thirds of its members, shall have invited to sign the Convention.

Article 68

(1) This Convention shall be subject to ratification, acceptance or approval by the signatory States in accordance with their respective constitutional procedures.
(2) This Convention shall enter into force 30 days after the date of deposit of the twentieth instrument of ratification, acceptance or approval. It shall enter into force for each State which subsequently deposits its instrument of ratification, acceptance or approval 30 days after the date of such deposit.

Article 69

Each Contracting State shall take such legislative or other measures as may be necessary for making the provisions of this Convention effective in its territories.

Article 70

This Convention Shall apply to all territories for whose international relations a Contracting State is responsible, except those which are excluded by such State by written notice to the depositary of this Convention either at the time of ratification, acceptance or approval or subsequently.

Article 71

Any Contracting State may denounce this Convention by written notice to the depositary of this Convention. The denunciation shall take effect six months after receipt of such notice.

Article 72

Notice by a Contracting State pursuant to Articles 70 or 71 shall not affect the rights or obligations under this Convention of that State or of any of its constituent subdivisions or agencies or of any national of that State arising out of consent to the jurisdiction of the Centre given by one of them before such notice was received by the depositary.

Article 73

Instruments of ratification, acceptance or approval of this Convention and of amendments thereto shall be deposited with the Bank which shall act as the depositary of this Convention. The depositary shall transmit certified copies of this Convention to States members of the Bank and to any other State invited to sign the Convention.

Article 74

The depositary shall register this Convention with the Secretariat of the United Nations in accordance with Article 102 of the Charter of the United Nations and the Regulations thereunder adopted by the General Assembly.

Article 75

The depositary shall notify all signatory States of the following:

(a) signatures in accordance with Article 67;

(b) deposits of instruments of ratification, acceptance and approval in accordance with Article 73;

(c) the date on which this Convention enters into force in accordance with Article 68;

(d) exclusions from territorial application pursuant to Article 70;

(e) the date on which any amendment of this Convention enters into force in accordance with Article 66; and

(f) denunciations in accordance with Article 71.

PARTIES TO THE WASHINGTON CONVENTION

Country	Signature	Deposit of Ratification	Entry into Force of Convention
Afghanistan	30 September 1966	25 June 1968	25 July 1968
Albania	15 October 1991	15 October 1991	14 November 1991
Argentina	21 May 1991		
Armenia	16 September 1992	16 September 1992	16 October 1992
Australia	24 March 1975	2 May 1991	1 June 1991
Austria	17 May 1966	25 May 1971	24 June 1971
Azerbaijan	18 September 1992	18 September 1992	18 October 1992
Bangladesh	20 November 1979	27 March 1980	26 April 1980
Barbados	13 May 1981	1 November 1983	1 December 1983
Belarus	10 July 1992	10 July 1992	9 August 1992
Belgium	15 December 1965	27 August 1970	26 September 1970
Belize	19 December 1986		
Benin	10 September 1965		
Bolivia	3 May 1991		
Botswana	15 January 1970	15 January 1970	14 February 1970
Bukina Faso	16 September 1965	29 August 1966	14 October 1966
Burundi	17 February 1967	5 November 1969	5 December 1969
Cambodia	5 November 1993		
Cameroon	23 September 1965	3 January 1967	2 February 1967
Central African Republic	26 August 1965	23 February 1966	14 October 1966
Chad	12 May 1966	29 August 1966	14 October 1966
Chile	25 January 1991		
China	9 February 1990	7 January 1993	6 February 1993
Columbia	16 May 1993		
Comoros	26 September 1978	7 November 1978	7 December 1978

Country	Signature	Deposit of Ratification	Entry into Force of Convention
Congo	27 December 1965	23 June 1966	14 October 1966
Costa Rica	29 September 1981		
Côte d'Ivoire	30 June 1965	16 February 1966	14 October 1966
Cyprus	9 March 1966	25 November 1966	25 December 1966
Czech Republic	23 March 1993	23 March 1993	22 April 1993
Denmark	11 October 1965	24 April 1968	24 May 1968
Ecuador	15 January 1986	15 January 1986	14 February 1986
Egypt	11 February 1972	3 May 1972	2 June 1972
El Salvador	9 June 1982	6 March 1984	5 April 1984
Estonia	23 June 1992	23 June 1992	22 July 1992
Ethiopia	21 September 1965		
Fiji	1 July 1977	11 August 1977	10 September 1977
Finland	14 July 1967	9 January 1969	8 February 1969
France	22 December 1965	21 August 1967	20 September 1967
Gabon	21 September 1965	4 April 1966	14 October 1966
Gambia	1 October 1974	27 December 1974	26 January 1975
Georgia	7 August 1992	7 August 1992	6 September 1992
Germany	27 January 1966	18 April 1969	18 May 1969
Ghana	26 November 1965	13 July 1966	14 October 1966
Greece	16 March 1966	21 April 1969	21 May 1969
Grenada	24 May 1991	24 May 1991	23 June 1991
Guinea	27 August 1968	4 November 1968	4 December 1968
Guinea-Bisseau	4 September 1991		
Guyana	3 July 1968	11 July 1969	10 August 1969
Haiti	30 January 1985		
Honduras	28 May 1986	14 February 1989	16 March 1989
Hungary	1 October 1986	4 February 1987	6 March 1987

Country	Signature	Deposit of Ratification	Entry into Force of Convention
Iceland	25 July 1966	25 July 1966	14 October 1966
Indonesia	16 February 1968	28 September 1968	28 October 1968
Ireland	30 August 1966	7 April 1981	7 May 1981
Israel	16 June 1980	22 June 1983	22 July 1983
Italy	18 November 1965	29 March 1971	28 April 1971
Jamaica	23 June 1965	9 September 1966	14 October 1966
Japan	23 September 1965	17 August 1967	16 September 1967
Jordan	14 July 1972	30 October 1972	29 November 1972
Kazakhstan	23 July 1992		
Kenya	24 May 1966	3 January 1967	2 February 1967
Korea (Republic)	18 April 1966	21 February 1967	23 March 1967
Kuwait	9 February 1978	2 February 1979	4 March 1979
Lesotho	19 September 1968	8 July 1969	7 August 1969
Liberia	3 September 1965	16 June 1970	16 July 1970
Lithuania	6 July 1992	6 July 1992	5 August 1992
Luxembourg	28 September 1965	30 July 1970	29 August 1970
Madagascar	1 June 1966	6 September 1966	14 October 1966
Malawi	9 June 1966	23 August 1966	14 October 1966
Malaysia	22 October 1965	8 August 1966	14 October 1966
Mali	9 April 1976	3 January 1978	2 February 1978
Mauritania	30 July 1965	11 January 1966	14 October 1966
Mauritius	2 June 1969	2 June 1969	2 July 1969
Moldova	12 August 1992		
Mongolia	14 June 1991	14 June 1991	14 July 1991
Morocco	11 October 1965	11 May 1967	10 June 1967
Nepal	28 September 1965	7 January 1969	6 February 1969
Netherlands	25 May 1966	14 September 1966	14 October 1966
New Zealand	2 September 1970	2 April 1980	2 May 1980

Country	Signature	Deposit of Ratification	Entry into Force of Convention
Nicaragua	4 February 1994		
Niger	23 August 1965	14 November 1966	4 December 1966
Nigeria	13 July 1965	23 August 1965	14 October 1966
Norway	24 June 1966	16 August 1967	15 September 1967
Pakistan	6 July 1965	15 September 1966	15 October 1966
Papua New Guinea	20 October 1978	20 October 1978	19 November 1978
Paraguay	27 July 1981	7 January 1983	6 February 1983
Peru	4 September 1991		
Philippines	26 September 1978	17 November 1978	17 December 1978
Portugal	4 August 1983	2 July 1984	1 August 1984
Romania	6 September 1974	12 September 1975	12 October 1975
Russia	16 June 1992		
Rwanda	21 April 1978	15 October 1979	14 November 1979
Saudi Arabia	28 September 1979	8 May 1980	7 June 1980
Senegal	26 September 1966	21 April 1967	21 May 1967
Seychelles	16 February 1978	20 March 1978	19 April 1978
Sierra Leone	27 September 1965	2 August 1966	14 October 1966
Singapore	2 February 1968	14 October 1968	13 November 1968
Slovakia	27 September 1992		
Slovenia	7 March 1994		
Solomon Islands	12 November 1979	8 September 1981	8 October 1981
Somalia	27 September 1965	29 February 1968	30 March 1968
Sri Lanka	30 August 1967	12 October 1967	11 November 1967
St. Lucia	4 June 1984	4 June 1984	4 July 1984
Sudan	15 March 1967	9 April 1973	9 May 1973
Swaziland	3 November 1970	14 June 1971	14 July 1971
Sweden	25 September 1965	29 December 1966	28 January 1967
Switzerland	22 September 1967	15 May 1968	14 June 1968

Country	Signature	Deposit of Ratification	Entry into Force of Convention
Tanzania	10 January 1992	18 May 1992	17 June 1992
Thailand	6 December 1985		
Togo	24 January 1966	11 August 1967	10 September 1967
Tonga	1 May 1989	21 March 1990	20 April 1990
Trinidad and Tobago	5 October 1966	3 January 1967	2 February 1967
Tunisia	5 May 1965	22 June 1966	14 October 1966
Turkey	24 June 1987	3 March 1989	2 April 1989
Turkmenistan	26 September 1992	26 September 1992	26 October 1992
Uganda	7 June 1966	7 June 1966	14 October 1966
United Arab Emirates	23 December 1981	23 December 1981	22 January 1982
United Kingdom	26 May 1965	19 December 1966	18 January 1967
United States of America	27 August 1965	10 June 1966	14 October 1966
Uruguay	28 May 1992		
Uzbekistan	17 March 1994		
Western Samoa	3 February 1978	25 April 1978	25 May 1978
Yugoslavia	21 March 1967	21 March 1967	25 May 1967
Zaire	29 October 1968	29 April 1970	29 May 1970
Zambia	17 June 1970	17 June 1970	17 July 1970
Zimbabwe	25 March 1991		

TERRITORIAL EXTENSIONS FOR WASHINGTON CONVENTION

The United Kingdom, pursuant to Article 70 of the Convention, excluded from its coverage the following territories for whose international relations it is responsible: Jersey, Isle of Man, British Indian Ocean Territory, Pitcairn Islands, British Antarctic Territory, Sovereign Base Areas of Cyprus. By notification received on June 27, 1979, and November 17, 1983, respectively, the United Kingdom extended the application of the Convention to Jersey as of July 1, 1979, and to the Isle of Man as of November 1, 1983.

5. Bilateral Commercial Treaties Signed by the United States Containing Arbitration Provisions.

Country	Signature	Date of Coming into Force	Citation
Belgium Arbitration Clause: Article 3	21 February 1961	3 October 1963	14 UST 1284; TIAS 5432; 480 UNTS 149.
Denmark Arbitration Clause: Art. V.	1 October 1951	30 July 1961	12 UST 908; TIAS 4797; 421 UNTS 105.
Federal Republic of Germany Arbitration Clause: Art. VI.	29 October 1954	14 July 1956	7 UST 1839; TIAS 3593; 273 UNTS 3.
France Arbitration Clause: Article III.	25 November 1959	21 December 1960	11 UST 2398; TIAS 4625; 401 UNTS 75.
Greece Arbitration Clause: Art. VI.	3 August 1951	13 October 1954	5 UST 1829; TIAS 3057; 224 UNTS 279.
Iran Arbitration Clause: Art. III.	15 August 1955	16 June 1957	8 UST 899; TIAS 3853; 284 UNTS 93.
Ireland Arbitration Clause: Art. X.	21 January 1950	14 September 1950	1 UST 785; TIAS 2155; 206 UNTS 269.
Israel Arbitration Clause: Art. V.	23 August 1951	3 April 1954	5 UST 550; TIAS 2948; 219 UNTS 237.

International Forum Selection

Country	Signature	Date of Coming into Force	Citation
Italy (Supplemental agreement to the Treaty of Feb. 2, 1948) Arbitration Clause: Art. VI.	26 September 1951	2 March 1961	12 UST 1341; TIAS 4685; 404 UNTS 326.
Japan Arbitration Clause: Art. IV.	2 April 1953	30 October 1953	4 UST 2063; TIAS 2863; 206 UNTS 143.
Korea Arbitration Clause: Art. V.	28 November 1956	7 November 1957	8 UST 2217; TIAS 3947; 302 UNTS 281.
Luxembourg Arbitration Clause: Art. III.	23 February 1962	28 March 1963	14 UST 251; TIAS 5306; 474 UNTS 3.
Netherlands Arbitration Clause: Art. V.	27 March 1956	5 December 1957	8 UST 2043; TIAS 3942; 285 UNTS 231.
Pakistan Arbitration Clause: Article V.	12 November 1959	12 February 1961	12 UST 110; TIAS 4683; 4094 UNTS 259.
Taiwan Arbitration Clause: Art. VI.	4 November 1946	30 November 1948	63 Stat. 1299; TIAS 1871; 25 UNTS 69.
Thailand Arbitration Clause: Article II.	29 May 1966	8 May 1968	19 UST 5843; TIAS 6540; 652 UNTS 253.

Country	Signature	Date of Coming into Force	Citation
Togo			
Arbitration Clause:			
Article III.	8 February 1966	5 February 1967	18 UST 1; TIAS 6193; 680 UNTS 159.
Vietnam			
Arbitration Clause:			
Article 2.	3 April 1961	30 November 1961	12 UST 1703; TIAS 4890; 424 UNTS 137.

The U.S. also has bilateral commercial treaties that do not contain arbitration provisions with the following countries: Argentina, Bolivia, Brunel, Columbia, Costa Rica, Estonia, Ethiopia, Finland, Honduras, India, Iraq, Latvia, Liberia, Madagascar, Morocco, Nepal, Norway, Oman, Paraguay, Saudi Arabia, Spain, Switzerland, Turkey, United Kingdom, Yemen and Yugoslavia.

6. BILATERAL INVESTMENT TREATIES SIGNED BY THE UNITED STATES CONTAINING ARBITRATION PROVISIONS.

Country	Signature	Entry into Force
Argentina Arbitration Clause: Art. VII, Art. VIII.	14 November 1991	20 October 1994
Armenia Arbitration Clause: Art. VI, Art. VII.	23 September 1992	
Bangladesh Arbitration Clause: Art. VII, Art. VIII.	12 March 1986	25 July 1989
Bulgaria Arbitration Clause: Art. VI, Art. VII.	23 September 1992	
Cameroon Arbitration Clause: Art. VI, Art. VII.	26 February 1986	6 April 1989
Congo Arbitration Clause: Art. VI, Art. VII.	12 February 1990	
Czechoslovakia Arbitration Clause: Art. VI, Art. VII.	22 October 1991	
Ecuador Arbitration Clause: Art. VI, VII.	10 September 1993	
Egypt Arbitration Clause: Art. VII, Art. VIII.	29 September 1982	27 June 1992
Grenada Arbitration Clause: Art. VI, Art. VII.	2 May 1986	3 March 1989
Haiti Arbitration Clause Art. VII, Art. VIII.	13 December 1983	

Country	Signature	Entry into Force
Kazakhstan Arbitration Clause: Art. VI, Art. VII.	19 May 1992	
Kyrgzstan Arbitration Clause: Art. VI, VII.	8 September 1993	
Moldova Arbitration Clause: Art. VI, VII.	21 April 1993	
Morocco Arbitration Clause: Art. VI, Art. VII.	22 July 1985	29 May 1991
Panama Arbitration Clause: Art. VII, Art. VIII.	27 October 1982	30 May 1991
Poland Arbitration Clause: Art. III, Art. IX, Art. X	21 March 1990	
Romania Arbitration Clause: Art. VI, VII.	28 May 1992	
Russia Arbitration Clause: Art. 5.	17 June 1992	
Senegal Arbitration Clause: Art. VII, Art. VIII.	6 December 1983	25 October 1990
Sri Lanka Arbitration Clause: Art. VI, Art. VII.	20 September 1991	
Tunisia Arbitration Clause: Art. VI, Art. VII.	15 May 1990	
Turkey Arbitration Clause: Art. VI, Art. VII.	3 December 1985	18 May 1990

Country	Signature	Entry into Force
Zaire Arbitration Clause: Art. VII, Art. VIII	3 August 1984	28 July 1989

The bilateral investment treaties with Armenia, Kazakhstan, Argentina, Moldova, Ecuador and Romania contain clauses that provide for optional jurisdiction of the courts in the host-states.

Appendix G

ARBITRATION STATUTES

1. AUSTRIA

a. Austrian Code of Civil Procedure 1895, as amended in 1983[1]

Arbitration Procedure — Arbitration Agreement

Article 577

(1) An agreement that a legal dispute shall be settled by one or more arbitrators (an arbitration agreement) is valid in so far as the parties are entitled to conclude a settlement concerning the subject matter of the dispute.

(2) An arbitration agreement submitting future disputes arising from a specified legal relationship to arbitration by one or more arbitrators is also valid.

(3) The arbitration agreement must be in writing or be contained in telegrams or telex exchanged by the parties.

Article 578

Judicial officers may not accept appointment as arbitrators during their tenure of judicial office.

Article 579

No one is obliged to accept appointment as arbitrator. If he has reasonable cause an arbitrator may resign even after accepting appointment.

Article 580

If the arbitration agreement contains neither the names of the arbitrators or [sic] a provision concerning number and appointment of arbitrators, each party shall appoint an arbitrator, and they in turn shall appoint the chairman of the arbitral tribunal.

---

1. From W. Melis, *A Guide to Commercial Arbitration in Austria* (Vienna 1983). Translation by Werner Melis and Richard Swetenham.

Article 581

(1) A party which is obliged to make an appointment of an arbitrator pursuant to an arbitration agreement can be required by the opposing party to appoint an arbitrator within 14 days and to give notice to the party making the demand. If the appointment is to be made by a third party, either party may make the demand. The demand may also be made if the arbitrator who has already been appointed pursuant to the arbitration agreement refuses to accept office as arbitrator or refuses to fulfill his obligations or dies or is challenged successfully or ceases to act for any other reason.

(2) If the party making the demand also has to appoint an arbitrator, the demand shall also give notice of the person appointed as arbitrator.

(3) The exchange of demands and notices can be made by post or through a public notary.

(4) A person who is called on to appoint an arbitrator is bound by an appointment made by him as soon as the opposing party or one of the parties has received notice of the appointment.

Article 582

(1) If an appointment is not made within the proper time or if the arbitrators cannot agree upon a chairman, the court shall upon application make the appointment. The application should be brought before the court which would have been competent to hear the dispute in first instance in the absence of an arbitration agreement; however, if a court has been indicated in the arbitration agreement as being competent for this purpose and if it would be possible for that court to be given competence by agreement of the parties (para. 104(1) and (2) Judicature Act), or if the arbitration agreement indicates the venue of the arbitral procedure, then that court is competent, or in the absence of such indication, the court under whose jurisdiction this venue comes. If there is no court with local jurisdiction, or if such court cannot be ascertained, the application should be brought before the court which has local jurisdiction for the 1st municipal district of Vienna, in so far as the arbitration agreement requires the arbitral tribunal to meet within Austria. The application may be made by the parties and under para. 580 by either of the arbitrators. The applicant does not need to be represented by an attorney, even before the Superior Court of First Instance.

(2) The order on the application is not subject to appeal.

Article 583

(1) If the parties cannot agree on the arbitrator to be appointed by them jointly, the court mentioned in para. 582 shall pronounce the rescission of the arbitration agreement.

(2) The same procedure shall be followed,

1. if named persons are appointed as arbitrators in the arbitration agreement and one of these arbitrators dies, ceases to act consequent upon a challenge or for any other reason, refuses to accept office as arbitrator or withdraws from the contract concluded with him because of his appointment; or

2. if an arbitrator who is named in the arbitration agreement or appointed by a party pursuant to the arbitration agreement or by the court pursuant to para. 582 refuses to fulfill the obligations assumed by his acceptance of office as arbitrator, or delays unreasonably in their fulfillment.

(3) If the arbitration agreement is concluded with reference to all disputes arising out of a particular legal relationship and the circumstances in which the court is to declare the arbitration agreement as rescinded are such that submission to arbitration of possible disputes arising in the future is not excluded, the court shall only declare the arbitration agreement of no effect for the case in question.

Article 584

(1) The decision on an application under para. 583 shall be made by order after an oral hearing. This decision and the decision on an application under para. 582 may be made in the Superior Court of First Instance by the President of the Court or by a judge authorized by him.

(2) An arbitrator who does not fulfill in time or at all the obligations assumed by his acceptance of office is liable to the parties for all the loss caused by his wrongful refusal or delay, without prejudice to the parties' rights to claim rescission of the arbitration agreement.

Article 585

The provisions of paras. 582 and 583 are not applicable in so far as the parties have agreed otherwise in the arbitration agreement or in a written agreement made after the conclusion of the arbitration agreement.

Article 586

(1) An arbitrator may be challenged for the same reasons that a judge may be challenged. (paras. 19 and 20 Judicature Act).

(2) A party which appoints an arbitrator alone or jointly with the opposing party is entitled to challenge him only if the reason for the challenge arose or became known to the party after the appointment.

Procedure before the arbitrators

Article 587

(1) The arbitrators shall hear the parties and investigate the facts of the case before making their award. The procedure shall be determined by the arbitrators in their discretion unless the parties have agreed otherwise in the arbitration agreement or in a subsequent written agreement.

(2) If a party refuses to attend the hearing before the arbitrators, the hearing shall continue in the presence of the other party.

Article 588

The arbitrators are not entitled to administer the oath to the parties, witnesses and experts, who appear voluntarily before them. They may not apply coercive measures or award punishments against parties or other persons.

Article 589

(1) Those judicial acts considered necessary by the arbitrators but which they have no jurisdiction to undertake will be carried out by the state court which has jurisdiction on the application of the arbitrators. In case of doubt the application is to be made to the district court in whose district the act is to be carried out or the evidence to be taken.

(2) The court to which the application is made shall accede to it in so far as it is not legally inadmissible. In particular the court shall also take those decisions regarding taking of evidence which are reserved by the present statute in the case of taking of evidence on commission to the court hearing the case.

Article 590

If more than two arbitrators are to decide, the award shall be made by an absolute majority unless the arbitration agreement contains anything to the contrary.

Article 591

(1) If the necessary majority for taking a decision, or where there are only two arbitrators, unanimity cannot be reached the arbitrators must inform the parties.

(2) If no other provision for this case is contained in the arbitration agreement or in a subsequent written agreement of the parties, any party may apply to the court mentioned in para. 582 for a declaration that the arbitration agreement is rescinded or of no effect in the particular case (para. 584).

Article 592

(1) Copies of the award shall be served on the parties either in person before the arbitral tribunal or by post or by a public notary.

(2) These copies and the original of the award shall mention the date of the making of the award and shall be signed by the arbitrators. The signatures of the majority of the arbitrators shall suffice if there is a statement in the award that the minority refuses to sign or if signature of the minority cannot be obtained because of an obstacle which cannot be overcome within a reasonable period of time.

Article 593

(1) The original award and documents recording the service of copies on the parties shall be kept in safe custody by the person named in the arbitration agreement. If no such agreement has been made or the named custodian has died, the arbitrators shall determine the method of deposit. In case of doubt these documents shall be deposited with a public notary of the district where the arbitral tribunal has its seat.

(2) The original of the award and the documents recording service are to be deemed documents common to the parties.

Article 594

(1) The arbitral award has the effect between the parties of a final and binding court judgment unless the parties have agreed in the arbitration agreement that there

shall be the possibility of an appeal against the award to a second-tier arbitral body.

(2) The chairman of the tribunal, or if he is unable to act, any other arbitrator, shall at the request of a party confirm in writing on a copy of the award the final and binding nature and the enforceability of the award.

Cancellation of the award

Article 595

The award shall be set aside,

(1)

1. if an arbitration agreement according to para. 577 does not exist, if the arbitration agreement has become invalid before the making of the award or has ceased to have effect for the particular case or if a party was unable to conclude the arbitration agreement because of its status.

2. if the party applying to have the award set aside was unable to present its case in the proceedings before the arbitrators or if required by statute to be represented by an agent or guardian was not so represented in those proceedings unless in the latter case the procedure has been subsequently properly ratified;

3. if statutory or contractual provisions regarding the composition of the arbitral tribunal or the method of reaching a decision have been infringed or if the original of the award has not been signed in accordance with the provisions of para. 592(2);

4. if a challenge to an arbitrator has been rejected unjustifiably by the arbitral tribunal;

5. if the arbitral tribunal dealt with matters beyond those referred to it;

6. if the award is incompatible with the basic principles of the Austrian legal system or if it infringes mandatory provisions of the law, the application of which cannot be set aside by a choice of law of the parties even in a case where a foreign contact according to para. 35 of the International Private Law Act is involved;

7. if the conditions are present in which a request can be made under para. 530(1) figures 1 to 7 for a court judgment to be set aside and the case reopened.

(2) In the cases set out in section (1) above, figures 2 to 7, the arbitration agreement will become invalid in respect of the subject-matter of the arbitration procedure if an arbitral award thereupon has been set aside twice by final and binding judgment.

Article 596

(1) If an application is made to set aside an award, the application shall be made to the court specified in para. 582.

(2) If the application is based on one of the grounds set out in para. 595(1) figures 1 to 6, it must be made within a time-limit of three months failing which the application will be time-barred. The time-limit begins to run on the day of service of the award on the party concerned, or, if the ground for rescission only came to the party's notice later, from the day when the party became aware of the said ground.

(3) The time-limit for applications under para. 595(1) figure 7 is governed by the provisions concerning the application to reopen the case.

Article 597

The procedure on an application to set aside the award shall be in accordance with the general provisions of the present statute.

Article 598

(1) A party cannot waive the application of paras. 586, 592 and 595, either in the arbitration agreement or any other agreement.

(2) If both parties have concluded the arbitration agreement as businessmen (para. 1(1) figure 1 of the Consumer Protection Act), they may waive the application of para. 595(1) figure 7.

Article 599

(1) The provisions of this chapter are applicable mutatis mutandis to arbitral tribunals constituted in ways permitted by statute whether by will or other dispositions not being based on the agreement of the parties to the dispute or by articles of association. The provisions of paras. 586, 592 and 595 may not be waived by unilateral dispositions or provisions of articles of association.

(2) Arbitral tribunals constituted in accordance with the Act for the Settlement of Differences in Associations 1951, Official Gazette No. 233/1951, are not subject to the provisions of this chapter.

Article 530

Application to re-open a case

(1) A case concluded by a judgment can be re-opened on application of a party,

1. if a document on which the judgment was based was completely or partially forged;

2. if a witness or expert of the opposing party has given false testimony during his examination (para. 288 Penal Code (P.C.)) and the judgment is based on this testimony;

3. if the judgment was given as a result of an act punishable at law, whether as wilful misrepresentation (para. 108 P.C.), embezzlement (para. 134 P.C.), fraud (para. 146 P.C.), forgery of documents (para. 223 P.C.), forgery of documents especially protected by the law (para. 224 P.C.), forgery of public seals (para. 225 P.C.), indirect false recording or certification (para. 228 P.C.), suppression of documents (para. 229 P.C.), or of displacement of boundary marks (para. 230 P.C.), on the part of the representative of the party, or of the opposing party or its representative;

4. if the judge has been guilty of criminal negligence of his official duties to the prejudice of the applicant in giving judgment or in a previous decision relating to the case on which the judgment is based;

5. if a decision by a criminal court on which the judgment is based has been set aside by a subsequent final judgment;

6. if the applicant discovers the existence of, or is placed in a position to use, a previous judgment concerning the same claim or the same legal relationship which is already final and which determines the rights of and between the parties of the case to be re-opened;

7. if the applicant has discovered or is placed in a position to use new facts or evidence which would have resulted in a more favourable decision for the applicant on the merits if they had been presented in the previous hearing.

(2) The re-opening of the case under figures 6 and 7 is only permissible if the applicant was unable without fault on his part to assert the finality of the judgment or the new facts or evidence before the end of the oral hearing after which the judgment of First Instance was given.

b. Austrian Judicature Act 1895, As Amended in 1983[2]

Challenges of Judges

Article 19

A judge can be challenged in civil cases,

(1) if he is excluded by statute from acting judicially in the particular case;

(2) if there is sufficient reason to doubt his impartiality.

Article 20

Judges are excluded from acting in civil cases,

(1) in cases where they are themselves a party or where in relation to the subject-matter of the case they have rights or liabilities in common with a party or are liable to indemnify a party;

(2) in cases concerning their spouses or persons directly related to the spouse by blood or marriage or persons related collaterally to the judge by blood to the fourth remove or by marriage to the second remove;

(3) in cases concerning their adoptive or foster-parents, adoptive or foster-children, and their wards;

(4) in cases in which they held or hold power of attorney from a party;

(5) in cases in which they took part in the making by a lower court of the judgment or decision appealed against.

Designation of the Appropriate Court by the Supreme Court

Article 28

(1) If for a civil action the conditions for the local jurisdiction of a domestic court within the meaning of this Act or of any other provisions are not fulfilled or cannot be ascertained, the Supreme Court shall designate a court which has subject-

2. From W. Melis, *A Guide to Commercial Arbitration in Austria* (Vienna 1983). Translation by Richard Swetenham.

matter jurisdiction and which shall be considered as having local jurisdiction for the case at hand if either

　　　1. Austria is obliged to exercise jurisdiction pursuant to a treaty under international law, or

　　　2. it would be impossible or unreasonable to bring the action abroad.

(2) This designation shall be made upon application by a party in civil actions, otherwise on the court's own motion. In civil actions the claimant shall allege and prove the presence of the conditions set out in figure 2.

Agreement on the Jurisdiction of Courts

Article 104

(1) The parties may submit to one or more courts of first instance of specially stated places by explicit agreement. The agreement must be proved to the courts by documents attached to the statement of claim.

(2) The agreement has legal effect only if it refers to a specific lawsuit or to disputes arising from a specific legal relationship. However, matters which are outside the sphere of action of the law courts cannot be brought before these courts by way of such agreements, legal cases belonging to a district court cannot be brought before a court of first instance and disputes exclusively assigned to courts of first instance cannot be brought before a district court.

c. Austrian Statute on Private International Law[3]

Public Policy Exclusion *(Ordre Public)*

Article 6

A provision of foreign law shall not be applied when its application would lead to a result irreconcilable with the basic tenets of the Austrian legal order. In its place, if necessary, the corresponding provision of Austrian law shall be applied.

Law of Obligations

General Rules

Article 35

(1) Obligations shall be judged according to the law expressly or impliedly selected by the parties (para. 11); if the circumstances reveal that the parties have assumed

---

3. Translation by Dr. Edith Palmer, Library of Congress, Law Library, 1978.

a particular legal order as determinative, this shall be equivalent to an implied selection.

(2) To the extent that a contractual choice of law was not made or that it is to be disregarded according to this Federal Statute, paras. 36 through 49 shall be determinative.

Consumer Contracts

Article 41

(1) Contracts for which the law of the state in which one party has his habitual residence grants this party special private law protection as a consumer shall be judged according to said law in those cases in which the contracts have resulted from an activity undertaken in that state and intended to result in such contracts by the entrepreneur or by persons employed by him for such purpose.

(2) To the extent that mandatory provisions of said law are involved, a contractual choice of law to the detriment of the consumer shall be disregarded.

Contracts Concerning the Use of Immovables

Article 42

(1) Contracts concerning the use of immovables or appurtenant structures shall be judged according to the law of the state in which the property is located.

(2) To the extent that mandatory provisions of said law concerning leases are involved, a contractual choice of law to the detriment of the lessee shall be disregarded.

Employment Contracts

Article 44

(1) Employment contracts shall be judged according to the law of the state in which the employee usually carries out his work. That law shall also remain determinative if the employee is sent to a place of work in another state.

(2) If the employee usually carries out his work in more than one state, or if he has no habitual place of work, the law of the state shall be determinative in which the employer has his habitual residence (his particular permanent business establishment, para. 36, second sentence).

(3) A contractual choice of law shall be taken into consideration only when it is made expressly. However, to the extent that mandatory provisions of the laws referred to in paras. 1 and 2 are involved, also an express contractual choice of law shall be disregarded, if it was made to the detriment of the employee.

2. BELGIUM

Articles 1676 to 1723 Code Judiciaire[1]

Article 1676
1. Any dispute which has arisen or may arise out of a specific legal relationship and in respect of which it is permissible to compromise may be the subject of an arbitration agreement.
2. With the exception of legal persons of public law, whosoever has the capacity or is empowered to compromise, may conclude an arbitration agreement. The state may conclude such an agreement when a treaty authorizes it to have recourse to arbitration.
3. The preceding provisions are applicable without prejudice to the exceptions provided for in the law.

Article 1677
An arbitration agreement shall be constituted by an instrument in writing signed by the parties or by other documents binding on the parties and showing their intention to have recourse to arbitration.

Article 1678
1. An arbitration agreement shall not be valid if it gives one of the parties thereto a privileged position with regard to the appointment of the arbitrator or arbitrators.
2. Without prejudice to the exceptions provided for in the law, an arbitration agreement concluded before a dispute has arisen, which dispute falls within the competence of the Labour Tribunal as determined in Articles 578 to 583 is *ipso jure* null.

Article 1679
1. The judge seized of a dispute which is the subject of an arbitration agreement shall, at the request of either party, declare that he has no jurisdiction, unless, insofar as concerns the dispute, the agreement is not valid or has terminated: this exception must be proposed *in limine litis*.
2. An application to the judicial authority for preservation or interim measures shall not be incompatible with an arbitration agreement and shall not imply a renunciation of the agreement.

Article 1680
An arbitrator may be any person who has the capacity to contract, except minors even when no longer under parental supervision, persons under guardianship and those who are either permanently or temporarily excluded from the right to vote.

---

1. Translation by Lambert Matvag and Dominque Grisay. International Handbook on Commercial Arbitration, Kluwer.

Article 1681

1. The arbitral tribunal shall be composed of an uneven number of arbitrators. There may be a sole arbitrator.

2. If the arbitration agreement provides for an even number of arbitrators, an additional arbitrator shall be appointed.

3. If the parties have not settled the number of arbitrators in the arbitration agreement and do not agree on the number, the arbitral tribunal shall be composed of three arbitrators.

Article 1682

The parties may, either in the arbitration agreement or subsequently thereto, appoint the sole arbitrator or the arbitrators or entrust the appointment to a third person. If the parties have not appointed the arbitrators and have not agreed on a method of appointment, each party shall, when the dispute arises, appoint an arbitrator or an equal number of arbitrators, as the case may be.

Article 1683

1. The party who intends bringing a dispute before an arbitral tribunal shall give notice to the other party. The notice shall refer to the arbitration agreement and specify the subject-matter of the dispute, unless the arbitration agreement already does so.

2. If there is more than one arbitrator, and if the parties are entitled to appoint them, the notice shall specify the arbitrator or arbitrators appointed by the party invoking the arbitration agreement; the other party shall be invited, in the notice, to appoint the arbitrator or arbitrators whom he is entitled to appoint.

3. If a third person has been entrusted with the appointment of a sole arbitrator or of arbitrators and has not done so, he also shall be given notice in accordance with paragraph 1 and invited to make the appointment.

4. The appointment of an arbitrator may not be withdrawn after notification of the appointment.

Article 1684

1. If the party or third person to whom notice has been given in accordance with Article 1683 has not, within a period of one month from the notice, appointed the arbitrator or arbitrators whom the party or third person is entitled to appoint, the President of the Court of First Instance shall make the nomination at the request of either party.

2. If the parties have agreed that there shall be a sole arbitrator and they have not appointed him by mutual consent within a period of one month from the notice under Article 1683, the appointment shall be made as determined in paragraph 1.

Article 1685

1. Where the arbitrators appointed or nominated in accordance with the foregoing provisions are even in number, they shall nominate another arbitrator to be president of the arbitral tribunal. If they do not agree and if the parties have not provided otherwise, the President of the Court of First Instance shall make the necessary nomi-

nation at the request of either party. The President may be seized after the expiration of a period of one month from the acceptance of his office by the last arbitrator or as soon as the failure to agree is established.

2. Where the arbitrators appointed are uneven in number they shall nominate one of themselves to be president of the arbitral tribunal unless the parties have agreed on another method of appointment. If the arbitrators do not agree, the nomination shall be made according to paragraph 1.

Article 1686

1. In the case dealt with under Articles 1684 and 1685, the decision taken by the President of the Court of First Instance is not subject to any other means of recourse.

2. The President's decision does not prejudice either the arbitrator's power to rule in respect of their own jurisdiction, or a party's right to invoke the arbitral tribunal's lack of jurisdiction.

Article 1687

1. If an arbitrator dies or cannot for a reason of law or fact perform his office, or if he refuses to accept it or does not carry it out, or if his office is terminated by mutual agreement of the parties, he shall be replaced in accordance with the rules governing his appointment or nomination. However, if the arbitrator or arbitrators are named in the arbitration agreement, the agreement shall terminate *ipso jure.*

2. A disagreement arising out of any case envisaged in paragraph 1 shall be brought before the Court of First Instance on the application of one of the parties. If the Court decides that there are grounds for replacing the arbitrator, it shall nominate his successor, taking into account the intention of the parties, as appearing from the arbitration agreement.

3. The parties may derogate from the provisions of this Article.

Article 1688

Unless the parties have agreed otherwise, neither the arbitration agreement nor the office of arbitrator shall be terminated by death of one of the parties.

Article 1689

The arbitrator who has accepted his office may not resign, unless so authorized by the Court of First Instance at his request. The Court decides after parties have been heard or summoned under judiciary notice by the clerk of the court. The Court's decision is not subject to any other means of recourse.

Article 1690

1. Arbitrators may be challenged on the same grounds as judges.

2. A party may not challenge an arbitrator appointed by him except on a ground of which the party becomes aware after the appointment.

Article 1691

1. The challenge shall, as soon as the challenger becomes aware of the ground of challenge, be notified to the arbitrators and, where applicable, to the third person who has, in pursuance of the arbitration agreement, appointed the arbitrator challenged. The arbitrators shall thereupon suspend further proceedings.

2. If, within a period of ten days of the notice of the challenge being given to him, the arbitrator challenged has not resigned, the arbitral tribunal shall so notify the challenger. The challenger shall, on pain of being barred, summon the arbitrator and the other parties to the Court of First Instance, within a period of ten days after receiving such notification, otherwise the proceedings before the arbitrators shall be *ipso jure* resumed. The appeal against the decision taken by the Court of First Instance will be judged according to Articles 843 to 847 of this Code.

3. If the arbitrator resigns or if the challenge is upheld by the judge, the arbitrator shall be replaced in accordance with the rules governing his appointment or nomination. However, if he has been named in the arbitration agreement, the agreement shall terminate *ipso jure*. The parties may derogate from the provisions of this paragraph.

Article 1692

1. The parties may in the arbitration agreement exclude certain categories of persons from being arbitrators.

2. If such an exclusion has been disregarded with respect to the composition of the arbitral tribunal, the irregularity shall be invoked in accordance with the provisions of Article 1691.

Article 1693

1. Without prejudice to the provisions of Article 1694, the parties may decide on the rules of the arbitral procedure and on the place of arbitration. If the parties do not indicate their intention before the first arbitrator has accepted his office, the decision shall be a matter for the arbitrators.

2. The president of the arbitral tribunal shall regulate the hearings and conduct the proceedings.

Article 1694

1. The arbitral tribunal shall give each party an opportunity of substantiating his claims and of presenting his case.

2. The arbitral tribunal shall make an award after oral proceedings. The parties may validly be summoned by registered letter, unless they have agreed upon any other method of summons. The parties may appear in person.

3. The procedure shall be in writing where the parties have so provided or insofar as they have waived oral proceedings.

4. Each party shall have the right to be represented by a lawyer or by a representative, in possession of a special power of attorney in writing, approved by the arbitral tribunal. Each party may be assisted by a lawyer or any person of his choice, approved

by the arbitral tribunal. Parties may not be represented or assisted by an *agent d'affaires.*

Article 1695

If, without legitimate cause, a party properly summoned does not appear or does not present his case within the period fixed, the arbitral tribunal may, unless the other party requests an adjournment, investigate the matter in dispute and make an award.

Article 1696

1. The arbitral tribunal may order a hearing of witnesses, an appraisal by experts, a visit to the site, the appearance of parties in person; the arbitral tribunal may accept an oath as being decisive or may request a supplementary oath. It may also order the production of documents held by a party according to the conditions provided in Article 877 of this code.

2. When the arbitral tribunal has ordered a hearing, and the witnesses do not appear voluntarily or refuse to take the oath or to testify, the arbitral tribunal will authorize the parties, or one of them, to request the Court of First Instance, within a fixed period, to appoint a *juge-commissaire*, to preside over the investigation. This hearing will take place according to the formalities for civil cases. The periods for arbitration are *ipso jure* suspended until the hearing is completed.

3. The arbitral tribunal may not order the verification of signatures nor rule on an objection relating to the production of documents or upon the alleged falseness of documents. In this case, it will leave it to the parties to bring the matter to the Court of First Instance within a determined period.

4. The periods for arbitration are *ipso jure* suspended until the day the tribunal receives notification by the most diligent party of the final decision concerning the incident.

Article 1697

1. The arbitral tribunal may rule in respect of its own jurisdiction and for this purpose, may examine the validity of the arbitration agreement.

2. A ruling that the contract is invalid shall not entail *ipso jure* the nullity of the arbitration agreement contained in it.

3. The arbitral tribunal's ruling that it has jurisdiction may not be contested before the judicial authority except at the same time as the award on the main issue and by the same procedure. The judicial authority may at the request of one of the parties decide whether a ruling that the arbitral tribunal has no jurisdiction is well founded.

4. The appointment of an arbitrator by a party shall not deprive that party of his rights to challenge the jurisdiction of the arbitral tribunal.

Article 1698

1. The parties may, up to the time of acceptance of office by the first arbitrator,

settle the period within which the award is to be made or provide for a method according to which the period is to be settled.

2. If the parties have not prescribed a period or a method of prescribing a period, if the arbitral tribunal delays in making the award and if a period of six months has elapsed from the date on which all the arbitrators accepted office in respect of the dispute submitted to arbitration, the Court of First Instance may, at the request of one of the parties, stipulate a period for the arbitral tribunal. The Court's decision is not subject to any means of recourse.

3. The office of arbitrator shall terminate if the award is not made within the relevant period unless that period is extended by agreement between the parties.

4. Where arbitrators are named in the arbitration agreement and the award is not made within the relevant period, the arbitration agreement shall terminate *ipso jure*, unless the parties have agreed otherwise.

Article 1699

Except where otherwise stipulated, an arbitral tribunal may make a final award in the form of one or more awards.

Article 1700

The arbitrators shall make their awards in accordance with the rules of law unless the contrary has been stipulated. To be valid, such stipulation must be made after the notification provided for in Article 1683.

Article 1701

1. An award shall be made after a deliberation in which all the arbitrators shall take part. The award shall be made by an absolute majority of votes, unless the parties have agreed on another majority.

2. The parties may also agree that, when a majority cannot be obtained, the president of the arbitral tribunal shall have a casting vote.

3. Except where otherwise stipulated, if the arbitrators are to award a sum of money, and a majority cannot be obtained for any particular sum, the votes for the highest sum shall be counted as votes for the next highest sum until a majority is obtained.

4. An award shall be set down in writing and signed by the arbitrators. If one or more of the arbitrators are unable or unwilling to sign, the fact shall be recorded in the award. However, the award shall bear a number of signatures which is at least equal to a majority of the arbitrators.

5. An award shall, in addition to the operative part, contain the following particulars:

(a) the names and permanent addresses of the arbitrators;

(b) the names and permanent addresses of the parties;

(c) the subject-matter of the dispute;

(d) the date on which the award was made;

(e) the place of arbitration and the place where the award was made.

6. The reasons for an award shall be stated.

Article 1702

1. The president of the arbitral tribunal shall give notice to each party of the award by sending him a copy thereof, signed in accordance with paragraph 4 of Article 1701.

2. The president of the arbitral tribunal shall deposit the original of the award with the registry of the court having jurisdiction; he shall notify the parties of the deposit.

3. The arbitrators' office ends when the award terminating the litigation has been notified and deposited according to the preceding provisions.

Article 1703

Unless the award is contrary to *ordre public* or the dispute was not capable of settlement by arbitration, an arbitral award has the authority of *res judicata* when it has been notified in accordance with paragraph 1 of Article 1702 and may no longer be contested before the arbitrators.

Article 1704

1. An arbitral award may be contested before a judicial authority only by way of an application to set aside and may be set aside only in the cases mentioned in this Article.

2. An arbitral award may be set aside:

(a) if it is contrary to *ordre public*;

(b) if the dispute was not capable of settlement by arbitration;

(c) if there is no valid arbitration agreement;

(d) if the arbitral tribunal has exceeded its jurisdiction or its powers;

(e) if the arbitral tribunal has omitted to make an award in respect of one or more points of the dispute and if the points omitted cannot be separated from the points in respect of which an award has been made;

(f) if the award was made by an arbitral tribunal irregularly constituted;

(g) if the parties have not been given an opportunity of substantiating their claims and presenting their case, or if there has been disregard of any other obligatory rule of the arbitral procedure, insofar as such disregard has had an influence on the arbitral award;

(h) if the formalities prescribed in paragraph 4 of Article 1701 have not been fulfilled;

(i) if the reasons for the award have not been stated;

(j) if the award contains conflicting provisions.

3. An award may also be set aside:

(a) if it was obtained by fraud;

(b) if it is based on evidence that has been declared false by a judicial decision having the force of *res judicata* or on evidence recognised as false;

(c) if, after it was made, there has been discovered a document or other piece of evidence which would have had a decisive influence on the award and which was withheld through the act of the other party.

4. A case mentioned in sub-paragraph (c), (d) or (f) of paragraph 2 shall be deemed not to constitute a ground for setting aside an award where the party availing himself of it had knowledge of it during the arbitration proceedings and did not invoke it at the time.

5. Grounds for the challenge and exclusion of arbitrators provided for under Articles 1690 and 1692 shall not constitute grounds for setting aside within the meaning of paragraph 2(f) of this Article, even when they become known only after the award is made.

Article 1705

If there are grounds for setting aside any part of an award, that part shall be set aside only if it can be separated from the other parts of the award.

Article 1706

1. The grounds for setting aside an arbitral award shall, on pain of being barred, be put forward by the party concerned in one and the same proceedings, except, however, in the case of a ground for setting aside provided for in paragraph 3 of Article 1704 where the ground is not known until later.

2. An application to set aside an award shall be admissible only where the award may no longer be contested before arbitrators.

Article 1707

1. An application to set aside an award, based on one of the grounds provided for in paragraph 2(c) to (j), of Article 1704 shall, on pain of being barred, be made within a period of three months from the date on which the award was notified. However, that period shall begin to run only from the date on which the award is no longer capable of contestation before arbitrators.

2. The defendant in an application to set aside an award may apply, in the same proceedings, for the award to be set aside, even if the period laid down in paragraph 1 has expired.

3. An application to set aside an award, based on one of the grounds provided for in paragraph 3 of Article 1704, shall be made within a period of three months from either the date of the discovery of the fraud, document or other piece of evidence, or the date on which the evidence was declared false or recognised as false, provided that a period of five years from the date on which the award was notified in accordance with paragraph 1 of Article 1702 has not expired.

4. The judicial authority seized of an application to set aside an award shall examine *proprio motu* whether the award is contrary to *ordre public* and whether the dispute was capable of settlement by arbitration.

Article 1708

1. If the arbitral tribunal has forgotten to decide on one or more points of the dispute that can be separated from the points on which it has ruled, this tribunal may, if so requested by a party, complete its award even if the period provided for in Article 1698 has expired, unless the other party contests that points have been omit-

ted or that the omitted points can be separated from the points on which a decision has been taken.

2. In this case the dispute is brought to the Court of First Instance by the most diligent party. The court refers the parties back to the arbitral tribunal in order to complete the award, if it decides that the omitted points can be separated from the points on which the arbitral tribunal has taken a decision.

Article 1709

The arbitrators may order provisional execution of their awards notwithstanding appeal and without prejudice to the rules of *"cantonnement"*. They may also subject the provisional execution to the establishment of a guarantee according to the rules of this Code.

Article 1710

1. The arbitral award may be enforced only after the enforcement formula has been apposed by the President of the Court of First Instance, on the application of the interested party. The party against whom enforcement is sought, cannot present his views at this stage of the procedure.

2. The President may only appose the enforcement formula on the award when the award is no longer capable of being contested before the arbitrators or if arbitrators have granted provisional enforcement notwithstanding appeal. The President's decision is enforceable notwithstanding any recourse without prejudice to the application of Article 1714.

3. The President shall refuse the application if the award or its enforcement is contrary to *ordre public* or if the dispute was not capable of settlement by arbitration.

4. Within the five days following the decision, the latter is notified, under judiciary cover by the clerk of the court to the petitioner.

Article 1711

1. If the application is denied, the petitioner may give notice of appeal to the Court of Appeal within a period of one month from notification. Appeal is notified to the party against whom enforcement is sought by a notification by means of a summons served by a bailiff [sic]

2. If this party seeks to secure the setting aside of the award without having previously made application for this, this party must on pain of being barred, make this application before the Court of First Instance, within a period of one month from the date of the service of the act of appeal. The court of appeal stays proceedings until a final judgment has been rendered concerning the application to set aside the award.

Article 1712

1. The decision granting exequatur must be served by the party who has applied for it to the other party. This decision is subject to an appeal brought before the Court of First Instance within a period of one month from the date on which the service has been made.

2. A party exercising this right of appeal and who seeks to secure the setting aside of the award without having previously made an application for this shall, on pain of being barred, make his application in the same proceedings and within the period prescribed in paragraph 1. A party who, while not exercising the right of appeal provided for in paragraph 1, seeks to secure the setting aside of an award shall, on pain of being barred, make his application for setting aside within the period prescribed in paragraph 1.

Article 1713
1. In the cases dealt with under Articles 1711 and 1712, the applications for setting aside based on the lack of a valid arbitration agreement are not subject to the period prescribed in paragraph 1 of Article 1707.
2. Without prejudice to the provisions of paragraph 3 of Article 1707, if, a party has become aware of one of the grounds for setting aside mentioned in paragraph 3 of Article 1704 only after the decision granting or refusing enforcement has been served upon him, that party may apply for the setting aside of the award on this ground, even if the period prescribed in Article 1711 and 1712 has expired.

Article 1714
1. In the case either of an appeal against the decision apposing an enforcement formula to an award or of an application for an award to be set aside, the judge may, at the request of one of the parties, order the enforcement of the award to be stayed, or that enforcement will depend on the constitution of a guarantee.
2. A decision apposing an enforcement formula to an award shall be without effect to the extent that the arbitral award has been set aside.

Article 1715
1. Where, before an arbitral tribunal, a compromise has been entered into between the parties in order to put an end to a dispute of which the tribunal is seized, that compromise may be recorded in an instrument prepared by the arbitral tribunal and signed by the arbitrators as well as by the parties. The instrument shall be subject to the provisions of paragraph 2 of Article 1702. The instrument may, on the application of the interested party, have an enforcement formula apposed to it by the President of the Court of First Instance.
2. The President of the Court of First Instance shall refuse the application if the compromise or its enforcement is contrary to *ordre public* or if the dispute was not capable of settlement by arbitration.
3. Within the five days following its pronouncement the decision is notified, under judiciary cover by the clerk of the court to the petitioner.

Article 1716
1. The decision apposing an enforcement formula to an instrument recording a compromise must be served by the party who has applied for it to the other party. This decision is open to appeal before the Court of First Instance within a period of one month from the date it was served.

2. If the application is denied, the petitioner may give notice of appeal according to Article 1711.

3. The decision apposing an enforcement formula to an instrument recording a compromise is void to the extent the compromise has been annulled.

Article 1717

1. Except in the case provided for in paragraph 2 of Article 1719, the court that is competent to apply part VI of this Code is the court designated by the arbitration agreement or in a later agreement, concluded before the designation of the place of arbitration.

2. If the parties have reached no agreement, the court of the place of arbitration has jurisdiction. If no place of arbitration has been designated, that court has jurisdiction in whose district the court is situated that would have been competent if the dispute had not been submitted to arbitration.

3. All this without prejudice to the provisions of Article 630 of this Code and international conventions.

4. The Belgian Court can take cognizance of an application to set aside only if at least one of the parties to the dispute decided in the arbitral award is either a physical person having Belgian nationality or residing in Belgium, or a legal person formed in Belgium or having a branch or some seat of operation there.

Article 1718

1. Where the appeal from a judgment of the Court of First Instance or of the Court of Commerce has been submitted to arbitration the arbitral award can only be enforced after the Court of Appeal has granted the enforcement formula, the party against whom execution is sought having been summoned.

2. If this party seeks to secure the setting aside of the award without having previously introduced a petition for this purpose, he must introduce his application to set aside during the same proceedings, on pain of being barred, without prejudice to the provisions of Article 1713.

3. The decisions taken by the Court of Appeal are not subject to appeal.

Article 1719

1. The President of the Court of First Instance decides, upon request, on the petition for exequatur of arbitral awards rendered abroad in pursuance of an arbitration agreement.

2. The petition is brought before the President of the Court of First Instance in whose jurisdiction the party against whom enforcement is sought has its domicile, and in default of domicile, its residence. If this party has neither domicile nor residence in Belgium, the petition will be brought to the President of the Court of First Instance of the place where the award must be enforced.

3. The petitioner elects domicile in the Court's district.

4. He joins to the request the original of the award as well as the arbitration agreement or copies thereof which fulfil the necessary conditions as to their authenticity.

5. The President of the Court verifies the petition and may for this purpose, summon the petitioner and the party against whom enforcement is sought to his chambers. The writ of summons is served to the parties under judiciary cover by the clerk of the court.

Article 1720

Within the five days following its pronouncement, the decision of the President of the Court of First Instance is notified, under judiciary cover by the clerk of the court to the petitioner.

Article 1721

If the application is denied, the petitioner may give notice of appeal to the Court of Appeal within a period of one month from notification of the decision. This appeal is introduced by service of a bailiff to the party against whom enforcement is sought containing a summons to appear before the court.

Article 1722

The decision granting exequatur must be served by the party who has applied for it to the other party. This decision may be appealed to the Court of First Instance within a period of one month from the date on which it has been served.

Article 1723

Except when a treaty between Belgium and the country where the award has been rendered is applicable, the President refuses to grant exequatur:

1. if the arbitral award is still open to appeal before the arbitrators and if the arbitrators have not ordered provisional enforcement notwithstanding appeal;

2. if the award or its enforcement is contrary to *ordre public*, or if the dispute is not capable of settlement by arbitration;

3. if there exists a ground for setting aside as provided in Article 1704.

3. ENGLAND

a. Arbitration Act, 1950

Part I: General Provisions as to Arbitration

1. Authority of arbitrators and umpires to be irrevocable.

The authority of an arbitrator or umpire appointed by or by virtue of an arbitration agreement shall, unless a contrary intention is expressed in the agreement, be irrevocable except by leave of the High Court or a judge thereof.

2. Death of party.

(1) An arbitration agreement shall not be discharged by the death of any party thereto, either as respects the deceased or any other party, but shall in such an event be enforceable by or against the personal representative of the deceased.

(2) The authority of an arbitrator shall be taken to affect the operation of any enactment or rule of law by virtue of which any right of action is extinguished by the death of a person.

3. Bankruptcy.

(1) Where it is provided by a term in a contract to which a bankrupt is a party that any differences arising thereout or in connection therewith shall be referred to arbitration, the said term shall, if the trustee in bankruptcy adopts the contract, be enforceable by or against him so far as relates to any such differences.

(2) Where a person who has been adjudged bankrupt had, before the commencement of the bankruptcy, become a party to an arbitration agreement, and any matter to which the agreement applies requires to be determined in connection with or for the purposes of the bankruptcy proceedings, then, if the case is one to which subsection (1) of this section does not apply, any other party to the agreement or, with the consent of the committee of inspection, the trustee in bankruptcy, may apply to the court having jurisdiction in the bankruptcy proceedings for an order directing that the matter in question shall be referred to arbitration in accordance with the agreement, and that court may, if it is of opinion that, having regard to all the circumstances of the case, the matter ought to be determined by arbitration, make an order accordingly.

4. Staying court proceedings where there is submission to arbitration.

(1) If any party to an arbitration agreement, or any person claiming through or under him, commences any legal proceedings in any court against any other party to the agreement, or any person claiming through or under him, in respect of any matter agreed to be referred, any party to those legal proceedings may at any time after appearance, and before delivering any pleadings or taking any other steps in the proceedings, apply to that court to stay the proceedings, and that court or a judge thereof, if satisfied that there is no sufficient reason why the matter should not be referred

in accordance with the agreement, and that the applicant was, at the time when the proceedings were commenced, and still remains, ready and willing to do all things necessary to the proper conduct of the arbitration, may make an order staying the proceedings.

(2) Notwithstanding anything in this Part of this Act, if any party to a submission to arbitration made in pursuance of an agreement to which the protocol set out in the First Schedule to this Act applies, or any person claiming through or under him, commences any legal proceedings in any court against any other party to the submission, or any person claiming through or under him, in respect of any matter agreed to be referred, any party to those legal proceedings may at any time after appearance, and before delivering any pleadings or taking any other steps in the proceedings, apply to that court to stay the proceedings, and that court or a judge thereof, unless satisfied that the agreement or arbitration has become inoperative or cannot proceed or that there is not in fact any dispute between the parties with regard to the matter agreed to be referred, shall make an order staying the proceedings.

5. Reference of interpleader issues to arbitration.

Where relief by way of interpleader is granted and it appears to the High Court that the claims in question are matters to which an arbitration agreement, to which the claimants are parties, applies, the High Court may direct the issue between the claimants to be determined in accordance with the agreement.

6. When reference is to a single arbitrator.

Unless a contrary intention is expressed therein, every arbitration agreement shall, if no other mode of reference is provided, be deemed to include a provision that the reference shall be to a single arbitrator.

7. Power of parties in certain cases to supply vacancy.

Where an arbitration agreement provides that the reference shall be to two arbitrators, one to be appointed by each party, then, unless a contrary intention is expressed therein —

(*a*) if either of the appointed arbitrators refuses to act, or is incapable of acting, or dies, the party who appointed him may appoint a new arbitrator in his place;

(*b*) if, on such a reference, one party fails to appoint an arbitrator, either originally, or by way of substitution as aforesaid, for seven clear days after the other party, having appointed his arbitrator, has served the party making default with notice to make the appointment, the party who has appointed an arbitrator may appoint that arbitrator to act as sole arbitrator in the reference and his award shall be binding on both parties as if he had been appointed by consent:

Provided that the High Court or a judge thereof may set aside any appointment made in pursuance of this section.

8. Umpires.

(1) Unless a contrary intention is expressed therein, every arbitration agreement

shall, where the reference is to two arbitrators, be deemed to include a provision that the two arbitrators shall appoint an umpire immediately after they are themselves appointed.

(2) Unless a contrary intention is expressed therein, every arbitration agreement shall, where such a provision is applicable to the reference, be deemed to include a provision that if the arbitrators have delivered to any party to the arbitration agreement, or to the umpire, a notice in writing stating that they cannot agree, the umpire may forthwith enter on the reference in lieu of the arbitrators.

(3) At any time after the appointment of an umpire, however appointed, the High Court may, on the application of any party to the reference and notwithstanding anything to the contrary in the arbitration agreement, order that the umpire shall enter upon the reference in lieu of the arbitrators and as if he were a sole arbitrator.

9. Agreements for reference to three arbitrators.

(1) Where an arbitration agreement provides that the reference shall be to three arbitrators, one to be appointed by each party and the third to be appointed by the two appointed by the parties, the agreement shall have effect as if it provided for the appointment of an umpire, and not for the appointment of a third arbitrator, by the two arbitrators appointed by the parties.

(2) Where an arbitration agreement provides that the reference shall be to three arbitrators to be appointed otherwise than as mentioned in subsection (1) of this section, the award of any two of the arbitrators shall be binding.

10. Power of court in certain cases to appoint an arbitrator or umpire.

In any of the following cases —

(*a*) where an arbitration agreement provides that the reference shall be to a single arbitrator, and all the parties do not, after differences have arisen, concur in the appointment of an arbitrator;

(*b*) if an appointed arbitrator refuses to act, or is incapable of acting, or dies, and the arbitration agreement does not show that it was intended that the vacancy should not be supplied and the parties do not supply the vacancy;

(*c*) where the parties or two arbitrators are at liberty to appoint an umpire or third arbitrator and do not appoint him, or where two arbitrators are required to appoint an umpire and do not appoint him;

(*d*) where an appointed umpire or third arbitrator refuses to act, or is incapable of acting, or dies, and the arbitration agreement does not show that it was intended that the vacancy should not be supplied, and the parties or arbitrators

do not supply the vacancy;

any party may serve the other parties or the arbitrators, as the case may be, with a written notice to appoint or, as the case may be, concur in appointing, an arbitrator, umpire or third arbitrator, and if the appointment is not made within seven clear days after the service of the notice, the High Court or a judge thereof may, on application by the party who gave the notice, appoint an arbitrator, umpire or third arbitrator who shall have the like powers to act in the reference and make an award as if he had been appointed by consent of all parties.

11. Reference to official referee.

Where an arbitration agreement provides that the reference to shall be to an official referee, any official referee to whom application is made shall, subject to any order of the High Court or a judge thereof as to transfer or otherwise, hear and determine the matters agreed to be referred.

12. Conduct of proceedings.

(1) Unless a contrary intention is expressed therein, every arbitration agreement shall, where such a provision is applicable to the reference, be deemed to contain a provision that the parties to the reference, and all persons claiming through them respectively, shall, subject to any legal objection, submit to be examined by the arbitrator or umpire, on oath or affirmation, in relation to the matters in dispute, and shall, subject as aforesaid, produce before the arbitrator or umpire all documents within their possession or power respectively which may be required or called for, and do all other things which during the proceedings on the reference the arbitrator or umpire may require.

(2) Unless a contrary intention is expressed therein, every arbitration agreement shall, where such a provision is applicable to the reference, be deemed to contain a provision that the witnesses on the reference shall, if the arbitrator or umpire thinks fit, be examined on oath or affirmation.

(3) An arbitrator or umpire shall, unless a contrary intention is expressed in the arbitration agreement, have power to administer oaths to, or take the affirmations of, the parties to and witnesses on a reference under the agreement.

(4) Any party to a reference under an arbitration agreement may sue out a writ of subpoena ad testificandum or a writ of subpoena duces tecum, but no person shall be compelled under any such writ to produce any document which he could not be compelled to produce on the trial of an action, and the High Court or a judge thereof may order that a writ of subpoena ad testificandum or of subpoena duces tecum shall issue to compel the attendance before an arbitrator or umpire of a witness wherever he may be within the United Kingdom.

(5) The High Court or a judge thereof may also order that a writ of habeas corpus ad testificandum shall issue to bring up a prisoner for examination before an arbitrator or umpire.

(6) The High Court shall have, for the purpose of and in relation to a reference, the same power of making orders in respect of —

    (*a*) security for costs;

    (*b*) discovery of documents and interrogatories;

    (*c*) the giving of evidence by affidavit;

    (*d*) examination on oath of any witness before an officer of the High Court or any other person, and the issue of a commission or request for the examination of a witness out of the jurisdiction;

(*e*) the preservation, interim custody or sale of any goods which are the subject matter of the reference;

(*f*) securing the amount in dispute in the reference;

(*g*) the detention, preservation or inspection of any property or thing which is the subject of the reference or as to which any question may arise therein, and authorising for any of the purposes aforesaid any persons to enter upon or into any land or building in the possession of any party to the reference, or authorising any samples to be taken or any observation to be made or experiment to be tried which may be necessary or expedient for the purpose of obtaining full information or evidence; and

(*h*) interim injunctions or the appointment of a receiver;

as it has for the purpose of and in relation to an action or matter in the High Court:

Provided that nothing in this subsection shall be taken to prejudice any power which may be vested in an arbitrator or umpire of making orders with respect to any of the matters aforesaid.

13. Time for making award.

(1) Subject to the provisions of subsection (2) of section twenty-two of this Act, and anything to the contrary in the arbitration agreement, an arbitrator or umpire shall have power to make an award at any time.

(2) The time, if any, limited for making an award, whether under this Act or otherwise, may from time to time be enlarged by order of the High Court or a judge thereof, whether that time has expired or not.

(3) The High Court may, on the application of any party to a reference, remove an arbitrator or umpire who fails to use all reasonable dispatch in entering on and proceeding with the reference and making an award, and an arbitrator or umpire who is removed by the High Court under this subsection shall not be entitled to receive any remuneration in respect of his services.

For the purposes of this subsection, the expression "proceeding with a reference" includes, in a case where two arbitrators are unable to agree, giving notice of that fact to the parties and to the umpire.

14. Interim awards.

Unless a contrary intention is expressed therein, every arbitration agreement shall, where such a provision is applicable to the reference, be deemed to contain a provision that the arbitrator or umpire may, if he thinks fit, make an interim award, and any reference in this Part of this Act to an award includes a reference to an interim award.

15. Specific performance.

Unless a contrary intention is expressed therein, every arbitration agreement shall, where such a provision is applicable to the reference, be deemed to contain a provision that the arbitrator or umpire shall have the same power as the High Court to order specific performance of any contract other than a contract relating to land or any interest in land.

16. Awards to be final.

Unless a contrary intention is expressed therein, every arbitration agreement shall, where such a provision is applicable to the reference, be deemed to contain a provision that the award to be made by the arbitrator or umpire shall be final and binding on the parties and the persons claiming under them respectively.

17. Power to correct slips.

Unless a contrary intention is expressed in the arbitration agreement, the arbitrator or umpire shall have power to correct in an award any clerical mistake or error arising from any accidental slip or omission.

18. Costs.

(1) Unless a contrary intention is expressed therein, every arbitration agreement shall be deemed to include a provision that the costs of the reference and award shall be in the discretion of the arbitrator or umpire, who may direct to and by whom and in what manner those costs or any part thereof shall be paid, and may tax or settle the amount of costs to be so paid or any part thereof, and may award costs to be paid as between solicitor and client.

(2) Any costs directed by an award to be paid shall, unless the award otherwise directs, be taxable in the High Court.

(3) Any provision in an arbitration agreement to the effect that the parties or any party thereto shall in any event pay their or his own costs of the reference or award or any part thereof shall be void, and this Part of this Act shall, in the case of an arbitration agreement containing any such provision, have effect as if that provision were not contained therein:

Provided that nothing in this subsection shall invalidate such a provision when it is a part of an agreement to submit to arbitration a dispute which has arisen before the making of that agreement.

(4) If no provision is made by an award with respect to the costs of the reference, any party to the reference may, within fourteen days of the publication of the award or such further time as the High Court or a judge thereof may direct, apply to the arbitrator for an order directing by and to whom those costs shall be paid, and thereupon the arbitrator shall, after hearing any party who may desire to be heard, amend his award by adding thereto such directions as he may think proper with respect to the payment of the costs of the reference.

(5) Section sixty-nine of the Solicitors Act, 1932 (which empowers a court before which any proceeding is being heard or is pending to charge property recovered or preserved in the proceeding with the payment of solicitors' costs) shall apply as if an arbitration were a proceeding in the High Court, and the High Court may make declarations and orders accordingly.

19. Taxation of arbitrator's or umpire's fees.

(1) If in any case an arbitrator or umpire refuses to deliver his award except on payment of the fees demanded by him, the High Court may, on an application for the purpose, order that the arbitrator or umpire shall deliver the award to the applicant on payment into court by the applicant of the fees demanded, and further that the fees demanded shall be taxed by the taxing officer and that out of the money paid into court there shall be paid out to the arbitrator or umpire by way of fees such sum as may be found reasonable on taxation and that the balance of the money, if any, shall be paid out to the applicant.

(2) An application for the purposes of this section may be made by any party to the reference unless the fees demanded have been fixed by a written agreement between him and the arbitrator or umpire.

(3) A taxation of fees under this section may be reviewed in the same manner as a taxation of costs.

(4) The arbitrator or umpire shall be entitled to appear and be heard on any taxation or review of taxation under this section.

20. Interest on awards

A sum directed to be paid by an award shall, unless the award otherwise directs, carry interest as from the date of the award and at the same rate as a judgment debt.

21. Statement of case.[1]

(1) An arbitrator or umpire may, and shall if so directed by the High Court, state —

> (*a*) any question of law arising in the course of the reference; or
>
> (*b*) an award or any part of an award,

in the form of a special case for the decision of the High Court.

(2) A special case with respect to an interim award or with respect to a question of law arising in the course of a reference may be stated, or may be directed by the High Court to be stated, notwithstanding that proceedings under the reference are still pending.

(3) A decision of the High Court under this section shall be deemed to be a judgment of the Court within the meaning of section twenty-seven of the Supreme Court of Judicature (Consolidation) Act, 1925 (which relates to the jurisdiction of the Court of Appeal to hear and determine appeals from any judgment of the High Court), but no appeal shall lie from the decision of the High Court on any case stated under paragraph (*a*) of subsection (1) of this section without the leave of the High Court or of the Court of Appeal.

---

1. Section 21 ceased to have effect by virtue of the Arbitration Act, 1979.

22. Power to remit award.

(1) In all cases of reference to arbitration the High Court or a judge thereof may from time to time remit the matters referred, or any of them, to the reconsideration of the arbitrator or umpire.

(2) Where an award is remitted, the arbitrator or umpire shall unless the order otherwise directs, make his award within three months after the date of the order.

23. Removal of arbitrator and setting aside of award.

(1) Where an arbitrator or umpire has misconducted himself or the proceedings, the High Court may remove him.

(2) Where an arbitrator or umpire has misconducted himself or the proceedings, or an arbitration or award has been improperly procured, the High Court may set the award aside.

(3) Where an application is made to set aside an award, the High Court may order that any money made payable by the award shall be brought into court or otherwise secured pending the determination of the application.

24. Power of court to give relief where arbitrator is not impartial or the dispute involves question of fraud.

(1) Where an agreement between any parties provides that disputes which may arise in the future between them shall be referred to an arbitrator named or designated in the agreement, and after a dispute has arisen any party applies, on the ground that the arbitrator so named or designated is not or may not be impartial, for leave to revoke the authority of the arbitrator or for an injunction to restrain any other party or the arbitrator from proceeding with the arbitration, it shall not be a ground for refusing the application that the said party at the time when he made the agreement knew, or ought to have known, that the arbitrator, by reason of his relation towards any other party to the agreement or of his connection with the subject referred, might not be capable of impartiality.

(2) Where an agreement between any parties provides that disputes which may arise in the future between them shall be referred to arbitration, and a dispute which so arises involves the question whether any such party has been guilty of fraud, the High Court shall, so far as may be necessary to enable that question to be determined by the High Court, have power to order that the agreement shall cease to have effect and power to give leave to revoke the authority of any arbitrator or umpire appointed by or by virtue of the agreement.

(3) In any case where by virtue of this section the High Court has power to order that an arbitration agreement shall cease to have effect or to give leave to revoke the authority of an arbitrator or umpire, the High Court may refuse to stay any action brought in breach of the agreement.

25. Power of court where arbitrator is removed or authority of arbitrator is revoked.

(1) Where an arbitrator (not being a sole arbitrator), or two or more arbitrators (not being all the arbitrators) or an umpire who has not entered on the reference is or

are removed by the High Court, the High Court may, on the application of any party to the arbitration agreement, appoint a person or persons to act as arbitrator or arbitrators or umpire in place of the person or persons so removed.

(2) Where the authority of an arbitrator or arbitrators or umpire is revoked by leave of the High Court, or a sole arbitrator or all the arbitrators or an umpire who has entered on the reference is or are removed by the High Court, the High Court may, on the application of any party to the arbitration agreement, either —

(*a*) appoint a person to act as sole arbitrator in place of the person or persons removed; or

(*b*) order that the arbitration agreement shall cease to have effect with respect to the dispute referred.

(3) A person appointed under this section by the High Court as an arbitrator or umpire shall have the like power to act in the reference and to make an award as if he had been appointed in accordance with the terms of the arbitration agreement.

(4) Where it is provided (whether by means of a provision in the arbitration agreement or otherwise) that an award under an arbitration agreement shall be a condition precedent to the bringing of an action with respect to any matter to which the agreement applies, the High Court, if it orders (whether under this section or under any other enactment) that the agreement shall cease to have effect as regards any particular dispute, may further order that the provision making an award a condition precedent to the bringing of an action shall also cease to have effect as regards that dispute.

26. Enforcement of award.

An award on an arbitration agreement may, by leave of the High Court or a judge thereof, be enforced in the same manner as a judgment or order to the same effect, and where leave is so given, judgment may be entered in terms of the award.

27. *Power of court to extend time for commencing arbitration proceedings.*

Where the terms of an agreement to refer future disputes to arbitration provide that any claims to which the agreement applies shall be barred unless notice to appoint an arbitrator is given or an arbitrator is appointed or some other step to commence arbitration proceedings is taken within a time fixed by the agreement, and a dispute arises to which the agreement applies, the High Court, if it is of opinion that in the circumstances of the case undue hardship would otherwise be caused, and notwithstanding that the time so fixed has expired, may, on such terms, if any, as the justice of the case may require, but without prejudice to the provisions of any enactment limiting the time for the commencement of arbitration proceedings, extend the time for such period as it thinks proper.

28. *Terms as to costs*

Any order made under this Part of this Act may be made on such terms as to costs or otherwise as the authority making the order thinks just:

Provided that this section shall not apply to any order made under subsection (2) of section four of this Act.

29. Extension of s. 496 of the Merchant Shipping Act, 1894.

(1) In subsection (3) of section four hundred and ninety-six of the Merchant Shipping Act, 1894 (which requires a sum deposited with a wharfinger by an owner of goods to be repaid unless legal proceedings are instituted by the shipowner), the expression "legal proceedings" shall be deemed to include arbitration.

(2) For the purposes of the said section four hundred and ninety-six, as amended by this section, an arbitration shall be deemed to be commenced when one party to the arbitration agreement serves on the other party or parties a notice requiring him or them to appoint or concur in appointing an arbitrator, or, where the arbitration agreement provides that the reference shall be to a person named or designated in the agreement, requiring him or them to submit the dispute to the person so named or designated.

(3) Any such notice as is mentioned in subsection (2) of this section may be served either —

(*a*) by delivering it to the person on whom it is to be served; or

(*b*) by leaving it at the usual or last known place of abode in England of that person; or

(*c*) by sending it by post in a registered letter addressed to that person at his usual or last known place of abode in England;

as well as in any other manner provided in the arbitration agreement; and where a notice is sent by post in manner prescribed by paragraph (*c*) of this subsection, service thereof shall, unless the contrary is proved, be deemed to have been effected at the time at which the letter would have been delivered in the ordinary course of post.

30. Crown to be bound.

This Part of this Act (except the provisions of subsection (2) of section four thereof) shall apply to any arbitration to which His Majesty, either in right of the Crown or of the Duchy of Lancaster or otherwise, or the Duke of Cornwall, is a party.

31. Application of Part I to statutory arbitrations.

(1) Subject to the provisions of section thirty-three of this Act, this Part of this Act, except the provisions thereof specified in subsection (2) of this section, shall apply to every arbitration under any other Act (whether passed before or after the commencement of this Act) as if the arbitration were pursuant to an arbitration agreement and as if that other Act were an arbitration agreement, except in so far as this Act is inconsistent with that other Act or with any rules or procedure authorised or recognised thereby.

(2) The provisions referred to in subsection (1) of this section are subsection (1) of section two, section three, subsection (2) of section four, section five, subsection (3) of section eighteen and sections twenty-four, twenty-five, twenty-seven and twenty-nine.

32. *Meaning of "arbitration agreement".*

In this Part of this Act unless the context otherwise requires, the expression "arbitration agreement" means a written agreement to submit present or future differences to arbitration, whether an arbitrator is named therein or not.

33. *Operation of PartI.*

This Part of this Act shall not affect any arbitration commenced (within the meaning of subsection (2) of section twenty-nine of this Act) before the commencement of this Act, but shall apply to an arbitration so commenced after the commencement of this Act under an agreement made before the commencement of this Act.

34. *Extent of Part I.*

Subsection (2) of section four of this Act shall

(*a*) extend to Scotland, with the omission of the words "Notwithstanding anything in this Part of this Act" and with the substitution, for references to staying proceedings, of references to existing proceedings; and

(*b*) extend to Northern Ireland, with the omission of the words "Notwithstanding anything in this Part of this Act";

but, save as aforesaid, none of the provisions of this Part of this Act shall extend to Scotland or Northern Ireland.

Part II: Enforcement of Certain Foreign Awards

35. *Awards to which Part II applies.*

(1) This Part of this Act applies to any award made after the twenty-eighth day of July, nineteen hundred and twenty-four

(*a*) in pursuance of an agreement for arbitration to which the protocol set out in the First Schedule to this Act applies; and

(*b*) between persons of whom one is subject to the jurisdiction of some one of such Powers as His Majesty, being satisfied that reciprocal provisions have been made, may by Order in Council declare to be parties to the convention set out in the Second Schedule to this Act, and of whom the other is subject to the jurisdiction of some other of the Powers aforesaid; and

(*c*) in one of such territories as His Majesty, being satisfied that reciprocal provisions have been made, may by Order in Council declare to be territories to which the the [sic] said convention applies;

and an award to which this Part of this Act applies is in this Part of this Act referred to as "a foreign award".

(2) His Majesty may by a subsequent Order in Council vary or revoke any Order previously made under this section.

(3) Any Order in Council under section one of the Arbitration (Foreign Awards) Act, 1930, which is in force at the commencement of this Act shall have effect as if it had been made under this section.

36. *Effect of foreign awards.*

(1) A foreign award shall, subject to the provisions of this Part of this Act, be enforceable in England either by action or in the same manner as the award of an arbitrator is enforceable by virtue of section twenty-six of this Act.

(2) Any foreign award which would be enforceable under this Part of this Act shall be treated as binding for all purposes on the persons as between whom it was made, and may accordingly be relied on by any of those persons by way of defence, set off or otherwise in any legal proceedings in England, and any references in this Part of this Act to enforcing a foreign award shall be construed as including references to relying on an award.

37. *Conditions for enforcement of foreign awards.*

(1) In order that a foreign award may be enforceable under this Part of this Act it must have —

(*a*) been made in pursuance of an agreement for arbitration which was valid under the law by which it was governed;

(*b*) been made by the tribunal provided for in the agreement or constituted in manner agreed upon by the parties;

(*c*) been made in conformity with the law governing the arbitration procedure;

(*d*) become final in the country in which it was made;

(*e*) been in respect of a matter which may lawfully be referred to arbitration under the law of England;

and the enforcement thereof must not be contrary to the public policy or the law of England.

(2) Subject to the provisions of this subsection, a foreign award shall not be enforceable under this Part of this Act if the court dealing with the case is satisfied that —

(*a*) the award has been annulled in the country in which it was made; or

(*b*) the party against whom it is sought to enforce the award was not given notice of the arbitration proceedings in sufficient time to enable him to present his case, or was under some legal incapacity and was not properly represented; or

(*c*) the award does not deal with all the questions referred or contains decisions on matters beyond the scope of the agreement for arbitration:

Provided that, if the award does not deal with all the questions referred, the court may, if it thinks fit, either postpone the enforcement of the award or order its enforcement subject to the giving of such security by the person seeking to enforce it as the court may think fit.

(3) If a party seeking to resist the enforcement of a foreign award proves that there is any ground other than the non-existence of the conditions specified in paragraphs (*a*), (*b*) and (*c*) of subsection (1) of this section, or the existence of the conditions specified in paragraphs (*b*) and (*c*) of subsection (2) of this section, entitling him to contest the validity of the award, the court may, if it thinks fit, either refuse to enforce the award or adjourn the hearing until after the expiration of such period as appears to the court to be reasonably sufficient to enable that party to take the necessary steps to have the award annulled by the competent tribunal.

38. *Evidence.*

(1) The party seeking to enforce a foreign award must produce —

(*a*) the original award or a copy thereof duly authenticated in manner required by the law of the country in which it was made; and

(*b*) evidence proving that the award has become final; and

(*c*) such evidence as may be necessary to prove that the award is a foreign award and that the conditions mentioned in paragraphs (*a*), (*b*) and (*c*) of subsection (1) of the last foregoing section are satisfied.

(2) In any case where any document required to be produced under subsection (1) of this section is in a foreign language, it shall be the duty of the party seeking to enforce the award to produce a translation certified as correct by a diplomatic or consular agent of the country to which that party belongs, or certified as correct in such other manner as may be sufficient according to the law of England.

(3) Subject to the provisions of this section, rules of court may be made under section ninety-nine of the Supreme Court of Judicature (Consolidation) Act, 1925, with respect to the evidence which must be furnished by a party seeking to enforce an award under this Part of this Act.

39. *Meaning of "final award".*

For the purposes of this Part of this Act, an award shall not be deemed final if any proceedings for the purpose of contesting the validity of the award are pending in the country in which it was made.

40. *Saving for other rights.*

Nothing in this Part of this Act shall —

(*a*) prejudice any rights which any person would have had of enforcing in England any award or of availing himself in England of any award if neither this Part of this Act nor Part I of the Arbitration (Foreign Awards) Act, 1930, had been enacted; or

(*b*) apply to any award made on an arbitration agreement governed by the law of England.

41. *Application of Part II to Scotland.*

(1) The following provisions of this section shall have effect for the purpose of the application of this Part of this Act to Scotland.

(2) For the references to England there shall be substituted references to Scotland.

(3) For subsection (1) of section thirty-six there shall be substituted the following subsection: —

> "(1) A foreign award shall, subject to the provisions of this Part of this Act, be enforceable by action, or, if the agreement for arbitration contains consent to the registration of the award in the Books of Council and Session for execution and the award is so registered, it shall, subject as aforesaid, be enforceable by summary diligence".

(4) For subsection (3) of section thirty-eight there shall be substituted the following subsection: —

> "(3) The Court of Session shall, subject to the provisions of this section, have power, exercisable by statutory instrument, to make provision by Act of Sederunt with respect to the evidence which must be furnished by a party seeking to enforce in Scotland an award under this Part of this Act, and the Statutory Instruments Act, 1946, shall apply to a statutory instrument containing an Act of Sederunt made under this subsection as if the Act of Sederunt had been made by a Minister of the Crown".

42. Application of Part II to Northern Ireland,

(1) The following provisions of this section shall have effect for the purpose of the application of this Part of this Act to Northern Ireland.

(2) For the references to England there shall be substituted references to Northern Ireland.

(3) For subsection (1) of section thirty-six there shall be substituted the following subsection: —

> "(1) A foreign award shall, subject to the provisions of this Part of this Act, be enforceable either by action or in the same manner as the award of an arbitrator under the provisions of the Common Law Procedure Amendment Act (Ireland), 1856, was enforceable at the date of the passing of the Arbitration (Foreign Awards) Act, 1930".

(4) For the reference, in subsection (3) of section thirty-eight, to section ninety-nine of the Supreme Court of Judicature (Consolidation) Act, 1925, there shall be substituted a reference to section sixty-one of the Supreme Court of Judicature (Ireland) Act, 1877, as amended by any subsequent enactment.

43. Saving for pending proceedings.

Any proceedings instituted under Part I of the Arbitration (Foreign Awards) Act, 1930, which are uncompleted at the commencement of this Act may be carried on and completed under this Part of this Act as if they had been instituted thereunder.

Part III: General

44. Short title, commencement and repeal.

(1) This Act may be cited as the Arbitration Act, 1950.

(2) This Act shall come into operation on the first day of September, nineteen hundred and fifty.

(3) The Arbitration Act, 1889, the Arbitration Clauses (Protocol) Act, 1924, and the Arbitration Act, 1934, are hereby repealed except in relation to arbitrations commenced (within the meaning of subsection (2) of section twenty-nine of this Act) before the commencement of this Act, and the Arbitration (Foreign Awards) Act, 1930, is hereby repealed; and any reference in any Act or other document to any enactment hereby repealed shall be construed as including a reference to the corresponding provision of this Act.

b. Arbitration Act, 1975

1. Staying court proceedings where party proves arbitration agreement

(1) If any party to an arbitration agreement to which this section applies, or any person claiming through or under him, commences any legal proceedings in any court against any other party to the agreement, or any person claiming through or under him, in respect of any matter agreed to be referred, any party to the proceedings may at any time after appearance, and before delivering any pleadings or taking any other steps in the proceedings, apply to the court to stay the proceedings; and the court, unless satisfied that the arbitration agreement is null and void, inoperative or incapable of being performed or that there is not in fact any dispute between the parties with regard to the matter agreed to be referred, shall make an order staying the proceedings.

(2) This section applies to any arbitration agreement which is not a domestic arbitration agreement; and neither section 4(1) of the Arbitration Act of 1950 nor section 4 of the Arbitration Act (Northern Ireland) 1937 shall apply to an arbitration agreement to which this section applies.

(3) In the application of this section to Scotland, for the references to staying proceedings there shall be substituted references to sisting[2] proceedings.

(4) In this section 'domestic arbitration agreement' means an arbitration agreement which does not provide, expressly or by implication, for arbitration in a State other than the United Kingdom and to which neither —

(a) an individual who is a national of, or habitually resident in, any State other than the United Kingdom; nor

(b) a body corporate which is incorporated in, or whose central management and control is exercised in, any State other than the United Kingdom;

is a party at the time the proceedings are commenced.

2. Replacement of former provisions

Sections 3 to 6 of this Act shall have effect with respect to the enforcement of Convention awards; and where a Convention award would, but for this section, be also a foreign award within the meaning of Part II of the Arbitration Act 1950, that Part shall not apply to it.

3. Effect of Convention Awards

(1) A Convention award shall, subject to the following provisions of this Act, be enforceable —

(a) in England and Wales, either by action or in the same manner as the award of an arbitrator is enforceable by virtue of section 26 of the Arbitration Act 1950;

(b) in Scotland, either by action or, in a case where the arbitration agreement contains consent to the registration of the award in the Books of Council and Session for execution and the award is so registered, by summary diligence;

2. Editor's Note. In Scottish procedure, to sist is to stop the progress of a case for a time.

(c) in Northern Ireland, either by action or in the same manner as the award of an arbitrator is enforceable by virtue of section 16 of the Arbitration Act (Northern Ireland) 1937.

(2) Any Convention award which would be enforceable under this Act shall be treated as binding for all purposes on the persons as between whom it was made, and may accordingly be relied on by any of those persons by way of defence, set off or otherwise in any legal proceedings in the United Kingdom; and any reference in this Act to enforcing a Convention award shall be construed as including references to relying on such an award.

4. Evidence

The party seeking to enforce a Convention award must produce —
(a) the duly authenticated original award or a duly certified copy of it; and
(b) the original arbitration agreement or a duly certified copy of it; and
(c) where the award or agreement is in a foreign language, a translation of it certified by an official or sworn translator or by a diplomatic or consular agent.

5. Refusal of enforcement

(1) Enforcement of a Convention award shall not be refused except in the cases mentioned in this section.

(2) Enforcement of a Convention award may be refused if the person against whom it is invoked proves —
(a) that a party to the arbitration agreement was (under the law applicable to him) under some incapacity; or
(b) that the arbitration agreement was not valid under the law to which the parties subject it or, failing any indication thereon, under the law of the country where the award was made; or
(c) that he was not given proper notice of the appointment of the arbitrator or of the arbitration proceedings or was otherwise unable to present his case; or
(d) (subject to subsection (4) of this section) that the award deals with a difference not contemplated by or not falling within the terms of the submission to arbitration or contains decisions on matters beyond the scope of the submission to arbitration; or
(e) that the composition of the arbitral authority or the arbitral procedure was not in accordance with the agreement of the parties or, failing such agreement, with the law of the country where the arbitration took place; or
(f) that the award has not yet become binding on the parties, or has been set aside or suspended by a competent authority of the country in which, or under the law of which, it was made.

(3) Enforcement of a Convention award may also be refused if the award is in respect of a matter which is not capable of settlement by arbitration, or if it would be contrary to public policy to enforce the award.

(4) A Convention award which contains decisions on matters not submitted to arbitration may be enforced to the extent that it contains decisions on matters submitted to arbitration which can be separated from those on matters not so submitted.

(5) Where an application for the setting aside or suspension of a Convention award has been made to such a competent authority as is mentioned in subsection (2)(f) of this section, the court before which enforcement of the award is sought may, if it thinks fit, adjourn the proceedings and may, on the application of the party seeking to enforce the award, order the other party to give security.

6. Saving

Nothing in this Act shall prejudice any right to enforce or rely on an award otherwise than under this Act or Party II of the Arbitration Act 1950.

7. Interpretation

(1) In this Act —

'arbitration agreement' means an agreement in writing (including an agreement contained in an exchange of letters or telegrams) to submit to arbitration present or future differences capable of settlement by arbitration;

'Convention award' means an award made in pursuance of an arbitration agreement in the territory of a State, other than the United Kingdom, which is a party to the New York [Arbitration] Convention; and

'the New York [Arbitration] Convention' means the Convention on the Recognition and Enforcement of Foreign Arbitral Awards adopted by the United Nations Conference on International Commercial Arbitration on 10th June 1958.

(2) If Her Majesty by Order in Council declares that any State specified in the Order is a party to the New York [Arbitration] Convention the Order shall, while in force, be conclusive evidence that that State is a party to that Convention.

(3) An Order in Council under this section may be varied or revoked by a subsequent Order in Council.

8. Short title, repeals, commencement and extent

(1) This Act may be cited as the Arbitration Act 1975.

(2) The following provisions of the Arbitration Act 1950 are hereby repealed, that is to say —

(a) section 4(2);

(b) in section 28 the proviso;

(c) in section 30 the words '(except the provisions of subsection (2) of section 4 thereof)';

(d) in section 31(2) the words 'subsection (2) of section 4'; and

(e) in section 34 the words from the beginning to 'save as aforesaid'.

(3) This Act shall come into operation on such date as the Secretary of State may by order made by statutory instrument appoint.

(4) This Act extends to Northern Ireland.

c. Arbitration Act, 1979

1. Judicial review of arbitration awards.

(1) In the Arbitration Act 1950 (in this Act referred to as 'the principal Act') section 21 (statement of case for a decision of the High Court) shall cease to have effect and, without prejudice to the right of appeal conferred by subsection (2) below, the High Court shall not have jurisdiction to set aside or remit an award on an arbitration agreement on the ground of errors of fact or law on the face of the award.

(2) Subject to subsection (3) below, an appeal shall lie to the High Court on any question of law arising out of an award made on an arbitration agreement; and on the determination of such an appeal the High Court may by order -

(a) confirm, vary or set aside the award; or

(b) remit the award to the reconsideration of the arbitrator or umpire together with the court's opinion on the question of law which was the subject of the appeal;

and where the award is remitted under paragraph (b) above the arbitrator or umpire shall, unless the order otherwise directs, make his award within three months after the date of the order.

(3) An appeal under this section may be brought by any of the parties to the reference -

(a) with the consent of the other parties to the reference; or

(b) subject to section 3 below, with the leave of the court.

(4) The High Court shall not grant leave under subsection (3)(b) above unless it considers that, having regard to all the circumstances, the determination of the question of law concerned could substantially affect the rights of one or more of the parties to the arbitration agreement; and the court may make any leave which it gives conditional upon the applicant complying with such conditions as it considers appropriate.

(5) Subject to subsection (6) below, if an award is made and, on an application made by any of the parties to the reference -

(a) with the consent of all the other parties to the reference, or

(b) subject to section 3 below, with the leave of the court,

it appears to the High Court that the award does not or does not sufficiently set out the reasons for the award, the court may order the arbitrator or umpire concerned to state the reasons for his award in sufficient detail to enable the court, should an appeal be brought under this section, to consider any question of law arising out of the award.

(6) In any case where an award is made without any reason being given, the High Court shall not make an order under subsection (5) above unless it is satisfied -

(a) that before the award was made one of the parties to the reference gave notice to the arbitrator or umpire concerned that a reasoned award would be required; or

(b) that there is some special reason why such a notice was not given.

(6A) Unless the High Court gives leave, no appeal shall lie to the Court of Appeal from a decision of the High Court -

(a) to grant or refuse leave under subsection 3(b) or 5(b) above; or

(b) to make or not to make an order under subsection (5) above.

(7) No appeal shall lie to the Court of Appeal from a decision of the High Court on an appeal under this section unless -

(a) the High Court or the Court of Appeal gives leave; and

(b) it is certified by the High Court that the question of law to which its decision relates either is one of general public importance or is one which for some other special reason should be considered by the Court of Appeal.

(8) Where the award of an arbitrator or umpire is varied on appeal, the award as varied shall have effect (except for the purposes of this section) as if it were the award of the arbitrator or umpire.

2. Determination of preliminary point of law by court.

(1) Subject to subsection (2) and section 3 below, on an application to the High Court made by any of the parties to a reference -

(a) with the consent of an arbitrator who has entered on the reference or, if an umpire has entered on the reference, with his consent, or

(b) with the consent of all the other parties,

the High Court shall have jurisdiction to determine any question of law arising in the course of the reference.

(2) The High Court shall not entertain an application under subsection (1)(a) above with respect to any question of law unless it is satisfied that -

(a) the determination of the application might produce substantial savings in costs to the parties; and

(b) the question of law is one in respect of which leave to appeal would be likely to be given under section 1(3)(b) above.

2(A) Unless the High Court gives leave, no appeal shall lie to the Court of Appeal from a decision of the High Court to entertain or not to entertain an application under subsection 1(a) above.

(3) A decision of the High Court under this section shall be deemed to be a judgment of the court within the meaning of section [16 of the Supreme Courts Act 1981] (appeals to the Court of Appeal), but no appeal shall lie from such a decision unless -

(a) the High Court or the Court of Appeal gives leave; and

(b) it is certified by the High Court that the question of law to which its decision relates either is one of general public importance or is one which for some other special reason should be considered by the Court of Appeal.

3. Exclusion agreements affecting rights under sections 1 and 2.

(1) Subject to the following provisions of this section and section 4 below -

(a) the High Court shall not, under section 1(3)(b) above, grant leave to appeal with respect to a question of law arising out of an award, and

(b) the High Court shall not, under section 1(5)(b) above, grant leave to make an application with respect to an award, and

(c) no application may be made under section 2(1)(a) above with respect to a question of law,

if the parties to the reference in question have entered into an agreement in writing (in this section referred to as an 'exclusion agreement') which excludes the right of appeal under section 1 above in relation to that award or, in a case falling within paragraph (c) above, in relation to an award to which the determination of the question of law is material.

(2) An exclusion agreement may be expressed so as to relate to a particular award, to awards under a particular reference or to any other description of awards, whether arising out of the same reference or not; and an agreement may be an exclusion agreement for the purposes of this section whether it is entered into before or after the passing of this Act and whether or not it forms part of an arbitration agreement.

(3) In any case where -

(a) an arbitration agreement, other than a domestic arbitration agreement, provides for disputes between the parties to be referred to arbitration, and

(b) a dispute to which the agreement relates involves the question whether a party has been guilty of fraud, and

(c) the parties have entered into an exclusion agreement which is applicable to any award made on the reference of that dispute,

then, except in so far as the exclusion agreement otherwise provides, the High Court shall not exercise its powers under section 24(2) of the principal Act (to take steps necessary to enable the question to be determined by the High Court) in relation to that dispute.

(4) Except as provided by subsection (1) above, sections 1 and 2 above shall have effect notwithstanding anything in any agreement purporting -

(a) to prohibit or restrict access to the High Court; or

(b) to restrict the jurisdiction of that court; or

(c) to prohibit or restrict the making of a reasoned award.

(5) An exclusion agreement shall be of no effect in relation to an award made on, or a question of law arising in the course of a reference under, a statutory arbitration, that is to say, such an arbitration as is referred to in subsection (1) of section 31 of the principal Act.

(6) An exclusion agreement shall be of no effect in relation to an award made on, or a question of law arising in the course of a reference under, an arbitration agreement which is a domestic arbitration agreement unless the exclusion agreement is entered into after the commencement of the arbitration in which the award is made or, as the case may be, in which the question of law arises.

(7) In this section 'domestic arbitration agreement' means an arbitration agreement which does not provide, expressly or by implication, for arbitration in a State other than the United Kingdom and to which neither -

(a) an individual who is a national of, or habitually resident in, any State other than the United Kingdom, nor

(b) a body corporate which is incorporated in, or whose central management and control is exercised in, any State other than the United Kingdom, is a party at the time the arbitration agreement is entered into.

4. Exclusion agreements not to apply in certain cases.

(1) Subject to subsection (3) below, if an arbitration award or a question of law arising in the course of a reference relates, in whole or in part; to -

(a) a question or claim falling within the Admiralty jurisdiction of the High Court, or

(b) a dispute arising out of a contract of insurance, or

(c) a dispute arising out of a commodity contract,

an exclusion agreement shall have no effect in relation to the award or question unless either -

(i) the exclusion agreement is entered into after the commencement of the arbitration in which the award is made or, as the case may be, in which the question of law arises, or

(ii) the award or question relates to a contract which is expressed to be governed by a law other than the law of England and Wales.

(2) In subsection (1)(c) above 'commodity contract' means a contract -

(a) for the sale of goods regularly dealt with on a commodity market or exchange in England or Wales which is specified for the purposes of this section by an order made by the Secretary of State; and

(b) of a description so specified.

(3) The Secretary of State may by order provide that subsection (1) above -

(a) shall cease to have effect; or

(b) subject to such conditions as may be specified in the order, shall not apply to any exclusion agreement made in relation to an arbitration award of a description so specified;

and an order under this subsection may contain such supplementary, incidental and transitional provisions as appear to the Secretary of State to be necessary or expedient.

(4) The power to make an order under subsection (2) or subsection (3) above shall be exercisable by statutory instrument which shall be subject to annulment in pursuance of a resolution of either House of Parliament.

(5) In this section 'exclusion agreement' has the same meaning as in section 3 above.

5. Interlocutory orders.

(1) If any party to a reference under an arbitration agreement fails within the time specified in the order or, if no time is so specified, within a reasonable time to comply with an order made by the arbitrator or umpire in the course of the reference, then, on the application of the arbitrator or umpire or of any party to the reference, the High Court may make an order extending the powers of the arbitrator or umpire as mentioned in subsection (2) below.

(2) If an order is made by the High Court under this section, the arbitrator or umpire shall have the power, to the extent and subject to any conditions specified in that order, to continue with the reference in default of appearance or of any other at

by one of the parties in like manner as a judge of the High Court might continue with proceedings in that court where a party fails to comply with an order of that court or a requirement of rules of court.

(3) Section 4(5) of the Administration of Justice Act 1970 (jurisdiction of the High Court to be exercisable by the Court of Appeal in relation to judge-arbitrators and judge-umpires) shall not apply in relation to the power of the High Court to make an order under this section, but in the case of a reference to a judge-arbitrator or judge-umpire that power shall be exercisable as in the case of any other reference to arbitration and also by the judge-arbitrator or judge-umpire himself.

(4) Anything done by a judge-arbitrator or judge-umpire in the exercise of the power conferred by subsection (3) above shall be done by him in his capacity as judge of the High Court and have effect as if done by that court.

(5) The preceding provisions of this section have effect notwithstanding anything in any agreement but do not derogate from any powers conferred on an arbitrator or umpire, whether by an arbitration agreement or otherwise.

(6) In this section `judge-arbitrator' and `judge-umpire' have the same meaning as in Schedule 3 to the Administration of Justice Act 1970.

6. Minor amendments relating to awards and appointments of arbitrators and umpires.

(1) In subsection (1) of section 8 of the principal Act (agreements where reference is to two arbitrators deemed to include provision that the arbitrators shall appoint an umpire immediately after their own appointment)

(a) for the words `shall appoint an umpire immediately' there shall be substituted the words 'may appoint an umpire at any time'; and

(b) at the end there shall be added the words `and shall do so forthwith if they cannot agree'.

(2) For section 9 of the principal Act (agreements for reference to three arbitrators) there shall be substituted the following section:

'9. Majority award of three arbitrators
Unless the contrary intention is expressed in the arbitration agreement, in any case where there is a reference to three arbitrators, the award of any two of the arbitrators shall be binding'.

(3) In section 10 of the principal Act (power of court in certain cases to appoint an arbitrator or umpire) in paragraph (c) after the word 'are', in the first place where it occurs, there shall be inserted the words 'required or are' and the words from 'or where' to the end of the paragraph shall be omitted.

(4) At the end of section 10 of the principal Act there shall be added the following subsection: -

'(2) In any case where -

(a) an arbitration agreement provides for the appointment of an arbitrator or umpire by a person who is neither one of the parties nor an existing arbitrator (whether the provision applies directly or in default of agreement by the parties or otherwise), and

(b) that person refuses to make the appointment or does not make it within the time specified in the agreement or, if no time is so specified, within a reasonable time,

any party to the agreement may serve the person in question with a written notice to appoint an arbitrator or umpire and, if the appointment is not made within seven clear days after the service of the notice, the High Court or a judge thereof may, on the application of the party who gave the notice, appoint an arbitrator or umpire who shall have the like powers to act in the reference and make an award as if he had been appointed in accordance with the terms of the agreement.'

7. Application and interpretation of certain provisions of Part I of principal Act.
(1) References in the following provisions of Part I of the principal Act to that Part of that Act shall have effect as if the preceding provisions of this Act were included in that Part, namely, -
    (a) section 14 (interim awards);
    (b) section 28 (terms as to costs of orders);
    (c) section 30 (Crown to be bound):
    (d) section 31 (application to statutory arbitration); and
    (e) section 32 (meaning of 'arbitration agreement').

(2) Subsections (2) and (3) of section 29 of the principal Act shall apply to determine when an arbitration is deemed to be commenced for the purposes of this Act.
(3) For the avoidance of doubt, it is hereby declared that the reference in subsection (1) of section 31 of the principal Act (statutory arbitrations) to arbitration under any other Act does not extend to arbitration under section 92 of the County Courts Act 1959 (cases in which proceedings are to be or may be referred to arbitration) and accordingly nothing in this Act or in Part I of the principal Act applies to arbitration under the said section 92.

8. Short title, commencement, repeals and extent.
(1) This Act may be cited as the Arbitration Act 1979.
(2) This Act shall come into operation on such day as the Secretary of State may appoint by order made by statutory instrument; and such an order -
    (a) may appoint different days for different provisions of this Act and for the purposes of the operation of the same provision in relation to different descriptions of arbitration agreement; and
    (b) may contain such supplementary, incidental and transitional provisions as appear to the Secretary of State to be necessary or expedient.

(3) In consequence of the preceding provisions of this Act, the following provisions are hereby repealed, namely -
    (a) in paragraph (c) of section 10 of the principal Act the words from 'or

where' to the end of the paragraph;
    (b) section 21 of the principal Act;
    (c) in paragraph 9 of Schedule 3 to the Administration of Justice Act 1970, in sub-paragraph (1) the words '21(1) and (2)' and sub-paragraph (2).

(4) This Act forms part of the law of England and Wales only.

4. FRANCE

Nouveau code de procédure civile.[1]

BOOK IV.
TITLE I - Arbitration Agreement.
Chapter I - The Arbitration Clause.

Article 1442

An arbitration clause is an agreement by which the parties to a contract undertake to submit to arbitration the disputes which may arise with respect to that contract.

Article 1443

An arbitration clause is null unless it is set forth in writing in the principal agreement or in a document to which the latter refers.

Subject to the same sanction, the arbitration clause must either appoint the arbitrator or arbitrators or set forth the manner in which they are to be appointed.

Article 1444

If, after the dispute has arisen, the constitution of the arbitral tribunal encounters a difficulty due to the acts of one of the parties or with respect to the functioning of the method of appointment, the President of the *Tribunal de Grande Instance* shall appoint the arbitrator or arbitrators.

Nevertheless, this appointment may be made by the President of the *Tribunal de Commerce* if the agreement expressly so provides.

If the arbitration clause is either manifestly null, or if it is not adequate for the purpose of constituting the arbitral tribunal, the President shall so determine and declare that no appointment is to be made.

Article 1445

The dispute shall be submitted to the arbitral tribunal either jointly by the parties, or by the most diligent party.

Article 1446

If null and void, the arbitration clause shall be considered not to have been written.

---

1. Translation by W. Laurence Craig, William W. Park and Jan A.S. Paulsson.

Chapter II - The Submission *(compromis)*.

Article 1447

A submission is an agreement by which the parties to an existing dispute refer the matter to arbitration by one or more persons.

Article 1448

A submission is null unless it establishes the object of the dispute.

Subject to the same sanction, it must either appoint the arbitrator or arbitrators or set forth the manner in which they are to be appointed.

A submission lapses if an arbitrator therein appointed does not accept the mission conferred on him.

Article 1449

A submission is to be in writing. It may take the form of minutes signed by the arbitrator and the parties.

Article 1450

The parties shall have the option of agreeing to arbitration even during the course of proceedings already instituted before another jurisdiction.

Chapter III - Common Rules

Article 1451

The mission of arbitrator may be entrusted only to a natural person, who must have full capacity to exercise his civil rights.

If the arbitration agreement designates a legal entity, the latter is empowered only to organize the arbitration.

Article 1452

The constitution of the arbitral tribunal is accomplished only if the arbitrator or arbitrators accept the mission with which they have been entrusted.

An arbitrator who has knowledge of a personal cause of disqualification shall so inform the parties. In such a case, he may accept his mission only with their agreement.

Article 1453

An arbitral tribunal may be composed of a sole arbitrator or of several arbitrators, uneven in number.

Article 1454

Whenever the parties appoint an even number of arbitrators, the arbitral tribunal shall be made complete by an arbitrator chosen either in accordance with the mechanism envisaged by the parties, or, in the absence of such mechanism, by the appointed arbitrators, or finally, in the absence of agreement by them, by the President of the *Tribunal de Grande Instance.*

Article 1455

Whenever a natural person or a legal entity is charged with organizing an arbitration, the arbitral mission shall be entrusted to one or several arbitrators accepted by all of the parties.

In the absence of such acceptance, the person or entity responsible for organizing the arbitration shall invite each party to appoint an arbitrator and shall, when appropriate, proceed to appoint the arbitrator required to complete the arbitral tribunal. If the parties do not appoint an arbitrator, this is to be done by the person or entity responsible for organizing the arbitration.

The arbitral tribunal may also be directly constituted according to the mechanisms set forth in the preceding paragraph.

The person or entity responsible for organizing the arbitration may provide that the arbitral tribunal render only a draft award and that if said draft is contested by one of the parties, the case shall be submitted to a second arbitral tribunal. In such a case, the members of the second tribunal shall be appointed by the person or entity responsible for organizing the arbitration, each of the parties having the possibility of having one of the thus appointed arbitrators replaced.

Article 1456

If the arbitration agreement does not establish a deadline, the mission of the arbitrators shall last only six months from the day the last arbitrator has accepted his mission.

The legal or contractual deadline may be extended either by agreement of the parties or, by a request of either of them or of the arbitral tribunal, by the President of the *Tribunal de Grande Instance* or, in the case contemplated by Article 1444, paragraph 2, by the President of the *Tribunal de Commerce.*

Article 1457

In the cases covered by Articles 1444, 1454, 1456, and 1463, the President of the court, seized as in urgent proceedings (*référé*) by a party or the arbitral tribunal, shall decide by non-appealable order.

Nevertheless, such order may be appealed if the President declares that no appointment is to be made for one of the reasons defined in Article 1444 (paragraph 3). The appeal is to be filed, examined, and decided in the same manner as with respect to jurisdictional disputes.

The President having jurisdiction is the President of the court designated by the arbitration agreement or, in the absence of such an agreement, the President of the court within the district where said agreement localized the arbitral proceedings. If the agreement is silent, the President having jurisdiction is the President of the court of the defendant's residence or of one of the defendants or, if the defendant does not reside in France, the President of the court in the place of the plaintiff's residence.

Article 1458

Whenever a dispute submitted to an arbitral tribunal by virtue of an arbitration agreement is brought before a court of the State, such court shall decline jurisdiction.

If the arbitral tribunal has not yet been seized of the matter, the court should also decline jurisdiction unless the arbitration agreement is manifestly null.

In neither case may the court determine its lack of jurisdiction on its own motion.

Article 1459

Any stipulation or agreement contrary to the rules set forth in the present Chapter shall be deemed void.

TITLE II - The Arbitral Proceedings

Article 1460

The arbitrators shall determine the procedure for the arbitration without being bound by the rules established for the courts, unless the parties have provided otherwise in the arbitration agreement.

Nevertheless, the guiding principles of litigation defined in Articles 4 to 10, 11 (paragraph 1) and 13 to 21 shall always be applicable to arbitral proceedings.

If a party is in possession of evidence, the arbitrator may also order him to produce it.

Article 1461

Procedural instructions and records of the proceedings are to be executed by all the arbitrators unless the submission authorizes them to delegate one arbitrator.

Third parties are to be heard without being sworn.

Article 1462

Arbitrators are to continue their mission until it is completed.

An arbitrator may not be dismissed except by the parties' unanimous consent.

Article 1463

An arbitrator may not decline to act or be challenged except for a ground of challenge revealed or having arisen subsequent to his appointment.

Difficulties in applying the present Article are to be brought before the President of the court having jurisdiction.

Article 1464

The arbitral proceedings end, except for specific agreement by the parties to the contrary:

    1. By the dismissal, death, or prevention of an arbitrator or by the loss of the full exercise of his civil rights;

2. By an arbitrator declining to act or being challenged;

3. By the expiry of the time limit for the arbitration.

Article 1465

Interruption of arbitral proceedings is governed by the provisions of Articles 369 to 376.

Article 1466

If one of the parties contests, before the arbitrator, the latter's jurisdiction, whether in principle or scope, it is for the arbitrator to decide on the validity or scope of his mission.

Article 1467

In the absence of an agreement to the contrary, the arbitrator is empowered to decide the claim for verification of a writing or of falsification of documents in conformity with Articles 287 to 294 and Article 299.

In the event that the objection of falsification has been raised (*en cas d'inscription de faux incidente*) Article 313 is to be applied by the arbitrator. The time limit for the arbitration shall continue to run from the day when the allegation has been ruled upon.

Article 1468

The arbitrator shall fix the date upon which the matter shall reach the stage of deliberation.

After this date, no claim may be made, nor any argument raised. No observation may be proffered, nor any document produced, except at the request of the arbitrator.

TITLE III - The Arbitral Award.

Article 1469

Arbitrator's deliberations are secret.

Article 1470

The arbitral award is to be rendered by majority vote.

Article 1471

The arbitral award shall succinctly set forth the respective claims and arguments of the parties.

The decision shall be reasoned.

Article 1472

The arbitral award should indicate:

-the names of the arbitrators who rendered it;
-its date;
-the place where it was rendered;
-the names, surnames, or appellation of the parties, as well as their domicile or corporate headquarters;
-wherever appropriate, the name of the attorneys or other persons who have represented or assisted the parties.

Article 1473

The award is to be signed by all of the arbitrators.

However, if a minority among them refuses to sign it, the others are to mention the fact and the award shall have the same effect as though it had been signed by all of the arbitrators.

Article 1474

The arbitrator is to decide the case in conformity with rules of law, unless the parties, in the arbitration agreement, have given him the authority to decide as *amiable compositeur.*

Article 1475

The award terminates the jurisdiction of the arbitrator with respect to the dispute which it decides.

Nevertheless, an arbitrator has the power to interpret the award, to rectify errors and material omissions which may affect it, and to complete it whenever he has omitted to rule on a element of the claim. Articles 461 to 463 are applicable. If the arbitral tribunal cannot be reconvened, this power shall be vested in the court which would have had jurisdiction in the absence of arbitration.

Article 1476

The award has, as of the moment it is rendered, *res judicata* effect with respect to the dispute which it decides.

Article 1477

The arbitral award may be forcibly executed only by virtue of an order of *exequatur* by the *Tribunal de Grande Instance* having jurisdiction at the place where the award was rendered. *Exequatur* shall be ordered by the enforcement judge of the Tribunal.

To this effect, the text of the award and a copy of the arbitration agreement shall be filed by one of the arbitrators or by the most diligent of the parties, at the Secretariat of the court.

Article 1478

Exequatur is inscribed on the text of the arbitral award.

An order refusing to grant *exequatur* must be reasoned.

Article 1479

The rules with respect to provisional execution of judgments are applicable to arbitral awards.

In the case of an appeal or an action to set aside, the First President or the magistrate supervising the case, once seized of a motion, may grant *exequatur* of the arbitral award declared provisionally enforceable. He may also order provisional execution under the conditions envisaged in Articles 525 and 526; his decision shall be deemed equivalent to *exequatur*.

Article 1480

An award is null unless it complies with the mandatory provisions of Article 1471 (paragraph 2), 1472, as to the names of the arbitrators and the date of the award, and 1473.

TITLE IV - Means of Recourse

Article 1481

An arbitral award may not be the object of *opposition* or appeal to the *Cour de Cassation*.

It may be the object of *tierce opposition* before the court which would have had jurisdiction but for arbitration, subject to the provisions of Article 588 (paragraph 1).

Article 1482

An arbitral award may be appealed unless the parties, in the arbitration agreement, waive their right to appeal. Nevertheless, it may not be appealed if the arbitrator has been empowered to act as *amiable compositeur*, unless the parties, in the arbitration agreement, expressly reserve the right to do so.

Article 1483

Whenever, in conformity with the distinctions made in Article 1482, the parties have not waived their right to appeal, or have expressly reserved said right in the arbitration agreement, only the normal procedure of appeal (*voie d'appel*) shall be open, whether the motion is to modify or to set aside the arbitral award. The appellate judge shall decide as *amiable compositeur* if the arbitrator had been so empowered.

Article 1484

Whenever, in conformity with the distinction made in Article 1482, the parties have waived their right to appeal, or have not expressly reserved said right in the arbitration agreement, a motion to set aside the document characterized as an arbitral award may nevertheless be raised irrespective of any stipulation to the contrary.

It may be granted only in the following cases:

    1. If the arbitrator decided in the absence of an arbitration agreement or on the basis of a void or expired agreement;

2. If the arbitral tribunal was irregularly composed or the sole arbitrator irregularly appointed.

3. If the arbitrator's decided in a manner incompatible with the mission conferred upon him;

4. Whenever due process (*le principe de la contradiction*) has not been respected;

5. In all cases of nullity defined in Article 1480;

6. If the arbitrator has violated public policy (*ordre public*).

Article 1485

Whenever a court seized of a motion to set aside does set the award aside, it decides on the merits of the case within the limits of the arbitrator's mission, unless the parties are agreed to the contrary.

Article 1486

Appeals and motions to set aside shall be brought before the Court of Appeal within whose district the arbitral award was rendered.

These means of recourse may be brought immediately following the rendering of the award, but are barred if they have not been made within one month following official notification of the award and its *exequatur* (*signification de la sentence revêtue de l'exequatur*).

Execution of the arbitral award is suspended for the period during which these means of recourse may be exercised. Exercise of such recourse has a suspensive effect as well.

Article 1487

Appeal and motions to set aside are to be filed, examined, and decided in accordance with the rules applicable to litigation before the Court of Appeal.

The characterization given by the parties to the means of recourse at the time when the declaration of appeal is made, may be modified or clarified up to the moment the Court of Appeal is seized of the matter.

Article 1488

An order granting exequatur may not be appealed in any manner.

Nevertheless, an appeal of the award or a motion to set aside the award encompasses *ipso jure*, within the limits of the terms of the action of which the Court of Appeal has been seized, appeal against the decision of a judge who has granted *exequatur* or declined jurisdiction in connection with *exequatur*.

Article 1489

An order refusing *exequatur* may be appealed within one month of its notification. In this case, the Court of Appeal shall, at the request of a party, consider such arguments as could have been made against the arbitral award, whether on appeal or in support of a motion to set aside.

Article 1490

Rejection of an appeal or a motion to set aside confers *exequatur* on the arbitral award, or on such of its dispositions as are not censored by the Court of Appeal.

Article 1491

A motion to revise the arbitral award may be brought in the same cases and under the same conditions as those that apply to court judgments.

Such a motion is to be brought before the Court of Appeal which would have had jurisdiction with respect to the other means of recourse against the award.

TITLE V - International Arbitration

Article 1492

Arbitration is international if it implicates international commercial interests.

Article 1493

The arbitration agreement may, directly or by reference to a set of arbitration rules, appoint one or more arbitrators or provide the manner for their appointment.

If any difficulty arises in the constitution of the arbitral tribunal with respect to an arbitration taking place in France, or to one for which the parties have agreed that French procedural law should apply, either party may, in the absence of a clause to the contrary, apply to the President of the *Tribunal de Grande Instance* of Paris in the manner set forth in Article 1457.

Article 1494

The arbitration agreement may, directly or by reference to a set of arbitration rules, define the procedure to be followed in the arbitral proceedings; it may also subject it to a given procedural law.

If the agreement is silent, the arbitrator, either directly or by reference to a law or a set of arbitration rules, shall establish such rules of procedure as may be necessary.

Article 1495

Whenever international arbitration is subject to French law, the provisions of Titles I, II, and III of the present Book shall apply only in the absence of specific agreement between the parties, and subject to Articles 1493 and 1494.

Article 1496

The arbitrator shall decide the dispute according to the rules of law chosen by the parties; in the absence of such a choice, he shall decide according to the rules he deems appropriate.

In all cases he shall take into account trade usages.

Article 1497

The arbitrator shall decide as *amiable compositeur* if the parties' agreement conferred this authority upon him.

TITLE VI - Recognition and Enforcement of, and Means of Recourse Against, Arbitral Awards REndered Abroad or In international Arbitration
Chapter I - Recognition and Enforcement of Arbitral Awards Rendered Abroad or in International Arbitration

Article 1498

Arbitral awards shall be recognized in France if their existence is proven by the party relying thereon and if such recognition is not manifestly contrary to international public policy (*ordre public*).

Subject to the same conditions, such awards shall be declared enforceable in France by the enforcement judge.

Article 1499

The existence of an arbitral award is established by the production of its original text together with the arbitration agreement, or by copies of said documents accompanied by proof of their authenticity.

If said documents are not in the French language, the party shall produce a translation certified by a translator on the list of court-appointed experts.

Article 1500

The provisions of Article 1476 through 1479 are applicable.

Chapter II - Means of Recourse Against ArbitraL Awards Rendered Abroad or in International Arbitration

Article 1501

A decision refusing recognition or enforcement of an award may be appealed.

Article 1502

An appeal against a decision granting recognition or enforcement may be brought only in the following cases:

1. If the arbitrator decided in the absence of an arbitration agreement on the basis of a void or expired agreement;

2. If the arbitral tribunal was irregularly composed or the sole arbitrator irregularly appointed;

3. If the arbitrator decided in a manner incompatible with the mission conferred upon him;

4. Whenever due process has not been respected;

5. If the recognition or enforcement is contrary to international public policy (*ordre public*).

Article 1503
The appeal provided in Articles 1501 and 1502 shall be made to the Court of Appeal having jurisdiction over the judge who rendered the decision. It may be brought within one month of notification of the judge's decision.

Article 1504
An arbitral award rendered in France in international arbitral proceedings is subject to an action to set aside on the grounds set forth in Article 1502.

An order to enforce such an award may not be appealed in any manner. However, the action to set aside encompasses *ipso jure*, within the limits of the terms of the action of which the Court of Appeal has been seized, appeal against the decision of the enforcement judge having issued such an order, or having declined jurisdiction.

Article 1505
Actions to set aside as provided in Article 1504 shall be brought before the Court of Appeal having jurisdiction in the place where the award was rendered. Such action may be heard as soon as the award has been rendered; it is barred if it has not been brought within the month following notification of the award and its *exequatur* ("*signification de la sentence revêtue de l'exequatur*").

Article 1506
Enforcement of the arbitral award is suspended during the time limit for exercising the means of recourse defined in Articles 1501, 1502 and 1504. The pendency of such an action brought within the time limit also has a suspensive effect.

Article 1507
The provisions of Title IV of the present Book, with the exception of those of the first paragraph of Article 1487 and of Article 1490, are not applicable to the means of recourse.

5. GERMANY

a. German Code of Civil Procedure (Zivilprozessordnung)[1]

Section 1025

(1) The agreement to submit a dispute to the decision of one or more arbitrators is legally valid to the extent that the parties are entitled to reach a settlement on the subject matter of the dispute.

(2) The arbitration agreement is invalid if one of the parties has taken advantage of its superior economic or social position to compel the other party to conclude this agreement or to accept any provisions that ensure a predominance over that other party in the arbitration procedure, particularly with regard to the appointment or challenge of arbitrators.

Section 1025a

An arbitration agreement concerning legal disputes over the existence of a rental relationship of residential property is invalid. This does not apply if the residential property is of the kind mentioned in section 556a paragraph 8 of the Civil Code.

Section 1026

An arbitration agreement concerning future disputes is invalid unless it refers to a definite legal relationship and to disputes arising therefrom.

Section 1027

(1) The arbitration agreement shall be concluded in explicit language and must be in writing; the document may not contain any agreement other than those that refer to the arbitration procedure. Pleadings on the merits of the case in the arbitral proceedings shall remedy any defect in the form.

(2) The provisions of paragraph 1 of this section shall not apply if the arbitration agreement is a commercial transaction for both parties and neither party belongs to the class of business professionals specified in section 4 of the Commercial Code.

(3) Insofar as paragraph 2 of this section does not require that the arbitration agreement be in writing, any of the parties may demand that a written document concerning the agreement be drawn up.

Section 1027a

The court shall dismiss as inadmissible any action regarding a dispute with respect to which the parties have concluded an arbitration agreement if the respondent invokes the agreement.

---

1. Law of Jan. 30, 1877 (RGBl 1877 at 83); Law of Sept. 12, 1950 [BGBl 1950 I at 533), as amended by art. 4 of the Law of July 25, 1986 (BGBl 1986 I at 1142, 1151). Translated by Luigi Fernando, Frank Koerner, and Russell Taylor. INTERNATIONAL HANDBOOK ON COMMERCIAL ARBITRATION, Kluwer.

Section 1028

If the arbitration agreement contains no provisions concerning the appointment of arbitrators, each party shall appoint an arbitrator.

Section 1029

(1) If both parties are entitled to appoint arbitrators, the initiating party shall communicate to the other party, in writing, the name of the arbitrator appointed by it, together with the request that the other party do the same within one week.

(2) If no appointment has been made by the expiration of this time limit, the court shall appoint the arbitrator at the request of the initiating party.

Section 1030

A party is bound by its appointment of an arbitrator, vis-à-vis the other party, as soon as the latter receives a notice of the appointment.

Section 1031

If an arbitrator who was not designated in the arbitration agreement dies, is unavailable for any reason, or refuses to assume or perform his function in the arbitral proceedings, the party that appointed him shall, at the request of the other party, appoint another arbitrator within a week. If an appointment has not been made on expiration of this time limit, the arbitrator shall be appointed, at the request of the initiating party, by the competent court.

Section 1032

(1) An arbitrator may be challenged on the same grounds and under the same conditions as a judge.

(2) An arbitrator who was not designated in the arbitration agreement may also be challenged for undue delay in the fulfillment of his duties.

(3) Minors, deaf and mute persons, and persons incapacitated by a court decision from holding public office may also be challenged.

Section 1033

Unless provisions are made by the parties for such a contingency, the arbitration agreement ceases to have effect if any of the following takes place:

(1) A person appointed as arbitrator in the arbitration agreement dies, is unavailable for any reason, refuses to assume the office, withdraws from the contract concluded with him, or unduly delays the fulfillment of his duties;

(2) The arbitrators notify the parties that they have reached a tie-vote.

Section 1034

(1) Before rendering the award, the arbitrators shall hear the parties and determine the facts pertaining to the subject matter of the dispute to such extent as they consider necessary. Lawyers may not be rejected as counsel; any agreements to the contrary shall be invalid. Persons excluded from oral argument in the ordinary courts under section 157 of this Code may be rejected.

(2) In all other matters, and insofar as the parties have not reached an agreement, the procedure shall be determined by the arbitrators at their discretion.

Section 1035

(1) Arbitrators may hear witnesses and experts who voluntarily appear before them.

(2) Arbitrators are not authorized to administer an oath to a witness, an expert, or a party.

Section 1036

(1) Judicial acts that are deemed necessary by the arbitrators, but that they are not authorized to perform, shall be performed by the competent court on the request of a party if such a request is deemed admissible.

(2) The court that has ordered the testimony of a witness or an expert, or has administered an oath, is also competent to make a decision in case of a refusal to either testify or give an expert opinion.

Section 1037

Arbitrators may continue arbitral proceedings and make the award even if it is asserted that the arbitral proceedings are inadmissible, particularly if it is claimed that there is no valid arbitration agreement, that the dispute does not fall within the terms of the arbitration agreement, or that an arbitrator is not authorized to act in that capacity.

Section 1038

If the award is to be rendered by several arbitrators, an absolute majority of votes shall be decisive unless the arbitration agreement provides otherwise.

Section 1039

(1) The award shall be dated and signed by the arbitrators. If the arbitral tribunal consists of more than two members and the signature of one of the arbitrators, although he participated in the voting on the award, cannot be obtained, the signature of the remaining arbitrators shall be sufficient. The presiding arbitrator shall make a note underneath the award that the signature of such arbitrator could not be obtained.

(2) A copy of the arbitral award shall be delivered to each party unless they have agreed to another means of notification.

(3) The award shall be deposited with the clerk of the competent court; however, except in the case of a declaration of enforceability, the parties may agree otherwise. The certificate of delivery or, if another means of notification has been agreed to, a proof of notification shall accompany the award.

Section 1040

The award has the legal effect for the parties of a final court judgment.

Section 1041

(1) An application to set aside an award may be made

1. if the award is not based on a valid arbitration agreement or it is based on an otherwise inadmissible procedure;
2. if the recognition of the award leads to a result that is obviously incompatible with the essential principles of German law, in particular, if the recognition violates basic constitutional rights;
3. if a party was not represented in the proceedings in accordance with the provisions of the law unless the party had consented to, or acquiesced in, the manner in which the proceedings were conducted;
4. if a party was not granted an opportunity to be heard in the course of the proceedings;
5. if the award does not state reasons;
6. if those conditions under which an action for judicial review may be brought, in accordance with the provisions of section 580, numbers 1 - 6, are fulfilled.

(2) An award shall not be set aside on the ground specified in number 5 of the preceding subsection if the parties have provided otherwise.

Section 1042

(1) An award can be enforced only if it has been declared enforceable.

(2) The application for a declaration of enforceability shall be denied and the award shall be set aside, should any ground specified in section 1041 for the setting aside of the award exist.

Section 1042a

(1) An application for a declaration of enforceability may be decided on without conducting a hearing and by court order; the respondent shall be heard before the decision is rendered. In case of a hearing, the decision shall take the form of a judgment.

(2) If a ground for setting aside the award is claimed, a hearing shall be ordered unless prompt denial of the application appears to be justified.

Section 1042b

(1) The application shall be accompanied by a requisite number of copies for service.

(2) If a hearing is ordered, the parties shall be notified of the date *ex officio*. In proceedings before the district court, the notification shall contain the request specified in section 215.

Section 1042c

(1) The order by which the award is declared enforceable shall be enforceable provisionally.

(2) The order is subject to objection. If an objection is raised, the decision on the

declaration of the enforceability of the award shall be made in the form of a judgment. The provisions of sections 707 to 717 shall apply accordingly.

(3) The decision denying an application for the declaration of enforceability is subject to immediate appeal.

Section 1042d

(1) The objection must be filed within two weeks of the service by submitting a written statement of objection. Paragraph 2 of section 339 shall apply accordingly. The statement of objection shall, at the same time, contain whatever is necessary to the preparation for the hearing.

(2) The parties shall be notified of the date of the hearing *ex officio*. The statement of objection shall be served on the opposing party *ex officio*, together with the notification.

Section 1043

(1) If the award has been declared enforceable and is final, it can be set aside only on the grounds specified in section 1041, paragraph 1, number 6; and the application can be made only if there is a basis to believe that the party, without being at fault, was unable to invoke such ground in the previous proceedings.

(2) The action must be commenced within a strict time limit of one month. This time period begins to run the day the party becomes aware of the existence of the ground for setting aside the award, but not before the decision on the declaration of enforceability has become final. After the expiration of a period of ten years from the day the decision became final, the application is inadmissible.

(3) If the award is set aside, the declaration of enforceability shall also be set aside.

Section 1044

(1) A foreign award that has become binding on the parties in accordance with the applicable law shall be enforced in accordance with the procedure prescribed for domestic awards, unless a treaty provides otherwise. Section 1039 shall not apply.

(2) The application for the declaration of enforceability shall be rejected if

1. the award is invalid; the validity of an award is determined by the law applicable to the arbitral proceedings, unless a treaty provides otherwise;

2. the recognition of the award leads to a result that is obviously incompatible with the essential principles of German law, in particular, if the recognition violates basic constitutional rights;

3. the party was not duly represented unless it had consented to, or acquiesced in, the manner in which the proceedings were conducted;

4. the party was not given the opportunity to be heard in the course of the proceedings.

(3) A declaration that recognition of the award has been denied in this country shall be issued in lieu of an order for the setting aside of the award.

(4) If an award is set aside abroad after it has been declared enforceable, an action for setting aside of the declaration of enforceability may be brought. The pro-

visions of paragraphs 2 and 3 of section 1043 shall apply analogously, subject to the condition that the strict time limit for such action shall commence on the day the party becomes aware of the final decision to set aside the award.

Section 1044a

(1) If the debtor in an arbitral settlement has consented to immediate enforcement, the settlement shall be enforced if it has been declared enforceable. A settlement may be declared enforceable only if it is dated and signed by the arbitrators and the parties, and if it is deposited with the clerk of the competent court.

(2) The declaration of enforceability shall be rejected if the settlement is invalid or its recognition violates public morals or public policy.

(3) The provisions of section 1042a to 1042d shall apply analogously; the claim of invalidity of the settlement has the same standing as the claim that there are grounds for setting aside the award.

Section 1045

(1) Jurisdiction with respect to judicial decisions on the appointment or the challenge of an arbitrator, on the termination of an arbitration agreement, or on the ordering of such court actions as are deemed necessary by the arbitrators is vested with the magistrate's court (Amtsgericht) or district court (Landgericht)

1. which is specified as such in the arbitration agreement; or
2. which would have jurisdiction were the claim to be asserted in court; or
3. in whose district the arbitral proceedings are taking place or have taken place.

(2) The decision may be rendered without an oral hearing. Prior to the decision, the opponent shall be heard.

(3) The decision is subject to immediate appeal.

Section 1046

The court designated in section 1045, paragraph 1 also has jurisdiction in matters concerning the declaration of enforceability of arbitral awards and settlements, as well as with regard to actions for the inadmissibility of arbitral proceedings, the setting aside of an award or of its declaration of enforceability, or the invalidity of a settlement.

Section 1047

From among several courts competent under sections 1045 and 1046, the court whose assistance was first sought by a party or the tribunal (section 1039) is and continues to be the competent court.

Section 1048

The provisions of this book shall apply analogously to arbitral tribunals that will lawfully be established by testamentary dispositions or dispositions not based on agreement.

b. German Law on Restrictive Trade Practices.[2]

Section 91

(1) Arbitration agreements with regard to future disputes arising out of agreements or decisions of the kind specified in sections 1 to 5b, 7, 8, 29, 99, paragraph 2, numbers 1a to 4, sections 100, 102, 102a, and 103, or claims within the meaning of section 35 are void if they do not grant each party the right in a particular case to seek a court decision in lieu of an arbitral decision. Arbitration agreements with regard to future disputes arising out of agreements or decisions of the kind specified in section 6 that do not grant each party the right in a particular case to seek a court decision in lieu of an arbitral tribunal decision are invalid unless the antitrust authority, on request, grants permission.

(2) Paragraphs 2 and 3 of section 1027 of the Code of Civil Procedure shall not apply to arbitration agreements within the meaning of paragraph 1 that are concluded with respect to existing legal disputes.

(3) Clause 3 of paragraph 1 of section 14 of the Law on Copyright and Other Protected Rights of September 9, 1965 (BGBl 1965 I at 1294) is not affected.

---

2. Gesetz gegen Wettbewerbsbeschränkungen (Kartell Gesetz) BGBl 1957 I at 1801, as modified by Law of September 9, 1980, BGBl. 1980 I at 1761. Translated by Luigi Fernando and Frank Koerner.

c. Decree on the Arbitration of Copyright Disputes[3]

On the basis of section 15 of the Copyright Protection Act as amended by Article 2, no. 8, of the Act of 24 June 1985, it is decreed as follows:

Section 1

(1) A written application for reference to the Arbitration Board pursuant to section 14(4) of the Copyright Protection Act must state the name and address of the defendant and a statement of the facts. The application should be lodged in duplicate.

(2) The Arbitration Board will serve the application on the defendant with a request to reply in writing within one month.

(3) If a copyright society seeks the conclusion of a global agreement the defendant may declare that he is not willing to enter into the agreement. If he gives this declaration, the proceedings are to be discontinued; they shall also be discontinued if he fails to reply within one month. The defendant must be informed of this.

Section 2

(1) The application may be withdrawn, but, in the case of proceedings where the parties are to be heard, this may be done without the defendant's consent only before the hearing begins.

(2) If the application is withdrawn, the claimant shall meet the costs of the proceedings and expenses necessarily incurred by the defendant.

Section 3

(1) In disputes concerning the conclusion or amendment of a global agreement the Arbitration Board shall decide on the basis of a hearing.

(2) If a hearing is not required by the parties it may be dispensed with.

Section 4

In disputes pursuant to section 14(1), No. 1, of the Copyright Protection Act the Arbitration Board shall decide by way of written proceedings. The board shall decide on the basis of a hearing if one of the parties requests it and the other consents or if, exceptionally, the board considers a hearing to agree to an attempt at conciliation without the arbitrators being present. The chairman must do so if this is requested by both parties.

Section 5

In disputes concerning the conclusion or amendment of a global agreement the chairman may, with the parties' consent, invite them prior to the hearing to agree to an attempt at conciliation without the arbitrators being present. The chairman must do so if this is requested by both parties.

---

3. BGBl 1985 I at 2543. Translation from 9 *Commercial Laws of Europe* 267 (1986). Reproduced with the permission of the publisher.

Section 6

(1) The parties are to be summoned to the hearing. At least two weeks' notice must be given.

(2) The hearing before the Arbitration Board shall not be in public. Representatives of the Federal Minister of Justice, the Supervisory Authority, and the Federal Cartel Office may attend.

(3) Section 157 of the Code of Civil Procedure shall apply by analogy to the dismissal of authorized representatives or advisers of the parties or to the prohibition of submission. It shall not be necessary to seek permission to make oral submissions before the Arbitration Board.

(4) A minute shall be taken of the hearing and signed by the chairman and the secretary.

(5) The parties need not be noticed verbally of the terms of the compromise proposal.

Section 7

(1) If the claimant does not appear at the hearing, the reference for arbitration will be deemed to have been withdrawn. However, the claimant may apply for restoration of the previous position. The provisions of the Code of Civil Procedure shall apply by analogy to restoration of the *status quo ante.*

(2) If the defendant does not appear at the hearing, the Arbitration Board may decide on the basis of the documents.

(3) Parties who fail to appear without being excused shall pay the costs incurred as a result of their nonappearance.

(4) The summons to the hearing must inform the parties of the consequences of failure to appear.

Section 8

(1) The Arbitration Board shall not be bound by offers of evidence. It shall make inquiries of its own motion and shall take such evidence as is necessary and appears appropriate. The parties shall be given an opportunity to state their observations on the results of the inquiries and evidence.

(2) Subject to subsection 3, the Arbitration Board may examine parties and witnesses, have experts' reports prepared, and obtain the opinion of associations of users and copyright societies that are not parties to the proceedings.

(3) The District Court (Amtsgericht) within whose jurisdiction the Arbitration Board sits shall, at the request of the Board, examine a witness who does not appear before the Arbitration Board voluntarily or refuses to make a statement, obtain a report from an expert who does not appear before the Board voluntarily or refuses to prepare a report, and administer an oath, if the Board considers this necessary, to a witness, expert or party.

(4) The provisions of the Organization of the Courts Act, particularly those concerning letters rogatory and those of the Code of Civil Procedure, shall apply by analogy.

Section 9

Rulings on the disqualification and challenging of members of the Arbitration Board shall be given by the District Court within whose jurisdiction the board sits. The application for discharge shall be submitted to the board. The provisions of the Code of Civil Procedure shall apply by analogy.

Section 10

In other respects the Board shall proceed according to its own discretion. In doing so, it shall act in conformity with the provisions of the Code of Civil Procedure.

Section 11

(1) If the Arbitration Board has honorary members, they shall receive, on application, remuneration in accordance with sections 2 to 5 and 9 to 11 of the Act on the Remuneration of Honorary Judges.

(2) Remuneration will be fixed by the supervisory authority.

(3) An honorary member may apply for remuneration to be fixed by the court. A ruling on the application shall be given by the District Court within whose jurisdiction the Board sits. The application must be submitted to the supervisory authority or placed on record at the registry. The supervisory authority may rectify the application. Costs are not recoverable.

Section 12

(1) Witnesses and experts shall receive remuneration pursuant to sections 2 to 6, 8 to 12 and 14 of the Act on the Remuneration of Witnesses and Experts section 7(1), (2), sentences 1 and 2, and section 15 of this Act shall apply by analogy.

(2) Section 11(2) and (3) shall apply by analogy.

(3) A decision fixing remuneration shall not take effect against the party liable for costs.

Section 13

(1) The supervisory authority shall charge a fee and expenses (costs) for proceedings before the Arbitration Board.

(2) The fee shall depend on the value of the subject matter in dispute and shall be determined according to the table in Annex 2 to the Court Costs Act. For the minimum fee, section 11(3) of that act shall apply by analogy.

(3) The value of the subject matter in dispute shall be determined by the board. It shall be calculated according to the provisions of the Code of Civil Procedure relating to proceedings before the ordinary courts.

(4) In proceedings pursuant to section 3, sentence 1, no fee shall be payable if the application is withdrawn or the proceedings are discontinued prior to a hearing. If the application is withdrawn before hearing of evidence, the fee shall be reduced to one third. In proceedings pursuant to section 3, sentence 2, and section 4, the board may waive or reduce the fee as it thinks fit if the application is withdrawn or the proceedings are discontinued.

(5) Expenses will be charged by applying numbers 1900 to 1912 of the tariffs schedule to the Court Costs Act.

(6) The fee shall be payable on termination of the proceedings and expenses immediately after they are incurred.

(7) Service of the application shall be conditional on the payment by the claimant of an advance equal to one third of the fee. In cases within section 1(3) the advance shall be demanded only when it is clear that the proceedings will be continued.

(8) The provisions of section 2(1), (2) and (4), sections 7, 8, 10, 49, 54, 56, 58, 59 and 68 of the Court Costs Act relating to exemption from costs, subsequent demand, nonrecovery and time-barring of costs, the party liable to pay the costs and advances for expenses, shall apply by analogy.

(9) Appeals against administrative acts in the execution of provisions on costs shall be decided, in proceedings relating to the conclusion or amendment of a global agreement, by the regional court of appeal (*Oberlandesgericht*); otherwise by the district court in whose jurisdiction the supervisory authority has its head office. Appeals shall be lodged with the Arbitration Board or the supervisory authority. Sections 4(3) and 5(3) and (4) of the Court Costs Act shall apply by analogy.

Section 14

(1) Unless otherwise provided, the Arbitration Board shall apportion the costs of the proceedings as it thinks fit. The board may order the expenses necessarily incurred by one party to be recovered entirely or partly from the other side if this is fair.

(2) The decision on costs may be challenged by an application for a court ruling, even if the Arbitration Board's compromise proposal is accepted. In proceedings relating to the conclusion or alteration of a global agreement the application shall be decided upon by the Regional Court of Appeal and otherwise the District Court in whose jurisdiction the Arbitration Board sits.

Section 15

(1) The costs of the proceedings (section 13) and the necessary expenses to be recovered by a party (section 14(1), sentence 2) shall be fixed by the supervisory authority. The party liable for costs must be notified of the amount fixed, and, where necessary expenses are fixed pursuant to section 14(1), sentence 2, the person entitled to reimbursement must also be notified of the amount.

(2) Any person affected may, within two weeks after service of the notice, apply for the amount of costs and recoverable necessary expenses to be fixed by the court. In the case of proceedings relating to the conclusion or alternation of a global agreement, the application shall be decided on by the regional court of appeal in whose jurisdiction the supervisory authority has its head office and in other cases by the District Court. The application must be submitted to the supervisory authority which may rectify it.

(3) The order fixing costs shall be enforced in accordance with the Code of Civil Procedure.

Section 16

Pursuant to section 14 of the Third Transference Act in conjunction with section 27 of the Copyright Protection Act, this decree shall also apply in Land Berlin.

Section 17

This decree shall come into force on January 1, 1986. At the same time, the Decree on the Arbitration Board by virtue of the Act on the Protection of Copyright and Related Rights of December 18, 1965, amended by the Decree of June 26, 1970, shall cease to have effect; however, it shall continue to apply to proceedings that were pending before January 1, 1986.

6. HONG KONG.

Laws of Hong Kong, Chapter 341, Arbitration

To make provision for arbitration in respect of civil matters.

PART I: Citation and Interpretation

1. Short title
This Ordinance may be cited as the Arbitration Ordinance.

2. Interpretation
(1) In this Ordinance, unless the context otherwise requires —

"arbitration agreement" has the same meaning as in article 7(1) of the UNCI-TRAL Model Law;

"Convention award" means an award to which Part IV applies, namely, an award made in pursuance of an arbitration agreement in a State or territory, other than Hong Kong, which is a party to the New York [Arbitration] Convention;

"Court" means the High Court;

"dispute" includes a difference;

"domestic arbitration agreement" means an arbitration agreement that is not an international arbitration agreement;

"foreign award" means an award to which Part III applies;

"international arbitration agreement" means an arbitration agreement pursuant to which an arbitration is, or would if commenced be, international within the meaning of article 1(3) of the UNCITRAL Model Law;

"the New York [Arbitration] Convention" means the Convention on the Recognition and Enforcement of Foreign Arbitral Awards adopted by the United Nations Conference on International Commercial Arbitration on 10 June 1958 the text of which is set out in the Third Schedule;

"the UNCITRAL Model Law" means the Model Law on International Trade Law adopted by the United Nations Commission on International Trade Law on 21 June 1985, the text of which is set out in the Fifth Schedule.

(2) Article 7(2) of the UNCITRAL Model Law shall apply to every arbitration agreement.

(3) In interpreting and applying the provisions of the UNCITRAL Model Law, regard shall be had to its international origin and to the need for uniformity in its interpretation, and regard may be had to the documents specified in the Sixth Schedule.

(4) In the UNCITRAL Model Law a reference to —

(*a*) "this State" shall be treated as being a reference to Hong Kong;

(*b*) "any agreement in force between this State and any other State or States" shall be treated as being a reference to any agreement that binds Hong Kong and any other place and that has the force of law in Hong Kong;

(*c*) "a State" shall be treated as including a reference to Hong Kong; and

(*d*) "different States" shall be treated as including a reference to Hong Kong and any other place.

PART IA: General

2A. Appointment of conciliator

(1) In any case where an arbitration agreement provides for the appointment of a conciliator by a person who is not one of the parties and that person refuses to make the appointment or does not make it within the time specified in the agreement or, if no time is so specified, within a reasonable time of being requested by any party to the agreement to make the appointment, the Court or a judge thereof may, on the application of any party to the agreement, appoint a conciliator who shall have the like powers to act in the conciliation proceedings as if he had been appointed in accordance with the terms of the agreement.

(2) Where an arbitration agreement provides for the appointment of a conciliator and further provides that the person so appointed shall act as an arbitrator in the event of the conciliation proceedings failing to produce a settlement acceptable to the parties —

(*a*) no objection shall be taken to the appointment of such person as an arbitrator, or to his conduct of the arbitration proceedings, solely on the ground that he had acted previously as a conciliator in connexion with some or all of the matters referred to arbitration;

(*b*) if such person declines to act as an arbitrator any other person appointed as an arbitrator shall not be required first to act as a conciliator unless a contrary intention appears in the arbitration agreement.

(3) Unless a contrary intention appears therein, an arbitration agreement which provides for the appointment of a conciliator shall be deemed to contain a provision that in the event of the conciliation proceedings failing to produce a settlement acceptable to the parties within 3 months, or such longer period as the parties may agree to, of the date of the appointment of the conciliator or, where he is appointed by name in the arbitration agreement, of the receipt by him of written notification of the existence of a dispute the proceedings shall thereupon terminate.

2B. Power of arbitrator to act as conciliator

(1) If all parties to a reference consent in writing, and for so long as no party withdraws in writing his consent, an arbitrator or umpire may act as a conciliator.

(2) An arbitrator or umpire acting as conciliator —

(*a*) may communicate with the parties to the reference collectively or separately;

(*b*) shall treat information obtained by him from a party to the reference as confidential, unless that party otherwise agrees or unless subsection (3) applies.

(3) Where confidential information is obtained by an arbitrator or umpire from a party to the reference during conciliation proceedings and those proceedings terminate without the parties reaching agreement in settlement of their dispute, the arbitrator or umpire shall, before resuming the arbitration proceedings, disclose to all other parties to the reference as much of that information as he considers is material to the arbitration proceedings.

(4) No objection shall be taken to the conduct of arbitration proceedings by an arbitrator or umpire solely on the ground that he had acted previously as a conciliator in accordance with this section.

2C. Settlement agreements

If the parties to an arbitration agreement reach agreement in settlement of their dispute and enter into an agreement in writing containing the terms of settlement (the "settlement agreement") the settlement agreement shall, for the purposes of its enforcement, be treated as an award on an arbitration agreement and may, by leave of the Court or a judge thereof, be enforced in the same manner as a judgment or order to the same effect and, where leave is so given, judgment may be entered in terms of the agreement.

2D. Proceedings to be heard otherwise than in open court

Proceedings under this Ordinance in the Court or Court of Appeal shall on the application of any party to the proceedings be heard otherwise than in open court.

2E. Restrictions on reporting of proceedings heard otherwise than in open court

(1) This section applies to proceedings under this Ordinance in the Court or Court of Appeal heard otherwise than in open court.

(2) A court in which proceedings to which this section applies are being heard shall, on the application of any party to the proceedings, give directions as to what information, if any, relating to the proceedings may be published.

(3) A court shall not give a direction under subsection (2) permitting information to be published unless —

   (a) all parties to the proceedings agree that such information may be published; or

   (b) the court is satisfied that the information, if published in accordance with such directions as it may give, would not reveal any matter, including the identity of any party to the proceedings, that any party to the proceedings reasonably wishes to remain confidential.

(4) Notwithstanding subsection (3), where a court gives a judgment in respect of proceedings to which this section applies and considers that judgment to be of major legal interest, it shall direct that reports of the judgment may be published in law reports and professional publications but, if any party to the proceedings reasonably wishes to conceal any matter, including the fact that he was such a party, the court shall —

   (a) give directions as to the action that shall be taken to conceal that matter in those reports; and (*b*) if it considers that a report published in accordance with directions given under paragraph (*a*) would be likely to reveal that matter, direct that no report shall be published until after the end of such period, not exceeding 10 years, as it considers appropriate.

2F. Representation and preparation work

For the avoidance of doubt, it is hereby declared that sections 44, 45 and 47 of the Legal Practitioners Ordinance (Cap. 159) do not apply to —

(*a*) arbitration proceedings;

(*b*) the giving of advice and the preparation of documents for the purpose of arbitration proceedings;

(*c*) any other thing done in relation to arbitration proceedings except where it is done in connection with court proceedings arising out of an arbitration agreement or arising in the course of, or resulting from, arbitration proceedings.

2G. Costs in respect of unqualified person

Section 50 of the Legal Practitioners Ordinance (Cap. 159), (which provides that no costs in respect of anything done by an unqualified person acting as a solicitor shall be recoverable in any action, suit or matter) shall not apply to the recovery of costs directed by an award.

2H. Enforcement of award

An award on an arbitration agreement may, by leave of the Court or a judge thereof, be enforced in the same manner as a judgment or order to the same effect and, where leave is so given, judgment may be entered in terms of the award.

2I. Crown to be bound

This Part and Parts II and IIA bind the Crown.

2J. Application to statutory arbitrations

(1) This Ordinance, except the provisions specified in subsection (2), shall apply to every arbitration under any other enactment, whether passed before or after the commencement of this Ordinance, as if the arbitration were pursuant to a domestic arbitration agreement and as if that other enactment were a domestic arbitration agreement, except in so far as —

(*a*) this Ordinance is inconsistent with that other enactment or with any rules or procedure authorized or recognized thereby; or

(*b*) that other enactment otherwise provides.

(2) The provisions referred to in subsection (1) are sections 4(1), 5, 7, 20(3), 26, 27 and 29.

2K. Governor in Council may amend Sixth Schedule

The Governor in Council may by order published in the Gazette amend the Sixth Schedule.

PART II: Domestic Arbitration

Application

2L. Application to domestic arbitration agreements

This Part applies to a domestic arbitration agreement and to an arbitration pursuant to a domestic arbitration agreement, except where a dispute has arisen and the parties to the dispute have subsequently agreed in writing —

(*a*) that Part IIA is to apply; or

(*b*) that the agreement is, or is to be treated as, an international arbitration agreement; or

(*c*) that the dispute is to be arbitrated as an international arbitration.

2M. Application to international arbitration agreements

This Part applies to an international arbitration agreement and to an arbitration pursuant to an international arbitration agreement if, but only if, the agreement provides or the parties to the reference agree in writing —

(*a*) that this Part is to apply; or

(*b*) that the agreement is, or is to be treated as, a domestic arbitration agreement; or

(*c*) that a dispute is to be arbitrated as a domestic arbitration.

Effect of Arbitration Agreements, etc.

3. Authority of arbitrators and umpires to be irrevocable

The authority of an arbitrator or umpire appointed by or by virtue of an arbitrator, agreement shall, unless a contrary intention is expressed in the agreement, be irrevocable except by leave of the Court or a judge thereof.

4. Death of party

(1) An arbitration agreement shall not be discharged by the death of any party thereto, either as respects the deceased or any other party, but shall in such an event be enforceable by or against the personal representative of the deceased.

(2) The authority of an arbitrator shall not be revoked by the death of any party by whom he was appointed.

(3) Nothing in this section shall be taken to affect the operation of any enactment or rule of law by virtue of which any right of action is extinguished by the death of a person.

5. Bankruptcy

(1) Where it is provided by a term in a contract to which a bankrupt is a party that any disputes arising thereout or in connexion therewith shall be referred to arbitration, the said term shall, if the trustee in bankruptcy adopts the contract, be

enforceable by or against him so far as relates to any such disputes. (*Amended 64 of 1989 s. 8*)

(2) Where a person who has been adjudged bankrupt had, before the commencement of the bankruptcy, become a party to an arbitration agreement, and any matter to which the agreement applies requires to be determined in connexion with or for the purposes of the bankruptcy proceedings, then, if the case is one to which subsection (1) does not apply, any other party to the agreement, or, with the consent of the committee of inspection, the trustee in bankruptcy, may apply to the Court for an order directing that the matter in question shall be referred to arbitration in accordance with the agreement, and the Court may, if it is of opinion that, having regard to all the circumstances of the case, the matter ought to be determined by arbitration, make an order accordingly.

6. Staying court proceedings where there is submission to arbitration

(1) If any party to an arbitration agreement, or any person claiming through or under him, commences any legal proceedings in any court against any other party to the agreement, or any person claiming through or under him, in respect of any matter agreed to be referred, any party to those legal proceedings may at any time after appearance, and before delivering any pleadings or taking any other steps in the proceedings, apply to that court to stay the proceedings, and that court or a judge thereof, if satisfied that there is no sufficient reason why the matter should not be referred in accordance with the agreement, and that the applicant was, at the time when the proceedings were commenced, and still remains, ready and willing to do all things necessary to the proper conduct of the arbitration, may make an order staying the proceedings.

6A. (Repealed 64 of 1989 s. 9)

6B. Consolidation of arbitrations

(1) Where in relation to two or more arbitration proceedings it appears to the Court —
(*a*) that some common question of law or fact arises in both or all of them, or
(*b*) that the rights to relief claimed therein are in respect of or arise out of the same transaction or series of transactions, or
(*c*) that for some other reason it is desirable to make an order under this section,
the Court may order those arbitration proceedings to be consolidated on such terms as it thinks just or may order them to be heard at the same time, or one immediately after another, or may order any of them to be stayed until after the determination of any other of them.

(2) Where the Court orders arbitration proceedings to be consolidated under subsection (1) and all parties to the consolidated arbitration proceedings are in agreement as to the choice of arbitrator or umpire for those proceedings the same shall be appointed by the Court but if all parties cannot agree the Court shall have power to appoint an arbitrator or umpire for those proceedings.

(3) Where the Court makes an appointment under subsection (2) of an arbitrator or umpire for consolidated arbitration proceedings, any appointment of any other arbitrator or umpire that has been made for any of the arbitration proceedings forming part of the consolidation shall for all purposes cease to have effect on and from the appointment under subsection (2).

7. Reference of interpleader issues to arbitration

Where relief by way of interpleader is granted and it appears to the Court that the claims in question are matters to which an arbitration agreement, to which the claimants are parties, applies, the Court may direct the issue between the claimants to be determined in accordance with the agreement.

Arbitrators and Umpires

8. When reference is to a single arbitrator

Unless a contrary intention is expressed therein, every arbitration agreement shall, if no other mode of reference is provided, be deemed to include a provision that the reference shall be to a single arbitrator.

9. Power of parties in certain cases to supply vacancy

Where an arbitration agreement provides that the reference shall be to 2 arbitrators, one to be appointed by each party, then, unless a contrary intention is expressed therein —

(*a*) if either of the appointed arbitrators refuses to act, or is incapable of acting, or dies, the party who appointed him may appoint a new arbitrator in his place;

(*b*) if, on such a reference, one party fails to appoint an arbitrator, either originally, or by way of substitution as aforesaid, for 7 clear days after the other party, having appointed his arbitrator, has served the party making default with notice to make the appointment, the party who has appointed an arbitrator may appoint that arbitrator to act as sole arbitrator in the reference and his award shall be binding on both parties as if he had been appointed by consent:

Provided that the Court or a judge thereof may set aside any appointment made in pursuance of this section.

10. Umpires

(1) Unless a contrary intention is expressed therein, every arbitration agreement shall, where the reference is to 2 arbitrators, be deemed to include a provision that the 2 arbitrators may appoint an umpire at any time after they are themselves appointed and shall do so forthwith if they cannot agree. (*Amended 10 of 1982 s. 4*)

(2) Unless a contrary intention is expressed therein, every arbitration agreement shall, where such a provision is applicable to the reference, be deemed to include a provision that if the arbitrators have delivered to any party to the arbitration agree-

ment, or to the umpire, a notice in writing stating that they cannot agree, the umpire may forthwith enter on the reference in lieu of the arbitrators.

(3) At any time after the appointment of an umpire, however appointed, the Court may, on the application of any party to the reference and notwithstanding anything to the contrary in the arbitration agreement, order that the umpire shall enter upon the reference in lieu of the arbitrators and as if he were a sole arbitrator.

11. *Majority award of 3 arbitrators*

Unless the contrary intention is expressed in the arbitration agreement, in any case where there is a reference to 3 arbitrators, the award of any 2 of the arbitrators shall be binding and in the event that no 2 of the arbitrators agree the award, the award of the arbitrator appointed by the arbitrators to be chairman shall be binding.

12. *Power of Court in certain cases to appoint an arbitrator or umpire*

(1) In any of the following cases —

(*a*) where an arbitration agreement provides that the reference shall be to a single arbitrator, and all the parties do not, after disputes have arisen, concur in the appointment of an arbitrator;

(*b*) if an appointed arbitrator refuses to act, or is incapable of acting, or dies, and the arbitration agreement does not show that it was intended that the vacancy should not be supplied and the parties do not supply the vacancy;

(*c*) where a party or an arbitrator is required or is at liberty to appoint, or concur in the appointment of, an umpire or an arbitrator and does not do so;

(*d*) where an appointed umpire or third arbitrator refuses to act, or is incapable of acting, or dies, and the arbitration agreement does not show that it was intended that the vacancy should not be supplied, and the parties or arbitrators do not supply the vacancy,

any party may serve the other parties or the arbitrators, as the case may be, with a written notice to appoint, or, as the case may be, concur in appointing, an arbitrator, umpire or third arbitrator, and if the appointment is not made within 7 clear days after the service of the notice, the Court or a judge thereof may, on application by the party who gave the notice, appoint an arbitrator, umpire or third arbitrator who shall have the like powers to act in the reference and make an award as if he had been appointed by consent of all parties.

(2) In any case where —

(*a*) an arbitration agreement provides for the appointment of an arbitrator or umpire by a person who is neither one of the parties nor an existing arbitrator (whether the provision applies directly or in default of agreement by the parties or otherwise); and

(*b*) that person refuses to make the appointment or does not make it within the time specified in the agreement or, if no time is so specified, within a reasonable time,

any party to the agreement may serve the person in question with a written notice to appoint an arbitrator or umpire and, if the appointment is not made within 7 clear days after the service of the notice, the Court or a judge thereof may, on the application of the party who gave the notice, appoint an arbitrator or umpire who shall have the like powers to act in the reference and make an award as if he had been appointed in accordance with the terms of the agreement.

13. (Repealed 52 of 1987 s. 45)

13A. Power of judges to take arbitrations

(1) Subject to the following provisions of this section a judge, District Judge, magistrate or public officer, may, if in all the circumstances he thinks fit, accept appointment as a sole or joint arbitrator, or as umpire, by or by virtue of an arbitration agreement.

(2) A judge, District Judge or magistrate shall not accept appointment as an arbitrator or umpire unless the Chief Justice has informed him that, having regard to the state of business in the courts, he can be made available to do so.

(3) A public officer shall not accept appointment as an arbitrator or umpire unless the Attorney General has informed him that he can be made available to do so.

(4) The fees payable for the services of a judge, District Judge, magistrate or public officer as an arbitrator or umpire shall be paid into the general revenue. (*Amended 64 of 1989 s. 11*)

(5) The Fourth Schedule shall have effect for modifying, and in certain cases replacing, provisions of this Ordinance in relation to arbitration by a judge as a sole arbitrator or umpire and, in particular, for substituting the Court of Appeal for the Court in provisions whereby arbitrators and umpires, their proceedings and awards, are subject to control and review by the Court.

(6) Subject to section 23C(3) any jurisdiction which is exercisable by the Court in relation to arbitrators and umpires otherwise than under this Ordinance shall, in relation to a judge appointed as a sole arbitrator or umpire, be exercisable instead by the Court of Appeal.

Conduct of Proceedings, Witnesses, etc.

14. Conduct of proceedings, witnesses, etc.

(1) Unless a contrary intention is expressed therein, every arbitration agreement shall, where such a provision is applicable to the reference, be deemed to contain a provision that the parties to the reference, and all persons claiming through them respectively, shall, subject to any legal objection, submit to be examined by the arbitrator or umpire, on oath or affirmation, in relation to the matters in dispute, and shall, subject as aforesaid, produce before the arbitrator or umpire all documents within their possession or power respectively which may be required or called for, and do all other things which during the proceedings on the reference the arbitrator or umpire may require.

(2) Unless a contrary intention is expressed therein, every arbitration agreement shall, where such a provision is applicable to the reference, be deemed to contain a

provision that the witnesses on the reference shall, if the arbitrator or umpire thinks fit, be examined on oath or affirmation.

(3) An arbitrator or umpire shall, unless a contrary intention is expressed in the arbitration agreement, have power to administer oaths to, or take the affirmations of, the parties to and witnesses on a reference under the agreement.

(3A) An arbitrator or umpire may receive any evidence that he considers relevant and shall not be bound by the rules of evidence.

(4) Any party to a reference under an arbitration agreement may sue out a writ of subpoena ad testificandum or a writ of subpoena duces tecum, but no person shall be compelled under any such writ to produce any document which he could not be compelled to produce on the trial of an action, and the Court or a judge thereof may order that a writ of subpoena ad testificandum or of subpoena duces tecum shall issue to compel the attendance before an arbitrator or umpire of a witness wherever he may be within Hong Kong.

(5) The Court or a judge thereof may also order that a writ of habeas corpus ad testificandum shall issue to bring up a prisoner for examination before an arbitrator or umpire.

(6) The Court shall have, for the purpose of and in relation to a reference, the same power of making orders in respect of —

(*a*) security for costs;

(*b*) discovery of documents and interrogatories;

(*c*) the giving of evidence by affidavit;

(*d*) examination on oath of any witness before an officer of the Court or any other person, and the issue of a commission or request for the examination of a witness out of the jurisdiction;

(*e*) the preservation, interim custody or sale of any goods which are the subject matter of the reference;

(*f*) securing the amount in dispute in the reference;

(*g*) the detention, preservation or inspection of any property or thing which is the subject of the reference or as to which any question may arise therein, and authorizing for any of the purposes aforesaid any person to enter upon or into any land or building in the possession of any party to the reference, or authorizing any samples to be taken or any observation to be made or experiment to be tried which may be necessary or expedient for the purpose of obtaining full information or evidence; and

(*h*) interim injunctions or the appointment of a receiver,

as it has for the purpose of and in relation to an action or matter in the Court: Provided that nothing in this subsection shall be taken to prejudice any power which may be vested in an arbitrator or umpire of making orders with respect to any of the matters aforesaid.

14A. *(Repealed 64 of 1989 s. 13)*

Provisions as to Awards

15. Time for making award

(1) Subject to the provisions of section 24(2) and anything to the contrary in the arbitration agreement, an arbitrator or umpire shall have power to make an award at any time.

(2) The time, if any, limited for making an award, whether under this Ordinance or otherwise, may from time to time be enlarged by order of the Court or a judge thereof, whether that time has expired or not.

(3) The Court may, on the application of any party to a reference, remove an arbitrator or umpire who fails to use all reasonable dispatch in entering on and proceeding with the reference and making an award, and an arbitrator or umpire who is removed by the Court under this subsection shall not be entitled to receive any remuneration in respect of his services.

For the purposes of this subsection, the expression "proceeding with a reference" includes, in a case where 2 arbitrators are unable to agree, giving notice of that fact to the parties and to the umpire.

16. Interim awards

Unless a contrary intention is expressed therein every arbitration agreement shall, where such a provision is applicable to the reference, be deemed to contain a provision that the arbitrator or umpire may, if he thinks fit, make an interim award, and any reference in this Part to an award includes a reference to an interim award.

17. Specific performance

Unless a contrary intention is expressed therein, every arbitration agreement shall, where such a provision is applicable to the reference, be deemed to contain a provision that the arbitrator or umpire shall have the same power as the Court to order specific performance of any contract other than a contract relating to land or any interest in land.

18. Awards to be filed

Unless a contrary intention is expressed therein, every arbitration agreement shall, where such a provision is applicable to the reference, be deemed to contain a provision that the award to be made by the arbitrator or umpire shall be final and binding on the parties and the persons claiming under them respectively.

19. Power to correct slips

Unless a contrary intention is expressed in the arbitration agreement, the arbitrator or umpire shall have power to correct in an award any clerical mistake or error arising from any accidental slip or omission.

Costs, Fees and Interest

20. Costs

(1) Unless a contrary intention is expressed therein, every arbitration agreement shall be deemed to include a provision that the costs of the reference and award shall be in the discretion of the arbitrator or umpire, who may direct to and by whom and in what manner those costs or any part thereof shall be paid, and may tax or settle the amount of costs to be so paid or any part thereof, and may award costs to be paid as between solicitor and client.

(2) Any costs directed by an award to be paid shall, unless the award otherwise directs, be taxable in the Court.

(2A) (*Repealed 64 of 1989 s. 14*)

(3) Any provision in an arbitration agreement to the effect that the parties or any party thereto shall in any event pay their or his own costs of the reference or award or any part thereof shall be void, and this Part shall, in the case of an arbitration agreement containing any such provision, have effect as if that provision were not contained therein:

Provided that nothing in this subsection shall invalidate such a provision when it is a part of an agreement to submit to arbitration a dispute which has arisen before the making of that agreement.

(4) If no provision is made by an award with respect to the costs of the reference, any party to the reference may, within 14 days of the publication of the award or such further time as the Court or a judge thereof may direct, apply to the arbitrator for an order directing by and to whom those costs shall be paid, and thereupon the arbitrator shall, after hearing any party who may desire to be heard, amend his award by adding thereto such directions as he may think proper with respect to the payment of the costs of the reference.

(5) Section 70 of the Legal Practitioners Ordinance (Cap. 159), which empowers a court before which any proceeding is being heard or is pending to declare a solicitor employed in the proceedings entitled to a charge on the property recovered or preserved in the proceedings, for his taxed costs in reference thereto, shall apply as if an arbitration were a proceeding in the Court, and the Court may make declarations and orders accordingly.

21. Taxation of arbitrator's or umpire's fees

(1) If in any case an arbitrator or umpire refuses to deliver his award except on payment of the fees demanded by him, the Court may, on an application for the purpose, order that the arbitrator or umpire shall deliver the award to the applicant on payment into court by the applicant of the fees demanded, and further that the fees demanded shall be taxed by the taxing officer and that out of the money paid into court there shall be paid out to the arbitrator or umpire by way of fees such sum as may be found reasonable on taxation and that the balance of the money, if any, shall be paid out to the applicant.

(2) An application for the purposes of this section may be made by any party to the reference unless the fees demanded have been fixed by a written agreement

between him and the arbitrator or umpire.

(3) A taxation of fees under this section may be reviewed in the same manner as a taxation of costs.

(4) The arbitrator or umpire shall be entitled to appear and be heard on any taxation or review of taxation under this section.

22. *Interest on awards*

A sum directed to be paid by an award shall, unless the award otherwise directs, carry interest as from the date of the award and at the same rate as a judgment debt.

22A. *Interest for period prior to payment*

(1) Unless a contrary intention is expressed therein, every arbitration agreement shall, where such a provision is applicable to the reference, be deemed to contain a provision that the arbitrator or umpire may, if he thinks fit, award interest at such rate as he thinks fit —

> (*a*) on any sum which is the subject of the reference but which is paid before the award, for such period ending not later than the date of payment as he thinks fit; and
>
> (*b*) on any sum which he awards, for such period ending not later than the date of payment of that sum as he thinks fit.

(2) The power to award interest conferred on an arbitrator or umpire by subsection (1) is without prejudice to any other power of an arbitrator or umpire to award interest.

Judicial Review, Determination of Preliminary Point of Law, Exclusion Agreements, Interlocutory Orders, Remission and Setting Aside of Awards, etc.

23. *Judicial review of arbitration awards*

(1) Without prejudice to the right of appeal conferred by subsection (2) the Court shall not have jurisdiction to set aside or remit an award on an arbitration agreement on the ground of errors of fact or law on the face of the award.

(2) Subject to subsection (3) an appeal shall lie to the Court on any question of law arising out of an award made on an arbitration agreement; and on the determination of such an appeal the Court may by order —

> (*a*) confirm, vary or set aside the award; or
>
> (*b*) remit the award to the reconsideration of the arbitrator or umpire together with the Court's opinion on the question of law which was the subject of the appeal;

and where the award is remitted under paragraph (*b*) the arbitrator or umpire shall, unless the order otherwise directs, make his award within 3 months after the date of the order.

(3) An appeal under this section may be brought by any of the parties to the reference —

> (*a*) with the consent of all the other parties to the reference; or

(*b*) subject to section 23B, with the leave of the Court.

(4) The Court shall not grant leave under subsection (3)(*b*) unless it considers that, having regard to all the circumstances, the determination of the question of law concerned could substantially affect the rights of one or more of the parties to the arbitration agreement; and the Court may make any leave which it gives conditional upon the applicant complying with such conditions as it considers appropriate.

(5) Subject to subsection (6), if an award is made and, on an application made by any of the parties to the reference —

(*a*) with the consent of all the other parties to the reference; or

(*b*) subject to section 23B, with the leave of the Court,

it appears to the Court that the award does not or does not sufficiently set out the reasons for the award, the Court may order the arbitrator or umpire concerned to state the reasons for his award in sufficient detail to enable the Court, should an appeal be brought under this section, to consider any question of law arising out of the award.

(6) In any case where an award is made without any reason being given, the Court shall not make an order under subsection (5) unless it is satisfied —

(*a*) that before the award was made one of the parties to the reference gave notice to the arbitrator or umpire concerned that a reasoned award would be required; or

(*b*) that there is some special reason why such a notice was not given.

(7) No appeal shall lie to the Court of Appeal from a decision of the Court on an appeal under this section unless the Court or the Court of Appeal gives leave.

(8) Where the award of an arbitrator or umpire is varied on appeal, the award as varied shall have effect (except for the purposes of this section) as if it were the award of the arbitrator or umpire.

23A. Determination of preliminary point of law by Court

(1) Subject to subsection (2) and section 23B, on an application to the Court made by any of the parties to a reference —

(*a*) with the consent of an arbitrator who has entered on the reference or, if an umpire has entered on the reference, with his consent, or

(*b*) with the consent of all the other parties,

the Court shall have jurisdiction to determine any question of law arising in the course of the reference.

(2) The Court shall not entertain an application under subsection (1)(*a*) with respect to any question of law unless it is satisfied that —

(*a*) the determination of the application might produce substantial savings in costs to the parties; and

(*b*) the question of law is one in respect of which leave to appeal would be likely to be given under section 23(3)(*b*).

(3) A decision of the Court under subsection (1) shall be deemed to be a judgment of the Court within the meaning of section 14 of the Supreme Court Ordinance (Cap. 4) (appeals to the Court of Appeal), but no appeal shall lie from such a decision

unless the Court or the Court of Appeal gives leave.

(4) (*Repealed 64 of 1989 s. 15*)

23B. Exclusion agreements affecting rights under sections 23 and 23A

(1) Subject to the following provisions of this section and section 23C —

(*a*) the Court shall not, under section 23(3)(*b*), grant leave to appeal with respect to a question of law arising out of an award; and

(*b*) the Court shall not, under section 23(5)(*b*), grant leave to make an application with respect to an award; and

(*c*) no application may be made under section 23A(1)(*a*) with respect to a question of law,

if the parties to the reference in question have entered into an agreement in writing (in this section referred to as an "exclusion agreement") which excludes the right of appeal under section 23 in relation to that award or, in a case falling within paragraph (*c*), in relation to an award to which the determination of the question of law is material.

(2) If the parties to an exclusion agreement subsequently enter into an agreement in writing to revoke the exclusion agreement the provisions of subsection (1) shall cease to apply to the reference or references in question until such time as a further exclusion agreement is entered into by the parties.

(3) An exclusion agreement may be expressed so as to relate to a particular award, to awards under a particular reference or to any other description of awards, whether arising out of the same reference or not; and an agreement may be an exclusion agreement for the purposes of this section whether it is entered into before or after the passing of this Ordinance and whether or not it forms part of an arbitration agreement.

(4) (*Repealed 64 of 1989 s. 16*)

(5) Except as provided by subsection (1), sections 23 and 23A shall have effect notwithstanding anything in any agreement purporting —

(*a*) to prohibit or restrict access to the Court; or

(*b*) to restrict the jurisdiction of that Court; or

(*c*) to prohibit or restrict the making of a reasoned award.

(6) An exclusion agreement shall be of no effect in relation to an award made on, or a question of law arising in the course of a reference under, a statutory arbitration, that is to say, such an arbitration as is referred to in section 33(1).

(7) An exclusion agreement shall be of no effect in relation to an award made on, or a question of law arising in the course of a reference under, an arbitration agreement unless the exclusion agreement is entered into after the commencement of the arbitration in which the award is made or, as the case may be, in which the question of law arises. (*Amended 64 of 1989 s. 16*)

(8) (*Repealed 64 of 1989 s. 16*)

23C. Interlocutory orders

(1) If any party to a reference under an arbitration agreement fails within the

time specified in the order or, if no time is so specified, within a reasonable time to comply with an order made by the arbitrator or umpire in the course of the reference, then, on the application of the arbitrator or umpire or of any party to the reference, the Court may make an order extending the powers of the arbitrator or umpire as mentioned in subsection (2).

(2) If an order is made by the Court under this section, the arbitrator or umpire shall have power, to the extent and subject to any conditions specified in that order, to continue with the reference in default of appearance or of any other act by one of the parties in like manner as a judge of the Court might continue with proceedings in that court where a party fails to comply with an order of that court or a requirement of rules of court.

(3) Section 13A(6) shall not apply in relation to the power of the Court to make an order under this section, but in the case of a reference to a judge-arbitrator or judge-umpire that power shall be exercisable as in the case of any other reference to arbitration and also by the judge-arbitrator or judge-umpire himself.

(4) Anything done by a judge-arbitrator or judge-umpire in the exercise of the power conferred by subsection (3) shall be done by him in his capacity as judge of the Court and have effect as if done by that court.

(5) The preceding provisions of this section have effect notwithstanding anything in any agreement but do not derogate from any powers conferred on an arbitrator or umpire, whether by an arbitration agreement or otherwise.

(6) In this section "judge-arbitrator" and "judge-umpire" have the same meaning as in the Fourth Schedule.

24. Power to remit award

(1) In all cases of reference to arbitration the Court or a judge thereof may from time to time remit the matters referred, or any of them, to the reconsideration of the arbitrator or umpire.

(2) Where an award is remitted, the arbitrator or umpire shall, unless the order otherwise directs, make his award within 3 months after the date of the order.

25. Removal of arbitrator and setting aside of award

(1) Where an arbitrator or umpire has misconducted himself or the proceedings, the Court may remove him.

(2) Where an arbitrator or umpire has misconducted himself or the proceedings, or an arbitration or award has been improperly procured, the Court may set the award aside.

(3) Where an application is made to set aside an award, the Court may order that any money made payable by the award shall be brought into court or otherwise secured pending the determination of the application.

26. Power of Count to give relief where arbitrator is not impartial or the dispute involves question of fraud

(1) Where an agreement between any parties provides that disputes which may

arise in the future between them shall be referred to an arbitrator named or designated in the agreement, and after a dispute has arisen any party applies, on the ground that the arbitrator so named or designated is not or may not be impartial, for leave to revoke the authority of the arbitrator or for an injunction to restrain any other party or the arbitrator from proceeding with the arbitration, it shall not be a ground for refusing the application that the said party at the time when he made the agreement knew, or ought to have known that the arbitrator, by reason of his relation towards any other party to the agreement or of his connexion with the subject referred, might not be capable of impartiality.

(2) Where an agreement between any parties provides that disputes which may arise in the future between them shall be referred to arbitration, and a dispute which so arises involves the question whether any such party has been guilty of fraud, the Court shall, so far as may be necessary to enable that question to be determined by the Court, have power to order that the agreement shall cease to have effect and power to give leave to revoke the authority of any arbitrator or umpire appointed by or by virtue of the agreement.

(3) In any case where by virtue of this section the Court has power to order that an arbitration agreement shall cease to have effect or to give leave to revoke the authority of an arbitrator or umpire, the Court may refuse to stay any action brought in breach of the agreement.

27. Power of Court where arbitrator is removed or authority of arbitrator is revoked

(1) Where an arbitrator, not being a sole arbitrator, or 2 or more arbitrators, not being all the arbitrators, or an umpire who has not entered on the reference is or are removed by the Court, the Court may, on the application of any party to the arbitration agreement, appoint a person or persons to act as arbitrator or arbitrators or umpire in place of the person or persons so removed.

(2) Where the authority of an arbitrator or arbitrators or umpire is revoked by leave of the Court, or a sole arbitrator or all the arbitrators or an umpire who has entered on the reference is or are removed by the Court, the Court may, on the application of any party to the arbitration agreement, either —

> (*a*) appoint a person to act as sole arbitrator in place of the person or persons removed; or
>
> (*b*) order that the arbitration agreement shall cease to have effect with respect to the dispute referred.

(3) A person appointed under this section by the Court as an arbitrator or umpire shall have the like power to act in the reference and to make an award as if he had been appointed in accordance with the terms of the arbitration agreement.

(4) Where it is provided, whether by means of a provision in the arbitration agreement or otherwise, that an award under an arbitration agreement shall be a condition precedent to the bringing of an action with respect to any matter to which the agreement applies, the Court, if it orders, whether under this section or under any other enactment, that the agreement shall cease to have effect as regards any particular dispute, may further order that the provision making an award a condition prece-

dent to the bringing of an action shall also cease to have effect as regards that dispute.

Enforcement of Award

28. (Repealed 64 of 1989 s. 17)

Miscellaneous

29. Power of Court to extend time for commencing arbitration proceedings
   Where the terms of an agreement to refer future disputes to arbitration provide that any claims to which the agreement applies shall be barred unless notice to appoint an arbitrator is given or an arbitrator is appointed or some other step to commence arbitration proceedings is taken within a time fixed by the agreement, and a dispute arises to which the agreement applies, the Court, if it is of opinion that in the circumstances of the case undue hardship would otherwise be caused, and notwithstanding that the time so fixed has expired, may, on such terms, if any, as the justice of the case may require, but without prejudice to the provisions of any enactment limiting the time for the commencement of arbitration proceedings, extend the time for such period as it thinks proper.

29A. Delay in prosecuting claims
   (1) In every arbitration agreement, unless the contrary be expressly provided therein, there is an implied term that in the event of a difference arising which is capable of settlement by arbitration it shall be the duty of the claimant to exercise due diligence in the prosecution of his claim.
   (2) Where there has been undue delay by a claimant in instituting or prosecuting his claim pursuant to an arbitration agreement, then, on the application of the arbitrator or umpire or of any party to the arbitration proceedings, the Court may make an order terminating the arbitration proceedings and prohibiting the claimant from commencing further arbitration proceedings in respect of any matter which was the subject of the terminated proceedings.
   (3) The Court shall not make an order under subsection (2) unless it is satisfied that —
      (*a*) the delay has been intentional and contumelious; or
      (*b*)(i) there has been inordinate and inexcusable delay on the part of the claimant or his advisers; and
      (ii) that such delay will give rise to a substantial risk that it is not possible to have a fair trial of the issues in the arbitration proceedings or is such as is likely to cause or to have caused serious prejudice to the other parties to the arbitration proceedings either as between themselves and the claimant or between each other or between them and a third party.
   (4) A decision of the Court under subsection (2) shall be deemed to be a judg-

ment of the Court within the meaning of section 14 of the Supreme Court Ordinance (Cap. 4) (appeals to the Court of Appeal) but no appeal shall lie from such a decision unless the Court or the Court of Appeal gives leave.

30. *Terms as to cost, etc.*

Any order made under this Part may be made on such terms as to costs or otherwise (including, in the case of an order under section 6B or 29A, the remuneration of the arbitrator or umpire in respect of his services) as the authority making the order thinks just.

31. *Commencement of arbitration*

(1) An arbitration shall be deemed to be commenced when one party to the arbitration agreement serves on the other party or parties a notice requiring him or them to appoint or concur in appointing an arbitrator, or, where the arbitration agreement provides that the reference shall be to a person named or designated in the agreement, requiring him or them to submit the dispute to the person so named or designated.

(2) Any such notice as is mentioned in subsection (1) may be served either —

  (a) by delivering it to the person on whom it is to be served; or
  (b) by leaving it at the usual or last known place of abode in Hong Kong of that
      person; or
  (c) by sending it by post in a registered letter addressed to that person at his
      usual or last known place of abode in Hong Kong,

as well as in any other manner provided in the arbitration agreement, and where a notice is sent by post in manner prescribed by paragraph (c), service thereof shall, unless the contrary is proved, be deemed to have been effected at the time at which the letter would have been delivered in the ordinary course of post. (*Amended 64 of 1989 s. 23*)

32. (*Repealed 64 of 1989 s. 18*)

33. (*Repealed 64 of 1989 s. 19*)

34. *Transitional — Part II*

This Part shall not affect any arbitration commenced, within the meaning of section 31(1), before the commencement of this Ordinance, but shall apply to an arbitration so commenced after the commencement of this Ordinance under an agreement made before the commencement of this Ordinance.

PART IIA: International Arbitration

Application

34A. Application to international arbitration agreements
  (1) Subject to subsection (2), this Part applies to an international arbitration agreement and to an arbitration pursuant to an international arbitration agreement.
  (2) This Part does not apply to an international arbitration agreement, or to an arbitration pursuant to an international arbitration agreement, to which, by virtue of section 2M, Part II applies.

34B. Application to domestic arbitration agreements
  This Part applies to a domestic arbitration agreement, and to an arbitration pursuant to a domestic arbitration agreement, to which, by virtue of section 2L, Part II does not apply.

Application of the UNCITRAL Model Law

34C. Application of UNCITRAL Model Law
  (1) An arbitration agreement and an arbitration to which this Part applies are governed by Chapters I to VII of the UNCITRAL Model Law.
  (2) Article 1(1) of the UNCITRAL Model Law shall not have the effect of limiting the application of the UNCITRAL Model Law to international commercial arbitrations.
  (3) The court that is competent to perform the functions specified in article 6 of the UNCITRAL Model Law is the High Court.

34D. Costs and interest.
  (1) For the avoidance of doubt it is declared that in the case of an arbitration governed by the UNCITRAL Model Law, unless it is otherwise agreed by the parties,
    (*a*) the costs of the reference and award shall be in the discretion of the arbitral tribunal, which may make such orders for the assessment and payment of those costs as it thinks fit; and
    (*b*) the arbitral tribunal may, if it thinks fit, award interest at such rate as it thinks fit —
      (i) on any sum which is the subject of the reference but which is paid before the award, for such period ending not later than the date of payment as it thinks fit; and
      (ii) on any sum which it awards, for such period ending not later than the date of payment of that sum as it thinks fit.
  (2) In this section, "arbitral tribunal" has the same meaning as in article 2 of the UNCITRAL Model Law.

PART III: Enforcement of Certain Foreign Awards

35. Awards to which Part III applies

This Part shall apply to any award made after 28 July 1924 —

(*a*) in pursuance of an agreement for arbitration to which the protocol set out in the First Schedule applies; and

(*b*) between persons of whom one is subject to the jurisdiction of some one of such Powers as Her Majesty, being satisfied that reciprocal provisions have been made, may by Order in Council declare to be parties to the convention set out in the Second Schedule, and of whom the other is subject to the jurisdiction of some other of the Powers aforesaid; and

(*c*) in one of such territories as Her Majesty, being satisfied that reciprocal provisions have been made, may by Order in Council declare to be territories to which the said convention applies.

36. Effect of foreign awards

(1) A foreign award shall, subject to the provisions of this Part, be enforceable in Hong Kong either by action or in the same manner as the award of an arbitrator is enforceable by virtue of section 2H.

(2) Any foreign award which would be enforceable under this Part shall be treated as binding for all purposes on the persons as between whom it was made, and may accordingly be relied on by any of those persons by way of defence, set off or otherwise in any legal proceedings in Hong Kong, and any references in this Part to enforcing a foreign award shall be construed as including references to relying on an award.

37. Conditions for enforcement of foreign awards

(1) In order that a foreign award may be enforceable under this Part it must have
—

> (*a*) been made in pursuance of an agreement for arbitration which was valid under the law by which it was governed;
> (*b*) been made by the tribunal provided for in the agreement or constituted in manner agreed upon by the parties;
> (*c*) been made in conformity with the law governing the arbitration procedure;
> (*d*) become final in the country in which it was made;
> (*e*) been in respect of a matter which may lawfully be referred to arbitration under the law of Hong Kong;

and the enforcement thereof must not be contrary to the public policy or the law of Hong Kong.

(2) Subject to the provisions of this subsection, a foreign award shall not be enforceable under this Part if the court dealing with the case is satisfied that —

> (*a*) the award has been annulled in the country in which it was made; or
> (*b*) the party against whom it is sought to enforce the award was not given notice of the arbitration proceedings in sufficient time to enable him to pre-

sent his case, or was under some legal incapacity and was not properly represented; or

(*c*) the award does not deal with all the questions referred or contains decisions on matters beyond the scope of the agreement for arbitration:

Provided that, if the award does not deal with all the questions referred, the Court may, if it thinks fit, either postpone the enforcement of the award or order its enforcement subject to the giving of such security by the person seeking to enforce it as the Court may think fit.

(3) If a party seeking to resist the enforcement of a foreign award proves that there is any ground other than the non-existence of the conditions specified in subsection (1)(*a*), (*b*) and (*c*), or the existence of the conditions specified in subsection (2)(*b*) and (*c*), entitling him to contest the validity of the award, the Court may, if it thinks fit, either refuse to enforce the award or adjourn the hearing until after the expiration of such period as appears to the Court to be reasonably sufficient to enable that party to take the necessary steps to have the award annulled by the competent tribunal.

38. Evidence

(1) The party seeking to enforce a foreign award must produce —

(*a*) the original award or a copy thereof duly authenticated in manner required by the law of the country in which it was made; and

(*b*) evidence proving that the award has become final; and

(*c*) such evidence as may be necessary to prove that the award is a foreign award and that the conditions mentioned in section 37(1)(*a*), (*b*) and (*c*) are satisfied.

(2) In any case where any document required to be produced under subsection (1) is in a foreign language, it shall be the duty of the party seeking to enforce the award to produce a translation certified as correct by a diplomatic or consular agent of the country to which that party belongs, or certified as correct in such other manner as may be sufficient according to the law of Hong Kong. (*Amended 64 of 1989 s. 23*)

(3) Subject to the provisions of this section, rules of court may be made under the Supreme Court Ordinance (Cap. 4) with respect to the evidence which must be furnished by a party seeking to enforce an award under this Part.

39. Meaning of "final award"

For the purposes of this Part, an award shall not be deemed final if any proceedings for the purpose of contesting the validity of the award are pending in the country in which it was made.

40. Saving for other rights, etc.

Nothing in this Part shall —

(*a*) prejudice any rights which any person would have had of enforcing in Hong Kong any award or of availing himself in Hong Kong of any award if this Part had not been enacted; or (*b*) apply to any award made on an arbitration agreement governed by the law of Hong Kong.

PART IV: Enforcement of Convention Awards

41. *Replacement of former provisions*
This Part shall have effect with respect to the enforcement of Convention awards; and where a Convention award would, but for this section, be also a foreign award within the meaning of Part III, that Part shall not apply to it.

42. *Effect of Convention awards*
(1) A Convention award shall, subject to this Part, be enforceable either by action or in the same manner as the award of an arbitrator is enforceable by virtue of section 2H. (*Amended 64 of 1989 s. 22*)

(2) Any Convention award which would be enforceable under this Part shall be treated as binding for all purposes on the persons as between whom it was made, and may accordingly be relied on by any of those persons by way of defence, set off or otherwise in any legal proceedings in Hong Kong and any reference in this Part to enforcing a Convention award shall be construed as including references to relying on such an award.

43. *Evidence*
The party seeking to enforce a Convention award must produce —
(*a*) the duly authenticated original award or a duly certified copy of it.
(*b*) the original arbitration agreement or a duly certified copy of it; and
(*c*) where the award or agreement is in a foreign language, a translation of it certified by an official or sworn translator or by a diplomatic or consular agent.

44. *Refusal of enforcement*
(1) Enforcement of a Convention award shall not be refused except in the cases mentioned in this section.

(2) Enforcement of a Convention award may be refused if the person against whom it is invoked proves —
(*a*) that a party to the arbitration agreement was (under the law applicable to him) under some incapacity; or
(*b*) that the arbitration agreement was not valid under the law to which the parties subjected it or, failing any indication thereon, under the law of the country where the award was made; or
(*c*) that he was not given proper notice of the appointment of the arbitrator or of the arbitration proceedings or was otherwise unable to present his case; or
(*d*) subject to subsection (4), that the award deals with a difference not con-templated by or not falling within the terms of the submission to arbitration

or contains decisions on matters beyond the scope of the submission to arbitration; or

(*e*) that the composition of the arbitral authority or the arbitral procedure was not in accordance with the agreement of the parties or, failing such agreement, with the law of the country where the arbitration took place; or

(*f*) that the award has not yet become binding on the parties, or has been set aside or suspended by a competent authority of the country in which, or under the law of which, it was made.

(3) Enforcement of a Convention award may also be refused if the award is in respect of a matter which is not capable of settlement by arbitration, or if it would be contrary to public policy to enforce the award.

(4) A Convention award which contains decisions on matters not submitted to arbitration may be enforced to the extent that it contains decisions on matters submitted to arbitration which can be separated from those on matters not so submitted.

(5) Where an application for the setting aside or suspension of a Convention award has been made to such a competent authority as is mentioned in subsection (2)(*f*), the court before which enforcement of the award is sought may, if it thinks fit, adjourn the proceedings and may, on the application of the party seeking to enforce the award, order the other party to give security.

45. *Saving*

Nothing in this Part shall prejudice any right to enforce or rely on an award otherwise than under this Part or Part III.

46. *Order to be conclusive evidence*

If the Governor by Order declares that any State or territory specified in the Order is a party to the New York [Arbitration] Convention the Order shall, while in force, be conclusive evidence that that State or territory is a party to that Convention.

7. Italy[1]

Codice di Procedura Civile (CPC)
Libro IV
Titolo VIII: Arbitration

CHAPTER I : Arbitration Agreement and Arbitration Clause

Article 806—Arbitration agreement

The parties may have the disputes arising between them decided by arbitrators, with the exception of the disputes provided for in Arts. 409 [labor disputes] and 442 [social security], those concerning issues of personal status and marital separation and those other disputes which may not be the subject of a settlement.

Article 807—Form of the arbitration agreement

The arbitration agreement shall be in writing and shall set out the subject matter of the dispute, under penalty of nullity.

The agreement shall be considered to be in writing where the intention of the parties is expressed in a telegram or telex.

The provisions regulating the validity of contracts exceeding the ordinary course of administration shall apply to the arbitration agreement.

Article 808—Arbitration Clause

The parties may establish in their contract or in a separate document that the disputes arising out of that contract be the subject of an arbitration agreement. The arbitration clause shall be contained in a document meeting the formal requirements for an arbitration agreement according to Art. 807, first and second paragraph.

Disputes ex Art. 409 may be decided by arbitrators may be decided by arbitrators only if this is provided for in collective labour contracts and agreements and if, under penalty of nullity, the parties' right to have recourse to the courts is not affected. The arbitration clause in collective labour contracts or agreements or in individual labour contracts is null and void where it authorizes the arbitrators to decide ex aequo et bono or declares that there will be no recourse against the award.

The validity of the arbitration clause shall be examined independently of the underlying contract; however, the power to stipulate a contract includes the power to agree on the arbitration clause.

Article 809—Number and appointment of arbitrators

There may be one or more arbitrators, provided that their number is uneven.

---

1. Unofficial translation of the Milan Chamber of Commerce.

The arbitration agreement or clause shall appoint the arbitrators or establish their number and manner of appointment.

Where an even number of arbitrators is indicated, one more arbitrator is appointed by the president of the court of first instance [tribunale] as provided for in Art. 810, unless the parties have agreed otherwise. Where the number of arbitrators is not indicated and the parties do not reach an agreement on this matter, there shall be three arbitrators and, failing appointment [by the parties], the president of the court of first instance shall proceed as provided for in Art. 810, unless the parties have agreed otherwise.

CHAPTER II: The Arbitrators

Article 810—Appointment of the arbitrators

Where, under the arbitration agreement or clause, the arbitrators are to be appointed by the parties, each party shall serve on the other a notice of his appointment(s) and request him to appoint his arbitrators. The party to whom the request is made shall notify the personal details of the arbitrator(s) he has appointed within the following twenty days.

Failing this, the party who has made the request may file a petition with the president of the court of first instance of the district in which the arbitration has its seat, requesting him to make the appointment. If the parties have not yet determined that seat, the petition shall be filed with the president of the court of first instance of the place in which the arbitration agreement or the contract to which the arbitration clause refers has been made or, if that place is abroad, to the president of the court of first instance of Rome. The president shall issue an order against which there shall be no appeal, after hearing the other party where necessary.

This provision shall also apply where the arbitration agreement or clause entrusts the appointment of one or more arbitrators to the courts or, where the appointment is entrusted to a third party, that third party fails to take the necessary action.

Article 811—Replacement of arbitrators

Where for whatever reason all or some of the appointed arbitrators are unable to act, they shall be replaced in the same manner laid down for their appointment in the arbitration agreement or clause. If the party concerned or the third party fails to take the necessary action, or the arbitration agreement or clause is silent on the matter, the provisions of the preceding article shall apply.

Article 812—Capacity to act as arbitrator

The arbitrators may be Italian or foreign nationals.

Minors, persons under a legal incapacity, bankrupts and those who have been disqualified from holding a public office may not act as arbitrators.

Article 813—Acceptance by and duties of the arbitrators

Acceptance by the arbitrators shall be given in writing and may be given by signing the arbitration agreement.

The arbitrators shall render their award within the time limit set by the parties or by law; if they fail to do so and the award is set aside on this ground, they shall be held liable in damages. They shall likewise be liable in damages if, after accepting their appointment, they renounce it without just cause.

Unless the parties have agreed otherwise, the arbitrator who fails to perform or postpones an act connected with his office may be replaced by agreement of the parties or by a third party entrusted with this task by the arbitration agreement or clause. Failing this, fifteen days after a notice to perform has been sent to the arbitrator by registered mail, any of the parties may file a petition with the president of the court of first instance of the district in which the arbitration has its seat. The president shall issue an order against which there shall be no appeal, after hearing the parties, and, where he ascertains that there has been failure to act or delay, he shall declare that the arbitrator is removed from office and shall proceed to replace him.

Article 814—Rights of the arbitrators

The arbitrators shall be entitled to reimbursement of their expenses and to a fee for services rendered, unless they have waived this right at the moment of acceptance or by a subsequent written statement. The parties shall be jointly and severally liable for payment, subject to the right of mutual recovery.

Where the arbitrators themselves fix the amount of their expenses and fees, that decision shall not be binding on the parties if they do not accept it. In this case, the amount of expenses and fees shall be fixed by an order of the president of the court of first instance referred to in Art. 810, second paragraph, against which there shall be no appeal, on petition by the arbitrators and after hearing the parties.

Article 815—Challenge of arbitrators

A party may refuse to accept an arbitrator whom he has not appointed, for the reasons laid down in Art. 51 [abstention of judges].

A challenge shall be made by petition to the president of the court of first instance referred to in Art. 810, second paragraph, within the peremptory time limit of ten days after the appointment has been notified or the ground for challenge has come to the party's knowledge, if later. The president issues an order against which there shall be no appeal, after hearing the challenged arbitrator and making summary inquiries where necessary.

CHAPTER III: The Proceedings

Article 816—Proceedings

The parties shall determine the seat of the arbitration in the territory of the Republic; otherwise the seat shall be determined by the Arbitrators at their first meeting.

The parties may establish the procedural rules to be followed by the arbitrators in the arbitration agreement, the arbitration clause or, provided that it is made before the commencement of the arbitration proceedings, in a separate written document.

Failing such provisions, the arbitrators may regulate the proceedings as they see fit.

They shall in any case set time limits for the parties to file documents, submissions and replies.

The arbitrators may delegate the taking of evidence to one of their number.

The arbitrators shall decide all issues arising in this course of the proceedings by an order which is not filed and may be revoked, with the exception of the case provided for in Art. 819.

Article 817—Objection of lack of jurisdiction

A party who, during the arbitration proceedings, fails to raise the objection that the pleadings of the other party exceed the limits of the arbitration agreement or clause, may not file a recourse for setting aside the award on this ground.

Article 818—Interim measures

The arbitrators may not grant sequestration orders or other interim measures.

Article 819—Incidental issues

If an issue arises during the proceedings which by law is not arbitrable, the arbitrators shall stay the proceedings where they deem that the decision entrusted to them depends on deciding that issue.

In all other cases, the arbitrators shall decide all issues arising in the arbitration proceedings.

In the case provided for in the first paragraph, the time limit set by Art. 820 shall be suspended until the day on which one of the parties notifies the judgment on the incidental issue to the arbitrators, once it has become res judicata; if less than sixty days remain, the time limit shall be extended by law to sixty days.

Article 819-bis—Connected cases [connessione]

The jurisdiction of the arbitrators is not excluded by the fact that the dispute referred to them is connected with an action pending before the court.

Article 819-ter—Hearing of witnesses

The arbitrators may hear the witness by requesting him to appear before them or decide to hear his statement at his home or office, if he agrees. They may further decide to hear the witness by requesting him to give written replies to questions within the time limit that they establish.

CHAPTER IV: The Award

Article 820—Time limit for the decision

Unless the parties have agreed otherwise, the arbitrators shall render their award within one hundred and eighty days of acceptance of their appointment. If there are several arbitrators and they did not all accept at the same time, the time limit begins to run from the last acceptance. The time limit is suspended where a petition for challenge is filed, until a decision thereon is rendered; it is, interrupted where replacement of the arbitrators is necessary.

Where evidence must be taken or an interlocutory award has been rendered, the arbitrators may extend the time limit once only and by not more than one hundred and eighty days.

In case of the death of one of the parties, the time limit is extended by thirty days.

The parties may agree in writing to an extension of the time limit.

Article 821—Relevance of the expiry of the time limit

The expiry of the time limit indicated in the preceding article may not be raised as a ground for setting aside the award if, before deliberation of the award as set out in the order [dispositivo] signed by the majority of the arbitrators, the party failed to notify to the other parties and to the arbitrators his intention to invoke the fact that the arbitrators' authority had thus been terminated.

Article 822—Rules for the deliberation [of the award]

The arbitrators shall decide according to the rules of law, unless the parties have authorized them, by whatever expression, to decide ex aequo et bono.

Article 823—Deliberation of and requirements for the award

The award shall be deliberated by a majority vote of the arbitrators meeting in personal conference and shall then be set down in writing.

It shall contain:

(1) the indication of the parties;

(2) the indication of the parties;

(3) the indication of the arbitration agreement or clause and of the issues submitted;

(4) a brief statement of reasons;

(5) the indication of the seat of the arbitration and the place or manner in which it was deliberated;

(6) the signatures of all the arbitrators, with an indication of their day, month and year; the arbitrators may sign in an place other than the place of deliberation, as well as abroad. If there is more than one arbitrator, they may sign in different places without having to meet in personal conference again.

However, an award signed only by the majority of the arbitrators shall be valid, provided that it is stated that it was deliberated in personal conference of all the arbitrators and that it is declared expressly that the other arbitrators were either unwilling or unable to sign it.

The award shall be binding on the parties from the date or the last signature.

Article 824—Place of rendition

Abrogated.

Art. 825—Filing of the award

The arbitrators shall draft the award in as many originals as the number of the parties and give notice of it to each party by handing over an original or sending it by registered mail within ten days of the date of the last signature.

The party intending to have the award enforced in the territory of the Republic shall file the original award or a certified copy thereof, together with the original arbitration agreement or document containing the arbitration clause or an equivalent document, or a certified copy thereof, with the Registry of the Magistrate's court [Pretura] of the district in which the arbitration has its seat.

The Magistrate, after ascertaining that the award meets all formal requirements, enforces it be decree. The award which has been enforced shall be registered in all cases where a judgment of the same content would be registered.

The Registry notifies the filing of the award and the decision of the Magistrate to the parties according to Art. 133, second paragraph.

A recourse against the decree denying enforcement of the award may be filed by petition with the court of first instance within thirty days of notification; the court of first instance, after hearing the parties, issues, in camera, an order against which there shall be no appeal.

Article 826—Correction of the award

On the request of a party, the award may be corrected by the same arbitrators who have rendered it, where there have been omissions, material errors or miscalculations.

The arbitrators shall take the necessary action within twenty days, after hearing the parties. Notice of the correction shall be given to the parties, also by registered mail, within ten days of the date of the last signature.

If the award has already been filed, the Magistrate of the place where the award has been filed shall be requested to correct the award. The provisions of Art. 288 shall apply insofar as they are compatible.

CHAPTER V: Means of Recourse

Article 827—Means of recourse

The award may only be subject to a recourse for setting aside, revocation or third party opposition.

A recourse may be filed irrespective of whether the award has been filed or not.

The award partially deciding on the merits of the dispute may be challenged immediately, whereas the award which decides some of the issues without resolving the dispute may be challenged only together with the final award.

Article 828—Recourse for setting aside

A recourse for setting aside may be filed with the court of appeal of the district in which the arbitration has its seat, within ninety days of notification of the award.

No recourse may be filed after one year from the date of the last signature.

The request to correct the award does not suspend the time limit for filing a recourse; however, the parts of the award which have been corrected may be challenged within the ordinary time limit, which begins to run after notification of the decision on the correction.

Article 829—Grounds for setting aside

Notwithstanding any waiver, a recourse for setting aside may be filed in the following cases:

(1) where the arbitration agreement is null and void;

(2) where the arbitrators have not been appointed according to the provisions laid down in Chapters I and II of this Title, provided that this ground for setting aside has been raised in the arbitration proceedings;

(3) where the award has been rendered by a person who could not be appointed arbitrator according to Art. 812;

(4) where the award exceeds the limits of the arbitration agreement, fails to decide any of the items of the arbitration agreement or contains contradictory provisions, provided that the provisions of Art. 817 are complied with;

(5)where the award does not meet the requirements indicated at nos. (3), (4), (5) and (6) of the second paragraph of Art. 823, provided that the provisions in the third paragraph of said article are complied with;

(6)where the award has been rendered after the expiry of the time limit indicated in Art. 820, provided that the provisions of Art. 821 are complied with;

(7)where the formalities laid down for proceedings under penalty of nullity have not been observed, when the parties had requested that they be complied with, according to Art. 816, and such defects have not been made good;

(8)where the award is contrary to a previous award against which there may be no recourse or to a previous judgment having the force of res judicata between the parties, provided that this objection has been raised in the arbitration proceedings;

(9)where the principles of due process [contraddittorio] has not been observed in the arbitration proceedings.

A recourse for setting aside may likewise be filed where the arbitrators did not decide according to law, unless the parties had authorized them to decide ex aequo et bono or had declared that there may be no recourse against the award.

In the cases ex Art. 808, second paragraph, the award may also be challenged for violation and misapplication of collective contracts and agreements.

Article 830—Decision on the recourse for setting aside

When granting the recourse, the court of appeal shall render a judgment stating that the award is null and void; where the defect only concerns a part of the award which is severable from the others, it shall state that the award is partially null and void.

Unless all the parties have declared a contrary intention, the court of appeal shall also decide on the merits, if the case is ready to be decided, or it shall make an order referring the case to the examining judge, where new evidence-taking is necessary for a decision on the merits.

While the case is pending, the court of appeal may, on the request of a party, make an order staying enforcement of the award.

Article 831—Revocation and third party opposition

Notwithstanding any waiver, the award may be revoked in the cases indicated at nos. (1), (2), (3), and (6) of Art. 395. Within the time limits and according to the formalities set out in the Second Book.

If the conditions mentioned in the first paragraph arise during the setting aside proceedings, the time limit for filing a request for revocation shall be suspended until notification of the judgment on the setting aside.

The award may be subject to third party opposition in the cases indicated in art. 404.

The request for revocation and third party opposition shall be filed with the court of appeal of the district in which the arbitration has its seat. The court of appeal may consolidate setting aside, revocation and third party opposition proceedings, unless the stage reached by the proceedings filed first does not allow an exhaustive examination of and decision o the other proceedings.

CHAPTER VI: International Arbitration

Article 832—International arbitration

Where at the date of signing the arbitration clause or agreement at least one of the parties has his domicile [residenza] or principal place of business [sede effettiva] abroad, or where a substantial part of the obligations arising out of the relationship to which the dispute refers must be performed abroad, the provisions of Chapters I to V of this title shall apply to arbitration insofar as they are not derogated from by this Chapter.

The provisions laid down in international conventions shall apply in any case.

Article 833—Form of the arbitration clause

An arbitration clause contained in general conditions or counteract or standard forms shall not be subject to the specific approval provided for in Arts. 1341 and 1342 of the Civil Code.

An arbitration clause contained in general conditions that are incorporated in an agreement in writing made by the parties shall be valid, if the parties knew of the clause or should have known of it by using ordinary diligence.

Article 834—Norms applicable to the merits

The parties may agree on the norms that the arbitrators shall apply to the merits of the dispute or provide that the arbitrators decide ex aequo et bono. If the parties are silent, the law with which the relationship has its closest connection shall apply.

In both cases the arbitrators shall take into account the provisions of the contract and trade usages.

Article 835—Language of the arbitration

Unless the parties have agreed otherwise, the language of the proceedings shall be determined by the arbitrators, taking into account the circumstances of the case.

Article 836—Challenge of arbitrators

The challenge of arbitrators is regulated by Art. 815, unless the parties have agreed otherwise.

Article 837—Deliberation of the award

The award shall be deliberated by a majority vote of the arbitrators meeting in personal conference or videoconference, unless the parties have agreed otherwise, and shall then be set down in writing.

Article 838—Recourse

The provisions of Art. 829, second paragraph, Art. 830, second paragraph and Art. 831 shall not apply to international arbitration, unless the parties have agreed otherwise.

CHAPTER VII: Foreign Awards

Article 839—Recognition and enforcement of foreign awards

The party wishing to enforce a foreign award in the Republic shall file a petition with the president of the court of appeal of the district in which the other party has his domicile; if that party has no domicile in Italy, the court of appeal of Rome shall have jurisdiction.

The petitioner shall supply the original award or a certified copy thereof, together with the original arbitration agreement or an equivalent document, or a certified copy thereof.

Where the documents mentioned in the second paragraph are not made in the Italian language, the petitioner shall also produce a certified translation.

The president of the court of appeal, where he ascertains that the award meets all formal requirements, enforces the foreign award in the Republic by decree, unless:

(1) the dispute could not be the subject of an arbitration agreement according to Italian law;

(2) the award contains provisions which are contrary to public policy.

Article 840—Opposition proceedings

An opposition may be filed against the decree granting or denying enforcement of the foreign award by filing a writ of summons with the court of appeal within thirty days of communication of the decree denying enforcement or notification of the decree granting enforcement.

Following such opposition, the proceedings shall be held according to Arts. 645 ff, insofar as they are applicable. The court of appeal shall render a judgment which may be appealed before the Supreme Court.

The court of appeal shall deny recognition or enforcement of the foreign award if in the opposition proceedings the party against whom the ward is invoked furnishes proof of the existence of one of the following circumstances.

(1)the parties to the arbitration agreement were, under the law applicable to them, under some incapacity, or the arbitration agreement is not valid under the law to which the parties have subjected it or, failing any indication thereon, under the law of the State where the award was made;

(2)the party against whom the award is invoked was not informed of the appointment of the arbitrator or of the arbitration proceedings or was otherwise unable to present his case in the proceedings;

(3)the award decides a dispute not contemplated by the arbitration agreement or clause; however, if the decisions in the award on matters submitted to arbitration can be separated from those not so submitted, the former may be recognized and enforced;

(4)the composition of the arbitration tribunal or the arbitration proceedings were not in accordance with the agreement of the parties or, failing such agreement, with the law of the place where the arbitration took place;

(5)the award has not yet become binding on the parties or has been set aside or suspended by a competent authority of the State in which, or under the law of which, it was made.

If an application for the setting aside or suspension of the effects of the award has been made to the competent authority indicated at no. (5) of the third paragraph, the court of appeal may adjourn the decision on the recognition or enforcement of the award; on the request of the party seeking enforcement it may, in the case of suspension, order the other party to give suitable security.

Recognition or enforcement of the foreign award shall likewise be denied if the court of appeal finds that:

(1)the dispute could not be the subject of an arbitration agreement under Italian law;

(2)the award contains provisions which are contrary to public policy.

The provisions laid down in international conventions shall apply in any case.

8. Netherlands

Dutch Code of Civil Procedure[1]

TITLE I: Arbitration in the Netherlands

Section One. Arbitration Agreement and Appointment of Arbitrators

Article 1020 — Arbitration agreements in general
1. Parties may agree to submit to arbitration disputes which have arisen or may arise between them out of a defined legal relationship, whether contractual or not.
2. The arbitration agreement mentioned in paragraph (1) includes both a submission by which the parties bind themselves to submit to arbitration an existing dispute between them and an arbitration clause under which parties bind themselves to submit to arbitration disputes which may arise in the future between them.
3. The arbitration agreement shall not serve to determine legal consequences of which the parties cannot freely dispose.
4. Parties may also agree to submit the following matters to arbitration:
    (*a*) the determination only of the quality or condition of goods;
    (*b*) the determination only of the quantum of damages or a monetary debt;
    (*c*) the filling of gaps in, or modification of, the legal relationship between the parties referred to in paragraph (1).
5. The term "arbitration agreement" includes an arbitration clause which is contained in articles of association or rules which bind the parties.
6. Arbitration rules referred to in an arbitration agreement shall be deemed to form part of that agreement.

Article 1021 — Form of arbitration agreement
The arbitration agreement must be proven by an instrument in writing. For this purpose an instrument in writing which provides for arbitration or which refers to standard conditions providing for arbitration is sufficient, provided that this instrument is expressly or impliedly accepted by or on behalf of the other party.

Article 1022 — Arbitration agreement and substantive claim before court;
arbitration agreement and interim measures by court
1. A court seized of a dispute in respect of which an arbitration agreement has been concluded shall declare that it has no jurisdiction if a party invokes the existence of the said agreement before submitting a defence, unless the agreement is invalid.
2. An arbitration agreement shall not preclude a party from requesting a court to grant interim measures of protection, or from applying to the President of the District Court for a decision in summary proceedings in accordance with the provisions of article 289. In the latter case the President shall decide the case in accordance with the provisions of article 1051.

1. Arbitration Act of 1 December 1986, translation from Albert Jan van den Berg, R. van Delden and H.J. Snijders, Netherlands Arbitration Law (1993).

Article 1023 — Who may be appointed as an arbitrator

Any natural person of legal capacity may be appointed as arbitrator. Unless the parties have agreed otherwise, no person shall be precluded from appointment by reason of his nationality.

Article 1024 — Submission agreement: commencement of arbitral proceedings

1. The submission agreement shall describe the matters which the parties wish to submit to arbitration.

2. The arbitration shall be deemed to have been commenced by the conclusion of the submission agreement, unless the parties have agreed to another method of commencement.

3. If the parties have agreed that a third person shall appoint the arbitrator or arbitrators, or any of them, either party shall send to the third person a copy of the submission agreement.

Article 1025 — Arbitration clause: commencement of arbitral proceedings

1. In the case of an arbitration clause, the arbitration shall be deemed to have been commenced on the day of receipt of a notice in writing in which a party informs the other that he is commencing arbitration. The said notice shall contain a description of the matters which the party commencing the arbitration wishes to submit to arbitration.

2. If the parties have agreed that a third person shall appoint the arbitrator or arbitrators, or any of them, the party who commences arbitration shall send to the third person a copy of the notice mentioned in paragraph (1).

3. The parties may agree that the arbitration shall be commenced in a different method from that provided for in this article.

Article 1026 — Number of arbitrators

1. The arbitral tribunal shall be composed of an uneven number of arbitrators. The arbitral tribunal may also consist of a sole arbitrator.

2. If the parties have not agreed on the number of arbitrators, or if the agreed method of determining that number is not carried out and the parties cannot reach agreement on the number, the number shall, at the request of either party, be determined by the President of the District Court.

3. If the parties have agreed on an even number of arbitrators, the arbitrators shall appoint an additional arbitrator who shall act as the chairman of the arbitral tribunal.

4. Failing agreement between the arbitrators in appointing the additional arbitrator, such arbitrator shall, unless the parties have agreed otherwise, be appointed, at the request of either party, by the President of the District Court.

Article 1027 — Appointment of arbitrators

1. The arbitrator or arbitrators shall be appointed by any method agreed by the parties. The parties may entrust to a third person the appointment of the arbitrator

or arbitrators or any of them. If no method of appointment is agreed upon, the arbitrator or arbitrators shall be appointed by consensus between the parties.

2. The appointment shall be made within two months after the commencement of the arbitration, unless the arbitrator or arbitrators have already been appointed. In the event, however, that any of the cases mentioned in article 1026(2) occurs, the period of two months shall start to run on the day on which the number of arbitrators is determined. The period for appointment shall be extended to three months if at least one of the parties is domiciled or has his actual residence outside the Netherlands. These periods may be shortened or extended by agreement between the parties.

3. If the appointment of the arbitrator or arbitrators is not made within the period prescribed in the preceding paragraph, the arbitrator shall, at the request of either party, be appointed by the President of the District Court. The other party shall be given an opportunity to be heard.

4. The President or the third person shall appoint the arbitrator or arbitrators without regard to the question whether or not there is a valid arbitration agreement. By participating in the appointment of the arbitrator or arbitrators, the parties do not forfeit the right to challenge the jurisdiction of the arbitral tribunal on the ground of absence of a valid arbitration agreement.

Article 1028 — Privileged position of a party in appointing arbitrators
If the arbitration agreement gives one of the parties a privileged position with regard to the appointment of the arbitrator or arbitrators, the other party may, despite the method of appointment laid down in that agreement, request the President of the District Court within one month after the commencement of the arbitration to appoint the arbitrator or arbitrators. The other party shall be given an opportunity to be heard. The provisions of article 1027(4) shall apply accordingly.

Article 1029 — Arbitrator's acceptance and release of mandate
1. An arbitrator shall accept his mandate in writing.

2. An arbitrator who has accepted his mandate may, at his own request, be released from his mandate either with the consent of the parties or a third person designated by the parties, or in the absence thereof, by the President of the District Court.

3. An arbitrator who has accepted his mandate may be released from his mandate by agreement between the parties.

4. An arbitrator who has accepted his mandate and who has become *de jure* or *de facto* unable to perform his mandate, may, at the request of either party, be released from his mandate by a third person designated by the parties, or in the absence of such third person, by the President of the District Court.

Article 1030 — Appointment of a substitute arbitrator
1. Unless the parties have agreed otherwise, an arbitrator who has been released from his mandate in accordance with the provisions of article 1029(2), (3) or (4)

shall be replaced pursuant to the rules applicable to the initial appointment. The same shall apply to an arbitrator who has died.

2. If the parties have named the arbitrator or arbitrators in the arbitration agreement, their replacement shall also take place in the cases prescribed in paragraph (1) above, unless the parties have agreed that the arbitration agreement shall terminate in such a case.

3. Unless the parties have agreed otherwise, the arbitral proceedings shall be suspended by operation of law in case of replacement. Unless the parties have agreed otherwise, the arbitral proceedings shall, after the suspension ceases, continue from the stage they had reached.

Article 1031 — Termination of the arbitral tribunal's mandate;
tribunal's failure to proceed
1. The parties may agree to terminate the mandate of the arbitral tribunal.

2. At the request of either party and after having heard the other party and the arbitrator or arbitrators, the third person designated by the parties, or in the absence thereof, the President of the District Court, may, having regard to all circumstances, terminate the mandate of the arbitral tribunal if, despite repeated reminders, the arbitral tribunal carries out its mandate in an unacceptably slow manner. In these circumstances, the jurisdiction of the court shall revive, unless the parties have agreed otherwise.

Article 1032 — Death of a party
1. Unless the parties have agreed otherwise, neither the arbitration agreement nor the mandate of the arbitral tribunal shall terminate by reason of the death of one of the parties.

2. The arbitral tribunal shall suspend the arbitral proceedings for such period as may be determined by it. The arbitral tribunal may, at the request of the legal successors of the deceased party, extend such period. The arbitral tribunal shall give the other party an opportunity to be heard in respect of such request.

3. Unless the parties have agreed otherwise, the arbitral proceedings shall, after any suspension, continue from the stage they had reached.

Article 1033 — Challenge of an arbitrator: grounds
1. An arbitrator may be challenged if circumstances exist that give rise to justifiable doubts as to his impartiality or independence. A secretary engaged by an arbitral tribunal may be challenged on the same grounds; the provisions of article 1035 shall apply accordingly to such a challenge.

2. A party may only challenge an arbitrator appointed by him on grounds of which he has become aware after the appointment has been made.

3. A party may not challenge an arbitrator appointed by a third person or the President of the District Court if he has acquiesced in this appointment, unless he has become aware of the ground for challenge after the appointment has been made.

Article 1034 — Duty to disclose

1. A prospective arbitrator or secretary who presumes that he could be challenged shall disclose in writing to the person who has approached him the existence of such grounds.

2. A person who has been appointed as arbitrator or secretary shall, if the parties have not previously been notified, immediately notify the parties as prescribed in the preceding paragraph.

Article 1035 — Challenge of an arbitrator: procedure

1. The challenge and the grounds therefor shall be notified in writing by the challenging party to the challenged arbitrator, the other members of the arbitral tribunal, the other party and, if a third person has appointed the challenged arbitrator, this third person. The arbitral tribunal may suspend the arbitral proceedings as of the day of receipt of the notification.

2. If the challenged arbitrator does not withdraw within two weeks after the day of receipt of the notification, the President of the District Court shall, at the request of either party, decide on the merits of the challenge. If such request is not made within four weeks after the day of receipt of the notification, the right to challenge shall be barred and the arbitral proceedings, if suspended, shall continue from the stage they had reached.

3. If the challenged arbitrator withdraws, or if the challenge is upheld by the President of the District Court, the arbitrator shall, unless the parties have agreed otherwise, be replaced in accordance with the rules governing his initial appointment. The provisions of article 1030(2) and (3) shall apply accordingly.

4. If the challenged arbitrator or one or both of the parties is domiciled or has his actual residence outside the Netherlands, the periods mentioned in paragraph (2) above shall be six and eight weeks respectively.

Section Two. The Arbitral Proceedings

Article 1036 — Determination of rules of procedure

Subject to the provisions of this Title, the arbitral proceedings shall be conducted in such manner as agreed between the parties or, to the extent that the parties have not agreed, as determined by the arbitral tribunal.

Article 1037 — Place of arbitration

1. The place of arbitration shall be determined by agreement of the parties, or failing such agreement, as determined by the arbitral tribunal. The determination of the place of arbitration establishes also the place where the award shall be made.

2. If the place of arbitration has not been determined either by the parties or the arbitral tribunal, the place of making the award as stated by the arbitral tribunal in the award shall be deemed to be the place of arbitration.

3. The arbitral tribunal may hold hearings, deliberate, and examine witnesses and experts at any other place, within or outside the Netherlands, which it deems appropriate.

Article 1038 — Representation and assistance

1. The parties may appear before the arbitral tribunal in person, be represented by a practising lawyer, or be represented by any other person expressly authorised in writing for this purpose.

2. The parties may be assisted in the arbitral proceedings by any persons they may choose.

Article 1039 — Equal treatment of parties; hearing; right to produce witnesses and experts; production of documents; rules of evidence

1. The parties shall be treated with equality. The arbitral tribunal shall give each party an opportunity to substantiate his claims and to present his case.

2. The arbitral tribunal shall, at the request of either party or on its own initiative, give the parties an opportunity of making an oral presentation.

3. The arbitral tribunal may, at the request of either party, allow a party to produce witnesses or experts. The arbitral tribunal shall have the power to designate one of its members to examine witnesses or experts.

4. The arbitral tribunal shall have the power to order the production of documents.

5. Unless the parties have agreed otherwise, the arbitral tribunal shall have discretion in the rules of evidence to be applied.

Article 1040 — Default of a party

1. If the claimant, without showing good cause, fails to communicate his statement of claim or duly to explain the claim, in spite of having had a reasonable opportunity to do so, the arbitral tribunal may terminate the arbitral proceedings by means of an arbitral award.

2. If the respondent, without showing good cause, fails to submit his defence, in spite of having been given a reasonable opportunity to do so, the arbitral tribunal may render an award forthwith.

3. In the circumstances mentioned in paragraph (2) above, the arbitral tribunal shall render an award in favour of the claimant, unless it considers the claim to be unlawful or unfounded. Before rendering an award, the arbitral tribunal may require the claimant to produce evidence in support of one or more of his allegations.

Article 1041 — Examination of witnesses

1. If an examination of witnesses takes place, the arbitral tribunal shall determine the time and place of the examination and the manner in which the examination shall proceed. If the arbitral tribunal deems it necessary, it shall examine the witnesses on oath or affirmation as provided in article 107(1).

2. If a witness does not appear voluntarily or, having appeared, refuses to give evidence, the arbitral tribunal may allow a party who so requests, within a period of time determined by the arbitral tribunal, to petition the President of the District Court to appoint a judge-commissary before whom the examination of the witness

shall take place. The examination shall take place in the same manner as in ordinary court proceedings. The Clerk of the District Court shall give the arbitrator or arbitrators an opportunity of attending the examination of the witness.

3. The Clerk of the District Court shall communicate without delay to the arbitral tribunal and the parties a copy of the record of the examination.

4. The arbitral tribunal may suspend the proceedings until the day on which it has received the record of the examination.

Article 1042 — Experts appointed by arbitral tribunal

1. The arbitral tribunal may appoint one or more experts to give advice. The arbitral tribunal shall communicate as soon as possible to the parties a copy of the appointment and the terms of reference of the experts.

2. The arbitral tribunal may require a party to provide the experts with the information required by them and to give them the necessary cooperation.

3. Upon receipt of the expert's report, the arbitral tribunal shall provide a copy of the report to the parties without delay.

4. At the request of either party, the experts shall be examined at a hearing. A party wishing to make such request shall inform the arbitral tribunal and the opposing party thereof without delay.

5. The arbitral tribunal shall give the parties an opportunity to examine the experts and to produce their own experts.

6. The provisions of article 1041(1) shall apply accordingly.

Article 1043 — Order for personal appearance of the parties

At any stage of the proceedings the arbitral tribunal may order the parties to appear in person for the purpose of providing information or attempting to arrive at a settlement.

Article 1044 — Request for information on foreign law

1. The arbitral tribunal may, through the intervention of the President of the District Court at The Hague, ask for information as mentioned in article 3 of the European Convention on Information on Foreign Law, concluded at London, 7 June 1968 (Dutch Treaty Series 1968, 142). The President shall, unless he considers the request to be without merit, send the request without delay to the agency mentioned in article 2 of said Convention and notify the arbitral tribunal thereof.

2. The arbitral tribunal may suspend the proceedings until the day on which it has received the answer to its request for information.

Article 1045 — Third parties

1. At the written request of a third party who has an interest in the outcome of the arbitral proceedings, the arbitral tribunal may permit such party to join the proceedings, or to intervene therein. The arbitral tribunal shall send without delay a copy of the request to the parties.

2. A party who claims to be indemnified by a third party may serve a notice of joinder on such a party. A copy of the notice shall be sent without delay to the arbitral tribunal and the other party.

3. The joinder, intervention or joinder for the claim of indemnity may only be permitted by the arbitral tribunal, having heard the parties, if the third party accedes by agreement in writing between him and the parties to the arbitration agreement.

4. On the grant of a request for joinder, intervention, or joinder for the claim of indemnity, the third party becomes a party to the arbitral proceedings. Unless the parties have agreed there on the arbitral tribunal shall determine the further conduct of the proceedings.

Article 1046 — Consolidation of arbitral proceedings

1. If arbitral proceedings have been commenced before an arbitral tribunal in the Netherlands concerning a subject matter which is connected with the subject matter of arbitral proceedings commenced before another arbitral tribunal in the Netherlands, any of the parties may, unless the parties have agreed otherwise, request the President of the District Court in Amsterdam to order a consolidation of the proceedings.

2. The President may wholly or partially grant or refuse the request, after he has given all parties and the arbitrators an opportunity to be heard. His decision shall be communicated in writing to all parties and the arbitral tribunals involved.

3. If the President orders consolidation in full, the parties shall in consultation with each other appoint one arbitrator or an uneven number of arbitrators and determine the procedural rules which shall apply to the consolidated proceedings. If, within the period of time prescribed by the President, the parties have not reached agreement on the above, the President shall, at the request of any of the parties, appoint the arbitrator or arbitrators and, if necessary, determine the procedural rules which shall apply to the consolidated proceedings. The President shall determine the remuneration for the work already carried out by the arbitrators whose mandate is terminated by reason of the full consolidation.

4. If the President orders partial consolidation, he shall decide which disputes shall be consolidated. The President shall, if the parties fail to agree within the period of time prescribed by him, at the request of any of the parties, appoint the arbitrator or arbitrators and determine which rules shall apply to the consolidated proceedings. In this event the arbitral tribunals before which arbitrations have already been commenced shall suspend those arbitrations. The award of the arbitral tribunal appointed for the consolidated arbitration shall be communicated in writing to the other arbitral tribunals involved. Upon receipt of this award, these arbitral tribunals shall continue the arbitrations commenced before them and decide in accordance with the award rendered in the consolidated proceedings.

5. The provisions of article 1027(4) shall apply accordingly in the cases mentioned in paragraphs (3) and (4) above.

6. An award rendered under paragraphs (3) and (4) above shall be subject to appeal to a second arbitral tribunal if and to the extent that all parties involved in the consolidated proceedings have agreed upon such an appeal.

Article 1047 — Section Two not applicable to quality arbitration

With the exception of the provisions of article 1037, the provisions of this Section shall not apply to arbitrations concerning the matters mentioned in article 1020(4)(*a*). In that case the proceedings shall be conducted in the manner agreed upon by the parties or, to the extent that the parties have not agreed thereon, as determined by the arbitral tribunal.

Article 1048 — Time limit for making the award

The arbitral tribunal is free to determine the time when the award shall be made.

Section Three. The Arbitral Award

Article 1049 — Types of award

The arbitral tribunal may render a final award, a partial final award, or an interim award.

Article 1050 — Appeal to second arbitral tribunal

1. An appeal from the arbitral award to a second arbitral tribunal is possible only if the parties have agreed thereto.

2. Unless the parties have agreed otherwise, an appeal to a second arbitral tribunal from a partial final award can be lodged only in conjunction with an appeal from the last final award.

3. Unless the parties have agreed otherwise, an appeal to a second arbitral tribunal from an interim award can be lodged only in conjunction with an appeal from a final or partial final award.

4. Unless the parties have agreed otherwise, an appeal to a second arbitral tribunal shall be lodged within three months after the date of deposit of the award with the Registry of the District Court.

Article 1051- Summary arbitral proceedings

1. The parties may agree to empower the arbitral tribunal or its chairman to render an award in summary proceedings, within the limits imposed by article 289(1).

2. In the event that, notwithstanding such agreement, the case is brought before the President of the District Court in summary proceedings, he may, if a party invokes the existence of the said agreement, taking into account all circumstances, declare to have no jurisdiction by referring the case to the agreed summary arbitral proceedings, unless the said agreement is invalid.

3. A decision rendered in summary arbitral proceedings shall be regarded as an arbitral award to which the provisions of Sections Three to Five inclusive of this Title shall be applicable.

4. In the case of a referral to the summary arbitral proceedings mentioned in paragraph (2) above, no appeal may be lodged against the decision of the President of the District Court.

Article 1052 — Pleas as to the jurisdiction of the arbitral tribunal

1. The arbitral tribunal shall have the power to decide on its own jurisdiction.

2. A party who appeared in the arbitral proceedings shall raise a plea that the arbitral tribunal lacks jurisdiction on the ground that there is no valid arbitration agreement, unless the plea is made on the ground that the dispute is not capable of settlement by arbitration by virtue of article 1020(3), before submitting a defence; thereafter that party will be barred from raising this plea in the arbitral proceedings or in proceedings before the court.

3. A party who has participated in the constitution of the arbitral tribunal may not, in the arbitral proceedings or in proceedings before the court, raise the plea that the arbitral tribunal lacks jurisdiction on the ground that the arbitral tribunal is constituted in violation of the applicable rules. A party who has made an appearance in the arbitral proceedings and who has not participated in the constitution of the arbitral tribunal, shall raise the plea that the arbitral tribunal lacks jurisdiction on the ground that the arbitral tribunal is constituted in violation of the applicable rules before submitting a defence; thereafter that party will be barred from raising this plea in the arbitral proceedings or in proceedings before the court.

4. Any decision in which the arbitral tribunal declares that it has jurisdiction can be challenged only by the means of recourse mentioned in article 1064(1) in conjunction with the challenge of a subsequent final or partial final award.

5. Unless the parties have agreed otherwise, the court shall have jurisdiction to try the case if the arbitral tribunal declares that it lacks jurisdiction.

6. Appeal to a second arbitral tribunal shall, if agreed, be allowed against both a decision of the arbitral tribunal that it has jurisdiction and a decision that it lacks jurisdiction. In such event the court shall have jurisdiction under paragraph (4) or (5) above only after a decision is made on appeal to the second arbitral tribunal or after the time limit for appeal has lapsed without the appeal having been lodged or earlier, if the right to appeal is renounced in writing.

Article 1053 — Separability of the arbitration clause

An arbitration agreement shall be considered and decided upon as a separate agreement. The arbitral tribunal shall have the power to decide on the validity of the contract of which the arbitration agreement forms part or to which the arbitration agreement is related.

Article 1054 — Rules applicable to the substance of the dispute

1. The arbitral tribunal shall make its award in accordance with the rules of law.

2. If a choice of law is made by the parties, the arbitral tribunal shall make its award in accordance with the rules of law chosen by the parties. Failing such choice of law, the arbitral tribunal shall make its award in accordance with the rules of law which it considers appropriate.

3. The arbitral tribunal shall decide as *amiable compositeur* if the parties by agreement have authorised it to do so.

4. In all cases the arbitral tribunal shall take into account any applicable trade usages.

Article 1055 — Enforceability of award notwithstanding arbitral appeal

Where an appeal from the award to a second arbitral tribunal is provided for, the arbitral tribunal may declare its award provisionally enforceable in cases where the court has the power to do so. The arbitral tribunal may determine that such enforceability of the award is subject to the giving of security.

Article 1056 — Penalty for non-compliance

The arbitral tribunal has the power to impose a penalty for non-compliance in cases where the court has such power. The provisions of articles 611*a* to 611*i* inclusive shall apply accordingly, although in the cases mentioned in article 611*d*, an application for the revocation, suspension or reduction of the penalty shall be made to the President of the District Court with whose Registry the original of the award shall be deposited in accordance with article 1058(1).

Article 1057 — Majority decision; refusal of minority to sign;
form and contents of award

1. Unless the parties have agreed otherwise, if the arbitral tribunal is composed of more than one arbitrator, it shall decide by a majority of votes.

2. The award shall be in writing and signed by the arbitrator or arbitrators.

3. If a minority of the arbitrators refuses to sign, the other arbitrators shall make mention thereof beneath the award signed by them. This statement shall be signed by them. A similar statement shall be made if a minority is incapable of signing and it is unlikely that this impediment will cease to exist within a reasonable time.

4. In addition to the decision, the award shall contain in any case:

   (*a*) the names and addresses of the arbitrator or arbitrators;

   (*b*) the names and addresses of the parties;

   (*c*) the date on which the award is made;

   (*d*) the place where the award is made:

   (*e*) the reasons for the decision, unless the award concerns merely the determination only of the quality or condition of goods as provided in article 1020(4)(*a*) or the recording of a settlement as provided in article 1069.

Article 1058 — Notification and deposit of award; termination of
mandate of arbitral tribunal

1. The arbitral tribunal shall ensure that without delay:

   (*a*) a copy of any award, signed by an arbitrator or the secretary of the arbitral tribunal, is communicated to the parties;

   (*b*) the original of the final or partial final award is deposited with the Registry of the District Court within whose district the place of arbitration is located.

2. Without prejudice to the provisions of articles 1060 and 1061, the mandate of the arbitral tribunal shall terminate upon the deposit of the last final award with the Registry.

Article 1059 — Res judicata of the award

1. Only a final or partial final arbitral award is capable of acquiring the force of *res judicata*. The award shall have such force from the day on which it is made.

2. If, however, an appeal to a second arbitral tribunal is provided for, the final or partial final award shall have the force of *res judicata* from the day on which the time limit for lodging appeal has lapsed or, if the appeal has been lodged, the day on which a decision is rendered on appeal, if and to the extent that the award rendered at first instance is affirmed on appeal.

Article 1060 — Rectification and correction of the award

1. Not later than thirty days after the date of deposit of the award with the Registry of the District Court, a party may request in writing that the arbitral tribunal rectify in the award a manifest computing or clerical error.

2. If the details referred to in article 1057(4)(*a*) to (*d*) inclusive are stated incorrectly or are partially or wholly absent from the award, a party may, not later than thirty days after the date of deposit of the award with the Registry of the District Court, request in writing that the arbitral tribunal correct the mistake or omission.

3. A copy of the request mentioned in paragraph (1) or (2) above shall be communicated by the arbitral tribunal to the other party.

4. An arbitral tribunal may, not later than thirty days after the date of deposit of the award with the Registry of the District Court, also make on its own initiative the rectification or the correction mentioned in paragraph (1) or (2) above.

5. In the event that the arbitral tribunal makes the rectification or correction, it shall record and sign it on the original and copies of the award, or set it out in a separately signed document, which shall be treated as forming part of the award. The provisions of articles 1057(1) to (3) inclusive and 1058(1) shall apply accordingly.

6. If the arbitral tribunal rejects the request for rectification or correction, it shall inform the parties thereof in writing.

7. A request under this article does not suspend the enforcement or setting aside of the award unless the President or the District Court deems that there are serious reasons for so doing while a decision on the request is pending.

Article 1061 — Additional award

1. If the arbitral tribunal has failed to decide on one or more matters which have been submitted to it, either party may, not later than thirty days after the date of deposit of the award with the Registry of the District Court, request the arbitral tribunal to render an additional award.

2. A copy of the request shall be communicated by the arbitral tribunal to the other party.

3. The arbitral tribunal shall give the parties an opportunity to be heard before deciding on the request.

4. An additional award shall be regarded as an arbitral award to which the provisions of Section Three to Five inclusive of this Title shall be applicable.

5. If the arbitral tribunal rejects a request for an additional award, it shall inform the parties accordingly in writing. A copy of this notification, signed by an arbitrator

or the secretary of the arbitral tribunal, shall be deposited with the Registry of the District Court, in accordance with the provisions of article 1058(1).

6. If an appeal to a second arbitral tribunal has been agreed, the arbitral award rendered at first instance may only be supplemented on appeal. Any request for supplementation shall be made within the period of time applicable to the lodging of the appeal.

Section Four. Enforcement of the Arbitral Award

Article 1062 — Granting leave for enforcement
1. Enforcement in the Netherlands of a final or partial final arbitral award which is not open to appeal to a second arbitral tribunal, or which is declared provisionally enforceable, or a final or partial award rendered on arbitral appeal, can take place only after the President of the District Court with whose Registry the original of the award shall be deposited by virtue of article 1058(1), has, in pursuance of a request of one of the parties, granted leave for enforcement.

2. Leave for enforcement shall be recorded on the original of the arbitral award or, if no deposit of the arbitral award has taken place, shall be laid down in a decision. The Court Clerk shall communicate without delay to the parties a certified copy of the arbitral award on which leave for enforcement is recorded or a certified copy of the decision in which leave for enforcement is granted.

3. If an appeal can be lodged from the award to a second arbitral tribunal, leave for enforcement of an award rendered at first instance which is not declared provisionally enforceable may be granted only after the time limit for lodging the appeal to a second arbitral tribunal has lapsed without the appeal having been lodged or earlier, if the right to appeal is renounced in writing.

4. If the President of the District Court grants leave for enforcement, the means of recourse mentioned in article 1064(1) shall be the only means of recourse available to the respondent. The setting aside or the revocation of an arbitral award causes by operation of law the annulment of any leave for enforcement.

Article 1063 — Refusal of leave for enforcement
1. Enforcement of an arbitral award may be refused by the President of the District Court only if the award or the manner in which it was made is manifestly contrary to public policy or good morals, or if enforcement is ordered notwithstanding the lodging of an appeal in violation of article 1055, or if a penalty for non-compliance is imposed in violation of article 1056. In the latter case, the refusal shall be limited to the enforcement of the penal sum.

2. The Court Clerk shall without delay send to the parties a certified copy of the President's decision to refuse leave for enforcement.

3. The petitioner may lodge an appeal to the Court of Appeal against refusal to grant leave for enforcement within two months after the date on which the decision is signed.

4. If refusal to grant leave for enforcement is affirmed on appeal, the time limit for recourse to the Supreme Court shall be two months after the date on which the decision on appeal is signed.

5. If leave for enforcement is granted on appeal or after recourse to the Supreme Court, the provisions of the first sentence of article 1062(4) shall apply accordingly.

Section Five. Setting Aside and Revocation of the Arbitral Award.

Article 1064 — Setting aside in general

1. Recourse to a court against a final or partial final arbitral award which is not open to appeal to a second arbitral tribunal, or a final or partial final award rendered on arbitral appeal, may be made only by an application for setting aside or revocation in accordance with this Section.

2. An application for setting aside shall be made to the District Court with whose Registry the original of the award shall be deposited by virtue of article 1058(1).

3. An application for setting aside may be made as soon as the award has acquired the force of *res judicata*. The right to make an application shall be extinguished three months after the date of deposit of the award with the Registry of the District Court. However, if the award together with leave for enforcement is officially served on the other party, that party may make an application for setting aside within three months after the said service, irrespective of whether the period of three months mentioned in the preceding sentence has lapsed.

4. An application to set aside an interim arbitral award may be made only in conjunction with an application for setting aside a final or partial final award.

5. All grounds for setting aside shall, on pain of being barred, be mentioned in the writ of summons.

Article 1065 — Grounds for setting aside

1. Setting aside of the award can take place only on one or more of the following grounds:
   (*a*) absence of a valid arbitration agreement;
   (*b*) the arbitral tribunal was constituted in violation of the rules applicable thereto;
   (*c*) the arbitral tribunal has not complied with its mandate;
   (*d*) the award is not signed or does not contain reasons in accordance with the provisions of article 1057;
   (*e*) the award, or the manner in which it was made, violates public policy or good morals.

2. The ground mentioned in paragraph (1)(*a*) above shall not constitute a ground for setting aside in the case mentioned in article 1052(2).

3. The ground mentioned in paragraph (1)(*b*) above shall not constitute a ground for setting aside in the cases mentioned in article 1052(3).

4. The ground mentioned in paragraph (1)(*c*) above shall not constitute a ground for setting aside if the party who invokes this ground has participated in the

arbitral proceedings without invoking such ground, although it was known to him that the arbitral tribunal did not comply with its mandate.

5. If the arbitral tribunal has awarded in excess of, or differently from, what was claimed, the arbitral award shall be partially set aside to the extent that the part of the award which is in excess of or different from the claim can be separated from the remaining part of the award.

6. If and to the extent that the arbitral tribunal has failed to decide one or more matters submitted to it, the application for setting aside on the ground mentioned in paragraph (1)(c) above shall be admissible only if an additional award mentioned in article 1061(1) is made, or the request for an additional award mentioned in article 1061(1) has wholly or partially been rejected.

7. Notwithstanding the provisions of the second sentence of article 1064(3), the time limit for making an application for setting aside mentioned in the preceding paragraph shall be three months from the date of deposit of the additional award or the copy of the notification mentioned in article 1061(5) with the Registry of the District Court.

Article 1066 — Suspension of enforcement
1. An application for setting aside shall not suspend the enforcement of the award.

2. However, the court which decides on an application for setting aside may, at the request of either party, if it considers the request to be justified, suspend enforcement until a final decision is made on the application for setting aside.

3. A copy of the request for suspension shall be communicated by the Court Clerk to the other party without delay.

4. The court shall decide on the request after the other party has been given an opportunity to be heard.

5. Upon granting the request, the court may order the petitioner to give security. Upon denying the request, the court may order the other party to give security.

6. If enforcement is suspended, either party may request the court to lift the suspension. The provisions of paragraphs (3) to (5) inclusive shall apply accordingly.

Article 1067 — Consequences of setting aside
Unless the parties have agreed otherwise, as soon as a decision setting aside the award has become final, the jurisdiction of the court shall revive.

Article 1068 — Revocation of the award in case of fraud, forgery or new documents
1. Revocation of the award can take place only on one or more of the following grounds:
- (a) the award is wholly or partially based on fraud which is discovered after the award is made and which is committed during the arbitral proceedings by or with the knowledge of the other party;
- (b) the award is wholly or partially based on documents which, after the award is made, are discovered to have been forged;

(*c*) after the award is made, a party obtains documents which would have had an influence on the decision of the arbitral tribunal and which were withheld as a result of the acts of the other party.

2. An application for revocation shall be brought before the Court of Appeal which would have had jurisdiction to decide on an appeal relating to the application for setting aside mentioned in article 1064, within three months after the fraud or forgery has become known or the party has obtained the new documents. The provisions of articles 1066 and 1067 shall apply accordingly.

3. Subject to the provisions of the preceding paragraphs, the provisions of the articles of Book One, Title Ten, shall apply accordingly.

Section Six. Arbitral Award on Agreed Terms

Article 1069

1. If during the arbitral proceedings the parties reach a settlement, the arbitral tribunal may, at the joint request of the parties, record the contents of the settlement in the form of an arbitral award. The arbitral tribunal may refuse the request without giving reasons.

2. An arbitral award on agreed terms shall be regarded as an arbitral award to which the provisions of Sections Three to Five inclusive of this Title shall be applicable, provided that:

(*a*) the award may be set aside only on the ground that it is contrary to public policy or good morals,

(*b*) notwithstanding the provisions of article 1057, the award does not need to contain reasons, and

(*c*) the award is also signed by the parties.

Section Seven. Final Provisions

Article 1070 — No appeal against certain decisions of President of District Court

No appeal may be lodged against the decisions of the President of the District Court mentioned in Sections One to Three inclusive of this Title.

Article 1071 — No attorney required for certain requests

In the cases mention [sic] in articles 1026(2) and (4), 1027(3), 1028, 1044(1), and 1062(1), the application and if applicable the answer need not be filed by an attorney.

Article 1072 — Agreement on competent President of District Court in certain cases

The parties may designate by agreement the President of a specific District Court as the President competent for the matters mentioned in articles 1026(2) and (4), 1027(3), 1028, 1029(2) and (4), 1031(2), 1035(2) and 1041(2).

444

Article 1073 — Applicability of Title One to arbitration within the Netherlands; appointment of arbitrators in case place of arbitration is unknown

1. The provisions of this Title shall apply if the place of arbitration is situated within the Netherlands.

2. If the parties have not determined the place of arbitration, the appointment or challenge of the arbitrator or arbitrators or the secretary engaged by an arbitral tribunal may take place in accordance with the provisions contained in Section One of this Title if at least one of the parties is domiciled or has his actual residence in the Netherlands.

TITLE TWO: Arbitration Outside the Netherlands

Article 1074 — Foreign arbitration agreement and substantive claim before Dutch court; foreign arbitration agreement and interim measures by Dutch court

1. A court in the Netherlands seized of a dispute in respect of which an arbitration agreement has been concluded under which arbitration shall take place outside the Netherlands shall declare that it has no jurisdiction if a party invokes the existence of the said agreement before submitting a defence, unless the agreement is invalid under the law applicable thereto.

2. The agreement mentioned in paragraph (1) shall not preclude a party from requesting a court in the Netherlands to grant interim measures of protection, or from applying to the President of the District Court for a decision in summary proceedings in accordance with the provisions of article 289.

Article 1075 — Recognition and enforcement of foreign award under treaties

An arbitral award made in a foreign State to which a treaty concerning recognition and enforcement is applicable may be recognised and enforced in the Netherlands. The provisions of articles 985 to 991 inclusive shall apply accordingly to the extent that the treaty does not contain provisions deviating therefrom and provided that the President of the District Court shall be substituted for the District Court and the time limit for appeal from his decision and for recourse to the Supreme Court shall be two months.

Article 1076 — Recognition and enforcement of foreign award without treaties

1. If no treaty concerning recognition and enforcement is applicable, or if an applicable treaty allows a party to rely upon the law of the country in which recognition or enforcement is sought, an arbitral award made in a foreign State may be recognised in the Netherlands and its enforcement may be sought in the Netherlands, upon submission of the original or a certified copy of the arbitration agreement and arbitral award, unless:

    (a) the party against whom recognition or enforcement is sought, asserts and proves that:

        (*i*) a valid arbitration agreement under the law applicable thereto is lacking;

(*ii*) the arbitral tribunal is constituted in violation of the rules applicable thereto;

(*iii*) the arbitral tribunal has not complied with its mandate;

(*iv*) the arbitral award is still open to an appeal to a second arbitral tribunal, or to a court in the country in which the award is made;

(*v*) the arbitral award has been set aside by a competent authority of the country in which that award is made;

(b) the court finds that the recognition or enforcement would be contrary to public policy.

2. The ground mentioned in paragraph (1)(A)(*a*) above shall not constitute a ground for refusal of recognition or enforcement if the party who invokes this ground has made an appearance in the arbitral proceedings and, before submitting a defence, has not raised the plea that the arbitral tribunal lacks jurisdiction on the ground that a valid arbitration agreement is lacking.

3. The ground mentioned in paragraph (1)(A)(*b*) above shall not constitute a ground for refusal of recognition or enforcement if the party who invokes this ground has participated in the constitution of the arbitral tribunal, or if he has not participated in the constitution of the arbitral tribunal, has made an appearance in the arbitral proceedings and, before submitting a defence, has not raised the plea that the arbitral tribunal lacks jurisdiction on the ground that the arbitral tribunal is constituted in violation of the applicable rules.

4. The ground mentioned in paragraph (1)(A)(*c*) above shall not constitute a ground for refusal of recognition or enforcement if the party who invokes this ground has participated in the arbitral proceedings without raising it, although it was known to him that the arbitral tribunal did not comply with its mandate.

5. If the award is in excess of, or different from, what was claimed, the arbitral award shall be capable of partial recognition or enforcement to the extent that the part of the award which is in excess of or different from the claim can be separated from the remaining part of the award.

6. The provisions of articles 985 to 991 inclusive shall apply accordingly, provided that the President of the District Court shall be substituted for the District Court, the time limit for appeal from his decision and for recourse to the Supreme Court shall be two months, and no documents need be submitted evidencing the enforceability of the arbitral award in the country in which it is made.

7. If an application for the setting aside of an award made in a foreign State is made to a competent authority of the country in which the award is made, the provisions of article 1066(2) to (6) inclusive shall apply accordingly when recognition or enforcement is sought in the Netherlands.

9. SWEDEN

a. Swedish Arbitration Act of 1929[1]

The Arbitration Agreement

Section 1

Any question in the nature of a civil matter which may be compromised by agreement, as well as any question of compensation for damage resulting from a crime may, when a dispute has arisen with regard thereto, be referred by agreement between the parties to the decision of one or more arbitrators. An arbitration agreement relating to any such question may also have reference to future disputes arising from a particular legal relationship specified in the agreement.

Arbitrators may not assume jurisdiction in respect of any question which is the subject of a pending court action or summary documentary process although such court action will not prevent arbitration proceedings if notice of withdrawal has been given to the presiding judge.

Section 2

If the arbitration agreement does not reserve the right of the parties to appeal from the award, they will be deemed to have consented to abide by it.

The present Act shall not apply to an arbitration agreement which provides for a right of appeal.

Section 3

If, after a request has been made for the application of an arbitration agreement, that request is rejected by a party, or a party fails in his duty to appoint an arbitrator, and the other party prefers to bring the dispute before a court of law rather than insist on an arbitration award, then the arbitration agreement shall be no bar to the jurisdiction of the court over the dispute.

Section 3a

In regard to disputes between business enterprises and consumers concerning products or services supplied in the main for private use, an arrangement made prior to the dispute to the effect that disputes shall be referred to arbitration without a right for the parties to appeal against the award may be invoked only if the value of the disputed matter matter [sic] exceeds the amount referred to in section 1 of the Small Claims Procedure Act (1974 No. 8) or if such Act does not apply pursuant to section 3 thereof.

The first paragraph does not apply if the dispute concerns an agreement between an insurer and an insured concerning insurance issued on the basis of collective bargaining contracts or of group agreements and are handled by representatives of the group, nor if an international obligation of Sweden to the contrary is in existence.

1. *Lag om skiljemän, 1929.* Translation by Stockholm Chamber of Commerce.

Section 4

No arbitration proceeding under this Act shall be instituted against any party who is resident outside Sweden and who is not subject to the jurisdiction of the Swedish courts in disputes of the nature in question, unless the arbitration agreement is to the effect that the proceedings are to take place in Sweden or the arbitrators or an arbitration institution, under powers conferred by the arbitration agreement, has decided that the proceedings are to take place in Sweden, or the party otherwise agrees to such proceedings taking place as aforesaid.

The Arbitrators and Their Appointment

Section 5

An arbitrator is not qualified to serve:

1. if he is a minor or has been declared incapable;

2. if, as a judge or otherwise by reason of public office, he has tried the dispute submitted to arbitration; if he has given evidence in the matter or submitted an expert opinion on the issue; if he himself, or one so related to him, either by blood or by marriage, as would debar a judge, has a personal interest in the matter or can expect any considerable advantage or disadvantage therefrom; or if he is a party in a similar case;

3. if he is so related to a party either by blood or by marriage, as would debar a judge; if he is involved in litigation against or is an obvious enemy of one of the parties; if he is in receipt of a salary or financial support from either party: if he is the subordinate of either party; if he has assisted one of the parties in preparing or conducting his case; or if he has accepted or stipulated for remuneration contrary to the provisions of section 23 of this Act;

4. if there is any other special circumstance which is likely to reduce the confidence in his honesty or impartiality; or

5. if he is prevented from performing his functions by any obstacle which is likely to prove of long duration. .

The receipt of a salary or financial support from the Crown does not disqualify an arbitrator in a case in which the Crown is a party, unless he is employed in or by the authority whose activities are directly concerned in the case.

An arbitrator shall not be disqualified merely because a person tries to provoke him or attacks him by word or deed in an attempt to disqualify him.

Section 6

If the parties do not agree on the choice of arbitrators and have made no agreement as to their number and the mode of their appointment, there shall be three arbitrators, one appointed by each party and the third by the two arbitrators so appointed.

Section 7

Where each party is to nominate an arbitrator or arbitrators and one party has given notice in writing to his opponent of his choice, the latter shall, unless otherwise agreed, within fourteen days notify the other party in writing of his choice.

A party who has given the other party notice of his choice of arbitrator may not revoke his choice without the consent of the other party.

Section 8

If a party who is bound to appoint an arbitrator fails to do his duty in that respect, or if the other arbitrators cannot agree on the choice of an arbitrator to be appointed by those others, then, unless otherwise agreed between the parties, an arbitrator shall be appointed by the District Court on the application of a party.

If an arbitrator is to be appointed by any person other than a party or other arbitrators but such person fails to make the appointment within a reasonable time, then, unless the parties have otherwise provided, the arbitration agreement shall terminate in so far as it applies to the dispute in question.

If a person who is designated as arbitrator in an arbitration agreement dies, the agreement shall terminate unless otherwise agreed between the parties. Where an arbitrator, who has been appointed in the manner aforesaid, resigns or becomes disqualified or is prevented for any other reason from performing his functions, then the same rule shall apply in relation to the dispute in question.

If an arbitrator who is designated in the arbitration agreement fails to perform his duties in an adequate manner, the District Court shall on the application of a party remove the arbitrator and shall, unless the parties have otherwise agreed, declare the arbitration agreement terminated.

Section 9

If a person who is designated as arbitrator in an arbitration agreement dies, the agreement shall lapse unless otherwise agreed between the parties. Where an arbitrator, who has been appointed in the manner aforesaid, resigns or becomes disqualified or is prevented for any other reason from performing his functions, then the same rule shall apply in relation to the dispute in question.

If an arbitrator who is designated in the arbitration agreement fails to perform his duties in an adequate manner, the District Court shall on the application of a party remove the arbitrator and shall, unless the parties have otherwise agreed, declare the arbitration agreement lapsed.

Section 10

If an arbitrator who is not named in the arbitration agreement resigns, then, unless the parties have otherwise provided, the District Court shall appoint another arbitrator on the application of a party.

Provided, however, that if the arbitrator has died or if his resignation is due to any disqualification or lawful excuse which has occurred after his appointment, then, unless the parties have otherwise provided, the person or persons who appointed the arbitrator shall appoint another in his place; to such appointment, the relevant provisions of Section 7 shall apply.

If an arbitrator who is not named in the arbitration agreement fails to perform his duties in an adequate manner, he shall on the application of a party be removed by the District Court and, unless the parties have otherwise provided, another person shall be appointed by the District Court in his place.

The Procedure

Section 11

Each party may call for the application of an arbitration agreement.

If the arbitration agreement has reference to an existing dispute but has not been made in writing clearly specifying the issue in the dispute, or if the agreement has reference to future disputes, the party invoking the agreement shall give notice in writing to his opponent of the question or questions as to which an arbitration award is requested. The present provision shall not prevent the arbitrators from deciding questions which the parties jointly refer to them in the course of the proceedings.

Section 12

When there are several arbitrators, one of them shall be chairman of the tribunal. Unless otherwise agreed, that arbitrator shall be chairman who has been appointed by the other arbitrators or by the District Court in place of such arbitrator.

The chairman shall fix a convenient place and time for any meeting of the arbitrators, arrange for summonses and other administrative work, and shall preside at any hearing.

Section 13

Subject to the procedural provisions hereinafter contained, the arbitrators shall act, as far as possible, in accordance with the instructions of the parties and shall otherwise deal with the case in an impartial, practical and speedy manner.

Section 14

The arbitrators shall give each party a sufficient opportunity to present his case orally or in writing. If a party fails without valid excuse to avail himself of such opportunity, then the arbitrators may decide the case on the existing material.

Section 15

Unless the parties otherwise provide, the arbitrators may take steps in order to promote the investigation of the matter, such as summoning a party or an expert or any other person to attend for examination, or call upon a party or any other person in possession of a written document or other object, which may be assumed to have importance as evidence, to produce the document or object. The arbitrators may not make orders on penalty of a fine, nor use other means of constraint, nor may they administer oaths or truth affirmations.

If a party wishes that a witness or an expert should be heard in court or that a party should be examined there on truth affirmation or that an order should be made for a party or any other person to produce as evidence a written document or an object on penalty of a fine, he shall apply to the District Court in whose area the person is present who is to be heard or is otherwise affected. If the arbitrators have considered the procedure necessary, and if the requisite information is made available, the court shall arrange for the examination or issue an order on penalty of a fine, provided that there is no legal obstacle to such procedure. The rules on evidence taken otherwise than at the trial in an ordinary action shall, to the extent relevant, apply to the procedures referred to above.

Section 16

All the arbitrators must take part in the resolution of a dispute. If there is a divergence of opinion among them, the opinion shared by more than one half of their number shall prevail, unless the parties have agreed otherwise. If the majority of the arbitrators do not agree on the resolution of a question which has been referred to them, the arbitration agreement shall terminate in respect of such question, unless the parties have otherwise agreed.

Section 17

The award shall be put down in writing and signed by the arbitrators.

The arbitrators should state in the award when and where it was given and, as soon as possible and not later than immediately after the giving of the award, notify the parties when and where it will be available.

Section 18

The parties may lay down a period within which the arbitration award must be given. If the award is not given within that period, the arbitration agreement shall terminate as regards the dispute which has been submitted to the arbitrators for decision.

Where the parties have not laid down any period for giving the award, then the award shall be given within six months reckoned from the date when the arbitration agreement was made or, where the arbitration agreement has reference to future disputes or has not been made in writing with a clear definition of the issue in dispute, from the date when the application of the agreement was called for in the manner provided in section 11 of this Act; but if proceedings concerning the validity or applicability of the arbitration agreement are commenced in any court of law within such time, the period for giving the award shall be reckoned from the date when the final decision was made in such proceedings. Provided, however, that the District Court may, for particular reasons, on the application of a party, extend the period referred to in this paragraph, but not, except for compelling reasons, for more than six months in the aggregate. The arbitration agreement shall terminate as regards the dispute in question on the expiration of the period fixed, unless before such time either an award has been given or application has been made for an extension of the period, which application is approved by the District Court. The provisions of this paragraph shall not apply in case the parties are, or one of them is, resident outside Sweden.

Section 19

Where several claims have been made in the matter, the arbitrators may give an award on one or more of such claims even if the parties have not concluded their cases concerning the remaining claims, provided that the rights of neither party be prejudiced thereby. Likewise the arbitrators may, where a party has partially admitted a claim, give a separate award on the part that has been admitted.

Void and Challengeable Awards

Section 20

The award is void:

1. if there was no valid arbitration agreement;
2. if the award has not been put down in writing and signed by the arbitrators; or
3. to the extent that the arbitrators have rendered a decision on a question which by law cannot be submitted to arbitration or if, when the award was given, the arbitration proceedings were inadmissible pursuant to the second paragraph of section 1 of this Act.

The absence of an arbitrator's signature on the award shall not, however, make the award void, if it has been signed by the majority of the arbitrators and if they have verified on the award that the arbitrator whose signature is absent took part in deciding the dispute.

If the award is void in part and, for such reason, cannot be enforced as regards the remainder, then the award shall be void in its entirety.

Section 21

At the request of a party an award shall be set aside by the court:

1. to the extent that the arbitrators have gone beyond the matters submitted to them or have given an award after the expiration of the period laid down in that behalf;
2. if the arbitrators have rendered a decision in a case in which the arbitration proceedings should not have taken place in this country;
3. if an arbitrator was disqualified or was not appointed in the proper manner; or,
4. if, through no fault of the party, any other irregularity of procedure has occurred, which in probability may be assumed to have influenced the decision.

A party may not rely on the existence of any irregularity of the aforesaid character if, by taking part in the proceedings without objection, or otherwise, he ought to be considered as having waived the irregularity.

An action to challenge the award must be commenced within sixty days from the time when the party received an original or a certified copy of the award. A party who fails to observe the said time limit forfeits his right to challenge the award.

Section 22

If an award is found by the execution authority to be so obscure as to make enforcement impossible, the existence of such award shall not debar a party from commencing an action in court concerning the question so decided by the arbitrators.

The Costs of Arbitration

Section 23

An arbitrator must not accept or stipulate for compensation from one party unless a similar benefit is due to him from the other party. An agreement to the contrary shall be void; and an arbitrator shall be bound to return what he has improperly received.

If no valid agreement has been made concerning the compensation of the arbitrators, the parties shall pay, jointly and severally, reasonable compensation to the arbitrators for their work and expenses. Unless otherwise agreed between the parties and the arbitrators, the arbitrators may fix, in the final award, the amount of the compensation due to each arbitrator and enjoin the parties to pay it.

Arbitrators may not withhold the award pending payment of their compensation.

Section 24

Unless otherwise agreed between the parties, the arbitrators may, at the request of either party, determine whether and to what extent the opposite party should reimburse the party the compensation due from the latter to the arbitrators, and his other costs in the proceedings.

Section 25

If a party is dissatisfied with a decision by the arbitrators relative to the compensation due to them, he may bring the matter before the court provided that he commences his action within sixty days from the time when he received the award. Each of the arbitrators has a similar right as regards compensation claimed by him; but the time for commencing action shall be reckoned from the day on which the award was given. The award shall clearly specify the procedure to be followed by a party wishing to proceed against the decision of the arbitrators.

Special Provisions

Section 26

In cases contemplated by section 21 of this Act, the competent court shall be the District Court which has jurisdiction over the defendant in civil actions concerning his person, and in cases contemplated by section 25 of this Act, the District Court in the place where the award was given. If there is no competent court according to this provisions, [sic] the action shall be tried by the Stockholm District Court.

Applications under sections 8, 9, 10 and 18 of this Act shall be entertained by the District Court in the place of residence of either party. If similar applications have been filed with more than one District Court, the District Court with which an application was first filed shall be competent and a decision made by any other District Court shall be void. If neither party is resident in Sweden, the Stockholm District Court shall be competent. No application must be granted until the other party has been given an opportunity to comment thereon. If an application contemplates the removal of an arbitrator, the latter should also be heard.

No appeal is allowed from a decision of a District Court appointing or dismissing an arbitrator or declaring an arbitration agreement terminated, or determining any question concerning prolongation of the period for giving an award.

Section 27

If the law provides that a party must commence proceedings within a certain time, but pursuant to an arbitration agreement his claim is to be settled by arbitration, then the party shall, within the specified period, call for the application of the arbitration agreement in the manner provided in section 11 of this Act.

If subsequently, through no fault of the party, there is an obstacle to a valid arbitration award being obtained, the party nevertheless retains his rights if he commences an action in the court within sixty days reckoned from the time when he was informed of such obstacle or, if the award has been set aside after having been challenged, from the time when the judgment to that effect has become non-appealable. Any such act or omission by the opponent as is contemplated by section 3 of this Act shall be considered equivalent to an obstacle of the type referred to above.

Section 28

With regard to the application of foreign arbitration agreements and foreign arbitral awards, the special provisions enacted for such purposes shall be observed.

b. Swedish Act of 1929 Concerning Foreign Arbitration Agreements and Awards[2]

Foreign Arbitration Agreements

Section 1

An arbitration agreement shall be considered as "foreign" if it stipulates that the proceedings are to take place outside Sweden.

An arbitration agreement which does not indicate whether the proceedings are to take place within or outside Sweden shall be considered as "foreign" if both parties were resident outside Sweden.

Section 2

If an arbitration agreement provides that the proceedings are to take place in a particular foreign State, the law of such State shall apply to the agreement.

Section 3

Swedish courts shall not, where objection is made, have jurisdiction to try any dispute which is subject to a foreign arbitration agreement, if the agreement is valid under the foreign law applicable to it and the dispute also is arbitrable under the law applicable to a Swedish arbitration agreement.

Section 4

No arbitration proceedings may, by virtue of a foreign arbitration agreement, take place in Sweden unless, in cases contemplated by the second paragraph of section 1 of this Act, the arbitrators or an arbitration institution, under powers conferred by the arbitration agreement, has decided that the proceedings are to take place in Sweden or the party against whom the agreement is invoked has become resident here after the making thereof. As regards the procedure in such cases, the provisions of the Swedish Arbitration Act (1929 No. 145) shall be observed.

Section 5

An arbitral award shall be considered as "foreign" if it was given abroad.

In applying this Act, an arbitral award shall be considered as given in the State where the arbitration proceedings have taken place.

Section 6

Foreign arbitral awards are valid in Sweden subject to such reservations as are hereinafter stated.

Section 7

A foreign arbitral award shall not be valid in Sweden if the person against whom the award is invoked shows:

2. *Lag om utländska skiljeavtal och skiljedomar, 1929.* Translation by Stockholm Chamber of Commerce.

1. that a party when the arbitration agreement was made lacked capacity to enter into such an agreement or was not properly represented or that the arbitration agreement is not valid under the law to which the parties have subjected it or, failing any indication thereof, under the law of the country where the award was given,

2. that he has not received proper notice of the appointment of an arbitrator or of the arbitration proceedings or that he for any other reason has been unable to present his case,

3. that the arbitrators have gone beyond the matters submitted to them and that by reason thereof the arbitral award is ineffective in the State where it was given or under whose law it was given,

4. that the appointment of the arbitral tribunal or its composition or the arbitration proceedings are in contravention of the agreement of the parties or, failing any agreement in this respect, in contravention of the law of the State where the proceedings took place, and by reason thereof the arbitral award is ineffective in the State where it was given or under whose law it was given, or

5. that the arbitration award has not yet become enforceable or otherwise binding on the parties in the State where it was given or under whose law it was given or that it has been set aside or suspended by a competent authority in the said State.

Moreover, a foreign arbitration award is not valid:

1. if the arbitration award comprises a decision of any question which under Swedish law is not arbitrable, or

2. if the implementation of the arbitration award would be patently incompatible with the basic principles of Swedish law.

Section 8

Any application for leave to enforce a foreign arbitral award shall be submitted to the Svea Court of Appeal.

There shall be attached to the application the original or a certified copy of the arbitral award and a certified translation into the Swedish language.

Section 9

The application referred to in section 8 of this Act may not be granted unless the other party has been given an opportunity to comment thereon.

Where the other party claims that he has applied to such authority as is referred to in sub-paragraph 5 of the first paragraph of section 7 of this Act in order to have the arbitral award set aside or to have its enforcement postponed, then the Court of Appeal may postpone its decision and, at the request of the applicant, require the other party to provide reasonable security on penalty that a decision to give leave of enforcement may otherwise be made.

If the Court of Appeal grants the application, the arbitration award shall be enforceable in the same manner as a final non-appealable judgment of a Swedish court, unless the Supreme Court on appeal against the decision of the Court of Appeal orders otherwise.

Section 10

If several claims have been referred to arbitration and the award does not cover them all, the Court of Appeal may, if there are reasons to do so, require the applicant to provide security for the repayment of any sums which he may have to refund by virtue of any subsequent award of the arbitrators. If the applicant is unable to provide the security requested by the Court, his application shall be refused.

Section 11

The provisions of this Act relating to foreign arbitral awards shall not apply to any decision by arbitrators who, independently of any arbitration agreement, have been appointed by virtue of a provision in any enactment or pursuant to a decision of a public authority.

Special Provisions

Section 12

The provisions of the second paragraph of section 15 of the Swedish Arbitration Act concerning the taking of evidence in the course of arbitration proceedings within Sweden shall also be applicable when proceedings take place outside Sweden under an arbitration agreement relating to a matter which is arbitrable according to Swedish law.

Section 13

If the provisions of any foreign law applicable to a cause or matter relating to a foreign arbitration agreement or arbitral award is not known to the court or other authority charged with applying the law, then the court or authority may require the party concerned to furnish proof in this respect.

10. Switzerland

a. Federal Conflict-of-Laws Act[1]

Chapter 12

I. Scope of Application. Seat of the Arbitral Tribunal.

Article 176
(1) The provisions of this chapter shall apply to any arbitration if the seat of the arbitral tribunal is in Switzerland and if, at the time when the arbitration agreement was concluded, at least one of the parties had neither its domicile nor its habitual residence in Switzerland.

(2) The provisions of this chapter shall not apply where the parties have in writing excluded its application and agreed to the exclusive application of the procedural provisions of cantonal law relating to arbitration.

(3) The seat of the arbitral tribunal shall be determined by the parties, or the arbitration institution designated by them, or, failing both, by the arbitrators.

II. Arbitrability.

Article 177
(1) Any dispute involving property may be the subject-matter of an arbitration.

(2) If a party to the arbitration agreement is a state or an enterprise or organisation controlled by it, it cannot rely on its own law in order to contest its capacity to be a party to an arbitration or the arbitrability of a dispute covered by the arbitration agreement.

III. Arbitration agreement.

Article 178
(1) As regards its form, an arbitration agreement shall be valid if made in writing, by telegram, telex, telecopier or any other means of communication which permits it to be evidenced by a text.

(2) As regards its substance, an arbitration agreement shall be valid if it conforms either to the law chosen by the parties, or to the law governing the subject-matter of the dispute, in particular the law governing the main contract, or if it conforms to Swiss law.

---

1. Entered into force 1 January 1989. Translation adopted by Association Suisse de l'Arbitrage, on the basis of text translated by Mssrs. Robert Brinier, Marc Blessing, Pierre Karrer, and Adam Samuel, with assistance from Clive Schmitthoff and Humphrey Lloyd.

(3) The validity of an arbitration agreement cannot be contested on the ground that the main contract may not be valid or that the arbitration agreement concerns disputes which have not yet arisen.

IV. Arbitral tribunal.

1. Constitution.

Article 179

(1) The arbitrators shall be appointed, removed or replaced in accordance with the agreement of the parties.

(2) In the absence of such an agreement, the matter may be referred to the court where the arbitral tribunal has its seat; the court shall apply by analogy the provisions of cantonal law concerning the appointment, removal or replacement of arbitrators.

(3) Where a court is called upon to appoint an arbitrator, it shall make the appointment, unless a summary examination shows that no arbitration agreement exists between the parties.

2. Challenge of Arbitrators.

Article 180

(1) An arbitrator may be challenged:
  a. if he does not meet the requirements agreed by the parties;
  b. if the arbitration rules agreed by the parties provide a ground for challenge; or
  c. if circumstances exist that give rise to justifiable doubts as to his independence.

(2) A party may challenge an arbitrator whom it has appointed or in whose appointment it has participated only on grounds of which it became aware after such appointment. The ground for challenge must be notified to the arbitral tribunal and to the other party without delay.

(3) In the event of a dispute and to the extent to which the parties have not determined the procedure for the challenge, the court of the seat of the arbitral tribunal shall decide; its decision is final.

V. Lis pendens

Article 181

The arbitral proceedings shall be pending from the time when one of the parties submits its request to the arbitrator or arbitrators designated in the arbitration agreement or, in the absence of such designation, from the time when one of the parties initiates the procedure for the constitution of the arbitral tribunal.

VI. Procedure.

1. Principle.

Article 182
(1) The parties may, directly or by reference to arbitration rules, determine the arbitral procedure; they may also submit it to a procedural law of their choice.

(2) Where the parties have not determined the procedure, the arbitral tribunal shall determine it to the extent necessary, either directly or by reference to a law or to arbitration rules.

(3) Whatever procedure is chosen, the arbitral tribunal shall ensure equal treatment of the parties and the right of the parties to be heard in an adversarial procedure.

2. Provisional and Protective Measures.

Article 183
(1) Unless the parties have agreed otherwise, the arbitral tribunal may, at the request of a party, order provisional or protective measures.

(2) If the party so ordered does not comply therewith voluntarily, the arbitral tribunal may request the assistance of the competent court. Such court shall apply its own law.

(3) The arbitral tribunal or the court may make the granting of provisional or protective measures subject to the provision of appropriate security.

3. Taking Evidence.

Article 184
(1) The arbitral tribunal shall itself take the evidence.

(2) Where the assistance of state authorities is needed for taking evidence, the arbitral tribunal or a party with the consent of the arbitral tribunal may request the assistance of the court of the seat of the arbitral tribunal. Such court shall apply its own law.

4. Other Judicial Assistance.

Article 185
For any further judicial assistance the court of the seat of the arbitral tribunal shall have jurisdiction.

VII. Jurisdiction.

Article 186
(1) The arbitral tribunal shall decide on its own jurisdiction.

(2) Any objection to its jurisdiction must be raised prior to any defence on the merits.

(3) The arbitral tribunal shall, in general, decide on its jurisdiction by a preliminary decision.

VIII. Decision on the Merits.

1. Applicable Law.

Article 187

(1) The arbitral tribunal shall decide the dispute according to the rules of law chosen by the parties or, in the absence of such a choice, according to the rules of law with which the case has the closest connection.

(2) The parties may authorize the arbitral tribunal to decide ex aequo et bono.

2. Partial Award.

Article 188

Unless the parties have agreed otherwise, the arbitral tribunal may make partial awards.

3. Arbitral Award.

Article 189

(1) The arbitral award shall be made in conformity with the rules of procedure and the form agreed by the parties.

(2) In the absence of such agreement, the award shall be made by a majority decision, or, in the absence of a majority, by the presiding arbitrator alone. It shall be in writing, reasoned, dated and signed. The signature of the presiding arbitrator shall suffice.

IX. Finality, Setting Aside.

1. Principle.

Article 190

(1) The award is final from the time when it is communicated.

(2) Proceedings for setting aside the award may only be initiated:
- (a) where the sole arbitrator has been incorrectly appointed or where the arbitral tribunal has been incorrectly constituted;
- (b) where the arbitral tribunal has wrongly declared itself to have or not to have jurisdiction;

(c) where the award has gone beyond the claims submitted to the arbitral tribunal, or failed to decide one of the claims;

(d) where the principle of equal treatment of the parties or their right to be heard in adversarial procedure has not been observed;

(e) where the award is incompatible with public policy.

(3) As regards preliminary decisions, setting aside proceedings can only be initiated on the grounds of the above paragraphs 2(a) and 2(b); the time-limit runs from the communication of the decision.

2. Competent Court.

Article 191

(1) Setting aside proceedings may only be brought before the Federal Supreme Court. The procedure is governed by the provisions of the Federal Judicial Organisation Act relating to public law appeals.

(2) However, the parties may agree that the court of the seat of the arbitral tribunal shall decide in lieu of the Federal Supreme Court; its decision is final. For this purpose the Cantons shall designate a sole Cantonal court.

X. Exclusion Agreements.

Article 192

(1) Where none of the parties has its domicile, its habitual residence, or a business establishment in Switzerland, they may, by an express statement in the arbitration agreement or by a subsequent agreement in writing, exclude all setting aside proceedings, or they may limit such proceedings to one or several of the grounds listed in Article 190, paragraph 2.

(2) Where the parties have excluded all setting aside proceedings and where the awards are to be enforced in Switzerland, the New York [Arbitration] Convention of 10 June, 1958 on the Recognition and Enforcement of Foreign Arbitral Awards shall apply by analogy.

XI. Deposit and Certificate of Enforceability.

Article 193

(1) Each party may at its own expense deposit a copy of the award with the Swiss court of the seat of the arbitral tribunal.

(2) At the request of a party, that court shall certify the enforceability of the award.

(3) At the request of a party, the arbitral tribunal shall certify that the award has been made in conformity with the provisions of this Act; such certificate has the same effect as the deposit of the award.

XII. Foreign Arbitral Awards.

Article 194

The recognition and enforcement of a foreign arbitral award is governed by the New York [Arbitration] Convention of 10 June, 1958 on the Recognition and Enforcement of Foreign Arbitral Awards.

b. Swiss Intercantonal Concordat on Arbitration[2]

Chapter I. General Provisions

Article 1 — Scope

1. This Concordat shall apply to any proceedings before an arbitral tribunal the seat of which is within one of the cantons party to this Concordat.

2. The application of arbitration agreements and rules of private or public institutions is reserved insofar as they do not violate mandatory provisions of this Concordat.

3. The following provisions of this Concordat are mandatory: Art. 2 subs. 2 and 3, Art. 4 to 9, 12, 13, 18 to 21, 22 subs. 2, Art. 25, 26 to 29, 31 subs. 1, Art. 33, subs. 1, a to f, 2 and 3, and Art. 36 to 46.

Article 2 — Seat of the Arbitral Tribunal

1. The seat of the arbitral tribunal is at the place chosen by agreement between the parties or by a decision of the body designated by them, or if there is none, by decision of the arbitrators.

2. If neither the parties nor the body designated by them nor the arbitrators have chosen the place of arbitration, the seat shall be at the place of the court which would have jurisdiction over the case but for arbitration.

3. If more than one court would have jurisdiction in the sense of the preceding subsection, the seat of the arbitral tribunal is at the place of the first judicial authority seized as provided in Art. 3.

Article 3 — Jurisdiction of Judicial Authority at the Seat of the Arbitral Tribunal

Subject to Art. 45 subsection 2, the superior court of common civil jurisdiction of the canton in which the seat of the arbitration is located has jurisdiction to:

(a) appoint arbitrators if they have not been designated by parties or by the body chosen by the parties;

(b) decide on challenges of arbitrators, their removal and placement;

(c) extend the term of the arbitrators;

(d) assist in executing measures for taking evidence on the arbitral tribunal's request;

(e) accept deposit of the arbitral award and notify it;

(f) give judgment on actions for annulment or revision of awards;

(g) declare the award enforceable.

Chapter II. Agreement to Arbitrate

Article 4 — Arbitration Agreements and Clauses

1. An agreement to arbitrate is made by an arbitration agreement or an arbitration clause.

2. Translation adopted by Association Suisse de l'Arbitrage.

2. In an arbitration agreement the parties submit an existing dispute to arbitration.

3. An arbitration clause may refer only to future disputes arising from a particular legal relationship.

Article 5 — Arbitrability

Any right at the free disposal of the parties is arbitrable unless the case is subject to the exclusive jurisdiction of a State authority pursuant to a mandatory legal provision.

Article 6 — Form

1. The agreement to arbitrate must be in writing.

2. It may result from a written declaration to adhere to the statutes of a juridical person provided that the declaration expressly refer to the arbitration clause contained in the statutes or rules made pursuant to them.

Article 7 — Exclusion of Lawyers

Any provision in an arbitration clause prohibiting the use of lawyers in an arbitration whether as arbitrators, secretaries or representatives of the parties is void.

Article 8 — Jurisdiction of the Arbitral Tribunal

1. If the validity of the agreement to arbitrate or its content or scope are challenged before the arbitral tribunal, it decides on its own jurisdiction by an interim or final award.

2. A plea of lack of jurisdiction of the arbitral tribunal must be raised prior to any defence on the merits.

Article 9 — Remedy as to Jurisdiction

An interim award whereby the arbitral tribunal accepts or declines jurisdiction may be challenged immediately by action for annulment as provided in Art. 30 (b).

Chapter III. Designation, Appointment and Term of Arbitrators. Lis Pendens

Article 10 — Number of Arbitrators

1. The arbitral tribunal shall consist of three arbitrators unless the parties have agreed on a different uneven number or on a sole arbitrator.

2. The parties may, however, agree to designate an even number of arbitrators without a chairman being designated.

Article 11 — Designation by the Parties

1. The parties may designate the arbitrator or arbitrators by common consent in the agreement to arbitrate itself or in a later agreement. They may also cause them to be designated by a body of their choice.

2. If an arbitrator is designated only by reference to his office, the designation shall be deemed to refer to the holder of the office at the time of acceptance of the mandate as arbitrator.

3. Unless otherwise agreed, each party designates an equal number of arbitrators, and the arbitrators so designated unanimously elect a chairman.

4. Where the arbitrators are even in number, the parties shall agree either to give a casting vote to the chairman, or to require an unanimous or qualified majority vote from the tribunal.

Article 12 — Appointment by the Judicial Authority

If the parties cannot agree on the designation of a sole arbitrator, if one of them fails to designate the arbitrator or arbitrators as required, or if the designated arbitrators cannot agree on a chairman, the judicial authority provided in Art. 3 shall make the appointment on petition by one of the parties, unless the agreement provides for another appointing body.

Article 13 — Lis Pendens

1. The arbitration is pending:
   (a) from the time when one of the parties seizes the arbitrator or arbitrators designated in an arbitrator clause; or
   (b) if there is no such designation in the arbitration clause, from the time when one of the parties commences the procedure for the designation of the arbitrators as provided in the arbitration clause; or
   (c) if there is no such provision in the arbitration clause, from the time when one of the parties petitions the competent judicial authority; or
   (d) if there is no arbitration clause, on the signing of the arbitration agreement.

2. If the arbitration rules accepted by the parties or the arbitration clause provide for a conciliation procedure, the commencement of this procedure shall be assimilated with the commencement of the arbitral proceedings.

Article 14 — Acceptance by the Arbitrators

1. The arbitrators must accept their mandate.

2. The arbitral tribunal shall be deemed to be properly constituted only when all the arbitrators have accepted their mandate with respect to the case submitted to them.

Article 15 — Secretary

1. With the agreement of the parties, the arbitral tribunal may designate a secretary.

2. Articles 18 to 20 shall be applicable to the challenge of a secretary.

Article 16 — Term

1. The parties may, either in an agreement to arbitrate or in a later agreement, impose a time limit on the authority of the arbitral tribunal.

2. In this case, the term may be extended each time for a certain period either by agreement between the parties, or by a decision of the judicial authority provided in Art. 3 on petition by one of the parties or by the arbitral tribunal.

3. If the petition is by one of the parties, the other party must be heard.

Article 17 — Unjustifiable Delay

The parties may at any time petition the judicial authority provided in Art. 3 with respect to unjustifiable delay on the part of the arbitral tribunal.

Chapter IV. Challenge, Removal and Replacement of Arbitrators

Article 18 — Challenge of Arbitrator

1. The parties may challenge an arbitrator on any grounds which the Statute on the Organization of the Federal Judiciary provides for the mandatory or voluntary withdrawal of the federal judges, and on any grounds in the arbitration rules to which the parties have submitted.

2. Any arbitrator who has been deprived of the exercise of civil rights or who has been sentenced to deprivation of liberty for an infamous crime or misdemeanor may also be challenged.

3. A party may not challenge an arbitrator designated by him unless the ground for such objection arises after such designation, or he establishes that he was not aware of it at the time of designation.

Article 19 — Challenge of the Arbitral Tribunal

1. The arbitral tribunal as such may be challenged if one of the parties has exercised an overriding influence on the designation of its members.

2. A new arbitral tribunal is established according to the method provided for in Art. 11.

3. The parties may still designate as an arbitrator any member of the tribunal that was challenged.

Article 20 — Time Limit

The challenge must be made before an appearance on the merits, or as soon as the challenging party has knowledge of the grounds for challenge.

Article 21 — Dispute

1. In case of dispute, the judicial authority provided for in Art. 3 shall decide on the challenge.

2. The parties may present evidence.

Article 22 — Removal

1. Any arbitrator may be removed by a written agreement of the parties.

2. The judicial authority provided for in Art. 3 on petition of one of the parties may also remove an arbitrator for cause.

Article 23 — Replacement

1. If an arbitrator dies, resigns, is challenged or removed he shall be replaced according to the method adopted for his designation or appointment.

2. If such replacement cannot take place, the new arbitrator shall be appointed by the judicial authority provided for in Art. 3, unless it follows from the agreement to arbitrate that it must be deemed to have lapsed.

3. Unless otherwise agreed, the judicial authority provided for in Art. 3, after consultation with the arbitral tribunal, shall determine the extent to which the proceedings in which the replaced arbitrator took part shall remain valid.

4. The replacement of one or several arbitrators shall not postpone the running of the time limit in which the arbitral tribunal may be required to make its award.

Chapter V. Procedure Before the Arbitrators

Article 24 — Determination

1. The rules of procedure before the arbitrators shall be determined by agreement between the parties, or if there is none, by decision of the arbitral tribunal.

2. If the rules of procedure have been determined neither by agreement between the parties nor by a decision of the arbitral tribunal, the Federal Code of Civil Procedure shall apply by analogy.

Article 25 — Right to Be Heard

The rules of procedure selected must in any case respect the principle of equality of the parties and permit both parties:

(a) to exercise their right to be heard and in particular to present their factual and legal arguments;

(b) to have sufficient time to become acquainted with the file;

(c) to participate at the hearings for taking of evidence or argument that the arbitral tribunal may conduct;

(d) to be represented or assisted by a representative of their choice.

Article 26 — Provisional Orders

1. The ordinary judicial authorities alone have jurisdiction to make provisional orders.

2. However, the parties may voluntarily submit to a provisional order proposed by the arbitral tribunal.

Article 27 — Assistance of the Judicial Authorities

1. The arbitral tribunal shall itself take evidence.

2. If necessary, the arbitral tribunal may request the assistance of the judicial authority provided for in Art. 3. That authority proceeds under cantonal law.

Article 28 — Third Party Practice

1. The intervention or calling of a third party may be admitted only by virtue of an agreement to arbitrate between the third party and the parties in dispute.

2. Moreover, third party practice is subject to the consent of the arbitral tribunal.

Article 29 — Set-off

1. Where one of the parties pleads a set-off on the basis of a legal relationship for which the arbitral tribunal lacks jurisdiction under the terms of the agreement to arbitrate, and the parties do not agree to extend the arbitration to that legal relationship, the proceedings shall be stayed, and a reasonable time shall be allowed to the party making the exception to establish it before the court having jurisdiction.

2. When the court having jurisdiction has made a determination, the proceedings are resumed upon motion of one of the parties.

3. If the arbitral tribunal has been given a time limit in which to make its award, such period shall not continue to run during the stay of proceedings.

Article 30 — Advance on Costs

1. The arbitral tribunal may order an advance of foreseeable costs and may make the procedural process dependent thereon. It shall determine the amount to be advanced by each party.

2. If one of the parties fails to advance the sums required the other party may either advance all the costs or forego the arbitration. In the latter course, the parties are no longer bound by the agreement to arbitrate with respect to the dispute in question.

Chapter VI. Arbitral Award

Article 31 — Deliberation and Award

1. All arbitrators must participate in all deliberations and decisions of the arbitral tribunals.

2. The award is made by a simple majority of votes, unless the agreement to arbitrate requires unanimity or a qualified majority. Art. 11 subsection 4 is reserved.

3. The arbitral tribunal decides according to the rules of the applicable law, unless the parties have, in the agreement to arbitrate, authorized it to judge ex aequo et bono.

4. The arbitral tribunal may not award a party more or other than claimed, unless a particular provision of law authorizes it to do so.

Article 32 — Partial Awards

Unless the parties agree otherwise, the arbitral tribunal may make several awards.

Article 33 — Content of the Award
1. The arbitral award shall specify:
    (a) the names of the arbitrators;
    (b) the designation of the parties;
    (c) the seat of the arbitration;
    (d) the relief prayed for by the parties or, in default of such, the question to be determined;
    (e) the factual, legal, and, as the case may be, ex aequo et bono reasons for the decision, unless the parties expressly waive this requirement;
    (f) the decision on the merits;
    (g) the decision as to the amount and burden of costs.
    2. The award shall be dated and signed by the arbitrators. The signature of the majority of the arbitrators shall suffice if there is a statement in the award that the minority refuses to sign.
    3. If the mandate of the arbitral tribunal is to designate one or more arbitrators, subs. 1 (c) of this article does not apply.

Article 34 — Consent Award
    If the parties settle their dispute in arbitration, the arbitral tribunal records this in the form of an award.

Article 35 — Deposit and Notification
    1. The arbitral tribunal shall attend to the deposit of the award with the judicial authority provided in Art. 3.
    2. The award shall be deposited in the original, where subsection 4 applies, together with as many copies as there are parties.
    3. If the award is not drafted in one of the official languages of the Swiss Confederation, the authority with whom it is deposited may require an authenticated translation of the award.
    4. Such authority shall notify the parties of the award and shall inform them of the date of deposit.
    5. The parties may waive deposit. They may likewise waive notification of the award by the judicial authority; in this case, the notification shall be attended to by the arbitral tribunal.

Chapter VII. Action for Annulment and Revision

I. Action for Annulment

Article 36 — Grounds
    An action for annulment of the arbitral award may be brought before the judicial authority provided for in Art. 3 where it is alleged that:
    (a) the arbitral tribunal was not properly constituted;

(b) that the arbitral tribunal mistakenly accepted or declined jurisdiction;

(c) that it awarded points not submitted to it or, subject to Art. 32, failed to make a determination on one of the items in the claim;

(d) that there was a breach of one of the mandatory procedural rules referred to in Art. 25;

(e) that the arbitral tribunal awarded to one of the parties more or other than claimed, without being authorized to do so by a provision of law;

(f) that the award is arbitrary in that it was based on findings which were manifestly contrary to the facts appearing in the file, or in that it constitutes a clear violation of law or fairness;

(g) that the arbitral tribunal made its award after the expiration of the time limit imposed upon it to accomplish its mission;

(h) that the conditions of Art. 33 were not complied with or that the order is unintelligible or contradictory;

(i) that the fees of the arbitrators fixed by the arbitral tribunal are manifestly excessive.

Article 37 — Deadline

1. The action for annulment must be brought within 30 days of the notification of the award.

2. The action shall be admissible only if all arbitral remedies provided in the agreement of the parties have been exhausted.

Article 38 — Suspensive Effect of Action

The action shall not have suspensive effect. However, the judicial authority provided for in Art. 3 may grant such effect on one of the parties' request.

Article 39 — Remand to the Arbitral Tribunal

The judicial authority seized of the action may, having heard the parties, and if it sees fit, remand the award to the arbitral tribunal and impose a deadline to amend or supplement the award.

Article 40 — Decision

1. If the judicial authority does not remand the award to the arbitral tribunal or if the award is not amended or supplemented within the deadline, the judicial authority shall give judgment on the action for annulment, and if it finds such action well-founded it may annul the award.

2. The annulment may relate only to certain items in the award, unless the other items are dependent on them.

3. If the action is based on Art. 36 letter (i), the award shall be annulled only in respect of the fees, and the judicial authority shall itself determine the amount of such fees.

4. If the award is annulled, the arbitrators shall decide anew, unless they are challenged on the ground that they participated in the previous proceedings or on some other ground.

II. Review

Article 41 — Grounds
    The award may be reviewed:
    (a) If it was influenced by acts that are punishable according to Swiss law. Such acts must be established in a criminal sentence unless the criminal proceedings could not result in a conviction for reasons other than lack of evidence.
    (b) If it was issued in ignorance of important facts in existence prior to the award or of evidence of decisive importance, and it was impossible for the petitioner to present such facts or evidence during the proceedings.

Article 42 — Deadline
    The action for revision must be brought before the judicial authority provided for in Art. 3 within 60 days of the date on which the petitioner became aware of the grounds for revision. However, it may not be brought later than five years after the notification of the award.

Article 43 — Remand to the Arbitral Tribunal
    1. If the action for revision succeeds, the judicial authority shall remand the case to the arbitral tribunal for new decision.
    2. Arbitrators unable to act shall be replaced in accordance with the provisions of Art. 3.
    3. If it is necessary to constitute a new arbitral tribunal, the arbitrators shall be designated or appointed in accordance with Art. 10 to 12.
    4. If the case is remanded to the arbitral tribunal, Art. 16 shall be applied by analogy.

Chapter VIII. Enforcement of Arbitral Awards

Article 44 — Declaration of Enforceability
    1. Upon petition of one of the parties, the judicial authority provided for in Art. 3 shall declare enforceable, to the same extent as a judgment, any arbitral award:
    (a) which the parties have formally accepted; or
    (b) in respect of which no action for annulment has been brought within the deadline stipulated in Art. 37 subsection 1; or
    (c) in respect of which an action for annulment has been brought within the deadline, but no suspensive effect was granted; or
    (d) in respect of which an action for annulment has been dismissed or is statute-barred. The declaration of enforceability may not be issued if the award is contrary to Art. 5.
    2. The certificate of enforceability of the arbitral award is affixed at the bottom of the award.
    3. The arbitral award may not be provisionally enforced.

Chapter IX. Final Provisions

Article 45 — Procedure

1. The cantons determine the procedure before the judicial authority provided in Art. 3. Decisions on appointment, removal and replacement of arbitrators are subject to summary procedure.

2. The cantons may vest jurisdiction in part or in whole, in accordance with Art. 3 a to e and g, in a judicial authority other than that provided for in that article. In this case, the parties may, nevertheless, submit their application to the superior court of common civil jurisdiction of the canton.

Article 46 — Consequence of Entry into Force

On entry into force of this Concordat in a canton, all statutory provisions of that canton concerning arbitration shall be abrogated. Article 45 is reserved.

11. UNITED STATES

a. Federal Arbitration Act.

Title 9, United States Code.

Chapter 1.

§ 1. *"Maritime transactions" and "commerce" defined; exceptions to operation of title*
"Maritime transactions", as herein defined, means charter parties, bills of lading of water carriers, agreements relating to wharfage, supplies furnished vessels or repairs to vessels, collisions, or any other matters in foreign commerce which, if the subject of controversy, would be embraced within admiralty jurisdiction; "commerce", as herein defined, means commerce among the several States or with foreign nations, or in any Territory of the United States or in the District of Columbia, or between any such Territory and another, or between any such Territory and any State or foreign nation, or between the District of Columbia and any State or Territory or foreign nation, but nothing herein contained shall apply to contracts of employment of seamen, railroad employees, or any other class of workers engaged in foreign or interstate commerce.

§ 2. *Validity, irrevocability, and enforcement of agreements to arbitrate*
A written provision in any maritime transaction or a contract evidencing a transaction involving commerce to settle by arbitration a controversy thereafter arising out of such contract or transaction, or the refusal to perform the whole or any part thereof, or an agreement in writing to submit to arbitration an existing controversy arising out of such a contract, transaction, or refusal, shall be valid, irrevocable, and enforceable, save upon such grounds as exist at law or in equity for the revocation of any contract.

§ 3. *Stay of proceeding where issue therein referable to arbitration*
If any suit or proceeding be brought in any of the courts of the United States upon any issue referable to arbitration under an agreement in writing for such arbitration, the court in which such suit is pending, upon being satisfied that the issue involved in such suit or proceeding is referable to arbitration under such an agreement, shall on application of one of the parties stay the trial of the action until such arbitration has been had in accordance with the terms of the agreement, providing the applicant for the stay is not in default in proceeding with such arbitration.

§ 4. *Failure to arbitrate under agreement; petition to United States court having jurisdiction for order to compel arbitration; notice and service thereof; hearing and determination*
A party aggrieved by the alleged failure, neglect, or refusal of another to arbitrate under a written agreement for arbitration may petition any United States district court which, save for such agreement, would have jurisdiction under title 28, in a civil

action or in admiralty of the subject matter of a suit arising out of the controversy between the parties, for an order directing that such arbitration proceed in the manner provided for in such agreement. Five days' notice in writing of such application shall be served upon the party in default. Service thereof shall be made in the manner provided by the Federal Rules of Civil Procedure. The court shall hear the parties, and upon being satisfied that the making of the agreement for arbitration or the failure to comply therewith is not in issue, the court shall make an order directing the parties to proceed to arbitration in accordance with the terms of the agreement. The hearing and proceedings, under such agreement shall be within the district in which the petition for an order directing such arbitration is filed. If the making of the arbitration agreement or the failure, neglect, or refusal to perform the same be in issue, the court shall proceed summarily to the trial thereof. If no jury trial be demanded by the party alleged to be in default, or if the matter in dispute is within admiralty jurisdiction, the court shall hear and determine such issue. Where such an issue is raised, the party alleged to be in default may, except in cases of admiralty, on or before the return day of the notice of application, demand a jury trial of such issue, and upon such demand the court shall make an order referring the issue or issues to a jury in the manner provided by the Federal Rules of Civil Procedure, or may specially call a jury for that purpose. If the jury find that no agreement in writing for arbitration was made or tha' there is no default in proceeding thereunder, the proceeding shall be dismissed. If the jury find that an agreement for arbitration was made in writing and that there is a default in proceeding thereunder, the court shall make an order summarily directing the parties to proceed with the arbitration in accordance with the terms thereof.

§ 5. Appointment of arbitrators or umpire

If in the agreement provision be made for a method of naming or appointing an arbitrator or arbitrators or an umpire, such method shall be followed; but if no method be provided therein, or if a method be provided and any party thereto shall fail to avail himself of such method, or if for any other reason there shall be a lapse in the naming of an arbitrator or arbitrators or umpire, or in filling a vacancy, then upon the application of either party to the controversy the court shall designate and appoint an arbitrator or arbitrators or umpire, as the case may require, who shall act under the said agreement with the same force and effect as if he or they had been specifically named therein; and unless otherwise provided in the agreement the arbitration shall be by a single arbitrator.

§ 6. Application heard as motion

Any application to the court hereunder shall be made and heard in the manner provided by law for the making and hearing of motions, except as otherwise herein expressly provided.

§ 7. Witness before arbitrators; fees; compelling attendance

The arbitrators selected either as prescribed in this title or otherwise, or a majority of them, may summon in writing any person to attend before them or any of them as a witness and in a proper case to bring with him or them any book, record, document or paper which may be deemed material as evidence in the case. The fees for such attendance shall be the same as the fees of witnesses before masters of the United States courts. Said summons shall issue in the name of the arbitrator or arbitrators, or a majority of them, and shall be signed by the arbitrators, or a majority of them, and shall be directed to the said person and shall be served in the same manner as subpoenas to appear and testify before the court; if any person or persons so summoned to testify shall refuse or neglect to obey said summons, upon petition the United States district court for the district in which such arbitrators, or a majority of them, are sitting may compel the attendance of such person or persons before said arbitrator or arbitrators, or punish said person or persons for contempt in the same manner provided by law for securing the attendance of witnesses or their punishment for neglect or refusal to attend in the courts of the United States.

§ 8. Proceedings begun by libel in admiralty and seizure of vessel or property

If the basis of jurisdiction be a cause of action otherwise justiciable in admiralty, then, notwithstanding anything herein to the contrary, the party claiming to be aggrieved may begin his proceeding hereunder by libel and seizure of the vessel or other property of the other party according to the usual course of admiralty proceedings, and the court shall then have jurisdiction to direct the parties to proceed with the arbitration and shall retain jurisdiction to enter its decree upon the award.

§ 9. Award of arbitrators; confirmation; jurisdiction; procedure

If the parties in their agreement have agreed that a judgment of the court shall be entered upon the award made pursuant to the arbitration, and shall specify the court, then at any time within one year after the award is made any party to the arbitration may apply to the court so specified for an order confirming the award, and thereupon the court must grant such an order unless the award is vacated, modified, or corrected as prescribed in sections 10 and 11 of this title. If no court is specified in the agreement of the parties, then such application may be made to the United States court in and for the district within which such award was made. Notice of the application shall be served upon the adverse party, and thereupon the court shall have jurisdiction of such party as though he had appeared generally in the proceeding. If the adverse party is a resident of the district within which the award was made, such service shall be made upon the adverse party or his attorney as prescribed by law for service of notice of motion in an action in the same court. If the adverse party shall be a nonresident, then the notice of the application shall be served by the marshal of any district within which the adverse party may be found in like manner as other process of the court.

§ 10. Same; vacation; grounds; rehearing

In either of the following cases the United States court in and for the district wherein the award was made may make an order vacating the award upon the application of any party to the arbitration--

(a) Where the award was procured by corruption fraud, or undue means.

(b) Where there was evident partiality or corruption in the arbitrators, or either of them.

(c) Where the arbitrators were guilty of misconduct in refusing to postpone the hearing, upon sufficient cause shown, or in refusing to hear evidence pertinent and material to the controversy; or of any other misbehavior by which the rights of any party have been prejudiced.

(d) Where the arbitrators exceeded their powers, or so imperfectly executed them that a mutual, final, and definite award upon the subject matter submitted was not made.

(e) Where an award is vacated and the time within which the agreement required the award to be made has not expired the court may, in its discretion, direct a rehearing by the arbitrators.

§ 11. Same; modification or correction; grounds; order

In either of the following cases the United States court in and for the district wherein the award was made may make any order modifying or correcting the award upon the application of any party to the arbitration--

(a) Where there was an evident material miscalculation of figures or an evident material mistake in the description of any person, thing, or property referred to in the award.

(b) Where the arbitrators have awarded upon a matter not submitted to them, unless it is a matter not affecting the merits of the decision upon the matter submitted.

(c) Where the award is imperfect in matter of form not affecting the merits of the controversy.

The order may modify and correct the award, so as to effect the intent thereof and promote justice between the parties.

§ 12. Notice of motions to vacate or modify; service; stay of proceeding

Notice of a motion to vacate, modify, or correct an award must be served upon the adverse party or his attorney within three months after the award is filed or delivered. If the adverse party is a resident of the district within which the award was made, such service shall be made upon the adverse party or his attorney as prescribed by law for service of notice of motion in an action in the same court. If the adverse party shall be a nonresident then the notice of the application shall be served by the marshal of any district within which the adverse party may be found in like manner as other process of the court. For the purposes of the motion any judge who might make an order to stay the proceedings in an action brought in the same court may make an order, to be served with the notice of motion, staying the proceedings of the adverse party to enforce the award.

§ 13. Papers filed with order on motions; judgment; docketing; force and effect; enforcement

The party moving for an order confirming, modifying, or correcting an award shall, at the time such order is filed with the clerk for the entry of judgment thereon, also file the following papers with the clerk:

(a) The agreement: the selection or appointment, if any, of an additional arbitrator or umpire; and each written extension of the time, if any, within which to make the award.

(b) The award.

(c) Each notice, affidavit, or other paper used upon an application to confirm, modify, or correct the award, and a copy of each order of the court upon such an application.

The judgment shall be docketed as if it was rendered in an action.

The judgment so entered shall have the same force and effect, in all respects, as, and be subject to all the provisions of law relating to, a judgment in an action; and it may be enforced as if it had been rendered in an action in the court in which it is entered.

§ 14. Contracts not affected

This title shall not apply to contracts made prior to January 1, 1926.

§ 15. Inapplicability of the Act of State doctrine

Enforcement of arbitral agreements, confirmation of arbitral awards, and execution upon judgments based on orders confirming such awards shall not be refused on the basis of the Act of State doctrine.

§ 16. Appeals

(a) An appeal may be taken from--

(1) an order--

(A) refusing a stay of any action under section 3 of this title,

(B) denying a petition under section 4 of this title to order arbitration to proceed,

(C) denying an application under section 206 of this title to compel arbitration,

(D) confirming or denying confirmation of an award or partial award, or

(E) modifying, correcting, or vacating an award;

(2) an interlocutory order granting, continuing, or modifying an injunction against an arbitration that is subject to this title; or

(3) a final decision with respect to an arbitration that is subject to this title.

(b) Except as otherwise provided in section 1292(b) of title 28, an appeal may not be taken from an interlocutory order--

(1) granting a stay of any action under section 3 of this title;

(2) directing arbitration to proceed under section 4 of this title;

(3) compelling arbitration under section 206 of this title; or

(4) refusing to enjoin an arbitration that is subject to this title.

Chapter 2.

§ 201. Enforcement of Convention
The Convention on the Recognition and Enforcement of Foreign Arbitral Awards of June 10, 1958, shall be enforced in United States courts in accordance with this chapter.

§ 202. Agreement or award falling under the Convention
An arbitration agreement or arbitral award arising out of a legal relationship, whether contractual or not, which is considered as commercial, including a transaction, contract, or agreement described in section 2 of this title, falls under the Convention. An agreement or award arising out of such a relationship which is entirely between citizens of the United States shall be deemed not to fall under the Convention unless that relationship involves property located abroad, envisages performance or enforcement abroad, or has some other reasonable relation with one or more foreign states. For the purpose of this section a corporation is a citizen of the United States if it is incorporated or has its principal place of business in the United States.

§ 203. Jurisdiction; amount in controversy
An action or proceeding falling under the Convention shall be deemed to arise under the laws and treaties of the United States. The district courts of the United States (including the courts enumerated in section 460 of title 28) shall have original jurisdiction over such an action or proceeding, regardless of the amount in controversy.

§ 204. Venue
An action or proceeding over which the district courts have jurisdiction pursuant to section 203 of this title may be brought in any such court in which save for the arbitration agreement an action or proceeding with respect to the controversy between the parties could be brought, or in such court for the district and division which embraces the place designated in the agreement as the place of arbitration if such place is within the United States.

§ 205. Removal of cases from State courts
Where the subject matter of an action or proceeding pending in a State court relates to an arbitration agreement or award falling under the Convention, the defendant or the defendants may, at any time before the trial thereof, remove such action or proceeding to the district court of the United States for the district and division embracing the place where the action or proceeding is pending. The procedure for removal of causes otherwise provided by law shall apply, except that the ground for removal provided in this section need not appear on the face of the complaint but may be shown in the petition for removal. For the purposes of Chapter 1 of this title any action or proceeding removed under this section shall be deemed to have been brought in the district court to which it is removed.

§ 206. Order to compel arbitration; appointment of arbitrators

A court having jurisdiction under this chapter may direct that arbitration be held in accordance with the agreement at any place therein provided for, whether that place is within or without the United States. Such court may also appoint arbitrators in accordance with the provisions of the agreement.

§ 207. Award of arbitrators; confirmation; jurisdiction; proceeding

Within three years after an arbitral award falling under the Convention is made, any party to the arbitration may apply to any court having jurisdiction under this chapter for an order confirming the award as against any other party to the arbitration. The court shall confirm the award unless it finds one of the grounds for refusal or deferral of recognition or enforcement of the award specified in the said Convention.

§ 208. Chapter l; residual application

Chapter 1 applies to actions and proceedings brought under this chapter to the extent that chapter is not in conflict with this chapter or the Convention as ratified by the United States.

Chapter 3

§ 301. Enforcement of Convention

The Inter-American Convention on International Commercial Arbitration of January 30, 1975, shall be enforced in United States courts in accordance with this chapter.

§ 302. Incorporation by reference

Sections, 202, 203, 204, 205, and 207 of this title shall apply to this chapter as if specifically set forth herein, except that for the purposes of this chapter "the Convention" shall mean the Inter-American Convention.

§ 303. Order to compel arbitration; appointment of arbitrators; locale

(a) A court having jurisdiction under this chapter may direct that arbitration be held in accordance with the agreement at any place therein provided for, whether that place is within or without the Untied States. The court may also appoint arbitrators in accordance with the provisions of the agreement.

(b) In the event the agreement does not make provision for the place of arbitration or the appointment of arbitrators, the court shall direct that the arbitration shall be held and the arbitrators be appointed in accordance with Article 3 of the Inter-American Convention.

§ 304. Recognition and enforcement of foreign arbitral decisions and awards; reciprocity

Arbitral decisions or awards made int he territory of a foreign State shall, on the basis of reciprocity, be recognized and enforced under this chapter only if that State has ratified or acceded to the Inter-American Convention.

§ 305. Relationship between the Inter-American Convention and the Convention on the Recognition and Enforcement of Foreign Arbitral Awards of June 10, 1958

When the requirements for application of both the Inter-American Convention and the Convention on the Recognition and Enforcement of Foreign Arbitral Awards of June 10, 1958, are met, determination as to which Convention applies shall, unless otherwise expressly agreed, be made as follows:

    (1) If a majority of the parties to the arbitration agreement are citizens of a State or States that have ratified or acceded to the Inter-American Convention and are member States of the Organization of American States, the Inter-American Convention shall apply.

    (2) In all other cases the Convention on the Recognition and Enforcement of Foreign Arbitral Awards of June 10, 1958, shall apply.

§ 306. Applicable rules of Inter-American Commercial Arbitration Commission

(a) For the purposes of this chapter the rules of procedure of the Inter-American Commercial Arbitration Commission referred to in Article 3 of the Inter-American Convention shall, subject to subsection (b) of this section, be those rules as promulgated by the Commission on July 1, 1988.

(b) In the event the rules of procedure of the Inter-American Commercial Arbitration Commission are modified or amended in accordance with the procedures for amendment of the rules of that Commission, the Secretary of State, by regulation in accordance with section 553 of title 5, consistent with the aims and purposes of this Convention, may prescribe that such modifications or amendments shall be effective for purposes of this chapter.

§ 307. Chapter 1; residual application

Chapter 1 applies to actions and proceedings brought under this chapter to the extent chapter 1 is not in conflict with this chapter or the Inter-American Convention as ratified by the United States.

b. Uniform Arbitration Act[1]

§ 1. *Validity of Arbitration Agreement*

A written agreement to submit any existing controversy to arbitration or a provision in a written contract to submit to arbitration any controversy thereafter arising between the parties is valid, enforceable and irrevocable, save upon such grounds as exist at law or in equity for the revocation of any contract. This act also applies to arbitration agreements between employers and employees or between their respective representatives [unless otherwise provided in the agreement].

§ 2. *Proceedings to Compel or Stay Arbitration*

(a) On application of a party showing an agreement described in Section 1, and the opposing party's refusal to arbitrate, the Court shall order the parties to proceed with arbitration, but if the opposing party denies the existence of the agreement to arbitrate, the Court shall proceed summarily to the determination of the issue so raised and shall order arbitration if found for the moving party, otherwise, the application shall be denied.

(b) On application, the court may stay an arbitration proceeding commenced or threatened on a showing that there is no agreement to arbitrate. Such an issue, when in substantial and bona fide dispute, shall be forthwith and summarily tried and the stay ordered if found for the moving party. If found for the opposing party, the court shall order the parties to proceed to arbitration.

(c) If an issue referable to arbitration under the alleged agreement is involved in an action or proceeding pending in a court having jurisdiction to hear applications under subdivision (a) of this Section, the application shall be made therein. Otherwise and subject to Section 18, the application may be made in any court of competent jurisdiction.

(d) Any action or proceeding involving an issue subject to arbitration shall be stayed if an order for arbitration or an application therefor has been made under this section or, if the issue is severable, the stay may be with respect thereto only. When

---

1. Some enactments of the Uniform Arbitration Act also provide for consolidation of multiparty arbitrators. For example, Section 2A of the Act as adopted in Massachusetts (Mass. Gen. Laws c.251) reads as follows:

> A party aggrieved by the failure or refusal of another to agree to consolidate one arbitration proceeding with another or others, for which the method of appointment of the arbitrator or arbitrators is the same, or to sever one arbitration proceeding from another or others, may apply to the superior court for an order for such consolidation or such severance. The court shall proceed summarily to the determination of the issue so raised. If a claimant under section twenty-nine of chapter one hundred and forty-nine applies for an order for consolidation or severance of such proceedings, the issue shall be decided under the applicable provisions of said section twenty-nine of said chapter one hundred and forty-nine governing consolidation or severance of such actions; otherwise the issue shall be decided under the Massachusetts Rules of Civil Procedure governing consolidation and severance of trials and the court shall issue an order accordingly. No provision in any arbitration agreement shall bar or prevent action by the court under this section.

the application is made in such action or proceeding, the order for arbitration shall include such stay.

(e) An order for arbitration shall not be refused on the ground that the claim in issue lacks merit or bona fides or because any fault or grounds for the claim sought to be arbitrated have not been shown.

§ 3. Appointment of Arbitrators by Court

If the arbitration agreement provides a method of appointment of arbitrators, this method shall be followed. In the absence thereof, or if the agreed method fails or for any reason cannot be followed, or when an arbitrator appointed fails or is unable to act and his successor has not been duly appointed, the court on application of a party shall appoint one or more arbitrators. An arbitrator so appointed has all the powers of one specifically named in the agreement.

§ 4. Majority Action by Arbitrators

The powers of the arbitrators may be exercised by a majority unless otherwise provided by the agreement or by this act.

§ 5. Hearing

Unless otherwise provided by the agreement:

(a) The arbitrators shall appoint a time and place for the hearing and cause notification to the parties to be served personally or by registered mail not less than five days before the hearing. Appearance at the hearing waives such notice. The arbitrators may adjourn the hearing from time to time as necessary and, on request of a party and for good cause, or upon their own motion may postpone the hearing to a time not later than the date fixed by the agreement for making the award unless the parties consent to a later date. The arbitrators may hear and determine the controversy upon the evidence produced notwithstanding the failure of a party duly notified to appear. The court on application may direct the arbitrators to proceed promptly with the hearing and determination of the controversy.

(b) The parties are entitled to be heard, to present evidence material to the controversy and to cross-examine witnesses appearing at the hearing.

(c) The hearing shall be conducted by all the arbitrators but a majority may determine any question and render a final award. If, during the course of the hearing, an arbitrator for any reason ceases to act, the remaining arbitrator or arbitrators appointed to act as neutrals may continue with the hearing and determination of the controversy.

§ 6. Representation by Attorney

A party has the right to be represented by an attorney at any proceeding or hearing under this act. A waiver thereof prior to the proceeding or hearing is ineffective.

§ 7. Witnesses, Subpoenas, Depositions

(a) The arbitrators may issue (cause to be issued) subpoenas for the attendance of witnesses and for the production of books, records, documents and other evidence, and shall have the power to administer oaths. Subpoenas so issued shall be served, and upon application to the Court by a party or the arbitrators, enforced, in the manner provided by law for the service and enforcement of subpoenas in a civil action.

(b) On application of a party and for use as evidence, the arbitrators may permit a deposition to be taken, in the manner and upon the terms designated by the arbitrators, of a witness who cannot be subpoenaed or is unable to attend the hearing.

(c) All provisions of law compelling a person under subpoena to testify are applicable.

(d) Fees for attendance as a witness shall be the same as for a witness in the .... Court.

§ 8. Award

(a) The award shall be in writing and signed by the arbitrators joining in the award. The arbitrators shall deliver a copy to each party personally or by registered mail, or as provided in the agreement.

(b) An award shall be made within the time fixed therefor by the agreement or, if not so fixed, within such time as the court orders on application of a party. The parties may extend the time in writing either before or after the expiration thereof. A party waives the objection that an award was not made within the time required unless he notifies the arbitrators of his objection prior to the delivery of the award to him.

§ 9. Change of Award by Arbitrators

On application of a party or, if an application to the court is pending under Sections 11, 12 or 13, on submission to the arbitrators by the court under such conditions as the court may order, the arbitrators may modify or correct the award upon the grounds stated in paragraphs (1) and (3) of subdivision (a) of Section 13, or for the purpose of clarifying the award. The application shall be made within twenty days after delivery of the award to the applicant. Written notice thereof shall be given forthwith to the opposing party, stating he must serve his objections thereto, if any, within ten days from the notice. The award so modified or corrected is subject to the provisions of Sections 11, 12 and 13.

§ 10. Fees and Expenses of Arbitration

Unless otherwise provided in the agreement to arbitrate, the arbitrators' expenses and fees, together with other expenses, not including counsel fees, incurred in the conduct of the arbitration, shall be paid as provided in the award.

§ 11. Confirmation of an Award

Upon application of a party, the Court shall confirm an award, unless within the time limits hereinafter imposed grounds are urged for vacating or modifying or correcting the award, in which case the court shall proceed as provided in Sections 12 and 13.

§ 12. Vacating an Award

(a) Upon application of a party, the court shall vacate an award where:

(1) The award was procured by corruption, fraud or other undue means;

(2) There was evident partiality by an arbitrator appointed as a neutral or corruption in any of the arbitrators or misconduct prejudicing the rights of any party;

(3) The arbitrators exceeded their powers;

(4) The arbitrators refused to postpone the hearing upon sufficient cause being shown therefor or refused to hear evidence material to the controversy or otherwise so conducted the hearing, contrary to the provisions of Section 5, as to prejudice substantially the rights of a party; or

(5) There was no arbitration agreement and the issue was not adversely determined in proceedings under Section 2 and the party did not participate in the arbitration hearing without raising the objection;

but the fact that the relief was such that it could not or would not be granted by a court of law or equity is not ground for vacating or refusing to confirm the award.

(b) An application under this Section shall be made within ninety days after delivery of a copy of the award to the applicant, except that, if predicated upon corruption, fraud or other undue means, it shall be made within ninety days after such grounds are known or should have been known.

(c) In vacating the award on grounds other than stated in clause (5) of Subsection (a) the court may order a rehearing before new arbitrators chosen as provided in the agreement, or in the absence thereof, by the court in accordance with Section 3, or if the award is vacated on grounds set forth in clauses (3) and (4) of Subsection (a) the court may order a rehearing before the arbitrators who made the award or their successors appointed in accordance with Section 3. The time within which the agreement requires the award to be made is applicable to the rehearing and commences from the date of the order.

(d) If the application to vacate is denied and no motion to modify or correct the award is pending, the court shall confirm the award. As amended Aug. 1956.

§ 13. Modification or Correction of Award

(a) Upon application made within ninety days after delivery of a copy of the award to the applicant, the court shall modify or correct the award where:

(1) There was an evident miscalculation of figures or an evident mistake in the description of any person, thing or property referred to in the award;

(2) The arbitrators have awarded upon a matter not submitted to them and the award may be corrected without affecting the merits of the decision upon the issues submitted; or

(3) The award is imperfect in a matter of form, not affecting the merits of the controversy.

(b) If the application is granted, the court shall modify and correct the award so as to effect its intent and shall confirm the award as so modified and corrected. Otherwise, the court shall confirm the award as made.

(c) An application to modify or correct an award may be joined in the alternative with an application to vacate the award.

§ 14. Judgment or Decree on Award

Upon the granting of an order confirming, modifying or correcting an award, judgment or decree shall be entered in conformity therewith and be enforced as any other judgment or decree. Costs of the application and of the proceedings subsequent thereto, and disbursements may be awarded by the court.

§ 15. Judgment Roll, Docketing

(a) On entry of judgment or decree, the clerk shall prepare the judgment roll consisting, to the extent filed, of the following:

(1) The agreement and each written extension of the time within which to make the award;

(2) The award;

(3) A copy of the order confirming, modifying or correcting the award; and

(4) A copy of the judgment or decree.

(b) The judgment or decree may be docketed as if rendered in an action.

§ 16. Applications to Court

Except as otherwise provided, an application to the court under this act shall be by motion and shall be heard in the manner and upon the notice provided by law or rule of court for the making and hearing of motions. Unless the parties have agreed otherwise, notice of an initial application for an order shall be served in the manner provided by law for the service of a summons in an action.

§ 17. Court, Jurisdiction

The term "court" means any court of competent jurisdiction of this State. The making of an agreement described in Section 1 providing for arbitration in this State confers jurisdiction on the court to enforce the agreement under this Act and to enter judgment on an award thereunder.

§ 18. Venue

An initial application shall be made to the court of the [county] in which the agreement provides the arbitration hearing shall be held or, if the hearing has been held, in the county in which it was held. Otherwise the application shall be made in the [county] where the adverse party resides or has a place of business or, if he has no residence or place of business in this State, to the court of any [county]. All subsequent applications shall be made to the court hearing the initial application unless the court otherwise directs.

§ 19. Appeals
(a) An appeal may be taken from:
  (1) An order denying an application to compel arbitration made under Section 2;
  (2) An order granting an application to stay arbitration made under Section 2(b);
  (3) An order confirming or denying confirmation of an award;
  (4) An order modifying or correcting an award;
  (5) An order vacating an award without directing a rehearing; or
  (6) A judgment or decree entered pursuant to the provisions of this act.
(b) The appeal shall be taken in the manner and to the same extent as from orders or judgments in a civil action.

§ 20. Act Not Retroactive
This act applies only to agreements made subsequent to the taking effect of this act.

§ 21. Uniformity of Interpretation
This act shall be so construed as to effectuate its general purpose to make uniform the law of those states which enact it.

§ 22. Constitutionality
If any provision of this act or the application thereof to any person or circumstance is held invalid, the invalidity shall not affect other provisions or applications of the act which can be given effect without the invalid provision or application, and to this end the provisions cf this act are severable.

§ 23. Short Title
This act may be cited as the Uniform Arbitration Act.

§ 24. Repeal
All acts or parts of acts which are inconsistent with the provisions of this act are hereby repealed.

§ 25. Time of Taking Effect
This act shall take effect.

Jurisdictions Where Uniform Arbitration Act Has Been Adopted:

Jurisdiction	Statutory Citation
Arizona	A.R.S. §§ 12-1501 to 12-1518.
Arkansas	Code 1987, §§ 16-108-201 to 16-108-224.
Colorado	C.R.S. 13-22-201 to 13-22-223.
Delaware	10 Del.C. §§ 5701 to 5725.
Dist. of Columbia	D.C. Code 1981, §§ 16-4301 to 16-4319.
Idaho	I.C. §§ 7-901 to 7-922.
Illinois	S.H.A. ch. 10, ¶¶ 101 to 123.
Indiana	West's A.I.C. 34-4-2-1 to 34-4-2-22.
Iowa	I.C.A. §§ 679A.1 to 679A.19.
Kansas	K.S.A. 5-401 to 5-422.
Maine	14 M.R.S.A. §§ 5927 to 5949.
Maryland	Code, Courts and Judicial Proceedings, §§ 3-201 to 3-234.
Massachusetts	M.G.L.A. c. 251, §§ 1 to 19.
Michigan	M.C.L.A. §§ 600.5001 to 600. 5035.
Minnesota	M.S.A. §§ 572.08 to 572.30.
Missouri	V.A.M.S. §§ 435.350 to 435.470.
Montana	MCA 27-5-111 to 27-5-324.
Nebraska	R.R.S. 1943, §§ 25-2601 to 25-2622.
Nevada	N.R.S. 38.015 to 38.205.
New Mexico	NMSA 1978, §§ 44-7-1 to 44-7-22.
North Carolina	G.S. §§ 1-567.1 to 1-567.20.
North Dakota	NDCC 32-29.2-01 to 32-29.2-20.
Oklahoma	15 Okl.St.Ann. §§ 801 to 818.
Pennsylvania	42 Pa.C.S.A. §§ 7301 to 7320.
South Carolina	Code 1976, §§ 15-48-10 to 15-48-240.
South Dakota	SDCL 21-25A-1 to 21-25A-38.
Tennessee	T.C.A. §§ 29-5-301 to 29-5-320.
Texas	Vernon's Ann.Texas Civ.St. arts. 224 to 238-6.
Utah	U.C.A.1953, 78-31a-1 to 78-31a-18.
Vermont	12 V.S.A. §§ 5651 to 5681.
Virginia	Code 1950, §§ 8.01-581.01 to 8.01-581.016.
Wyoming	W.S.1977, §§ 1-36-101 to 1-36-119.

c. New York Civil Practice Law & Rules.

§ 7501. *Effect of arbitration agreement*

A written agreement to submit any controversy thereafter arising or any existing controversy to arbitration is enforceable without regard to the justiciable character of the controversy and confers jurisdiction on the courts of the state to enforce it and to enter judgment on an award. In determining any matter arising under this article, the court shall not consider whether the claim with respect to which arbitration is sought is tenable, or otherwise pass upon the merits of the dispute.

§ 7502. *Applications to the court; venue; statutes of limitation; provisional remedies*

(a) **Applications to the court; venue.**

A special proceeding shall be used to bring before a court the first application arising out of an arbitrable controversy which is not made by motion in a pending action. The proceeding shall be brought in the court and county specified in the agreement; or, if none be specified, in a court in the county in which one of the parties resides or is doing business, or, if there is no such county, in a court in any county; or in a court in the county in which the arbitration was held. All subsequent applications shall be made by motion in the pending action or the special proceeding.

(b) **Limitation of time.**

If, at the time that a demand for arbitration was made or a notice of intention to arbitrate was served, the claim sought to be arbitrated would have been barred by limitation of time had it been asserted in a court of the sate, a party may assert the limitation as a bar to the arbitration on an application to the court as provided in section 7503 or subdivision (b) of section 7511. The failure to assert such bar by such application shall not preclude its assertion before the arbitrators, who may, in their sole discretion, apply or not apply the bar. Except as provided in subdivision (b) of section 7511, such exercise of discretion by the arbitrators shall not be subject to review by a court on an application to confirm, vacate or modify the award.

(c) **Provisional remedies.**

The supreme court in the county in which an arbitration is pending, or, if not yet commenced, in a county specified in subdivision (a), may entertain an application for an order of attachment or for a preliminary injunction in connection with an arbitrable controversy, but only upon the ground that the award to which the applicant may be entitled may be rendered ineffectual without such provisional relief. The provisions of articles 62 and 63 of this chapter shall apply to the application, including those relating to undertakings and to the time for commencement of an action (arbitration shall be deemed an action for this purpose) if the application is made before commencement, except that the sole ground for the granting of the remedy shall be as stated above. The form of the application shall be as provided in subdivision (a).

§ 7503. *Application to compel or stay arbitration; stay of action; notice of intention to arbitrate*

(a) **Application to compel arbitration; stay of action.**

A party aggrieved by the failure of another to arbitrate may apply for an order compelling arbitration. Where there is no substantial question whether a valid agreement was made or complied with, and the claim sought to be arbitrated is not barred by limitation under subdivision (b) of section 7502, the court shall direct the parties to arbitrate. Where any such question is raised, it shall be tried forthwith in said court. If an issue claimed to be arbitrable is involved in an action pending in a court having jurisdiction to hear a motion to compel arbitration, the application shall be made by motion in that action. If the application is granted, the order shall operate to stay a pending or subsequent action, or so much of it as is referable to arbitration.

(b) **Application to stay arbitration.**

Subject to the provisions of subdivision (c), a party who has not participated in the arbitration and who has not made or been served with an application to compel arbitration, may apply to stay arbitration on the ground that a valid agreement was not made or has not been complied with or that the claim sought to be arbitrated is barred by limitation under subdivision (b) of section 7502.

(c) **Notice of intention to arbitrate.**

A party may serve upon another party a demand for arbitration or a notice of intention to arbitrate, specifying the agreement pursuant to which arbitration is sought and the name and address of the party serving the notice, or of an officer or agent thereof if such party is an association or corporation, and stating that unless the party served applies to stay the arbitration within twenty days after such service he shall thereafter be precluded from objecting that a valid agreement was not made or has not been complied with and from asserting in court the bar of a limitation of time. Such notice or demand shall be served in the same manner as a summons or by registered or certified mail, return receipt requested. An application to stay arbitration must be made by the party served within twenty days after service upon him of the notice or demand, or he shall be so precluded. Notice of such application shall be served in the same manner as a summons or by registered or certified mail, return receipt requested. Service of the application may be made upon the adverse party, or upon his attorney if the attorney's name appears on the demand for arbitration or the notice of intention to arbitrate. Service of the application by mail shall be timely if such application is posted within the prescribed period. Any provision in an arbitration agreement or arbitration rules which waives the right to apply for a stay of arbitration is hereby declared null and void.

§ 7504. *Court appointment of arbitrator*

If the arbitration agreement does not provide for a method of appointment of an arbitrator, or if the agreed method fails or for any reason is not followed, or if an arbitrator fails to act and his successor has not been appointed, the court, on application of a party, shall appoint an arbitrator.

§ 7505. *Powers of arbitrator*

An arbitrator and any attorney of record in the arbitration proceeding has the power to issue subpoenas. An arbitrator has the power to administer oaths.

§ 7506. *Hearing*

(a) **Oath of arbitrator.**

Before hearing any testimony, an arbitrator shall be sworn to hear and decide the controversy faithfully and fairly by an officer authorized to administer an oath.

(b) **Time and place.**

The arbitrator shall appoint a time and place for the hearing and notify the parties in writing personally or by registered or certified mail not less than eight days before the hearing. The arbitrator may adjourn or postpone the hearing. The court, upon application of any party, may direct the arbitrator to proceed promptly with the hearing and determination of the controversy.

(c) **Evidence.**

The parties are entitled to be heard, to present evidence and to cross-examine witnesses. Notwithstanding the failure of a party duly notified to appear, the arbitrator may hear and determine the controversy upon the evidence produced.

(d) **Representation by attorney.**

A party has the right to be represented by an attorney and may claim such right at any time as to any part of the arbitration or hearings which have not taken place. This right may not be waived. If a party is represented by an attorney, papers to be served on the party shall be served upon his attorney.

(e) **Determination by majority.**

The hearing shall be conducted by all the arbitrators, but a majority may determine any question and render an award.

(f) **Waiver.**

Except as provided in subdivision (d), a requirement of this section may be waived by written consent of the parties and it is waived if the parties continue with the arbitration without objection.

§ 7507. *Award; form; time; delivery*

Except as provided in section 7508, the award shall be in writing, signed and affirmed by the arbitrator making it within the time fixed by the agreement, or, if the time is not fixed, within such time as the court orders. The parties may in writing extend the time either before or after its expiration. A party waives the objection that an award was not made within the time required unless he notifies the arbitration in writing of his objection prior to the delivery of the award to him. The arbitrator shall deliver a copy of the award to each party in the manner provided in the agreement, or, if no provision is so made, personally or by registered or certified mail, return receipt requested.

§ 7508. *Award by confession*

(a) **When available.**

An award by confession may be made for money due or to become due at any time before an award is otherwise made. The award shall be based upon a statement, verified by each party, containing an authorization to make the award, the sum of the award or the method of ascertaining it, and the facts constituting the liability.

(b) **Time of award.**

The award may be made at any time within three months after the statement is verified.

(c) **Person or agency making award.**

The award may be made by an arbitrator or by the agency or person named by the parties to designate the arbitrator.

§ 7509. Modification of award by arbitrator

On written application of a party to the arbitrators within twenty days after delivery of the award to the applicant, the arbitrators may modify the award upon the grounds stated in subdivision (c) of section 7511. Written notice of the application shall be given to other parties to the arbitration. Written objection to modification must be served on the arbitrators and other parties to the arbitration within ten days of receipt of the notice. The arbitrators shall dispose of any application made under this section in writing, signed and acknowledged by them, within thirty days after either written objection to modification has been served on them or the time for serving said objection has expired, whichever is earlier. The parties may in writing extend the time for such disposition either before or after its expiration.

§ 7510. Confirmation of award

The court shall confirm an award upon application of a party made within one year after its delivery to him, unless the award is vacated or modified upon a ground specified in section 7511.

§ 7511. Vacating or modifying award

(a) **When application made.**

An application to vacate or modify an award may be made by a party within ninety days after its delivery to him.

(b) **Grounds for vacating.**

1. The award shall be vacated on the application of a party who either participated in the arbitration or was served with a notice of intention to arbitrate if the court finds that the rights of that party were prejudiced by:

    (i) corruption, fraud or misconduct in procuring the award; or

    (ii) partiality of an arbitrator appointed as a neutral, except where the award was by confession; or

    (iii) an arbitrator, or agency or person making the award exceeded his power or so imperfectly executed it that a final and definite award upon the subject matter submitted was not made; or

    (iv) failure to follow the procedure of this article, unless the party applying to vacate the award continued with the arbitration with notice of the defect and without objection.

2. The award shall be vacated on the application of a party who neither participated in the arbitration nor was served with a notice of intention to arbitrate if the court finds that:

(i) the rights of that party were prejudiced by one of the grounds specified in paragraph one; or

(ii) a valid agreement to arbitrate was not made; or

(iii) the agreement to arbitrate had not been complied with; or

(iv) the arbitrated claim was barred by limitation under subdivision (b) of section 7502.

(c) **Grounds for modifying.**

The court shall modify the award if:

1. there was a miscalculation of figures or a mistake in the description of any person, thing or property referred to in the award; or

2. the arbitrators have awarded upon a matter not submitted to them and the award may be corrected without affecting the merits of the decision upon the issues submitted; or

3. the award is imperfect in a matter of form, not affecting the merits of the controversy.

(d) **Rehearing.**

Upon vacating an award, the court may order a rehearing and determination of all or any of the issues either before the same arbitrator or before a new arbitrator appointed in accordance with this article. Time in any provision limiting the time for a hearing or award shall be measured from the date of such order or rehearing, whichever is appropriate, or a time may be specified by the court.

(e) **Confirmation.**

Upon the granting of a motion to modify, the court shall confirm the award as modified; upon the denial of a motion to vacate or modify, it shall confirm the award.

§ 7512. *Death or incompetency of a party*

Where a party dies after making a written agreement to submit a controversy to arbitration, the proceedings may be begun or continued upon the application of, or upon notice to, his executor or administrator or, where it relates to real property, his distributee or devisee who has succeeded to his interest in the real property. Where a committee of the property or of the person of a party to such an agreement is appointed, the proceedings may be continued upon the application of, or notice to, the committee. Upon the death or incompetency of a party, the court may extend the time within which an application to confirm, vacate or modify the award or to stay arbitration must be made. Where a party has died since an award was delivered, the proceedings thereupon are the same as where a party dies after a verdict.

§ 7513. *Fees and expenses*

Unless otherwise provided in the agreement to arbitrate, the arbitrators' expenses and fees, together with other expenses, not including attorney's fees, incurred in the conduct of the arbitration, shall be paid as provided in the award. The court, on application, may reduce or disallow any fee or expense it finds excessive or allocate it as justice requires.

§ 7514. Judgment on an award
(a) Entry.
A judgment shall be entered upon the confirmation of an award.
(b) Judgment-roll.
The judgment-roll consists of the original or a copy of the agreement and each written extension of time within which to make an award; the statement required by section 7508 where the award was by confession; the award; each paper submitted to the court and each order of the court upon an application under sections 7510 and 7511; and a copy of the judgment.

12. UNCITRAL MODEL LAW

United Nations Commission on International Trade Law.

Model Law on International Commercial Arbitration.
Adopted 21 June 1985

CHAPTER I. General Provisions

Article 1 — Scope of application
   (1) This Law applies to international commercial arbitration, subject to any agreement in force between this State and any other State or States.
   (2) The provisions of this Law, except articles 8, 9, 35 and 36, apply only if the place of arbitration is in the territory of this State.
   (3) An arbitration is international if:
   (a) the parties to an arbitration agreement have, at the time of the conclusion of that agreement, their places of business in different States; or
   (b) one of the following places is situated outside the State in which the parties have their places of business:
   (i) the place of arbitration if determined in, or pursuant to, the arbitration agreement;
   (ii) any place where a substantial part of the obligations of the commercial relationship is to be performed or the place with which the subject-matter of the dispute is most closely connected; or
   (c) the parties have expressly agreed that the subject-matter of the arbitration agreement relates to more than one country.
   (4) For the purposes of paragraph (3) of this article:
   (a) if a party has more than one place of business, the place of business is that which has the closest relationship to the arbitration agreement;
   (b) if a party does not have a place of business, reference is to be made to his habitual residence.
   (5) This Law shall not affect any other law of this State by virtue of which certain disputes may not be submitted to arbitration or may be submitted to arbitration only according to provisions other than those of this Law.

Article 2 — Definitions and rules of interpretation
   For the purposes of this Law:
   (a) "arbitration" means any arbitration whether or not administered by a permanent arbitral institution;
   (b) "arbitral tribunal" means a sole arbitrator or a panel of arbitrators;
   (c) "court" means a body or organ of the judicial system of a State;
   (d) where a provision of this Law, except article 28, leaves the parties free to determine a certain issue, such freedom includes the right of the parties to authorize a third party, including an institution, to make that determination;

(e) where a provision of this Law refers to the fact that the parties have agreed or that they may agree or in any other way refers to an agreement of the parties, such agreement includes any arbitration rules referred to in that agreement;

(f) where a provision of this Law, other than in articles 25(*a*) and 32(2)(*a*), refers to a claim, it also applies to a counter-claim, and where it refers to a defence, it also applies to a defence to such counter-claim.

Article 3 — Receipt of written communications

(1) Unless otherwise agreed by the parties:

(a) any written communication is deemed to have been received if it is delivered to the addressee personally or if it is delivered at his place of business, habitual residence or mailing address; if none of these can be found after making a reasonable inquiry, a written communication is deemed to have been received if it is sent to the addressee's last-known place of business, habitual residence or mailing address by registered letter or any other means which provides a record of the attempt to deliver it;

(b) the communication is deemed to have been received on the day it is so delivered.

(2) The provisions of this article do not apply to communications in court proceedings.

Article 4 — Waiver of right to object

A party who knows that any provision of this Law from which the parties may derogate or any requirement under the arbitration agreement has not been complied with and yet proceeds with the arbitration without stating his objection to such non-compliance without undue delay or, if a time-limit is provided therefor, within such period of time, shall be deemed to have waived his right to object.

Article 5 — Extent of court intervention

In matters governed by this Law, no court shall intervene except where so provided in this Law.

Article 6 — Court or other authority for certain functions of arbitration assistance and supervision

The functions referred to in articles 11(3), 11(4), 13(3), 14, 16(3) and 34(2) shall be performed by ... [Each State enacting this model law specifies the court, courts or, where referred to therein, other authority competent to perform these functions.]

CHAPTER II. Arbitration Agreement

Article 7 — Definition and form of arbitration agreement

(1) "Arbitration agreement" is an agreement by the parties to submit to arbitra-

tion all or certain disputes which have arisen or which may arise between them in respect of a defined legal relationship, whether contractual or not. An arbitration agreement may be in the form of an arbitration clause in a contract or in the form of a separate agreement.

(2) The arbitration agreement shall be in writing. An agreement is in writing if it is contained in a document signed by the parties or in an exchange of letters, telex, telegrams or other means of telecommunication which provide a record of the agreement, or in an exchange of statements of claim and defence in which the existence of an agreement is alleged by one party and not denied by another. The reference in a contract to a document containing an arbitration clause constitutes an arbitration agreement provided that the contract is in writing and the reference is such as to make that clause part of the contract.

Article 8 — Arbitration agreement and substantive claim before court
(1) A court before which an action is brought in a matter which is the subject of an arbitration agreement shall, if a party so requests not later than when submitting his first statement on the substance of the dispute, refer the parties to arbitration unless it finds that the agreement is null and void, inoperative or incapable of being performed.

(2) Where an action referred to in paragraph (1) of this article has been brought, arbitral proceedings may nevertheless be commenced or continued, and an award may be made, while the issue is pending before the court.

Article 9 — Arbitration agreement and interim measures by court
It is not incompatible with an arbitration agreement for a party to request, before or during arbitral proceedings, from a court an interim measure of protection and for a court to grant such measure.

CHAPTER III. Composition of Arbitral Tribunal

Article 10 — Number of arbitrators
(1) The parties are free to determine the number of arbitrators.
(2) Failing such determination, the number of arbitrators shall be three.

Article 11 — Appointment of arbitrators
(1) No person shall be precluded by reason of his nationality from acting as an arbitrator, unless otherwise agreed by the parties.
(2) The parties are free to agree on a procedure of appointing the arbitrator or arbitrators, subject to the provisions of paragraphs (4) and (5) of this article.
(3) Failing such agreement,
    (a) in an arbitration with three arbitrators, each party shall appoint one arbitrator, and the two arbitrators thus appointed shall appoint the third arbitrator; if a party fails to appoint the arbitrator within thirty days of receipt of a

request to do so from the other party, or if the two arbitrators fail to agree on the third arbitrator within thirty days of their appointment, the appointment shall be made, upon request of a party, by the court or other authority specified in article 6;

    (b) in an arbitration with a sole arbitrator, if the parties are unable to agree on the arbitrator, he shall be appointed, upon request of a party, by the court or other authority specified in article 6.

  (4) Where, under an appointment procedure agreed upon by the parties,

    (a) a party fails to act as required under such procedure, or

    (b) the parties, or two arbitrators, are unable to reach an agreement expected of them under such procedure, or

    (c) a third party, including an institution, fails to perform any function entrusted to it under such procedure, any party may request the court or other authority specified in article 6 to take the necessary measure, unless the agreement on the appointment procedure provides other means for securing the appointment.

  (5) A decision on a matter entrusted by paragraph (3) or (4) of this article to the court or other authority specified in article 6 shall be subject to no appeal. The court or other authority, in appointing an arbitrator, shall have due regard to any qualifications required of the arbitrator by the agreement of the parties and to such considerations as are likely to secure the appointment of an independent and impartial arbitrator and, in the case of a sole or third arbitrator, shall take into account as well the advisability of appointing an arbitrator of a nationality other than those of the parties.

Article 12 — Grounds for challenge

  (1) When a person is approached in connection with his possible appointment as an arbitrator, he shall disclose any circumstances likely to give rise to justifiable doubts as to his impartiality or independence. An arbitrator, from the time of his appointment and throughout the arbitral proceedings, shall without delay disclose any such circumstances to the parties unless they have already been informed of them by him.

  (2) An arbitrator may be challenged only if circumstances exist that give rise to justifiable doubts as to his impartiality or independence, or if he does not possess qualifications agreed to by the parties. A party may challenge an arbitrator appointed by him, or in whose appointment he has participated, only for reasons of which he becomes aware after the appointment has been made.

Article 13 — Challenge procedure

  (1) The parties are free to agree on a procedure for challenging an arbitrator, subject to the provisions of paragraph (3) of this article.

  (2) Failing such agreement, a party who intends to challenge an arbitrator shall, within fifteen days after becoming aware of the constitution of the arbitral tribunal or after becoming aware of any circumstance referred to in article 12(2), send a written statement of the reasons for the challenge to the arbitral tribunal. Unless the chal-

lenged arbitrator withdraws from his office or the other party agrees to the challenge, the arbitral tribunal shall decide on the challenge.

(3) If a challenge under any procedure agreed upon by the parties or under the procedure of paragraph (2) of this article is not successful, the challenging party may request, within thirty days after having received notice of the decision rejecting the challenge, the court or other authority specified in article 6 to decide on the challenge, which decision shall be subject to no appeal; while such a request is pending, the arbitral tribunal, including the challenged arbitrator, may continue the arbitral proceedings and make an award.

Article 14 — Failure or impossibility to act
(1) If an arbitrator becomes *de jure* or *de facto* unable to perform his functions or for other reasons fails to act without undue delay, his mandate terminates if he withdraws from his office or if the parties agree on the termination. Otherwise, if a controversy remains concerning any of these grounds, any party may request the court or other authority specified in article 6 to decide on the termination of the mandate, which decision shall be subject to no appeal.

(2) If, under this article or article 13(2), an arbitrator withdraws from his office or a party agrees to the termination of the mandate of an arbitrator, this does not imply acceptance of the validity of any ground referred to in this article or article 12(2).

Article 15 — Appointment of substitute arbitrator
Where the mandate of an arbitrator terminates under article 13 or 14 or because of his withdrawal from office for any other reason or because of the revocation of his mandate by agreement of the parties or in any other case of termination of his mandate, a substitute arbitrator shall be appointed according to the rules that were applicable to the appointment of the arbitrator being replaced.

CHAPTER IV. Jurisdiction of Arbitral Tribunal

Article 16 — Competence of arbitral tribunal to rule on its jurisdiction
(1) The arbitral tribunal may rule on its own jurisdiction, including any objections with respect to the existence or validity of the arbitration agreement. For that purpose, an arbitration clause which forms part of a contract shall be treated as an agreement independent of the other terms of the contract. A decision by the arbitral tribunal that the contract is null and void shall not entail *ipso jure* the invalidity of the arbitration clause.

(2) A plea that the arbitral tribunal does not have jurisdiction shall be raised not later than the submission of the statement of defence. A party is not precluded from raising such a plea by the fact that he has appointed, or participated in the appointment of, an arbitrator. A plea that the arbitral tribunal is exceeding the scope of its authority shall be raised as soon as the matter alleged to be beyond the scope of its

authority is raised during the arbitral proceedings. The arbitral tribunal may, in either case, admit a later plea if it considers the delay justified.

(3) The arbitral tribunal may rule on a plea referred to in paragraph (2) of this article either as a preliminary question or in an award on the merits. If the arbitral tribunal rules as a preliminary question that it has jurisdiction, any party may request, within thirty days after having received notice of that ruling, the court specified in article 6 to decide the matter, which decision shall be subject to no appeal; while such a request is pending, the arbitral tribunal may continue the arbitral proceedings and make an award.

Article 17 — Power of arbitral tribunal to order interim measures

Unless otherwise agreed by the parties, the arbitral tribunal may, at the request of a party, order any party to take such interim measure of protection as the arbitral tribunal may consider necessary in respect of the subject-matter of the dispute. The arbitral tribunal may require any party to provide appropriate security in connection with such measure.

CHAPTER V. Conduct of Arbitral Proceedings

Article 18 — Equal treatment of parties

The parties shall be treated with equality and each party shall be given a full opportunity of presenting his case.

Article 19 — Determination of rules of procedure

(1) Subject to the provisions of this Law, the parties are free to agree on the procedure to be followed by the arbitral tribunal in conducting the proceedings.

(2) Failing such agreement, the arbitral tribunal may, subject to the provisions of this Law, conduct the arbitration in such manner as it considers appropriate. The power conferred upon the arbitral tribunal includes the power to determine the admissibility, relevance, materiality and weight of any evidence.

Article 20 — Place of arbitration

(1) The parties are free to agree on the place of arbitration. Failing such agreement, the place of arbitration shall be determined by the arbitral tribunal having regard to the circumstances of the case, including the convenience of the parties.

(2) Notwithstanding the provisions of paragraph (1) of this article, the arbitral tribunal may, unless otherwise agreed by the parties, meet at any place it considers appropriate for consultation among its members, for hearing witnesses, experts or the parties, or for inspection of goods, other property or documents.

Article 21 — Commencement of arbitral proceedings

Unless otherwise agreed by the parties, the arbitral proceedings in respect of a particular dispute commence on the date on which a request for that dispute to be referred to arbitration is received by the respondent.

Article 22 — Language

(1) The parties are free to agree on the language or languages to be used in the arbitral proceedings. Failing such agreement, the arbitral tribunal shall determine the language or languages to be used in the proceedings. This agreement or determination, unless otherwise specified therein, shall apply to any written statement by a party, any hearing and any award, decision or other communication by the arbitral tribunal.

(2) The arbitral tribunal may order that any documentary evidence shall be accompanied by a translation into the language or languages agreed upon by the parties or determined by the arbitral tribunal.

Article 23 — Statements of claim and defence

(1) Within the period of time agreed by the parties or determined by the arbitral tribunal, the claimant shall state the facts supporting his claim, the points at issue and the relief or remedy sought, and the respondent shall state his defence in respect of these particulars, unless the parties have otherwise agreed as to the required elements of such statements. The parties may submit with their statements all documents they consider to be relevant or may add a reference to the documents or other evidence they will submit.

(2) Unless otherwise agreed by the parties, either party may amend or supplement his claim or defence during the course of the arbitral proceedings, unless the arbitral tribunal considers it inappropriate to allow such amendment having regard to the delay in making it.

Article 24 — Hearings and written proceedings

(1) Subject to any contrary agreement by the parties, the arbitral tribunal shall decide whether to hold oral hearings for the presentation of evidence or for oral argument, or whether the proceedings shall be conducted on the basis of documents and other materials. However, unless the parties have agreed that no hearings shall be held, the arbitral tribunal shall hold such hearings at an appropriate stage of the proceedings, if so requested by a party.

(2) The parties shall be given sufficient advance notice of any hearing and of any meeting of the arbitral tribunal for the purposes of inspection of goods, other property or documents.

(3) All statements, documents or other information supplied to the arbitral tribunal by one party shall be communicated to the other party. Also any expert report or evidentiary document on which the arbitral tribunal may rely in making its decision shall be communicated to the parties.

Article 25 — Default of a party

Unless otherwise agreed by the parties, if, without showing sufficient cause,

    (a) the claimant fails to communicate his statement of claim in accordance

with article 23(1), the arbitral tribunal shall terminate the proceedings;
  (b) the respondent fails to communicate his statement of defence in accordance with article 23(1), the arbitral tribunal shall continue the proceedings without treating such failure in itself as an admission of the claimant's allegations;
  (c) any party fails to appear at a hearing or to produce documentary evidence, the arbitral tribunal may continue the proceedings and make the award on the evidence before it.

Article 26 — Expert appointed by arbitral tribunal
  (1) Unless otherwise agreed by the parties, the arbitral tribunal
  (a) may appoint one or more experts to report to it on specific issues to be determined by the arbitral tribunal;
  (b) may require a party to give the expert any relevant information or to produce, or to provide access to, any relevant documents, goods or other property for his inspection.

  (2) Unless otherwise agreed by the parties, if a party so requests or if the arbitral tribunal considers it necessary, the expert shall, after delivery of his written or oral report, participate in a hearing where the parties have the opportunity to put questions to him and to present expert witnesses in order to testify on the points at issue.

Article 27 — Court assistance in taking evidence
  The arbitral tribunal or a party with the approval of the arbitral tribunal may request from a competent court of this State assistance in taking evidence. The court may execute the request within its competence and according to its rules on taking evidence.

CHAPTER VI. Making of Award and Termination of Proceedings

Article 28 — Rules applicable to substance of dispute
  (1) The arbitral tribunal shall decide the dispute in accordance with such rules of law as are chosen by the parties as applicable to the substance of the dispute. Any designation of the law or legal system of a given State shall be construed, unless otherwise expressed, as directly referring to the substantive law of that State and not to its conflict of laws rules.

  (2) Failing any designation by the parties, the arbitral tribunal shall apply the law determined by the conflict of laws rules which it considers applicable.

  (3) The arbitral tribunal shall decide *ex aequo et bono* or as *amiable compositeur* only if the parties have expressly authorized it to do so.

  (4) In all cases, the arbitral tribunal shall decide in accordance with the terms of the contract and shall take into account the usages of the trade applicable to the transaction.

Article 29 — Decision making by panel of arbitrators

In arbitral proceedings with more than one arbitrator, any decision of the arbitral tribunal shall be made, unless otherwise agreed by the parties, by a majority of all its members. However, questions of procedure may be decided by a presiding arbitrator, if so authorized by the parties or all members of the arbitral tribunal.

Article 30 — Settlement

(1) If, during arbitral proceedings, the parties settle the dispute, the arbitral tribunal shall terminate the proceedings and, if requested by the parties and not objected to by the arbitral tribunal, record the settlement in the form of an arbitral award on agreed terms.

(2) An award on agreed terms shall be made in accordance with the provisions of article 31 and shall state that it is an award. Such an award has the same status and effect as any other award on the merits of the case.

Article 31 — Form and contents of award

(1) The award shall be made in writing and shall be signed by the arbitrator or arbitrators. In arbitral proceedings with more than one arbitrator, the signatures of the majority of all members of the arbitral tribunal shall suffice, provided that the reason for any omitted signature is stated.

(2) The award shall state the reasons upon which it is based, unless the parties have agreed that no reasons are to be given or the award is an award on agreed terms under article 30.

(3) The award shall state its date and the place of arbitration as determined in accordance with article 20(1). The award shall be deemed to have been made at that place.

(4) After the award is made, a copy signed by the arbitrators in accordance with paragraph (1) of this article shall be delivered to each party.

Article 32 — Termination of proceedings

(1) The arbitral proceedings are terminated by the final award or by an order of the arbitral tribunal in accordance with paragraph (2) of this article.

(2) The arbitral tribunal shall issue an order for the termination of the arbitral proceedings when:

(a) the claimant withdraws his claim, unless the respondent objects thereto and the arbitral tribunal recognizes a legitimate interest on his part in obtaining a final settlement of the dispute;

(b) the parties agree on the termination of the proceedings;

(c) the arbitral tribunal finds that the continuation of the proceedings has for any other reason become unnecessary or impossible.

(3) The mandate of the arbitral tribunal terminates with the termination of the arbitral proceedings, subject to the provisions of articles 33 and 34(4).

Article 33 — Correction and interpretation of award; additional award

(1) Within thirty days of receipt of the award, unless another period of time has been agreed upon by the parties:

(a) a party, with notice to the other party, may request the arbitral tribunal to correct in the award any errors in computation, any clerical or typographical errors or any errors of similar nature;

(b) if so agreed by the parties, a party, with notice to the other party, may request the arbitral tribunal to give an interpretation of a specific point or part of the award.

If the arbitral tribunal considers the request to be justified, it shall make the correction or give the interpretation within thirty days of receipt of the request. The interpretation shall form part of the award.

(2) The arbitral tribunal may correct any error of the type referred to in paragraph (1)(a) of this article on its own initiative within thirty days of the date of the award.

(3) Unless otherwise agreed by the parties, a party, with notice to the other party, may request, within thirty days of receipt of the award, the arbitral tribunal to make an additional award as to claims presented in the arbitral proceedings but omitted from the award. If the arbitral tribunal considers the request to be justified, it shall make the additional award within sixty days.

(4) The arbitral tribunal may extend, if necessary, the period of time within which it shall make a correction, interpretation or an additional award under paragraph (1) or (3) of this article.

(5) The provisions of article 31 shall apply to a correction or interpretation of the award or to an additional award.

CHAPTER VII. Recourse Against Award

Article 34 — Application for setting aside as exclusive recourse against arbitral award

(1) Recourse to a court against an arbitral award may be made only by an application for setting aside in accordance with paragraphs (2) and (3) of this article.

(2) An arbitral award may be set aside by the court specified in article 6 only if:

(a) the party making the application furnishes proof that:

(i) a party to the arbitration agreement referred to in article 7 was under some incapacity; or the said agreement is not valid under the law to which the parties have subjected it or, failing any indication thereon, under the law of this State; or

(ii) the party making the application was not given proper notice of the appointment of an arbitrator or of the arbitral proceedings or was otherwise unable to present his case; or

(iii) the award deals with a dispute not contemplated by or not falling within the terms of the submission to arbitration, or contains decisions on matters beyond the scope of the submission to arbitration, provided that, if the decisions on matters submitted to arbitration can be separated from those not so submitted, only that part of the award which contains decisions on matters not submitted to arbitration may be set aside; or

(iv) the composition of the arbitral tribunal or the arbitral procedure was not in accordance with the agreement of the parties, unless such agreement was in conflict with a provision of this Law from which the parties cannot derogate, or, failing such agreement, was not in accordance with this Law; or

(b) the court finds that:

(i) the subject-matter of the dispute is not capable of settlement by arbitration under the law of this State; or

(ii) the award is in conflict with the public policy of this State.

(3) An application for setting aside may not be made after three months have elapsed from the date on which the party making that application had received the award or, if a request had been made under article 33, from the date on which that request had been disposed of by the arbitral tribunal.

(4) The court, when asked to set aside an award, may, where appropriate and so requested by a party, suspend the setting aside proceedings for a period of time determined by it in order to give the arbitral tribunal an opportunity to resume the arbitral proceedings or to take such other action as in the arbitral tribunal's opinion will eliminate the grounds for setting aside.

CHAPTER VIII. REcognition and Enforcement of Awards

Article 35 — Recognition and enforcement

(1) An arbitral award, irrespective of the country in which it was made, shall be recognized as binding and, upon application in writing to the competent court, shall be enforced subject to the provisions of this article and of article 36.

(2) The party relying on an award or applying for its enforcement shall supply the duly authenticated original award or a duly certified copy thereof, and the original arbitration agreement referred to in article 7 or a duly certified copy thereof. If the award or agreement is not made in an official language of this State, the party shall supply a duly certified translation thereof into such language.

Article 36 — Grounds for refusing recognition or enforcement

(1) Recognition or enforcement of an arbitral award irrespective of the country in which it was made, may be refused only:

(a) at the request of the party against whom it is invoked, if that party furnishes to the competent court where recognition or enforcement is sought proof that:

(i) a party to the arbitration agreement referred to in article 7 was under some incapacity; or the said agreement is not valid under the law to which the parties have subjected it or, failing any indication thereon, under the law of the country where the award was made; or

(ii) the party against whom the award is invoked was not given proper notice of the appointment of an arbitrator or of the arbitral proceedings or was otherwise unable to present his case; or

(iii) the award deals with a dispute not contemplated by or not falling within the terms of the submission to arbitration, or it contains decisions on matters beyond the scope of the submission to arbitration, provided that, if the decisions on matters submitted to arbitration can be separated from those not so submitted, that part of the award which contains decisions on matters submitted to arbitration may be recognized and enforced; or

(iv) the composition of the arbitral tribunal or the arbitral procedure was not in accordance with the agreement of the parties or, failing such agreement, was not in accordance with the law of the country where the arbitration took place; or

(v) the award has not yet become binding on the parties or has been set aside or suspended by a court of the country in which, or under the law of which, the award was made; or

(b) if the court finds that:

(i) the subject-matter of the dispute is not capable of settlement by arbitration under the law of this State: or

(ii) the recognition or enforcement of the award would be contrary to the public policy of this State.

(2) If an application for setting aside or suspension of an award has been made to a court referred to in paragraph (1)(a)(v) of this article, the court where recognition or enforcement is sought may, if it considers it proper, adjourn its decision and may also, on the application of the party claiming recognition or enforcement of the award, order the other party to provide appropriate security.

Appendix H

INTERNATIONAL ARBITRATION RULES

1. AMERICAN ARBITRATION ASSOCIATION

a. AAA Commercial Arbitration Rules.

1. Agreement of Parties

The parties shall be deemed to have made these rules a part of their arbitration agreement whenever they have provided for arbitration by the American Arbitration Association (hereinafter AAA) or under its Commercial Arbitration Rules. These rules and any amendment of them shall apply in the form obtaining at the time the demand for arbitration or submission agreement is received by the AAA. The parties, by written agreement, may vary the procedures set forth in these rules.

2. Name of Tribunal

Any tribunal constituted by the parties for the settlement of their dispute under these rules shall be called the Commercial Arbitration Tribunal.

3. Administrator and Delegation of Duties

When parties agree to arbitrate under these rules, or when they provide for arbitration by the AAA and an arbitration is initiated under these rules, they thereby authorize the AAA to administer the arbitration. The authority and duties of the AAA are prescribed in the agreement of the parties and in these rules, and may be carried out through such of the AAA's representatives as it may direct.

4. National Panel of Arbitrators

The AAA shall establish and maintain a National Panel of Commercial Arbitrators and shall appoint arbitrators therefore as hereinafter provided.

5. Regional Offices

The AAA may, in its discretion, assign the administration of an arbitration to any of its regional offices.

6. Initiation under an Arbitration Provision in a Contract

Arbitration under an arbitration provision in a contract shall be initiated in the following manner:

(a) The initiating party (hereinafter claimant) shall, within the time period, if any, specified in the contract(s), give written notice to the other party (hereinafter respondent) of its intention to arbitrate (demand), which notice shall contain a statement setting forth the nature of the dispute, the amount involved, if any, the remedy sought, and the hearing locale requested, and

(b) Shall file at any regional office of the AAA three copies of the notice and three copies of the arbitration provisions of the contract, together with the appropriate administrative fee as provided in the Administrative Fee Schedule.

The AAA shall give notice of such filing to the respondent or respondents. A respondent may file an answering statement in duplicate with the AAA within ten days after notice from the AAA, in which event the respondent shall at the same time send a copy of the answering statement to the claimant. If a counterclaim is asserted, it shall contain a statement setting forth the nature of the counterclaim, the amount involved, if any, and the remedy sought. If a counterclaim is asserted, it shall contain a statement setting forth the nature of the counterclaim, the amount involved, if any, and the remedy sought. If a counterclaim is made in the answering statement, the appropriate fee provided in the Administrative Fee Schedule shall be forwarded to the AAA with the answering statement. If no answering statement is filed within the stated time, it will be treated as a denial of the claim. Failure to file an answering statement shall not operate to delay the arbitration.

7. Initiation under a Submission

Parties to any existing dispute may commence an arbitration under these rules by filing at any regional office of the AAA three copies of a written submission to arbitrate under these rules, signed by the parties. It shall contain a statement of the matter in dispute, the amount of money involved, if any, the remedy sought, and the hearing locale requested, together with the appropriate administrative fee as provided in the Administrative Fee Schedule.

8. Changes of Claim

After filing of a claim, if either party desires to make any new or different claim or counterclaim, same shall be made in writing and filed with the AAA, and a copy shall be mailed to the other party, who shall have a period of ten days from the date of such mailing within which to file an answer with the AAA. After the arbitrator is appointed, however, no new or different claim may be submitted except with the arbitrator's consent.

9. Applicable Procedures

Unless the AAA in its discretion determines otherwise, the Expedited Procedures shall be applied in any case where no disclosed claim or counterclaim exceeds $25,000, exclusive of interest and arbitration costs. Parties may also agree to the Expedited Procedures in cases involving claims in excess of $25,000. The Expedited Procedures shall be applied as described in Sections 53 through 57 of these rules.

10. Administrative Conference, Preliminary Hearing, and Mediation Conference

At the request of any party or at the discretion of the AAA, an administrative conference with the AAA and the parties and/or their representatives will be scheduled in appropriate cases to expedite the arbitration proceedings.

In large or complex cases, at the request of any party or at the discretion of the arbitrator or the AAA, a preliminary hearing with the parties and/or their representatives and the arbitrator may be scheduled by the arbitrator to specify the issues to be resolved, to stipulate to uncontested facts, and to consider any other matters that will expedite the arbitration proceedings. Consistent with the expedited nature of arbitration, the arbitrator may, at the preliminary hearing, establish (i) the extent of and schedule for the production of relevant documents and other information, (ii) the identification of any witnesses to be called, and (iii) a schedule for further hearings to resolve the dispute.

With the consent of the parties, the AAA at any stage of the proceeding may arrange a mediation conference under the Commercial Mediation Rules, in order to facilitate settlement. The mediator shall not be an arbitrator appointed to the case. Where the parties to a pending arbitration agree to mediate under the AAA's rules, no additional administrative fee is required to initiate the mediation.

11. Fixing of Locale

The parties may mutually agree on the locale where the arbitration is to be held. If any party requests that the hearing be held in a specific locale and the other party files no objection thereto within ten days after notice of the request has been mailed to it by the AAA, the locale shall be the one requested. If a party objects to the locale requested by the other party, the AAA shall have the power to determine the locale and its decision shall be final and binding.

12. Qualifications of an Arbitrator

Any neutral arbitrator appointed pursuant to Section 13, 14, 15, or 54, or selected by mutual choice of the parties or their appointees, shall be subject to disqualification for the reasons specified in Section 19. If the parties specifically so agree in writing, the arbitrator shall not be subject to disqualification for those reasons.

Unless the parties agree otherwise, an arbitrator selected unilaterally by one party is a party-appointed arbitrator and is not subject to disqualification pursuant to Section 19.

The term "arbitrator" in these rules refers to the arbitration panel, whether composed of one or more arbitrators and whether the arbitrators are neutral or party appointed.

13. Appointment from Panel

If the parties have not appointed an arbitrator and have not provided any other method of appointment, the arbitrator shall be appointed in the following manner: immediately after the filing of the demand or submission, the AAA shall submit simultaneously to each party to the dispute an identical list of names of persons chosen from the panel.

Each party to the dispute shall have ten days from the mailing date in which to cross off any names objected to, number the remaining names in order of preference, and return the list to the AAA. If a party does not return the list within the time specified, all persons named therein shall be deemed acceptable. From among the persons who have been approved on both lists, and in accordance with the designated order of mutual preference, the AAA shall invite the acceptance of an arbitrator to serve. If the parties fail to agree on any of the persons named, or if acceptable arbitrators are unable to act, or if for any other reason the appointment cannot be made from the submitted lists, the AAA shall have the power to make the appointment from among other members of the panel without the submission of additional lists.

14. Direct Appointment by a Party

If the agreement of the parties names an arbitrator or specifies a method appointing an arbitrator, that designation or method shall be followed. The notice of appointment, with the name and address of the arbitrator, shall be filed with the AAA by the appointing party. Upon the request of any appointing party, the AAA shall submit a list of members of the panel from which the party may, if it so desires, make the appointment.

If the agreement specifies a period of time within which an arbitrator shall be appointed and any party fails to make the appointment within that period, the AAA shall make the appointment.

If no period of time is specified in the agreement, the AAA shall notify the party to make the appointment. If within ten days thereafter an arbitrator has not been appointed by a party, the AAA shall make the appointment.

15. Appointment of Neutral Arbitrator by Party-Appointed Arbitrators

If the parties have selected party-appointed arbitrators, or if such arbitrators have been appointed as provided in Section 14, and the parties have authorized them to appoint a neutral arbitrator within a specified time and no appointment is made within that time or any agreed extension thereof, the AAA may appoint a neutral arbitrator, who shall act as chairperson.

If no period of time is specified for appointment of the neutral arbitrator and the party-appointed arbitrators do not make the appointment within ten days from the date of the appointment of the last party-appointed arbitrator, the AAA may appoint the neutral arbitrator, who shall act as chairperson.

If the parties have agreed that their party-appointed arbitrators shall appoint the neutral arbitrator from the panel, the AAA shall furnish to the party-appointed arbitrators, in the manner prescribed in Section 13, a list selected from the panel, and the appointment of the neutral arbitrator shall be made as prescribed in that section.

16. Nationality of Arbitrator in International Arbitration

Where the parties are nationals or residents of different countries, any neutral arbitrator shall, upon the request of either party, be appointed from among the nationals of a country other than that of any of the parties. The request must be made prior to the time set for the appointment of the arbitrator as agreed by the parties or set by these rules.

17. Number of Arbitrators

If the arbitration agreement does not specify the number of arbitrators, the dispute shall be heard and determined by one arbitrator, unless the AAA, in its discretion, directs that a greater number of arbitrators be appointed.

18. Notice to Arbitrator of Appointment

Notice of the appointment of the neutral arbitrator, whether appointed mutually by the parties or by the AAA, shall be mailed to the arbitrator by the AAA, together with a copy of these rules, and the signed acceptance of the arbitrator shall be filed with the AAA prior to the opening of the first hearing.

19. Disclosure and Challenge Procedure

Any person appointed as neutral arbitrator shall disclose to the AAA any circumstance likely to affect impartiality, including any bias or any financial or personal interest in the result of the arbitration or any past or present relationship with the parties or their representatives. Upon receipt of such information from the arbitrator or another source, the AAA shall communicate the information to the parties and, if it deems it appropriate to do so, to the arbitrator and others. Upon objection of a party to the continued service of a neutral arbitrator, the AAA shall determine whether the arbitrator should be disqualified and shall inform the parties of its decision, which shall be conclusive.

20. Vacancies

If for any reason an arbitrator should be unable to perform the duties of the office, the AAA may, on proof satisfactory to it, declare the office vacant. Vacancies shall be filled in accordance with the applicable provisions of these rules.

In the event of a vacancy in a panel of neutral arbitrators after the hearings have commenced, the remaining arbitrator or arbitrators may continue with the hearing and determination of the controversy, unless the parties agree otherwise.

21. Date, Time, and Place of Hearing

The arbitrator shall set the date, time, and place for each hearing. The AAA shall mail to each party notice thereof at least ten days in advance, unless the parties by mutual agreement waive such notice or modify the terms thereof.

22. Representation

Any party may be represented by counsel or other authorized representative. A party intending to be so represented shall notify the other party and the AAA of the name and address of the representative at least three days prior to the date set for the hearing at which that person is first to appear. When such a representative initiates an arbitration or responds for a party, notice is deemed to have been given.

23. Stenographic Record

Any party desiring a stenographic record shall make arrangements directly with a stenographer and shall notify the other party of these arrangements in advance of the hearing. The requesting party or parties shall pay the cost of the record. If the transcript is agreed by the parties to be, or determined by the arbitrator to be, the official record of the proceeding, it must be made available to the arbitrator and to the other parties for inspection, at a date, time, and place determined by the arbitrator.

24. Interpreters

Any party wishing an interpreter shall make all arrangements directly with the interpreter and shall assume the costs of the service.

25. Attendance at Hearings

The arbitrator shall maintain the privacy of the hearings unless the law provides to the contrary. Any person having a direct interest in the arbitration is entitled to attend hearings. The arbitrator shall otherwise have the power to require the exclusion of any witness, other than a party or other essential person, during the testimony of any other witness. It shall be discretionary with the arbitrator to determine the propriety of the attendance of any other person.

26. Postponements

The arbitrator for good cause shown may postpone any hearing upon the request of a party or upon the arbitrator's own initiative, and shall also grant such postponement when all of the parties agree thereto.

27. Oaths

Before proceeding with the first hearing, each arbitrator may take an oath of office and, if required by law, shall do so. The arbitrator may require witnesses to testify under oath administered by any duly qualified person and, if it is required by law or requested by any party, shall do so.

28. Majority Decision

All decisions of the arbitrators must be by a majority. The award must also be made by a majority unless the concurrence of all is expressly required by the arbitration agreement or by law.

29. Order of Proceedings and Communication with Arbitrator

A hearing shall be opened by the filing of the oath of the arbitrator, where required; by the recording of the date, time, and place of the hearing, and the presence of the arbitrator, the parties, and their representatives, if any; and by the receipt by the arbitrator of the statement of the claim and the answering statement, if any.

The arbitrator may, at the beginning of the hearing, ask for statements clarifying the issues involved. In some cases, part or all of the above will have been accomplished at the preliminary hearing conducted by the arbitrator pursuant to Section 10.

The complaining party shall then present evidence to support its claim. The defending party shall then present evidence supporting its defense. Witnesses for each party shall submit to questions or other examination. The arbitrator has the discretion to vary this procedure but shall afford a full and equal opportunity to all parties for the presentation of any material and relevant evidence.

Exhibits, when offered by either party, may be received in evidence by the arbitrator.

The names and addresses of all witnesses and a description of the exhibits in the order received shall be made a part of the record.

There shall be no direct communication between the parties and a neutral arbitrator other than at oral hearing, unless the parties and the arbitrator agree otherwise. Any other oral or written communication from the parties to the neutral arbitrator shall be directed to the AAA for transmittal to the arbitrator.

30. Arbitration in the Absence of a Party or Representative

Unless the law provides to the contrary, the arbitration may proceed in the absence of any party or representative who, after due notice, fails to be present or fails to obtain a postponement. An award shall not be made solely on the default of a party. The arbitrator shall require the party who is present to submit such evidence as the arbitrator may require for the making of an award.

31. Evidence

The parties may offer such evidence as is relevant and material to the dispute and shall produce such evidence as the arbitrator may deem necessary to an understanding and determination of the dispute. An arbitrator or other person authorized by law to subpoena witnesses or documents may do so upon the request of any party or independently.

The arbitrator shall be the judge of the relevance and materiality of the evidence offered, and conformity to legal rules of evidence shall not be necessary. All evidence shall be taken in the presence of all of the arbitrators and all of the parties, except where any of the parties is absent in default or has waived the right to be present.

32. Evidence by Affidavit and Post-hearing Filing of Documents or Other Evidence

The arbitrator may receive and consider the evidence of witnesses by affidavit, but shall give it only such weight as the arbitrator deems it entitled to after consideration of any objection made to its admission.

If the parties agree or the arbitrator directs that documents or other evidence be submitted to the arbitrator after the hearing, the documents or other evidence shall be filed with the AAA for transmission to the arbitrator. All parties shall be afforded an opportunity to examine such documents or other evidence.

33. Inspection or Investigation

An arbitrator finding it necessary to make an inspection or investigation in connection with the arbitration shall direct the AAA to so advise the parties. The arbitrator shall set the date and time and the AAA shall notify the parties. Any party who so desires may be present at such an inspection or investigation. In the event that one or all parties are not present at the inspection or investigation, the arbitrator shall make a verbal or written report to the parties and afford them an opportunity to comment.

34. Interim Measures

The arbitrator may issue such orders for interim relief as may be deemed necessary to safeguard the property that is the subject matter of the arbitration without prejudice to the rights of the parties or to the final determination of the dispute.

35. Closing of Hearing

The arbitrator shall specifically inquire of all parties whether they have any further proofs to offer or witnesses to be heard. Upon receiving negative replies or if satisfied that the record is complete, the arbitrator shall declare the hearing closed and a minute thereof shall be recorded. If briefs are to be filed, the hearing shall be declared closed as of the final date set by the arbitrator for the receipt of briefs. If documents are to be filed as provided in Section 32 and the date set for their receipt is later than that set for the receipt of briefs, the later date shall be the date of closing the hearing. The time limit within which the arbitrator is required to make the award shall commence to run, in the absence of other agreements by the parties, upon the closing of the hearing.

36. Reopening of Hearing

The hearing may be reopened on the arbitrator's initiative, or upon application of a party, at any time before the award is made. If reopening the hearing would prevent the making of the award within the specific time agreed on by the parties in the contract(s) out of which the controversy has arisen, the matter may not be reopened unless the parties agree on an extension of time. When no specific date is fixed in the contract, the arbitrator may reopen the hearing and shall have thirty days from the closing of the reopened hearing within which to make an award.

37. Waiver of Oral Hearing

The parties may provide, by written agreement, for the waiver of oral hearings in any case. If the parties are unable to agree as to the procedure, the AAA shall specify a fair and equitable procedure.

38. Waiver of Rules

Any party who proceeds with the arbitration after knowledge that any provision or requirement of these rules has not been complied with and who fails to state an objection thereto in writing shall be deemed to have waived the right to object.

39. Extensions of Time

The parties may modify any period of time by mutual agreement. The AAA or the arbitrator may for good cause extend any period of time established by these rules, except the time for making the award. The AAA shall notify the parties of any extension.

40. Serving of Notice

Each party shall be deemed to have consented that any papers, notices, or process necessary or proper for the initiation or continuation of an arbitration under these rules; for any court action in connection therewith; or for the entry of judgment on any award made under these rules may be served on a party by mail addressed to the party or its representative at the last known address or by personal service, in or outside the state where the arbitration is held, provided that reasonable opportunity to be heard with regard thereto has been granted to the party.

The AAA and the parties may also use facsimile transmission, telex, telegram, or other written forms of electronic communication to give the notices required by these rules.

41. Time of Award

The award shall be made promptly by the arbitrator and, unless otherwise agreed by the parties or specified by law, no later than thirty days from the date of closing the hearing, or, if oral hearings have been waived, from the date of the AAA's transmittal of the final statements and proofs to the arbitrator.

42. Form of Award

The award shall be in writing and shall be signed by a majority of the arbitrators. It shall be executed in the manner required by law.

43. Scope of Award

The arbitrator may grant any remedy or relief that the arbitrator deems just and equitable and within the scope of the agreement of the parties, including, but not limited to, specific performance of a contract. The arbitration shall, in the award, assess arbitration fees, expenses, and compensation as provided in Sections 48, 49, and 50 in favor of any party and, in the event that any administrative fees or expenses are due the AAA, in favor of the AAA.

44. Award upon Settlement

If the parties settle their dispute during the course of the arbitration, the arbitrator may set forth the terms of the agreed settlement in an award. Such an award is referred to as a consent award.

45. Delivery of Award to Parties

Parties shall accept as legal delivery of the award the placing of the award or a true copy thereof in the mail addressed to a party or its representative at the last known address, personal service of the award, or the filing of the award in any other manner that is permitted by law.

46. Release of Documents for Judicial Proceedings

The AAA shall, upon the written request of a party, furnish to the party, at its expense, certified copies of any papers in the AAA's possession that may be required in judicial proceedings relating to the arbitration.

47. Applications to Court and Exclusion of Liability

(a)No judicial proceeding by a party relating to the subject matter of the arbitration shall be deemed a waiver of the party's right to arbitrate.

(b)Neither the AAA nor any arbitrator in a proceeding under these rules is a necessary party in judicial proceedings relating to the arbitration.

(c)Parties to these rules shall be deemed to have consented that judgment upon the arbitration award may be entered in any federal or state court having jurisdiction thereof.

(d)Neither the AAA nor any arbitrator shall be liable to any party for any act or omission in connection with any arbitration conducted under these rules.

48. Administrative Fee

As a not-for-profit organization, the AAA shall prescribe an Administrative Fee Schedule and a Refund Schedule to compensate it for the cost of providing administrative services. The schedule in effect at the time the demand for arbitration or submission agreement is received shall be applicable.

The administrative fee shall be advanced by the initiating party or parties, subject to final apportionment by the arbitrator in the award.

When a claim or counterclaim is withdrawn or settled, the refund shall be made in accordance with the Refund Schedule.

The AAA may, in the event of extreme hardship on the part of any party, defer or reduce the administrative fee.

49. Expenses

The expenses of witnesses for either side shall be paid by the party producing such witnesses. All expenses of the arbitration, including required travel and other expenses of the arbitrator, AAA representatives, and any witness and the cost of any proof produced at the direct request of the arbitrator, shall be borne equally by the parties, unless they agree otherwise or unless the arbitrator in the award assesses such expenses or any part thereof against any specified party or parties.

50. Neutral Arbitrator's Fee

Unless the parties agree otherwise, members of the National Panel of Commercial Arbitrators appointed as neutrals will serve without compensation for the first day of service.

Thereafter, compensation shall be based on the amount of service involved and the number of hearings. An appropriate daily rate and other arrangements will be discussed by the administrator with the parties and the arbitrator. If the parties fail to agree to the terms of compensation, an appropriate rate shall be established by the AAA and communicated in writing to the parties.

Any arrangement for the compensation of a neutral arbitrator shall be made through the AAA and not directly between the parties and the arbitrator. The terms of compensation of neutral arbitrators on a panel shall be identical.

51. Deposits

The AAA may require the parties to deposit in advance of any hearings such sums of money as it deems necessary to defray the expense of the arbitration, including the arbitrator's fee, if any, and shall render an accounting to the parties and return any unexpended balance at the conclusion of the case.

52. Interpretation and Application of Rules

The arbitrator shall interpret and apply these rules insofar as they relate to the arbitrator's powers and duties. When there is more than one arbitrator and a difference arises among them concerning the meaning or application of these rules, it shall be decided by a majority vote. If that is unobtainable, either an arbitrator or a party may refer the question to the AAA for final decision. All other rules shall be interpreted and applied by the AAA.

EXPEDITED PROCEDURES

53. Notice by Telephone

The parties shall accept all notices from the AAA by telephone. Such notices by the AAA shall subsequently be confirmed in writing to the parties. Should there be a failure to confirm in writing any notice hereunder, the proceeding shall nonetheless be valid if notice has, in fact, been given by telephone.

54. Appointment and Qualifications of Arbitrator

Where no disclosed claim or counterclaim exceeds $25,000 exclusive of interest and arbitration costs, the AAA shall submit simultaneously to each party an identical list of five proposed arbitrators drawn from the National Panel of Commercial Arbitrators, from which one arbitrator shall be appointed.

Each party may strike two names from the list on a peremptory basis. The list is returnable to the AAA within seven days from the date of the AAA's mailing to the parties.

If for any reason the appointment of an arbitrator cannot be made from the list, the AAA may make the appointment from among other members of the panel without the submission of additional lists.

The parties will be given notice by telephone by the AAA of the appointment of the arbitrator, who shall be subject to disqualification for the reasons specified in Section 19. The parties shall notify the AAA, by telephone, within seven days of any objection to the arbitrator appointed. Any objection by a party to the arbitrator shall be confirmed in writing to the AAA with a copy to the other party or parties.

55. Date, Time, and Place of Hearing

The arbitrator shall set the date, time, and place of the hearing. The AAA will notify the parties by telephone, at least seven days in advance of the hearing date. A formal Notice of Hearing will be sent by the AAA to the parties.

56. The Hearing

Generally, the hearing shall be completed within one day, unless the dispute is resolved by submission of documents under Section 37. The arbitrator, for good cause shown, may schedule an additional hearing to be held within seven days.

57. Time of Award

Unless otherwise agreed by the parties, the award shall be rendered not later than fourteen days from the date of the closing of the hearing.

b. AAA International Arbitration Rules.

Article 1

1. Where parties have agreed in writing to arbitrate disputes under these [American Arbitration Association] International Arbitration Rules, the arbitration shall take place in accordance with their provisions, as in effect at the date of commencement of the arbitration, subject to whatever modifications the parties may adopt in writing.

2. These rules govern the arbitration, except that, where any such rule is in conflict with any provision of the law applicable to the arbitration from which the parties cannot derogate, that provision shall prevail.

3. These rules specify the duties and responsibilities of the administrator, the American Arbitration Association. The administrator may provide services through its own facilities or through the facilities of arbitral institutions with whom it has agreements of cooperation.

I. COMMENCING THE ARBITRATION

Notice of Arbitration and Statement of Claim

Article 2

1. The party initiating arbitration ("claimant") shall give written notice of arbitration to the administrator and to the party or parties against whom a claim is being made ("respondent(s)").

2. Arbitral proceedings shall be deemed to commence on the date on which the notice of arbitration is received by the administrator.

3. The notice of arbitration shall include the following:
   (a) a demand that the dispute be referred to arbitration;
   (b) the names and addresses of the parties;
   (c) a reference to the arbitration clause or agreement that is invoked;
   (d) a reference to any contract out of or in relation to which the dispute arises;
   (e) a description of the claim and an indication of the facts supporting it;
   (f) the relief or remedy sought and the amount claimed; and
   (g) may include proposals as to the number of arbitrators, the place of arbitration and the language(s) of the arbitration.

Upon receipt of such notice, the administrator will communicate with all parties with respect to the arbitration, including the matters set forth in (g) above, if the parties have not already agreed on these matters, and will acknowledge the commencement of the arbitration.

Statement of Defense and Counterclaim
Article 3

1. Within forty-five days after the date of the commencement of the arbitration, a respondent shall file a statement of defense in writing with the claimant and any other parties, and with the administrator for transmittal to the tribunal when appointed.

2. At the time a respondent submits its statement of defense, a respondent may make counterclaims or assert set-offs as to any claim covered by the agreement to arbitrate, as to which the claimant shall within forty-five days file a statement of defense.

3. A respondent shall respond to the administrator, the claimant and other parties within forty-five days as to any proposals the claimant may have made as to the number of arbitrators, the place of the arbitration or the language(s) of the arbitration, except to the extent that the parties have previously agreed as to these matters.

Amendments to Claims
Article 4

During the arbitral proceedings, any party may amend or supplement its claim, counterclaim or defense, unless the tribunal considers it inappropriate to allow such amendment because of the party's delay in making it or of prejudice to the other parties or any other circumstances. A claim or counterclaim may not be amended if the amendment would fall outside the scope of the agreement to arbitrate.

II. The Tribunal

Number of Arbitrators
Article 5

If the parties have not agreed on the number of arbitrators, one arbitrator shall be appointed unless the administrator determines in its discretion that three arbitrators are appropriate because of the large size, complexity or other circumstances of the case.

Appointment of Arbitrators
Article 6

1. The parties may mutually agree upon any procedure for appointing arbitrators and shall inform the administrator as to such procedure.

2. The parties may mutually designate arbitrators, with or without the assistance of the administrator. When such designations are made, the parties shall notify the administrator so that notice of the appointment can be communicated to the arbitrators, together with a copy of these rules.

3. If within sixty days after the commencement of the arbitration, all of the parties have not mutually agreed on a procedure for appointing the arbitrator(s) or have not mutually agreed on the designation of the arbitrator(s), the administrator shall, at the written request of any party, appoint the arbitrator(s) and designate the presiding arbitrator. If all of the parties have mutually agreed upon a procedure for appointing the arbitrator(s), but all appointments have not been made within the time limits provided in that procedure, the administrator shall, at the written request of any party, perform all functions provided for in that procedure.

4. In making such appointments, the administrator, after inviting consultation with the parties, shall endeavor to select suitable arbitrators. At the request of any party or on its own initiative, the administrator may appoint nationals of a country other than that of any of the parties.

Challenge of Arbitrators
Article 7

Unless the parties agree otherwise, arbitrators acting under these rules shall be impartial and independent. Prior to accepting appointment, a prospective arbitrator shall disclose to the administrator any circumstance likely to give rise to justifiable doubts as to the arbitrator's impartiality or independence. Once appointed, an arbitrator shall disclose any additional such information to the parties and to the administrator. Upon receipt of such information from an arbitrator or a party, the administrator shall communicate it to the parties and to the arbitrator.

Article 8

1. A party may challenge any arbitrator whenever circumstances exist that give rise to justifiable doubts as to the arbitrator's impartiality or independence. A party wishing to challenge an arbitrator shall send notice of the challenge to the administrator within fifteen days after being notified of the appointment of the arbitrator, or within fifteen days after the circumstances giving rise to the challenge became known to that party.

2. The challenge shall state in writing the reasons for the challenge.

3. Upon receipt of such a challenge, the administrator shall notify the other parties of the challenge. When an arbitrator has been challenged by one party, the other parties may agree to the acceptance of the challenge and, if there is agreement, the arbitrator shall withdraw. The challenged arbitrator may also withdraw from office in the absence of such agreement. In neither case does this imply acceptance of the validity of the grounds for the challenge.

Article 9

If the other party or parties do not agree to the challenge or the challenged arbitrator does not withdraw, the decision on the challenge shall be made by the administrator in its sole discretion.

Replacement of an Arbitrator
Article 10

If an arbitrator withdraws after a challenge, or the administrator sustains the challenge, or the administrator determines that there are sufficient reasons to accept the resignation of an arbitrator, or an arbitrator dies, a substitute arbitrator shall be appointed pursuant to the provisions of Article 6, unless the parties otherwise agree.

Article 11

1. If an arbitrator on a three-person tribunal fails to participate in the arbitration, the two other arbitrators shall have the power in their sole discretion to continue the arbitration and to make any decision, ruling or award, notwithstanding the failure of the third arbitrator to participate. In determining whether to continue the arbitration or to render any decision, ruling or award without the participation of an arbitrator, the two other arbitrators shall take into account the stage of the arbitration, the reason, if any, expressed by the third arbitrator for such nonparticipation, and such other matters as they consider appropriate in the circumstances of the case. In the event that the two other arbitrators determine not to continue the arbitration without the participation of the third arbitrator, the administrator on proof satisfactory to it shall declare the office vacant, and a substitute arbitrator shall be appointed pursuant to the provisions of Article 6, unless the parties otherwise agree.

2. If a substitute arbitrator is appointed, the tribunal shall determine at its sole discretion whether all or part of any prior hearings shall be repeated.

III. General Conditions

Representation
Article 12

Any party may be represented in the arbitration. The names, addresses and telephone numbers of representatives shall be communicated in writing to the other parties and to the administrator. Once the tribunal has been established, the parties or their representatives may communicate in writing directly with the tribunal.

Place of Arbitration
Article 13

1. If the parties disagree as to the place of arbitration, the place of arbitration may initially be determined by the administrator, subject to the power of the tribunal to determine finally the place of arbitration within sixty days after its constitution. All such determinations shall be made having regard for the contentions of the parties and the circumstances of the arbitration.

2. The tribunal may hold conferences or hear witnesses or inspect property or documents at any place it deems appropriate. The parties shall be given sufficient written notice to enable them to be present at any such proceedings.

Language
Article 14

If the parties have not agreed otherwise, the language(s) of the arbitration shall be that of the documents containing the arbitration agreement, subject to the power of the tribunal to determine otherwise based upon the contentions of the parties and the circumstances of the arbitration. The tribunal may order that any documents delivered in another language shall be accompanied by a translation into such language or languages.

Pleas as to Jurisdiction
Article 15

1. The tribunal shall have the power to rule on its own jurisdiction, including any objections with respect to the existence or validity of the arbitration agreement.

2. The tribunal shall have the power to determine the existence or validity of a contract of which an arbitration clause forms a part. Such an arbitration clause shall be treated as an agreement independent of the other terms of the contract.

3. Objections to the arbitrability of a claim must be raised no later than forty-five days after the commencement of the arbitration and, in respect to a counterclaim, no later than forty-five days after filing the counterclaim.

Conduct of the Arbitration
Article 16

1. Subject to these rules, the tribunal may conduct the arbitration in whatever manner it considers appropriate, provided that the parties are treated with equality and that each party has the right to be heard and is given a fair opportunity to present its case.

2. Documents or information supplied to the tribunal by one party shall at the same time be communicated by that party to the other party or parties.

Further Written Statements
Article 17

The tribunal may decide whether any written statements, in addition to statements of claims and counterclaims and statements of defense, shall be required from the parties or may be presented by them, and shall fix the periods of time for submitting such statements.

Periods of Time
Article 18

The periods of time fixed by the tribunal for the communication of written statements should not exceed forty-five days. However, the tribunal may extend such time limits if it considers such an extension justified.

Notices
Article 19

1. Unless otherwise agreed by the parties or ordered by the tribunal, all notices, statements and written communications may be served on a party by air mail or air courier addressed to the party or its representative at the last known address or by personal service. Facsimile transmission, telex, telegram, or other written forms of electronic communication may be used to give any such notices, statements or written communications.

2. For the purpose of calculating a period of time under these rules, such period shall begin to run on the day following the day when a notice, statement or written communication is received. If the last day of such period is an official holiday at the

place received, the period is extended until the first business day which follows. Official holidays occurring during the meeting of the period of time are included in calculating the period.

Evidence
Article 20

1. Each party shall have the burden of proving the facts relied on to support its claim or defense.

2. The tribunal may order a party to deliver to the tribunal and to the other parties a summary of the documents and other evidence which that party intends to present in support of its claim, counterclaim or defense.

3. At any time during the proceedings, the tribunal may order parties to produce other documents, exhibits or other evidence it deems necessary or appropriate.

Hearings
Article 21

1. The tribunal shall give the parties at least thirty days' advance notice of the date, time and place of the initial oral hearing. The tribunal shall give reasonable notice of subsequent hearings.

2. At least fifteen days before the hearings, each party shall give the tribunal and the other parties the names and addresses of any witnesses it intends to present, the subject of their testimony and the languages in which such witnesses will give their testimony.

3. At the request of the tribunal or pursuant to mutual agreement of the parties, the administrator shall make arrangements for the interpretation of oral testimony or for a record of the hearing.

4. Hearings are private unless the parties agree otherwise or the law provides to the contrary. The tribunal may require any witness or witnesses to retire during the testimony of other witnesses. The tribunal may determine the manner in which witnesses are examined.

5. Evidence of witnesses may also be presented in the form of written statements signed by them.

6. The admissibility, relevance, materiality and weight of the evidence offered by any party shall be determined by the tribunal.

Interim Measures of Protection
Article 22

1. At the request of any party, the tribunal may take whatever interim measures it deems necessary in respect of the subject-matter of the dispute, including measures

for the conservation of the goods which are the subject-matter in dispute, such as ordering their deposit with a third person or the sale of perishable goods.

2. Such interim measures may be taken in the form of an interim award and the tribunal may require security for the costs of such measures.

3. A request for interim measures addressed by a party to a judicial authority shall not be deemed incompatible with the agreement to arbitrate or a waiver of the right to arbitrate.

Experts
Article 23

1. The tribunal may appoint one or more independent experts to report to it, in writing, on specific issues designated by the tribunal and communicated to the parties.

2. The parties shall provide such an expert with any relevant information or produce for inspection any relevant documents or goods that the expert may require. Any dispute between a party and the expert as to the relevance of the requested information or goods shall be referred to the tribunal for decision.

3. Upon receipt of an expert's report, the tribunal shall send a copy of the report to all parties, who shall be given an opportunity to express, in writing, their opinion on the report. A party may examine any document on which the expert has relied in such a report.

4. At the request of any party, the parties shall be given an opportunity to question the expert at a hearing. At this hearing, parties may present expert witnesses to testify on the points at issue.

Default
Article 24

1. If a party fails to file a statement of defense within the time established by the tribunal without showing sufficient cause for such failure, as determined by the tribunal, the tribunal may proceed with the arbitration.

2. If a party, duly notified under these rules, fails to appear at a hearing without showing sufficient cause for such failure, as determined by the tribunal, the tribunal may proceed with the arbitration.

3. If a party, duly invited to produce evidence, fails to do so within the time established by the tribunal without showing sufficient cause for such failure, as determined by the tribunal, the tribunal may make the award on the evidence before it.

Closure of Hearing
Article 25

1. After asking the parties if they have any further testimony or evidentiary submissions and upon receiving negative replies or if satisfied that the record is complete, the tribunal may declare the hearings closed.

2. If it considers it appropriate, on its own motion or upon application of a party, the tribunal may reopen the hearings at any time before the award is made.

Waiver of Rules
Article 26

A party who knows that any provision of the rules or requirement under the rules has not been complied with, but proceeds with the arbitration without promptly stating an objection in writing thereto, shall be deemed to have waived the right to object.

Awards, Decisions and Rulings
Article 27

1. When there is more than one arbitrator, any award, decision or ruling of the arbitral tribunal shall be made by a majority of the arbitrators.

2. When the parties or the tribunal so authorize, decisions or rulings on questions of procedure may be made by the presiding arbitrator, subject to revision by the tribunal.

Form and Effect of the Award
Article 28

1. Awards shall be made in writing, promptly by the tribunal, and shall be final and binding on the parties. The parties undertake to carry out any such award without delay.

2. The tribunal shall state the reasons upon which the award is based, unless the parties have agreed that no reasons need be given.

3. An award signed by a majority of the arbitrators shall be sufficient. Where there are three arbitrators and one of them fails to sign, the award shall be accompanied by a statement of whether the third arbitrator was given the opportunity to sign.

4. The award shall contain the date and the place where the award was made, which shall be the place designated pursuant to Article 13.

5. An award may be made public only with the consent of all parties or as required by law.

6. Copies of the award shall be communicated to the parties by the administrator.

7. If the arbitration law of the country where the award is made requires the award to be filed or registered, the tribunal shall comply with such requirement.

8. In addition to making a final award, the tribunal may make interim, interlocutory, or partial orders and awards.

Applicable Laws
Article 29

1. The tribunal shall apply the substantive law or laws designated by the parties as applicable to the dispute. Failing such a designation by the parties, the tribunal shall apply such law or laws as it determines to be appropriate.

2. In arbitrations involving the application of contracts, the tribunal shall decide in accordance with the terms of the contract and shall take into account usages of the trade applicable to the contract.

3. The tribunal shall not decide as amiable compositeur or ex aequo et bono unless the parties have authorized it to do so.

Settlement or Other Reasons for Termination
Article 30

1. If the parties settle the dispute before an award is made, the tribunal shall terminate the arbitration and, if requested by all parties, may record the settlement in the form of an award on agreed terms. The tribunal is not obliged to give reasons for such an award.

2. If the continuation of the proceedings becomes unnecessary or impossible for any other reason, the tribunal shall inform the parties of its intention to terminate the proceedings. The tribunal shall thereafter issue an order terminating the arbitration, unless a party raises justifiable grounds for objection.

Interpretation or Correction of the Award
Article 31

1. Within thirty days after the receipt of an award, any party, with notice to the other parties, may request the tribunal to interpret the award or correct any clerical, typographical or computation errors or make an additional award as to claims presented but omitted from the award.

2. If the tribunal considers such a request justified, after considering the contentions of the parties, it shall comply with such a request within thirty days after the request.

Costs
Article 32

The tribunal shall fix the costs of arbitration in its award. The tribunal may apportion such costs among the parties if it determines that such apportionment is reasonable, taking into account the circumstances of the case. Such costs may include:

     (a) the fees and expenses of the arbitrators;
     (b) the costs of assistance required by the tribunal, including its experts;
     (c) the fees and expenses of the administrator;
     (d) the reasonable costs for legal representation of a successful party.

Compensation of Arbitrators
Article 33

Arbitrators shall be compensated based upon their amount of service, taking into account the size and complexity of the case. An appropriate daily or hourly rate, based on such considerations, shall be arranged by the administrator with the parties and the arbitrators prior to the commencement of the arbitration. If the parties fail to agree on the terms of compensation, an appropriate rate shall be established by the administrator and communicated in writing to the parties.

Deposit of Costs
Article 34

1. When claims are filed, the administrator may request the filing party to deposit appropriate amounts, as an advance for the costs referred to in Article 32, paragraphs (a), (b) and (c).

2. During the course of the arbitral proceedings, the tribunal may request supplementary deposits from the parties.

3. If the deposits requested are not paid in full within thirty days after the receipt of the request, the administrator shall so inform the parties, in order that one or the other of them may make the required payment. If such payments are not made, the tribunal may order the suspension or termination of the proceedings.

4. After the award has been made, the administrator shall render an accounting to the parties of the deposits received and return any unexpended balance to the parties.

Confidentiality
Article 35

Confidential information disclosed during the proceedings by the parties or by witnesses shall not be divulged by an arbitrator or by the administrator. Unless otherwise agreed by the parties, or required by applicable law, the members of the tribunal and the administrator shall keep confidential all matters relating to the arbitration or the award.

Exclusion of Liability
Article 36

The members of the tribunal and the administrator shall not be liable to any party for any act or omission in connection with any arbitration conducted under these rules, except that they may be liable to a party for the consequences of conscious and deliberate wrongdoing.

Interpretation of Rules
Article 37

The tribunal shall interpret and apply these rules insofar as they relate to its powers and duties. All other rules shall be interpreted and applied by the administrator.

2. Austrian International Arbitral Centre

Rules of Arbitration and Conciliation of the International Arbitral Centre of the Federal Economic Chamber, Vienna.

a. Arbitration Rules.

General Provisions

Jurisdiction

Article 1

1. The International Arbitral Centre of the Federal Economic Chamber in Vienna ("the Centre") has jurisdiction to settle disputes of a commercial nature if a valid arbitration agreement exists and if at least one party has its place of business outside the territory of the Republic of Austria.

2. If parties all of which have their place of business in Austria agree to the jurisdiction of the Centre, the Permanent Arbitral Tribunal of the Vienna Chamber of Commerce or, if another venue in Austria has been agreed, the Permanent Arbitral Tribunal of the Chamber of Commerce within whose territorial jurisdiction the agreed arbitration venue is situated, shall have jurisdiction. The latter tribunal shall conduct the proceedings in accordance with the rules of arbitration for the Permanent Arbitral Tribunals of the Chambers of Commerce.

3. Arbitration proceedings shall be conducted at the seat of the Centre in Vienna. Nevertheless, the parties can agree that the proceedings be conducted at a different place.

Organization

Article 2

1. The organs of the Centre are the Board, consisting of the Chairman and at least four other members, and the Secretary.

2. The arbitrators to whom arbitration proceedings are entrusted are also members of the Centre for the duration of their mandate.

Article 3

1.The Chairman and the other members of the Board of the Centre are appointed for a period of office of five years by the Board of the Federal Economic Chamber; they can be reappointed.

2. The meetings of the Board are presided over by the Chairman, or in his absence by the most senior member present. The Board can validly take decisions if an absolute majority of its members is present. The Board shall take decisions by a simple majority. In the event of a tie in voting, the Chairman shall have a casting vote.

3. Members of the Board who are parties to particular arbitration proceedings in any capacity whatsoever shall be excluded from decisions pertaining to those proceedings.

4. The members of the Board must perform their duties to the best of their ability and are not subject to any directives in that respect. They are bound to secrecy on all matters coming to their notice in the course of their duties.

Article 4

1. The Secretary shall be appointed by the Board of the Federal Economic Chamber for a period of office of five years; he can be reappointed.

2. The Secretary shall direct the activities of the Secretariat; the latter shall perform the administrative tasks of the Centre.

3. The Secretary must perform his duties to the best of his ability and is not subject to any directives in that respect. He is bound to secrecy on all matters coming to his notice in the course of his duties.

4. The Secretary shall attend the meetings of the Board in an advisory capacity.

Arbitrators

Article 5

1. Arbitrators should have specific knowledge and experience in legal, commercial or other pertinent matters. They need not be Austrian citizens.

2. The names of persons qualified to act as arbitrators can be placed upon a list of arbitrators to be kept by the Secretary. The Board shall decide upon any addition to or deletion from that list and shall prepare a new list of arbitrators every three years.

3. Inclusion in the list of arbitrators is not a prerequisite for acting as an arbitrator. Insofar as the present rules authorize them to nominate or appoint arbitrators, the parties, the arbitrators nominated by the parties and the Board can nominate or appoint any qualified person as arbitrator.

4. A member of the Board may act only as Chairman of an arbitral tribunal or sole arbitrator.

5. The arbitrators must perform their duties in complete independence and impartiality, to the best of their ability, and are not subject to any directives in that respect. They are bound to observe secrecy in respect of all matters that come to their notice in the course of their duties.

Arbitral Proceedings

Commencement of the Proceedings

Article 6

1. The arbitral proceedings are commenced when a statement of claims drawn up in German or in one of the languages of the arbitration agreement is filed with the Secretariat. The proceedings become pending on receipt of the statement of claims by the Secretariat.

2. One copy of the statement of claims together with enclosures must be submitted for each Defendant, each arbitrator and the Secretariat.

3. The statement of claims must include:
—the designation of the parties and their addresses;
—the document or documents giving evidence of the jurisdiction of the Centre;
—a specific statement of claims and the particulars and supporting documents on which the claims are based;
—the amount in dispute at the time of submission of the statement of claims, unless the claims are not related exclusively to a specific sum of money;
—particulars regarding the number of arbitrators in accordance with Article 9, if a decision by three arbitrators is requested, the nomination of an arbitrator and the address of that person.

4. If the statement of claims is defective or incomplete or if copies of documents or enclosures are missing, the Secretary shall call upon the Claimant to remedy the defect or to submit the necessary copies of documents or enclosures, setting a time-limit; the provisions of the second sentence of paragraph 1 of the present Article shall not be affected thereby.

Article 7

The Secretary shall make service to the Defendant of the statement of claims and one copy each of the rules of arbitration and the list of arbitrators and shall invite the Defendant to submit a memorandum in reply within a period of thirty days, including where appropriate a counter-claim accompanied by the number of copies required in accordance with Article 6 paragraph 2, and to state his wishes with regard to the number of arbitrators in accordance with Article 9. If a decision by three arbitrators is requested, an arbitrator shall also be nominated in the memorandum in reply and the address of that person shall be stated.

Time-Limits, Service and Communications

Article 8

1. Time-limits provided for in the rules of arbitration or set by the Secretary can be prolonged by the latter on request or on his own initiative — possibly also after their expiry — if he considers that the reasons that are presented or that come to his notice in other ways are worthy of consideration.

2. Communications shall be considered as having been validly served if they are forwarded by registered letter, telex or telefax to the addresses indicated by the parties or if the document to be served has been demonstrably delivered.

Nomination and Appointment of Arbitrators

Article 9

1. The parties can agree that their dispute is to be decided either by a sole arbitrator or by a tribunal composed of three arbitrators.

2. When no such agreement has been made and the parties do not agree on the number of arbitrators, the Board shall determine whether the dispute is to be decided by one or three arbitrators.

3. The parties shall be notified of the decision of the Board pursuant to paragraph 2 of the present Article; in the event that proceedings before a sole arbitrator are decided upon, the parties shall be requested to agree on a sole arbitrator and to indicate that person's name and address within thirty days after service of the request. If no such indication is made within that period, the sole arbitrator shall be appointed by the Board.

4. If the dispute is to be decided by three arbitrators, the party that has not yet nominated an arbitrator shall be requested to indicate the name and address of an arbitrator within thirty days after service of the request. If no such indication is made within that period, the arbitrator for the defaulting party shall be appointed by the Board.

5. If the dispute is to be decided by three arbitrators, the arbitrators nominated by the parties or appointed by the Board shall be requested to agree on a Chairman

and to indicate his name and address within thirty days after service of the request. If no such indication is made within that period, the Chairman shall be appointed by the Board.

Article 10

1. Two or more Claimants or two or more Defendants shall mutually agree whether they wish the dispute to be decided by a sole arbitrator or by three arbitrators and, if a decision by three arbitrators is wished, they shall jointly nominate an arbitrator.

2. If there is no agreement among the Claimants or among the Defendants concerning the number of arbitrators, the said Claimants or Defendants shall be requested by the Secretary to agree on the number of arbitrators within thirty days after delivery of the statement of claims.

3. If no agreement as to the number of arbitrators is reached within the period indicated in paragraph 2 of the present Article, the Board shall determine whether the dispute is to be decided by one or three arbitrators.

4. If the Claimants or the Defendants have agreed that the dispute is to be decided by three arbitrators, without having nominated an arbitrator, they shall be requested by the Secretary to indicate the name and address of an arbitrator within thirty days after delivery of the request.

5. If no arbitrator is nominated within the period indicated in paragraph 4 of the present Article, and if the dispute is to be decided by three arbitrators, the arbitrator for the defaulting Claimants or Defendants shall be appointed by the Board.

Challenge of Arbitrators

Article 11

1. An arbitrator may be challenged if there are sufficient grounds for doubting his independence or impartiality.

2. If a party challenges an arbitrator, it must inform the Secretary thereof stating the grounds for challenge after the latter have come to its notice.

3. A challenge is inadmissible if the party making the challenge has taken part in the proceedings notwithstanding the knowledge which it already had thought to have had of the grounds of challenge relied upon. A challenge is also inadmissible if the grounds of challenge relied upon come to the knowledge of the party making the challenge in the course of the proceedings but that party made them known with undue delay.

4. The Board shall decide upon the challenge.

Termination of the Mandate of Arbitrators

Article 12

1. Any party may request the termination of the mandate of an arbitrator who does not perform his duties or unduly delays the proceedings. The request must be submitted to the Secretariat. The Board shall decide upon the request.

2. If the inability of an arbitrator to perform the duties of his mandate is not merely temporary, the Board shall terminate his mandate at the request of a party. If an arbitrator is obviously unable to perform his duties, the Board may terminate his mandate even without a request from a party.

Article 13

1. If the challenge of an arbitrator is allowed, if his mandate is terminated, if he has resigned his mandate or has died, then,

(a) if that arbitrator is a sole arbitrator, the parties shall be requested to agree within thirty days on the nomination of a replacement and to indicate his name and address;

(b) if that arbitrator is the Chairman of an arbitral tribunal, the remaining arbitrators shall be requested to agree within thirty days on t he nomination of a replacement and to indicate his name and address; and

(c) if that arbitrator has been nominated by a party or has been appointed for a party, the party that nominated him or for whom he was appointed shall be requested to nominate a replacement within thirty days and to indicate his name and address.

If no such nomination is received within that period, the new arbitrator shall be appointed by the Board.

2. The new arbitrator shall take over the arbitration proceedings at the point which they had reached on the termination of the previous arbitrator's mandate. If necessary, the arbitral tribunal can order the repetition of individual steps of the proceedings.

Conduct of the Proceedings

Article 14

1. The proceedings may be oral or only in writing. Hearings shall take place at the request of one party or if the sole arbitrator or arbitral tribunal to which the case has been referred considers it necessary.

2. The date of hearings shall be fixed by the sole arbitrator or the Chairman of the arbitral tribunal. Hearings shall not be public. A record of the results of the hearings shall be made.

3. If the arbitrators consider it necessary, they may on their own initiative collect evidence, and in particular may question parties or witnesses, may request the parties to submit documents and may call in experts.

Article 15

The parties shall have the right to be represented by authorized agents of their choice in the proceedings before the arbitrators.

Article 16

1. The arbitrators shall apply the substantive law designated by the parties. Failing such a designation by the parties, the arbitrators shall apply the law that is designated in the choice of law rules that they consider to be authoritative. In any case, the arbitrators shall observe the contract and the usages of trade applicable to the transaction.

2. The arbitrators may not base their decisions on equity unless they have been expressly empowered by the parties.

Article 17

The parties must pursue the proceedings with due expedition. Interruptions of the proceedings for indefinite or unduly long periods shall not be permitted, even at the joint request of the parties. The Board may strike off the list of cases proceedings that are not pursued by the parties with due expedition, there being no adequate grounds; the pendency of the proceedings and the mandate of the arbitrators shall thereby be terminated.

The Award

Article 18

1. Awards shall be drawn up in writing and all the necessary copies shall be signed by the arbitrators. The signatures of the majority of the arbitrators shall suffice if the award contains a statement that an arbitrator refuses to sign or that his signature cannot be obtained because of an obstacle which cannot be overcome within a

reasonable period of time. If an arbitral tribunal makes an award by a majority decision, mention thereof shall be made at the request of the arbitrator who is in a minority.

2. Awards are confirmed on all the necessary copies by the signature of the Secretary and the stamp of the Centre and served on to the parties.

3. The Chairman or if he is prevented another arbitrator shall confirm on a copy at the request of a party the finality and enforceability of the award.

4. By their agreement to the Vienna Rules, the parties undertake to implement the award.

5. A copy of the award shall be deposited with the Secretariat of the Centre.

Article 19

The cost of the arbitration fixed by the Secretary in accordance with Article 23 paragraph 1 shall be stated in the award that terminates the proceedings. The arbitrators shall decide on the proportions in which these costs as well as the costs duly incurred by the parties in respect of legal representation and any further expenses for due prosecution of legal claims shall be borne by the parties.

Article 20

The parties can require that an award be issued concerning the content of any settlement reached between them.

Article 21

If an award or a settlement is to be enforced, the Secretary may provide the prosecuting party with the information that is known to him regarding the law on enforcement and the enforcement practice of the State in which the award or the settlement are to be enforced free of charge, but without guaranteeing the correctness or completeness of such information.

Costs of the Proceedings

Costs and Deposits

Article 22

1. The Claimant (Counter-claimant) shall pay the registration fee; that fee is intended to cover the costs up to the submission of the files to the arbitrators. If high-

er outlay is incurred, an additional sum may be prescribed.

2. If there are more than two parties to the proceedings, the registration fee shall be increased by 10% for each additional party.

3. The registration fee shall not be repayable. The registration fee, as well as any additional amount required in accordance with paragraph 1 of the present Article shall be deducted from the Claimant's (Counter-claimant's) share of the deposit against costs of arbitration.

4. Service of the statement of claims (counter-claims) will not be made unless the prescribed registration fee has been paid.

Article 23

1. The costs of arbitration (administrative costs, arbitrators' fees, cash outlay on such as experts' fees, travelling and subsistence expenses of arbitrators and experts, rental amounts, costs of minuting, interpretation and translation) shall be fixed by the Secretary.

2. As soon as it is known whether the dispute is to be decided by a sole arbitrator or by an arbitral tribunal, the Secretary shall fix the amount of the deposit against the expected costs of arbitration. That deposit shall be paid in equal shares by the parties before transmission of the files to the arbitrators and within thirty days after service of the payment request.

3. If the Claimant (Counter-claimant) fails to pay its share within the period fixed, the Secretary may delete the claim or counter-claim from the list of cases of the Centre. He shall inform the parties thereof. The claim (counter-claim) can be resubmitted in accordance with Article 6.

4. If the share of the Defendant (Counter-defendant) is not received within the period fixed, the Secretary shall inform the Claimant (Counter-claimant) thereof and shall request the Claimant or Counter-claimant to pay the failing share of the deposit within thirty days after service of the request. If this amount is not received within the period fixed, the Secretary can delete the claim (counter-claim) from the list of cases to the Centre. He shall inform the parties thereof. The claim (counter-claim) can be resubmitted in accordance with Article 6.

5. If it should be necessary to increase the deposit against costs in the course of the proceedings because of an increase in the amount in dispute, a procedure analogous to that provided for in paragraphs 2 to 4 of the present Article shall be adopted. Until payment of the additional deposit, the increase of the amount in dispute shall not be taken into account in the arbitral proceedings.

6. If it should be necessary to increase the deposit against costs in the course of the proceedings because the amount fixed for cash outlay is not sufficient, a procedure analogous to that provided for in paragraphs 2 to 4 of the present Article shall be adopted.

7. Reductions in the amount in dispute shall be taken into account in the calculation of arbitrators' fees and administrative costs only if they occurred before trans-

mission of the files to the arbitrators.

8. If the proceedings should be terminated otherwise than by an award or a settlement, the Secretary shall fix the arbitrators' fees and administrative costs at an appropriate level and shall determine the cash outlay.

9. If the arbitrators consider it to be necessary to appoint experts, they shall inform the Secretary thereof, indicating the expected costs. The Secretary will proceed by analogy with the provisions of paragraphs 2 to 4 of the present Article. The arbitrators may appoint an expert only after the deposit against the expected fees and expenses of the expert has been paid to the Secretariat or the payment of the fees and expenses has been ensured by means of a service contract between the experts and the parties. The preceding provisions shall also apply to the appointment of interpreters and translators.

Article 24

1. The administrative costs of the Centre and the arbitrators' fees shall be fixed on the basis of the amount in dispute according to the schedules of costs attached to these Rules. Cash outlays (such as experts' fees, travelling and subsistence expenses of arbitrators and experts, rental amounts, costs of minuting, interpretation and translation) shall be determined according to the actual expenditure.

2. For the purpose of calculating the administrative costs and the arbitrators' fees, the amounts in dispute in respect of the claim and counter-claim shall be added if the parties each pay half of the deposit against costs fixed by the Secretary. If that is not the case, the deposits against costs in respect of the claim and counter-claim shall be calculated separately.

3. A separate calculation shall also be made if the claims presented in the counter-claim bear no relation to the claims presented in the statement of claims.

4. If there are more than two parties to proceedings, the rates for the administrative costs of the Centre and the arbitrators' fees contained in the schedules attached to these Rules shall be increased by 10% for each additional party.

5. In the case of proceedings conducted concerning a number of individual claims or counter-claims, the Secretary may make a separate calculation of the arbitrators' fees according to the amounts in dispute in respect of the individual claims.

6. The rates quoted in the schedule for arbitrators' fees are the fees for sole arbitrators. In any case they shall be raised to two-and-a-half times the amounts quoted if an arbitral tribunal is appointed and up to three times those amounts in the event of the particular difficulty of a case.

ARBITRATION COSTS
REGISTRATION FEES AS 10,000
Administrative Charges

Amount in Dispute in Schillings

up to	1,000,000		10,000
1,000,001 to	2,000,000	10,000+1.5% of excess over	1,000,000
2,000,001 to	5,000,000	25,000+1.0% of excess over	2,000,000
5,000,001 to	10,000,000	55,000+0.5% of excess over	5,000,000
10,000,001 to	20,000,000	80,000+0.2% of excess over	10,000,000
20,000,001 to	50,000,000	100,000+0.1% of excess over	20,000,000
50,000,001 to	100,000,000	130,000+0.05% of excess over	50,000,000
over	100,000,000	155,000+0.01% of excess over	100,000,000

FEES FOR SOLE ARBITRATORS2

Amount in Dispute in Schillings

up to	1,000,000	6% — minimum fee 10,000		
1,000,001 to	2,000,000	60,000 + 3%	of excess over	1,000,000
2,000,001 to	5,000,000	90,000 + 2.5%	of excess over	2,000,000
5,000,001 to	10,000,000	165,000 + 2%	of excess over	5,000,000
10,000,001 to	20,000,000	265,000 + 1%	of excess over	10,000,000
20,000,001 to	50,000,000	365,000 + 0.6%	of excess over	20,000,000
50,000,001 to	100,000,000	545,000 + 0.4%	of excess over	50,000,000
100,000,001 to	200,000,000	745,000 + 0.2%	of excess over	100,000,000
200,000,001 to	1,000,000,000	945,000 + 0.1%	of excess over	200,000,000
over	1,000,000,000	1,745,000 + 0.01%	of excess over	1 billion

b. Austrian International Arbitral Center Conciliation Rules

Article 1

At the request of a party, conciliation proceedings can be conducted where the Centre may have jurisdiction as to the subject matter. They are not subject to the existence of a valid arbitration agreement.

Article 2

The request for the opening of conciliation proceedings shall be filed with the Secretariat of the Centre. The latter shall invite the opposing party or parties to reply within thirty days after service of the request. If a party refuses to participate in the conciliation proceedings or does not reply within that period, the attempted conciliation shall be considered as having failed.

Article 3

When the opposing party or parties accepts/accept recourse to conciliation, the Board shall nominate one of its members or another qualified person to act as conciliator. The latter shall study the documents submitted by the parties, shall convene them to a hearing and shall then submit proposals for the amicable settlement of the dispute.

Article 4

If agreement is reached, that shall be the subject of a record signed by the parties and the conciliator. If a valid arbitration agreement exists, the Board shall appoint the conciliator as sole arbitrator, provided that all parties so request. The sole arbitrator must authenticate the agreement in the form of a settlement or, if the parties so wish, make an award on the basis of the agreement.

Article 5

If no agreement is reached, the conciliation shall be considered as having failed. Declaration made by the parties in the course of conciliation proceedings shall not bind them in later arbitration proceedings. Except under the conditions set forth in Article 4 of these Rules, the conciliator may not be appointed as an arbitrator in subsequent arbitration proceedings.

Article 6

The costs of the conciliation proceedings and those of any activity of the conciliator under the conditions set forth in Article 4 shall be fixed by the Secretary at an appropriate share of the costs applicable for arbitration proceedings on the basis of the corresponding amount in dispute (Article 24 paragraph 1 of the Rules of Arbitration). The same shall apply to the deposits against costs to be fixed by the Secretary.

3. CENTER FOR PUBLIC RESOURCES.

Rules for Non-Administered Arbitration of International Disputes.

A. General and Introductory Rules

Rule 1. Scope of Application

1.1 Where the parties to a contract have provided for arbitration under the Rules, they shall be deemed to have made these Rules a part of their arbitration agreement, except to the extent that they have agreed in writing, or on the record during the course of the arbitral proceeding, to modify these Rules. Unless the parties otherwise agree, these Rules, and any amendment thereof adopted by CPR, shall apply in the form obtaining at the time the arbitration is commenced.

1.2 These Rules shall govern the conduct of the arbitration except that where any of these Rules is in conflict with a mandatory provision of applicable procedural law of the seat of arbitration, that provision of law shall prevail.

Rule 2. Notices

2.1 Notices shall be given in writing at the address specified in writing by the recipient or, if no address has been specified, to the then business or residence address of the recipient. Notices may be given by mail, courier, telex or facsimile transmission. Notices shall be deemed to be effective as of the date of receipt. Proof of transmission shall be deemed prima facie proof of receipt of any notice given under these Rules.

2.2 The Arbitral Tribunal (the "Tribunal") shall give the parties at least thirty days' advance notice of the date, time and place of the initial pre-hearing conference pursuant to Rule. 9.4. The Tribunal shall give reasonable notice of subsequent hearings.

2.3 Time periods specified by these Rules or established by the Tribunal shall start to run on the day a notice is received, unless the Tribunal shall specifically provide otherwise.

Rule 3. Commencement of Arbitration

3.1 The party commencing arbitration (the "Claimant") shall address to the other party (the "Respondent") a notice of arbitration.

3.2 The arbitration shall be deemed commenced on the date on which the notice of arbitration is received by the Respondent.

3.3 The notice of arbitration shall include in the text or in attachments thereto:

(a) The full names, descriptions and addresses of the parties;

(b) A demand that the dispute be referred to arbitration pursuant to the Rules;

(c) The text or a summary of the arbitration clause or the separate arbitration agreement that is involved;

(d) A statement of the Claimant's claim;

(e) The relief or remedy sought; and

(f) The name and address of the arbitrator appointed by the Claimant, unless the parties have agreed that neither shall appoint an arbitrator.

3.4 Within thirty days after receipt of the notice of arbitration, the Respondent shall deliver to the Claimant a notice of defense. Failure to deliver a notice of defense shall not delay the arbitration; in the event of such failure, all claims set forth in the demand shall be deemed denied.

3.5 The notice of defense shall include:

(a) Any comment on items (a), (b), and (c) of the notice of arbitration that the Respondent may deem appropriate;

(b) A statement of the Respondent's defense; and

(c) The name and address of the arbitrator appointed by the Respondent, unless the parties have agreed that neither shall appoint an arbitrator.

3.6 The Respondent may include in its notice of defense any counterclaim within the scope of the arbitration clause. If it does so, the counterclaim in the notice of defense shall include items (a), (b), (c), (d) and (e) of Rule 3.3.

3.7 If a counterclaim is asserted, within thirty days after receipt of the notice of defense, the Claimant shall deliver to the Respondent a reply to counterclaim which shall have the same elements as provided in Rule 3.5 for the notice of defense.

3.8 Claims or counterclaims within the scope of the arbitration clause may be freely added or amended prior to the establishment of the Tribunal and thereafter with the consent of the Tribunal. Notices of defense or replies to amended claims or counterclaims shall be delivered within twenty days after the addition or amendment.

3.9 If a dispute is submitted to arbitration pursuant to a submission agreement, Rule 3 shall apply to the extent that it is not inconsistent with the submission agreement.

Rule 4. Representation

4.1 The parties may be represented or assisted by persons of their choice.

4.2 Each party shall communicate the name, address and function of such persons in writing to the other party and to the Tribunal.

B. Rules with Respect to the Tribunal

Rule 5. Selection of Arbitrators by the Parties

5.1 Unless the parties have agreed in writing on a Tribunal consisting of a sole arbitrator or of three arbitrators not appointed by parties, the Tribunal shall consist of two arbitrators appointed by the parties and a third arbitrator, who shall chair the Tribunal, selected as provided in Rule 5.2.

5.2 As soon as possible after the appointment of two party-appointed arbitrators and delivery of the notice of defense provided for in Rule 3.4 and in any event within twenty days thereafter, the party-appointed arbitrators shall discuss potential candidates for the third arbitrator and shall proceed to select the third arbitrator. They shall attempt to make their selection within twenty days of their initial discussion, but they may extend their selection process until one or both of them have concluded, and have so advised the appointing parties, that a deadlock has been reached. In this event, the third arbitrator shall be selected as provided in Rule 6.

5.3 If the parties have agreed on a Tribunal consisting of a sole arbitrator or of three arbitrators none of whom shall be appointed by either party, as soon as possible after delivery of the notice of defense provided for in Rule 3.4 and in any event within twenty days thereafter, the parties' representatives shall discuss potential candidates for the arbitrator(s) and shall proceed to select the arbitrator(s). They shall attempt to make their selection within twenty days of their initial discussion, but they may extend their selection process until one or both of them have concluded that a deadlock has been reached. In this event, the arbitrator(s) shall be selected as provided in Rule 6.

Rule 6. Selection of Arbitrator(s) by Neutral Organization

6.1 Whenever (i) a party has failed to appoint the arbitrator to be appointed by it; (ii) the parties have failed to appoint the arbitrator(s) to be appointed by them acting jointly; (iii) the party appointed arbitrators have failed to appoint the third arbitrator; or (iv) the parties have provided that one or more arbitrators shall be appointed by a neutral organization agreed on by the parties (the Neutral Organization), the arbitrator(s) required to complete the Tribunal shall be selected as provided in Rule 6, and either party may request the Neutral Organization in writing, with copy to the other party, to proceed pursuant to Rule 6.

6.2 The written request may be made as follows:

(a) If a party has failed to appoint the arbitrator to be appointed by it, or the parties have failed to appoint the arbitrator(s) to be appointed by them through agreement, at any time after such failure has occurred.

(b) If the party-appointed arbitrators have failed to appoint the third arbitrator, as soon as the procedure contemplated by Rule 5.2 has been completed.

(c) If the arbitrator(s) are to be appointed by the Neutral Organization, as soon as the arbitration has been commenced.

6.3 The written request shall include complete copies of the notice of arbitration and the notice of defense or, if the dispute is submitted under a submission agreement, a copy of the agreement supplemented by the notice of arbitration and notice of defense if they are not part of the agreement.

6.4 The Neutral Organization shall then submit to the parties a list of not less than three candidates if one arbitrator remains to be selected, and of not less than seven candidates if two or three arbitrators are to be selected. If either party shall so request, a majority of such candidates shall be of a nationality other than the nationality of the parties. Such list shall include a brief statement of each candidate's qualifications. Each party shall number the candidates in order of preference, shall note any objection it may have to any candidate, and shall deliver the list so marked to the Neutral Organization and to the other party. Any party failing without good cause to return the candidate list so marked within ten days after receipt shall be deemed to have assented to all candidates listed thereon. The Neutral Organization shall designate as arbitrator(s) the nominee(s) willing to serve for whom the parties collectively have indicated the highest preference and who appear to meet the standards set forth in Rule 7. If a tie should result between two candidates, the Neutral Organization may designate either candidate. If this procedure for any reason should fail to result in designation of the required number of arbitrators, the Neutral Organization shall appoint a person or persons whom it deems qualified to fill any remaining vacancy, who, if either party shall so request, shall be of a nationality other than the nationality of the parties.

Rule 7. Qualifications, Challenges and Replacement of Arbitrators

7.1 Each arbitrator shall be independent and impartial.

7.2 By accepting appointment, each arbitrator shall be deemed to be bound by these Rules.

7.3 Each arbitrator shall disclose in writing to the Tribunal and the parties at the time of his or her appointment and promptly upon their arising during the course of the arbitration any circumstances that might cause doubt regarding the arbitrator's independence or impartiality. Such circumstances include bias, interest in the result of the arbitration, and past or present relations with a party.

7.4 Any arbitrator may be challenged if circumstances exist or arise that give rise to justifiable doubt regarding that arbitrator's independence or impartiality, provided, that a party may challenge an arbitrator whom it has appointed only for reasons of which it becomes aware after the appointment has been made.

7.5 A party may challenge an arbitrator only by a notice in writing to the Tribunal, with copy to the other party, given no later than fifteen days after (i) the parties have been notified that the Tribunal has been constituted, or (ii) the challenging party has become aware of the circumstances specified in Rule 7.4, whichever shall last occur. The notice shall state the reasons for the challenge with specificity.

7.6 When an arbitrator has been challenged by a party, the other party may agree to the challenge or the arbitrator may voluntarily withdraw. Neither of these actions implies acceptance of the validity of the challenge.

7.7 If neither agreed disqualification nor voluntary withdrawal occurs, the challenge shall be decided as follows:

(a) By unanimous vote of the remaining members of the Tribunal;

(b) If the Tribunal consists of a sole Arbitrator or fails or refuses to decide the challenge, by the Neutral Organization.

7.8 In the event of death, resignation or successful challenge of an arbitrator not appointed by a party, a substitute arbitrator shall be selected pursuant to the procedure by which the arbitrator being replaced was selected. In the event of the death, resignation or successful challenge of an arbitrator appointed by a party, that party may appoint a substitute arbitrator; provided, however, that should that party fail to notify the Tribunal and the other party of its appointment within twenty days from the date on which the opening arose, that party's right of appointment shall lapse and the Tribunal shall promptly request the Neutral Organization to appoint a substitute arbitrator forthwith.

7.9 In the event that an arbitrator fails to act or is de jure or de facto prevented from duly performing the functions of an arbitrator, the procedures provided in Rule 7.8 shall apply to the selection of a replacement. If the Tribunal consists of a sole arbitrator and the parties do not agree on whether the arbitrator has failed to act or is prevented from performing the functions of an arbitrator, either party may request the Neutral Organization to make that determination forthwith. If the Tribunal consists of three arbitrators and the parties do not so agree, such determination shall be made by a majority of the Tribunal.

7.10 If the sole arbitrator or the chairman of the Tribunal is replaced, the successor shall decide the extent to which any hearings held previously shall be repeated. If any other arbitrator is replaced, the Tribunal in its discretion may require that some or all prior hearings be repeated.

Rule 8. Challenges to the Jurisdiction of the Tribunal

8.1 The Tribunal shall have the power to hear and determine challenges to its jurisdiction.

8.2 The Tribunal shall have the power to determine the existence, validity or scope of the contract of which an arbitration clause forms a part, and/or of the arbitration clause itself. For the purposes of challenges to the jurisdiction of the Tribunal, the arbitration clause shall be considered as separable from any contract of which it forms a part.

8.3 Any challenges to the jurisdiction of the Tribunal, except challenges based on the award itself, shall be made not later than the notice of defense or, with respect to a counterclaim, the reply to the counterclaim; provided, however, that if a claim or counterclaim is later added or amended such a challenge may be made not later than the reply to such claim or counterclaim.

C. Rules with Respect to the Conduct of the Arbitral Proceedings

Rule 9. General Provisions

9.1 Subject to these Rules, the Tribunal may conduct the arbitration in such manner as it shall deem appropriate. The chairman shall be responsible for the organization of arbitral conferences and hearings and arrangements with respect to the functioning of the Tribunal.

9.2 The proceedings shall be conducted in an expeditious manner. The Tribunal is empowered to impose time limits it considers reasonable on each phase of the proceeding, including without limitation the time allotted to each party for presentation of its case and for rebuttal.

9.3 Except as otherwise provided in these Rules or permitted by the Tribunal, no party or anyone acting on its behalf shall have any ex parte communication with any arbitrator with respect to any matter of substance relating to the proceeding, or on any matter with the arbitrator it appointed, except that a party and the arbitrator it appointed may confer regarding the selection of the chairman of the Tribunal.

9.4 The Tribunal shall hold an initial pre-hearing conference for the planning and scheduling of the proceeding. Such conference shall be held as promptly as possible after the selection of the Tribunal, unless it is of the view that further submissions from the parties are appropriate prior to such conference. The objective of this conference shall be to discuss all elements of the arbitration with a view to planning for its future conduct. Matters to be considered in the initial pre-hearing conference may include, inter alia, the following:

(a) Procedural matters such as the timing and manner of any required disclosure; the desirability of bifurcation or other separation of the issues in the arbitration; the desirability and practicability of consolidating the arbitration with any other proceeding; the scheduling of conferences and hearings; the scheduling of pre-hearing memoranda; the need for and type of record of conferences and hearings, including the need for transcripts; the amount of time allotted to each party for presentation of its case and for rebuttal; the mode, manner and order for presenting proof; the need for expert witnesses and how expert testimony should be presented; and the necessity for any on-site inspection by the Tribunal;

(b) The early identification and narrowing of the issues in the arbitration;

(c) The possibility of stipulations of fact and admissions by the parties solely for purposes of the arbitration, as well as simplification of document authentication; and

(d) The possibility of appointment of an independent expert by the Tribunal;

(e) The possibility of the parties engaging in settlement negotiations, with or without the assistance of a mediator or arbitrator.

After the initial conference, further pre-hearing or other conferences may be held as the Tribunal deems appropriate.

9.5 In order to define the issues to be heard and determined, the Tribunal may inter alia make pre-hearing orders for the arbitration and instruct the parties to file more detailed statements of claim and of defense and pre-hearing memoranda.

9.6 Unless the parties have agreed upon the seat of arbitration, the Tribunal shall fix the seat of arbitration. The award shall be deemed made at such place. Hearings may be held and the Tribunal may schedule meetings, including telephone meetings, wherever it deems appropriate.

9.7 If the parties have not agreed otherwise, the language(s) of the arbitration shall be that of the documents containing the arbitration agreement, subject to the power of the Tribunal to determine otherwise based upon the contentions of the parties and the circumstances of the arbitration. The Tribunal may order that any documents submitted in other languages shall be accompanied by a translation into such language or languages.

Rule 10. Applicable Laws

10.1 The Tribunal shall apply the substantive law designated by the parties as applicable to the dispute. Failing such a designation by the parties, the Tribunal shall apply such law or laws as it determines to be appropriate.

10.2 Subject to Rule 10.1, in arbitrations involving the application of contracts, the Tribunal shall decide in accordance with the terms of the contract and shall take into account usages of the trade applicable to the contract.

10.3 The Tribunal shall not decide as amiable compositeur or ex aequo et bono unless the parties have authorized it to do so.

Rule 11. Disclosure

The Tribunal shall permit and facilitate such disclosure as it shall determine is appropriate in the circumstances, taking into account the needs of the parties and the desirability of making disclosure expeditious and cost-effective. The Tribunal may issue orders to protect the confidentiality of proprietary information, trade secrets and other sensitive information disclosed.

Rule 12. Evidence and Hearings

12.1 The Tribunal shall determine the manner in which the parties shall present their cases. Unless otherwise determined by the Tribunal or agreed by the parties, the presentation of a party's case shall include the submission of a pre-hearing memorandum including the following elements:

(a) A statement of facts;

(b) A statement of each claim being asserted;

(c) A statement of the applicable law upon which the party relies;

(d) A statement of the relief requested, including the basis for any damages claimed; and

(e) A statement of the evidence to be presented, including the name, capacity and subject of testimony of any witnesses to be called, the language in which each witness will testify and an estimate of the amount of time required for the witness' direct testimony.

12.2 Evidence may be presented in written or oral form as the Tribunal may determine is appropriate. The Tribunal is not required to apply the rules of evidence used in judicial proceedings. The Tribunal shall determine the applicability of any privilege or immunity and the admissibility, relevance, materiality and weight of the evidence offered.

12.3 The Tribunal, in its discretion, may require the parties to produce evidence in addition to that initially offered. It may also appoint experts whose testimony shall be subject to cross examination and rebuttal.

12.4 The Tribunal shall determine the manner in which witnesses are to be examined. If a witness testifies in a language other than the language of the proceeding, the party producing such witness will arrange at its expense for interpretation of the testimony. The Tribunal shall have the right to exclude witnesses from hearings during the testimony of other witnesses.

Rule 13. Interim Measures of Protection

13.1 At the request of a party, the Tribunal may take such interim measures as it deems necessary in respect of the subject matter of the dispute, including measures for the preservation of assets, the conservation of goods or the sale of perishable goods. The Tribunal may require security for the costs of such measures.

13.2 A request for interim measures by a party to a court shall not be deemed incompatible with the agreement to arbitrate or as a waiver of that agreement.

Rule 14. The Award

14.1 The Tribunal may make final, interim, interlocutory and partial orders or awards. The Tribunal may grant any remedy or relief, including but not limited to specific performance of a contract, within the scope of the agreement of the parties, which is permissible under the law or laws applicable to the dispute pursuant to Rule 10.1, or, if the parties have authorized the Tribunal to decide as amiable compositeur or ex aequo et bono, any remedy or relief which the Tribunal deems just and equitable. With respect to any interim, interlocutory or partial award, the Tribunal may state in its award whether or not it views the award as final, for purposes of any judicial proceedings in connection therewith.

14.2 All awards shall be in writing and shall state the reasoning on which the award rests unless the parties agree otherwise. The award shall be deemed to be made at the seat of arbitration and shall contain the date on which the award was made. When there are three arbitrators, the award shall be made and signed by at least a majority of the arbitrators; and if the award decides a number of issues, the part of the award relating to each issue shall be made and signed by at least a majority of the arbitrators. When one of three arbitrators does not sign, the award shall be accompanied by a statement of whether the third arbitrator was given the opportunity to sign.

14.3 A member of the Tribunal who does not join in an award may file a dissenting opinion. Such opinion shall not constitute part of the award.

14.4 Executed copies of awards and of any dissenting opinion shall be delivered by the Tribunal to the parties. If the arbitration law of the country where the award is made requires the award to be filed or registered, the Tribunal shall comply with such requirement.

14.5 Within twenty days after receipt of the award, either party, with notice to the other party, may request the Tribunal to correct in an award any errors in computation, any clerical or typographical errors, or any errors of a similar nature. Within thirty days after the delivery of an award to the parties or of a request by a party for a correction, the Tribunal may make corrections on its own initiative and corrections requested by either party. All such corrections shall be in writing, and the provisions of Rule 14 shall apply to them.

14.6 After expiration of the thirty-day period provided in Rule 14.5, the award shall be final and binding on the parties, and the parties undertake to carry out the award without delay.

14.7 The dispute should in most circumstances be heard and be submitted to the Tribunal for decision within nine months after the initial pre-hearing conference required by Rule 9.4. The final award should in most circumstances be rendered within three months thereafter. The parties and the arbitrators shall use their best efforts to comply with this schedule.

D. Miscellaneous Rules

Rule 15. Failure to Comply with Rules

Whenever a party fails to comply with these Rules in a manner deemed material by the Tribunal, the Tribunal shall fix a reasonable period of time for compliance and, if the party does not comply within said period, the Tribunal may impose a remedy it deems just, including an award on default. Prior to entering an award on default the Tribunal shall require the non-defaulting party to produce such evidence and legal argument in support of its contentions, as the Tribunal may deem appropriate. The Tribunal may receive such evidence and argument without the defaulting party's presence or participation.

Rule 16. Costs

16.1 Each arbitrator shall be compensated on a reasonable basis determined at the time of appointment for serving as an arbitrator and shall be reimbursed for any travel and other expenses.

16.2 Subject to any agreement between the parties to the contrary, the Tribunal may apportion the costs of arbitration between or among the parties in such manner as it deems reasonable taking into account the circumstances of the case, the conduct of the parties during the proceeding, and the result of the arbitration.

16.3 For the purposes of Rule 16.2 the costs of arbitration include:

(a) The fees and expenses of members of the Tribunal;

(b) The costs of expert advice and other assistance engaged by the Tribunal;

(c) The travel, translation, and other expenses of witnesses to such extent as the Tribunal may deem appropriate;

(d) The costs for legal representation and assistance and experts incurred by a party to such extent as the Tribunal may deem appropriate;

(e) The charges and expenses of the Neutral Organization with respect to the arbitration;

(f) The costs of a transcript, if any; and

(g) The costs of meeting and hearing facilities.

16.4 The Tribunal may require each party to deposit an equal amount as an advance for the costs referred to in Rule 16.3 except those specified in subparagraph (d), and, during the course of the proceeding, it may require supplementary deposits from the parties. Any such funds shall be held and disbursed in such a manner as the Tribunal may deem appropriate.

16.5 If the required deposits are not paid in full within twenty days after receipt of the request, the Tribunal shall so inform the parties in order that jointly or severally they may make the required payment. If such payment is not made, the Tribunal may suspend or terminate the proceedings.

16.6 After the proceeding has been concluded, the Tribunal shall return any unexpended balance from deposits made to the parties as may be appropriate.

Rule 17. Confidentiality

The parties and the arbitrators shall treat the proceedings, any related disclosure and the decisions of the Tribunal, as confidential, except in connection with a judicial challenge to, or enforcement of, an award, and unless otherwise required by law.

Rule 18. Settlement and Mediation

18.1 Either party may propose settlement negotiations to the other party at any time. The Tribunal may suggest that the parties explore settlement at such times as the Tribunal may deem appropriate and shall suggest that they do so at or before conclusion of the hearing, unless the Tribunal concludes that settlement discussions would be inappropriate or unproductive.

18.2 With the consent of the parties, the Tribunal at any stage of the proceeding may arrange for mediation of the claims asserted in the arbitration by a mediator acceptable to the parties. The Mediator shall be a person other than a member of the Tribunal. The Tribunal may provide the Mediator with whatever factual and legal material developed in the arbitration it deems appropriate.

18.3 The Tribunal will not be informed of any settlement offers or other statements made during settlement negotiations or a mediation between the parties, unless both parties consent.

Rule 19. Actions against the Neutral Organization or Arbitrators

Neither the Neutral Organization nor any arbitrator shall be liable to any party for any act or omission in connection with any arbitration conducted under these Rules, except that they may be liable to a party for the consequences of conscious and deliberate wrongdoing.

Rule 20. Waiver

A party knowing of a failure to comply with any provision of these Rules and neglecting to state its objections promptly waives any objection thereto.

4. Geneva: Chamber of Commerce and Industry("CCIG").

A. General Provisions

1. Scope of the Rules

1.1 These Rules apply whenever the parties have agreed to submit their disputes to CCIG arbitration.

1.2 Arbitration agreements referring to the Arbitration Directives of the CCIG of June 1, 1980 are considered as referring to the present Rules unless one of the parties objects.

2. Arbitration Committee

2.1 The CCIG shall provide all necessary assistance to the parties for the organization of the arbitration pursuant to these Rules.

2.2 For this purpose, the CCIG shall appoint an Arbitration Committee which shall perform the functions of the CCIG according to these Rules. The Arbitration Committee shall consist of three to five members, one of which shall be an officer or employee o the CCIG. The members of the Arbitration Committee shall be appointed by the CCIG for three years. Such members may not serve as arbitrators or counsel in CCIG arbitrations.

3. Place of Arbitration

Unless otherwise agreed, the place of arbitration shall be Geneva.

4. Confidentiality

CCIG arbitration is confidential. The parties, the arbitrators and the CCIG undertake not to disclose to third parties any facts or other information relating to the dispute or the arbitral proceedings. The parties, the arbitrators and the CCIG shall refrain from publishing or causing others to publish the award, unless the parties to the arbitration agree to such publication.

5. Notifications

The awards and orders of the arbitral tribunal as well as other decisions of the arbitral tribunal and those of the CCIG shall be notified to the parties at the address shown in the request for arbitration, or at any other address subsequently specified, by any means of communication permitting proof of receipt.

6. Time Limits

The CCIG may extend the time limits provided in the present Rules if the circumstances so justify.

B. Commencing the Arbitration Proceedings

7. Request for Arbitration

7.1 The party wishing to initiate an arbitration under these Rules shall deliver its request to the CCIG. Such request shall contain:
    a) the names, capacities and addresses of the parties, including telephone and telefax or telex numbers;
    b) a copy of the contract containing the arbitration agreement or any other document showing that the arbitration is governed by these Rules;
    c) a statement of the facts and legal argument on which the claimant's case is based, together with supporting documents;
    d) the claimant's prayer for relief, i.e. a brief and precise description of each claim;
    e) an estimate of the amount in dispute, if no definite sum of money is claimed;
    f) relevant information regarding the number and choice of the arbitrators within the meaning of Articles 10 and 11.
7.2 The request shall be delivered in as many copies as there are other parties, together with an additional copy for each arbitrator and for the CCIG. The CCIG shall send the request to the respondent.

8. Answer

8.1 The respondent shall communicate its answer to the CCIG within thirty days from the receipt of the request. The answer shall contain:
    a) a statement of the defenses, together with supporting documents, including any objection concerning the arbitration agreement;
    b) any counterclaim, together with the information provided in Article 7.1 d)—e);
    c) relevant information regarding the number and choice of the arbitrators within the meaning of Articles 10 and 11.
8.2 The answer shall be delivered in as many copies as there are other parties, together with an additional copy for each arbitrator and for the CCIG. The CCIG shall send the answer to the claimant.
8.3 The provisions of this Article are subject to Article 18 with respect to the participation of a third party.
    C. Formation of the Arbitral Tribunal

9. Agreement to Arbitrate

The CCIG shall proceed with the formation of the arbitral tribunal, unless it is apparent from the outset that there is manifestly no agreement to arbitrate referring to the CCIG.

10. Independence and Qualifications of the Arbitrators

10.1 Every arbitrator, whether a sole arbitrator, chairperson or a coarbitrator, shall be and remain independent from the parties and has the obligation to disclose immediately any circumstances likely to affect independence with respect to the parties or nay one of them.

10.2 Every arbitrator shall have the qualifications agreed by the parties and the availability required to conduct the arbitration to an expeditious completion.

10.3 The sole arbitrator or the chairperson may not have the same nationality as one of the parties unless the parties agree otherwise or have the same nationality.

11. Number of Arbitrators

11.1 The parties are free to agree that the arbitral tribunal shall consist of a sole arbitrator or of three arbitrators.

11.2 In the absence of such an agreement, the tribunal shall consist of a sole arbitrator, unless the CCIG decides to form a tribunal of three arbitrators on account of the amount in dispute, of the nature and of the complexity of the dispute.

12. Appointment of the Arbitrators

12.1 Sole Arbitrator

The parties may select the sole arbitrator by mutual agreement. In the absence of such a selection within a thirty-day time limit set by the CCIG, the CCIG shall appoint the sole arbitrator.

12.2 Tribunal of Three Arbitrators

If the agreement to arbitrate provides for a tribunal of three arbitrators, each party shall select a coarbitrator respectively in the request for arbitration and in the answer. In the absence of a selection by a party, the CCIG shall appoint the coarbitrator.

If the CCIG decides to form a tribunal of three arbitrators pursuant to Article 11.2, each party shall select a coarbitrator upon the request of the CCIG. Failing such a selection by a party within a thirty-day time limit set by the CCIG, the CCIG shall appoint the coarbitrator.

Within a thirty-day time limit starting from the date when the coarbitrators learned from the CCIG of their appointment, the coarbitrators shall select a chairperson. Failing such selection of a chairperson, the CCIG shall appoint the chairperson.

12.3 Confirmation of the Arbitrators

Every arbitrator selected by the parties, either separately or jointly, or by the coarbitrators, shall be deemed to be appointed only upon confirmation by the CCIG. The CCIG may refuse the confirmation, without indicating any reasons, if it considers that the arbitrator does not fulfill the requirements of Article 10.

13. Challenge

13.1 An arbitrator may be challenged upon the ground that he or she does not fulfill the requirements of Article 10.1, that he or she does not possess the qualifications agreed by the parties, or that he or she manifestly does not have the availability required to conduct the arbitration to an expeditious completion.

13.2 Challenges are within the exclusive jurisdiction of the CCIG. The challenge petition shall be submitted to the CCIG immediately after the party making such challenge becomes aware of the relevant facts. It shall specify the facts and circumstances upon which the challenge is based.

13.3 The CCIG shall ask the other parties, the challenged arbitrator and the other arbitrators to submit written observations and shall render a decision summarily stating reasons.

13.4 In domestic arbitrations, the mandatory provisions of the Swiss Intercantonal Arbitration Convention of 27 March 1969 are reserved.

14. Removal

14.1 An arbitrator may be removed by written agreement of the parties.

14.2 An arbitrator can also be removed by the CCIG if he or she refuses to carry out his or her functions or is manifestly unable to do so. The CCIG invites the parties, the contested arbitrator and the other arbitrators to submit written observations and shall render a decision summarily motivated.

14.3 In domestic arbitrations, the mandatory provisions of the Swiss Intercantonal Arbitration Convention of 27 March 1969 are reserved.

15. Replacement

15.1 In case of death, removal, successful challenge or resignation of an arbitrator, such arbitrator shall be replaced pursuant to the provisions of Article 12.

15.2 Unless otherwise agreed by the parties or otherwise decided by the arbitral tribunal, the proceeding shall continue with the new arbitrator from the point where the previous arbitrator ceased to perform his or her duties.

D. Multiple Requests for Arbitration, Multiparty Arbitration

16. Multiple Requests

16.1 If an arbitration is initiated between parties already involved in another arbitration governed by these Rules, the CCIG may assign the second case to the arbitral tribunal appointed to decide the first case, in which case the parties shall be deemed to have waived their right to select an arbitrator in the second case.

16.2 In order to decide upon such assignment, the CCIG shall take into account all the circumstances, including the links between the two cases and the progress already made in the first case.

17. Multiparty Arbitration in General

17.1 In arbitration proceedings comprising more than two parties, including in case of participation of a third party within the meaning of Article 18, the number of arbitrators shall be determined in accordance with Article 11.

17.2 The parties may agree on a method of selection of the coarbitrators. In the absence of such an agreement, the coarbitrators shall be appointed by the CCIG, which shall take into account any proposals by the parties.

17.3 The chairperson or the sole arbitrator shall be appointed in accordance with Article 12.

18. Participation of a Third Party

18.1 If a respondent intends to cause a third party to participate in the arbitration, it shall so state in its answer and shall state the reasons for such participation. The respondent shall deliver to the CCIG an additional copy of its answer.

18.2 The CCIG shall send the answer to the third party whose participation is sought, the provisions of Articles 8 and 9 being applicable by analogy.

18.3 Upon receipt of the third party's answer, the CCIG shall decide on the participation of the third party in the already pending proceeding, taking into account all of the circumstances. If the CCIG accepts the participation of the third party, it shall proceed with the formation of the arbitral tribunal in accordance with Article 17; if it does not accept the participation, it shall proceed according to Article 12.

18.4 The decision of the CCIG regarding the participation of third parties shall not prejudice the decision of the arbitrators on the same subject. Regardless of the decision of the arbitrators on such participation, the formation of the arbitral tribunal cannot be challenged.

E. Procedure before the Arbitral Tribunal

19. Applicable Rules

Unless otherwise agreed by the parties, the procedure before the arbitral tribunal shall be governed by the provisions in this chapter and any additional rules established by the parties or, if none, by the arbitrators.

20. Communications

Subject to Article 5 of these Rules, the arbitral tribunal shall determine the means of communication between itself and the parties.

21. Conciliation

The arbitral tribunal may at any time seek to conciliate the parties. Any settlement may be embodied in an arbitral award rendered by consent of the parties.

22. Assistance

Each party has the right to be assisted by the counsel of its choice, regardless of the nationality or residence of such counsel.

23. Provisional or Conservatory Measures

23.1 Each party may request provisional or conservatory measures from a state authority having jurisdiction or from the arbitral tribunal.

23.2 The arbitral tribunal shall request the respondent party to state its position and shall render an order based on an adversarial proceeding within a short time.

23.3 In case of utmost urgency, the arbitral tribunal may order provisional or conservatory measures upon mere presentation of the request, provided that the other party shall be heard subsequently.

23.4 In domestic arbitrations, the mandatory provisions of the Swiss Intercantonal Arbitration Convention of 27 March 1969 are reserved.

24. Additional Briefs

At the request of a party or upon its own initiative, the arbitral tribunal shall order the exchange of additional briefs if the circumstances so justify.

25. Documents

25.1 Each party shall produce the documents upon which it relies in conjunction with the written pleadings provided in Articles 7, 8 and 24.

25.2 Exceptionally, the arbitral tribunal may permit the production of new documents if the parties so agree, if the party wishing to produce the new document could not do so within the applicable time limit, or if the relevance of the document did not become apparent until after expiry of the time limit.

25.3 Each party may request in due course the production of documents in the custody of the opponent. If the parties disagree, the arbitral tribunal may order production of the documents, on condition that the requesting party demonstrates the likely existence and relevance of such documents.

26. Witnesses

26.1 The party wishing to have a witness heard shall deliver a preliminary statement signed by such witness, unless the witness refuses. Unless otherwise decided by the arbitral tribunal, the preliminary statements shall be delivered at the latest fifteen days before the hearing at which evidence is to be taken.

26.2 At the hearing at which evidence is taken, each party shall examine its witnesses, if it deems necessary in order to complete the preliminary statements. The opponent shall thereafter ask the questions that it deems relevant. The arbitrators may ask their own questions at any time.

27. Experts

27.1 Each party may consult and present one or more experts of its choice to be heard by the arbitral tribunal. The provisions regarding the examination of witnesses shall apply by analogy.

27.2 The arbitral tribunal may, of its own motion or at the request of a party, appoint one or more experts. The arbitral tribunal shall consult the parties with respect to the appointment and terms of reference of such experts.

28. Records

The examination of witnesses, experts and parties shall be recorded by a stenographer. At the request of the parties or if it deems appropriate, the arbitral tribunal may substitute any process permitting the preservation of the entire statements or of their essential elements.

F. Award

29. Reasons

Unless otherwise agreed by the parties, the award shall state reasons in a concise manner. It shall confirm the undertaking of confidentiality contained in Article 4 of these Rules.

30. Notification

The CCIG shall notify the award to the parties provided that all the costs of arbitration have been paid. The CCIG shall keep a copy of the award for ten years.

G. Expedited Procedure

31. Special Provisions

If the parties so agree, the arbitration shall be conducted according to an expedited procedure. Such arbitrations shall be governed by the foregoing provisions, subject to the following changes:
 a) the CCIG may shorten the time limits for the appointment of arbitrators;
 b) upon deposit of the request for Arbitration, each party may state its position only once in writing on the claims asserted against it;
 c) unless the parties authorize the arbitral tribunal to decide on the basis of the documentary evidence only, the arbitral tribunal shall hold a single hearing for the examination of the parties, witnesses and expert witnesses as well as for oral argument.
 d) the award shall be rendered within six months from the date when the CCIG hands the file over to the arbitrators;
 e) the award shall summarily state reasons, unless the parties waive the requirement of reasons.

H. Costs of Arbitration

32. Definition of Costs

The costs of arbitration include the fees and disbursements of the CCIG as well as the fees and expenses of the arbitral tribunal.

33. Fees and Disbursements of the CCIG

33.1 The fees of the CCIG shall be CHF 4000 for arbitrations where the amount in dispute does not exceed CHF 2 000 000 and CHF 6000 for arbitrations involving a higher amount. The CCIG may amend these charges should the cost of administering arbitrations so require.

33.2 The fees of the CCIG shall be paid at the time of filing the request for Arbitration, failing which the CCIG shall not proceed with the case.

33.3 The CCIG shall assess an additional charge when an arbitrator is challenged.

33.4 The disbursements of the CCIG include the actual costs incurred by the CCIG, such as telephone, telefax, photocopies and courier services.

34. Fees and Expenses of the Arbitral Tribunal

34.1 The fees of the arbitrators shall in principle be computed according to the time reasonably spent on the resolution of the dispute at an hourly rate subject to limits established in proportion to the amount in dispute. The CCIG schedule in force at the time of the filing of the request shall apply.

34.2 The expenses of the arbitral tribunal include the actual expenses incurred by the arbitral tribunal, such as the costs of travel, meeting room rental, the remuneration of interpreters, the recording and transcribing of hearings, telephone, telefax, photocopies and courier services.

35. Advance

35.1 When the arbitral tribunal is being formed, the CCIG shall determine the amount of the advance towards the costs of arbitration, subject to possible changes during the arbitration. The filing of a counterclaim or a new claim shall result in the determination of separate advances.

35.2 The advance shall be paid in two installments of 50% each. The first instalment shall be paid at the beginning of the proceeding or following the filing of a new claim within the time limits set by the CCIG. The CCIG shall hand over the file to the arbitral tribunal as soon as the first instalment is paid. The second instalment shall be paid during the proceeding at a date to be set by the CCIG in agreement with the arbitrators.

35.3 Each instalment shall be payable in equal shares by the claimant and the respondent. If a party does not pay its share, the other party may substitute for it; if the share is not paid, the claim to which such share relates, after notice, shall be deemed to be withdrawn.

35.4 Any supplementary advance fixed by the CCIG in agreement with the arbitrators shall be paid in a single instalment in conformity with Article 35.3.

35.5 The advance shall bear interest at a usual rate. Such interest is included in the final computation of the arbitration costs in favor of the parties having advanced the amounts bearing interest.

35.6 If the arbitral tribunal orders an expert report, the expert shall commence work only after payment by the parties, or by one of them, of an advance determined by the arbitral tribunal and intended to cover the costs of the expertise.

36. Assessment of the Costs of Arbitration in the Award

36.1 At the end of the proceeding, the CCIG shall determine the final amount of the costs of arbitration. Such costs shall be stated in the arbitral award, which shall also determine which party shall bear such costs or in which proportion the parties shall share them.

36.2 In addition, the arbitral tribunal shall in principle adjudge that the losing party contribute towards the attorney's fees of the other party.

SCHEDULE FOR ARBITRATORS FEES

1. Pursuant to article 34.1 of the Arbitration Rules, the fees of the arbitrators shall in principle be computed according to the time reasonably spent on the resolution of the dispute at an hourly rate established on the basis of the amount in dispute, as follows:

Amount in Dispute		Hourly Rate
— up to Fr.	500 000.—	200.—
— from Fr.	500 000.— to 1 000 000.—	250.—
— from Fr.	1 000 000.— to 2 000 000.—	300.—
— more than Fr.	2 000 000.—	350.—
Travel time is count at one-half value.		

2. In any case, the total amount of arbitrator's fees shall not exceed a certain percentage of the amount in dispute, as follows:

Amount in Dispute sole arbitrator	three arbitrators		Maximum Fee Percentage	
10%	16%	— up to Fr		500 000.—
6%	10%	— from Fr.	500 001.— to	1 000 000.—
5%	7.5%	— from Fr.	1 000 001.— to	2 000 000.—
3%	6%	— from Fr.	2 000 001.— to	5 000 000.—
2%	3%	— more than Fr.		5 000 001.—

5. International Centre for the Settlement of Investment Disputes.

a. ICSID Institution Rules.

Rules of Procedure for the Institution of Conciliation and Arbitration Proceedings

Rule 1
The Request

(1) Any Contracting State or any national of a Contracting State wishing to institute conciliation or arbitration proceedings under the Convention shall address a request to that effect in writing to the Secretary-General at the seat of the Centre. The request shall indicate whether it relates to a conciliation or an arbitration proceeding. It shall be drawn up in an official language of the Centre, shall be dated, and shall be signed by the requesting party.

(2) The request may be made jointly by the parties to the dispute.

Rule 2
Contents of the Request

(1) The request shall:

(a) designate precisely each party to the dispute and state the address of each;

(b) state, if one of the parties is a constituent subdivision or agency of a Contracting State, that it has been designated to the Centre by that State pursuant to Article 25(1) of the Convention;

(c) indicate the date of consent and the instruments in which it is recorded, including, if one party is a constituent subdivision or agency of a Contracting State, similar date on the approval of such consent by that State unless it had notified the Centre that no such approval is required;

(d) indicate with respect to the party that is a national of a Contracting State;

    (i) its nationality on the date of consent; and

    (ii) if the party is a natural person;

        (A) his nationality on the date of the request; and

        (B) that he did not have the nationality of the Contracting State party to the dispute either on the date of consent or on the date of the request; or

    (iii) if the party is a juridical person which on the date of consent had the nationality of the Contracting State party to the dispute, the agreement of the parties that it should be treated as a national of another

Contracting State for the purposes of the Convention; and
>   (e) contain information concerning the issues in dispute indicating that there is, between the parties, a legal dispute arising directly out of an investment.

(2) The information required by subparagraphs (1)(c) and (1)(d)(iii) shall be supported by documentation.

(3) "Date of consent" means the date on which the parties to the dispute consented in writing to submit it to the Centre; if both parties did not act on the same day, it means the date on which the second party acted.

Rule 3
Optional Information in the Request

The request may in addition set forth any provisions agreed by the parties regarding the number of conciliators or arbitrators and the method of their appointment, as well as any other provisions agreed concerning the settlement of the dispute.

Rule 4
Copies of the Request

(1) The request shall be accompanied by five additional signed copies. The Secretary-General may require such further copies as he may deem necessary.

(2) Any documentation submitted with the request shall conform to the requirements of Administrative and Financial Regulation 30.

Rule 5
Acknowledgement of the Request

(1) On receiving a request the Secretary-General shall:
>   (a) send an acknowledgement to the requesting party;
>   (b) take no other action with respect to the request until he has received payment of the prescribed fee.

(2) As soon as he has received a fee for lodging the request, the Secretary-General shall transmit a copy of the request and of the accompanying documentation to the other party.

Rule 6
Registration of the Request

(1) The Secretary-General shall, subject to Rule 5(1)(b), as soon as possible, either:

(a) register the request in the Conciliation or the Arbitration Register and on the same day notify the parties of the registration; or

(b) if he finds, on the basis of the information contained in the request, that the dispute is manifestly outside the jurisdiction of the Centre, notify the parties of his refusal to register the request and of the reasons therefor.

(2) A proceeding under the Convention shall be deemed to have been instituted on the date of the registration of the request.

Rule 7
Notice of Registration

The notice of registration of a request shall:

(a) record that the request is registered and indicate the date of the registration and of the dispatch of that notice;

(b) notify each party that all communications and notices in connection with the proceeding will be sent to the address stated in the request, unless another address is indicated to the Centre;

(c) unless such information has already been provided, invite the parties to communicate to the Secretary-General any provisions agreed by them regarding the number and the method of appointment of the conciliators or arbitrators;

(d) invite the parties to proceed, as soon as possible, to constitute a Conciliation Commission in accordance with Articles 29 to 31 of the Convention, or an Arbitral Tribunal in accordance with Articles 37 to 40; and

(e) be accompanied by a list of the members of the Panel of Conciliators or of Arbitrators of the Centre.

Rule 8
Withdrawal of the Request

The requesting party may, by written notice to the Secretary-General, withdraw the request before it has been registered. The Secretary-General shall promptly notify the other party, unless, pursuant to Rule 5(1)(b), the request had not been transmitted to it.

Rule 9
Final Provisions

(1) The texts of these Rules in each official language of the Centre shall be equally authentic.

(2) These Rules may be cited as the "Institution Rules" of the Centre.

b. ICSID Arbitration Rules.

Rules of Procedure for Arbitration Proceedings

Chapter I

Establishment of the Tribunal

Rule 1
General Obligations

(1) Upon notification of the registration of the request for arbitration, the parties shall, with all possible dispatch, proceed to constitute a Tribunal, with due regard to Section 2 of Chapter IV of the Convention.

(2) Unless such information is provided in the request, the parties shall communicate to the Secretary-General as soon as possible any provisions agreed by them regarding the number of arbitrators and the method of their appointment.

(3) Except if each member of the Tribunal is appointed by agreement of the parties, nationals of the State party to the dispute or of the State whose national is a party to the dispute may be appointed by a party only if appointment by the other party to the dispute of the same number of arbitrators of either of these nationalities would not result in a majority of arbitrators of these nationalities.

(4) No person who had previously acted as a conciliator or arbitrator in any proceeding for the settlement of the dispute may be appointed as a member of the Tribunal.

Rule 2
Method of Constituting the Tribunal in the Absence of Previous Agreement

(1) If the parties, at the time of the registration of the request for arbitration, have not agreed upon the number of arbitrators and the method of their appointment, they shall, unless they agree otherwise, follow the following procedure:

(a) the requesting party shall, within 10 days after the registration of the request, propose to the other party the appointment of a sole arbitrator or of a specified uneven number of arbitrators and specify the method proposed for their appointment;

(b) within 20 days after receipt of the proposals made by the requesting party, the other party shall:

(i) accept such proposals; or

(ii) make other proposals regarding the number of arbitrators and the method of their appointment;

(c) within 20 days after receipt of the reply containing any such other proposals, the requesting party shall notify the other party whether it accepts or rejects such proposals.

(2) The communications provided for in paragraph (1) shall be made or promptly confirmed in writing and shall either be transmitted through the Secretary-General or directly between the parties with a copy to the Secretary-General. The parties shall promptly notify the Secretary-General of the contents of any agreement reached.

(3) At any time 60 days after the registration of the request, if no agreement on another procedure is reached, either party may inform the Secretary-General that it chooses the formula provided for in Article 37(2)(b) of the Convention. The Secretary-General shall thereupon promptly inform the other party that the Tribunal is to be constituted in accordance with that Article.

Rule 3
Appointment of Arbitrators to a Tribunal Constituted in Accordance with Convention

Article 37 (2)(b)

(1) If the Tribunal is to be constituted in accordance with Article 37(2)(b) of the Convention:

(a) either party shall in a communication to the other party:

(i)name two persons, identifying one of them, who shall not have the same nationality as nor be a national of either party, as the arbitrator appointed by it, and the other as the arbitrator proposed to be the President of the Tribunal; and

(ii) invite the other party to concur in the appointment of the arbitrator proposed to be the President of the Tribunal and to appoint another arbitrator.

(b) promptly upon receipt of this communication the other party shall, in its reply;

(i) name a person as the arbitrator appointed by it, who shall not have the same nationality as nor be a national of either party; and

(ii) concur in the appointment of the arbitrator proposed to be the President of the Tribunal or name another person as the arbitrator proposed to be President;

(c) promptly upon receipt of the reply containing such a proposal, the initiating party shall notify the other party whether it concurs in the appointment of the arbitrator proposed by that party to be the President of the Tribunal.

(2) The communications provided for in this Rule shall be made or promptly confirmed in writing and shall either be transmitted through the Secretary-General or directly between the parties with a copy to the Secretary-General.

Rule 4
Appointment of Arbitrators by the Chairman of the Administrative Council

(1) If the Tribunal is not constituted within 90 days after the dispatch by the Secretary-General of the notice of registration, or such other period as the parties may agree, either party may, through the Secretary-General, address to the Chairman of the Administrative Council a request in writing to appoint the arbitrator or arbitrators not yet appointed and to designate an arbitrator to be the President of the Tribunal.

(2) The provision of paragraph (1) shall apply mutatis mutandis in the event that the parties have agreed that the arbitrators shall elect the President of the Tribunal and they fail to do so.

(3) The Secretary-General shall forthwith send a copy of the request to the other party.

(4) The Chairman shall, with due regard to Articles 38 and 40(1) of the Convention, and after consulting both parties as far as possible, comply with that request within 30 days after its receipt.

(5) The Secretary-General shall promptly notify the parties of any appointment or designation made by the Chairman.

Rule 5
Acceptance of Appointments

(1) The party or parties concerned shall notify the Secretary-General of the appointment of each arbitrator and indicate the method of his appointment.

(2) As soon as the Secretary-General has been informed by a party or the Chairman of the Administrative Council of the appointment of an arbitrator, he shall seek an acceptance from the appointee.

(3) If an arbitrator fails to accept his appointment within 15 days, the Secretary-General shall promptly notify the parties, and if appropriate the Chairman, and invite them to proceed to the appointment of another arbitrator in accordance with the method followed for the previous appointment.

Rule 6 Constitution of the Tribunal

(1) The Tribunal shall be deemed to be constituted and the proceeding to have begun on the date the Secretary-General notifies the parties that all the arbitrators have accepted their appointment.

(2) Before or at the first session of the Tribunal, each arbitrator shall sign a declaration in the following form:

"To the best of my knowledge there is no reason why I should not serve on the Arbitral Tribunal constituted by the International Center for Settlement of Investment Disputes with respect to a dispute between .... and ....

"I shall keep confidential all information coming to my knowledge as a result of my participation in this proceeding, as well as the contents of any award made by the Tribunal.

"I shall judge fairly as between the parties, according to the applicable law, and shall not accept any instruction or compensation with regard to the proceeding from any source except as provided in the Convention on the Settlement of Investment Disputes and in the Regulations and Rules made pursuant thereto.

"A statement of my past and present professional, business and other relationships (if any) with the parties is attached hereto."

Any arbitrator failing to sign a declaration by the end of the first session of the Tribunal shall be deemed to have resigned.

Rule 7
Replacement of Arbitrators

At any time before the Tribunal is constituted, each party may replace any arbitrator appointed by it and the parties may by common consent agree to replace any arbitrator. The procedure of such replacement shall be in accordance with Rules 1, 5 and 6.

Rule 8
Incapacity or Resignation of Arbitrators

(1) If an arbitrator becomes incapacitated or unable to perform the duties of his office, the procedure in respect of the disqualification of arbitrators set forth in Rule 9 shall apply.

(2) An arbitrator may resign by submitting his resignation to the other members of the Tribunal and the Secretary-General. If the arbitrator was appointed by one of the parties, the Tribunal shall promptly consider the reasons for his resignation and decide whether it consents thereto. The Tribunal shall promptly notify the Secretary-General of its decision.

Rule 9
Disqualification of Arbitrators

(1) A party proposing the disqualification of an arbitrator pursuant to Article 57 of the Convention shall promptly, and in any event before the proceeding is declared closed, file its proposal with the Secretary-General, stating its reasons therefor.

(2) The Secretary-General shall forthwith:

(a) transmit the proposal to the members of the Tribunal and, if it relates to a sole arbitrator or to a majority of the members of the Tribunal, to the Chairman of the Administrative Council; and

(b)notify the other party of the proposal.

(3) The arbitrator to whom the proposal relates may, without delay, furnish explanations to the Tribunal or the Chairman, as the case may be.

(4)Unless the proposal relates to a majority of the members of the Tribunal, the other members shall promptly consider and vote on the proposal in the absence of the arbitrator concerned. If those members are equally divided, they shall, through the Secretary-General, promptly notify the Chairman of the proposal, of any explanation furnished by the arbitrator concerned and of their failure to reach a decision.

(5) Whenever the Chairman has to decide on a proposal to disqualify an arbitrator, he shall take that decision within 30 days after he has received the proposal.

(6) The proceeding shall be suspended until a decision has been taken on the proposal.

Rule 10
Procedure during a Vacancy on the Tribunal

(1) The Secretary-General shall forthwith notify the parties and, if necessary, the Chairman of the Administrative Council of the disqualification, death, incapacity or resignation of an arbitrator and of the consent, if any, of the Tribunal to a resignation.

(2) Upon the notification by the Secretary-General of a vacancy on the Tribunal, the proceeding shall be or remain suspended until the vacancy has been filled.

Rule 11
Filling Vacancies on the Tribunal

(1) Except as provided in paragraph (2), a vacancy resulting from the disqualification, death, incapacity or resignation of an arbitrator shall be promptly filled by the same method by which his appointment had been made.

(2) In addition to filling vacancies relating to arbitrators appointed by him, the Chairman of the Administrative Council shall appoint a person from the Panel of Arbitrators:

(a) to fill a vacancy caused by the resignation, without the consent of the Tribunal, of an arbitrator appointed by a party; or

(b) at the request of either party, to fill any other vacancy, if no new appointment is made and accepted within 30 days of the notification of the vacancy by the Secretary-General.

(3) The procedure for filling a vacancy shall be in accordance with Rules 1, 4(4), 4(5), 5 and, mutatis mutandis, 6(2).

Rule 12
Resumption of Proceeding after Filling a Vacancy

As soon as a vacancy on the Tribunal has been filled, the proceeding shall continue from the point it had reached at the time the vacancy occurred. The newly appointed arbitrator may, however, require that the oral procedure be recommenced, if this had already been started.

Chapter II

Working of the Tribunal

Rule 13
Sessions of the Tribunal

(1) The Tribunal shall hold its first session within 60 days after its constitution or such other period as the parties may agree. The dates of that session shall be fixed by the President of the Tribunal after consultation with its members and the Secretary-General. If upon its constitution the Tribunal has no President because the parties have agreed that the President shall be elected by its members, the Secretary-General shall fix the dates of that session. In both cases, the parties shall be consulted as far as possible.

(2) The dates of subsequent sessions shall be determined by the Tribunal, after consultation with the Secretary-General and with the parties as far as possible.

(3) The Tribunal shall meet at the seat of the Centre or at such other place as may have been agreed by the parties in accordance with Article 63 of the Convention. If the parties agree that the proceeding shall be held at a place other than the Centre or an institution with which the Centre has made the necessary arrangements, they shall consult with the Secretary-General and request the approval of the Tribunal. Failing such approval, the Tribunal shall meet at the seat of the Centre.

(4) The Secretary-General shall notify the members of the Tribunal and the parties of the dates and place of the sessions of the Tribunal in good time.

Rule 14
Sittings of the Tribunal

(1) The President of the Tribunal shall conduct its hearings and preside at its deliberations.

(2) Except as the parties otherwise agree, the presence of a majority of the members of the Tribunal shall be required at its sittings.

(3) The President of the Tribunal shall fix the date and hour of its sittings.

Rule 15
Deliberations of the Tribunal

(1) The deliberations of the Tribunal shall take place in private and remain secret.

(2) Only members of the Tribunal shall take part in its deliberations. No other person shall be admitted unless the Tribunal decides otherwise.

Rule 16
Decisions of the Tribunal

(1) Decisions of the Tribunal shall be taken by a majority of the votes of all its members. Abstention shall count as a negative vote.

(2) Except as otherwise provided by these Rules or decided by the Tribunal, it may take any decision by correspondence among its members, provided that all of them are consulted. Decisions so taken shall be certified by the President of the Tribunal.

Rule 17
Incapacity of the President

If at any time the President of the Tribunal should be unable to act, his functions shall be performed by one of the other members of the Tribunal, acting in the order in which the Secretary-General had received the notice of their acceptance of their appointment to the Tribunal.

Rule 18
Representation of the Parties

(1) Each party may be represented or assisted by agents, counsel or advocates whose names and authority shall be notified by that party to the Secretary-General, who shall promptly inform the Tribunal and the other party.

(2) For the purposes of these Rules, the expression "party" includes, where the contexts so admits, an agent, counsel or advocate authorized to represent that party.

Chapter III

General Procedural Provisions

Rule 19
Procedural Orders

The Tribunal shall make the orders required for the conduct of the proceeding.

Rule 20
Preliminary Procedural Consultation

(1) As early as possible after the constitution of a Tribunal, its President shall endeavor to ascertain the views of the parties regarding questions of procedure. For this purpose he may request the parties to meet him. He shall, in particular, seek their views on the following matters:

(a) the number of members of the Tribunal required to constitute a quorum at its sittings;

(b) the language or languages to be used in the proceeding;

(c) the number and sequence of the pleadings and the time limits within which they are to be filed;

(d) the number of copies desired by each party of instruments filed by the other;

(e) dispensing with the written or the oral procedure;

(f) the manner in which the cost of the proceeding is to be apportioned; and

(g) the manner in which the record of the hearings shall be kept.

(2) In the conduct of the proceeding the Tribunal shall apply any agreement between the parties on procedural matters, except as otherwise provided in the Convention or the Administrative and Financial Regulations.

Rule 21
Pre-Hearing Conference

(1) At the request of the Secretary-General or at the discretion of the President of the Tribunal, a pre-hearing conference between the Tribunal and the parties may be held to arrange for an exchange of information and the stipulation of uncontested facts in order to expedite the proceeding.

(2) At the request of the parties, a pre-hearing conference between the Tribunal and the parties, duly represented by their authorized representatives, may be held to consider the issues in dispute with a view to reaching an amicable settlement.

Rule 22
Procedural Languages

(1) The parties may agree on the use of one or two languages to be used in the proceeding, provided, that, if they agree on any language that is not an official language of the Centre, the Tribunal, after consultation with the Secretary-General, gives its approval. If the parties do not agree on any such procedural language, each of them may select one of the official languages (i.e. English, French and Spanish) for this purpose.

(2) If two procedural languages are selected by the parties, any instruments may be filed in either language. Either language may be used at the hearings, subject, if the Tribunal so requires, to translation and interpretation. The orders and the award of the Tribunal shall be rendered and the record kept in both procedural languages, both versions being equally authentic.

Rule 23
Copies of Instruments

Except as otherwise provided by the Tribunal after consultation with the parties and the Secretary-General, every request, pleading, application, written observation, supporting documentation, if any, or other instrument shall be filed in the form of a signed original accompanied by the following number of additional copies:

(a) before the number of members of the Tribunal has been determined: five;

(b) after the number of members of the Tribunal has been determined: two more than the number of its members.

Rule 24
Supporting Documentation

Supporting documentation shall ordinarily be filed together with the instrument to which it relates, and in any case within the time limit fixed for the filing of such instrument.

Rule 25
Correction of Errors

An accidental error in any instrument or supporting document may, with the consent of the other party or by leave of the Tribunal, be corrected at any time before the award is rendered.

Rule 26
Time Limits

(1) Where required, time limits shall be fixed by the Tribunal by assigning dates for the completion of the various steps in the proceeding. The Tribunal may delegate this power to its President.

(2) The Tribunal may extend any time limit it has fixed. If the Tribunal is not in session, this power shall be exercised by its President.

(3) Any step taken after expiration of the applicable time limit shall be disregarded unless the Tribunal, in special circumstances and after giving the other party an opportunity of stating its views, decides otherwise.

Rule 27
Waiver

A party which knows or should have known that a provision of the Administrative and Financial Regulations, of these Rules, of any other rules or agreement applicable to the proceeding, or of an order of the Tribunal has not been complied with and which fails to state promptly its objections thereto, shall be deemed—subject to Article 45 of the Convention—to have waived its right to object.

Rule 28
Cost of Proceeding

(1) Without prejudice to the final decision on the payment of the cost of the proceeding, the Tribunal may, unless otherwise agreed by the parties, decide:

(a) at any stage of the proceeding, the portion which each party shall pay, pursuant to Administrative and Financial Regulation 14, of the fees and expenses of the Tribunal and the charges for the use of the facilities of the Centre.

(b) with respect to any part of the proceeding, that the related costs (as determined by the Secretary-General) shall be borne entirely or in a particular share by one of the parties.

(2) Promptly after the closure of the proceeding, each party shall submit to the Tribunal a statement of costs reasonably incurred or borne by it in the proceeding and the Secretary-General shall submit to the Tribunal an account of all amounts paid by each party to the Centre and of all costs incurred by the Centre for the proceeding. The Tribunal may, before the award has been rendered, request the parties and the Secretary-General to provide additional information concerning the cost of the proceeding.

Chapter IV

Written and Oral Procedures

Rule 29
Normal Procedures

Except if the parties otherwise agree, the proceeding shall comprise two distinct phases: a written procedure followed by an oral one.

Rule 30
Transmission of the Request

As soon as the Tribunal is constituted, the Secretary-General shall transmit to each member a copy of the request by which the proceeding was initiated, of the supporting documentation, of the notice of registration and of any communication received from either party in response thereto.

Rule 31
The Written Procedure

(1) In addition to the request for arbitration, the written procedure shall consist of the following pleadings, filed within time limits set by the Tribunal:
    (a) a memorial by the requesting party;
    (b) a counter-memorial by the other party; and, if the parties so agree or the Tribunal deems it necessary;
    (c) a reply by the requesting party; and
    (d) a rejoinder by the other party.
(2) If the request was made jointly, each party shall, within the same time limit determined by the Tribunal, file its memorial and, if the parties so agree or the Tribunal deems it necessary, its reply; however, the parties may instead agree that one of them shall, for the purposes of paragraph (1), be considered as the requesting party.
(3) A memorial shall contain: a statement of the relevant facts; a statement of law; and the submissions. A counter-memorial, reply or rejoinder shall contain an admission or denial of the facts stated in the last previous pleading; any additional facts, if necessary; observations concerning the statement of law in the last previous pleading; a statement of law in answer thereto; and the submissions.

Rule 32
The Oral Procedure

(1) The oral procedure shall consist of the hearing by the Tribunal of the parties, their agents, counsel and advocates, and of witnesses and experts.

(2) The Tribunal shall decide, with the consent of the parties, which other persons besides the parties, their agents, counsel and advocates, witnesses and experts during their testimony, and officers of the Tribunal may attend the hearings.

(3) The members of the Tribunal may, during the hearings, put questions to the parties, their agents, counsel and advocates, and ask them for explanations.

Rule 33
Marshalling of Evidence

Without prejudice to the rules concerning the production of documents, each party shall, within time limits fixed by the Tribunal, communicate to the Secretary-General, for transmission to the Tribunal and the other party, precise information regarding the evidence which it intends to produce and that which it intends to request the Tribunal to call for, together with an indication of the points to which such evidence will be directed.

Rule 34
Evidence: General Principles

(1) The Tribunal shall be the judge of the admissibility of any evidence adduced and of its probative value.

(2) The Tribunal may, if it deems it necessary at any stage of the proceeding:

(a)call upon the parties to produce documents, witnesses and experts; and

(b) visit any place connected with the dispute or conduct inquiries there.

(3) The parties shall cooperate with the Tribunal in the production of the evidence and in the other measures provided for in paragraph (2). The Tribunal shall take formal note of the failure of a party to comply with its obligations under this paragraph and of any reasons given for such failure.

(4) Expenses incurred in producing evidence and in taking other measures in accordance with paragraph (2) shall be deemed to constitute part of the expenses incurred by the parties within the meaning of Article 61(2) of the Convention.

Rule 35
Examination of Witnesses and Experts

(1) Witnesses and experts shall be examined before the Tribunal by the parties under the control of its President. Questions may also be put to them by any member of the Tribunal.

(2) Each witness shall make the following declaration before giving his evidence:

"I solemnly declare upon my honour and conscience that I shall speak the truth, the whole truth and nothing but the truth."

(3) Each expert shall make the following declaration before making his statement:

"I solemnly declare upon my honour and conscience that my statement will be in accordance with my sincere belief."

Rule 36
Witnesses and Experts: Special Rules

Notwithstanding Rule 35 the Tribunal may:

(a) admit evidence given by a witness or expert in a written deposition; and

(b) with the consent of both parties, arrange for the examination of a witness or expert otherwise than before the Tribunal itself. The Tribunal shall define the subject of the examination, the time limit, the procedure to be followed and other particulars. The parties may participate in the examination.

Rule 37
Visits and Inquiries

If the Tribunal considers it necessary to visit any place connected with the dispute or to conduct an inquiry there, it shall make an order to this effect. The order shall define the scope of the visit or the subject of the inquiry, the time limit, the procedure to be followed and other particulars. The parties may participate in any visit or inquiry.

Rule 38
Closure of the Proceeding

(1) When the presentation of the case by the parties is completed, the proceeding shall be declared closed.

(2) Exceptionally, the Tribunal may, before the award has been rendered, reopen the proceeding on the ground that new evidence is forthcoming of such a nature as to constitute a decisive factor, or that there is a vital need for clarification on certain specific points.

Chapter V

Particular Procedures

Rule 39
Provisional Measures

(1) At any time during the proceeding a party may request that provisional measures for the preservation of its rights be recommended by the Tribunal. The request shall specify the rights to be preserved, the measures the recommendation of which is requested, and the circumstances that require such measures.

(2) The Tribunal shall give priority to the consideration of a request made pursuant to paragraph (1).

(3) The Tribunal may also recommend provisional measures on its own initiative or recommend measures other than those specified in a request. It may at any time modify or revoke its recommendations.

(4) The Tribunal shall only recommend provisional measures, or modify or revoke its recommendations, after giving each party an opportunity of presenting its observations.

(5) Nothing in this Rule shall prevent the parties, provided that they have so stipulated in the agreement recording their consent, from requesting any judicial or other authority to order provisional measures, prior to the institution of the proceeding, or during the proceeding, for the preservation of their respective rights and interests.

Rule 40
Ancillary Claims

(1) Except as the parties otherwise agree, a party may present an incidental or additional claim or counter-claim arising directly out of the subject-matter of the dispute, provided that such ancillary claim is within the scope of the consent of the parties and is otherwise within the jurisdiction of the Centre.

(2) An incidental or additional claim shall be presented not later than in the reply and a counter-claim no later than in the counter-memorial, unless the Tribunal, upon justification by the party presenting the ancillary claim and upon considering any objection of the other party, authorizes the presentation of the claim at a later stage in the proceeding.

(3) The Tribunal shall fix a time limit within which the party against which an ancillary claim is presented may file its observations thereon.

Rule 41
Objections to Jurisdiction

(1) Any objection that the dispute or any ancillary claim is not within the juris-diction of the Centre or, for other reasons, is not within the competence of the Tribunal shall be made as early as possible. A party shall file the objection with the Secretary-General no later than the expiration of the time limit fixed for the filing of the counter-memorial, or, if the objection relates to an ancillary claim, for the filing of the rejoinder—unless the facts on which the objection is based are unknown to the party at that time.

(2) The Tribunal may on its own initiative consider, at any stage of the proceed-ing, whether the dispute or any ancillary claim before it is within the jurisdiction of the Centre and within its own competence.

(3) Upon formal raising of an objection relating to the dispute, the proceeding on the merits shall be suspended. The President of the Tribunal, after consultation with its other members, shall fix a time limit within which the parties may file obser-vations on the objection.

(4) The Tribunal shall decide whether or not the future procedures relating to the objection shall be oral. It may deal with the objection as a preliminary question or join it to the merits of the dispute. If the Tribunal overrules the objection or joins it to the merits, it shall once more fix time limits for the future procedures.

(5) If the Tribunal decides that the dispute is not within the jurisdiction of the Centre or not within its own competence, it shall render an award to that effect.

Rule 42
Default

(1) If a party (in this Rule called the "defaulting party") fails to appear or to pre-sent its case at any stage of the proceeding, the other party may, at any time prior to the discontinuance of the proceeding, request the Tribunal to deal with the questions submitted to it and to render an award.

(2) The Tribunal shall promptly notify the defaulting party of such a request. Unless it is satisfied that that party does not intend to appear or to present its case in the proceeding, it shall, at the same time, grant a period of grace and to this end:

(a) if that party had failed to file a pleading or any other instrument within the time limit fixed therefor, fix a new time limit for its filing; or

(b) if that party had failed to appear or present its case at a hearing, fix a new date for the hearing.

The period of grace shall not, without the consent of the other party, exceed 60 days.

(3) After the expiration of the period of grace or when, in accordance with para-graph (2), no such period is granted, the Tribunal shall resume the consideration of the dispute. Failure of the defaulting party to appear or to present its case shall not be deemed an admission of the assertions made by the other party.

(4) The Tribunal shall examine the jurisdiction of the Centre and its own competence in the dispute and, if it is satisfied, decide whether the submissions made are well-founded in fact and in law. To this end, it may, at any stage of the proceeding, call on the party appearing to file observations, produce evidence or submit oral explanations.

Rule 43
Settlement and Discontinuance

(1) If, before the award is rendered, the parties agree on a settlement of the dispute or otherwise to discontinue the proceeding, the Tribunal, or the Secretary-General if the Tribunal has not yet been constituted, shall, at their written request, in an order take note of the discontinuance of the proceeding.

(2) If the parties file with the Secretary-General the full and signed text of their settlement and in writing request the Tribunal to embody such settlement in an award, the Tribunal may record the settlement in the form of its award.

Rule 44
Discontinuance at Request of a Party

If a party requests the discontinuance of the proceeding, the Tribunal, or the Secretary-General if the Tribunal has not yet been constituted, shall in an order fix a time limit within which the other party may state whether it opposes the discontinuance. If no objection is made in writing within the time limit, the other party shall be deemed to have acquiesced in the discontinuance and the Tribunal, or if appropriate the Secretary-General, shall in an order take note of the discontinuance of the proceeding. If objection is made, the proceeding shall continue.

Rule 45
Discontinuance for Failure of Parties to Act

If the parties fail to take any steps in the proceeding during six consecutive months or such period as they may agree with the approval of the Tribunal, or of the Secretary-General if the Tribunal has not yet been constituted, they shall be deemed to have discontinued the proceeding and the Tribunal, or if appropriate the Secretary-General, shall, after notice to the parties, in an order take note of the discontinuance.

Chapter VI

The Award

Rule 46
Preparation of the Award

The award (including any individual or dissenting opinion) shall be drawn up and signed within 60 days after the closure of the proceeding. The Tribunal may, however, extend this period by a further 30 days if it would otherwise be unable to draw up the award.

Rule 47
The Award

(1) The award shall be in writing and shall contain:
(a) a precise designation of each party;
(b) a statement that the Tribunal was established under the Convention, and a description of the method of its constitution;
(c) the name of each member of the Tribunal, and an identification of the appointing authority of each;
(d) the names of the agents, counsel and advocates of the parties;
(e) the dates and place of the sittings of the Tribunal;
(f) a summary of the proceeding;
(g) a statement of the facts as found by the Tribunal;
(h) the submissions of the parties;
(i) the decision of the Tribunal on every question submitted to it, together with reasons upon which the decision is based; and
(j) any decision of the Tribunal regarding the cost of the proceeding.
(2) The award shall be signed by the members of the Tribunal who voted for it; the date of each signature shall be indicated.
(3) Any member of the Tribunal may attach his individual opinion to the award, whether he dissents from the majority or not, or a statement of his dissent.

Rule 48
Rendering of the Award

(1) Upon signature by the last arbitrator to sign, the Secretary-General shall promptly:
(a) authenticate the original text of the award and deposit it in the archives of the Centre, together with any individual opinions and statements of dissent; and

(b) dispatch a certified copy of the award (including individual opinions and statements of dissent) to each party, indicating the date of dispatch on the original text and on all copies.

(2) The award shall be deemed to have been rendered on the date on which the certified copies were dispatched.

(3) The Secretary-General shall, upon request, make available to a party additional certified copies of the award.

(4) The Centre shall not publish the award without the consent of the parties. The Centre may, however, include in its publications excerpts of the legal rules applied by the Tribunal.

Rule 49
Supplementary Decisions and Rectification

(1) Within 45 days after the date on which the award was rendered, either party may request, pursuant to Article 49(2) of the Convention, a supplementary decision on, or the rectification of, the award. Such a request shall be addressed in writing to the Secretary-General. The request shall:
(a) identify the award to which it relates;
(b) indicate the date of the request;
(c) state in detail:
(i) any question which, in the opinion of the requesting party, the Tribunal omitted to decide in the award; and
(ii) any error in the award which the requesting party seeks to have rectified; and
(d) be accompanied by a fee for lodging the request.

(2) Upon receipt of the request and of the lodging fee, the Secretary-General shall forthwith:
(a) register the request;
(b) notify the parties of the registration;
(c) transmit to the other party a copy of the request and of any accompanying documentation; and
(d) transmit to each member of the Tribunal a copy of the notice of registration, together with a copy of the request and of any accompanying documentation.

(3) The President of the Tribunal shall consult the members on whether it is necessary for the Tribunal to meet in order to consider the request. The Tribunal shall fix a time limit for the parties to file their observations on the request and shall determine the procedure for its consideration.

(4) Rules 46-48 shall apply, mutatis mutandis, to any decision of the Tribunal pursuant to this Rule.

(5) If a request is received by the Secretary-General more than 45 days after the award was rendered, he shall refuse to register the request and so inform forthwith the requesting party.

Chapter VII

Interpretation, Revision and Annulment of the Award

Rule 50
The Application

(1) An application for the interpretation, revision or annulment of an award shall be addressed in writing to the Secretary-General and shall:
    (a) identify the award to which it relates;
    (b) indicate the date of the application;
    (c) state in detail:
        (i) in an application for interpretation, the precise points in dispute;
        (ii) in an application for revision, pursuant to Article 51(1) of the Convention, the change sought in the award, the discovery of some fact of such a nature as decisively to affect the award, and evidence that when the award was rendered that fact was unknown to the Tribunal and to the applicant, and that the applicant's ignorance of that fact was not due to negligence;
        (iii) in an application for annulment, pursuant to Article 52(1) of the Convention, the grounds on which it is based. These grounds are limited to the following:
    •that the Tribunal was not properly constituted;
    •that the Tribunal has manifestly exceeded its powers;
    •that there was corruption on the part of a member of the Tribunal;
    •that there has been a serious departure from a fundamental rule of procedure;
    •that the award has failed to state the reasons on which it is based;
    (d) be accompanied by the payment of a fee for lodging the application.
(2) Without prejudice to the provisions of paragraph (3), upon receiving an application and the lodging fee, the Secretary-General shall forthwith:
    (a) register the application;
    (b) notify the parties of the registration; and
    (c) transmit to the other party a copy of the application and of any accompanying documentation.
(3) The Secretary-General shall refuse to register an application for:
    (a) revision, if, in accordance with Article 51(2) of the Convention, it is not made within 90 days after the discovery of the new fact and in any event within three years after the date on which the award was rendered (or any subsequent decision or correction);
    (b) annulment, if, in accordance with Article 52(2) of the Convention, it is not made:
        (i) within 120 days after the date on which the award was rendered (or any subsequent decision or correction) if the application is based on any of the following grounds:

•the Tribunal was not properly constituted;
•the Tribunal has manifestly exceeded its powers;
•there has been a serious departure from a fundamental rule of procedure;
•the award has failed to state the reasons on which it is based;

> (ii) in the case of corruption on the part of a member of the Tribunal, within 120 days after discovery thereof, and in any event within three years after the date on which the award was rendered (or any subsequent decision or correction).

(4) If the Secretary-General refuses to register an application for revision, or annulment, he shall forthwith notify the requesting party of his refusal.

Rule 51
Interpretation or Revision: Further Procedures

(1) Upon registration of an application for the interpretation or revision of an award, the Secretary-General shall forthwith:

(a) transmit to each member of the original Tribunal a copy of the notice of registration, together with a copy of the application and of any accompanying documentation; and

(b) request each member of the Tribunal to inform him within a specified time limit whether that member is willing to take part in the consideration of the application.

(2) If all members of the Tribunal express their willingness to take part in the consideration of the application, the Secretary-General shall so notify the members of the Tribunal and the parties. Upon dispatch of these notices the Tribunal shall be deemed to be reconstituted.

(3) If the Tribunal cannot be reconstituted in accordance with paragraph (2), the Secretary-General shall so notify the parties and invite them to proceed, as soon as possible, to constitute a new Tribunal, including the same number of arbitrators, and appointed by the same method, as the original one.

Rule 52
Annulment: Further Procedures

(1) Upon registration of an application for the annulment of an award, the Secretary-General shall forthwith request the Chairman of the Administrative Council to appoint an ad hoc Committee in accordance with Article 52(3) of the Convention.

(2) The Committee shall be deemed to be constituted on the date the Secretary-General notifies the parties that all members have accepted their appointment. Before or at the first session of the Committee, each member shall sign a declaration conforming to that set forth in Rule 62(2).

Rule 53
Rules of Procedure

The provisions of these Rules shall apply mutatis mutandis to any procedure relating to the interpretation, revision or annulment of an award and to the decision of the Tribunal or Committee.

Rule 54
Stay of Enforcement of the Award

(1) The party applying for the interpretation, revision or annulment of an award may in its application, and either party may at any time before the final disposition of the application, request a stay in the enforcement of part or all of the award to which the application relates. The Tribunal or Committee shall give priority to the consideration of such a request.

(2) If an application for the revision or annulment of an award contains a request for a stay of its enforcement, the Secretary-General shall, together with the notice of registration, inform both parties of the provisional stay of the award. As soon as the Tribunal or Committee is constituted it shall, if either party requests, rule within 30 days on whether such stay should be continued; unless it decides to continue the stay, it shall automatically be terminated.

(3) If a stay of enforcement has been granted pursuant to paragraph (1) or continued pursuant to paragraph (2), the Tribunal or Committee may at any time modify or terminate the stay at the request of either party. All stays shall automatically terminate on the date on which a final decision is rendered on the application, except that a Committee granting the partial annulment of an award may order the temporary stay of enforcement of the unannulled portion in order to give either party an opportunity to request any new Tribunal constituted pursuant to Article 52(6) of the Convention to grant a stay pursuant to Rule 55(3).

(4) A request pursuant to paragraph (1), (2) (second sentence) or (3) shall specify the circumstances that require the stay or its modification or termination. A request shall only be granted after the Tribunal or Committee has given each party an opportunity of presenting its observations.

(5) The Secretary-General shall promptly notify both parties of the stay of enforcement of any award and of the modification or termination of such a stay, which shall become effective on the date on which he dispatches such notification.

Rule 55
Resubmission of Dispute after an Annulment

(1) If a Committee annuls part or all of an award, either party may request the resubmission of the dispute to a new Tribunal. Such a request shall be addressed in writing to the Secretary-General and shall:

(a) identify the award to which it relates;

(b) indicate the date of the request;

(c) explain in detail what aspect of the dispute is to be submitted to the Tribunal; and

(d) be accompanied by a fee for lodging the request.

(2) Upon receipt of the request and of the lodging fee, the Secretary-General shall forthwith:

(a)register it in the Arbitration Register;

(b) notify both parties of the registration;

(c) transmit to the other party a copy of the request and of any accompanying documentation; and

(d) invite the parties to proceed, as soon as possible, to constitute a new Tribunal, including the same number of arbitrators, and appointed by the same method, as the original one.

(3) If the original award had only been annulled in part, the new Tribunal shall not reconsider any portion of the award not so annulled. It may, however, in accordance with the procedures set forth in Rule 54, stay or continue to stay the enforcement of the unannulled portion of the award until the date its own award is rendered.

(4) Except as otherwise provided in paragraphs (1)—(3), these Rules shall apply to a proceeding on a resubmitted dispute in the same manner as if such dispute had been submitted pursuant to the Institution Rules.

Chapter VIII

General Provisions

Rule 56
Final provisions

(1) The texts of these Rules in each official language of the Centre shall be equally authentic.

(2) These Rules may be cited as the "Arbitration Rules" of the Centre.

6. INTERNATIONAL CHAMBER OF COMMERCE.

a. I.C.C. Rules of Optional Conciliation.

Article 1

All business disputes of an international character may be submitted to conciliation by a sole conciliator appointed by the International Chamber of Commerce.

Article 2

The party requesting conciliation shall apply to the Secretariat of the Court of the International Chamber of Commerce setting out succinctly the purpose of the request and accompanying it with the fee required to open the file, as set out in Appendix III hereto.

Article 3

The Secretariat of the Court shall, as soon as possible, inform the other party of the request for conciliation. That party will be given a period of 15 days to inform the Secretariat whether it agrees or declines to participate in the attempt to conciliate.

If the other party agrees to participate in the attempt to conciliate it shall so inform the Secretariat within such period.

In the absence of any reply within such period or in the case of a negative reply the request for conciliation shall be deemed to have been declined. The Secretariat shall, as soon as possible, so inform the party which had requested conciliation.

Article 4

Upon receipt of an agreement to attempt conciliation, the Secretary General of the Court shall appoint a conciliator as soon as possible. The conciliator shall inform the parties of his appointment and set a time-limit for the parties to present their respective arguments to him.

Article 5

The conciliator shall conduct the conciliation process as he thinks fit, guided by the principles of impartiality, equity and justice.

With the agreement of the parties, the conciliator shall fix the place for conciliation.

The conciliator may at any time during the conciliation process request a party to submit to him such additional information as he deems necessary.

The parties may, if they so wish, be assisted by counsel of their choice.

Article 6

The confidential nature of the conciliation process shall be respected by every person who is involved in it in whatever capacity.

Article 7

The conciliation process shall come to an end:

a) Upon the parties signing an agreement. The parties shall be bound by such agreement. The agreement shall remain confidential unless and to the extent that its execution or application require disclosure.

b) Upon the production by the conciliator of a report recording that the attempt to conciliate has not been successful. Such report shall not contain reasons.

c) Upon notification to the conciliator by one or more parties at any time during the conciliation process of an intention no longer to pursue the conciliation process.

Article 8

Upon termination of the conciliation, the conciliator shall provide the Secretariat of the Court with the settlement agreement signed by the parties or with his report of lack of success or with a notice from one or more parties of the intention no longer to pursue the conciliation process.

Article 9

Upon the file being opened, the Secretariat of the Court shall fix the sum required to permit the process to proceed, taking into consideration the nature and importance of the dispute. Such sum shall be paid in equal shares by the parties.

This sum shall cover the estimated fees of the conciliator, expenses of the conciliation, and the administrative expenses as set out in Appendix III hereto.

In any case where, in the course of the conciliation process, the Secretariat of the Court shall decide that the sum originally paid is insufficient to cover the likely total costs of the conciliation, the Secretariat shall require the provision of an additional amount which shall be paid in equal shares by the parties.

Upon termination of the conciliation, the Secretariat shall settle the total costs of the process and advise the parties in writing.

All the above costs shall be borne in equal shares by the parties except and insofar as a settlement agreement provides otherwise.

A party's other expenditures shall remain the responsibility of the party.

Article 10

Unless the parties agree otherwise, a conciliator shall not act in any judicial or arbitration proceeding relating to the dispute which has been the subject of the conciliation process whether as an arbitrator, representative or counsel of a party.

The parties mutually undertake not to call the conciliator as a witness in any such proceedings, unless otherwise agreed between them.

Article 11

The parties agree not to introduce in any judicial or arbitration proceeding as evidence or in any manner whatsoever:

a) any views expressed or suggestions made by any party with regard to the possible settlement of the dispute;

b) any proposals put forward by the conciliator;

c) the fact that a party had indicated that it was ready to accept some proposal for a settlement put forward by the conciliator.

b. I.C.C. Rules of Arbitration.

Article 1—Court of Arbitration

1. The Court of Arbitration of the International Chamber of Commerce is the international arbitration body attached to the International Chamber of Commerce. Members of the Court are appointed by the Council of the International Chamber of Commerce. The function of the Court is to provide for the settlement by arbitration of business disputes of an international character in accordance with these Rules.

2. In principle, the Court meets once a month. It draws up its own internal regulations.

3. The Chairman of the Court of Arbitration or his deputy shall have power to take urgent decisions on behalf of the Court, provided that any such decision shall be reported to the Court at its next session.

4. The Court may, in the manner provided for in its internal regulations, delegate to one or more groups of its members the power to take certain decisions provided that any such decision shall be reported to the Court at its next session.

5. The Secretariat of the Court of Arbitration shall be at the Headquarters of the International Chamber of Commerce.

Article 2—The arbitral tribunal

1. The Court of Arbitration does not itself settle disputes. Insofar as the parties shall not have provided otherwise, it appoints, or confirms the appointments of, arbitrators in accordance with the provisions of this Article. In making or confirming such appointment, the Court shall have regard to the proposed arbitrator's nationality, residence and other relationships with the countries of which the parties or the other arbitrators are nationals.

2. The disputes may be settled by a sole arbitrator or by three arbitrators. In the following Articles the word "arbitrator" denotes a single arbitrator or three arbitrators as the case may be.

3. Where the parties have agreed that the disputes shall be settled by a sole arbitrator, they may, by agreement, nominate him for confirmation by the Court. If the parties fail so to nominate a sole arbitrator within 30 days from the date when the Claimant's Request for Arbitration has been communicated to the other party, the sole arbitrator shall be appointed by the Court.

4. Where the dispute is to be referred to three arbitrators, each party shall nominate in the Request for Arbitration and the Answer thereto respectively one arbitrator for confirmation by the Court. Such person shall be independent of the party nominating him. If a party fails to nominate an arbitrator, the appointment shall be made by the Court.

The third arbitrator, who will act as chairman of the arbitral tribunal, shall be appointed by the Court, unless the parties have provided that the arbitrators nominated by them shall agree on the third arbitrator within a fixed time-limit. In such a case the Court shall confirm the appointment of such third arbitrator. Should the two arbitrators fail, within the time-limit fixed by the parties or the Court, to reach agreement on the third arbitrator, he shall be appointed by the Court.

5. Where the parties have not agreed upon the number of arbitrators, the Court shall appoint a sole arbitrator, save where it appears to the Court that the dispute is such as to warrant the appointment of three arbitrators. In such a case the parties shall each have a period of 30 days within which to nominate an arbitrator.

6. Where the Court is to appoint a sole arbitrator or the chairman of an arbitral tribunal, it shall make the appointment after having requested a proposal from a National Committee of the ICC that it considers to be appropriate. If the Court does not accept the proposal made, or if said National Committee fails to make the proposal requested within the time-limit fixed by the Court, the Court may repeat its request or may request a proposal from another appropriate National Committee.

Where the Court considers that the circumstances so demand, it may choose the sole arbitrator or the chairman of the arbitral tribunal from a country where there is no National Committee, provided that neither of the parties objects within the time-limit fixed by the Court.

The sole arbitrator or the chairman of the arbitral tribunal shall be chosen from a country other than those of which the parties are nationals. However, in suitable circumstances and provided that neither of the parties objects within the time-limit fixed by the Court, the sole arbitrator or the chairman of the arbitral tribunal may be chosen from a country of which any of the parties is a national.

Where the Court is to appoint an arbitrator on behalf of a party which has failed to nominate one, it shall make the appointment after having requested a proposal from the National Committee of the country of which the said party is a national. If the Court does not accept the proposal made, or if said National Committee fails to make the proposal requested within the time-limit fixed by the Court, or if the country of which the said party is a national has no National Committee, the Court shall be at liberty to choose any person whom it regards as suitable, after having informed the National Committee of the country of which such person is a national, if one exists.

7. Every arbitrator appointed or confirmed by the Court must be and remain independent of the parties involved in the arbitration.

Before appointment or confirmation by the Court, a prospective arbitrator shall disclose in writing to the Secretary General of the Court any facts or circumstances which might be of such a nature as to call into question the arbitrator's independence in the eyes of the parties. Upon receipt of such information, the Secretary General of the Court shall provide it to the parties in writing and fix a time-limit for any comments from them.

An arbitrator shall immediately disclose in writing to the Secretary General of the Court and the parties any facts or circumstances of a similar nature which may arise between the arbitrator's appointment or confirmation by the Court and the notification of the final award.

8. A challenge of an arbitrator, whether for an alleged lack of independence or otherwise, is made by the submission to the Secretary General of the Court of a written statement specifying the facts and circumstances on which the challenge is based.

For a challenge to be admissible, it must be sent by a party either within 30 days from receipt by that party of the notification of the appointment or confirmation of the arbitrator by the Court; or within 30 days from the date when the party making the challenge was informed of the facts and circumstances on which the challenge is based, if such date is subsequent to the receipt of the aforementioned notification.

9. The Court shall decide on the admissibility, and at the same time if need be on the merits, of a challenge after the Secretary General of the Court has accorded an opportunity for the arbitrator concerned, the parties and any other members of the arbitral tribunal to comment in writing within a suitable period of time.

10. An arbitrator shall be replaced upon his death, upon the acceptance by the Court of a challenge, or upon the acceptance by the Court of the arbitrator's resignation.

11. An arbitrator shall also be replaced when the Court decides that he is prevented de jure or de facto from fulfilling his functions, or that he is not fulfilling his functions in accordance with the Rules or within the prescribed time-limits.

When, on the basis of information that has come to its attention, the Court considers applying the preceding subparagraph, it shall decide on the matter after the Secretary General of the Court has provided such information in writing to the arbitrator concerned, the parties and any other members of the arbitral tribunal, and accorded an opportunity to them to comment in writing within a suitable period of time.

12. In each instance where an arbitrator is to be replaced, the procedure indicated in the preceding paragraphs 3, 4, 5 and 6 shall be followed. Once reconstituted, and after having invited the parties to comment, the arbitral tribunal shall determine if and to what extent prior proceedings shall again take place.

13. Decisions of the Court as to the appointment, confirmation, challenge or replacement of an arbitrator shall be final.

The reasons for decisions by the Court as to the appointment, confirmation, challenge, or replacement of an arbitrator on the grounds that he is not fulfilling his functions in accordance with the Rules or within the prescribed time-limits, shall not be communicated.

Article 3—Request for arbitration

1. A party wishing to have recourse to arbitration by the International Chamber of Commerce shall submit its Request for Arbitration to the Secretary of the Court, through its National Committee or directly. In this latter case the Secretariat shall bring the Request to the notice of the National Committee concerned.

The date when the Request is received by the Secretariat of the Court shall, for all purposes, be deemed to be the date of commencement of the arbitral proceedings.

2. The Request for Arbitration shall inter alia contain the following information:

    a) names in full, description, and addresses of the parties,

    b) a statement of the Claimant's case,

    c) the relevant agreements, and in particular the agreement to arbitrate, and such documentation or information as will serve clearly to establish the circumstances of the case,

    d) all relevant particulars concerning the number of arbitrators and their choice in accordance with the provisions of Art. 2 above.

3. The Secretariat shall send a copy of the Request and the documents annexed thereto to the Defendant for his Answer.

Article 4—Answer to the request

1. The Defendant shall within 30 days from the receipt of the documents referred to in paragraph 3 of Art. 3 comment on the proposals made concerning the number of arbitrators and their choice and, where appropriate, nominate an arbitrator. He shall at the same time set out his defence and supply relevant documents. In exceptional circumstances the Defendant may apply to the Secretariat for an extension of time for the filing of his defence and his documents. The application must, however, include the Defendant's comments on the proposals made with regard to the number of arbitrators and their choice and also, where appropriate, the nomination of an arbitrator. If the Defendant fails so to do, the Secretariat shall report to the Court, which shall proceed with the arbitration in accordance with these Rules.

2. A copy of the Answer and of the documents annexed thereto, if any, shall be communicated to the Claimant for his information.

Article 5—Counter-claim

1. If the Defendant wishes to make a counter-claim, he shall file the same with the Secretariat, at the same time as his Answer as provided for in Art. 4.

2. It shall be open to the Claimant to file a Reply with the Secretariat within 30 days from the date when the counter-claim was communicated to him.

Article 6—Pleadings and written statements, notifications or communications

1. All pleadings and written statements submitted by the parties, as well as all documents annexed thereto, shall be supplied in a number of copies sufficient to provide one copy for each party, plus one for each arbitrator, and one for the Secretariat.

2. All notifications or communications from the Secretariat and the arbitrator shall be validly made if they are delivered against receipt or forwarded by registered

post to the address or last known address of the party for whom the same are intended as notified by the party in question or by the other party as appropriate.

3. Notification or communication shall be deemed to have been effected on the day when it was received, or should, if made in accordance with the preceding paragraph, have been received by the party itself or by its representative.

4. Periods of time specified in the present Rules or in the Internal Rules or set by the Court pursuant to its authority under any of these Rules shall start to run on the day following the date a notification or communication is deemed to have been effected in accordance with the preceding paragraph. When, in the country where the notification or communication is deemed to have been effected, the day next following such date is an official holiday or a non-business day, the period of time shall commence on the first following working day. Official holidays and non-working days are included in the calculation of the period of time. If the last day of the relevant period of time granted is an official holiday or a non-business day in the country where the notification or communication is deemed to have been effected, the period of time shall expire at the end of the first following working day.

Article 7—Absence of agreement to arbitrate

Where there is no prima facie agreement between the parties to arbitrate or where there is an agreement but it does not specify the International Chamber of Commerce, and if the Defendant does not file an Answer within the period of 30 days provided by paragraph 1 of Art. 4 or refuses arbitration by the International Chamber of Commerce, the Claimant shall be informed that the arbitration cannot proceed.

Article 8—Effect of the agreement to arbitrate

1. Where the parties have agreed to submit to arbitration by the International Chamber of Commerce, they shall be deemed thereby to have submitted ipso facto to the present Rules.

2. If one of the parties refuses or fails to take part in the arbitration, the arbitration shall proceed notwithstanding such refusal or failure.

3. Should one of the Parties raise one or more pleas concerning the existence or validity of the agreement to arbitrate, and should the Court be satisfied of the prima facie existence of such an agreement, the Court may, without prejudice to the admissibility or merits of the plea or pleas, decide that the arbitration shall proceed. In such a case any decision as to the arbitrator's jurisdiction shall be taken by the arbitrator himself.

4. Unless otherwise provided, the arbitrator shall not cease to have jurisdiction by reason of any claim that the contract is null and void or allegation that it is inexistent provided that he upholds the validity of the agreement to arbitrate. He shall continue to have jurisdiction, even though the contract itself may be inexistent or null

and void, to determine the respective rights of the parties and to adjudicate upon their claims and pleas.

5. Before the file is transmitted to the arbitrator, and in exceptional circumstances even thereafter, the parties shall be at liberty to apply to any competent judicial authority for interim or conservatory measures, and they shall not by so doing be held to infringe the agreement to arbitrate or to affect the relevant powers reserved to the arbitrator. Any such application and any measures taken by the judicial authority must be notified without delay to the Secretariat of the Court of Arbitration. The Secretariat shall inform the arbitrator thereof.

Article 9—Advance to cover costs of arbitration

1. The Court shall fix the amount of the advance on costs in a sum likely to cover the costs of arbitration of the claims which have been referred to it. Where, apart from the principal claim one or more counter-claims are submitted, the Court may fix separate advances on costs for the principal claim and he counter-claim or counter-claims.

2. The advance on costs shall be payable in equal shares by the Claimant or Claimants and the Defendant or Defendants. However, any one party shall be free to pay the whole of the advance on costs in respect of the claim or the counter-claim should the other party fail to pay its share.

3. The Secretariat may make the transmission of the file to the arbitrator conditional upon the payment by the parties or one of them of the whole or part of the advance on costs to the International Chamber of Commerce.

4. When the Terms of Reference are communicated to the Court in accordance with the provisions of Art. 13, the Court shall verify whether the requests for the advance on costs have been complied with.

The Terms of Reference shall only become operative and the arbitrator shall only proceed in respect of those claims for which the advance on costs has been duly paid to the International Chamber of Commerce.

Article 10—Transmission of the file to the arbitrator

Subject to the provisions of Art. 9, the Secretariat shall transmit the file to the arbitrator as soon as it has received the Defendant's Answer to the Request for Arbitration, at the latest upon the expiry of the time-limits fixed in Arts. 4 and 5 above for the filing of these documents.

Article 11—Rules governing the proceedings

The rules governing the proceedings before the arbitrator shall be those resulting from these Rules and, where these Rules are silent, any rules which the parties (or, failing them, the arbitrator) may settle, and whether or not reference is thereby made to a municipal procedural law to be applied to the arbitration.

Article 12—Place of arbitration

The place of arbitration shall be fixed by the Court, unless agreed upon by the parties.

Article 13—Terms of reference

1. Before proceeding with the preparation of the case, the arbitrator shall draw up, on the basis of the documents or in the presence of the parties and in the light of their most recent submissions, a document defining his Terms of Reference. This document shall include the following particulars:
    a) the full names and description of the parties,
    b) the addresses of the parties to which notifications or communications arising in the course of the arbitration may validly be made,
    c) a summary of the parties' respective claims,
    d) definition of the issues to be determined,
    e) the arbitrator's full name, description and address,
    f) the place of arbitration,
    g) particulars of the applicable procedural rules and, if such is the case, reference to the power conferred upon the arbitrator to act as amiable compositeur.
    h) such other particulars as may be required to make the arbitral award enforceable in law, or may be regarded as helpful by the Court of Arbitration or the arbitrator.

2. The document mentioned in paragraph 1 of this Article shall be signed by the parties and the arbitrator. Within two months of the date when the file has been transmitted to him, the arbitrator shall transmit to the Court the said document signed by himself and by the parties. The Court may, pursuant to a reasoned request from the arbitrator or if need be on its own initiative, extend this time-limit if it decides it is necessary to do so.

Should one of the parties refuse to take part in the drawing up of the said document or to sign the same, the Court, if it is satisfied that the case is one of those mentioned in paragraphs 2 and 3 of Art. 8, shall take such action as is necessary for its approval. Thereafter the Court shall set a time-limit for the signature of the statement by the defaulting party and on expiry of that time-limit the arbitration shall proceed and the award shall he made.

3. The parties shall be free to determine the law to be applied by the arbitrator to the merits of the dispute. In the absence of any indication by the parties as to the applicable law, the arbitrator shall apply the law designated as the proper law by ICC rule of conflict which he deems appropriate.

4. The arbitrator shall assume the powers of an amiable compositeur if the parties are agreed to give him such powers.

5. In all cases the arbitrator shall take account of the provisions of the contract and the relevant trade usages.

Article 14—The arbitral proceedings

1. The arbitrator shall proceed within as short a time as possible to establish the facts of the case by all appropriate means. After study of the written submissions of the parties and of all documents relied upon, the arbitrator shall hear the parties together in person if one of them so requests; and failing such a request he may of his own motion decide to help them.

In addition, the arbitrator may decide to hear any other person in the presence of the parties or in their absence provided they have been duly summoned.

2. The arbitrator may appoint one or more experts, define their Terms of Reference, receive their reports and/or hear them in person.

3. The arbitrator may decide the case on the relevant documents alone if the parties so request or agree.

Article 15

1. At the request of one of the parties or if necessary on his own initiative, the arbitrator, giving reasonable notice, shall summon the parties to appear before him on the day and at the place appointed by him and shall so inform the Secretariat of the Court.

2. If one of the parties, although duly summoned, fails to appear, the arbitrator, if he is satisfied that the summons was duly received and the party is absent without valid excuse, shall have power to proceed with the arbitration, and such proceedings shall be deemed to have been conducted in the presence of all parties.

3. The arbitrator shall determine the language or languages of the arbitration, due regard being paid to all the relevant circumstances and in particular to the language of the contract.

4. The arbitrator shall be in full charge of the hearings, at which all the parties shall be entitled to be present. Save with the approval of the arbitrator and of the parties, persons not involved in the proceedings shall not be admitted.

5. The parties may appear in person or through duly accredited agents. In addition, they may be assisted by advisers.

Article 16

The parties may make new claims or counter-claims before the arbitrator on condition that these remain within the limits fixed by the Terms of Reference provided for in Art. 13 or that they are specified in a rider to that document, signed by the parties and communicated to the Court.

Article 17—Award by consent

If the parties reach a settlement after the file has been transmitted to the arbitrator in accordance with Art. 10, the same shall be recorded in the form of an arbitral award made by consent of the parties.

Article 18—Time-limit for award

1. The time-limit within which the arbitrator must render his award is fixed at six months. Once the terms of Art. 9(4) have been satisfied, such time-limit shall start to run from the date of the last signature by the arbitrator or of the parties of the document mentioned in Art. 13, or from the expiry of the time-limit granted to a party by virtue of Art. 13(2), or from the date that the Secretary General of the Court notifies the arbitrator that the advance on costs is paid in full, if such notification occurs later.

2. The Court may, pursuant to a reasoned request from the arbitrator or if need be on its own initiative, extend this time-limit if it decides it is necessary to do so.

3. Where no such extension is granted and, if appropriate, after application of the provisions of Art. 2(11), the Court shall determine the manner in which the dispute is to be resolved.

Article 19—Award by three arbitrators

When three arbitrators have been appointed, the award is given by a majority decision. If there be no majority, the award shall be made by the Chairman of the arbitral tribunal alone.

Article 20—Decision as to costs of arbitration

1. The arbitrator's award shall, in addition to dealing with the merits of the case, fix the costs of the arbitration and decide which of the parties shall bear the costs or in what proportions the costs shall be borne by the parties.

2. The costs of the arbitration shall include the arbitrator's fees and the administrative costs fixed by the Court in accordance with the scale annexed to the present Rules, the expenses, if any, of the arbitrator, the fees and expenses of any experts, and the normal legal costs incurred by the parties.

3. The Court may fix the arbitrator's fees at a figure higher or lower than that which would result from the application of the annexed scale if in the exceptional circumstances of the case this appears to be necessary.

Article 21—Scrutiny of award by the Court

Before signing an award, whether partial or definitive, the arbitrator shall submit it in draft form to the Court. The Court may lay down modifications as to the form of the award and, without affecting the arbitrator's liberty of decision, may also draw his attention to points of substance. No award shall be signed until it has been approved by the Court as to its form.

Article 22—Making of award

The arbitral award shall be deemed to be made at the place of the arbitration proceedings and on the date when it is signed by the arbitrator.

Article 23—Notification of award to parties

1. Once an award has been made, the Secretariat shall notify to the parties the text signed by the arbitrator; provided always that the costs of the arbitration have been fully paid to the International Chamber of Commerce by the parties or by one of them.

2. Additional copies certified true by the Secretary General of the Court shall be made available, on request and at any time, to the parties but to no one else.

3. By virtue of the notification made in accordance with paragraph 1 of this article, the parties waive any other form of notification or deposit on the part of the arbitrator.

Article 24—Finality and enforceability of award

1. The arbitral award shall be final.

2. By submitting the dispute to arbitration by the International Chamber of Commerce, the parties shall be deemed to have undertaken to carry out the resulting award without delay and to have waived their right to any form of appeal insofar as such waiver can validly be made.

Article 25—Deposit of award

An original of each award made in accordance with the present Rules shall be deposited with the Secretariat of the Court. The arbitrator and the Secretariat of the Court shall assist the parties in complying with whatever further formalities may be necessary.

Article 26—General rule

In all matters not expressly provided for in these Rules, the Court of Arbitration and the arbitrator shall act in the spirit of these Rules and shall make every effort to make sure that the award is enforceable at law.

I.C.C. APPENDIX I—STATUTES OF THE ICC COURT OF ARBITRATION

Article 1—Appointment of members

The members of the Court of Arbitration of the International Chamber of Commerce are appointed for a term of three years by the Council of that Chamber pursuant to Art. 5.3i of the Constitution, on the proposal of each National Committee.

Article 2—Composition

The Court of Arbitration shall be composed of a Chairman, of eight Vice-Chairmen, of a Secretary General and of one or several Technical Advisers chosen by the Council of the International Chamber of Commerce either from among the members of the Court or apart from them, and of one member for, and appointed by, each National Committee.

The chairmanship may be exercised by two Co-Chairmen; in this case, they shall have equal rights, and the expression "the Chairman", used in the Rules of Conciliation and Arbitration, shall apply to either of them equally.

When a member of the Court does not reside in the city where International Headquarters of the International Chamber of Commerce is situated, the Council may appoint an alternate member.

If the Chairman is unable to attend a session of the Court, he shall be replaced by one of the Vice-Chairmen.

Article 3—Function and powers

The function of the Court of Arbitration is to ensure the application of the Rules of Conciliation and Arbitration of the International Chamber of Commerce, and the Court has all the necessary powers for that purpose. It is further entrusted, if need be, with laying before the Commission on International Arbitration any proposals for modifying the Rules of Conciliation and Arbitration of the International Chamber of Commerce which it considers necessary.

Article 4—Deliberations and quorum

The decisions of the Court shall be taken by a majority vote, the Chairman having a casting vote in the event of a tie. The deliberations of the Court shall be valid when at least six members are present.

The Secretary General of the International Chamber of Commerce, the Secretary General of the Court and the Technical Adviser or Advisers shall attend in an advisory capacity only.

I.C.C. APPENDIX II—INTERNAL RULES OF THE ICC COURT OF ARBITRATION

Role of the Court of Arbitration

1. The Court of Arbitration may accept jurisdiction over business disputes not of an international business nature, if it has jurisdiction by reason of an arbitration agreement.

Confidential character of the work of the Court of Arbitration

2. The work of the Court of Arbitration is of a confidential character which must be respected by everyone who participates in that work in whatever capacity.

3. The sessions of the Court of Arbitration, whether plenary or those of a Committee of the Court, are open only to its members and to the Secretariat.

However, in exceptional circumstances and, if need be, after obtaining the opinion of members of the Court, the Chairman of the Court of Arbitration may invite honorary members of the Court and authorize observers to attend. Such persons must respect the confidential character of the work of the Court.

4. The documents submitted to the Court of Arbitration or drawn up by it in the course of the proceedings it conducts are communicated only to the members of the Court and to the Secretariat.

The Chairman or the Secretary General of the Court may nevertheless authorize researchers undertaking work of a scientific nature on international trade law to acquaint themselves with certain documents of general interest, with the exception of memoranda, notes, statements and documents remitted by the parties within the framework of arbitration proceedings.

Such authorization shall not be given unless the beneficiary has undertaken to respect the confidential character of the documents made available and to refrain from any publication in their respect without having previously submitted the text for approval to the Secretary General of the Court.

Participation of members of the Court of Arbitration in ICC arbitration

5. Owing to the special responsibilities laid upon them by the ICC Rules of Arbitration, the Chairman, the Vice-Chairmen and the Secretariat of the Court of Arbitration may not personally act as arbitrators or as counsel in cases submitted to ICC arbitration.

The members of the Court of Arbitration may not be directly appointed as co-arbitrators, sole arbitrator or Chairman of an arbitral tribunal by the Court of Arbitration. They may however be proposed for such duties by one or more of the parties, subject to confirmation by the Court.

6. When the Chairman, a Vice-Chairman or a member of the Court of Arbitration is involved, in any capacity whatsoever, in proceedings pending before the Court, he must inform the Secretary General of the Court as soon as he becomes aware of such involvement.

He must refrain from participating in the discussions or in the decisions of the Court concerning the proceedings and he must be absent from the courtroom whenever the matter is considered.

He will not receive documentation or information submitted to the Court of Arbitration during the proceedings.

Relations between the members of the Court and the ICC National Committees

7. By virtue of their capacity, the members of the Court are independent of the ICC National Committees which proposed them for nomination by the ICC Council.

Furthermore, they must regard as confidential, vis-à-vis the said National Committees, any information concerning individual disputes with which they have become acquainted in their capacity as members of the Court except when they have been requested, by the Chairman of the Court or by its Secretary General, to communicate that information to their respective National Committees.

Committee of the Court

8. In accordance with the provisions of Art. 1(4) of the ICC Rules of Arbitration, the Court of Arbitration hereby establishes a Committee of the Court composed as follows, and with the following powers.

9. The Committee consists of a Chairman and two members. The Chairman of the Court of Arbitration acts as the Chairman of the Committee. He may nevertheless designate a Vice-Chairmen of the Court to replace him during a session of the Committee.

The other two members of the Committee are appointed by the Court of Arbitration from among the Vice-Chairman or the other members of the Court. At each meeting of the Court it appoints the members who are to attend the meeting of the Committee to be held before the next plenary session of the Court.

10. The Committee meets when convened by its Chairman, in principle twice a month.

11.

a) The Committee is empowered to take any decision within the jurisdiction of the Court of Arbitration, with the exception of decisions concerning challenges of arbitrators (Arts. 2(8) and 2(9) of the ICC Rules of Arbitration), allegations that an arbitrator is not fulfilling his functions (Art. 2 (11) of the ICC Rules of Arbitration) and approval of draft awards other than awards made with the consent of the parties.

b) The decisions of the Committee are taken unanimously.

c) When the Committee cannot reach a decision or deems it preferable to abstain, it transfers the case to the next plenary session of the Court of Arbitration, making any suggestions it deems appropriate.

d) The Committee's proceedings are brought to the notice of the Court of Arbitration at its next plenary session.

Absence of an arbitration agreement

12. Where there is no prima facie arbitration agreement between the parties or where there is an agreement but it does not specify the ICC, the Secretariat draws the attention of the Claimant to the provisions laid down in Art. 7 of the Rules of Arbitration. The Claimant is entitled to require the decision to be taken by the Court of Arbitration.

This decision is of an administrative nature. If the Court decides that the arbitration solicited by the Claimant cannot proceed, the parties retain the right to ask the competent jurisdiction whether or not they are bound by an arbitration agreement in the light of the law applicable.

If the Court of Arbitration considers prima facie that the proceedings may take place, the arbitrator appointed has the duty to decide as to his own jurisdiction and, where such jurisdiction exists, as to the merits of the dispute.

Joinder of claims in arbitration proceedings

13. When a party presents a Request for Arbitration in connection with a legal relationship already submitted to arbitration proceedings by the same parties and pending before the Court of Arbitration, the Court may decide to include that claim in the existing proceedings, subject to the provisions of Art. 16 of the ICC Rules of Arbitration.

Advances to cover costs of arbitration

14. When the Court of Arbitration has set separate advances on costs for a specific case in accordance with Art. 9(1) (sub para. 2) of the ICC Rules of Arbitration, the Secretariat requests each of the parties to pay the amount corresponding to its claims, without prejudice to the right of the parties to pay the said advances on costs in equal shares, if they deem it advisable.

15. When a request for an advance on costs has not been complied with, the Secretariat may set a time-limit, which must not be less than 30 days, on the expiry of which the relevant claim, whether principal claim or counter-claim, shall be considered as withdrawn. This does not prevent the party in question from lodging a new claim at a later date.

Should one of the parties wish to object to this measure, he must make a request, within the aforementioned period, for the matter to be decided by the Court of Arbitration.

16. If one of the parties claims a right to a set-off with regard to either a principal claim or counter-claim, such set-off is taken into account in determining the advance to cover the costs of arbitration, in the same way as a separate claim, insofar as it may require the arbitrators to consider additional matters.

Arbitral awards: form

17. When it scrutinizes draft arbitral awards in accordance with Art. 21 of the ICC Rules of Arbitration, the Court of Arbitration pays particular attention to the respect of the formal requirements laid down by the law applicable to the proceedings and, where relevant, by the mandatory rules of the place of arbitration, notably with regard to the reasons for awards, their signature and the admissibility of dissenting opinions.

Arbitrators' fees

18. In setting the arbitrators' fees on the basis of the scale attached to the ICC Rules of Arbitration, the Court of Arbitration takes into consideration the time spent, the rapidity of the proceedings and the complexity of the dispute, so as to arrive at a figure within the limits specified or, when circumstances require, higher or lower than those limits (Art. 20(3) of the ICC Rules of Arbitration).

I.C.C. APPENDIX III—SCHEDULE OF ICC CONCILIATION AND ARBITRATION COSTS (in force as from January 1, 1993)

1. Costs of conciliation

a) The administrative expenses for a conciliation procedure shall be fixed at one-quarter of the amount calculated in accordance with the scale of administrative expenses hereinafter set out. Where the sum in dispute in a conciliation procedure is not stated, the Secretary General of the Court of Arbitration shall fix the administrative expenses at his discretion.

b) The fee of the conciliator to be paid by the parties shall be fixed by the Secretary General of the Court of Arbitration. Such fee shall be reasonable in amount, taking into consideration the time spent, the complexity of the dispute and any other relevant circumstances.

2. Costs of arbitration

a) The advance on costs fixed by the Court of Arbitration comprises the fee(s) of the arbitrator(s), any personal expenses of the arbitrator(s) and the administrative expenses.

b) The submission of any claim or counter-claim to the arbitrator(s) shall be made only after at least half of the advance on costs fixed by the Court has been satisfied. Terms of Reference shall only become operative and the arbitrator(s) shall only proceed in respect of those claims and counter-claims for which the totality of the advance on costs fixed by the Court has been satisfied.

c) The Court shall fix the administrative expenses of each arbitration in accordance with the scale hereinafter set out or, where the sum in dispute is not stated, at its discretion. If exceptional circumstances so require, the Court may fix the administrative expenses at a lower figure than that which would result from application of said scale.

d) Subject to Art. 20(3) of the ICC Rules of Arbitration, the Court shall fix the fee(s) of the arbitrator(s) in accordance with the scale hereinafter set out or, where the sum in dispute is not stated, at its discretion.

e) When a case is submitted to more than one arbitrator, the Court, at its discretion, shall have the right to increase the total fees up to a maximum of three times the fee payable to one arbitrator.

f) When arbitration is preceded by attempted conciliation, one-half of the administrative expenses paid in respect of the said attempt shall be credited to the administrative expenses of the arbitration.

g) Before any expertise can be commenced, the parties, or one of them, shall pay an advance on costs fixed by the arbitrator(s) sufficient to cover the expected fee and expenses of the expert as determined by the arbitrator(s).

3. Advance on administrative expenses

a) Each party to a dispute submitted to conciliation under the Rules of Optional Conciliation of the ICC is required to make an advance payment of US$ 500 on the administrative expenses.

b) Each request to open an arbitration pursuant to the ICC Rules of Arbitration must be accompanied by an advance payment of US$ 2,000 on the administrative expenses.

c) No request for conciliation or arbitration will be entertained unless accompanied by the appropriate payment. This payment is not recoverable and becomes the property of the ICC. Such payment by a party shall be credited to its portion of the administrative expenses for the conciliation or arbitration, as the case may be.

4. Appointment of arbitrators

A registration fee of US$ 2,000 is payable by the requesting party in respect of each request made to the ICC to appoint an arbitrator for any arbitration not conducted under the ICC Rules of Arbitration. No request for appointment of an arbitrator will be entertained unless accompanied by said fee, which is not recoverable and becomes the property of the ICC.

Such fee shall cover any additional services rendered by the ICC regarding the appointment, such as decisions on a challenge of the arbitrator and the appointment of a substitute arbitrator.

5. Scales of administrative expenses and of arbitrator's fees

To calculate the administrative expenses and the arbitrator's fees, the amounts calculated for each successive slice of the sum in dispute must be added together, except that where the sum in dispute is over US$ 80 million, a flat amount of US$ 65,500 shall constitute the entirety of the administrative expenses.

A. Administrative Expenses

SUM IN DISPUTE (IN US DOLLARS)	ADMINISTRATIVE EXPENSES
UP TO 50,000	$2,000
FROM 50,000 to 100,000	3.00%
FROM 100,001 to 500,000	1.50%
FROM 500,001 to 1,000,000	1.00%
FROM 1,000,001 to 2,000,000	0.50%
FROM 2,000,001 to 5,000,000	0.20%
FROM 5,000,001 to 10,000,000	0.10%
FROM 10,000,001 to 80,000,000	0.05%
OVER 80,000,000	$65,500

B. Arbitrator's Fees

SUM IN DISPUTE (IN US DOLLARS)	MINIMUM	MAXIMUM
UP TO 50,000	$ 2,000	15.00%
FROM 50,001 to 100,000	1.50%	10.00%
FROM 100,001 to 500,000	0.80%	5.00%
FROM 500,001 to 1,000,000	0.50%	3.00%
FROM 1,000,001 to 2,000,000	0.30%	2.50%
FROM 2,000,001 to 5,000,000	0.20%	0.80%
FROM 5,000,001 to 10,000,000	0.10%	0.50%
FROM 10,000,001 to 50,000,000	0.05%	0.15%
FROM 50,000,001 to 100,000,000	0.02%	0.10%
OVER 100,000,000	0.01%	0.05%

7. LONDON COURT OF INTERNATIONAL ARBITRATION.

Article 1—Request for Arbitration

Any party wishing to commence an arbitration under these Rules ("the Claimant") shall send to the Registrar of the Court ("the Registrar") a written request for arbitration ("the Request") which shall include, or be accompanied by:

(a) the names and addresses of the parties to the arbitration;

(b) copies of the contractual documents in which the arbitration clause is contained or under which the arbitration arises;

(c) a brief statement describing the nature and circumstances of the dispute, and specifying the relief claimed;

(d) a statement of any matters (such as the place or language of the arbitration, or the number of arbitrators, or their qualifications or identities) on which the parties have already agreed in relation to the conduct of the arbitration, or with respect to which the requesting party wishes to make a proposal;

(e) if the arbitration agreement calls for party nomination of arbitrators, the name and address (and telephone and telex numbers, if known) of the Claimant's nominee;

(f) the fee prescribed in the Schedule of Costs; and shall confirm to the Registrar that copies have been served on the other parties. The date of receipt by the Registrar of the Request for Arbitration shall be deemed to be the date on which the arbitration has commenced.

Article 2—Response by Respondent

2.1 For the purpose of facilitating the choice of arbitrators, within 30 days of receipt of its copy of the Request for Arbitration the Respondent may send to the Registrar a Response containing:

(a) confirmation or denial of all or part of the claims;

(b) a brief statement of the nature and circumstances of any envisaged counter-claims;

(c) comment in response to any statements contained in the Request, as called for under Article 1(d), on matters relating to the conduct of the arbitration:

(d) if the arbitration agreement calls for party nomination of arbitrators, the name and address (and telephone and telex numbers if known) of the Respondent's nominee; and shall confirm to the Registrar that copies have been served on the other parties.

2.2 Failure to send a Response shall not preclude the Respondent from denying the claim nor from setting out a counterclaim in its Statement of Defence. However, if the arbitration agreement calls for party nomination of arbitrators, failure to send a Response or to nominate an arbitrator in it shall constitute a waiver of the opportunity to nominate an arbitrator.

Article 3—The Arbitral Tribunal

3.1 In these Rules, the expression "the Tribunal" includes a sole arbitrator or all the arbitrators where more than one is appointed. All arbitrators (whether or not nominated by the parties) conducting an arbitration under these Rules shall be and remain at all times wholly independent and impartial, and shall not act as advocates for any party. Before appointment by the Court, if the Registrar so requests, any arbitrator shall furnish a resume of his past and present professional positions (which will be communicated to the parties). In any event every arbitrator shall sign a declaration to the effect that there are no circumstances likely to give rise to any justified doubts as to his impartiality or independence, and that he will forthwith disclose any such circumstances to the Court and to all the parties if they should arise after that time and before the arbitration is concluded.

3.2 The Court will appoint the Tribunal to determine the dispute as soon as practicable after receipt by the Registrar of the Response, or after the expiry of 30 days following receipt by the Respondent of the Request if no Response is received, provided that the Registrar is satisfied that the Request has been properly served. A sole arbitrator will be appointed unless the parties have agreed otherwise, or unless the Court determines that in view of all the circumstances of the case a three-member tribunal is appropriate.

3.3 The Court alone is empowered to appoint arbitrators and such appointment will be made in the name of the Court by the President or any Vice President of the Court. The Court will appoint arbitrators with due regard for any particular method or criteria of selection agreed by the parties. In selecting arbitrators consideration will be given, so far as possible, to the nature of the contract, the nature and circumstances of the dispute, and the nationality, location and languages of the parties. Where the parties are of different nationalities, then unless they have agreed otherwise, sole arbitrators or chairmen are not to be appointed if they have the same nationality as any party (the nationality of parties being understood to include that of

C. Illustrative Calculation of I.C.C. Fees and Expenses

Sum in Dispute (in US Dollars)	A. Administrative Expenses (in U.S. Dollars)	B. Arbitrator's Fees (in U.S. Dollars)	
		Minimum	Maximum
Up to 50,000	2,000	2,000	15.00% of the Sum in Dispute
FROM 50,001 to 100,000	2,000 + 3.00% of Amt. over 50,000	2,000 + 1.5% of Amt. Over 50,000	7,500 + 10.00% of Amt. Over 50,000
FROM 100,001 to 500,000	3,500 + 1.50% of Amt. over 100,000	2,750 + 0.80% of Amt. over 100,000	12,500 + 5.00% of Amt. over 100,000
FROM 500,001 to 1,000,000	9,500 + 1.00% of Amt. over 500,000	5,950 + 0.50% of Amt. over 500,000	32,500 + 3.00% of Amt. over 500,000
FROM 1,000,001 to 2,000,000	14,500 + 0.5% of Amt. over 1,000,000	8,450 + 0.30% of Amt. over 1,000,000	47,500 + 2.5% of Amt. over 1,000,000
FROM 2,000,001 to 5,000,000	19,500 + 0.20% of Amt. over 2,000,000	11,450 + 0.20% of Amt. over 2,000,000	72,500 + 0.80% of Amt. over 2,000,000
FROM 5,000,001 to 10,000,000	25,000 + 0.10% of Amt. over 5,000,000	17,450 + 0.10% of Amt. over 5,000,000	96,500 + 0.50% of Amt. over 5,000,000
FROM 10,000,001 to 50,000,000	30,500 + 0.05% of Amt. over 10,000,000	22,450 + 0.05% of Amt. over 10,000,000	121,500 + 0.15% of Amt. over 10,000,000
FROM 50,000,001 to 80,000,000	50,500 + 0.05% of Amt. over 50,000,000	42,450 + 0.02% of Amt. over 50,000,000	181,500 + 0.10% of Amt. over 50,000,000
FROM 80,000,001 to 100,000,000	65,500	48,450 + 0.02% of Amt. over 80,000,000	211,500 + 0.10% of Amt. over 80,000,000
OVER 100,000,000	65,500	52,450 + 0.01% of Amt. over 100,000,000	231,500 + 0.05% of Amt. over 100,000,000

controlling shareholders or interests). If the parties have agreed that they are to nominate arbitrators themselves, or to allow two arbitrators, or a third party, to nominate an arbitrator, the Court may refuse to appoint such nominees if it determines that they are not suitable or independent or impartial. In the case of a three-member Tribunal the Court will designate the Chairman, who will not be a party-nominated arbitrator.

3.4 If the arbitration agreement calls for party nominations, and the Respondent fails to make such a nomination within the time limit established by Article 2, the Court will forthwith appoint an arbitrator in place of the arbitrator to be nominated by the Respondent. If the Request does not contain a nomination by the Claimant, and the Claimant fails to make such a nomination with the same time limit, the Court will likewise make that appointment.

3.5 In the event that the Court determines that a nominee is not suitable or independent or impartial, or if an appointed arbitrator is to be replaced, the Court shall have discretion to decide whether or not to follow the original nominating process. If it so decides any opportunity for renomination shall be waived if not exercised within 30 days, after which the Court shall appoint the replacement as soon as practicable.

3.6 If any arbitrator, after appointment, dies, refuses, or in the opinion of the Court becomes unable or unfit to act, the Court will, upon request by a party or by the remaining arbitrators, appoint another in accordance with the provisions of Article 3.5. If in the opinion of the Court an arbitrator acts in manifest violation of these Rules, or does not conduct the proceedings with reasonable diligence, he will be considered unfit.

3.7 An arbitrator may be challenged if circumstances exist that give rise to justifiable doubts as to his impartiality or independence. A party may challenge an arbitrator it has nominated, or in whose appointment it has participated, only for reasons of which it becomes aware after the appointment has been made.

3.8 A party who intends to challenge an arbitrator shall, within fifteen days of the constitution of the Tribunal or after becoming aware of any circumstances referred to in Article 3.6 or 3.7, whichever is the later, send a written statement of the reasons for the challenge to the Court. Unless the challenged arbitrator withdraws or the other party agrees to the challenge within 15 days of receipt of the written statement of challenge, the Court shall decide on the challenge.

3.9 The decision of the Court with respect to all matters referred to in this Article shall be final. Such decisions are deemed to be administrative in nature, and the Court shall not be required to give reasons for them. To the extent permitted by the law of the place of arbitration the parties shall be taken to have waived any right of appeal in respect of any such decisions to a court of law or other judicial authority. If such appeals remain possible due to mandatory provisions of the law of the place of arbitration, the Court shall, subject to the provisions of the applicable law, decide whether the arbitral proceedings are to continue notwithstanding an appeal.

Article 4—Communications between Parties and the Tribunal

4.1 Until the Tribunal is finally constituted and the Court determines that it would be appropriate for the parties and the Tribunal to communicate directly, all communications between parties and arbitrators shall be made through the Registrar. If and when the Court directs that communication shall take place directly between the Tribunal and the parties (with simultaneous copies to the Registrar) all further reference in these Rules to the Registrar shall thereafter be read as references to the Tribunal.

4.2 Where the Registrar, on behalf of the Tribunal, sends any communication to one party, he shall send a copy to each of the other parties.

4.3 Where any party sends any communication (including Statements under Article 6) to the Registrar, it shall include a copy for each arbitrator, and it shall also send copies to all the other parties and confirm to the Registrar in writing that it has done so.

4.4 The addresses of the parties for the purpose of all communications during the proceedings shall be those set out in the Request, or as any party may at any time notify to the Registrar and to the other parties.

Article 5—Conduct of the Proceedings

5.1 The parties may agree on the arbitral procedure, and are encouraged to do so.

5.2 In the absence of procedural rules agreed by the parties or contained herein, the Tribunal shall have the widest discretion allowed under such law as may be applicable to ensure the just, expeditious, economical, and final determination of the dispute.

5.3 In the case of a three-member tribunal the Chairman may, after consulting the other arbitrators, make procedural rulings alone.

Article 6—Submission of Written Statements and Documents

6.1 Subject to any procedural rules agreed by the parties or determined by the Tribunal under Article 5, the written stage of the proceedings shall be as set out in this Article.

6.2 Within 30 days of receipt of notification from the Court of the appointment of the Tribunal, the Claimant shall send to the Registrar a Statement of Case setting out in sufficient detail the facts and any contentions of law on which it relies, and the relief claimed.

6.3 Within 40 days of receipt of the Statement of Case, the Respondent shall send to the Registrar a Statement of Defence stating in sufficient detail which of the facts and contentions of law in the Statement of Case it admits or denies, on what grounds, and on what other facts and contentions of law it relies. Any counterclaims shall be submitted with the Statement of Defence in the same manner as claims are set out in the Statement of Case.

6.4 Within 40 days of receipt of the Statement of Defence, the Claimant may send to the Registrar a Statement of Reply which, where there are counterclaims, shall include a Defence to Counterclaims.

6.5 If the Statement of Reply contains a Defence to Counterclaims, the Respondent has a further 40 days to send to the Registrar a Statement of Reply regarding Counterclaims.

6.6 All Statements referred to in this Article shall be accompanied by copies (of, if they are especially voluminous, lists) of all essential documents on which the party concerned relies and which have not previously been submitted by any party, and (where appropriate) by any relevant samples.

6.7 As soon as practicable following completion of the submission of the Statements specified in this Article, the Tribunal shall proceed in such a manner as has been agreed by the parties, or pursuant to its authority under these Rules. If the Respondent fails to submit a Statement of Defence, or if at any point any party fails to avail itself of the opportunity to present its case in the manner directed by the Tribunal, the Tribunal may nevertheless proceed with the arbitration and make the award.

Article 7—Place of Arbitration

7.1 The parties may choose the place of arbitration. Failing such a choice, the place of arbitration shall be London, unless the Tribunal determines in view of all the circumstances of the case that another place is more appropriate.

7.2 The Tribunal may hold hearings and meetings anywhere convenient, subject to the provisions of Article 10.2 and provided that the award shall be made at the place of arbitration.

Article 8—Language of Arbitration

8.1 The language(s) of the arbitration shall be that of the document(s) containing the arbitration agreement, unless the parties have agreed otherwise.

8.2 If a document is drawn up in a language other than the language(s) of the arbitration, and no translation of such document is submitted by the party producing the document, the Tribunal, or, if the Tribunal has not been appointed the Court, may order that party to submit a translation in a form to be determined by the Tribunal or the Court.

Article 9—Party Representatives

Any party may be represented by legal practitioners or any other representatives, subject to such proof of authority as the Tribunal may require.

Article 10—Hearings

10.1 Any party has the right to be heard before the Tribunal, unless the parties have agreed on documents-only arbitration.

10.2 The Tribunal shall fix the date, time and place of any meetings and hearings in the arbitration, and the Registrar shall give the parties reasonable notice thereof.

10.3 The Tribunal may in advance of hearings submit to the parties a list of questions which it wishes them to treat with special attention.

10.4 All meetings and hearings shall be in private unless the parties agree otherwise.

Article 11—Witnesses

11.1 Before any hearing, the Tribunal may require any party to give notice of the identity of witnesses it wishes to call, as well as the subject matter of their testimony and its relevance to the issues.

11.2 The Tribunal has discretion to allow, refuse or limit the appearance of witnesses, whether witnesses of fact or expert witnesses.

11.3 Any witness who gives oral evidence may be questioned by each of the parties or their legal practitioners, under the control of the Tribunal. The Tribunal may put questions at any stage of the examination of the witnesses.

11.4 The testimony of witnesses may be presented in written form, either as signed statements or by duly sworn affidavits. Subject to Article 11.2 any party may request that such a witness should attend for oral examination at a hearing. If he fails to attend, the Tribunal may place such weight on the written testimony as it thinks fit, or exclude it altogether.

11.5 Subject to the mandatory provisions of any applicable law it shall be proper for any party or its legal practitioners to interview any witness or potential witness prior to his appearance at any hearing.

Article 12—Experts Appointed by the Tribunal

12.1 Unless otherwise agreed by the parties, the Tribunal:

(a) may appoint one or more experts to report to the Tribunal on specific issues;

(b) may require a party to give any such expert any relevant information or to produce, or to provide access to, any relevant documents, goods or property for inspection by the expert.

12.2 Unless otherwise agreed by the parties, if a party so requests or if the Tribunal considers it necessary, the expert shall, after delivery of his written or oral report, participate in a hearing at which the parties shall have the opportunity to question him, and to present expert witnesses in order to testify on the points at issue.

Article 13—Additional Powers of the Tribunal

13.1 Unless the parties at any time agree otherwise, and subject to any mandatory limitations of any applicable law, the Tribunal shall have the power, on the application of any party or of its own motion, but in either case only after giving the parties a proper opportunity to state their views, to:

(a) determine what are the rules of law governing or applicable to any contract, or arbitration agreement or issue between the parties.

(b) order the correction of any such contract or arbitration agreement, but only to the extent required to rectify any mistake which he determines to be common to all the parties and then only if and to the extent to which the rules of law governing or applicable to the contract permit such correction;

(c) allow other parties to be joined in the arbitration with their express consent, and make a single final award determining all disputes between them;

(d) allow any party, upon such terms (as to costs and otherwise) as it shall determine, to amend claims or counterclaims;

(e) extend or abbreviate any time limits provided by these Rules or by its directions;

(f) conduct such enquiries as may appear to the Tribunal to be necessary or expedient;

(g) order the parties to make any property or thing available for inspection, in their presence, by the Tribunal or any expert;

(h) order the preservation, storage, sale or other disposal of any property or thing under the control of any party;

(i) order any party to produce to the Tribunal, and to the other parties for inspection, and to supply copies of, any documents or classes of documents in their possession or power which the Tribunal determines to be relevant.

13.2 By agreeing to arbitration under these Rules the parties shall be taken to have agreed to apply only to the Tribunal, and not to any court of law or other judicial authority, for an order under Article paragraphs (g), (h) or (i) of Article 13.1.

Article 14—Jurisdiction of the Tribunal

14.1 The Tribunal shall have the power to rule on its own jurisdiction, including any objections with respect to the existence or validity of the arbitration agreement.

For that purpose, an arbitration clause which forms part of a contract shall be treated as an agreement independent of the other terms of the contract. A decision by the Tribunal that the contract is null and void shall not entail ipso jure the invalidity of the arbitration clause.

14.2 A plea that the Tribunal does not have jurisdiction shall be raised not later than in the Statement of Defence. A plea that the Tribunal is exceeding the scope of its authority shall be raised promptly after the Tribunal has indicated its intention to decide on the matter alleged to be beyond the scope of its authority. In either case the Tribunal may nevertheless admit a late plea under this paragraph if it considers the delay justified.

14.3 In addition to the jurisdiction to exercise the powers defined elsewhere in these Rules, the Tribunal shall have jurisdiction to determine any question of law arising in the arbitration; proceed in the arbitration notwithstanding the failure or refusal of any party to comply with these Rules or with the Tribunal's orders or directions, or to attend any meeting or hearing, but only after giving that party written notice that it intends to do so; and to receive and take into account such written or oral evidence as it shall determine to be relevant, whether or not strictly admissible in law.

Article 15—Deposits and Security

15.1 The Tribunal may direct the parties, in such proportions as it deems just, and subject to the confirmation of the Court that the amounts are in conformity with the Schedule of Costs, to make one or several interim or final payments on account of the costs of the arbitration. Such deposits shall be made to and held by the Court to the order of the Chairman of the Tribunal or sole arbitrator, and may be drawn from as required by the Tribunal. Interest on sums deposited, if any, shall be accumulated to the deposits.

15.2 The Tribunal shall have the power to order any party to provide security for the legal or other costs of any other party by way of deposit or bank guarantee or in any other manner the Tribunal thinks fit.

15.3 By agreeing to arbitration under these Rules the parties shall be taken to have agreed to apply only to the Tribunal, and not to any court of law or other judicial authority, for an order under Article 15.1, or for an order for security for costs under Article 15.2.

15.4 Without prejudice to the right of any party to apply to a competent court for preaward conservatory measures (except those referred to in Articles 15.1 and 15.2), the Tribunal shall also have the power to order any party to provide security for all or part of any amount in dispute in the arbitration.

15.5 In the event that orders under paragraphs 1, 2 and 4 of this Article are not complied with, the Tribunal may disregard claims or counterclaims by the noncomplying party, although it may proceed to determine claims or counterclaims by complying parties.

Article 16—The Award

16.1 The Tribunal shall make its award in writing and, unless all the parties agree otherwise, shall state the reasons upon which its award is based. The award shall state its date and shall be signed by the arbitrator or arbitrators.

16.2 If any arbitrator refuses or fails to comply with the mandatory provisions of any applicable law relating to the making of the award, having been given a reasonable opportunity to do so, the remaining arbitrators shall proceed in his absence.

16.3 Where there is more than one arbitrator and they fail to agree on any issue, they shall decide by a majority. Failing a majority decision on any issue, the Chairman of the Tribunal shall make the award alone as if he were sole arbitrator. If an arbitrator refuses or fails to sign the award, the signatures of the majority shall be sufficient, provided that the reason for the omitted signature is stated.

16.4 The sole arbitrator or Chairman shall be responsible for delivering the award to the Court, which shall transmit certified copies to the parties provided that the costs of the arbitration have been paid to the Court in accordance with Article 18.

16.5 Awards may be expressed in any currency, and the Tribunal may award that simple or compound interest shall be paid by any party on any sum which is the subject of the reference at such rates as the Tribunal determines to be appropriate without being bound by legal rates of interest, in respect of any period which the Tribunal determines to be appropriate ending not later than the date upon which the award is complied with.

16.6 The Tribunal may make separate final awards on different issues at different times, which shall be subject to correction under the procedure specified in Article 17. Such awards shall be enforceable.

16.7 In the event of a settlement, the Tribunal may render an award recording the settlement if any party so requests. If the parties do not require a consent award, then on confirmation in writing by the parties to the Court that a settlement has been reached the Tribunal shall be discharged and the reference to arbitration concluded, subject to payment by the parties of any outstanding costs of the arbitration in accordance with Article 18.

16.8 By agreeing to arbitration under these Rules, the parties undertake to carry out the award without delay, and waive their right to any form of appeal or recourse to a court of law or other judicial authority, insofar as such waiver may be validly made. Awards shall be final and binding on the parties as from the date they are made.

Article 17—Correction of Awards and Additional Awards

17.1 Within thirty days of receipt of the award, unless another period of time has been agreed upon by the parties, a party may by notice to the Registrar request the Tribunal to correct in the award any errors in computation, any clerical or typographical errors or any errors of similar nature. If the Tribunal considers the request to be justified, it shall make the corrections within thirty days of receipt of the request. Any correction, which shall take the form of a separate memorandum, shall become part of the award.

17.2 The Tribunal may correct any error of the type referred to in Article 17.1 on its own initiative within thirty days of the date of the award.

17.3 Unless otherwise agreed by the parties, a party may request, within thirty days of receipt of the award, and with notice to the other party or parties, the Tribunal to make an additional award as to claims presented in the arbitral proceedings but not dealt with in the award. If the Tribunal considers the request to be justified, it shall make the additional award within sixty days.

17.4 The provisions of Article 16 shall apply mutatis mutandis to a correction of the award and to any additional award.

Article 18—Costs

18.1 The costs of the arbitration (other than the legal or other costs incurred by the parties themselves) shall be in accordance with the Schedule of Costs applicable to these Rules as of the date of the Request for Arbitration.

18.2 The Tribunal shall specify in the award the total amount of the costs of the arbitration, subject to the confirmation of the Court that the amount is in conformity with the Schedule of Costs. Unless the parties shall agree otherwise, the Tribunal shall determine the proportions in which the parties shall pay all or part of them to the Court. If the Tribunal has determined that all or any part of the costs of the arbitration shall be paid by any party other than a party which has already paid them to the Court, the latter shall have the right to recover the appropriate amount from the former.

18.3 The Tribunal shall have the authority to order in its award that all or a part of the legal or other costs of a party (apart from the costs of the arbitration) be paid by another party.

18.4 If the arbitration is abandoned, suspended or concluded, by agreement or otherwise, before the final award is made, the parties shall be jointly and severally liable to pay to the Court the costs of the arbitration as determined by the Tribunal, subject to the confirmation by the Court that the amount is in conformity with the Schedule of Costs. In the event that the costs so determined are less than the deposits made, there shall be a refund in such proportions as the parties may agree, or, failing agreement, in the same proportions as the deposits were made.

Article 19—Exclusion of Liability

19.1 Neither the Court nor any arbitrator shall be liable to any party for any act or omission in connection with any arbitration conducted under these Rules, save that arbitrators (but not the Court) may be liable for the consequences of conscious and deliberate wrongdoing.

19.2 fter the award has been made and the possibilities of correction and additional awards referred to in Article 17 have lapsed or been exhausted, neither the Court nor any arbitrator shall be under any obligation to make any statement to any person about any matter concerning the arbitration, nor shall any party seek to make any arbitrator or any officer of the Court a witness in any legal proceedings arising out of the arbitration.

Article 20—General Rules

20.1 A party who knows that any provision of, or requirement under, these Rules has not be [sic] complied with and yet proceeds with the arbitration without promptly stating its objection to such non-compliance, shall be deemed to have waived its right to object.

20.2 In all matters not expressly provided for in these Rules, the Court and the Tribunal shall act in the spirit of these Rules and shall make every reasonable effort to ensure that the award is legally enforceable.

8. ARBITRATION RULES OF THE STOCKHOLM CHAMBER OF COMMERCE.

I. Organisation of the Institute

Article 1

The Arbitration Institute of the Stockholm Chamber of Commerce ("the Institute") is an organ within the Stockholm Chamber of Commerce ("the Chamber") for dealing with matters of arbitration. Its objects are:

• to assist in the settlement of domestic and international disputes in accordance with the Rules of the Institute set forth in Articles 5-34 hereof,

• to assist in the settlement of disputes in accordance with other rules adopted by the Institute.

• to assist, pursuant to its own decision in each case, in proceedings which take place in a manner that differs wholly or partly from that contemplated by the rules referred to above, and

• to provide information concerning arbitration matters.

Article 2

The Institute shall have a Board composed of three members who shall be appointed for a period of three years by the Executive Committee of the Chamber. One of the members, who shall act as Chairman, shall be a judge having experience of business disputes, while one of the others shall be a practising lawyer, and once a person who enjoys the confidence of the business community.

Each member shall have a personal deputy appointed by the Executive Committee for the same three-year period as the member. The deputy shall have the same qualifications as the member for whom he is a deputy.

For special reasons, the Executive Committee may remove a member or a deputy.

If a member or a deputy resigns or is removed during his term of office, the Executive Committee will nominate another person to serve as member or deputy during the balance of the term.

References below to "the Chairman" or "members" apply equally to a deputy serving in the place of the Chairman or a member.

Article 3

Two members of the Board shall form a quorum. If no majority is attained, the Chairman shall have a casting vote. Decisions of the Board are final and cannot be reviewed by the Chamber.

Article 4

The Institute shall have a secretariat composed of one or several persons employed by the Chamber. The secretariat shall be under the direction of a Secretary-General who shall be a lawyer.

II.Arbitration Rules of the Institute

A. Composition of Arbitral Tribunals

Article 5—Number of arbitrators and manner of their appointment

If the parties have not agreed on the number of arbitrators, they shall be three in number.

If the parties have agreed that the dispute is to be decided by a sole arbitrator, then the appointment shall be made by the Institute. In other cases each party shall appoint an equal number of arbitrators and the Institute one arbitrator, who shall be chairman of the tribunal.

If the parties have so agreed, the Institute shall appoint all members of the tribunal.

If an arbitrator appointed by a party dies, such party shall appoint another arbitrator in his place. If the arbitrator had been appointed by the Institute, the Institute shall appoint another arbitrator in his place.

If an arbitrator resigns or is discharged, the Institute shall appoint another arbitrator. If the arbitrator had been appointed by a party, such party shall be consulted by the Institute.

If a party fails to appoint an arbitrator within the time prescribed by the Institute, then the Institute shall make the appointment.

Article 6—Duty of an arbitrator to disclose grounds for his disqualification

A person who is asked whether he wishes to accept appointment as an arbitrator shall disclose to the person approaching him any circumstances which might be deemed to diminish trust in his impartiality or independence (disqualification). If he is nevertheless appointed, he shall at once make the same disclosure to the parties and the other arbitrators.

An arbitrator who becomes aware in the course of the arbitral proceedings of any circumstances which may disqualify him must immediately inform the parties and the other arbitrators thereof.

Article 7—Challenge of arbitrators

If a party wishes to challenge an arbitrator he shall do so in writing. Such a challenge shall state the reasons thereof and shall be notified to the Institute, the arbitrators and each other party.

Any challenge by a party of an arbitrator must be made immediately but in any event within thirty days of the date on which the allegedly disqualifying circumstance becomes known to the party. A party who fails to notify a challenge within the prescribed time is deemed to have waived his right to make such challenge.

Decisions of challenges will be made by the Institute.

Article 8—Discharge of arbitrators

If the Institute finds that an arbitrator is disqualified it shall discharge him.

The Institute may also decide to discharge an arbitrator on the ground of any lawful excuse or failure to perform his duties in an adequate manner.

Before a decision on discharge is made the Institute shall solicit the views of the parties and the arbitrators.

B. Initiation of Proceedings. Procedures of the Institute

Article 9—Request for arbitration

Arbitration is initiated by the filing by a party with the Institute of a request for arbitration which shall include:

(a) A statement of the names and addresses of the parties;

(b) An account of the dispute;

(c) A preliminary statement of the relief claimed by the claimant;

(d) A copy of the agreement on which the claim is based and of the arbitration agreement if the latter is not included in the former; and, where applicable,

(e) A statement identifying the arbitrator or arbitrators appointed by the claimant.

Article 10—Dismissal

If it is obvious that the Institute lacks competence over the dispute, the claimant's request for arbitration shall be dismissed.

Article 11—The respondent's reply, etc.

If it is not obvious that jurisdiction is lacking, the request shall be communicated by the Institute to the respondent. The respondent shall be asked to submit a reply to the Institute which shall include:

(a) A statement commenting on the request made by the claimant; and, where applicable,

(b) A statement identifying the arbitrator or arbitrators appointed by the respondent.

If the respondent desires to raise any objection concerning the validity or applicability of the arbitration agreement, such objection shall be made in the reply together with a statement of the grounds therefor.

If the respondent desires to make a counterclaim or plead a set-off, a statement to that effect shall be made in the reply, including an account of the dispute and a preliminary statement of the relief claimed. A counterclaim or a plea by way of set-off must be comprised by the arbitration agreement.

The respondent's reply shall be communicated to the claimant. The claimant shall be given an opportunity to comment on any objections and pleas advanced by the respondent.

Failure by the respondent to submit a reply shall not prevent the proceedings in the case from continuing.

Article 12—Amplification. Time limits

The Institute may request a party to amplify any submission to the Institute. If the claimant fails to comply with such a request, the Institute may decide to dismiss the case. If the respondent fails to do so, such failure shall not prevent the proceedings in the case from continuing.

If the respondent should fail to amplify his counterclaim or plea for a set-off, with claim or plea may be dismissed by the Institute.

If the Institute has requested a party to perform any act within a specified time, such time limit may be extended by the Institute.

Article 13—Security for costs

The Institute shall fix a sum which shall be paid to the Institute and which, together with accrued interest, shall constitute security for the costs of the proceedings. The amount thereof is fixed in accordance with regulations issued by the Institute. The Institute may fix separate sums for a counterclaim and a plea by way of set-off. After notification by the arbitral tribunal the Institute may in the course of the proceedings decide to increase the sums to be paid.

Each party shall as a rule contribute half of such sums of money as are referred to in the preceding paragraph. One party may, however, pay the entire sum.

If a party fails to make a required payment the Institute shall afford the other party an opportunity to do so. If, this notwithstanding, the required payment is not made, the case shall be wholly or partly dismissed or stayed.

The Institute may, both in the course of the proceedings and thereafter, draw on the security to pay fees to the arbitrators and other costs of the proceedings.

The Institute may decide that the security may partly consist of a bank guarantee or other security.

Article 14—Decision of the Institute

When the exchange of written submissions pursuant to Articles 9-12 has been concluded, then, unless it is obvious that jurisdiction is lacking, the Institute shall:

(a) Appoint a chairman of the arbitral tribunal and, if necessary, another arbitrator pursuant to Article 5;

(b) Determine the place of arbitration unless the parties have done so; and

(c) Fix the amount of the security and the time within which each party shall pay his share thereof.

Article 15—Referral of a case to the arbitral tribunal

As soon as the arbitral tribunal has been appointed and the security been provided, the Institute shall refer the case to the arbitral tribunal.

C. The Proceedings Before the Arbitral Tribunal

Article 16—The procedure before the arbitral tribunal

The arbitral tribunal shall determine the manner in which the proceedings will be conducted. In so doing, the arbitral tribunal shall comply with the stipulations of the parties in the arbitration agreement and these Rules and shall have regard to the wishes of the parties.

The arbitral tribunal shall deal with the case in an impartial, practical and speedy fashion. Each party shall be given a sufficient opportunity to present his case.

If the arbitral tribunal is composed of three or more members, the Chairman may, if the other arbitrators have so authorised him, decide questions of procedure on his own.

Article 17—Language

Unless the parties have agreed on the language or languages to be used in the proceedings, the arbitral tribunal shall make a determination in such respect.

Article 18—Statement of claim and defence

1. The claimant shall submit a statement of claim which, unless such information has already been provided in the case, shall include:

(a) The specific relief claimed.

(b) The circumstances which constitute the material facts on which the claimant relies in support of his claim.

The statement of claim in addition ought to include a preliminary statement of the evidence which the claimant desires to adduce.

2. The respondent shall submit a defence, which, unless such information has previously been provided in the case, shall include:

(a) A statement as to whether and to what extent the respondent accepts or opposes the relief claimed by the claimant;

(b) If the claim is denied in whole or in part, the circumstances which constitute the material facts on which such denial is based and specifying whether the respondent admits or denies the material facts relied upon by the claimant; and, if he respondent so pleads,

(c) A specific plea by way of set-off or counterclaim and the grounds on which it is based.

The defence further ought to include a preliminary statement of the evidence which the respondent desires to adduce.

3.The arbitral tribunal may decide on the submission by the parties of additional written statements.

Article 19—Amendment to claim or defence

A party may amend his claim or defence in the course of the proceedings if his case, as amended, is still comprised by the arbitration agreement and unless the arbitral tribunal considers it inappropriate having regard to the point of time at which the request is made, the prejudice that may be caused to the other party or other circumstances.

The provisions of the preceding paragraph shall apply equally to the right of a party to introduce a plea for a set-off or a counterclaim.

Article 20—Oral hearing

An oral hearing shall, as a rule, be arranged. Guided by the wishes of the parties, the arbitral tribunal shall determine the time at which such a hearing shall take place, its duration and how it shall be organized, including the manner in which evidence is to be presented.

If an arbitrator is replaced in the course of the proceedings, the newly composed tribunal shall decide whether and to what extent a prior oral hearing shall be repeated.

Article 21—Evidence

At the request of the arbitral tribunal, the parties shall state the evidence on which they wish to rely, specifying what they wish to prove with each piece of evidence, and shall produce the documentary evidence on which they rely.

The arbitral tribunal determines whether written affidavits may be submitted.

The arbitral tribunal may refuse to accept evidence offered to it if it considers that such evidence is not required or is irrelevant or that proof can be established by other means in a considerably simpler fashion or at considerably lesser expense.

After having conscientiously scrutinised and evaluated everything that has occurred in the proceedings, the arbitral tribunal shall determine what has been proved in the case.

Article 22—Expert

Unless the parties provide otherwise, the arbitral tribunal may appoint an expert to give his opinion on a particular matter.

Article 23—Failure of a party to appear, etc.

If one of the parties, without showing valid cause, fails to appear at a hearing or otherwise to comply with an order of the arbitral tribunal, such failure will not prevent the arbitral tribunal from proceeding with the case and rendering an award.

Article 24—Waiver of procedural irregularities

A party who fails during the proceedings to object within a reasonable time to any deviation from provisions of the arbitration agreement or other rules applicable to the proceedings shall be deemed to have waived his right to invoke such irregularity.

Article 25—Voting

When a vote is taken, that opinion shall prevail which has received more votes than any other opinion. If such a majority is not attained the opinion of the chairman shall prevail.

D. The Award

Article 26—Time for making an award

An award shall be made not later than one year after the case has been referred to the arbitral tribunal. At the request of the arbitral tribunal, the Institute may, however, if appropriate extend this period.

Article 27—Separate award

A separate issue or part of the matter in dispute between the parties may, at the request of a party, be decided by a separate award. If any party objects, such an award may be rendered only if there are special reasons therefor.

Where a party has partially admitted a claim, the arbitral tribunal may give a separate award on the part that has been admitted.

Article 28—Award

The award shall be rendered at the place of arbitration. The award shall contain an order or declaration and the reasons therefor and shall be signed by all the arbitrators. An award may be rendered even in the absence of the signature of an arbitrator provided that the award has been signed by a majority of the arbitrators and contains a verification by them that the arbitrator whose signature is missing took part in deciding the dispute.

An arbitrator may attach a dissenting opinion to the award.

If a settlement is made the arbitral tribunal may at the request of the parties confirm such settlement in an award.

Article 29—Costs

The arbitral tribunal shall decide in the award which amounts of compensation are due to the Institute and the arbitrators, respectively. The parties are jointly and severally liable for the payment of such sums.

The losing party shall be ordered to pay such compensation and costs as well as the costs of the other party unless the circumstances call for a different result.

If a case is terminated before an award has been rendered, the arbitral tribunal may decide that the parties shall pay compensation to the Institute and the arbitrators. If a case is terminated before it has been referred to the arbitral tribunal, the Institute will determine the amount of compensation due to it.

An award may be rendered even if it deals only with costs.

Article 30—Fees of arbitrators

The fees of arbitrators shall be reasonable in amount and shall be determined taking into account the time spent by the arbitrators, the complexity of the case, the amount in dispute and other circumstances.

Article 31—Correction of an award, etc.

Any obvious miscalculation or clerical error in an award shall be corrected by the arbitral tribunal.

If a party so requests within thirty days of receiving the award the tribunal may decide a question which should have been decided in the award but which was not decided therein.

If a party so requests within thirty days of receiving the award the arbitral tribunal may provide an interpretation thereof in writing.

Before the arbitral tribunal takes any action, the parties shall be afforded an opportunity to express their views.

E. Miscellaneous Provisions

Article 32—Compensation due to the Institute
The amount of compensation due to the Institute will be determined in accordance with regulations issued by the Institute.

Article 33—Filing of awards, etc.
An arbitral tribunal must after the close of the proceedings submit to the Institute one copy of each award and written order issued in the case as well as of all recorded minutes therein.

Article 34—Effectiveness
These Rules shall enter into force on 1 January 1988 and will replace the former Rules of the Institute.

If an arbitration agreement has been concluded prior to 1 January 1988, the former Statutes or former Rules of the Institute shall apply unless the parties agree otherwise.

9. United Nations Commission on International Trade Law (UNCITRAL).

Section I. Introductory Rules

Scope of Application

Article 1

1. Where the parties to a contract have agreed in writing that disputes in relation to that contract shall be referred to arbitration under the UNCITRAL Arbitration Rules, then such disputes shall be settled in accordance with these Rules subject to such modification as the parties may agree in writing.

2. These Rules shall govern the arbitration except that where any of these Rules is in conflict with a provision of the law applicable to the arbitration from which the parties cannot derogate, that provision shall prevail.

Notice, Calculation of Periods of Time

Article 2

1. For the purposes of these Rules, any notice, including a notification, communication or proposal, is deemed to have been received if it is physically delivered to the addressee or if it is delivered at his habitual residence, place of business or mailing address, or, if none of these can be found after making reasonable inquiry, then at the addressee's last-known residence or place of business. Notice shall be deemed to have been received on the day it is so delivered.

2. For the purposes of calculating a period of time under these Rules, such period shall begin to run on the day following the day when a notice, notification, communication or proposal is received. If the last day of such period is an official holiday or a non-business day at the residence or place of business of the addressee, the period is extended until the first business day which follows. Official holidays or non-business days occurring during the running of the period of time are included in calculating the period.

Notice of Arbitration

Article 3

1. The party initiating recourse to arbitration (hereinafter called the "claimant") shall give to the other party (hereinafter called the "respondent") a notice of arbitration.

2. Arbitral proceedings shall be deemed to commence on the date on which the notice of arbitration is received by the respondent.

3. The notice of arbitration shall include the following:
   a. a demand that the dispute be referred to arbitration;
   b. the names and addresses of the parties;

c. a reference to the arbitration clause or the separate arbitration agreement that is invoked;

d. a reference to the contract out of or in relation to which the dispute arises;

e. the general nature of the claim and an indication of the amount involved, if any;

f. the relief or remedy sought;

g. a proposal as to the number of arbitrators (i.e. one or three), if the parties have not previously agreed thereon.

4. The notice of arbitration may also include:

a. the proposals for the appointments of a sole arbitrator and an appointing authority referred to in article 6, paragraph 1;

b. the notification of the appointment of an arbitrator referred to in article 7;

c. the statement of claim referred to in article 18.

Representation and Assistance

Article 4

The parties may be represented or assisted by persons of their choice. The name and addresses of such persons must be communicated in writing to the other party; such communication must specify whether the appointment is being made for purposes of representation or assistance.

Section II. Composition of theArbitral Tribunal

Number of Arbitrators

Article 5

If the parties have not previously agreed on the number of arbitrators (i.e., one or three), and if within fifteen days after the receipt by the respondent of the notice of arbitration the parties have not agreed that there shall be only one arbitrator, three arbitrators shall be appointed.

Appointment of Arbitrators

Article 6

1. If a sole arbitrator is to be appointed, either party may propose to the other:

a. the names of one or more persons, one of whom would serve as the sole arbitrator; and

b. if no appointing authority has been agreed upon by the parties, the name or names of one or more institutions or persons, one of whom would serve as appointing authority.

2. If within thirty days after receipt by a party of a proposal made in accordance with paragraph 1 the parties have not reached agreement on the choice of a sole arbitrator, the sole arbitrator shall be appointed by the appointing authority agreed upon by the parties. If no appointing authority has been agreed upon by the parties, or if the appointing authority agreed upon refuses to act or fails to appoint the arbitrator within sixty days of the receipt of a party's request therefor, either party may request the Secretary-General of the Permanent Court of Arbitration at The Hague to designate an appointing authority.

3. The appointing authority shall, at the request of one of the parties, appoint the sole arbitrator as promptly as possible. In making the appointment the appointing authority shall use the following list-procedure, unless both parties agree that the list-procedure should not be used or unless the appointing authority determines in its discretion that the use of the list-procedure is not appropriate for the case:

    a. at the request of one of the parties the appointing authority shall communicate to both parties an identical list containing at least three names;

    b. within fifteen days after the receipt of this list, each party may return the list to the appointing authority after having deleted the name or names to which he objects and numbered the remaining names on the list in the order of his preference;

    c. after the expiration of the above period of time the appointing authority shall appoint the sole arbitrator from among the names approved on the lists returned to it and in accordance with the order of preference indicated by the parties;

    d. if for any reason the appointment cannot be made according to this procedure, the appointing authority may exercise its discretion in appointing the sole arbitrator.

4.In making the appointment, the appointing authority shall have regard to such considerations as are likely to secure the appointment of an independent and impartial arbitrator and shall take into account as well the advisability of appointing an arbitrator of a nationality other than the nationalities of the parties.

Article 7

1. If three arbitrators are to be appointed, each party shall appoint one arbitrator. The two arbitrators thus appointed shall choose the third arbitrator who will act as the presiding arbitrator of the tribunal.

2. If within thirty days after the receipt of a party's notification of the appointment of an arbitrator the other party has not notified the first party of the arbitrator he has appointed:

    a. the first party may request the appointing authority previously designated by the parties to appoint the second arbitrator; or

    b. if no such authority has been previously designated by the parties, or if the appointing authority previously designated refuses to act or fails to appoint the arbitrator within thirty days after receipt of a party's request therefor, the first party may request the Secretary-General of the

Permanent Court of Arbitration at The Hague to designate the appointing authority. The first party may then request the appointing authority so designated to appoint the second arbitrator. In either case, the appointing authority may exercise its discretion in appointing the arbitrator.

3. if within thirty days after the appointment of the second arbitrator the two arbitrators have not agreed on the choice of the presiding arbitrator, the presiding arbitrator shall be appointed by an appointing authority in the same way as a sole arbitrator would be appointed under article 6.

Article 8

1. When an appointing authority is requested to appoint an arbitrator pursuant to article 6 or article 7, the party which makes the request shall send to the appointing authority a copy of the notice of arbitration, a copy of the contract out of or in relation to which the dispute has arisen and a copy of the arbitration agreement if it is not contained in the contract. The appointing authority may require from either party such information as it deems necessary to fulfill its function.

2. Where the names of one or more persons are proposed for appointment as arbitrators, their full names, addresses and nationalities shall be indicated, together with a description of their qualifications.

Challenge of Arbitrators

Article 9

A prospective arbitrator shall disclose to those who approach him in connection with his possible appointment any circumstances likely to give rise to justifiable doubts as to his impartiality or independence. An arbitrator, once appointed or chosen, shall disclose such circumstances to the parties unless they have already been informed by him of these circumstances.

Article 10

1. Any arbitrator may be challenged if circumstances exist that give rise to justifiable doubts as to the arbitrator's impartiality or independence.

2 .A party may challenge the arbitrator appointed by him (only for reasons of which he becomes aware after the appointment has been made.

Article 11

1. A party who intends to challenge an arbitrator shall send notice of his challenge within fifteen days after the appointment of the challenged arbitrator has been notified to the challenging party or within fifteen days after the circumstances mentioned in articles 9 and 10 became known to that party.

2. The challenge shall be notified to the other party, to the arbitrator who is challenged and to the other members of the arbitral tribunal. The notification shall be in writing and shall state the reasons for the challenge.

3. When an arbitrator has been challenged by one party, the other party may

agree to the challenge. The arbitrator may also, after the challenge, withdraw from his office. In neither case does this imply acceptance of the validity of the grounds for the challenge. In both cases the procedure provided in article 6 or 7 shall be used in full for the appointment of the substitute arbitrator, even if during the process of appointing the challenged arbitrator a party had failed to exercise his right to appoint or to participate in the appointment.

Article 12

1. If the other party does not agree to the challenge and the challenged arbitrator does not withdraw, the decision on the challenge will be made:
   a. when the initial appointment was made by an appointing authority, by that authority;
   b. when the initial appointment was not made by an appointing authority, but an appointing authority has been previously designated, by that authority;
   c. in all other cases, by the appointing authority to be designated in accordance with the procedure for designating an appointing authority as provided for in article 6.

2. If the appointing authority sustains the challenge, a substitute arbitrator shall be appointed or chosen pursuant to the procedure applicable to the appointment or choice of an arbitrator as provided in articles 6 to 9 except that, when this procedure would call for the designation of an appointing authority, the appointment of the arbitrator shall be made by the appointing authority which decided on the challenge.

Replacement of an Arbitrator

Article 13

1. In the event of the death or resignation of an arbitrator during the course of the arbitral proceedings, a substitute arbitrator shall be appointed or chosen pursuant to the procedure provided for in articles 6 to 9 that was applicable to the appointment or choice of the arbitrator being replaced.

2. In the event that an arbitrator fails to act or in the event of the de jure or de facto impossibility of his performing his functions, the procedure in respect of the challenge and replacement of an arbitrator as provided in the preceding articles shall apply.

Repetition of Hearings in the Event of the Replacement of an Arbitrator

Article 14

If under articles 11 to 13 the sole or presiding arbitrator is replaced, any hearings held previously shall be repeated; if any other arbitrator is replaced, such prior hearings may be repeated at the discretion of the arbitral tribunal.

Section III. Arbitral Proceedings

General Provisions

Article 15

1. Subject to these Rules, the arbitral tribunal may conduct the arbitration in such manner as it considers appropriate, provided that the parties are treated with equality and that at any stage of the proceedings each party is given a full opportunity of presenting his case.

2. If either party so requests at any stage of the proceedings, the arbitral tribunal shall hold hearings for the presentation of evidence by witnesses, including expert witnesses, or for oral argument. In the absence of such a request, the arbitral tribunal shall decide whether to hold such hearings or whether the proceedings shall be conducted on the basis of documents and other materials.

3. All documents or information supplied to the arbitral tribunal by one party shall at the same time be communicated by that party to the other party.

Place of Arbitration

Article 16

1. Unless the parties have agreed upon the place where the arbitration is to be held, such place shall be determined by the arbitral tribunal, having regard to the circumstances of the arbitration.

2. The arbitral tribunal may determine the locale of the arbitration within the country agreed upon by the parties. It may hear witnesses and hold meetings for consultation among its members at any place it deems appropriate, having regard to the circumstances of the arbitration.

3. The arbitral tribunal may meet at any place it deems appropriate for the inspection of goods, other property or documents. The parties shall be given sufficient notice to enable them to be present at such inspection.

4. The award shall be made at the place of arbitration.

Language

Article 17

1.Subject to an agreement by the parties, the arbitral tribunal shall, promptly after its appointment, determine the language or languages to be used in the proceedings. This determination shall apply to the statement of claim, the statement of defence, and any further written statements and, if oral hearings take place, to the language or languages to be used in such hearings.

2. The arbitral tribunal may order that any documents annexed to the statement of claim or statement of defence, and any supplementary documents or exhibits submitted in the course of the proceedings, delivered in their original language, shall be accompanied by a translation into the language or languages agreed upon by the parties or determined by the arbitral tribunal.

Statement of Claim

Article 18

1. Unless the statement of claim was contained in the notice of arbitration, within a period of time to be determined by the arbitral tribunal, the claimant shall communicate his statement of claim in writing to the respondent and to each of the arbitrators. A copy of the contract, and of the arbitration agreement if not contained in the contract, shall be annexed thereto.

2. The statement of claim shall include the following particulars:
   a. the names and addresses of the parties;
   b. a statement of the facts supporting the claim;
   c. the points at issue;
   d. the relief or remedy sought.

The claimant may annex to his statement of claim all documents he deems relevant or may add a reference to the documents or other evidence he will submit.

Statement of Defence

Article 19

1. Within a period of time to be determined by the arbitral tribunal, the respondent shall communicate his statement of defence in writing to the claimant and to each of the arbitrators.

2. The statement of defence shall apply to the particulars (b), (c), and (d) of the statement of claim (article 18, para. 2). The respondent may annex to his statement the documents on which he relies for his defence or may add a reference to the documents or other evidence he will submit.

3. In his statement of defence, or at a later stage in the arbitral proceedings if the arbitral tribunal decides that the delay was justified under the circumstances, the respondent may make a counterclaim arising out of the same contract or rely on a claim arising out of the same contract for the purpose of a set-off.

4. The provisions of article 18, paragraph 2, shall apply to a counter-claim and a claim relied on for the purpose of a set-off.

Amendments to the Claim or Defence

Article 20

During the course of the arbitral proceedings either party may amend or supplement his claim or defence unless the arbitral tribunal considers it inappropriate to allow such amendment having regard to the delay in making it or prejudice to the other party or any other circumstances. However, a claim may not be amended in such a manner that the amended claim falls outside the scope of the arbitration clause or separate arbitration agreement.

Pleas as to the Jurisdiction of the Arbitral Tribunal

Article 21
1. The arbitral tribunal shall have the power to rule on objections that it has no jurisdiction, including any objections with respect to the existence or validity of the arbitration clause or of the separate arbitration agreement.
2. The arbitral tribunal shall have the power to determine the existence or validity of the contract of which an arbitration clause forms a part. For the purposes of article 21, an arbitration clause which forms part of a contract and which provides for arbitration under these Rules shall be treated as an agreement independent of the other terms of the contract. A decision by the arbitral tribunal that the contract is null and void shall not entail ipso jure the invalidity of the arbitration clause.
3. A plea that the arbitral tribunal does not have jurisdiction shall be raised not later than in the statement of defence or, with respect to a counter-claim, in the reply to the counter-claim.
4. In general, the arbitral tribunal should rule on a plea concerning jurisdiction as a preliminary question. However, the arbitral tribunal may proceed with the arbitration and rule on such a plea in their final award.

Further Written Statements

Article 22
The arbitral tribunal shall decide which further written statements, in addition to the statement of claim and the statement of defence, shall be required from the parties or may be presented by them and shall fix the periods of time for communicating such statements.

Periods of Time

Article 23
The periods of time fixed by the arbitral tribunal for the communication of written statements (including the statement of claim and statement of defence) should not exceed forty-five days. However, the arbitral tribunal may extend the time-limits if it concludes that an extension is justified.

Evidence and Hearings

Article 24
1. Each party shall have the burden of proving the facts relied on to support his claim or defence.
2. The arbitral tribunal may, if it considers it appropriate, require a party to deliver to the tribunal and to the other party, within such a period of time as the arbitral tribunal shall decide, a summary of the documents and other evidence which that party intends to present in support of the facts in issue set out in his statement of claim or statement of defence.

3. At any time during the arbitral proceedings the arbitral tribunal may require the parties to produce documents, exhibits or other evidence within such a period of time as the tribunal shall determine.

Article 25

1. In the event of an oral hearing, the arbitral tribunal shall give the parties adequate advance notice of the date, time and place thereof.

2. If witnesses are to be heard, at least fifteen days before the hearing each party shall communicate to the arbitral tribunal and to the other party the names and addresses of the witnesses he intends to present, the subject upon and the languages in which such witnesses will give their testimony.

3. The arbitral tribunal shall make arrangements for the translation of oral statements made at a hearing and for a record of the hearing if either is deemed necessary by the tribunal under the circumstances of the case, or if the parties have agreed thereto and have communicated such agreement to the tribunal at least fifteen days before the hearing.

4. Hearings shall be held in camera unless the parties agree otherwise. The arbitral tribunal is free to determine the manner in which witnesses are examined.

5. Evidence of witnesses may also be presented in the form of written statements signed by them.

6. The arbitral tribunal shall determine the admissibility, relevance, materiality, and weight of the evidence offered.

Interim Measures of Protection

Article 26

1. At the request of either party, the arbitral tribunal may take any interim measures it deems necessary in respect of the subject-matter of the dispute, including measures for the conservation of the goods forming the subject-matter in dispute, such as ordering their deposit with a third person or the sale of perishable goods.

2. Such interim measures may be established in the form of an interim award. The arbitral tribunal shall be entitled to require security for the costs of such measures.

3. A request for interim measures addressed by any party to a judicial authority shall not be deemed incompatible with the agreement to arbitrate, or as a waiver of that agreement.

Experts

Article 27

1. The arbitral tribunal may appoint one or more experts to report to it, in writing, on specific issues to be determined by the tribunal. A copy of the expert's terms of references, established by the arbitral tribunal, shall be communicated to the parties.

2. The parties shall give the expert any relevant information or produce for his inspection any relevant documents or goods that he may require of them. Any dis-

pute between a party and such expert as to the relevance of the required information or production shall be referred to the arbitral tribunal for decision.

3. Upon receipt of the expert's report, the arbitral tribunal shall communicate a copy of the report to the parties who shall be given the opportunity to express, in writing, their opinion on the report. A party shall be entitled to examine any document on which the expert has relied in his report.

4. At the request of either party the expert, after delivery of the report, may be heard at a hearing where the parties shall have the opportunity to be present and to interrogate the expert. At this hearing either party may present expert witnesses in order to testify on the points at issue. The provisions of article 25 shall be applicable to such proceedings.

Default

Article 28

1. If, within the period of time fixed by the arbitral tribunal the claimant has failed to communicate his claim without showing sufficient cause for such failure, the arbitral tribunal shall issue an order for the termination of the arbitral proceedings. If, within the period of time fixed by the arbitral tribunal, the respondent has failed to communicate his statement of defence without showing sufficient cause for such failure, the arbitral tribunal shall order that the proceedings continue.

2. If one of the parties, duly notified under these Rules, fails to appear at a hearing, without showing sufficient cause for such failure, the arbitral tribunal may proceed with the arbitration.

3. If one of the parties, duly invited to produce documentary evidence, fails to do so within the established period of time, without showing sufficient cause for such failure, the arbitral tribunal may make the award on the evidence before it.

Closure of Hearings

Article 29

1. The arbitral tribunal may inquire of the parties if they have any further proof to offer or witnesses to be heard or submissions to make and, if there are none, it may declare the hearings closed.

2. The arbitral tribunal may, if it considers it necessary owing to exceptional circumstances, decide, on its own motion or upon application of a party, to reopen the hearings at any time before the award is made.

Waiver of Rules

Article 30

A party who knows that any provision of, or requirement under, these Rules has not been complied with and yet proceeds with the arbitration without promptly stating his objection to such non-compliance, shall be deemed to have waived his right to object.

Section IV. The Award

Article 31

1. When there are three arbitrators, any reward or other decision of the arbitral tribunal shall be made by a majority of the arbitrators.

2. In the case of questions of procedure, when there is no majority or when the arbitral tribunal so authorizes, the presiding arbitrator may decide on his own, subject to revision, if any, by the arbitral tribunal.

Form and Effect of the Award

Article 32

1. In addition to making a final award, the arbitral tribunal shall be entitled to make interim, interlocutory, or partial awards.

2. The award shall be made in writing and shall be final and binding on the parties. The parties undertake to carry out the award without delay.

3. The arbitral tribunal shall state the reasons upon which the award is based, unless the parties have agreed that no reasons are to be given.

4. An award shall be signed by the arbitrators and it shall contain the date on which and the place where the award was made. Where there are three arbitrators and one of them fails to sign, the award shall state the reason for the absence of the signature.

5. The award may be made public only with the consent of both parties.

6. Copies of the award signed by the arbitrators shall be communicated to the parties by the arbitral tribunal.

7. If the arbitration law of the country where the award is made requires that the award be filed or registered by the arbitral tribunal, the tribunal shall comply with this requirement within the period of time required by law.

Applicable Law, Amiable Compositeur

Article 33

1. The arbitral tribunal shall apply the law designated by the parties as applicable to the substance of the dispute. Failing such designation by the parties, the arbitral tribunal shall apply the law determined by the conflict of laws rules which it considers applicable.

2. The arbitral tribunal shall decide as amiable compositeur or ex aequo et bono only if the parties have expressly authorized the arbitral tribunal to do so and if the law applicable to the arbitral procedure permits such arbitration.

3. In all cases, the arbitral tribunal shall decide in accordance with the terms of the contract and shall take into account the usages of the trade applicable to the

transaction.

Settlement or Other Grounds for Termination

Article 34

1. If, before the award is made, the parties agree on a settlement of the dispute, the arbitral tribunal shall either issue an order for the termination of the arbitral proceedings or, if requested by both parties and accepted by the tribunal, record the settlement in the form of an arbitral award on agreed terms. The arbitral tribunal is not obliged to give reasons for such an award.

2. If, before the award is made, the continuation of the arbitral proceedings becomes unnecessary or impossible for any reason not mentioned in paragraph 1, the arbitral tribunal shall inform the parties of its intention to issue an order for the termination of the proceedings. The arbitral tribunal shall have the power to issue such an order unless a party raises justifiable grounds for objection.

3. Copies of the order for termination of the arbitral proceedings or of the arbitral award on agreed terms, signed by the arbitrators, shall be communicated by the arbitral tribunal to the parties. Where an arbitral award on agreed terms is made, the provisions of article 32, paragraphs 2 and 4 to 7, shall apply.

Interpretation of the Award

Article 35

1. Within thirty days after the receipt of the award, either party, with notice to the other party, may request that the arbitral tribunal give an interpretation of the award.

2. The interpretation shall be given in writing within forty-five days after the receipt of the request. The interpretation shall form part of the award and the provisions of article 32, paragraphs 2 to 7, shall apply.

Correction of the Award

Article 36

1. Within thirty days after the receipt of the award, either party, with notice to the other party, may request the arbitral tribunal to correct in the award any errors in computation, any clerical or typographical errors, or any errors of similar nature. The arbitral tribunal may within thirty days after the communication of the award make such corrections on its own initiative.

2. Such corrections shall be in writing, and the provisions of article 32, paragraphs 2 to 7, shall apply.

Additional Award

Article 37

1. Within thirty days after the receipt of the award, either party, with notice to the other party, may request the arbitral tribunal to make an additional award as to claims presented in the arbitral proceedings but omitted from the award.

2. If the arbitral tribunal considers the request for an additional award to be justified and considers that the omission can be rectified without any further hearings or evidence, it shall complete its award within sixty days after the receipt of the request.

3. When an additional award is made, the provisions of article 32, paragraphs 2 to 7, shall apply.

Costs

Article 38

The arbitral tribunal shall fix the costs of arbitration in its award. The term "costs" includes only:

   a. the fees of the arbitral tribunal to be stated separately as to each arbitrator and to be fixed by the tribunal itself in accordance with article 39;
   b. the travel and other expenses incurred by the arbitrators;
   c. the costs of expert advice and of other assistance required by the arbitral tribunal;
   d. the travel and other expenses of witnesses to the extent such expenses are approved by the arbitral tribunal;
   e. the costs for legal representation and assistance of the successful party if such costs were claimed during the arbitral proceedings, and only to the extent that the arbitral tribunal determines that the amount of such costs is reasonable;
   f. any fees and expenses of the appointing authority as well as the expenses of the Secretary-General of the Permanent Court of Arbitration at The Hague.

Article 39

1. The fees of the arbitral tribunal shall be reasonable in amount, taking into account the amount in dispute, the complexity of the subject-matter, the time spent by the arbitrators, and any other relevant circumstances of the case.

2. If an appointing authority has been agreed upon by the parties or designated by the Secretary-General of the Permanent Court of Arbitration at The Hague, and if that authority has issued a schedule of fees for arbitrators in international cases which it administers, the arbitral tribunal in fixing its fees shall take that schedule of fees into account to the extent that it considers appropriate in the circumstances of the case.

3. If such appointing authority has not issued a schedule of fees for arbitrators in international cases, any party may at any time request the appointing authority to furnish a statement setting forth the basis for establishing fees which is customarily followed in international cases in which the authority appoints arbitrators. If the appointing authority consents to provide such a statement, the arbitral tribunal in fixing its fees shall take such information into account to the extent that it considers

appropriate in the circumstances of the case.

4. In cases referred to in paragraphs 2 and 3, when a party so requests and the appointing authority consents to perform the function, the arbitral tribunal shall fix its fees only after consultation with the appointing authority which may make any comment it deems appropriate to the arbitral tribunal concerning the fees.

Article 40

1. Except as provided in paragraph 2, the costs of arbitration shall in principle be borne by the unsuccessful party. However, the arbitral tribunal may apportion each of such costs between the parties if it determines that apportionment is reasonable, taking into account the circumstances of the case.

2. With respect to the costs of legal representation and assistance referred to in article 38 paragraph (e), the arbitral tribunal, taking into account the circumstances of the case, shall be free to determine which party shall bear such cost or may apportion such costs between the parties if it determines that apportionment is reasonable.

3. When the arbitral tribunal issues an order for the termination of the arbitral proceedings or makes an award on agreed terms, it shall fix the costs of arbitration referred to in article 38 and article 39, paragraph 1, in the text of that order or award.

4. No additional fees may be charged by an arbitral tribunal for interpretation or correction or completion of its award under articles 35 to 37.

Deposits of Costs

Article 41

1. The arbitral tribunal, on its establishment, may request each party to deposit an equal amount as an advance for the costs referred to in article 38, paragraphs (a), (b) and (c).

2. During the course of the arbitral proceedings the arbitral tribunal may request supplementary deposits from the parties.

3. If an appointing authority has been agreed upon by the parties or designated by the Secretary-General of the Permanent Court of Arbitration at The Hague, and when a party so requests and the appointing authority consents to perform the function, the arbitral tribunal shall fix the amounts of any deposits or supplementary deposits only after consultation with the appointing authority which may make any comments to the arbitral tribunal which it deems appropriate concerning the amount of such deposits a supplementary deposits.

4. If the required deposits are not paid in full within 30 days after the receipt of the request, the arbitral tribunal shall so inform the parties in order that one or another of them may make the required payment. If such payment is not made, the arbitral tribunal may order the suspension or termination of the arbitral proceedings.

5. After the award has been made, the arbitral tribunal shall render an accounting to the parties of the deposits received and return any unexpected balance to the parties.

Appendix I

CONSTRAINTS ON PARTY AUTONOMY

1. ROME CONVENTION

European Convention on the Law Applicable to Contractual Obligations, 19 June 1980.[1]

Article 5: Certain Consumer Contracts

1. This Article applies to a contract the object of which is the supply of goods or services to a person (the consumer) for a purpose which can be regarded as being outside his trade or profession, or a contract for the provision of credit for that object.

2. Notwithstanding the provisions of Article 3, a choice of law made by the parties shall not have the result of depriving the consumer of the protection afforded to him by the mandatory rules of the law of the country in which he has his habitual residence:

—if in that country the conclusion of the contract was preceded by a specific invitation addressed to him or by advertising, and he had taken in that country all the steps necessary on his part for the conclusion of the contract, or

—if the other party or his agent received the consumer's order in that country, or

—if the contract is for the sale of goods and the consumer travelled from that country to another country and there gave his order, provided that the consumer's journey was arranged by the seller for the purpose of inducing the consumer to buy.

3. Notwithstanding the provisions of Article 4, a contract to which this Article applies shall, in the absence of choice in accordance with Article 3, be governed by the law of the country in which the consumer has his habitual residence if it is entered into in the circumstances described in paragraph 2 of this Article.

4. This Article shall not apply to:

(a) a contract of carriage;

(b) a contract for the supply of services where the services are to be supplied to the consumer exclusively in a country other than that in which he has his habitual residence.

---

1. Official Journal of the European Communities, L266, Vol. 23, 9 October 1980. Reprinted in 19 I.L.M. 1492 (1980).

5. Notwithstanding the provisions of paragraph 4, this Article shall apply to a contract which, for an inclusive price, provides for a combination of travel and accommodation.

Article 7: Mandatory Rules

1. When applying under this Convention the law of a country, effect may be given to the mandatory rules of the law of another country with which the situation has a close connection, if and so far as, under the law of the latter country, those rules must be applied whatever the law applicable to the contract. In considering whether to give effect to these mandatory rules, regard shall be had to their nature and purpose and to the consequences of their application or non-application.

2. Nothing in this Convention shall restrict the application of the rules of the law of the forum in a situation where they are mandatory irrespective of the law otherwise applicable to the contract.

2. RESTATEMENT (SECOND) CONFLICT OF LAWS.

§187. Law of the State Chosen by the Parties

(1) The law of the state chosen by the parties to govern their contractual rights and duties will be applied if the particular issue is one which the parties could have resolved by an explicit provision in their agreement directed to that issue.

(2) The law of the state chosen by the parties to govern their contractual rights and duties will be applied, even if the particular issue is one which the parties could not have resolved by an explicit provision in their agreement directed to that issue, unless either

(a) the chosen state has no substantial relationship to the parties or the transaction and there is no other reasonable basis for the parties' choice, or

(b) application of the law of the chosen state would be contrary to a fundamental policy of a state which has a materially greater interest than the chosen state in the determination of the particular issue and which, under the rule of §188, would be the state of the applicable law in the absence of an effective choice of law by the parties.

(3) In the absence of a contrary indication of intention, the reference is to the local law of the state of the chosen law.

3. Swiss Federal Conflict-of-Laws Act [1]

Article 15

1. The law designated by this Statute is, by way of exception, not applicable if, under all the circumstances, the case clearly has only a slight connection with the designated law, and has a much closer connection with another law.

2. This provision is not applicable where the parties have made a choice of law.

Article 17 (Swiss Public Policy Exception)

The application of provisions of a foreign law is excluded if the outcome is incompatible with Swiss public policy.

Article 18

Provisions of Swiss law which, in view of their special policy, must be applied without regard to the law designated by this Statute remain reserved.

Article 19

1. A provision of a law other than the one designated by this Statute that is meant to be applied mandatorily may be taken into account if interests of a party that are according to Swiss views legitimate and clearly overriding so require and the case is closely connected to that law.

2. Whether such a provision should be taken into account depends on its policy and its consequences for a judgment that is fair according to Swiss views.

Article 116

1. Contracts are governed by the law chosen by the parties.

2. The choice of law must be explicit or clearly evident from the agreement or from the circumstances. Moreover, it is governed by the chosen law.

3. The choice of law can be made or altered at any time. If made or altered after the conclusion of the contract, it takes effect retroactively from the time of the conclusion of the contract. The rights of third parties are reserved.

---

1. Translated and annotated by Pierre A. Karrer, Karl W. Arnold, and Paolo Michele Patocchi, Switzerland's Private International Law (2d ed. 1994). Footnotes have been omitted.

Article 120 (Contracts with Consumers)

1. Contracts for goods and services for the current personal or family consumption or use of a consumer not connected with the professional or business activity of the consumer are governed by the law of the country in which the consumer has his habitual residence:
   (a) if the marketer received the order in that country;
   (b) if in that country an offer or advertisement preceded the making of the contract and the consumer performed in that country the legal actions required to make the contract, or
   (c) if the marketer prompted the consumer to go abroad and make his order there.
2. A choice of law is excluded.

Appendix J

FOREIGN JUDGMENTS

1. UNIFORM FOREIGN MONEY JUDGMENTS ACT.

§ 1. [Definitions]

As used in this Act:

(1) "foreign state" means any governmental unit other than the United States, or any state, district, commonwealth, territory, insular possession thereof, or the Panama Canal Zone, the Trust Territory of the Pacific Islands, or the Ryukyu Islands;

(2) "foreign judgment" means any judgment of a foreign state granting or denying recovery of a sum of money, other than a judgment for taxes, a fine or other penalty, or a judgment for support in matrimonial or family matters.

§ 2. [Applicability]

This Act applies to any foreign judgment that is final and conclusive and enforceable where rendered even though an appeal therefrom is pending or it is subject to appeal.

§ 3. [Recognition and Enforcement]

Except as provided in section 4, a foreign judgment meeting the requirements of section 2 is conclusive between the parties to the extent that it grants or denies recovery of a sum of money. The foreign judgment is enforceable in the same manner as the judgment of a sister state which is entitled to full faith and credit.

§ 4. [Grounds for Non-recognition]

(a) A foreign judgment is not conclusive if

(1) the judgment was rendered under a system which does not provide impartial tribunals or procedures compatible with the requirements of due process of law;

(2) the foreign court did not have personal jurisdiction over the defendant; or

(3) the foreign court did not have jurisdiction over the subject matter.

(b) A foreign judgment need not be recognized if

(1) the defendant in the proceedings in the foreign court did not receive notice of the proceedings in sufficient time to enable him to defend;

(2) the judgment was obtained by fraud;

(3) the [cause of action] [claim for relief] on which the judgment is based is repugnant to the public policy of this state;

(4) the judgment conflicts with another final and conclusive judgment;

(5) the proceeding in the foreign court was contrary to an agreement between the parties under which the dispute in question was to be settled otherwise than by proceedings in that court; or

(6) in the case of jurisdiction based only on personal service, the foreign court was a seriously inconvenient forum for the trial of the action.

§ 5. [Personal Jurisdiction]

(a) The foreign judgment shall not be refused recognition for lack of personal jurisdiction if

(1) the defendant was served personally in the foreign state;

(2) the defendant voluntarily appeared in the proceedings, other than for the purpose of protecting property seized or threatened with seizure in the proceedings or of contesting the jurisdiction of the court over him;

(3) the defendant prior to the commencement of the proceedings had agreed to submit to the jurisdiction of the foreign court with respect to the subject matter involved;

(4) the defendant was domiciled in the foreign state when the proceedings were instituted, or, being a body corporate had its principal place of business, was incorporated, or had otherwise acquired corporate status, in the foreign state;

(5) the defendant had a business office in the foreign state and the proceedings in the foreign court involved a [cause of action] [claim for relief] arising out of business done by the defendant through that office in the foreign state; or

(6) the defendant operated a motor vehicle or airplane in the foreign state and the proceedings involved a [cause of action] [claim for relief] arising out of such operation.

(b) The courts of this state may recognize other bases of jurisdiction.

§ 6. [Stay in Case of Appeal]

If the defendant satisfies the court either that an appeal is pending or that he is entitled and intends to appeal from the foreign judgment, the court may stay the proceedings until the appeal has been determined or until the expiration of a period of time sufficient to enable the defendant to prosecute the appeal.

§ 7. [Saving Clause]

This Act does not prevent the recognition of a foreign judgment in situations not covered by this Act.

§ 8. [Uniformity of Interpretation]

This Act shall be so construed as to effectuate its general purpose to make uniform the law of those states which enact it.

§ 9. [Short Title]

This Act may be cited as the Uniform Foreign Money-Judgments Recognition Act.

UNIFORM FOREIGN MONEY-JUDGMENTS RECOGNITION ACT
JURISDICTIONS WHERE ACT HAS BEEN ADOPTED

Jurisdiction	Statutory Citation
Alaska	AS 90.30.100 to 09.30.180
California	Cal.C.C.P. §§ 1713 to 1713.8.
Colorado	C.R.S.A. §§ 13-62-101 to 13-62-109.
Connecticut	C.G.S.A. §§ 50a-30 to 50a-38.
Georgia	O.C.G.A. §§ 9-12-110 to 9-12-117.
Idaho	I.C. §§ 10-1401 to 10-1409.
Illinois	S.H.A. 735 ILCS 5/12-618 to 5/12-626.
Iowa	I.C.A. §§ 626B.1 to 626B.8.
Maryland	Code, Courts and Judicial Proceedings, §§ 10-701 to 1-709.
Massachusetts	M.G.L. c. 235, § 23A.
Michigan	M.C.L. §§ 691.1151 to 691.1159.
Minnesota	M.S.A. § 548.35.
Missouri	V.A.M.S. §§ 511.770 to 511.787.
New Mexico	NMSA 1978, §§ 39-4B-1 to 39-4B-9.
New York	CPLR 5301 to 5309.
Ohio	R.C. §§ 2329.90 to 2329.94.
Oklahoma	12 Okl.St.Ann. § 710 to 718.
Oregon	ORS 24.200 to 24.255.
Pennsylvania	42 P.S. §§ 22001 to 22009.
Texas	V.T.C.A., Civil Practice and Remedies Code §§ 36.001 to 36.008.
Virgin Islands	5 V.I.C. §§ 561b to 569.
Virginia	Code 1950, §§ 8.01-465.6 to 8.01-465.13.
Washington	RCWA 6.40.010 to 6.40.915.

2. SWISS FEDERAL CONFLICT-OF-LAWS ACT.[1]

Section 5: Recognition and Enforcement of Foreign Decisions

Article 25

A foreign decision is recognized in Switzerland:

(a) if jurisdiction lay with the judicial or administrative authorities of the country in which the decision was rendered;

(b) if no ordinary judicial remedy can any longer be brought against the decision or if the decision is final, and

(c) if no ground for non-recognition under Article 27 exists.

Article 26

Jurisdiction lies with a foreign authority,

(a) if a provision of this Statute so provides or, if there is no such provision, if the defendant had his domicile, in the country where the decision was rendered;

(b) if, in disputes of financial interest the parties by an agreement valid under this Statute subjected themselves to the jurisdiction of the authority, that rendered the decision;

(c) if in a dispute of financial interest the defendant entered an unconditional appearance, or

(d) if, in the case of a counterclaim, the authority that rendered the decision had jurisdiction over the principal claim, and the two claims are factually connected.

Article 27

1. A foreign decision is not recognized in Switzerland if its recognition would be clearly incompatible with Swiss public policy.

2. A foreign decision is also not recognized if a party proves:

(a) that neither according to the law of its domicile nor according to the law of its habitual residence, was the party properly served with process, unless the party entered an unconditional appearance in the proceedings.

(b) that the judgment was rendered in violation of essential principles of Swiss procedural law, especially, the party was denied the right to be heard;

(c) that a lawsuit between the same parties concerning the same case was first commenced or decided in Switzerland, or was first decided in a third country, provided that the prerequisites for the recognition of that decision are met.

---

1. Translation by Pierre Karrer, Karl W. Arnold, and Paolo Michele Patocchi, SWITZERLAND'S PRIVATE INTERNATIONAL LAW (2d ed. 1994). Footnotes have been omitted.

3. In no other respects may the foreign decision be reviewed on the merits.

Article 28

A decision recognized pursuant to Articles 25 to 27 is declared enforceable on petition by the interested party.

Article 29

1. A petition for recognition or declaration of enforceability must be directed to the competent authority of the canton in which the foreign decision is invoked. The following must be attached to the petition:
(a) a complete and certified original of the decision;
(b) a certificate that no ordinary judicial remedy can any longer be brought against the decision or that the decision is final; and
(c) in case of a decision by default, a document establishing that the losing party was properly and timely served with process, and had a reasonable opportunity to defend itself.
2. The party opposing the petition must be heard; the party may present evidence.
3. If a foreign decision is invoked on a preliminary point, the authority seized may itself decide on recognition.

Article 30

Articles 25 to 29 also apply to a settlement in court if in the country in which it was made the settlement is considered equivalent to a judgment.

Article 31

Articles 25 to 29 apply by analogy to the recognition and enforcement of a judgment or document of noncontentious jurisdiction.

Article 32

1. A foreign decision or document concerning civil status is recorded in the Register of Civil Status if it is so ordered by the cantonal supervisory authority.
2. Registration is permitted if the conditions of Articles 25 to 27 are met.
3. If it is unclear whether the procedural rights of the parties were sufficiently safeguarded in the foreign rendering country, the interested parties must be heard.

3. United Kingdom.

Foreign Judgments (Reciprocal Enforcement) Act. 13 April 1933

Section: 1

Power to extend Part I of Act to foreign countries giving reciprocal treatment

(1) If, in the case of any foreign country, Her Majesty is satisfied that, in the event of the benefits conferred by this Part of this Act being extended to, or to any particular class of, judgments given in the courts of that country or in any particular class of those courts, substantial reciprocity of treatment will be assured as regards the enforcement in that country of similar judgments given in similar courts of the United Kingdom, She may by Order in Council direct—

(a) that this Part of this Act shall extend to that country;

(b) that such courts of that country as are specified in the Order shall be recognised courts of that country for the purposes of this Part of this Act; and

(c) that judgments of any such recognised court, or such judgments of any class so specified, shall, if within subsection (2) of this section, be judgments to which this Part of this Act applies.

(2) Subject to subsection (2A) of this section, a judgment of a recognized court is within this subsection if it satisfies the following conditions, namely—

(a) it is either final and conclusive as between the judgment debtor and the judgment creditor or requires the former to make an interim payment to the latter; and

(b) there is payable under it a sum of money, not being a sum payable in respect of taxes or other charges of a like nature or in respect of a fine or other penalty; and

(c) it is given after the coming into force of the Order in Council which made that court a recognised court.

(2A) The following judgments of a recognised court are not within subsection (2) of this section—

(a) a judgment given by that court on appeal from a court which is not a recognised court;

(b) a judgment or other instrument which is regarded for the purposes of its enforcement as a judgment of that court but which was given or made in another country;

(c) a judgment given by that court in proceedings founded on a judgment of a court in another country and having as their object the enforcement of that judgment.

(3) For the purposes of this section, a judgment shall be deemed to be final and conclusive notwithstanding that an appeal may be pending against it, or that it may

still be subject to appeal, in the courts of the country of the original court.

(4) His Majesty may be a subsequent Order in Council vary or revoke any Order previously made under this section.

(5) Any Order in Council made under this section before its amendment by the Civil Jurisdiction and Judgments Act 1982 which deems any court of a foreign country to be a superior court of that country for the purposes of this Part of this Act shall (without prejudice to subsection (4) of this section) have effect from the time of that amendment as if it provided for that court to be a recognised court of that country for those purposes, and for any final and conclusive judgment of that court, if within subsection (2) of this section, to be a judgment to which this Part of this Act applies.

Section: 2

Application for, and effect of, registration of foreign judgment

(1) A person, being a judgment creditor under a judgment to which this Part of this Act applies, may apply to the High Court at any time within six years after the date of the judgment, or, where there have been proceedings by way of appeal against the judgment, after the date of the last judgment given in those proceedings, to have the judgment registered in the High Court, and on any such application the court shall, subject to proof of the prescribed matters and to the other provisions of this Act, order the judgment to be registered:

Provided that a judgment shall not be registered if at the date of the application—

(a) it has been wholly satisfied; or

(b) it could not be enforced by execution in the country of the original court.

(2) Subject to the provisions of this Act with respect to the setting aside of registration—

(a) a registered judgment shall, for the purposes of execution, be of the same force and effect; and

(b) proceedings may be taken on a registered judgment; and

(c) the sum for which a judgment is registered shall carry interest; and

(d) the registering court shall have the same control over the execution of a registered judgment; as if the judgment had been a judgment originally given in the registering court and entered on the date of registration:

Provided that execution shall not issue on the judgment so long as, under this Part of the Act and the Rules of Court made thereunder, it is competent for any party to make an application to have the registration of the judgment set aside, or, where such an application is made, until after the application has been finally determined.

(3) [Omitted]

(4) If at the date of the application for registration the judgment of the original court has been partly satisfied, the judgment shall not be registered in respect of the whole sum payable under the judgment of the original court, but only in respect of the balance remaining payable at that date.

(5) If, on an application for the registration of a judgment, it appears to the registering court that the judgment is in respect of different matters and that some, but not all, of the provisions of the judgment are such that if those provisions had been contained in separate judgments those judgments could properly have been registered, the judgment may be registered in respect of the provisions aforesaid but not in respect of any other provisions contained therein.

(6) In addition to the sum of money payable under the judgment of the original court, including any interest which by the law of the country of the original court becomes due under the judgment up to the time of registration, the judgment shall be registered for the reasonable costs of and incidental to registration, including the costs of obtaining a certified copy of the judgment from the original court.

Section: 3: Rules of Court

(1) The power to make rules of court under section [84 of the Supreme Court Act 1981], shall, subject to the provisions of this section, include power to make rules for the following purposes—

(a) For making provision with respect to the giving of security for costs by persons applying for the registration of judgments;

(b) For prescribing the matters to be proved on an application for the registration of a judgment and for regulating the mode of proving those matters;

(c) For providing for the service on the judgment debtor of notice of the registration of a judgment;

(d) For making provision with respect to the fixing of the period within which an application may be made to have the registration of the judgment set aside and with respect to the extension of the period so fixed;

(e) For prescribing the method by which any question arising under this Act whether a foreign judgment can be enforced by execution in the country of the original court, or what interest is payable under a foreign judgment under the law of the original court, is to be determined;

(f) For prescribing any matter which under this Part of this Act is to be prescribed.

(2) Rules made for the purposes of this Part of this Act shall be expressed to have, and shall have, effect subject to any such provisions contained in Order in Council made under section one of this Act as are declared by the said Orders to be necessary for giving effect to agreements made between His Majesty and foreign countries in relation to matters with respect to which there is power to make rules of court for the purposes of this Part of this Act.

Section: 4: Cases in which registered judgments must, or may, be set aside

(1) On an application in that behalf duly made by any party against whom a registered judgment may be enforced, the registration of the judgment—

    (a) shall be set aside if the registering court is satisfied—

        (i) that the judgment is not a judgment to which this Part of this Act applies or was registered in contravention of the foregoing provisions of this Act; or

        (ii) that the courts of the country of the original court had no jurisdiction in the circumstances of the case; or

        (iii) that the judgment debtor, being the defendant in the proceedings in the original court, did not (notwithstanding that process may have been duly served on him in accordance with the law of the country of the original court) receive notice of those proceedings in sufficient time to enable him to defend the proceedings and did not appear; or

        (iv) that the judgment was obtained by fraud; or

        (v) that the enforcement of the judgment would be contrary to public policy in the country of the registering court; or

        (vi) that the rights under the judgment are not vested in the person by whom the application for registration was made;

    (b) may be set aside if the registering court is satisfied that the matter in dispute in the proceedings in the original court had previously to the date of the judgment in the original court been the subject of a final and conclusive judgment by a court having jurisdiction in the matter.

(2) For the purposes of this section the courts of the country of the original court shall, subject to the provisions of subsection (3) of this section, be deemed to have had jurisdiction—

    (a) in the case of a judgment given in an action in personam—

        (i) if the judgment debtor, being a defendant in the original court, submitted to the jurisdiction of that court by voluntarily appearing in the proceedings . . . ; or

        (ii) if the judgment debtor was plaintiff in, or counter-claimed in, the proceedings in the original court; or

        (iii) if the judgment debtor, being a defendant in the original court, had before the commencement of the proceedings agreed, in respect of the subject matter of the proceedings, to submit to the jurisdiction of that court or of the courts of the country of that court; or

        (iv) if the judgment debtor, being a defendant in the original court, was at the time when the proceedings were instituted resident in, or being a body corporate had its principal place of business in, the country of that court; or

        (v) if the judgment debtor, being a defendant in the original court, had an office or place of business in the country of that court and the proceedings in that court were in respect of a transaction effected through or at that office or place;

(b) in the case of a judgment given in an action of which the subject matter was immovable property or in an action in rem of which the subject matter was movable property, if the property in question was at the time of the proceedings in the original court situate in the country of that court;

(c) in the case of a judgment given in an action other than any such action as is mentioned in paragraph (a) or paragraph (b) of this subsection, if the jurisdiction of the original court is recognised by the law of the registering court.

(3) Notwithstanding anything in subsection (2) of this section, the courts of the country of the original court shall not be deemed to have had jurisdiction—

(a) if the subject matter of the proceedings was immovable property outside the country of the original court; or

(b) [Omitted]

(c) if the judgment debtor, being a defendant in the original proceedings, was a person who under the rules of public international law was entitled to immunity from the jurisdiction of the courts of the country of the original court and did not submit to the jurisdiction of that court.

Section: 5: Powers of registering court on application to set aside registration

(1) If, on an application to set aside the registration of a judgment, the applicant satisfies the registering court either that an appeal is pending, or that he is entitled and intends to appeal, against the judgment, the court, if it thinks fit, may, on such terms as it may think just, either set aside the registration or adjourn the application to set aside the registration until after the expiration of such period as appears to the court to be reasonably sufficient to enable the applicant to take the necessary steps to have the appeal disposed of by the competent tribunal.

(2) Where the registration of a judgment is set aside under the last foregoing subsection, or solely for the reason that the judgment was not at the date of the application for registration enforceable by execution in the country of the original court, the setting aside of the registration shall not prejudice a further application to register the judgment when the appeal has been disposed of or if and when the judgment becomes enforceable by execution in that country, as the case may be.

(3) Where the registration of a judgment is set aside solely for the reason that the judgment, notwithstanding that it had at the date of the application for registration been partly satisfied, was registered for the whole sum payable thereunder, the registering court shall, on the application of the judgment creditor, order judgment to be registered for the balance remaining payable at that date.

Section: 6 : Foreign judgments which can be registered not to be enforceable otherwise

No proceedings for the recovery of a sum payable under a foreign judgment, being a judgment to which this Part of this Act applies, other than proceedings by way of registration of the judgment, shall be entertained by any court in the United Kingdom.

Section: 7: Power to apply Part I of Act to British dominions, protectorates and mandated territories

(1) His Majesty may by Order in Council direct that this Part of this Act shall apply to His Majesty's dominions outside the United Kingdom and to judgments obtained in the courts of the said dominions as it applies to foreign countries and judgments obtained in the courts of foreign countries, and in the event of His Majesty so directing, this Act shall have effect accordingly and Part II of the Administration of Justice Act 1920, shall cease to have effect except in relation to those parts of the said dominions to which it extends at the date of the Order.

(2) If at any time after His Majesty has directed as aforesaid an Order in Council is made under section one of this Act extending Part I of this Act to any part of His Majesty's dominions to which the said Part II extends as aforesaid, the said Part II shall cease to have effect in relation to that part of His Majesty's dominions.

(3) References in this section to His Majesty's dominions outside the United Kingdom shall be construed as including references to any territories which are under His Majesty's protection and to any territories in respect of which a mandate under the League of Nations has been accepted by His Majesty.

Section: 8
General effect of certain foreign judgments

(1) Subject to the provisions of this section, a judgment to which Part I of this Act applies or would have applied if a sum of money had been payable thereunder, whether it can be registered or not, and whether, if it can be registered, it is registered or not, shall be recognised in any court in the United Kingdom as conclusive between the parties thereto in all proceedings founded on the same cause of action and may be relied on by way of defence or counterclaim in any such proceedings.

(2) This section shall not apply in the case of any judgment—

(a) where the judgment has been registered and the registration thereof has been set aside on some ground other than—

(i) that a sum of money was not payable under the judgment; or

(ii) that the judgment had been wholly or partly satisfied; or

(iii) that at the date of the application the judgment could not be enforced by execution in the country of the original court; or

(b) where the judgment has not been registered, it is shown (whether it could have been registered or not) that if it had been registered the registration thereof would have been set aside on an application for that purpose on some ground other than one of the grounds specified in paragraph (a) of this subsection.

(3) Nothing in this section shall be taken to prevent any court in the United Kingdom recognising any judgment as conclusive of any matter of law or fact decided therein if that judgment would have been so recognised before the passing of this Act.

Section: 9: Power to make foreign judgments unenforceable in United Kingdom if no reciprocity

(1) If it appears to His Majesty that the treatment in respect of recognition and enforcement accorded by the courts of any foreign country to judgments given in the . . . courts of the United Kingdom is substantially less favourable than that accorded by the courts of the United Kingdom to judgments of the . . . courts of that country, His Majesty may by Order in Council apply this section to that country.

(2) Except in so far as His Majesty may by Order in Council under this section otherwise direct, no proceedings shall be entertained in any court in the United Kingdom for the recovery of any sum alleged to be payable under a judgment given in a court of a country to which this section applies.

(3) His Majesty may by a subsequent Order in Council vary or revoke any Order previously made under this section.

Section: 10: Provision for issue of copies of, and certificates in connection with, UK judgments

(1) Rules may make provision for enabling any judgment creditor wishing to secure the enforcement in a foreign country to which Part I of this Act extends of a judgment to which this subsection applies, to obtain, subject to any conditions specified in the rules—
(a) a copy of the judgment; and
(b) a certificate giving particulars relating to the judgment and the proceedings in which it was given.

(2) Subsection (1) applies to any judgment given by a court or tribunal in the United Kingdom under which a sum of money is payable, not being a sum payable in respect of taxes or other charges of a like nature or in respect of a fine or other penalty.

(3) In this section "rules"—
(a) in relation to judgments given by a court, means rules of court;
(b) in relation to judgments given by any other tribunal, means rules or regulations made by the authority having power to make rules or regulations regulating the procedure of that tribunal.

Section: 10A: Arbitration awards

The provisions of this Act, except sections 1(5) and 6, shall apply as they apply to a judgment, in relation to an award in proceedings on an arbitration which has, in pursuance of the law in force in t he place where it was made, become enforceable in the same manner as a judgment given by a court in that place.

Section: 11: Interpretation

(1) In this Act, unless the context otherwise requires, the following expressions have the meanings hereby assigned to them respectively, that is to say—

"Appeal" includes any proceeding by way of discharging or setting aside a judgment or an application for a new trial or a stay of execution;

"Country of the original court" means the country in which the original court is situated;

"Judgment" means a judgment or order given or made by a court in any civil proceedings, or a judgment or order given or made by a court in any criminal proceedings for the payment of a sum of money in respect of compensation or damages to an injured party;

"Judgment creditor" means the person in whose favour the judgment was given and includes any person against whom the judgment is enforceable under the law of the original court;

"Original court" in relation to any judgment means the court by which the judgment was given;

"Prescribed" means prescribed by rules of court;

"Registration" means registration under Part I of this Act, and the expressions "register" and "registered" shall be construed accordingly;

"Registering court" in relation to any judgment means the court to which an application to register the judgment is made.

(2) For the purposes of this Act, the expression "action in personam" shall not be deemed to include any matrimonial cause or any proceedings in connection with any of the following matters, that is to say, matrimonial matters, administration of the estates of deceased persons, bankruptcy, winding up of companies, lunacy, or guardianship of infants.

Section: 12: Application to Scotland

This Act in its application to Scotland shall have effect subject to the following modifications:—

(a) For any reference to the High Court (except in section eleven of this Act) there shall be substituted a reference to the Court of Session:

(b) The Court of Session shall, subject to the provisions of subsection (2) of section three of this Act, have power by Act of Sederunt to make rules for the purposes specified in subsection (1) of the said section:

(c) Registration under Part I of this Act shall be effected by registering in the Books of Council and Session or in such manner as the Court of Session may by Act of Sederunt prescribe:

(d) For any reference to section two hundred and thirteen of the Supreme Court of Judicature (Consolidation) Act, 1925, there shall be substituted a reference to the Courts of Law Fees (Scotland) Act, 1895:

(e) For any reference to the entering of a judgment there shall be substituted a reference to the signing of the interlocutor embodying the judgment.

Section: 13: Application to Northern Ireland

This Act in its application to Northern Ireland shall have effect subject to the following modifications:—

(a) References to the High Court shall, unless the context otherwise requires, be construed as references to the High Court in Northern Ireland:

(b) For the references to section ninety-nine of the Supreme Court of Judicature (Consolidation) Act 1925, there shall be substituted references to sections 55 ... of the Judicature (Northern Ireland) Act 1978.

Section: 14: Short title

This Act may be cited as the Foreign Judgments (Reciprocal Enforcement) Act 1933.

Appendix K

ANALYTIC TABLE OF SELECTED JUDICIAL DECISIONS

I. FEDERAL CASES.

A. Cases Failing to Honor Forum Selection Clauses.

1. Red Bull Assoc. v. Best Western, 862 F.2d 963 (2d Cir. 1988).
2. Union Ins. Soc. of Canton, Ltd. v. S.S. Elikon, 642 F.2d 721 (4th Cir. 1981).
3. Hoffman v. Minuteman Press Int'l Inc., 747 F. Supp. 552 (W.D. Mo. 1990).
4. Van's Supply & Equipment v. Echo, 711 F.Supp. 497 (W.D.Wis. 1989).
5. Continental Grain Export Corp. v. Ministry of War-Etka Co., 603 F.Supp. 724 (S.D.N.Y. 1984).
6. McDonnell Douglas Corp. v. Islamic Republic of Iran, 591 F. Supp. 293 (E.D. Mo. 1984).
7. Leasewell, Ltd. v. Jack Shelton Ford, Inc., 423 F.Supp. 1011 (S.D.W.Va. 1976).

B. Cases Commending Forum Selection Clauses in Order to Dispatch Parties to Another Forum.

1. Stewart Organization Inc. v. Ricoh Corp., 487 U.S. 22 (1988).
2. The Bremen v. Zapata Off-Shore Co., 407 U.S. 1 (1972).
3. Lambert v. Kysar, 983 F.2d 1110 (1st Cir. 1993).
4. Roby v. Corporation of Lloyd's, 996 F.2d 1353 (2nd Cir. N.Y. 1993).
5. Milanovich v. Costa Crorciere, S.p.A., 964 F.2d 763 (D.C.Cir. 1992).
6. Riley v. Kingsley Underwriting Agencies, Ltd., 969 F.2d 953 (10th Cir. 1992).
7. Trinidad Foundry and Fabricating, Ltd. v. M/V K.A.S. Camilla, 966 F.2d 613 (11th Cir. 1992).
8. Royal Bed and Spring Co., Inc. v Famossul Industria e Commercio de Moveis Ltda., 906 F.2d 45 (1st Cir. 1990).
9. Taag Linhas Aeras de Angola v. Transamerica Airlines, Inc., 915 F.2d 1351 (9th Cir. 1990).
10. Forsythe v. Saudi Arabian Airlines Corp., 885 F.2d 285 (5th Cir. 1989).
11. Instrumentation Assoc. v. Madsen Electronics (Canada) Ltd., 859 F.2d 4 (3rd Cir. 1988).
12. Manetti-Farrow, Inc. v. Gucci, 858 F.2d 509 (9th Cir. 1988).

13. Sterling Forest Associates, Ltd. v. Barnett-Range Corp., 840 F.2d 249 (4th Cir. 1988).
14. Andrews v. Heinhold Commodities, Inc., 771 F.2d 184 (7th Cir. 1985).
15. AVC Nederland B.V. v. Atrium Inv. Partnership, 740 F.2d 148 (2nd Cir. 1984).
16. General Elec. Co. v. G. Siempelkimp GmbH & Co., 809 F. Supp. 1306 (S.D. Ohio 1993).
17. Lawler v. Schumacher Filters America, Inc., 832 F. Supp. 1044 (E.D. Va. 1993).
18. Bonny v. Society of Lloyd's, 784 F.Supp. 1350 (N.D.Ill. 1992).
19. Water Energizers Ltd. v. Water Energizers Inc., 788 F. Supp. 208 (S.D.N.Y. 1992).
20. Weiss v. Columbia Pictures Television, Inc., 801 F. Supp. 1276 (S.D.N.Y. 1992).
21. Best Buy Co. v. Onkyo U.S.A. No CIV.A.4-90-677, 1991 WL 156571 (D.Minn. 1991).
22. Compton v. A.G. Edwards & Sons, Inc., 728 F. Supp. 629 (D. Or. 1990).
23. Medoil v. Citicorp, 729 F.Supp. 1456 (S.D.N.Y. 1990).
24. Advent Electronics v. Samsung Semiconductors, 709 F.Supp. 843 (N.D.Ill. 1989).
25. Page Construction v. Perini Construction, 712 F.Supp. 9 (D.R.I. 1989).
26. Ritchie v. Carvel, 714 F.Supp. 700 (S.D.N.Y. 1989).
27. L.A. Pipeline Const. Co. v. Texas Eastern Products Pipeline Co., 699 F. Supp. 266 (S.D.Ind. 1988).
28. Lexington Investment Co. v. Southwest Stainless, Inc., 697 F. Supp. 139 (S.D.N.Y. 1988).
29. TUC v. Eagle Telephones, 698 F.Supp. 35 (D.Conn. 1988).
30. Falcoal, Inc. v. Trukiye Komur Isletmeleri Kurumu, 660 F.Supp. 1536 (S.D.Tex. 1987).
31. Hughes Drilling Fluides v. M/V Luo Fu Shan, No. CIV.A. 86-1844, 1987 WL 12595, (E.D.La. 1987).
32. Tisdale v. Shell Oil Co., 723 F.Supp. 653 (M.D.Ala. 1987).
33. Benge v. Software Galaria, Inc., 608 F. Supp. 601 (E.D. Mo. 1985).
34. Karlberg European Transpa, Inc. v. Jk-Josef Kratz Vertriegbsgesellschaft mbH, 618 F.Supp. 344 (N.D.Ill. 1985).
35. Adelson v. World Transportation, Inc., 631 F. Supp. 504 (S.D. Fla. 1984).
36. Cuevas v. Reading & Bates Corp., 577 F.Supp. 462 (S.D. Tex 1983).
37. D'Antruono v. CCH Computax Systems, Inc., 570 F. Supp. 708 (D. R.I. 1983).
38. Richardson Engineering Co. v. International Business Machines Corp., 554 F. Supp. 467 (D.Vt. 1981).
39. Staco Energy Products Co. v. Driver-Harris CO., 509 F. Supp. 1226 (S.D. Ohio 1981).
40. Hoes of America, Inc. V. Hoes, 493 F.Supp. 1205 (C.D.Ill. 1979).

41. Wellmore Coal Corp. v. Gates Learjet Corp., 475 F. Supp. 1140 (W.D. Va. 1979).

C. Cases Recognizing Forum Selection Clauses in Order to Hear the Dispute.

1. Heller Financial, Inc. v. Midwhey Powder Co., Inc., 883 F.2d 1286 (7th Cir. 1989).
2. Submersible Systems Technology, Inc. v. 21st Century Film Corp., 767 F. Supp. 266 (S.D. Fla. 1991).
3. Paribas Corp. v. Shelton Ranch Corp., 742 F. Supp. 1483 (S.D.N.Y. 1990).
4. First Interstate Leasing v. Sagge, 697 F.Supp. 744 (S.D.N.Y. 1988).
5. St. Paul Fire and Marine v. Travellers Indemnity, 401 F. Supp. 927 (D. Mass. 1975).

II. STATE CASES.

A. Cases Failing to Honor Forum Selection Clauses.

1. Ernest and Norman Hart Bros. Inc. v. Town Contractors, 18 Mass. App.Ct. 60, 463 N.E.2d 355 (1984).
2. High Life Sales Co. v. Brown-Forman Corp., 823 S.W.2d 493 (Mo. 1992).
3. Tandy Computer Leasing, Div. of Tandy Electronics, Inc. v. Terina's Pizza, Inc., 105 Nev. 841, 784 P.2d 7 (1989).
4. Dancart Corp. v. St. Albans Rubber Co., 124 N.H. 598, 474 A.2d 1020 (1984).
5. Credit Francais Int'l S.A. v. Sociedad Financiere de Comerico, C.A., 490 N.Y.S.2d 670, 128 Misc.2d 564 (1985).
6. United Standard Management v. Mahoney Valley Solar, 16 Ohio App.3d 476, 476 N.E.2d 724 (1984).
7. United Standard Management Corp. v. Mahoning Valley Solar Resources, Inc., 16 Ohio App.3d 476, 476 N.E.2d 724 (1984).
8. Eads v. Woodmen of the World Life Ins. Co., 785 P.2d 328 (Okl.App. 1989).
9. Dyersburg Machine Works, Inc. v. Rentenbach Eng'g Co., 650 S.W.2d 378 (Tenn. 1983).
10. Exum v. Vantage Press Co., 17 Wash. App. 477, 563 P.2d 1314 (1977).

B. Cases Commending Forum Selection Clauses in Order to Dispatch Parties to Another Forum.

1. Volkswagenwerk, A.G. v. Klippan, GMBH, 611 P.2d 498 (Alaska 1980).
2. Societe Jean Nichoas et Fils v. Mousseux, 123 Ariz. 59, 597 P.2d 541 (1979).

3. Smith, Valentino & Smith, Inc. v. Super. Ct. of Los Angeles County, 17 Cal.3d 491, 131 Cal. Rptr. 374, 551 P.2d 1206 (1976).
4. ABC Mobile Systems, Inc. v. Harvey, 701 P.2d 137 (Colo. Ct. App. 1985).
5. Funding Systems Leasing Corp. v. Diaz, 34 Conn.Supp. 99, 378 A.2d 108 (1977).
6. Elia Corp. v. Paul N. Howard Co., 391 A.2d 214 (Del. Super. Ct. 1978).
7. Manrique v. Fabbri, 11 Fla. L. Week. 430, 493 So.2d 437 (1986).
8. Calanca v. D & S Mfg. Co., 157 Ill. App. 3d 85, 510 N.E.2d 21 (1987).
9. Prudential Resources Corp. v. Plunkett, 583 S.W.2d 97 (Ky. Ct. App. 1979).
10. James v. Midland County Agr. and Horticultural Soc., 107 Mich.App. 1, 308 N.W.2d 688 (Mich.App. 1981).
11. Hauenstein & Bermeister, Inc. v. Met-Fab Indus., Inc., 216 Neb. 426, 344 N.W.2d 454 (1984).
12. Air Economy Corp. v. Aero-Flow Dynamics, Inc., 122 N.J. Super. 456, 300 A.2d 856 (1973).
13. Reeves v. Chem. Indus. Co., 262 Or. 95, 495 P.2d 729 (1972).
14. Central Contracting Co. v. C.E. Youngdahl & Co., 418 Pa. 122, 209 A.2d 810 (1965).
15. St. John's Episcopal Center v. South Carolina Dep't of Social Serv., 276 S.C. 507, 280 S.E.2d 207 (1981).
16. Green v. Clinic Master, Inc., 272 N.W.2d 813 (S.D. 1978).

C. Cases Recognizing Forum Selection Clauses in Order to Hear the Dispute.

1. SD Leasing, Inc. v. Al Spain and Assocs., 277 Ark. 178, 640 S.W.2d 451 (1982).
2. Kimco Leasing, Inc. v. Ransom Junior High School, 61 Ed. Law Rep. 721, 556 N.E.2d 1371 (Ind.App. 1990).
3. Vanier (Jerry D.), d/b/a Vanier v. Ponsoldt (William R.), d/b/a Pegasus Ranch, Pegasus Ranch, Inc., Bethesda Farm, Inc., 251 Kan. 88, 833 P.2d 949 (1992).
4. Electrical Prod. Consol. v. Bodell, 132 Mont. 243, 69 A.L.R.2d 1318, 316 P.2d 788 (1957).
5. International Collection Serv., Inc. v. Gibbs, 147 Vt. 105, 510 A.2d 1325 (1986).
6. Kuhn, State ex rel. v. Luchsinger, 231 Wis. 533, 286 N.W. 72 (1939).

Appendix L

TABLE OF CASES SITED

Principal cases discussed are in bold type. Other cases cited are in roman type. Page references follow the case citation.

1. COURTS IN THE UNITED STATES.

2. Foreign Tribunals.

3. Decisions of Arbitral and International Tribunals.

Appendix M

SELECTED BIBLIOGRAPHY

Book titles appear in capitals, while the titles of articles are listed in italics.

Abi-Saab, Georges, *De l'arbitrage dans ses rapports avec la justice internationale,* in ETUDES DE DROIT INTERNATIONAL EN L'HONNEUR DE PIERRE LALAIVE 377 (C. Dominicé, R. Patry & C. Reymond, eds., 1993).

Abrams, Douglas E., *Arbitrability in Recent Federal Civil Rights Legislation: The Need for Amendment,* 26 Connecticut Law Review 521 (1994).

Abrams, Roger I., Frances Abrams and Dennis Nolan, *Arbitral Therapy,* 46 RUTGERS LAW REVIEW 1751 (1994).

Aksen, Gerald, *American Arbitration Accession Arrives in the Age of Aquarius: United States Implements United Nations Convention on the Recognition and Enforcement of Foreign Arbitral Awards,* 3 SOUTHWESTERN UNIVERSITY LAW REVIEW 1 (1971).

Aksen, Gerald, *Application of the New York Convention by United States Courts,* IV YEARBOOK COMMERCIAL ARBITRATION 341 (1979).

Aksen, Gerald, *Consolidated Arbitrations,* in WIDE WORLD OF ARBITRATION: AN ANTHOLOGY 64 (C. Gold & S. Mackenzie, eds., 1978).

Aksen, Gerald, *Multi-Party Arbitrations in the United States,* in ARBITRATION AND THE LICENSING PROCESS (R. Goldscheider & M. de Haas, eds., 1984).

Alexander, Larry and Emily Sherwin, *The Deceptive Nature of Rules,* 142 U. PENN. LAW REVIEW 1191 (1994).

Alzamora, Carlos, *Reflections on the U.N. Compensation Commission,* 9 ARB. INT'L 349 (1993).

American Arbitration Association, *Party Appointed Arbitrators,* 16 LAWYERS' ARB. LETTER (No. 4) (Vicki Young, ed., Winter 1992/93).

American Arbitration Association, *Consolidation and the Arbitration Agreement,* 18 LAWYERS' ARB. LETTER (No. 1) (Vicki Young, ed., Spring 1994).

Antaki, N., *L'Amiable composition,* in ACTES DU 1ER COLLOQUE SUR L'ARBITRAGE COMMERCIAL INTERNATIONAL (ed. N. Antaki & A. Prujiner, 1985).

Arkin, Harry, *International Ad Hoc Arbitration: A Practical Alternative,* 15 INT'L BUSINESS LAWYER 5 (1987).

Arkin, Harry, *Pre-Arbitration Dispute Resolution: What is it, Where is it, and Why?,* INTERNATIONAL BUSINESS LAWYER 373, September 1993.

Armfelt, Andrew, *Avoiding the Arbitration Trap*, FINANCIAL TIMES, 27 October 1992, at 17, cols. 1-4.

Arnaldez, Jean-Jacques, Yves Derains and Sigvard Jarvin (eds.), COLLECTION OF ICC ARBITRAL AWARDS, Volume I — Awards 1974-85 (1990) and Volume II — Awards 1986-90 (1994).

Arnold, Karl, Pierre Karrer and Paolo Michele Patocchi, SWITZERLAND'S PRIVATE INTERNATIONAL LAW (2nd Ed. 1994).

Arnold, Tom and Dan Hubert, *Focus Points in Effective Arbitration Practice*, in INTERNATIONAL ALTERNATIVE DISPUTE RESOLUTION (CORPORATE COUNSEL'S GUIDE) Chapter 20 (Business Laws, Inc., 1993).

Audit, Bernard, *A National Codification of International Commercial Arbitration: The French Decree of May 12, 1981*, in RESOLVING TRANSNATIONAL DISPUTES THROUGH ARBITRATION 117 (Thomas Carbonneau ed., 1984).

Audit, Bernard, *Droit International Privé: Compétence Internationale*, in 1986 RECUEIL DALLOZ SIREY, 26éme Cahier, Informations rapides 265.

Audit, Bernard, TRANSNATIONAL ARBITRATION AND STATE CONTRACTS (1987, Hague Academy of International Law).

Audit, Bernard, DROIT INTERNATIONAL PRIVE (1991).

Audit, Bernard, *Arbitration and the Brussels Convention,* 9 ARB. INT'L 1 (1993).

Audit, Bernard, Observations C.S.E.E. v. SORELEC, D. 1986 I.R. 265, GRANDS ARRETS DE LA JURISPRUDENCE DE DROIT INTERNATIONAL PRIVE (22e Ed.) No. 68.

Audit, Bernard, FRAUDE A LA LOI (1974). Audit, Bernard, *Les `Accords' d'Alger du 19 janvier 1981 tendant au règlement des différends entre les Etats-Unis et l'Iran,* 108 JOURNAL DU DROIT INT'L (CLUNET) 713 (1981).

Audit, Bernard, *Qualification et Droit International Privé,* 18 DROITS — REVUE FRANCAISE DE THEORIE JURIDIQUE 55 (1993).

Audit, Bernard, *Le Tribunal des Différends Irano-Américains (1981-1984)*, 112 JOURNAL DU DROIT INT'L (CLUNET) 791 (1985).

Auerbach, Jerold, JUSTICE WITHOUT LAW (1983).

Auerback, Raymond, *Governing Law Issues in International Financial Transactions,* 27 INTERNATIONAL LAWYER 303 (1993).

Ayres, Ian and Jennifer Gerarda Brown, *Economic Rationales For Mediation,* 80 VIRGINIA LAW REVIEW 323 (1994).

Badr, Gamal Moursi, STATE IMMUNITY (1984).

Baker, Stewart and Mark Davis, THE UNCITRAL ARBITRATION RULES IN PRACTICE (1994).

Ball, Markham, *Just Do It — Drafting the Arbitration Clause in an International Agreement,* 10 J. INT. ARB.(No. 4) 29 (1993).

Ball, Markham, *The Iraq Claims Process — A Progress Report,* 9 J. INT'L ARB. (No. 1) 37 (1992).

Barclay, Cedric, *The Other Side of the Coin,* 51 ARB. 270 (1985).

Barist, Jeffrey, *Commercial Arbitration Law and Clauses: A Drafter's Guide* (1994)

Batiffol, Henri and P. Lagarde, DROIT INTERNATIONAL PRIVE (5th Ed. 1970).

Battiffol, Henri, *Arbitrage international et immunités de juridiction et d'éxécution: les conditions d'application de la Convention de New York,* 1974 REVUE DE L'ARBI-TRAGE 326.

Baum, Axel, *Arbitration and Court Intervention,* 1 INT'L ARB. REP. 449 (1986).

Beam, Alex, *McJustice on Trial,* BOSTON GLOBE, 30 November 1992, p. 11.

Becker, Joseph D., *Attachments and International Arbitration — An Addendum,* 2 ARB. INT'L 365 (1986).

Becker, Joseph D., *Attachment in Aid of Arbitration: The American Position,* 1 ARB. INT'L 40 (1985).

Beechey, John, *International Arbitration and The Award of Security for Costs in England,* 12 BULL ASS. SUISSE ARB. 179 (1994).

Bedjaoui, Mohammed, *Des fortes vérités de Cassandre aux modestes correctifs de Némésis,* in ETUDES DE DROIT INTERNATIONAL EN L'HONNEUR DE PIERRE LALAIVE 385 (C. Dominicé, R. Patry & C. Reymond, eds., 1993).

Bellet, Pierre, *Des arbitres neutres et non-neutres,* in ETUDES DE DROIT INTERNA-TIONAL EN L'HONNEUR DE PIERRE LALAIVE 399 (C. Dominicé, R. Patry & C. Reymond, eds., 1993).

Bellet, Pierre, MULTIPARTY ARBITRATION (1994).

Bellet, Pierre & E. Mezger, *L'arbitrage international dans le nouveau code de procédure civile,* 70 REVUE CRITIQUE DE DROIT INT'L PRIVE 611 (1981).

Bellet, Pierre, *Le symposium international de Varsovie sur l'arbitrage international dans les litiges commerciaux multilatéraux,* 1981 REVUE DE L'ARBITRAGE 50.

Ben-Menahem, Hanina, JUDICIAL DEVIATION IN TALMUDIC LAW: GOV-ERNED BY MEN, NOT BY RULES (Jewish Law in Context, Neil Hecht, ed., 1991)

Beniassadi, Mohammad Reza, *Do Mandatory Rules of Public Law Limit Choice of Law in International Commercial Arbitration?,* 10 INT'L TAX & BUS. L. 59 (1992).

Benjamin, P., *The European Convention on International Commercial Arbitration,* 37 BRITISH YEARBOOK ON INT'L LAW 478 (1961).

Berg, Albert Jan van den, *Annulment of Awards in International Arbitration,* in INTERNATIONAL ARBITRATION IN THE 21ST CENTURY: TOWARDS "JUDICIALIZATION" AND UNIFORMITY? 133 (Richard Lillich & Charles Brower, eds., 1994).

Berg, Albert Jan van den, THE NEW YORK ARBITRATION CONVENTION OF 1958: TOWARDS A UNIFORM JUDICIAL INTERPRETATION (1981).

Berg, Albert Jan van den and Pieter Sanders, ARBITRATION IN THE NETHER-LANDS (1989).

Berg, Albert Jan van den, R. van Delden and Henk J. Snijders, NETHERLANDS ARBITRATION LAW (1994).

Berg, Albert Jan van den, *Consolidated Arbitrations: The New York Arbitration Convention and the Dutch Arbitration Act 1986 — A Replique to Mr. Jarvin,* 3 Arbitration International 257 (1987).

Berg, Albert Jan van den, *The Efficiency of Awards in International Commercial Arbitration,* 58 ARB. 267 (1992).

Berg, Albert Jan van den, *Consolidated Arbitration and the New York Arbitration Convention,* 2 ARBITRATION INTERNATIONAL 367 (1986).

Berg, A.J. van den, *The Netherlands Arbitration Act 1986,* 15 INT'L BUSINESS LAWYER 356 (1987).

Berg, Albert Jan van den, *When is an Arbitral Award Non-Domestic Under the New York Convention of 1958?,* 6 PACE LAW REVIEW 25 (1985).

Berg, Albert Jan van den, *Non-Domestic Arbitral Awards Under the 1958 New York Convention,* 2 ARBITRATION INTERNATIONAL 191 (1986).

Berger, Klaus Peter, INTERNATIONAL ECONOMIC ARBITRATION (1993).

Berglin, R.H., *The Application in United States Courts of the Public Policy Provision of the Convention on the Recognition and Enforcement of Foreign Arbitral Awards,* 4 DICKINSON J. INT'L LAW 167 (1986).

Berman, Harold Joseph, *The Law of International Commercial Transactions (Lex Mercatoria),* 2 EMORY JOURNAL OF INT. DISPUTE RESOLUTION 235 (1988).

Berman, Harold Joseph, LAW AND REVOLUTION (1983).

Bernardini, Piero, *The Arbitration Clause of an International Contract,* 9 JOURNAL OF INTERNATIONAL ARBITRATION (No. 2) 45 (1992).

Bernardini, Piero, *Considerations pratiques sur le règlement des différends relatifs aux investissements: le point de vue des utilisateurs,* 21 RASSEGNA DELL'ARBITRATO 7 (1981).

Bernardini, Piero, L'Arbitrage en Italié aprés la reforme, 1994 REV. ARB. 479.

Bernet, Martin & Nicolas Ulmer, *Recognition and Enforcement of Foreign Civil Judgments in Switzerland,* 27 INTERNATIONAL LAWYER 315 (1993).

Bernini, G., *Domestic and International Arbitration in Italy After the Legislative Reform,* 5 PACE L. REV. 543 (1985).

Bernini, G., *Observations Regarding Recognition and Enforcement of Foreign Arbitral Awards in Italy* in COMMERCIAL ARBITRATION: ESSAYS IN MEMORIAM EUGENIO MINOLI 39 (ed. Associazioni Italiana per Arbitrato, Unione Tipographico, Turin 1974).

Bernstein, Lisa, *Understanding the Limits of Court-Connected ADR: A Critique of Federal Court-Annexed Arbitration Programs,* 141 U. PENN. L. REV. 2169 (1993).

Bernstein, Lisa, *Opting Out of the Legal System: Extralegal Contractual Relations in the Diamond Industry,* 21 J. LEGAL STUDIES 115 (1992).

Bingham, Thomas, *Reasons and Reasons for Reasons: Differences Between a Court Judgment and an Arbitration Award,* 4 ARB. INT'L 141 (1988).

Blessing, Marc, *The New International Arbitration Law in Switzerland,* 5 J. INT'L ARB. 9 (June 1988).

Blessing, Marc, *Drafting Arbitration Clauses, presented at General Meeting of the Swiss Arbitration Association,* Basel, 17 June 1994.

Blumberg, Philip I., *The Corporate Entity in an Era of Multinational Corporations,* 15 DELAWARE J. CORP. LAW 283 (1990).

Blumberg, Philip I., THE LAW OF CORPORATE GROUPS (Vol. I, 1983; Vol. II, 1985).

Blumberg, Philip I., THE MULTINATIONAL CHALLENGE TO CORPORATION LAW: THE SEARCH FOR A NEW CORPORATE PERSONALITY (1993).

Böckstiegel, Karl-Heinz and Carl Heymans, eds., COMMERCIAL ARBITRATION IN ENGLAND AND THE FEDERAL REPUBLIC OF GERMANY (1987).

Böckstiegel, Karl-Heinz, ARBITRATION AND STATE ENTERPRISES (1984).

Böckstiegel, Karl-Heinz, *Experiences as an Arbitrator Using the UNCITRAL Rules,* in ETUDES DE DROIT INTERNATIONAL EN L'HONNEUR DE PIERRE LALAIVE 423 (C. Dominicé, R. Patry & C. Reymond, eds., 1993).

Böckstiegel, Karl-Heinz, *The Legal Rules Applicable in Internal Commercial Arbitration Involving States or States-Controlled Enterprises,* in 60 YEARS OF ICC ARBITRATION: A LOOK AT THE FUTURE 117 (International Chamber of Commerce, ed., 1984).

Böckstiegel, Karl-Heinz, *Public Policy and Arbitrability,* in COMPARATIVE ARBITRATION PRACTICE AND PUBLIC POLICY IN ARBITRATION 177 (ed. P. Sanders, 1987).

Böckstiegel, Karl-Heinz, *Relevance of National Arbitration Law for Arbitrations Under the UNCITRAL Rules,* 1 J. INT'L ARB. 223 (1984).

Bogdon, *Recognition in Sweden of Money Judgments in Civil and Commercial Matters,* NORDISK TIDSSKRIFT FOR INTERNATIONAL RET 85 (1985).

Bond, Stephen R., How to Draft an ICC Arbitration Clause, 7 ICSID REVIEW — FOREIGN INVESTMENT LAW JOURNAL 153 (1992).

Bond, Sephen R., *The 1986 Reform of ICC's Practice Relating to Costs and Payments,* 2 ARB. INT'L 358 (1986).

Bone, Robert G., *Rethinking the Day in Court Ideal and Nonparty Preclusion,* 67 N.Y.U. L. REV. 193 (1992).

Borchers, Patrick, *Forum Selection Agreements in the Federal Courts after Carnival Cruise,* 67 WASH. L. REV. 55 (1992).

Borchers, Patrick, *Choice of Law in American Courts in 1992,* 42 AM. J. COMP. LAW 125 (1994).

Born, Gary B., INTERNATIONAL COMMERCIAL ARBITRATION IN THE UNITED STATES (1994).

Born, Gary B., *A Reappraisal of the Extraterritorial Reach of U.S. Law,* 24 LAW & POL. INT'L BUS. 1 (1992).

Born, Gary B. and David Westin, INTERNATIONAL CIVIL LITIGATION IN UNITED STATES COURTS (2d Ed. 1992).

Boyd, Stewart and Michael Mustill, COMMERCIAL ARBITRATION (2d Edition 1989).

Brand, Ronald A., *Enforcement of Foreign Money Judgments in the United States: In Search of Uniformity and International Acceptance,* 67 NOTRE DAME L.REV. 353 (1991).

Brand, Ronald (ed.), ENFORCING FOREIGN JUDGMENTS IN THE UNITED STATES AND UNITED STATES JUDGMENTS ABROAD (1992).

Branson, D. and W.M. Tupman, *Selecting an Arbitral Forum: A Guide to Cost Effective International Arbitration,* 24 VA. J. INT'L L. 917 (1984).

Breckenridge, Jonathan, *Bargaining Unfairness and Agreements to Arbitrate: Judicial and Legislative Application of Contract Defenses to Arbitration Agreements,* 1991 ANNUAL SURVEY OF AMERICAN LAW 925.

Bredin, Jean-Denis, *Note on Société Impex c/ Société P.A.Z. Malteria Adriatica, Malteria Tirena, Cour de cassation, 18 May 1971,* 1972 DALLOZ 37.

Brilmayer, Lea, *The Extraterritorial Application of American Law: A Methodological and Constitutional Appraisal,* 50 LAW & CONTEMPORARY PROBLEMS 11 (1987).

Brilmayer, Lea and Charles Norchi, *Federal Extraterritoriality and Fifth Amendment Due Process,* 105 HARV. L. REV. 1217 (1992).

Briner, Robert, *Arbitration Under the ICC-Rules in Switzerland and the Concordat,* in RECUEIL DE TRAVAUX SUISSES SUR L'ARBITRAGE INTERNATIONAL 127 (ed. C. Reymond & E. Bucher, 1984).

Briner, Robert, *La revision des sentences arbitrales dans les cantons faisant partie du Concordat intercantonal sur l'arbitrage,* RECUEIL DE TRAVAUX SUISSES SUR L'ARBITRAGE INTERNATIONAL 285 (Claude Reymond & Eugene Bucher, eds., 1984).

Broches, Aaron, *A Model Law on International Commercial Arbitration? A Progress Report on the Work Undertaken Within the U.N. Commission on International Trade Law (UNCITRAL),* 18 GEORGE WASHINGTON J. OF INT'L LAW & ECONOMICS 79 (1984).

Broches, Aaron, *Award Rendered Pursuant to the ICSID Convention: Binding Force, Finality, Recognition, Enforcement, Execution,* 2 ICSID REVIEW: FOREIGN INVESTMENT LAW JOURNAL 287 (1987).

Broches, Aaron, *On the Finality of Awards: A Reply to Michael Reisman,* 8 ICSID REVIEW 92 (1993).

Broches, Aaron, *Recourse Against the Award: Recognition and Enforcement of the Award,* in UNCITRAL'S PROJECT FOR A MODEL LAW ON INTERNATIONAL COMMERCIAL ARBITRATION 201 (ed. P. Sanders, 1984).

Broches, Aaron, *Settlement of Disputes Arising Out of Investments in Developing Countries,* 11 INTERNATIONAL BUSINESS LAWYER 206 (1984).

Broches, Aaron, *The Convention on the Settlement of Investment Disputes between States and Nationals of Other States: Applicable Law and Default Procedure,* in INTERNATIONAL ARBITRATION: LIBER AMICORUM FOR MARTIN DOMKE 12 (ed. P. Sanders, Martinus Nijhoff, The Hague 1967).

Brönnimann,J. and G. W. Bosch Walters (eds.), INTERNATIONALE SCHIEDS-GERICHTSBARKEIT IN DER SCHWEIZ (1991).

Brower, Charles and Richard Lillich, INTERNATIONAL ARBITRATION IN THE 21ST CENTURY (1994).

Brower, Charles and W.M. Tupman, *Court-Ordered Provisional Measures Under the New York Convention,* 80 AMERICAN J. OF INT'L LAW 24 (1986).

Brown, Frederick and Amy A. Meldrum, *International Arbitration Provisions for Emerging Companies Going International,* in COUNSELING EMERGING COMPANIES IN GOING INTERNATIONAL (Alan S. Gutterman, ed., 1994).

Brunet, Edward J., *Arbitration and Constitutional Rights,* 71 N.C. L. REV. 81 (1992).

Brunet, Edward J., *Questioning the Quality of Alternate Dispute Resolution,* 62 TUL. L. REV. 1 (1987).

Bucheit, Lee, *Negotiating the Submission to Jurisdiction Clause,* INTERNATIONAL FINANCIAL LAW REVIEW 27 (November 1993).

Bucher, Eugene and Claude Reymond (eds.), RECUEIL DE TRAVAUX SUISSES SUR L'ARBITRAGE INTERNATIONAL (1984).

Bucher, Andreas & P.-Y. Tschanz, INTERNATIONAL ARBITRATION IN SWITZERLAND (1989).

Bucher, Andreas, LE NOUVEL ARBITRAGE INTERNATIONAL EN SUISSE (1988).

Bucher, Andreas, *Le Premier Amendement de la LDIP,* in ETUDES DE DROIT INTERNATIONAL EN L'HONNEUR DE PIERRE LALAIVE 3 (C. Dominicé, R. Patry & C. Reymond, eds., 1993).

Bucher, Andreas, *Court Intervention in Arbitration,* in INTERNATIONAL ARBITRATION IN THE 21ST CENTURY: TOWARD "JUDICIALIZATION" AND UNIFORMITY? 29 (Richard Lillich & Charles Brower, eds., 1994).

Bucher, Andreas, *Les voies de recours,* 1989 REVUE DE DROIT DES AFFAIRES INTERNATIONALES 771.

Bucher, Eugene, *Arbitration under the ICC Rules in Switzerland,* RECUEIL DE TRAVAUX SUISSES SUR L'ARBITRAGE INTERNATIONAL 127 (Claude Reymond & Eugene Bucher, eds., 1984).

Buckley, Colin, *Issue Preclusion and Issues of Law: A Doctrinal Framework Based on Rules of Recognition, Jurisdiction and Legal History,* 24 HOUS. L. REV. 875 (1987).

Budin, R., *La nouvelle loi suisse sur l'arbitrage international,* 1988 REVUE DE L'ARBITRAGE 51.

Budin, R., *La suspension dans l'arbitrage international: dispositions applicables en Suisse sous le régime du Concordat intercantonal sur l'arbitrage (C.I.A.),* 1986 REVUE DE L'ARBITRAGE 415.

Bühring-Uhle, Christian, MEDIATION AND ARBITRATION IN INTERNATIONAL BUSINESS (Scheduled for publication, 1995).

Burley, Anne-Marie, *Law Among Liberal States: Liberal Internationalism and the Act of State Doctrine,* 92 COLUMBIA L. REV. 1907 (1992).

Butler, James R., ARBITRATION IN BANKING (R.M.A. 1988).

Carbonneau, Thomas E. and Jean Robert, THE FRENCH LAW OF ARBITRATION (1983).

Carbonneau, Thomas E. (ed.), LEX MERCATORIA AND ARBITRATION (1990).

Carbonneau, Thomas E., ALTERNATIVE DISPUTE RESOLUTION: MELTING THE LANCES AND DISMOUNTING THE STEEDS (1989).

Carbonneau, Thomas E., *Arbitral Adjudication: A Comparative Assessment of its Remedial and Substantive Status in Transnational Commerce,* 19 TEXAS INT'L L.J. 33 (1984).

Carbonneau, Thomas E., Mitsubishi: *The Folly of Quixotic Internationalism,* 2 ARB. INT'L 166 (1986).

Carbonneau, Thomas E., *National Law and the Judicialization of Arbitration: Manifest Destiny, Manifest Disregard or Manifest Error*, in INTERNATIONAL ARBITRATION IN THE 21ST CENTURY: TOWARDS "JUDICIALIZATION" AND UNIFORMITY? 115 (Richard Lillich & Charles Brower, eds., 1994).

Carbonneau, Thomas E., *Rendering Arbitral Awards with Reasons: The Elaboration of a Common Law of International Transactions*, 23 COLUMBIA J. TRANSNAT'L LAW 579 (1985).

Carpinello, George P., *Testing the Limits of Choice of Law Clauses: Franchise Contracts As a Case Study*, 74 MARQ. L. REV. 57 (1990).

Carter, P.B., *Transnational Recognition and Enforcement of Foreign Public Law*, 1989 CAMBRIDGE L. J. 417 (1989).

Carter, P. B., *Choice of Law: Methodology or Mythology*, in ETUDES DE DROIT INTERNATIONAL EN L'HONNEUR DE PIERRE LALAIVE 11 (C. Dominicé, R. Patry & C. Reymond, eds., 1993).

Carter, James H., *Dispute Resolution and International Agreements*, in INTERNATIONAL ALTERNATIVE DISPUTE RESOLUTION (CORPORATE COUNSEL'S GUIDE) Chapter 4 (Business Laws, Inc., 1993).

Casad, Robert, CIVIL JUDGEMENT RECOGNITION (1981).

Cass, Ronald, *Judicial Decisionmaking and Judges' Incentives, Manuscript Presented to Boston University Faculty Workshop*, 11 November 1993.

Cato, D. Mark, ARBITRATION PRACTICE AND PROCEDURE (1992).

Cavers, David, *A Critique of Choice of Law Problems*, 47 HARV. L. REV. 173 (1933).

Cavers, David, THE CHOICE-OF-LAW PROCESS (1965).

Cervens, Jeanne de, Howard Classen, Robert Rowell & James Wise, *Survey of the Legality of Confessed Judgment Clauses in Commercial Transactions*, 47 BUS. LAW. 729 (1992).

Chang, Robert, *Toward An Asian-America Legal Scholarship: Critical Race Theory, Post-Structuralism and Narrative Space*, 81 CAL. L. REV. 1243 (1993).

Chatterjee, S.K., *Do Disputes Arise "out of" or "under" or "out of and under" a Contract?*, 60 ARBITRATION 117 (1994).

Cheung, Andrew Kui-Nung, *Enforcement of Foreign Arbitral Awards in the People's Republic of China*, 34 AM. J. COMPL. L. 295 (1986).

Chow, Daniel C.K., *Rethinking the Act of State Doctrine*, 62 WASH. L. REV. 397 (1987).

Christie, R.H., *Amiable Composition in French and English Law*, 58 ARB. 259 (1992).

Classen, Howard, Jeanne de Cervens, Robert Rowell and James Wise, *Survey of the Legality of Confessed Judgment Clauses in Commercial Transactions*, 47 BUS. LAW. 729 (1992).

Coase, Ronald, *The Problem of Social Costs*, 3 J. LAW & ECON. 1 (1960).

Cohen, Michael, *Hague Conference to Draft Convention on Enforcing Foreign Judgments*, A.B.A. NEWSLETTER FOR SECTION ON INT'L BUS. L. 4 (Winter, 92/93).

Cooper, Laura and Dennis Nolan, LABOR ARBITRATION: A COURSEBOOK (1994).

Corr, John B., *Thoughts On the Vitality of Erie*, 41 AM. U. L.REV. 1087 (1992).

Coulson, Robert, BUSINESS ARBITRATION (4th Ed., 1991).

Coulson, Robert, *An American Critique of the IBA's Ethics for International Arbitrators*, 4 J. INT'L ARB. (No.2) 103

Coulson, Robert, *Do We Know How Arbitration Panels Decide?*, 6 J. INT'L ARB. (No. 2) 7 (1989).

Coulson, Robert, *The Future Growth of Institutional Administration in International Commercial Arbitration*, in THE ART OF ARBITRATION, ESSAYS ON INTER-NATIONAL ARBITRATION, LIBER AMICORUM PIETER SANDERS (ed. J.C. Schultsz & A.J. van den Berg, 1982).

Coulson, Robert, *The Practical Advantages of Administered Arbitration*, NIDR FORUM 41 (Winter 1993).

Coulson, Robert, *Medaloa: A Practical Technique for Resolving International Business Disputes*, 11 (No.2) JOURNAL OF INTERNATIONAL ARBITRATION 1111 (1994).

Coulson, Robert, *So Far, So Good: Enforcement of Foreign Commercial Arbitration Awards in United States Courts*, in CONTEMPORARY PROBLEMS IN INTER-NATIONAL ARBITRATION 353 (1986).

Covey, Anne E. and Michael S. Morris, *The Enforceability of Agreements Providing for Forum and Choice of Law Selection*, 61 DENV. L.J. 837 (1988).

Craig, W. Laurence, William W. Park and Jan Paulsson, INTERNATIONAL CHAM-BER OF COMMERCE ARBITRATION (2d. Ed. 1990).

Craig, W. Laurence, Jan Paulsson and William W. Park, *French Codification of a Legal Framework for International Commercial Arbitration*, 13 GEORGETOWN JOUR-NAL OF LAW & POLICY IN INTERNATIONAL BUSINESS 727 (1981).

Craig, W. Laurence, *The Final Chapter in the Pyramids Case: Discounting an ICSID Award for Annulment Risk*, 8 FOREIGN INVESTMENT L.J. 264 (1993).

Craig, W. Laurence, *International Ambition and National Restraint in ICC Arbitration*, 1 ARB. INT'L 19 (1985).

Craig, W. Laurence, *Uses and Abuses of Appeal from International Arbitration Awards*, in PRIVATE INVESTORS ABROAD: PROBLEMS AND SOLUTIONS IN INTERNATIONAL BUSINESS IN 1987 (ed. J. Moss, Mathew Bender, 1988), Cap. 14.

Cremades, Bernardo & Steven Plehn, *The New Lex Mercatoria and the Harmonization of the Laws of International Commercial Arbitration: Is It Still a Conflict of Laws Problem?*, 16 INT'L LAWYER 613 (1982).

Cremades, Bernardo & Steven Plehn, *The New Lex Mercatoria and the Harmonization of the Laws of International Commercial Transaction*, 2 B.U. INT'L L.J. 317 (1984).

Cremades, Bernardo, *Is Exclusion of Concurrent Courts' Jurisdiction over Conservative Measures to be Introduced through a Revision of the New York Convention?*, 3 J. INT'L ARB. (No. 3) 105 (1989).

Cremades, Bernardo, *The Impact of International Arbitration on the Development of Business Law*, 31 AMERICAN J. COMPARATIVE L. 526 (1983).

Cromie, Stephen, INTERNATIONAL COMMERCIAL LITIGATION (W.D. Park, Consulting Editor, 1990).

Currie, Brainard, SELECTED ESSAYS ON THE CONFLICT OF LAWS (1963).

Dana, Jane and William T. Lake, *Judicial Review of Awards of the Iran-United States Claims Tribunal: Are the Tribunal's Awards Dutch?*, 16 LAW & POLICY INT'L BUS. 755 (1984).

Dannemann, Gerhard, *Jurisdiction Based on the Presence of Assets in Germany: A Case Note*, 41 INT'L & COMP. L.Q. 632 (1992).

Dasser, Feloc, INTERNATIONALE SCHIEDSGERICHTE UND LEX MERCATORIA, RECHTSVERGLEICHENDER BEITRAG ZUR DISKUSSION UBER EIN NICHTSTAATLICHES HANDELSRECHT (Zurich, 1989).

Davenport, Brian, *The New English Draft Arbitration Bill*, 10 ARB. INT'L 163 (1994).

David, René, ARBITRATION IN INTERNATIONAL TRADE (1985).

Davidson, Fraser, *Where is an Arbitral Award Made?*, 41 INTERNATIONAL & COMPARATIVE LAW QUARTERLY 637 (1992).

Davis, Kenneth Culp, DISCRETIONARY JUSTICE: A PRELIMINARY INQUIRY (1969).

Davis, Kenneth Culp, *No Law to Apply*, 25 SAN DIEGO L. REV. 1 (1988).

Davis, Mark and Stewart Baker, THE UNCITRAL ARBITRATION RULES IN PRACTICE (1994).

De Boisseson, Matthieu, DROIT FRANCAIS DE L'ARBITRAGE (2d. ed., 1990).

De Ly, Filip, *The Place of Arbitration in the Conflict of Laws of International Commercial Arbitration: An Exercise in Arbitration Planning*, 12 N.W. J. INT'L L. & BUS. 48 (1991).

De Ly, Filip, INTERNATIONAL BUSINESS LAW AND LEX MERCATORIA (1992).

Delaume, Georges R., TRANSNATIONAL CONTRACTS: APPLICABLE LAW AND SETTLEMENT OF DISPUTES (1975).

Delaume, Georges R., LAW AND PRACTICE OF TRANSNATIONAL CONTRACTS (1988).

Delaume, Georges R., *ICSID Arbitration and the Courts*, 77 AM. J. INT. L. 784 (1983).

Delaume, Georges R., *The Proper Law of State Contracts and the Lex Mercatoria*, 3 FOR. INVESTMENT L.J. 79 (1988).

Delaume, Georges R., *ICSID Arbitration*, in CONTEMPORARY PROBLEMS IN INTERNATIONAL ARBITRATION 23 (J. Lew, ed., 1987).

Delaume, Georges R., *Sovereign Immunity and Public Debt*, 23 INT'L LAW. 811 (1989).

Delaume, Georges R., *Enforcement of State Contract Awards: Jurisdictional Pitfalls and Remedies*, 8 ICSID REVIEW (No.1) 29 (1993).

Delaume, Georges R., *The Pyramids Stand — the Pharaohs Can Rest in Peace*, 8 FOREIGN INVESTMENT L.J. 231 (1993).

Delaume, Georges R., *The Foreign Sovereign Immunities Act and Public Debt Litigation: Some Fifteen Years Later*, 88 AM. J. INT'L LAW 257 (1994).

Delaume, Georges R., *ICSID Arbitration in Practice*, 2 INTERNATIONAL TAX AND BUSINESS LAW 58 (1984).

Delaume, Georges R., *ICSID Arbitration: Practical Considerations*, 1 J. OF INT'L ARB. 21 (1984).

Delaume, Georges R., *L'Affaire du Plateau des Pyramides et le CIRDI*, 1994 REVUE DE L'ARBITRAGE 39.

Delaume, Georges R., *De l'efficacité des sentences transnationales intéressant un Etat: une pondération s'impose*, in ETUDES DE DROIT INTERNATIONAL EN L'HONNEUR DE PIERRE LALAIVE 469 (C. Dominicé, R. Patry & C. Reymond, eds., 1993).

Delden, R. van, A.H. van den Berg and Henk J. Sijders, NETHERLANDS ARBITRATION LAW (1994).

Dellett, S., *Arbitration, Forum Selection, and Choice of Law Agreements in International Securities Transactions*, 42 WASHINGTON & LEE L. REV. 1069 (1985).

Delvolvé, Jean-Louis, *Multipartism: The Dutco Decision of the French Cour de cassation*, 9 ARBITRATION INTERNATIONAL 197 (1993).

Delvolvé, Jean-Louis, ARBITRATION IN FRANCE (1982).

De Mello, X., *Arbitrage et ordre public national découlant des règles de concurrence*, 1979 REVUE DE L'ARBITRAGE 101.

Demenlenaere, Bernadette and Marcel Storme, INTERNATIONAL ARBITRATION IN BELGIUM (1989).

Demont, Jean-François, *Ingénieur Epfl et François Vermeille, L'arbitrage, son tribunal, sa procédure vus par l'expert*, RECUEIL DE TRAVAUX SUISSES SUR L'ARBITRAGE INTERNATIONAL 235 (Claude Reymond & Eugene Bucher, eds., 1984).

Derains, Yves, Sigvard Jarvin and Jean-Jacques Arnaldez (eds.), COLLECTION OF ICC ARBITRAL AWARDS, Volume I — Awards 1974-85 (1990) and Volume II — Awards 1986-90 (1994).

Derains, Yves, *Arbitrage et droit de la concurrence*, 14 REVUE SUISSE DU DROIT INTERNATIONAL DE LA CONCURRENCE 39 (1982).

Derains, Yves, *L'Application Cumulative par L'Arbitre des Systèmes de Conflict de Lois Intéressés au Litige*, 1972 REV. ARB. 99.

Derains, Yves, *Les Normes d'Application Immediate dans la Jurisprudence Arbitrale Internationale*, in LE DROIT DES RELATIONS ECONOMIQUES INTERNATIONALES: ETUDES OFFERTES A BERTHOLD GOLDMAN (P. Fouchard, P. Kahn & A. Lyon-Caen, eds., 1982).

Dessemontet, François, ed., LE NOUVEAU DROIT INTERNATIONAL PRIVE SUISSE (1989).

Devolvé, J.-L., *L'Arbitrage et les tier — le droit de l'arbitrage — les solutions contractuelles: la clause d'arbitrage multipartite*, 1988 REVUE DE L'ARBITRAGE 501.

Dicey, A.V. & J.H.C. Morris, THE CONFLICT OF LAWS (L. Collins ed., 11th Ed. 1987).

Dominicé, Christian, *L'Arbitrage et les immunités des organisations internationales*, in ETUDES DE DROIT INTERNATIONAL EN L'HONNEUR DE PIERRE LALAIVE 483 (C. Dominicé, R. Patry & C. Reymond, eds., 1993).

Domke, Martin, DOMKE ON COMMERCIAL ARBITRATION (Gabriel Wilner, ed., 1991).

Donahey, M. Scott, *The Independence and Neutrality of Arbitrators,* 9 J. INT'L ARB. 31 (1992).

Donaldson, John, *The 1979 Arbitration Act,* 45 ARB. 147 (1979).

Donaldson, John, *Relationship Between the Courts and Arbitration Under the Common Law Systems,* 47 ARB. 72 (1981).

Donoghue, Joan E., *Taking "Sovereign" Out of the Foreign Sovereign Immunities Act: A Functional Approach to the Commercial Activity Exception,* 17 YALE J. INT'L L. 489 (1992).

Dore, Isaak, ARBITRATION AND CONCILIATION UNDER THE UNCITRAL RULES: A TEXTUAL ANALYSIS (1986).

Dore, Isaak, THEORY AND PRACTICE OF MULTIPARTY COMMERCIAL ARBI-TRATION (1990).

Dore, Isaak, THE UNCITRAL FRAMEWORK FOR ARBITRATION IN CONTEM-PORARY PERSPECTIVE (1993).

Dougherty, Francis M., *Validity of Contractual Provision Limiting Place or Court in Which Action May Be Brought,* 31 A.L.R. 4th 404 (1984).

Droz, Georges, COMPETENCE JUDICIAIRE ET EFFETS DES JUGEMENTS DANS LE MARCHE COMMUN (1972).

Droz, Georges, *Problèmes provoqués par l'imbrication des Conventions de Bruxelles, de Lugano et de San Sebastian,* in ETUDES DE DROIT INTERNATIONAL EN L'HONNEUR DE PIERRE LALAIVE 21 (C. Dominicé, R. Patry & C. Reymond, eds., 1993).

Dutoit, Bernard, *Le nouveau droit international privé suisse des contrats à l'aune de la Convention de Rome du 19 juin sur la loi applicable aux obligations contractuelles,* in ETUDES DE DROIT INTERNATIONAL EN L'HONNEUR DE PIERRE LALAIVE 31 (C. Dominicé, R. Patry & C. Reymond, eds., 1993).

Ebb, Lawrence, *A Tale of Three Cities: Arbitrator Misconduct by Abuse of Retainer and Committment-Fee Arrangement,* 3 THE AMERICAN REVIEW OF INTERNA-TIONAL ARBITRATION: ESSAYS IN HONOR OF HANS SMIT 177 (1992).

Ebb, Lawrence, *Reflections on Indian Enforcement of the GE/Renusagar Award,* 10 ARB. INT'L 141 (1994).

Edwards, Harry T., *Alernative Dispute Resolution: Panacea or Anathema,* 99 HARV. L. REV. 668 (1986).

Eiseman, Frédéric, *La clause d'arbitrage pathologique,* in ARBITRAGE COMMER-CIAL: ESSAIS IN MEMORIAM EUGENIO MINOLI 129 (1974).

Eisemann, Frédéric, *Arbitration Under the International Chamber of Commerce Rules,* 15 INT'L AND COMPARATIVE L. QUART. 726 (1966).

El-Hakim, Jacques, *Should the Key Terms Award, Commercial and Binding be Defined in the New York Convention?,* 6 J. INT'L ARB. (No. 1) 161 (1989).

El-Hakim, Jacques, *Litiges multilateraux dans le cadre des projets en moyen-orient,* 1981 REVUE DE L'ARBITRAGE 86.

Epfl, Ingénieur, *Jean-François Demont et François Vermeille, L'arbitrage, son tribunal, sa procédure vus par l'expert*, RECUEIL DE TRAVAUX SUISSES SUR L'ARBITRAGE INTERNATIONAL 235 (Claude Reymond & Eugene Bucher, eds., 1984).

Epstein, David & Jeffrey Snyder, INTERNATIONAL LITIGATION: GUIDE TO JURISDICTION PRACTICE & STRATEGY (1989).

Erickson, Julia L., *Forum Selection Clauses in Light of the Erie Doctrine and Federal Common Law: Stewart Organization v. Ricoh Corp.*, 72 MINN. L. REV. 1090 (1988).

Farnsworth, E. Allan, *Good Faith Performance and Commercial Reasonableness Under the Uniform Commercial Code*, 30 U. CHI. L.REV. 666 (1963).

Feldman, M., *The Annulment Proceedings and the Finality of ICSID Arbitral Awards*, 2 ICSID REVIEW: FOREIGN INVESTMENT L.J. 85 (1987).

Feller, David, *End of the Trilogy: The Declining State of Labor Arbitration*, 48 ARBITRATION JOURNAL (No. 3) 18 (1993).

Fentiman, Richard, *Jurisdiction, Discretion and the Brussels Convention*, 26 CORNELL INTERNATIONAL LAW JOURNAL 59 (1993).

Fini, Tom, *The Scope of the Van Dusen Rule in Federal-Question Transfers*, 1992/1993 ANNUAL SURVEY OF AMERICAN LAW 49 (1993).

Finkin, Matthew, *Commentary on "Arbitration of Employment Disputes Without Unions,"* 66 CHI. KENT L. REV. 799 (1990).

Fiss, Owen, *Against Settlement*, 93 YALE L.J. 1073 (1984).

FitzGibbon, Scott and Donald Glazer, LEGAL OPINIONS (1992).

Fitzpatrick, Peter, *Arbitration and Governing Law*, in INTERNATIONAL ALTERNATIVE DISPUTE RESOLUTION (CORPORATE COUNSEL'S GUIDE) Chapter 7 (Business Laws, Inc., 1993).

Fouchard, Philippe, L'ARBITRAGE COMMERCIAL INTERNATIONAL (1964).

Fouchard, Philippe, *Lex travaux de la C.N.U.D.C.I.: le réglement d'arbitrage*, 106 J. DU DROIT INTERNATIONAL (CLUNET) 816 (1979).

Fouchard, Philippe, *Les institutions permanents d'arbitrage devant le juge étatiques (à propos d'une jurisprudence récente)*, 1987 REVUE DE L'ARBITRAGE 225.

Fouchard, Philippe, *Une Initiative Contestable de la CNUDCI*, 1994 REVUE DE L'ARBITRAGE 461.

Fouchard, Philippe, *Note on Hecht c/ Soc. Buisman's, Cour d'appel de Paris*, 19 June 1970, 1972 REVUE DE L'ARBITRAGE 67.

Fouchard, Philippe, *Adaptation of Contracts to the Economic Climate*, in ARBITRATION AND THE LICENSING PROCESS 6-73 (ed. R. Goldscheider & M. de Haas, 1984).

Fouchard, Philippe, L'ARBITRAGE INTERNATIONAL COMMERCIAL (1964).

Fouchard, Philippe, *Un arbitrage quand est-il international?*, 1970 REVUE DE L'ARBITRAGE 59.

Francescakis, *Quelques précisions sur les "lois d'application immédiate" et leurs rapports avec les règles de conflit de lois*, 1966 R.C.D.I.P. 1.

Frank, E., Stephen Goldberg, A. Sander, & Nancy H. Rogers, DISPUTE RESOLUTION: NEGOTIATION, MEDIATION AND OTHER PROCESSES (2nd Ed. 1992).

Fried, Charles, CONTRACT AS PROMISE: A THEORY OF CONTRACTUAL OBLIGATION (1981).

Friedland, P., *Provisional Measures in ICSID Arbitration*, 2 ARBITRATION INTERNATIONAL 335 (1986).

Friedler, Edith, *Party Autonomy Revisited: A Statutory Solution to A Choice-of-Law Problem*, 37 KANSAS L. REV. 471 (1989).

Fuller, Lon, *The Forms and Limits of Adjudication*, 92 HARV. L. REV. 353 (1978).

Gaffney, Terrence J. and David L. Johnson, *Lender Liability: Perspectives on Risk and Prevention*, 105 BANKING L.J. 325 (1988).

Gaillard, Emmanuel, *Présentation de la résolution de l'ILA sur l'application de règles transnationals par les arbitres du commerce international (Cairo, April 1992)*, 1994 REVUE DE L'ARBITRAGE 212.

Gaillard, Emmanuel and Carlo Poncet, *Introductory Note and Translations to the Swiss LDIP*, 27 I.L.M. 37 (1988).

Gaillard, Emmanuel and Robert B. von Mehren, INTERNATIONAL COMMERCIAL ARBITRATION: RECENT DEVELOPMENTS, Vols. I and II, (Practicing Law Institute Seminar, October 1988).

Gaillard, Emmanuel, *A Foreign View of the New Swiss Law on International Arbitration*, 4 ARB. INT'L 25 (1988).

Gaillard, Emmanuel, *L'affaire Sofidif ou les difficultés de l'arbitrage multipartite*, 1987 REVUE DE L'ARBITRAGE 275.

Gaillard, Emmanuel, *L'arbitrage multipartite et la consolidation des procédures connexes*, in INTERNAT'L LAW ASSOC.: WARSAW CONFERENCE (1988) 14.

Gaillard, Emmanuel, *Belgium: Statute on the Setting Aside of Arbitral Awards*, 25 INT'L LEGAL MATERIALS 725 (1985).

Gaillard, Emmanuel, *The UNCITRAL Model Law and Recent Statutes on International Arbitration in Europe and North America*, 2 ICSID REVIEW: FOREIGN INVESTMENT LAW JOURNAL 424 (1987).

Gantner, Richard A., Note, 22 SETON HALL L.REV. 505 (1992).

Gaudemet-Tallon, Hélène, *Le Forum Non Conveniens: Une menace pour la Convention de Bruxelles?* 80 REV. CRIT. DR. INT. PRIVE 491 (1991).

Gaudemet-Tallon, Hélène, *Les régimes relatifs au refus d'exercer la compétence juridictionnelle en matière civile et commerciale*, prepared for the 14th International Congress on Comparative Law, Athens, August 1994, publication in 1994 REVUE INTERNATIONALE DE DROIT COMPARE (No. 2) 423.

Gaudet, M., *The International Chamber of Commerce Court of Arbitration*, 4 INT'L TAX & BUSINESS LAWYER 213 (1986).

Geimer, Reinhold, *Internationales Zivilprozessrecht*, ZIVILPROZESSORDNUNG 3 (Richard Zoeller, ed., 17th Ed. 1991).

Gerarda Brown, *Jennifer & Ian Ayres, Economic Rationales For Mediation*, 80 VIRGINIA LAW REVIEW 323 (1994).

Gerstenhaber, Rachel, *Freezer Burn: United States Extraterritorial Freeze Orders and the Case for Efficient Risk Allocation*, 140 U. PENN. L. REV. 2333 (1992).

Gillette, Clayton P., *Commercial Relationships and the Selection of Default Rules for Remote Risks*, 19 J. LEGAL STUD. 535 (1990).

Gillette, Clayton P., *Limitations on the Obligation of Good Faith,* 1981 DUKE L.J. 619 (1981).

Gillette, Clayton P., *Commercial Rationality and the Duty to Adjust Long-Term Contracts,* 69 MINN. L. REV. 521 (1985).

Glazer, Donald and Scott FitzGibbon, LEGAL OPINIONS (1992).

Glendon, Mary Ann, *Tradition and Creativity in Culture and Law,* 27 FIRST THINGS 13 (1992).

Glossner, Otto, *The Influence of the International Chamber of Commerce on Modern Arbitration,* SIXTY YEARS OF ICC ARBITRATION: A LOOK AT THE FUTURE 399 (1984).

Glossner, Otto, *The Rules of Conciliation and Arbitration of the International Chamber of Commerce: Some Observations,* in COMMERCIAL ARBITRATION: ESSAYS IN MEMORIAM EUGENIO MINOLI 219 (ed. Associazioni Italiana per Arbitrato, 1974).

Goekjian, S., *ICC Arbitration from a Practitioner's Perspective,* 14 J.INT'L LAW AND ECONOMICS 407 (1980).

Goldberg, Kenneth L., Lender Liability and Good Faith, 68 B.U. L. REV. 653 (1988).

Goldberg, Stephen, Frank E., A. Sander, & Nancy H. Rogers, DISPUTE RESOLUTION: NEGOTIATION, MEDIATION AND OTHER PROCESSES (2nd Ed. 1992).

Goldman, Berthold, *Nouvelles réflexions sur la Lex Mercatoria,* in ETUDES DE DROIT INTERNATIONAL EN L'HONNEUR DE PIERRE LALAIVE 241 (C. Dominicé, R. Patry & C. Reymond, eds., 1993).

Goldman, Berthold, *Les conflits de lois dans l'arbitrage international de droit privé,* II RECUEIL DES COURS DE L'ACADEMIE DE DROIT INTERNATIONAL DE LA HAYE 347 (1963).

Goldman, Berthold, *La lex mercatoria dans les contrats et l'arbitrage internationaux: réalité et perspectives,* 1977-1979 TRAVAUX DU COMITE FRANÇAIS DE DROIT INTERNATIONAL PRIVE 221.

Goldman, Berthold, *The Applicable Law: General Principles of Law: The Lex Mercatoria,* in CONTEMPORARY PROBLEMS IN INTERNATIONAL ARBITRATION 113 (ed. J. Lew, 1985).

Goldman, Berthold, *Une bataille judiciaire autour de la lex mercatoria,* 1983 REVUE DE L'ARBITRAGE 379.

Goldman, Berthold, *Frontières dur droit et "lex mercatoria,"* 9 ARCHIVES DE PHILOSOPHIE DE DROIT 177 (1964).

Goldman, Berthold, *Les problèmes spécifiques de l'arbitrage international,* 1980 REVUE DE L'ARBITRAGE 323.

Goldman, Berthold, *La lex mercatoria dans les contrats et l'arbitrage internationaux: réalité et perspectives,* 106 J. DU DROIT INTERNATIONAL (CLUNET) 475 (1979).

Goldman, Lee, *My Way and the Highway: The Law and Economics of Choice of Forum Clauses in Consumer Form Contracts,* 86 NORTHWESTERN UNIVERSITY LAW REVIEW 700 (1992).

Golsong, H., *L'arrangement relatif à l'application de la convention européenne sur l'arbitrage commercial international*, VIII ANNUAIRE FRANCAIS DE DROIT INTERNATIONAL 742 (1962).

Golsong, H., *A Guide to Procedural Issues in International Arbitration*, 18 INT'L LAWYER 663 (1984).

Goodman, Ron, *Arbitrability and Antitrust: Mitsubishi Motors Corp. v. Soler Chrysler-Plymouth*, 23 COLUM. J. OF TRANSNAT'L L. 655 (1985).

Gordley, James Russell and Arthur Taylor Von Mehren, THE CIVIL LAW SYSTEM (1977).

Gordon, Michael Wallace, Mary Ann Glendon and Chris Osakwe, COMPARATIVE LEGAL TRADITION (1982).

Gottesman, Michael H., *Draining the Dismal Swamp: The Case for Federal Choice of Law Statutes*, 80 GEO. L.J. 1 (1991).

Graham, William C., *Dispute Resolution in the Canada-U.S. Free Trade Agreement*, 37 MCGILL L.R. 544 (1992).

Gravel, Serge, *Arbitration Within the NAFTA Area, 4 (No. 2)* ICC INTERNATIONAL COURT OF ARBITRATION BULLETIN 22 (1993).

Gray, Christine & Benedict Kingsbury, *Developments in Dispute Settlement: Inter-State Arbitration Since 1945*, 1992 BRITISH YEARBOOK OF INTERNATIONAL LAW 97 (1993).

Greenawalt, Kent, *The Enduring Significance of Neutral Principles*, 78 COLUMBIA L. REV. 982 (1978).

Greenawalt, Kent, *How Law Can Be Determinate*, 38 UCLA L. REV. 1 (1990).

Greenberg, Mark D., *The Appropriate Source of Law for Forum Non Conveniens Decisions in International Cases: A Proposal for the Development of Federal Common Law*, 4 INT'L TAX & BUS. LAW. 155 (1986).

Grigera-Naón, Horacio, *Arbitration in Latin America: Overcoming Traditional Hostility*, 22 INTER-AMERICAN LAW REVIEW 203 (1991).

Grigera-Naón, Horacio, CHOICE OF LAW PROBLEMS IN INTERNATIONAL COMMERCIAL ARBITRATION (1992).

Grigera-Naón, Horacio, *Enforceability of Awards based on Transnational Rules under the New York, Panama, Geneva and Washington Conventions*, REPORT OF THE SIXTY-FIFTH CONFERENCE OF THE INTERNATIONAL LAW ASSOCIATION (CAIRO, EGYPT) 119 (1992).

Grillo, Trina, *The Mediation Alternative: Process Dangers for Women*, 100 YALE L.J. 1545 (1991).

Gruson, Michael, *Forum-Selection Clauses in International and Interstate Commercial Agreements*, 1982 U. ILL. L. REV. 133 (1982).

Gruson, Michael, *Governing-Law Clauses in International and Interstate Loan Agreements: New York's Approach*, 1982 U. ILL. L. REV. 207 (1982).

Gruson, Michael, FORUM SELECTION CLAUSES IN INTERNATIONAL AND INTERSTATE COMMERCIAL AGREEMENTS (P.L.I. No. A4-4437, 1993)

Gruson, Michael, *Controlling Site of Litigation*, in SOVEREIGN LENDING: MANAGING LEGAL RISK 29 (M. Gruson & R. Reisner, eds., 1984).

Guedj, Thomas G., *The Theory of the Lois de Police, A Functional Trend in Continental Private International Law—A Comparative Analysis With Modern American Theories,* 39 AM. J. COMP. L. 661 (1991).

Hacking, David, *Where We Are Now: Trends and Developments Since the Arbitration Act (1979),* 2 J. INT'L ARB. 7 (1985).

Hadenfeldt, Reimer and Thomas Ruede, SCHWEIZERISCHES SCHIEDSGERICHT-SRECHT: NACH KNOKORDAT UND IPRG (1993).

Hafter, Peter, *Gespräche zwischen Schiedsgericht und Parteien — Ein Beitrag zur Technik der Führung von Schiedsgerichten,* RECUEIL DE TRAVAUX SUISSES SUR L'ARBITRAGE INTERNATIONAL 203 (Claude Reymond & Eugene Bucher, eds., 1984).

Hague Conference on Private International Law, RECUEIL DES CONVENTIONS: 1951-1988.

Hall, Marc and William Honey, *Bases for Recognition of Foreign Nation Money Judgments in the United States and Need for Federal Intervention,* 16 SUFFOLK TRANSNATIONAL LAW REVIEW 405 (1993).

Hall and Newton, *International Arbitration Bodies,* N.Y.L.J., 16 June 1992, at 1, col.1.

Hancock, T.M. de, *The ICC Court of Arbitration,* 1 J. INT'L ARB. 21 (1984).

Hardee, Lee R., *Comment, Enforcing Forum Selection Clauses,* 1990 J. DISP. RESOL. 401.

Harper, Michael, *Limiting 301 Preemption: Three Cheers for the Trilogy, Only One for Lingle and Lueck,"* 66 CHICAGO KENT L. REV. 685 (1990).

Harper, Conrad, *Arbitration in U.S. Foreign Relations,* DISPUTE RESOLUTION JOURNAL 8 (June 1984).

Hascher, Dominique, *Consolidation of Arbitration by American Courts: Fostering or Hampering International Commercial Arbitration,* 1 J. OF INT'L ARB. 127 (1984).

Hascher, Dominique, *Chronique des Sentences Arbitral,* 1993 JOURNAL DE DROIT INTERNATIONAL 1001.

Hascher, Dominique, *Chronique de Jurisprudence Francaise,* Société Unichips Finanziara v Gesnouin (Cour d'Appeal de Paris, 1993), 1993 REV. ARB. 255.

Hay, Peter and Robert Walker, *The Proposed Recognition-of-Judgments Convention Between the United States and the United Kingdom,* 11 TEX. INT'L L.J. 421 (1976).

Hay, Peter, *Reflections on Conflict-of-Laws Methodology,* 32 HASTINGS L.J. 1644 (1981).

Hay, Peter, *Comments on `Self-Limited Rules of Law' in Conflicts Methodology,* 30 AM. J. COMP. L. 127 (1982).

Hay, Peter, *The Recognition and Enforcement of American Money Judgments in Germany,* 40 AM. J. COMP. L. 729 (1992).

Hay, Peter, Maurice Rosenberg and Willis Reese (eds.), CONFLICT OF LAWS (9th Ed. 1990).

Heiser, Walter, *Forum Selection Clauses in State Courts: Limitations on Enforcement after Stewart and Carnival Cruise,* 45 FLORIDA L. REV. 361 (1993).

Hermann, A.H., *Bill Pulls the Wrong Punches*, FINANCIAL TIMES, 15 February 1994, page 12.

Hermann, A.H., *U.S. Court Rejects ITC's Claim to Sovereign Immunity*, FINANCIAL TIMES, 11 February 1988, at 9.

Hermann, A.H., *The Draft English Bill: Pulling the Wrong Punches*, 10 ARB. INT'L. 185 (1994).

Herrmann, Gerold, *Background and Salient Features of the United Nations Convention on International Bills of Exchange and International Promissory Notes*, 10 U. PA. J. INT'L BUS. L. 517 (1988).

Herrmann, Gerold, *The Role of the Courts Under the UNCITRAL Model Law Script*, in CONTEMPORARY PROBLEMS IN INTERNATIONAL ARBITRATION 164 (ed. J. Lew, 1985).

Herrmann, Gerold, *The UNCITRAL Model Law on International Commercial Arbitration — Its Salient Features and Prospects*, in ACTES DU 1ER COLLOQUE SUR L'ARBITRAGE COMMERCIAL INTERNATIONAL 351 (ed. N. Antaki & A. Prujiner, 1986).

Herrmann, Gerold, *The UNCITRAL Model Law — Its Background, Salient Features and Purposes*, 1 ARB. INT'L 6 (1985).

Herrmann, Gerold, *UNCITRAL Adopts Model Law on International Commercial Arbitration*, 2 ARB. INT'L 2 (1986).

Herrmann, Gerold, *UNCITRAL's Work Towards a Model Law on International Commercial Arbitration*, 4 PACE L. REV. 537 (1984).

Heuzé, Vincent, *La Morale, L'Arbitre et le Juge*, 1993 REVUE DE L'ARBITRAGE 179.

Hill, Alfred, *Judicial Function in Choice-of-Law*, 85 COLUMBIA L.REV. 1585 (1985).

Hirsch, Alain, *Les arbitres peuvent-ils connaître les avocats des parties? Critique d'une nouvelle notion de l'indépendance des arbitres dans les arbitrages CCI*, 8 ASA BULL. 7 (1990).

Hirsch, Alain, *The Place of Arbitration and the Lex Arbitri*, 34 ARB. J. 43 (1979).

Hirsch, Moshe, THE ARBITRATION MECHANISMS OF THE INTERNATIONAL SETTLEMENT OF INVESTMENT DISPUTES (1993).

Hjerner, L., *On Partial Awards, Orders and Other Decisions in Arbitral Proceedings, in Particular with Respect to Arbitration in Sweden*, 1984 SWEDISH AND INTERNAT'L ARB. 31.

Hjerner, L., *On Partial Awards, Orders and Other Decisions in Arbitral Proceedings, in Particular with respect to Arbitration in Sweden*, 1984 SWEDISH AND INT'L ARB. 31.

Hoellering, Michael, *Alternative Dispute Resolution and International Trade*, 14 NEW YORK UNIVERSITY REV. OF LAW & SOCIAL CHANGE 785 (1986).

Hoellering, Michael, *Arbitration of Patent Disputes*, 1987-1988 ARB. AND THE LAW 163.

Hoellering, Michael, *How to Draft an AAA Arbitration Clause*, 1991-92 ARBITRATION AND THE LAW 166 (1992).

Hoellering, Michael, *Interim Relief in Aid of International Commercial Arbitration*, 3 WISCONSIN INT'L L.J. 1 (1984).

Hoellering, Michael, *Remedies in Arbitration,* 1985 ARB. AND THE LAW 516.

Hoffman, David A., *Drafting ADR Contract Provisions: A Checklist and Sample Clauses,* 22 MASS. LAWYERS WEEKLY 921 (1994).

Holtzmann, Howard and Joseph Newhaus, GUIDE TO THE UNCITRAL MODEL LAW ON INTERNATIONAL COMMERCIAL ARBITRATION (1989).

Holtzmann, Howard and Robert Coulson, *L'Administation de la Preuve dans les Arbitrages Commerciaux Americains,* 1974 REVUE D'ARBITRAGE 128.

Holtzmann, Howard, *Balancing the Need for Certainty and Flexibility in International Arbitration Procedures,* in INTERNATIONAL ARBITRATION IN THE 21ST CENTURY: TOWARDS "JUDICIALIZATION" AND UNIFORMITY? 3 (Richard Lillich & Charles Brower, eds., 1994).

Holtzmann, Howard, *Dispute Resolution Procedures in East-West Trade,* 13 INT'L LAWYER 233 (1979).

Holtzmann, Howard, *First Code of Ethics for Arbitration in Commercial Disputes,* 33 BUS. LAWYER 309 (1977).

Holtzmann, Howard, *National Reports,* U.S., II YEARBOOK OF INTERNATIONAL ARBITRATION (1977).

Holtzmann, Howard, *Some Lessons of the Iran-United States Claims Tribunal,* in PRIVATE INVESTORS ABROAD: PROBLEMS AND SOLUTIONS IN INTERNATIONAL BUSINESS IN 1987 (ed. J. Moss, Mathew Bender, New York 1988) Cap. 16.

Honey, William & Marc Hall, *Bases for Recognition of Foreign Nation Money Judgments in the United States and Need for Federal Intervention,* 16 SUFFOLK TRANSNATIONAL LAW REVIEW 405 (1993).

Horsmans, Guy, *Actualité et evolution du droit Belge de l'arbitrage,* REVUE DE L'ARBITRAGE 417 (1992).

Horsmans, Guy, *L'arbitrage et l'ordre public interne,* 1978 REVUE DE L'ARBITRAGE 79.

Horvath, Eva, *Arbitration in Central and Eastern Europe,* 11 (No. 2) JOURNAL OF INTERNATIONAL ARBITRATION 5 (1994).

Houssaye, Isabella de la, *Manifest Disregard of the Law in International Commercial Arbitrations,* 28 COLUMBIA J. TRANSNAT'L L. 449 (1990).

Hubert, Dan & Tom Arnold, *Focus Points in Effective Arbitration Practice,* in INTERNATIONAL ALTERNATIVE DISPUTE RESOLUTION (CORPORATE COUNSEL'S GUIDE) Chapter 20 (Business Laws, Inc., 1993).

Hunter, J. Martin & Jan A.S. Paulsson, *A Code of Ethics for Arbitrators in International Commercial Arbitration?,* 1985 INT'L BUS. L. 153.

Hunter, J. Martin & Jan A.S. Paulsson, *Commentary on the 1985 Rules of the LCIA,* X YEARBOOK: COMMERCIAL ARBITRATION 167 (1985).

Hunter, J. Martin, Jan A.S. Paulsson, Nigel Rawling, & Alan Redfern, FRESHFIELDS GUIDE TO ARBITRATION AND ADR (1993).

Hunter, J. Martin & Alan Redfern, INTERNATIONAL COMMERCIAL ARBITRATION (2nd Edition 1991).

Hunter, J. Martin, *Achievement of the Intention of the Parties: Arbitration Agreements and the First Procedural Steps in International Arbitration*, 48 ARBITRATION 213 (1982).

Hunter, J. Martin, *UNCITRAL Model Law — Which Road Should London Take?*, 50 ARB. 288 (1984).

Ismail, Hilny, *Forum Non Conveniens, United States Multinational Corporations, and Personal Injuries in the Third World: Your Place or Mine?*, 11 B.C. THIRD WORLD L.J. 249 (1991).

Janis, Mark, AN INTRODUCTION TO INTERNATIONAL LAW (1988).

Jarrosson, Charles, *Arbitrage et Expertise*, 1993 REVUE DE L'ARBITRAGE 779.

Jarrosson, Charles, *Note on Société Hilmarton v. OTV*, 1994 REV. ARB. 327.

Jarvin, Sigvard, *Yves Derains & Jean-Jacques Arnaldez (eds.)*, COLLECTION OF ICC ARBITRAL AWARDS, Volume I — Awards 1974-85 (1990) and Volume II — Awards 1986-90 (1994).

Jarvin, Sigvard, *Comments on a September 1982 Decision by the Chairman*, VIII YEARBOOK: COMMERCIAL ARBITRATION 206 (1983).

Jarvin, Sigvard, *Choosing the Place of Arbitration: Where Do We Stand?*, 16 INT'L BUS. LAWYER 417 (1988).

Jarvin, Sigvard, *Consolidated Arbitration, the New York Arbitration Convention and the Dutch Arbitration Act 1986 — A Critique of Dr. van den Berg*, 3 ARB. INT'L 254 (1987).

Jarvin, Sigvard, *The ICC Arbitral Process: The Place of Arbitration*, 4 ICC INTERNATIONAL COURT OF ARBITRATION BULLETIN (No. 2) 7 (1993).

Jarvin, Sigvard, *The Sources and Limits of an Arbitrator's Powers*, 2 ARB. INT'L 140 (1986).

Johnson, David L. & Terrence J. Gaffney, *Lender Liability: Perspectives on Risk and Prevention*, 105 BANKING L.J. 325 (1988).

Jolidon, Pierre, COMMENTAIRE DU CONCORDAT SUISSE SUR L'ARBITRAGE (1984).

Jolidon, P., *Les motifs de recours en nullité selon le Concordat suisse sur l'arbitrage*, 1979 BERNER FESTGABE ZUM SCHWEIZERISCHEN JURISTENTAG 311.

Joly, Françoise, *Le règlement d'arbitrage international de l'Association Américaine d'Arbitrage*, 1993 REVUE DE L'ARBITRAGE 401.

Jones, D. Lloyd, *The Iran-United States Claims Tribunal: Private Rights and State Responsibility*, 24 VIRGINIA J. INT'L L. 259 (1984).

Juenger, Friedrich K., CHOICE OF LAW AND MULTISTATE JUSTICE (1993).

Juenger, Friedrich K., *An International Transaction in the American Conflict of Laws*, 7 FLORIDA J. INT'L L. 383 (1992), at 385.

Juenger, Friedrich K., *Forum Shopping, Domestic and International*, 63 TUL. L. REV. 553 (1989).

Juenger, Friedrich K., *Supreme Court Validation of Forum-Selection Clauses*, 19 WAYNE L. REV. 49 (1972).

Juenger, Friedrich K., *Recognition of Money Judgments in Civil and Commercial Matters*, 36 AM. J. COMP. L. 1 (1988).

Juenger, Friedrich K., *General Course on Private International Law*, 193 RECUEIL DES COURS 119 (1983).

Juenger, Friedrich K., *Localising Provisions in International Contracts*, 68 AUSTRALIAN LAW JOURNAL 649 (1994).

Kaden, Lewis B., *Judges and Arbitrators: Observations on the Scope of Judicial Review*, 80 COLUMBIA L. REV. 267 (1980).

Kahn, Philippe, *Droit international économique, droit du développement, lex mercatoria: concept unique ou pluralisme des ordres juridiques?*, in LE DROIT DES RELATIONS ECONOMIQUES INTERNATIONALES: ETUDES OFFERTES A BERTHOLD GOLDMAN 97 (ed. P. Fouchard, P. Kahn & A. Lyon-Caen, 1982).

Kahn, Philippe, *Les principes généraux du droit devant les arbitres du commerce international*, 116 J. DU DROIT INTERNATIONAL (CLUNET) 305 (1989).

Kane, Mary Kay, *Suing Foreign Sovereigns: A Procedural Compass*, 34 STAN. L. REV. 385 (1982).

Kanowitz, Leo, ALTERNATIVE DISPUTE RESOLUTION (1986).

Kaplan, Charles, *L'arbitrabilité des litiges commerciaux en matière de droit de la concurrence*, 1988 DROIT ET PRACTIQUE DU COMMERCE INTERNATIONAL 403 (1988).

Kaplan, Neil, *Hong Kong and the UNCITRAL Model Law*, 54 ARB. 173 (1988).

Karrer, Pierre, *Starting International Arbitration — Pitfalls in the Runway*, RECUEIL DE TRAVAUX SUISSES SUR L'ARBITRAGE INTERNATIONAL 139 (Claude Reymond & Eugene Bucher, eds., 1984).

Karrer, Pierre, Karl Arnold and Paolo Michele Patocchi, SWITZERLAND'S PRIVATE INTERNATIONAL LAW (2nd Ed. 1994).

Kassis, Antoine, REFLEXIONS SUR LE REGLEMENT D'ARBITRAGE DE LA CHAMBRE DE COMMERCE INTERNATIONAL (1988).

Kassis, Antoine, *The Questionable Validity of Arbitration and Awards Under the Rules of the International Chamber of Commerce*, 6 J. INT'L ARB. (No. 2), 79 (1989).

Kassis, Antoine, *L'arbitrage multipartite et les clauses de consolidation*, 14 DROIT ET PRATIQUE DU COMMERCE INTERNAT'L 221 (1988).

Kassis, Antoine, PROBLEMES DE BASE DE L'ARBITRAGE EN DROIT COMPARE ET EN DROIT INTERNATIONAL: TOME I ARBITRAGE JURIDICTIONNEL ET ARBITRAGE CONTRACTUEL (1987).

Kaster, *Note on the Consequences of a Broad Arbitration Clause Under the Federal Arbitration Act*, 52 BOSTON UNIVERSITY LAW REVIEW 571 (1972).

Kaufmann, Gabrielle, LES CLAUSES D'ELECTION DE FOR DANS LES CONTRAS INTERNATIONAUX (1980).

Kaufmann, Gabrielle, *Specificity of International Arbitration*, RECUEIL DE TRAVAUX SUISSES SUR L'ARBITRAGE INTERNATIONAL 297 (Claude Reymond & Eugene Bucher, eds., 1984).

Kaufmann, Gabrielle, *The Geneva Chamber of Commerce and Industry Adopts Revised Arbitration Rules*, 9 JOURNAL OF INTERNATIONAL ARBITRATION (No. 2) 72 (1992).

Kellner, F. and D. Rivkin, *In Support of the FAA: An Argument Against U.S. Adoption of the UNCITRAL Model Law*, 1 AM. REV. INT'L ARB. 535.

Kennedy, Lionel, *Enforcing International Commercial Arbitration Agreements and Awards Not Subject to the New York Convention*, 23 VIRGINIA J. INT'L L. 75 (1982).

Kerr, Michael, ARBITRATION LAWS AND COURTS: INTERNATIONAL CONFLICTS (Singapore Conference on Arbitration and the Changing World of the Nineties, 1994).

Kerr, Michael, *Arbitration and the Courts: The UNCITRAL Model Law*, 34 INTERNAT'L AND COMPARATIVE L. QUART. 1 (1985).

Kerr, Michael, *Arbitration v. Litigation*, 3 ARB. INT'L 79 (1987).

Kerr, Michael, *Arbitration v. Litigation: The Macao Sardine Case*, 15 INT'L BUSINESS LAWYER 152 (1987).

Kerr, Michael, *Equity Arbitration in England*, 2 AMERICAN REVIEW OF INTERNATIONAL ARBITRATION 377 (1993).

Kerr, Michael, *International Arbitration v. Litigation*, 1980 J. OF BUSINESS LAW 164.

Kessedjian, Catherine, LA RECONNAISSANCE ET L'EXECUTION DES JUGEMENTS EN DROIT INTERNATIONAL PRIVE AUX ETATS-UNIS (1987).

Kessedjian, Catherine, *Towards a Worldwide Covention on Jurisdiction and Enforcement*, INTERNATIONAL LITIGATION NEWS (I.B.A.), August 1994, at 8.

Kingsbury, Benedict and Christine Gray, *Developments in Dispute Settlement: Inter-State Arbitration Since 1945*, 1992 BRITISH YEARBOOK OF INTERNATIONAL LAW 97 (1993).

Kirby, John McKinley, *Consumer's Right to Sue at Home Jeopardized Through Forum Selection Clause in Carnival Cruise Lines v. Shute*, 70 N.C. L. REV. 888 (1992).

Klein, F.-E., CONSIDERATIONS SUR L'ARBITRAGE EN DROIT INTERNATIONAL PRIVE (1955).

Klein, F.-E., *A propos de l'éxécution en Suisse des sentences arbitrales étrangères*, 1985 BERNER FESTGABE ZUM SCHWEIZERISCHEN JURISTENTAG 157.

Klein, F.-E., *La Convention europénne sur l'arbitrage commercial international*, 51 REVUE CRITIQUE DE DROIT INTERNATIONAL PRIVE 621 (1962).

Knapp, Blaise, *Le droit suisse est applicable au présent contrat*, in ETUDES DE DROIT INTERNATIONAL EN L'HONNEUR DE PIERRE LALAIVE 81 (C. Dominicé, R. Patry & C. Reymond, eds., 1993).

Knoepfler, François, and Philippe Schweizer, PRECIS DE DROIT INTERNATIONAL PRIVE SUISSE (Bern 1990).

Knoepfler, Françous & Philippe Schweitzer, *Les mesure provisoires et l'arbitrage*, in RECUEIL DE TRAVAUX SUISSES SUR L'ARBITRAGE INTERNATIONAL 221 (ed. C. Reymond & E. Bucher, 1984).

Knoepfler, François, *L'Article 19 LDIP est-il adapté à l'arbitrage international?*, in ETUDES DE DROIT INTERNATIONAL EN L'HONNEUR DE PIERRE LALAIVE 531 (C. Dominicé, R. Patry & C. Reymond, eds., 1993).

Knoepfler, François, *Le contrat dans le nouveau droit international privé suisse*, in LE

NOUVEAU DROIT INTERNATIONAL PRIVE SUISSE 79 (François Dessemontet, ed., 1989).

Kornhauser, Louis & Lawrence Sager, *The One and the Many: Adjudication in Collegial Courts,* 81 CAL. L. REV. 1 (1993).

Kötz, Hein and Konrad Zweigert, INTRODUCTION TO COMPARATIVE LAW (Tony Weir, trans. 1987).

Lagarde, Paul and H. Batiffol, DROIT INTERNATIONAL PRIVE (5th Ed. 1970).

Lagarde, Paul, *Approche critique de la lex mercatoria,* in LE DROIT DES RELATIONS ECONOMIQUE INTERNATIONALES: ETUDES OFFERTES A BERTHOLD GOLDMAN (ed. P. Fouchard, P. Kahn & A. Lyon-Caen, 1982).

Lake, William T. and Jane Dana, *Judicial Review of Awards of the Iran-United States Claims Tribunal: Are the Tribunal's Awards Dutch?,* 16 LAW & POLICY INT'L BUS. 755 (1984).

Lalive, Pierre, Jean Francois Poudret and Claude Reymond, LE DROIT DE L'ARBI-TRAGE (1989).

Lalive, Pierre, *Codification et arbitrage international,* in LE DROIT DES RELATIONS ECONOMIQUES INTERNATIONALES: ETUDES OFFERTES A BERTHOLD GOLDMAN 151 (ed. P. Fouchard, P. Kahn & A. Lyon-Caen, 1982).

Lalive, Pierre, *Les Regles de Conflit de Lois Appliquées au Fond du Litige par L'Arbitre International Siégeant en Suisse,* 1976 REVUE DE L'ARBITRAGE 155.

Lalive, Pierre, *L'Importance de l'arbitrage commercial international,* in ACTES DU 1ER COLLOQUE SUR L'ARBITRAGE COMMERCIAL INTERNATIONAL 15 (ed. N. Antaki & A. Prujiner, 1986).

Lalive, Pierre, *The New Swiss Law on International Arbitration,* 4 ARB. INT'L 2 (1988).

Lalive, Pierre, *On the Neutrality of the Arbitrator and the Place of Arbitration,* RECUEIL DE TRAVAUX SUISSES SUR L'ARBITRAGE INTERNATIONAL 22 (C. Reymond & E. Bucher, eds., 1984).

Lalive, Pierre, *Problèmes relatifs à l'arbitrage international commercial,* 120 RECUEIL DES COURS 569 (1967-I).

Lasswell, Harold D. and Myres S. McDougal, *Criteria for a Theory About Law,* 44 S. CALIF. L. REV. 362 (1971).

Launders, Rachel and Andrew Rogers, *Separability — The Indestructible Arbitration Clause,* 10 ARB. INT'L (No. 1) 77

Lebedev, Sergei, *The 1977 Optional Clause for Soviet-American Contracts,* 27 AMER. J. COMP. L. 469 (1979).

Leboulanger, Philippe, Etat, *Politique et Arbitrage — L'Affaire de Plateau des Pyramides,* 1986 REV. DE L'ARBITRAGE 3 (1986).

Lederman, Leandra, *Viva Zapata: Toward a Rational System of Forum-Selection Clause Enforcement in Diversity Cases,* 66 N.Y.U. LAW REV. 422 (1991).

Leeson, Susan M. & Bryan M. Johnson, ENDING IT: DISPUTE RESOLUTION IN AMERICA (1988).

Leflar, R., AMERICAN CONFLICTS LAW (1986).

Leflar, Robert, *Conflicts Law: More Choice-Influencing Considerations,* 54 S. CAL. L. REV. 1584 (1966).

Leflar, Robert, *Choice Influencing Considerations in Conflicts Law,* 41 N.Y.U.L. REV.267 (1966).

Legall, Jean Pierre, *Fiscalité et Arbitrage,* 1994 REV. ARB. 3 (Part I) & 253 (Part II).

Legoff, Jacques, LA BOURSE ET LA VIE (1986).

Lester, Gillian, *Toward the Feminization of Collective Bargaining Law,* 36 MCGILL L.J. 1181 (1991).

Lévy, Laurent, *Dissenting Opinions in International Arbitration in Switzerland,* 5 ARBITRATION INTERNATIONAL 35 (1989).

Lévy, Laurent and William W. Park, *A Swiss-American Perspective of a Franco-American Treatise,* 2 ARBITRATION INTERNATIONAL 266 (1986).

Lew, Julian D. (ed.), THE IMMUNITY OF ARBITRATORS (1990).

Lew, Julian D. (ed.), THE ART OF ARBITRATION (1982).

Lew, Julian D., APPLICABLE LAW IN INTERNATIONAL COMMERCIAL ARBITRATION (1978).

Lew, Julian D. (ed.), CONTEMPORARY PROBLEMS IN INTERNATIONAL COMMERCIAL ARBITRATION (1986).

Lew, Julian D., *A Questions of Costs,* FINANCIAL TIMES, 28 June 1994, at 16.

Lew, Julian D. *The Arbitration Act of 1975,* 24 INT'L COMPARATIVE L. QUARTERLY 870 (1975).

Lew, Julian D., *The Recognition and Enforcement of Arbitration Awards in England,* 10 THE INT'L LAWYER 425 (1976).

Lewis, Charles J., STATE AND DIPLOMATIC IMMUNITY (3d Ed. 1990).

Lillich, Richard & Charles Brower (eds.), INTERNATIONAL ARBITRATION IN THE 21ST CENTURY: TOWARDS "JUDICIALIZATION" AND UNIFORMITY? (1994).

Lillich, Richard, *The Law Governing Disputes Under Economic Development Agreements: Reexamining the Concept of "Internationalization,* in INTERNATIONAL ARBITRATION IN THE 21ST CENTURY: TOWARDS "JUDICIALIZATION" AND UNIFORMITY? 61 (Richard Lillich & Charles Brower, eds., 1994).

Lillich, Richard, ed., THE U.N. COMPENSATION COMMISSION (1995).

Lionnet, Klaus, *Should the Procedural Law Applicable to International Arbitration Be De-nationalized or Unified? The Answer of the UNCITRAL Model Law,* 8 JOURNAL OF INTERNATIONAL ARBITRATION (No.8) 5 (1991).

Lipstein, Kurt, *One Hundred Years of Hague Conferences on Private International Law,* 42 INTERNATIONAL AND COMPARATIVE LAW QUARTERLY 553 (1993).

Litman, Harry, *Considerations of Choice of Law in the Doctrine of Forum Non Conveniens,* 74 CAL. L. REV. 565 (1986).

Littman, Mark, *England Reconsiders `The Stated Case',* 13 INT'L LAWYER 253 (1979).

Lombardini, Carlo, *Jurisdictional Clause in Contract,* FINANCIAL L. REV. 42 (Jan. 1991).

Lookofsky, Joseph, TRANSNATIONAL LITIGATION AND COMMERCIAL ARBITRATION (1992).

Loquin, Eric, L'AMIABLE COMPOSITION EN DROIT COMPARE ET INTERNA-TIONAL (1980).

Loquin, Eric, *Les pouvoirs des arbitres internationaux à la lumière de l'évolution récente du droit international*, 110 J. DU DROIT INTERNAT'L (CLUNET) 298 (1983).

Loumiet, Carlos, *Introductory Note: Florida International Arbitration Act*, 26 INT'L LEGAL MATERIALS 949 (1987).

Loussouarn, Yvon and Pierre Bourel, DROIT INTERNATIONAL PRIVE (1978).

Lowenfeld, Andreas F. (ed.), INTERNATIONAL LITIGATION AND ARBITRA-TION (1993).

Lowenfeld, Andreas F., *The Free Trade Agreement Meets Its First Challenge*, 37 MCGILL L. R. 597 (1992).

Lowenfeld, Andreas F., *The Mitsubishi Case: Another View*, 2 ARB. INT'L 116 (1986).

Lowenfeld, Andreas F., *Thoughts About A Multinational Judgments Convention*, 57 LAW & CONTEMPORARY PROBLEMS 289 (1994).

Lowenfeld, Andreas F., *Singapore and the Local Bar: Aberration or Ill Omen?*, 5 J. INT'L ARB. (No. 1) 71 (1988).

Lutz, Robert, *Enforcement of Foreign Judgments, Part I: A Selected Bibliography on United States Enforcement of Judgments Rendered Abroad and Enforcement of Foreign Judgments, Part II: A Selected Bibliography on Enforcement of U.S. Judgments in Foreign Countries*, 27 INTERNATIONAL LAWYER 471 and 1029 (1993).

Machina, Mark and Michael Rothchild, *Risk*, in UTILITY AND PROBABILITY (THE NEW PALGRAVE DICTIONARY OF ECONOMICS) 277 (J. Eatwell, M. Milgate, & P. Newman, eds., 1990).

Macneil, Ian, AMERICAN ARBITRATION LAW (1992).

Macneil, Ian, Richard Speidel, & Thomas Stipanowich, FEDERAL ARBITRATION LAW (1994).

Magyar, Jennifer, *Statutory Civil Rights Claims in Arbitration*, 72 B.U. L. REV. 641 (1992).

Maier, Harold G. and Thomas R. McCoy, *A Unifying Theory for Judicial Jurisdiction and Choice of Law*, 39 AM. J. COMP. L. 249 (1991).

Maniruzzaman, A.F.M., *Conflict of Laws Issues in International Arbitration: Practice and Trends*, 9 ARBITRATION INTERNATIONAL 371 (1993).

Maniruzzaman, A.F.M., *International Commercial Arbitration: The Conflict of Laws Issues in Determining the Applicable Substantive Law in the Context of Investment Agreements*, XL NETHERLANDS INTERNATIONAL LAW REVIEW 201 (1993).

Mann, Francis A., *England Rejects "Delocalized" Contracts and Arbitration*, 33 INT'L & COMP. L.Q. 193 (1984).

Mann, Francis A., *Introduction to LEX MERCATORIA AND ARBITRATION* xxi (Thomas Carbonneau, ed., 1990).

Mann, Francis A., *New Dangers of Arbitration in Switzerland*, FINANCIAL TIMES 43 (24 Nov. 1988).

Mann, Francis A., *Lex Facit Arbitrum,* in INTERNATIONAL ARBITRATION: LIBER AMICORUM FOR MARTIN DOMKE 157 (1967); reprinted in 2 ARB. INT'L 241 (1986).

Mann, Francis A., *Private Arbitration and Public Policy,* 4 CIV. JUST. Q. 257 (1985).

Mann, Francis A., *Foreign Investment in the International Court of Justice,* 86 AM. J. INT'L L. 92 (1992).

Mann, Francis A., *Sovereign Immunity Under English Law,* in SOVEREIGN LENDING: MANAGING LEGAL RISK 103 (M. Gruson & R. Reisner, eds., 1984).

Mann, Francis A., *State Contracts and International Arbitration,* 43 BRITISH YEARBOOK OF INTERNAT'L LAW 1 (1967).

Mann, Francis A., *Where is an Award `Made'?,* 1 ARB. INT'L 107 (1985).

Martin, James (ed.), PERSPECTIVES ON CONFLICT OF LAWS (1980).

Marville, H. and L. Scalbert, *Les clauses compromissoires pathologiques,* 1998 REVUE D'ARBITRAGE 117.

Mayer, Pierre, *Le principle de bonne foi devant les arbitres du commerce international,* in ETUDES DE DROIT INTERNATIONAL EN L'HONNEUR DE PIERRE LALAIVE 543 (C. Dominicé, R. Patry & C. Reymond, eds., 1993).

Mayer, Pierre, *Les Lois de Police Etrangères,* 1981 J. DR. INT'L 277.

Mayer, Pierre, *L'autonomie de l'arbitre international dans l'appréciation de sa propre compétence,* 217 HAGUE ACADEMY RECUEIL DES COURS (1989).

Mayer, Pierre, *Mandatory Rules of Law in International Arbitration,* 2 ARB. INT'L 274 (1986).

Mayer, Pierre, DROIT INTERNATIONAL PRIVE (1987).

Mayer, Pierre, *La Sentence Contraire à L'Ordre Public au Fond,* 1994 REV. ARB. 615.

McClendon, J. Stewart (ed.), SURVEY OF INTERNATIONAL ARBITRATION SITES (2d. Edition, 1988).

McClendon, J. Stewart, *Arbitration Clauses in International Contracts,* in SURVEY OF INTERNATIONAL ARBITRATION SITES 127 (J.S. McClendon, ed., 3rd Ed., 1993).

McClendon, J. Stewart, *Enforcement of Foreign Arbitral Awards in the United States,* 4 NORTHWESTERN J. OF INT'L LAW & BUSINESS 58 (1982).

McCoy, Thomas R. and Harold G. Maier, *A Unifying Theory for Judicial Jurisdiction and Choice of Law,* 39 AM. J. COMP. L. 249 (1991).

McDougal, Myres S. and Harold D. Lasswell, *Criteria for a Theory About Law,* 44 S. CALIF. L. REV. 362 (1971).

McWhinney, Edward, *The International Arbitral and Judicial Processes and the Atrophy of the Permanent Court of Arbitration,* in ETUDES DE DROIT INTERNATIONAL EN L'HONNEUR DE PIERRE LALAIVE 577 (C. Dominicé, R. Patry & C. Reymond, eds., 1993).

Meagher, Robert F., AN INTERNATIONAL REDISTRIBUTION OF WEALTH AND POWER (1979).

Meldrum, Amy A. and Frederick Brown, *International Arbitration Provisions for Emerging Companies Going International,* COUNSELING EMERGING COMPANIES IN GOING INTERNATIONAL 361 (Alan S. Gutterman, ed., 1994).

Melis, Werner, *Force Majeure and Hardship Clauses in International Commercial Contracts: A View of the Practice of the ICC Court of Arbitration*, 1 J. INT'L ARB. 213 (1984).

Meltzer, Bernard, *After the Labor Arbitration Award: The Public Policy Defense*, 10 INDUS. REL. L.J. 241 (1988).

Mentschikoff, Soia, *Commercial Arbitration*, 61 COLUMBIA L. REV. 846 (1960).

Merkin, Robert, ARBITRATION LAW (1991).

Meyer, Philip, *Convicts, Criminals, Prisoners and Outlaws: A Course in Popular Storytelling*, 42 J. LEGAL ED. 129 (1992).

Mezger, E., *Compétemce-compétence des arbitres et indépendance de la convention arbitrale dans la Convention dite Européenne sur l'Arbitrage Commercial International de 1961*, in COMMERCIAL ARBITRATION: ESSAYS IN MEMORIAM EUGENIO MINOLI 315 (ed. Associazioni Italiana per Arbitrato, Unione Tipographico, Turin 1974).

Mezger, E., *Dix questions relatives au titre VI du livre IV NCPC*, 1981 REVUE DE L'ARBITRAGE 543.

Mezger, E., *De l'autonomie de la clause compromissoire, de la `compétence-compétence' de l'arbitre, et d'autres problèmes fondamentaux de l'arbitrage dans la plus récente jurisprudence allemande,'* 1978 REVUE DE L'ARBITRAGE 548.

Mezger, E., *La jurisprudence française relative aux sentences arbitrales étrangères et la doctrine de l'autonomie de la volonté en matière d'arbitrage international de droit privé*, in MELANGES OFFERTS A JACQUES MAURY 273 (1960).

Mijs, Wim and Sam Muller (eds.), THE FLAME REKINDLED: NEW HOPES FOR INTERNATIONAL ARBITRATION (1994).

Mills, William III, *State International Arbitration Statutes and the U.S. Arbitration Act: Unifying the Availability of Interim Relief*, in INTERNATIONAL ALTERNATIVE DISPUTE RESOLUTION (CORPORATE COUNSEL'S GUIDE) Chapter 8 (Business Laws, Inc., 1993).

Mnookin, Robert, *Why Negotiations Fail: An Exploration of Barriers to the Resolution of Conflict*, 8 OHIO STATE J. DISPUTE RESOLUTION 235 (1993).

Moghaddam, Alexander and Alan Nakazawa, *COGSA and Choice of Foreign Law Clauses in Bills of Lading*, TUL. MARITIME L.J. 1 (1992).

Moreau, Bertrand, *Savoir-faire, non-respect du secret et arbitrage*, 1979 REVUE DE L'ARBITRAGE 52.

Morris, Michael S. and Anne E. Covey, *The Enforceability of Agreements Providing for Forum and Choice of Law Selection*, 61 DENV. L.J. 837 (1988).

Morris, J.H.C. and A.V. Dicey, THE CONFLICT OF LAWS (L. Collins, ed., 11th Ed. 1987).

Mullenix, Linda S., *Another Choice of Forum, Another Choice of Law: Consensual Adjudicatory Procedure in Federal Court*, 57 FORDHAM L. REV. 291 (1988).

Mullenix, Linda S., *The Counter-Reformation in Procedural Justice*, 77 MINN. L. REV. 375 (1992).

Mullenix, Linda S., *Another Easy Case, More Bad Law: Carnival Cruise Lines and Contractual Personal Jurisdiction*, 27 TEX. INT'L L.J. 323 (1992).

Muller, Sam and Wim Mijs (eds.), THE FLAME REKINDLED: NEW HOPES FOR INTERNATIONAL ARBITRATION (1994).

Murphy, Ewell Jr., *Transnational Arbitration As a Means of Managing Foreign Corporate Risks* in INTERNATIONAL ALTERNATIVE DISPUTE RESOLUTION (CORPORATE COUNSEL'S GUIDE) Chapter 3.1 (Business Laws, Inc., 1993).

Murphy, Ewell Jr., *How to Draft a Transnational Arbitration Clause: The Four Languages of Charles V*, in INTERNATIONAL ALTERNATIVE DISPUTE RESOLUTION (CORPORATE COUNSEL'S GUIDE) Chapter 3 (Business Laws, Inc., 1993).

Murray, John, Alan Rau and Edward Sherman, PROCESSES OF DISPUTE RESOLUTION: THE ROLE OF LAWYERS (1989).

Mustill, Michael and Stewart Boyd, COMMERCIAL ARBITRATION (2d Edition 1989).

Mustill, Michael, *Cedric Barclay Memorial Lecture*, 58 ARBITRATION 159 (1992).

Mustill, Michael, *Multipartite Arbitration: An Agenda for Law-Makers*, 7 ARB. INT'L 393 (1991).

Mustill, Michael, The New Lex Mercatoria: The First Twenty Five Years, 4 ARB. INT'L 86, reprinted from LIBER AMICORUM FOR LORD WILBERFORCE (1987).

Mustill, Michael, *Transnational Arbitration in English Law*, 37 CURRENT LEGAL PROBLEMS 133 (1984).

Najar, Jean-Claude & M. Polkinghorne, *Australia's Adoption of the UNCITRAL Model Law*, 3 INT'L ARB. REPORT 21 (1989).

Nakazawa, Alan and Alexander Moghaddam, *COGSA and Choice of Foreign Law Clauses in Bills of Lading*, 17 TUL. MARITIME L.J. 1 (1992).

Nanda, Ved and David Pansius, LITIGATION OF INTERNATIONAL DISPUTES IN U.S. COURTS (1993 Edition).

Nariman, Fali S., *Foreign Arbitral Awards in India: Problems, Pitfalls and Progress*, 6 J. OF INT'L ARB. (No. 1) 25.

Nariman, Fali S., *International Commercial Arbitration in India*, 10 ARBITRATION INTERNATIONAL 373 (1994).

Newhaus, Joseph and Howard Holtzmann, GUIDE TO THE UNCITRAL MODEL LAW ON INTERNATIONAL COMMERCIAL ARBITRATION (1989).

Nettesheim, Patrick and Henning Stahl, *Bundesgerichtshof Rejects Enforcement of United States Punitive Damages Award*, 28 TEXAS INTERNATIONAL LAW JOURNAL 416 (1993).

Newman, Lawrence & M. Burrows, *International Litigation*, NEW YORK L.J., December 26, 1984.

Newman, Perry B., *Forum Selection Clauses in Commercial Loan Documents: Unimpeachable or Unenforceable?*, 107 BANKING L. J. 547 (1990).

Newhaus, Joseph and Howard Holtzmann, GUIDE TO THE UNCITRAL MODEL LAW ON INTERNATIONAL COMMERCIAL ARBITRATION (1989).

Newton and Hall, *International Arbitration Bodies*, N.Y.L.J., 16 June 1992, at 1, col.1.

Neyroud, Philippe and William W. Park, *Predestination and Swiss Arbitration Law: Geneva's Application of the International Concordat*, 2 B.U. INT'L L.J. 1 (1983-84).

Ngongi, Ikomi, PRIVATIZATION IN CAMEROON: LEGAL AND INSTITUTIONAL PREREQUISITES (1991).

Nichol, Victor and Benjamin Wolkinson, *Religious Discrimination: Arbitrating the Grievances*, 48 DISPUTE RESOLUTION JOURNAL 54 (December 1993).

Nichols, Bruce, *Sovereign Debtors Under U.S. Immunity Law*, in SOVEREIGN LENDING: MANAGING LEGAL RISK 81 (M. Gruson & R. Reisner, eds., 1984).

Nicklisch, Fritz, *Agreement to Arbitrate to Fill Contractual Gaps*, 5 J. INT'L ARB. 35 (1988).

Nolan, Dennis, and Laura Cooper, LABOR ARBITRATION: A COURSEBOOK (1994).

North, P.M., *The Draft U.K./U.S. Judgments Convention: A British Viewpoint*, 1 N.W. J. INT'L. & BUS. 219 (1979).

O'Neill, Philip D. Jr., *American Legal Developments in Commercial Arbitration involving Foreign States and State Enterprises*, in INTERNATIONAL COMMERCIAL ARBITRATION, Vol. II, 225 (Emmanuel Gaillard and Robert B. von Mehren, eds., Practicing Law Institute Seminar, October 1988).

O'Neill, Philip D., Jr., *American Legal Developments in Commercial Arbitration Involving Foreign States and State Enterprises*, 6 J. INT'L ARB. (No. 1) 117 (1989).

O'Neill, Philip D., Jr., *Recent Developments in International Commercial Arbitration: An American Perspective*, 4 J. INT'L ARB. (No. 1), 7 (1987).

Oppetit, Bruno, Arbitrage, *médiation et conciliation*, 1984 REVUE DE L'ARBITRAGE 307.

Oppetit, Bruno, *L'arbitrage et les contrats commerciaux à long terme*, 1976 REVUE DE L'ARBITRAGE 91.

Oppetit, Bruno, *Sur le concept d'arbitrage*, in LE DROIT DES RELTIONS ECONOMIQUES INTERNATIONALES: ETUDES OFFERTES A BERTHOLD GOLDMAN 229 (ed. P. Fouchard, P. Kahn & A. Lyon-Caen, 1982).

Palmer, Gerald, *Enforcing Arbitral Decisions*, NATIONAL LAW JOURNAL 25 (February 1994).

Panchaud, André, *Le siège de l'arbitrage international de droit privé*, 61 SCHWEIZERISCHES JURISTEN-ZEITUNG 369 (1965); 1966 REVUE DE L'ARBITRAGE 2.

Pansius, David and Ved Nanda, LITIGATION OF INTERNATIONAL DISPUTES IN U.S. COURTS (1993 Edition).

Park, William W., W. Laurence Craig, and Jan Paulsson, INTERNATIONAL CHAMBER OF COMMERCE ARBITRATION (2d. Ed. 1990).

Park, William W., W. Laurence Craig and Jan Paulsson, *French Codification of a Legal Framework for International Commercial Arbitration*, 13 GEORGETOWN JOURNAL OF LAW & POLICY IN INTERNATIONAL BUSINESS 727 (1981).

Park, William W. and Jan Paulsson, *Arbitrage Commercial et Contrats Internationaux*, 45 REVUE DU BARREAU 215 (1985).

Park, William W. and Jan Paulsson, *The Binding Force of International Arbitral Awards*, 23 VIRGINIA JOURNAL OF INTERNATIONAL LAW 253 (1983).

Park, William W. and Laurent Lévy, *A Swiss-American Perspective of a Franco-American Treatise*, 2 ARBITRATION INTERNATIONAL 266 (1986).

Park, William W. and Philippe Neyroud, *Predestination and Swiss Arbitration Law*, 2 BOSTON UNIVERSITY INTERNATIONAL LAW JOURNAL 1 (1983).

Park, William W., *Arbitration of International Contract Disputes*, 39 BUSINESS LAWYER 1783 (1984).

Park, William W., *El arbitraje comercial internacional y la lex loci arbitri*, 2 REVISTA DE LA CORTE ESPANOLA DE ARBITRAJE 57 (1985).

Park, William W., *Finality and Fairness in Tax Arbitration*, 11 JOURNAL OF INTERNATIONAL ARBITRATION (No. 2) 19 (1994).

Park, William W., *International Products Liability Litigation: Choosing the Applicable Law*, 12 INTERNATIONAL LAWYER 845 (1978).

Park, William W., *Judicial Controls in the Arbitral Process*, 5 ARBITRATION INTERNATIONAL 230 (1989).

Park, William W., *Particularités de l'arbitrage en matière bancaire et financière*, 116 SEMAINE JUDICIAIRE (No. 35) 621 (1994).

Park, William W., *Judicial Supervision of Transnational Commercial Arbitration*, 21 HARVARD INTERNATIONAL LAW JOURNAL 87 (1980).

Park, William W., *L'Arbitrage et le recouvrement des prêts consentis à des débiteurs étrangers*, 37 MCGILL LAW JOURNAL 375 (1992).

Park, William W., *Legal Issues in the Third World's Economic Development*, 61 BOSTON UNIVERSITY LAW REVIEW 1321 (1981).

Park, William W., *Legal Policy Conflicts in International Banking*, 50 OHIO STATE LAW JOURNAL 1067 (1989).

Park, William W., *National Law and Commercial Justice*, 63 TULANE LAW REVIEW 647 (1989).

Park, William W., *National Legal Systems and Private Dispute Resolution*, 82 AMERICAN JOURNAL OF INTERNATIONAL LAW 616 (1988).

Park, William W., *Private Adjudicators and the Public Interest: The Expanding Scope of International Arbitration*, 12 BROOKLYN JOURNAL OF INTERNATIONAL LAW 629 (1986).

Park, William W., Reviews of INTERNATIONAL COMMERCIAL ARBITRATION AND THE COURTS and GUIDE TO INTERNATIONAL ARBITRATION AND ARBITRATORS (Parker School of Foreign and Comparative Law), 85 AMERICAN JOURNAL OF INTERNATIONAL LAW 586 (1991).

Park, William W., *When the Borrower and the Banker Are at Odds: Arbitration and International Finance*, 65 TULANE LAW REVIEW 1323 (1991).

Park, William W., *The Influence of National Legal Systems on International Commercial Arbitration*, in RESOLVING TRANSNATIONAL DISPUTES THROUGH ARBITRATION 80 (T. Carbonneau, ed., 1984).

Park, William W., *The International Currency of Arbitral Awards: Choosing an Arbitral Situs*, COUNSELING EMERGING COMPANIES IN GOING INTERNATIONAL 391 (Alan S. Gutterman, ed., 1994).

Park, William W., *The Lex Loci Arbitri and International Commercial Arbitration*, 32 INTERNATIONAL & COMPARATIVE LAW QUARTERLY 21 (1983).

Partan, Daniel, THE INTERNATIONAL LAW PROCESS (1992).

Patocchi, Paolo Michele, Karl Arnold and Pierre Karrer, SWITZERLAND'S PRIVATE INTERNATIONAL LAW (2nd Ed. 1994).

Patrikis, Ernest, *Immunity of Central Bank Assets Under U.S. Law*, in SOVEREIGN LENDING: MANAGING LEGAL RISK 89 (M. Gruson & R. Reisner, eds., 1984).

Paul, Joel, *Comity in International Law*, 32 HARV. INT'L L.J. 1 (1991).

Paul, Jeremy, *A Bedtime Story*, 74 VA. L. REV. 914 (1988).

Paulsson, Jan and William W. Park, *Arbitrage Commercial et Contrats Internationaux*, 45 REVUE DU BARREAU 215 (1985).

Paulsson, Jan, Nigel Rawling, Alan Redfern and Martin Hunter, FRESHFIELDS GUIDE TO ARBITRATION AND ADR (1993).

Paulsson, Jan, *Extent of Independence of Arbitration from the Law of the Situs*, in CONTEMPORARY PROBLEMS IN INTERNATIONAL ARBITRATION 141 (J. Lew, ed., 1987).

Paulsson, Jan, *Third World Participation in International Investment Arbitration, Vol 2 (No. 1)* ICSID REVIEW — FOREIGN INVESTMENT LAW JOURNAL 19 (1987).

Paulsson, Jan, *The New York Convention's Misadventures in India*, 7 INTERNATIONAL ARBITRATION REPORT (No. 6) 3 (1992).

Paulsson, Jan, *Standards of Conduct for Counsel in International Arbitration*, 3 AMERICAN REVIEW OF INTERNATIONAL ARBITRATION 214 (1992).

Paulsson, Jan, W. Laurence Craig, and William W. Park, INTERNATIONAL CHAMBER OF COMMERCE ARBITRATION (2d. Ed. 1990).

Paulsson, Jan, *Delocalization of International Commercial Arbitration*, 32 INT'L & COMP. L.Q. 53 (1983).

Paulsson, Jan, William W. Park and W. Lawrence Craig, *French Codification of a Legal Framework for International Commercial Arbitration*, 13 GEORGETOWN JOURNAL OF LAW & POLICY IN INTERNATIONAL BUSINESS 727 (1981).

Paulsson, Jan and William W. Park, *The Binding Force of International Arbitral Awards*, 23 VIRGINIA JOURNAL OF INTERNATIONAL LAW 253 (1983).

Paulsson, Jan, *Arbitration Unbound: An Award Detached from the Law of its Country of Origin*, 30 INT'L & COMP. L.Q. 358 (1981).

Paulsson, Jan, *Arbitration Under the Rules of the International Chamber of Commerce*, in RESOLVING TRANSNATIONAL DISPUTES THROUGH INTERNATIONAL ARBITRATION 235 (ed. T. Carbonneau, 1984).

Paulsson, Jan, *Arbitre et juge en Suede: Exposé générale et reflexions sur la delocalisation des sentence arbitrales*, 1980 REV. ARB. 476.

Paulsson, Jan, *The ICSID Klöckner v. Cameroon Award: The Duties of Partners in North-South Economic Development Agreements*, 1 J. INT'L ARB. 145 (1984).

Paulsson, Jan, *May a State Invoke Its International Law to Repudiate Consent to International Arbitration?*, 2 ARBITRATION INTERNATIONAL 90 (1986).

Paulsson, Jan, *La réforme de la loi de l'arbitrage de Hong Kong*, 1984 REVUE DE L'ARBITRAGE 325.

Paulsson, Jan, *The Role of the Swedish Courts in Transnational Commercial Arbitration,* 21 VIRGINIA J. OF INT'L LAW 211 (1981).

Paulsson, Jan, *The Role of the Swedish Courts in Transnational Commercial Arbitration,* 21 VIRGINIA J. OF INT'L L. 211 (1981).

Peace, Nancy, *Letter from the President, 1 SPIDR NEWS (No. 2) 1 (Society of Professionals in Dispute Resolution,* Winter 1993).

Pearson, Todd L., *Limiting Lender Liability: The Trend Toward Written Credit Agreement Statutes,* 76 MINN. L. REV. 295 (1991).

Pechota, Vratislav, *International Economic Arbitration in the USSR and Eastern Europe,* 8 N.Y.L. SCH. J. INT'L COMP. L. 377 (1987).

Perret, François, *Les conclusions et leur cause juridique au regard de la règle "ne eat judex ultra petita partium,* in ETUDES DE DROIT INTERNATIONAL EN L'HONNEUR DE PIERRE LALAIVE 595 (C. Dominicé, R. Patry & C. Reymond, eds., 1993).

Perrin, Jean-François, *Théorie de l'incorporation et cohérence de l'ordre juridique,* in ETUDES DE DROIT INTERNATIONAL EN L'HONNEUR DE PIERRE LALAIVE 141 (C. Dominicé, R. Patry & C. Reymond, eds., 1993).

Peter, Wolfgang, ARBITRATION AND RENEGOTIATION OF INTERNATIONAL INVESTMENT AGREEMENTS (Second Edition, 1995.).

Philip, A., *The Significance of the Place of Arbitration in International Arbitration,* 1986 SWEDISH AND INTERNATIONAL ARBITRATION 37.

Philippe, Denis, *"Pacta sunt servanda" et "Rebus sic stantibus,"* in L'APPORT DE LA JURISPRUDENCE ARBITRALE 181 (1986), International Chamber of Commerce Pub. No. 440/1.

Pisar, Samuel, *The United Nations Convention on Foreign Arbitral Awards,* 1959 J. BUSINESS LAW 156.

Platto, C., ed., ENFORCEMENT OF FOREIGN JUDGMENTS WORLDWIDE (1989).

Plehn, Steven and Bernardo Cremades, *The New Lex Mercatoria and the Harmonization of the Laws of International Commercial Transaction,* 2 B.U. INT'L L.J. 317 (1984).

Polak, Maurice and Rene Vam Rooij, PRIVATE INTERNATIONAL LAW IN THE NETHERLANDS.

Polkinghorne, M., *The Right of Representation in a Foreign Venue,* 4 ARB. INT'L 333 (1988).

Poncet, Charles & Emmanuel Gaillard, *Switzerland: Statute on International Arbitration,* 27 INT'L LEGAL MATERIALS 37 (1988).

Polinsky, A. Mitchell, *Risk Sharing Through Breach of Contract Remedies,* 12 J. LEG. STUD. 427 (1983).

Poncet, Carlo and Emmanuel Gaillard, *Introductory Note and Translations to the Swiss LDIP,* 27 I.L.M. 37 (1988).

Posner, Richard, *The Summary Jury Trial and Other Methods of Alternative Dispute Resolution: Some Cautionary Observations,* 53 U. CHICAGO L. REV. 366 (1986).

Poudret, Jean François, Pierre Lalive and Claude Reymond, LE DROIT DE L'ARBI-
TRAGE (1989).

Poudret, Jean-François, *La clause arbitrale par référence selon la Convention de New
York et l'art. 6 du Concordat sur l'arbitrage*, in MELANGES GUY FLATTET 523
(ed. B. Dutoit, J. Hofstetter & P. Piot, 1985).

Poudret, Jean-François, *Le droit applicable à la convention d'arbitrage, manuscript presented at General Meeting of the Swiss Arbitration Association*, Basel, 17 June 1994.

Poudret, Jean-François, *Expertise et droit d'être entendu dans l'arbitrage international*,
in ETUDES DE DROIT INTERNATIONAL EN L'HONNEUR DE PIERRE
LALAIVE 607 (C. Dominicé, R. Patry & C. Reymond, eds., 1993).

Poudret, Jean-François, *L'interpétation des sentences arbitrales*, RECUEIL DE
TRAVAUX SUISSES SUR L'ARBITRAGE INTERNATIONAL 269 (Claude
Reymond & Eugene Bucher, eds., 1984).

Purcell, Edward Jr., *Geography as a Litigation Weapon: Consumers, Forum-Selection
Clauses, and the Rehnquist Court*, 40 UCLA LAW REVIEW 423 (1992).

Quigley, L., *Accession by the United States to the United Nations Convention on the
Recognition and Enforcement of Foreign Awards*, 70 YALE L.J. 1049 (1971).

Rahmann, Detlef, *Arbitrability of Antitrust Issues*, 1990 COMPARATIVE LAW
YEARBOOK OF INTERNATIONAL BUSINESS 97.

Rashkover, Barry W., *Title 14, New York Choice of Law Rule for Contractual Disputes:
Avoiding the Unreasonable Results*, 71 CORNELL L.REV. 227 (1985).

Rau, Alan, John Murray and Edward Sherman, PROCESSES OF DISPUTE RESOLU-
TION: THE ROLE OF LAWYERS (1989).

Rawling, Nigel, Alan Redfern, Martin Hunter and Jan Paulsson, FRESHFIELDS
GUIDE TO ARBITRATION AND ADR 1-2 (1993).

Redfern, Alan, Martin Hunter, Jan Paulsson and Nigel Rawling, FRESHFIELDS
GUIDE TO ARBITRATION AND ADR (1993).

Redfern, Alan and Martin Hunter, INTERNATIONAL COMMERCIAL ARBITRA-
TION (2d Ed. 1992).

Redfern, Alan, *Arbitration and the Courts: Interim Measures of Protection — Is the
Tide About to Turn?*, scheduled for publication in TEXAS J. INTERNATIONAL
LAW (1994).

Redfern, Alan, *ICSID — Losing its Appeal?*, 3 ARB. INT'L 98 (1987).

Redfern, Alan, *The Importance of the Forum in International Commercial Arbitration*,
1980 THE INTERNATIONAL CONTRACT: LAW AND FINANCE REVIEW
YEARBOOK 484.

Reese, W., Maurice Rosenberg, and Peter Hay (eds.), CONFLICT OF LAWS (9th Ed.
1990).

Reichert, Douglas, *Enforcement of Foreign Arbitral Awards Under the United Nations
Convention of 1958: A Survey of Recent Federal Case Law*, 11 MARYLAND J. OF
INT'L LAW AND TRADE 13 (1987).

Reisman, W. Michael, *The Breakdown of the Control Mechanism in ICSID Arbitration*,
1989 DUKE L. J. 739.

Reisman, W. Michael and Aaron Schreiber, JURISPRUDENCE: UNDERSTANDING
AND SHAPING LAW (1987).

Reisman, W. Michael, *Criteria for Use of Force in International Law,* 10 YALE J. INT'L L. 279 (1985).

Reisman, W. Michael, *Repairing ICSID's Control System: Some Comments on Aaron Broches' "Observations on the Finality of ICSID Awards,"* 7 ICSID REVIEW 196 (1992).

Reisman, W. Michael, NULLITY AND REVISION (1971).

Reisman, W. Michael, SYSTEMS OF CONTROL IN INTERNATIONAL ADJUDI-CATION AND ARBITRATION (1992).

Resnick, Judith, *On the Bias: Feminist Reconsideration of the Aspirations for Our Judges,* 61 S. CAL. L. REV. 1877 (1988).

Resnick, Judith, *Failing Faith: Adjudicatory Procedure in Decline,* 53 U. CHICAGO L. REV. 494 (1986).

Reuland, Robert, *The Recognition of Judgments in the European Community: The Twenty-fifth Anniversary of the Brussels Convention,* 14 MICHIGAN J. INTER-NATIONAL LAW 559 (1993).

Reyes, Ramon E., *Medoil Corp v. Citicorp: Uncertainty Requires an Indepth Inquiry into Forum Selection Clause Enforceability Issues,* 17 BROOKLYN J. INT'L L. 687 (1991).

Reymond, Claude, *The Channel Tunnel Case and the Law of Int'l Arb'n,* 109 L.Q.R. 337 (1993).

Reymond, Claude, *Common Law and Civil Law Procedures: Which Is the More Inquisitorial?,* 55 ARB. 155 (1989).

Reymond, Claude, *Problèmes actuels de l'arbitrage commercial international,* 1982 REVUE ECONOMIQUE ET SOCIALE 5

Reymond, Claude, *Where is an Arbitral Award Made?,* 108 LAW QUARTERLY REVIEW 1 (1992).

Reymond, Claude, *Security for Costs in International Arbitration,* 110 LAW QUAR-TERLY REVIEW 501 (1994).

Reymond, Claude, *Soverainté de l'Etat et Participation à l'Arbitrage,* 1985 REVUE DE L'ARBITRAGE 517.

Reymond, Claude and Eugene Bucher (eds.), RECUEIL DE TRAVAUX SUISSES SUR L'ARBITRAGE INTERNATIONAL (1984).

Reymond, Claude, Jean Francois Poudret and Pierre Lalive, LE DROIT DE L'ARBI-TRAGE (1989).

Reynolds, Michael, ARBITRATION (1993).

Rhodes, J. & L. Sloan, *The Pitfalls of International Commercial Arbitration,* 17 VAN-DERBILT J. OF INT'L LAW 19 (1984).

Rifkin, D., *Keeping Lawyers Out of International Arbitration,* 9 INT'L FIN. L.R. 2, 11 (1990).

Riskin, Leonard and James Westbrook, DISPUTE RESOLUTION AND LAWYERS (1987).

Rivkin, David and F. Kellner, *In Support of the FAA: An Argument Against U.S. Adoption of the UNCITRAL Model Law,* 1 AM. REV. INT'L ARB. 535 (1990).

Rivkin, David, *Enforceability of Arbitral Awards Based on Lex Mercatoria,* 9 ARB. INT'L 67 (1993).

Robert, Jean and Thomas Carbonneau, THE FRENCH LAW OF ARBITRATION (1983).

Robert, Jean, *De la place de la loi dans l'arbitrage,* in INTERNATIONAL ARBITRATION: LIBER AMICORUM FOR MARTIN DOMKE 226 (ed. P. Sanders, 1967).

Robine, Eric, *What Companies Expect of International Commercial Arbitration,* 9 J. INT'L ARB'N (No. 2) 31 (1992).

Roebuck, Derek, *A Short History of Arbitration,* in HONG KONG AND CHINA ARBITRATION CASES AND MATERIALS (Kaplan, Spruce & Moser, eds. 1994).

Rogers, Andrew, *Arbitrability,* 10 ARB'N INT'L 263 (1994).

Rogers, Andrew and Rachel Launders, *Separability — The Indestructible Arbitration Clause,* 10 ARB. INT'L (No. 1) 77 (1994).

Rogers, Nancy H., E. Frank, Stephen Goldberg and A. Sander, DISPUTE RESOLUTION: NEGOTIATION, MEDIATION AND OTHER PROCESSES (2nd Ed. 1992).

Rokison, Ken, *The Sources and Limits of the Arbitrator's Powers in England,* in CONTEMPORARY PROBLEMS IN INTERNATIONAL ARBITRATION 86 (ed. J. Lew, 1985).

Rosenberg, Maurice, W. Reese and P. Hay (eds.), CONFLICT OF LAWS (9th Ed. 1990).

Rosenberg, Maurice, *Comment on Reich v. Purcell,* 15 U.C.L.A. L. REV. 641 (1968).

Roth, Peter M., *Reasonable Extraterritoriality: Correcting the "Balance of Interests",* 41 INT'L & COMP. L.Q. 245 (1992).

Rothchild, Michael and Mark Machina, *Risk,* in UTILITY AND PROBABILITY (THE NEW PALGRAVE DICTIONARY OF ECONOMICS) 277 (J. Eatwell, M. Milgate, & P. Newman, eds., 1990).

Rovine, Arthur, *"Fast Track" Arbitration: A Step Away From Judicialization of International Arbitration,* in INTERNATIONAL ARBITRATION IN THE 21ST CENTURY: TOWARDS "JUDICIALIZATION" AND UNIFORMITY? 45 (Richard Lillich & Charles Brower, eds., 1994).

Rowell, Robert, Jeanne de Cervens, Howard Classen and James Wise, *Survey of the Legality of Confessed Judgment Clauses in Commercial Transactions,* 47 BUS. LAW. 729 (1992).

Rubin, Alfred, *Enforcing the Rules of International Law,* 34 HARV. INT. L. J. 149 (1993).

Ruede, Thomas and Reimer Hadenfeldt, SCHWEIZERISCHES SCHIEDSGERICHTSRECHT: NACH KNOKORDAT UND IPRG (1993).

Sager, Lawrence and Louis Kornhauser, *The One and the Many: Adjudication in Collegial Courts,* 81 CAL. L. REV. 1 (1993).

Sammartano, Mauro Rubino, *Amiable Compositeur (Joint Mandate to Settle) and Ex Bono et Aequo (Discretional Authority to Mitigate Strict Law,* 9 J. INT'L ARB. (No.1) 5 (1992).

Sammartano, Mauro Rubino, *Multy Party Arbitration: Disputes Arising from One or More Contractual Relationship,* 9 INT'L BUSINESS LAWYER 436 (1981).

Sammartano, Mauro Rubino, *Le `tronc commun' des lois nationales en présence (Réflexions sur le droit applicable par l'arbitre international)*, 1987 REVUE DE L'ARBITRAGE 113.

Sampson, John, *Distant Forum Abuse in Consumer Transactions: A Proposed Solution*, 51 TEX. L. REV. 269 (1973).

Samuel, Adam, *A Taste of Alternative Dispute Resolution: Anglo-American Style*, PERMEABILITE DES ORDRES JURIDIQUES/OSMOSE ZWISCHEN RECHTSORDNUNGEN/THE RESPONSIVENESS OF LEGAL SYSTEMS TO FOREIGN INFLUENCES 373 Schultehess Polygraphischer Verlag, Zurich 1992).

Samuel, Adam, *The Recognition and Enforcement of Judicial Awards in England with a Comparative Look at the United States of America*, LE JURIST SUISSE FAC AU DROIT ET AUX JUGEMENTS ETRANGER 105 (F. Knoepfler, ed., edition Universitaire Fribourg Suisse, 1988).

Samuel, Adam, JURISDICTIONAL PROBLEMS IN INTERNATIONAL COMMERCIAL ARBITRATION (1989).

Samuel, Adam, *Developments in English Arbitration Law*, 5 J INT'L ARB. (1988).

Sander, Frank A., Nancy H. Rogers, E. Frank and Stephen Goldberg, DISPUTE RESOLUTION: NEGOTIATION, MEDIATION AND OTHER PROCESSES (2nd Ed. 1992).

Sanders, Gerard, *Rethinking Arbitral Preclusion*, 24 LAW & POLICY INT. BUS. 101 (1992).

Sanders, Pieter and Albert Jan Van Den Berg, ARBITRATION IN THE NETHERLANDS (1989).

Sanders, Pieter, *L'Autonomie de la clause compromissoire*, in HOMMAGE A FREDERIC EISEMANN 31 (1978).

Sanders, Pieter, *Commentary on UNCITRAL Arbitration Rules*, II YEARBOOK: COMMERCIAL ARBITRATION 172 (1977).

Sanders, Pieter, *International Commercial Arbitration*, in COMMERCIAL ARBITRATION: ESSAYS IN MEMORIAM EUGENIO MINOLI 467 (ed. Associazioni Italiana per Arbitrato, Unione Tipographico, 1974).

Sanders, Pieter, *The New Dutch Arbitration Act*, 3 ARB. INT'L 194 (1987).

Sanders, Pieter, *Trends in International Commercial Arbitration*, 145 RECUEIL DES COURS 207 (1975-II).

Sandrock, Otto, *Arbitration Agreements and Groups of Companies*, in ETUDES DE DROIT INTERNATIONAL EN L'HONNEUR DE PIERRE LALAIVE 625 (C. Dominicé, R. Patry & C. Reymond, eds., 1993).

Sandrock, Otto, *Arbitration Agreements and Groups of Companies*, 27 INTERNATIONAL LAWYER 941 (1993).

Sandrock, Otto, *Welche Verfahrensregeln hat ein Internationales Schiedsgericht zu befolgen?*, FESTSCHRIFT FUR OTTOARNDT GLOSSNER ZUM 70. GEBURTSTAG (Verlag Recht und Wirschaft GmbH, Heidelberg)

Sandrock, Otto, *How Much Freedom Should an International Arbitration Enjoy?*, 3 AM. REV. INT'L ARB. 30 (1992).

Sandrock, Otto, *Is International Arbitration Inept to Solve Disputes Arising Out of International Loan Agreements,* 11 (No. 3) JOURNAL OF INTERNATIONAL ARBITRATION 33 (1994).

Sandrock, Otto, *Internationale Kredite und die Internationale Schielsgerichts barkeit,* ZEITSCHRIFT FÜR WIRTSCHAFTS-UND BANKRECHT 405 (12 & 19 March 1994).

Scalbert, H. and L. Marville, *Les clauses compromissoires pathologiques,* 1998 REVUE D'ARBITRAGE 117.

Schauer, Fred, *Rules and the Rule of Law,* 14 HARV. J. L. & PUB. POL'Y 645 (1991).

Schlag, Pierre, *Le Hors de Texte C'est Moi: the Politics of Form and the Domestication of Deconstruction,* 11 CARDOZO L. REV. 1631 (1990).

Schmitthoff, Clive, *Arbitration and EEC Law,* 24 COMMON MARKET L.R. 143 (1987).

Schmitthoff, Clive, *Extrajudicial Dispute Settlement,* in FORUM INTERNATIONALE (Kluwer, Deventer, No. 3).

Schneider, Michael, *Le lieu ou la jurisprudence est rendue,* 9 BULLETIN DE L'ASSO-CIATION SUISSE DE L'ARBITRAGE 279 (1991).

Schneider, Michael, *Lean Arbitration: Cost Control and Efficiency Through Progressive Identification of Issues and Separate Pricing of Arbitration Services,* 10 ARB. INT'L 119 (1994).

Schönle, Herbert, *Les Fondements Constitutionels de la Liberté Contractuelle,* in PRES-ENCE ET ACTUALITE DE LA CONSTITUTION DANS L'ORDRE JURIDIQUE: MELANGES OFFERTS A LA SOCIETE SUISSE DES JURISTES POUR SON CONGRES 1991 A GENEVE 61 (1991).

Schönle, Herbert, *La Bonne Foi (Rapport Suisse),* in XLIII JOURNEES LOUISIANAISES (1994).

Schönle, Herbert, *Intérêts moratoirs, intérêts compensatoires et dommages-intérêts de retard en arbitrage international,* in ETUDES DE DROIT INTERNATIONAL EN L'HONNEUR DE PIERRE LALAIVE 649 (C. Dominicé, R. Patry & C. Reymond, eds., 1993).

Schorn, Hubert, DIE GESETZGEBUNG DES NATIONALSOZIALISMUS ALS MIT-TEL DER MACHTPOLITIK (1963).

Schorn, Hubert, DER RICHTER IM DRITTEN REICH (1959).

Schreiber, Aaron and W. Michael Reisman, JURISPRUDENCE: UNDERSTANDING AND SHAPING LAW (1987).

Schütze, Rolf, *The Precedental Effects of Arbitration Decisions,* 11 (No. 3) J. INT. ARB. 69 (1994).

Schwartz, Eric, *Multi-Party Arbitration and the ICC — In the Wake of Dutco,* 10 JOURNAL OF INTERNATIONAL ARBITRATION (No. 3) 5 (1993).

Schwebel, Stephen, INTERNATIONAL ARBITRATION: THREE SALIENT PROB-LEMS (1987).

Schwebel, Stephen, *The Majority Vote of an International Arbitral Tribunal,* in ETUDES DE DROIT INTERNATIONAL EN L'HONNEUR DE PIERRE LALAIVE 671 (C. Dominicé, R. Patry & C. Reymond, eds., 1993).

Schweizer, Philippe and Francois Knoepfler, PRECIS DE DROIT INTERNATIONAL PRIVE SUISSE (Bern 1990).

Scoles and Hay, CONFLICT OF LAWS (1984).

Scott, Robert E., *Conflict and Cooperation in Long-Term Contracts*, 75 CALIF. L. REV. 2005 (1987).

Sealey, Len, *Arbitration — Contract Alleged Void — Jurisdiction of Arbitrator*, 1962 CAMBRIDGE L.J. 14.

Sesser, Gary, *Choice of Law, Forum Selection and Arbitration Clauses in International Contracts: The Promise and the Reality*, A U.S. View, 1992 INT'L BUS. LAW. 397.

Shenton, David and Gordon Toland, *London As a Venue for International Arbitration: The Arbitration Act 1979*, 12 LAW AND POLICY IN INT'L BUSINESS 643 (1980).

Shenton, David, *Arbitral Impartiality: The Attitude of the English Courts*, 8 INT'L BUSINESS LAWYER 76 (1980).

Sher, Michael, *Can Lawyers Save the Rainforest: Enforcing the Second Generation of Debt for Nature Swaps*, 17 HARV. ENVTL. L.REV. 1 (1993).

Sherman, Edward F., Alan Rau and John Murray, PROCESSES OF DISPUTE RESOLUTION: THE ROLE OF LAWYERS (1989).

Sherman, Edward F., *Court-Mandated Alternative Dispute Resolution: What Form of Participation Should be Required?*, 46 SMU LAW REVIEW 2079 (1993).

Sidel, M. & M. Tong, *China: Recognition and Enforcement of Foreign Arbitral Awards Under the New York Convention*, 10 EAST ASIAN EXECUTIVE REPORTS 5, 14 (1988).

Siegel, Martha, *A Practioner's Guide to Feminist Jurisprudence*, BOSTON BAR JOURNAL 6 (September/October 1993).

Siehr, Kurt, *Rules for Declining Jurisdiction in Civil and Commercial Matters*, in RAPPORTS SUISSES PRESENTES AU XIVè CONGRES INTERNATIONAL DU DROIT COMPARE 163 (Institut Suisse Droit Comparé, Schultess Zurich, 1994).

Silberman, Linda J., *Developments in Jurisdiction and Forum Non Conveniens in International Litigation: Thoughts on Reform and a Proposal for a Uniform Standard*, 28 TEXAS INT. L. J. 501 (1993).

Simmonds, K., *International Arbitration between States: The Future Prospects*, 14 NORTHERN KENTUCKY L.R. 1 (1987).

Singer, Joseph W., *Real Conflicts*, 69 B. U. L. REV. 1 (1989).

Singer, Joseph W., *The Player and the Cards: Nihilism and Legal Theory*, 94 YALE L.J. 1 (1984).

Smit, Hans, *Introduction to Symposium: Achieving Justice in Arbitration*, 65 TUL. L. REV. 1309 (June, 1991).

Smit, Hans, *The Future of International Commercial Arbitration: A Single Transnational Institution?*, 25 COLUMBIA J. TRANSNAT'L L. 9 (1986).

Smit, Hans, *Mitsubishi: It Is Not What It Seems To Be*, 4 J. INT'L ARB. 7 (Sept. 1987).

Snijders, Henk J., A.H. van den Berg and R. van Delden, NETHERLANDS ARBITRATION LAW (1994).

Snyder, Jeffrey and David Epstein, INTERNATIONAL LITIGATION: GUIDE TO JURISDICTION PRACTICE & STRATEGY (1989).

Sommer, Joseph H., *The Subsidiary: Doctrine Without A Cause?*, 59 FORDHAM L. REV. 227 (1990).

Sorkowitz, Alan, *Enforcing Judgments Under the Uniform Foreign Money-Judgments Recognition Act*, 37 PRACTICAL LAWYER (No. 5) 57 (1991).

Speidel, Richard E., *Court Imposed Price Adjustments Under Long-Term Supply Contracts*, 76 N.W. U.L. REV. 369 (1981).

Speidel, Richard E., *Arbitration of Statutory Rights Under the Federal Arbitration Act: The Case for Reform*, 4 OHIO ST.J. DISP. RESOL. 157 (1989).

Stahl, Henning and Patrick Nettesheim, *Bundesgerichtshof Rejects Enforcement of United States Punitive Damages Award*, 28 TEXAS INTERNATIONAL LAW JOURNAL 416 (1993).

Stein, Steven and David Wotman, *The Arbitration Hearing*, in INTERNATIONAL COMMERCIAL ARBITRATION IN NEW YORK 87 (J. McClendon & R. Goodman, eds., 1986).

Stein, Steven & David Wotman, *International Commercial Arbitration in the 1980's: A Comparison of the Major Arbitral Systems and Rules*, 38 BUSINESS LAWYER 1685 (1983).

Stern, Brigitte, *Lex Mercatoria et arbitrage international: A propos des Mélanges Goldman*, 2 ARB. INT'L 294 (1986).

Stern, Brigitte, *Trois arbitrages: un même problème, trois solutions*, 1980 REVUE DE L'ARBITRAGE 3.

Stern, Brigitte *Changements de circonstonces et clauses d'élection de for devant le Tribunal des différands irano-américains*, XXIX ANNUAIRE FRANCAIS DE DROIT INTERNATIONAL 313 (1983).

Stewart, David. *The Iran-United States Claims Tribunal: A Review of Developments 1983-84*, 16 LAW & POLICY INT'L BUS. 677 (1984).

Stewart, Margaret G., *Forum Non Conveniens: A Doctrine in Search of a Role*, 74 CAL. L. REV. (1986).

Steyn, Johan, *Arbitration in England: The Current Issues*, 15 INT'L BUSINESS LAWYER 432 (1987).

Steyn, Johan, *Arbitration and the English Courts*, 48 ARB. 162 (1982).

Steyn, Johan, *England's Response to the Model Law of Arbitration (1993 Freshfields Arbitration Lecture)*, 10 ARB. INT'L (No. 1) 1 (1994) and 60 ARBITRATION 184 (1994).

Stipanowich, Thomas, *Rethinking American Arbitration*, 63 INDIANA L.J. 425 (1988).

Stipanowich, Thomas, *Punitive Damages in Arbitration: Garrity v. Lyle Stuart Revisited*, 66 B.U. L. REV. 953 (1986).

Storme, Marcel and Bernadette Demenlenaere, INTERNATIONAL ARBITRATION IN BELGIUM (1989).

Storme, Marcel, *Belgium: A Paradise for International Commercial Arbitration*, 14 INT'L BUS. LAWYER 294 (1986).

Storme, Marcel, *Proposition de loi relative à l'annulation des sentences arbitrales,* 1985 REVUE DE L'ARBITRAGE 461.

Summers, Robert, *Good Faith in General Contract Law and the Sales Provisions of the Uniform Commercial Code,* 54 VA. L.REV. 195 (1968).

Svernlov, C., *What Isn't, Ain't,* 8 JOURNAL OF INTERNATIONAL ARBITRATION (No. 4) 37 (1991).

Teitz, Louise, *Taking Multiple Bites at the Apple: A Proposal to Resolve Conflicts of Jurisdiction and Multiple Proceedings,* 26 INT'L LAW. 21 (1992).

Thieffrey, J., *International Commercial Arbitration Agreements and the Enforcement of Foreign Arbitral Awards — A Commentary on the Arbitration Act 1975,* 1981 LLOYD'S MARITIME COMMERCIAL L. QUARTERLY 17.

Thomas, Rhidian D., THE LAW AND PRACTICE RELATING TO APPEALS FROM ARBITRAL AWARDS (1994).

Thompson, D., `Detachment' from the National Law in International Commercial Arbitration,* 48 ARB. 105 (1982).

Thorens, Justin, *L'arbitre international au point de rencontre des traditions du droit civil et de la common law,* in ETUDES DE DROIT INTERNATIONAL EN L'HONNEUR DE PIERRE LALAIVE 693 (C. Dominicé, R. Patry & C. Reymond, eds., 1993).

Timmons, John, *Where is an Arbitration Award Made and What Are the Consequences?,* ARBITRATION (May 1992).

Tschanz, P.-Y., *La convention d'arbitrage,* 1989 REVUE DE DROIT DES AFFAIRES INTERNATIONALES 749.

Tupman, W.M., and D. Branson, *Selecting an Arbitral Forum: A Guide to Cost Effective International Arbitration,* 24 VA. J. INT'L L. 917 (1984).

Tupman, W.M., *Staying Enforcement of Arbitral Awards Under the New York Convention,* 3 ARB. INT'L 209 (1987).

Ughi, G., *Attachments and Other Interim Court Remedies in Support of Arbitration: Italy,* 12 INT'L BUSINESS LAWYER 115 (1984).

Ulmer, Nicholas and Martin Bernet, *Recognition and Enforcement of Foreign Civil Judgments in Switzerland,* 27 INTERNATIONAL LAWYER 315 (1993).

Ulmer, Nicholas, *Drafting Arbitration Clauses,* 1975 J. BUSINESS LAW 9.

UNIDROIT PRINCIPLES OF INTERNATIONAL COMMERCIAL CONTRACTS (International Institute for Unification of Private Law, Rome, 1994).

Vagts, Detlev, TRANSNATIONAL BUSINESS PROBLEMS (1986).

Vagts, Detlev, *Dispute Resolution Mechanisms in International Business,* 203 RECUEIL DES COURS (Hague Academy of International Law 1987).

Vam Rooij, Rene and Maurice Polak, PRIVATE INTERNATIONAL LAW IN THE NETHERLANDS.

Veeder, V.V., *Chronique de jurisprudence anglaise: L'Arret Channel Tunnel,* 1993 REVUE DE L'ARBITRAGE 705 (1993).

Veeder, V. V., *Mr. Justice Lawrence: The "True Begetter" of the English Commercial Court,* 110 LAW QUARTERLY REVIEW 292 (1994).

Veeder, V.V., *Multi-party Disputes: Consolidation Under English Law, The Vimeira — a Sad Forensic Tale*, 2 ARB. INT'L 310 (1986).

Vermeille, François, *Ingénieur Epfl, and Jean-François Demont, L'arbitrage, son tribunal, sa procédure vus par l'expert*, RECUEIL DE TRAVAUX SUISSES SUR L'ARBITRAGE INTERNATIONAL 235 (Claude Reymond & Eugene Bucher, eds., 1984).

Verveniotis, George, *Arbitration and Contractual Gaps*, 5 J. INT'L ARB. 103 (1988).

Volken, *Conflits de juridictions, entraide judiciaire, reconnaissance et exécution des jugements étrangers*, in LE NOUVEAU DROIT INTERNATIIONAL PRIVE SUISSE (François Dessemontet, ed., 1989) 245.

Volmer, Andrew, and Gary Born, *The Effect of the Revised Federal Rules of Civil Procedure on Personal Jurisdiction, Service and Discovery in International Cases*, 150 FEDERAL RULES DECISIONS 221 (1993).

Von Mehren, Arthur Taylor, *Recognition and Enforcement of Foreign Judgments—General Theory and the Role of Jurisdictional Requirements*, 1980-II HAGUE RECUEIL.

Von Mehren, Arthur Taylor, *To what Extent Is International Commercial Arbitration Autonomous?*, LE DROIT DES RELATIONS ECONOMIQUES INTERNATIONALES: ETUDES OFFERTES A BERTHOLD GOLDMAN (P. Fouchard, P. Kahn & A. Lyon-Caen, eds., 1982).

Von Mehren, Arthur Taylor and James Russell Gordley, THE CIVIL LAW SYSTEM (1977).

Von Mehren, Arthur, *Recognition and Enforcement of Foreign Judgments: A new Approach for the Hague Conference*, 57 LAW & CONTEMPORARY PROBLEMS 271, (1994).

Von Mehren, Arthur Taylor, *Jurisdiction to Adjudicate: reflections on the Role and Scope of Specific Jurisdiction*, in ETUDES DE DROIT INTERNATIONAL EN L'HONNEUR DE PIERRE LALAIVE 557 (C. Dominicé, R. Patry & C. Reymond, eds., 1993).

Von Mehren, Arthur Taylor, *International Commercial Arbitration: The Contribution of the French Jurisprudence*, 46 LOUISIANA L. REV. 1045 (1986).

Von Mehren, Robert, *The Iran-U.S.A. Arbitral Tribunal*, 31 AMERICAN J. COMPARATIVE L. 713 (1983).

Von Mehren, Robert & P. Kourides, *International Arbitrations between States and Foreign Private Parties: The Libyan Nationalization Cases*, 75 AMERICAN J. OF INT'L LAW 476 (1981).

Von Overbeck, Alfred E., in LES LEGISLATIONS DE DROIT INTERNATIONAL PRIVE 167 (Asser Institute, ed., 1971).

Walker, Robert and Peter Hay, *The Proposed Recognition-of-Judgments Convention Between the United States and the United Kingdom*, 11 TEX. INT'L L.J. 421 (1976).

Waller, Spencer Weber, *Bringing Meaning to Interest Balancing in Transnational Litigation*, 23 VAND. J. TRANSNAT'L L. 925 (1991).

Walters, G. W. Bosch, and J. Brönnimann (eds.), INTERNATIONALE SCHIEDSGERICHTSBARKEIT IN DER SCHWEIZ (1991).

Wehrli, Olivier, *Recognition in Switzerland of Foreign Bankruptcy Judgments*, 2/3 EUROPEAN REPORT 5 (1992).

Weintraub, Russell, INTERNATIONAL LITIGATION AND ARBITRATION (1994).

Weintraub, Russell, *The Need for Awareness of International Standards When Construing Multilateral Conventions: The Arbitration, Evidence and Service Conventions*, 28 TEXAS INTERNATIONAL LAW JOURNAL 441 (1993).

Werner, Jacques, ADR: *Will European Brains Be Set On Fire?*, 10 J. INT. ARB. (No. 4) 45 (1993).

Westbrook, James and Leonard Riskin, DISPUTE RESOLUTION AND LAWYERS (1987).

Westbrook, Jay, *Extraterritoriality, Conflict of Laws, and the Regulation of Transnational Business*, 25 TEXAS INT'L L.J. 71 (1990).

Westbrook, Jay, *The Coming Encounter: International Arbitration and Bankruptcy*, 67 MINNESOTA L.R. 595 (1983).

Westberg, Jay, INTERNATIONAL TRANSACTIONS AND CLAIMS INVOLVING GOVERNMENT PARTIES: CASE LAW OF THE IRAN-U.S. CLAIMS TRIBUNAL (1991).

Westin, David and Gary B. Born, INTERNATIONAL CIVIL LITIGATION IN UNITED STATES COURTS (2d Ed. 1992).

Wetter, J. Gillis and Charl Priem, *The 1993 General Electric Case: The Supreme Court of India Reaffirms Pro-Enforcement Policy Under the 1958 New York Convention*, INTERNATIONAL ARBITRATION REPORT (1993).

Wetter, J. Gillis, Review of W. CRAIG, W. PARK AND J. PAULSSON, INTERNATIONAL CHAMBER OF COMMERCE ARBITRATION in SVENSK JURIST-TIDNING 156 (1984).

Wetter, J. Gillis, *Issues of Corruption Before Arbitral Tribunals*, 10 ARBITRATION INTERNATIONAL 277 (1994).

Wetter, J. Gillis, *The Importance of Having a Connection*, 3 ARB. INT'L 329 (1987).

Wetter, J. Gillis, *A Multi-party Arbitration Scheme for International Joint Ventures*, 3 ARB. INT'L 2 (1987).

Wetter, J. Gillis, *Salient Features of Swedish Arbitration Clauses*, 1983 SWEDISH AND INTERNAT'L ARB. 33.

Whitte, Ralph, *Developments in the Erie Doctrine*, 40 AMERICAN J. COMPARATIVE LAW 967 (1992).

Wiener, P.R. (ed.), ENFORCING MONEY JUDGMENTS (1991).

Wilner, Gabriel (ed.), DOMKE ON COMMERCIAL ARBITRATION (1991).

Wilner, Gabriel, *Determining the Law Governing Performance in International Commercial Arbitration*, 19 RUTGERS L. REV. 646 (1965).

Wise, James, Robert Rowell, Jeanne de Cervens and Howard Classen, *Survey of the Legality of Confessed Judgment Clauses in Commercial Transactions*, 47 BUS. LAW. 729 (1992).

Woodward, David, *Reciprocal Recognition and Enforcement of Civil Judgments in the United States*, 8 N.C. J. INT'L LAW & COM. REG. 298 (1983).

Wotman, Daniel R. and Steven Stein, *The Arbitration Hearing,* in INTERNATIONAL COMMERCIAL ARBITRATION IN NEW YORK 87-98 (J. McClendon & R. Goodman, eds., 1986).

Wright, Charles Alan, THE LAW OF FEDERAL COURTS (4th ed. 1983).

Young, Vicki (ed.), *Consolidation and the Arbitration Agreement,* 18 LAWYERS' ARB. LETTER (No. 1), Spring 1994).

Young, Vicki (ed.), *Party Appointed Arbitrators,* 16 LAWYERS' ARB. LETTER (No. 4), 1 Winter 1992/93.

Zweigert, Konrad and Hein Kötz, INTRODUCTION TO COMPARATIVE LAW (Tony Weir, trans. 1987).

INDEX

(References are to page numbers)